Footprint Western Canada

Matthew Gardner
3rd edition

Canada is more than a canoe route after all. Canada is a road trip. And like any road trip worthy of the name, it is ultimately about freedom in its purest form.

Will Ferguson, author, Beauty Tips from Moose Jaw: Travels in Search of Canada (2004).

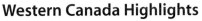

Western Canada Highlights

See colour maps at back of book

❶ Dempster Highway
The last great frontier road to the frozen north, page 353.

❷ Dawson City
The site of history's biggest Gold Rush, preserved as a living Wild West museum, page 347.

❸ Rafting the Tatshenshini in Kluane National Park
The ultimate trip down a pristine river, page 344.

❹ Atlin
A remote ramshackle frontier-style village in a stunning setting, page 331.

❺ Gwaii Haanas National Park
Haida villages and totem stands on this remote and magical island, page 234.

❻ Whale watching and Hot Springs Cove
A popular excursion from Tofino, page 116.

❼ Victoria's parks and gardens
Magnificent and diverse oases of calm, with great views and access to trails, page 93.

❽ Salt Spring Island Saturday market
An unmissable market, excellent for local crafts, page 105.

❾ Museum of Anthropology, Vancouver
An overwhelming collection of Northwest Coast native carvings, page 53.

❿ Hiking in Garibaldi Provincial Park
Expansive views of ice and peaks, something suitable for all levels of fitness, page 152.

ALASKA
USA

Dawson City ❷

Yukon

YUKON

Yukon Plateau

❸ ❹ ○ Whitehorse

○ Atlin

BRITISH COLUMBIA

Pacific Ocean

Prince Rupert ○

Haida Gwaii

❺

Coast Mountains

Inter Plateau

Mackenzie Mountains

Vancouver Island

❻

Whistler ❿

Vancouver ❾

Victoria ❼ ❽

N

100 km
100 miles

Beaufort Sea

Great Bear
Lake

NORTHERN
TERRITORIES

Great Slave
Lake

Fort
Saint John

ALBERTA

Edmonton

Jasper

Lake Louise

Kamloops

Banff

Calgary

Kelowna

Penticton

Nelson

Medicine Hat

Lethbridge

A

Contents

The beautiful Coast Mountains provide a breathtaking backdrop to Vancouver's city skyline.

An inukshuk stands sentry over Whistler and Blackcomb mountain, a traditional Inuit symbol of hospitality and friendship it is the official logo for the 2010 Winter Olympics.

Flores Island
Dense rainforest, rocky bays and countless islands are what you'll find at Clayoquot Sound.

Into the Wild
Jasper National Park is the place for long backcountry hikes.

A foot in the door

Travellers who choose to visit Western Canada are characteristically nature lovers or sports enthusiasts who enjoy direct interaction with the great outdoors. This is an area bigger than Mexico, but inhabited by fewer people than Switzerland, almost all of them squeezed into one small corner. The remaining wilderness is as diverse as it is vast, containing row upon row of lofty ice-capped mountains, huge lakes, mighty rivers, dense forests, broad valleys and plateaux, wide open prairie, steep-sided canyons, glaciers and ice fields, Arctic tundra and even the odd patch of cactus-spattered desert or bizarre Badlands moonscape. The lush coastline is punctuated by long, narrow fjords and fringed with islands of all sizes.

As this was one of the last places on Earth to be 'discovered' by Europeans, previously occupied solely by peoples defined by a reverence and respect for their environment, prophets of sustainability, this paradise has not yet been spoilt. It is one of the last remaining, easily accessible places on Earth where nature can be experienced in her most wild and pristine state, replete with ancient trees and increasingly rare large mammals.

With a few notable exceptions, the region's small towns are a let-down after their sublime surroundings, and there's little culture or history beside those of the First Nations and the many gold rushes. The people, however, display a distinctive 'West Coast' character. Humbled and clearly delighted by their spacious land, Western Canadians tend to be polite, tolerant and easy-going, opposed to oppression, war and corporate culture. All this makes travel here easy, safe and relaxing, but the stronger dollar means it is not as affordable as it used to be, and with the approach of the 2010 Winter Olympics hosted by Vancouver and Whistler, this is not likely to change.

The 2010 Winter Olympics

Hordes of the homeless notwithstanding, Vancouver, and most of BC in fact, is booming. Unemployment is low, the construction machine is roaring, real estate has gone crazy, and the provincial premier has recently announced a $14 billion, 12-year transit upgrade plan, most of it for Vancouver. The ubiquitous symbol, if not catalyst, of these apparent glory days is the city's selection, with Whistler, as host of the 2010 Winter Olympic and Paralympic Games. The 123-km highway that connects the towns is now one long construction zone, a frenzied, four year, $600 million scramble to conquer geography and accommodate the mobile masses. Meanwhile, gaping industrial trenches like science fiction sets have taken over whole blocks of Downtown Vancouver, while a giant mechanical mole burrows its way towards the airport, digging out the new Canada Line, a $1.9 billion underground expansion of the light railway system.

The Olympics are a serious business, in every sense. They're also something of a gamble: some cities come away with egg-covered faces and fleeced wallets; others turn handsome profits, boost local businesses and economies, and get to keep a complete bonus set of matching infrastructure goodies. Sure of their hand, the province

Ski the Canadian Rockies
The Rockies are a premier attraction and every outdoor activity is persued here.

has put $310 million on the table, the federal government almost $600 million, and domestic sponsors have signed $709 million-worth of agreements. The cream of national performers are being recruited so that, at the opening and closing ceremonies, self-effacing Canada might for once emerge Cinderella-like from the shadow of her overbearing sister to the south and estranged stepmother across the Atlantic, and bedazzle an expected three billion television viewers around the world. The Canadian Security Intelligence Service has already started infiltrating activist organisations lest they draw the world's attention to the environmental damage, the destruction of local indigenous peoples' traditional homelands, the eviction of poor people from their Eastside homes. BC Place Stadium is getting a new roof for the occasion: a big-top would seem appropriate.

To lessen the inevitable bedlam of the big month – yes, all this for 27 days – the organizing committee is considering asking Vancouverites to leave their cars at home, work different hours and maybe go and stay with friends or family elsewhere. The chips are down, the circus is coming to town, Canada is going to the ball! Everyone has their own version of the story but, love it or hate it, you certainly can't ignore it.

Modern classics
Sleek glass, chrome and granite skyscrapers contribute to an eclectic mix of architecture.

1 *The world famous resort of Whistler will co-host the 2010 Winter Olympics.* ▸▸ *See page 156.*

2 *Trains no longer run on the Kettle Valley Railway, but some 600 km are suitable for hiking and biking.* ▸▸ *See page 193.*

3 *Hoodoos are tall sandstone sculptures carved by wind and water.* ▸▸ *See page 311.*

4 *Khutzeymateen Grizzly Bear Sanctuary is the only protected grizzly habitat in Canada.* ▸▸ *See page230.*

5 *Dawson City, site of the biggest gold stampede, is a living museum with clapboard houses, boardwalks and saloons.* ▸▸ *See page 348.*

6 *Originally totem poles portrayed actual characters, depicted to provoke ridicule and contempt from those passing by.* ▸▸ *See page 382.*

7 *Tatshenshini-Alsek Wilderness Park is best reached on a guided rafting trip.* ▸▸ *See page 343.*

8 *The Okanagan Valley receives the most sun and least rain in Canada, an ideal climate for orchards and vineyards.* ▸▸ *See page 188.*

9 *Vancouver Public Library , an example of the city's eclectic architecture.* ▸▸ *See page 45.*

10 *This striking longhouse at Vetter Creek houses the Nisga'a Park Visitor Centre.* ▸▸ *See page 229.*

11 *Cowboys and rodeos can still be seen in parts of Western Canada.* ▸▸ *See page 259.*

12 *Waterton Lakes National Park is a UNESCO World Heritage Site and an interesting juxtaposition of prairies and mountain.* ▸▸ *See page 317.*

Convivial pursuits

We're guessing that most people visit Western Canada for the natural beauty, but outdoor pursuits comes a close second. Indeed, the two go together, for what better way to appreciate the scenic splendour than by playing in it. Hiking is the ultimate activity, and often the only way to reach the tastiest offerings of this sensory feast. The Rockies present the most outstanding collection of hikes, and you really can't go wrong as every major park has exceptional hikes of all lengths. Thanks to a string of campgrounds and hostels, this chunk of paradise can also be surprisingly affordable. Calgary, gateway to the Rockies, is a young, wealthy city, with a fine museum, and plenty of good art and restaurants. To the east, Drumheller is surrounded by extraordinary Badlands scenery, and boasts a world-class dinosaur museum. Only slightly less spectacular than the Rockies, however, are the Coast Mountains around Vancouver, the Sea to Sky Highway and the great peaks up around Stewart or Atlin. The Kluane Range in the Yukon has the biggest mountains of all and massive glaciers, and then there are the Columbia Mountains around Revelstoke and the West Kootenays. Every single region in this book has first-class hiking, and so much more besides.

Coasting along

Vancouver is a top destination in its own right, with a multi-layered personality that includes a jamboree bag of architectural styles, a fascinating blend of European, Asian and Native American cultures, numerous neighbourhoods with distinctive characters, the 28-kilometre seawall promenade, some great beaches and parks, the world-class Museum of Anthropology, three ski hills and world-renowned diving. Nearby is the Sea to Sky Highway, offering the best in all outdoor pursuits, and Vancouver Island, a relatively compact destination with plenty of

attractions on offer. Victoria is a beautiful town of gardens, beaches and parks set around a picturesque harbour and Tofino is a particularly good West-Coast base for whale-watching, trips to Hot Springs Cove, hiking through temperate rainforest, beach-combing, surfing, storm watching and kayaking. On the Gulf Islands, an exceptionally laid-back pace has attracted an unusual blend of artists, hippies and eccentrics.

Interior motives and northern exposure (or Wine Country and Wilderness)

For those whose idea of Canada is moose and lumberjack shirts, the biggest surprise is the Okanagan, which gets more sun and higher temperatures than most famous resorts to the south. Hills covered in wineries, orchards and sagebrush slope down to beaches heaving with bronzed bathers. A spirit similar to that of the Gulf Islands is also found in the West Kootenays, a string of attractive former mining communities with the odd ghost town and several hot springs. In Northern BC, frontier roads built for gold stampeders lead through increasingly broad horizons. Tweedsmuir Provincial Park and Bella Coola offer unforgettable tastes of true wilderness, while Haida Gwaii boasts a fantastic new cultural centre and the roadless Gwaii Haanas National Park, where ancient abandoned Haida villages are slowly being reclaimed by the lush rainforest. The Yukon is a land of friendly characters, midnight sun, northern lights and minimal landscapes that explode into late-summer colours. Besides the inevitable hiking, there are long canoe trips, rafting on the awesome Tatshenshini River, crazy roads to quaint little towns and the ultimate gold-mining boomtown of Dawson City, a rare still-living taste of the Wild West.

*Left: The most famous icon in the Rockies, Lake Louise in Banff National Park. **Above:** The very British-looking Parliament Buildings are but one example of Victoria's grandiose architecture.*

The Dempster Highway
Driving this frontier road across the tundra into the arctic circle is a challenge and an adventure

Essentials

❖ Footprint features

Planning your trip

Where to go

Western Canada is vast. Unless you have lots of time and like road-trips, be selective about what you want from your trip and focus on one or two geographical regions. Whether or not you have your own vehicle will also be a significant factor: buses take much longer than driving and some areas – like the Kootenays – are almost impossible to appreciate without wheels. Unless you're pursuing specialized interests, Vancouver, Victoria and Banff make the most obvious bases. Vancouver is the obvious, most convenient starting point and it's a great year-round destination in its own right. If you want to concentrate on the Rockies, however, you would be well advised to start in Calgary. Combining this and the following section with the calendar of events on page 31 will help you to get the most out of your trip.

One week

Those with only a week definitely have to focus on one area. For a taste of the **Gulf Islands** and two very different but equally enticing towns, hop from Vancouver to Victoria (Vancouver Island) via Galiano and Salt Spring islands, maybe squeezing in a hike along the East Sooke or Juan de Fuca trails. For outdoor pursuits, take the Sea to Sky Highway from Vancouver to the **Coast Mountains** around Squamish, Garibaldi Park and Whistler. Drivers could return via the dramatic **Fraser Canyon**. For big trees, whale watching, hot springs, endless beaches, sea kayaking and a lively seaside scene, head straight to **Tofino** (Vancouver Island). If time allows, squeeze in a trip to Gabriola Island from Nanaimo.

Alternatively, fly into Calgary and spend the whole week in the **Rockies**. Concentrate on Banff, Lake Louise and Yoho, but try to drive as far north as the Columbia Icefield. Those drawn to the north could take an internal flight to Whitehorse, hire a vehicle and drive a wonderfully scenic loop of the **Yukon**, including Kluane National Park, the Top of the World Highway, Dawson City, the Dempster Highway as far as the Tombstone Mountains, then back to Whitehorse on the Klondike Highway.

Two weeks

With two weeks or more, you could combine the above **Gulf Islands** and **Tofino** trips, with a brief stop in **Chemainus**. Return to Vancouver via **Nanaimo**, or continue north to Courtenay, catch a ferry to Powell River and drive south along the **Sunshine Coast**. Alternatively, combine either of these coastal trips with a week in the **Coast Mountains**. Fast drivers could potentially see a lot of British Columbia's southern interior. From Vancouver, take the Sea to Sky Highway or Fraser Canyon routes to Salmon Arm, then spend some time in the wineries, orchards and beaches of the **Okanagan**, returning via the Crowsnest Highway. Or continue on the TransCanada Highway to Revelstoke, head south through the **West Kootenays** and back on the Crowsnest, maybe getting a taste of the Okanagan on the way. With an open-jaw ticket flying out of Calgary, you could get a taste of the Coast Mountains, Okanagan or the West Kootenays, and the Rockies.

Consider spending all of your time in the **Rockies**. Work north from Banff to the Columbia Icefield, then on the way back down do the Lake Louise-Yoho-Kootenay Park loop. A great longer loop, for those with itchy feet, would involve driving the whole Icefields Parkway to Jasper, then heading west to Mount Robson, south to Kamloops via Wells Gray Park, then back to Calgary on the TransCanada Highway via Revelstoke and Yoho Park. The **Yukon** loop described above would make a great

⁞ How big is your footprint?

Responsible tourism is largely a matter of common sense, but a few points are worth underlining.
→ When hiking, always stick to trails and never pick wild flowers.
→ Practise 'no trace' camping: take out everything you take in. Where no outhouses are available, bury waste and toilet paper in the ground away from paths and at least 30 m from a water source.
→ Never feed or approach any wild animals. The correct disposal of litter and storage of foodstuffs is a key issue. Bears that dine well once due to a camper's laziness will keep coming back until they eventually have to be exterminated.
→ Every summer, British Columbia experiences a number of forest fires that rage out of control destroying vast tracts of land. Keep an eye out for fire bans, never light a fire other than in the designated place, never leave a fire burning and be especially careful when extinguishing

cigarettes; one spark taken by the wind to the tinder-dry brush is all it takes.
→ Whale-watching and bear-watching tours are major draws in Canada, and most operators are respectful towards the animals; still, there will always be the odd unscrupulous guide who oversteps the line. Don't encourage them. Visitors who come to Canada to hunt or fish should be aware of, and respect, the laws and limitations; they are there to protect the future of the species.
→ Equally open to abuse are Canada's First Nations. Canada's native populations do not necessarily enjoy the attention of tourists. Please respect any First Nations sights such as burial grounds that are held as sacred and are off-limits to outsiders. Never photograph a native American without asking their permission first.

two- or three-week trip. If time allows, add a short canoe trip or a diversion to Haines, Alaska or Atlin, BC.

One month

The Gulf Islands-Victoria-Tofino-Courtenay-Sunshine Coast loop could be combined with a tour of the **southern interior** including the Coast Mountains and Okanagan. Or head to the north of Vancouver Island, take the **Inside Passage** up the ruggedly beautiful West Coast to Prince Rupert; visit **Haida Gwaii** and take a kayak tour to abandoned First Nations villages; head across on the Yellowhead Highway to Mount Robson and Jasper; drive through the **Rockies** to Banff, then back to Vancouver taking in parts of southern BC. The even more ambitious could continue north from Prince Rupert to Skagway on an Alaska ferry, do a tour of the **Yukon**, then drive south on the Cassiar Highway, taking a diversion to see the glaciers on the way to Stewart.

A fantastic **inland loop** would be to drive the Crowsnest Highway to Osoyoos, then head north through the Okanagan Valley to Vernon, drive east to Nakusp, do the West Kootenays loop of New Denver-Slocan Valley-Nelson-Kaslo-New Denver, then return to Nakusp and continue north to Revelstoke; head east to the Rockies, then north up the Icefields Parkway to Jasper; return to Vancouver via Mount Robson, Wells Gray Park, Kamloops, and the Sea to Sky Highway.

For an **Alberta-based loop**, drive from Calgary to Drumheller, south to the Dinosaur Park, then take in Head-Smashed-In Buffalo Jump, Cardston and Waterton Lakes Park; cross the Crowsnest Pass and head north through the West Kootenays, finally looping back to the Rockies. A month in the **Yukon** would allow you to do some

⫶ Don't forget your toothbrush

Canada's weather is extremely changeable, so bring clothes for all occasions. For hiking and other outdoor pursuits bring plenty of layers of thin synthetic fibres, preferably long-sleeved for protection against bugs (which are less attracted to light colours); a good pair of boots and waterproof clothing are equally important. A camera is essential and binoculars can be useful for spotting wildlife. Many situations call for a tent, sleeping bag and lightweight camp-stove. A Swiss Army knife, torch and compass are also key. Visitors staying in hostels may want to bring a sleeping sheet and padlock, though such things are usually supplied. Everything you may need can be bought in Canada, often at a lower price than at home.

hikes in Kluane National Park and the Tombstone Mountains, and take a longer canoe trip such as the two-week paddle up the Yukon River, or drive the Dempster Highway to Inuvik and visit the frozen north.

When to go

Western Canada's weather is fickle, unpredictable and highly localized. The Okanagan and Thompson valleys, for instance, are so dry as to be nearly desert, yet can get very cold in winter, while the West Coast receives copious amounts of rain year-round, but is blessed with Canada's mildest winters and earliest springs. Weather in the mountains can change from blazing sunshine to blizzards in a single day, even in July.

With so much water to play in and around, an uninterrupted string of great festivals, outdoor pursuits galore, and (usually) as much sun as you could want, summer is the obvious time to visit Western Canada. Most hikes in the Rockies and other mountain regions are only snow-free between July and September, which is also the most reliable time to see those snowy peaks free of cloud. Many attractions, campgrounds and Visitor Centres only open from Victoria Day (third Monday in May) to Labour Day (first Monday in September). When we say 'summer' or 'May-Sep', this is what we mean. In the Yukon, the summer days are extremely long, with the sun barely setting at all around the summer solstice.

Many places (the Rockies in particular) are overrun with tourists during the summer. Accommodation rates are higher and coastal ferries tend to get booked up, so reservations for both are highly recommended. The best overall time is mid-August to September: the crowds are thinning, the trails are still open and the autumn colours are spectacular in the mountains and the Yukon. Spring is a good time for visitors concentrating on the coast, as the blossoms are out in Victoria and Vancouver, and the whales are migrating past Tofino.

Winter in Canada is a different matter entirely. Tourism is still very much alive, but attracting a different group of people: those who come to ski or snowboard. Canada offers some of the best, most affordable skiing in the world, as well as many other snow-related activities. Most sights are closed in winter, however, and transportation can be slow. Late February to March are the best months for skiing: the days are getting longer and warmer but the snow is still at its best. Vancouver, which has three ski hills, makes an excellent year-round destination.

Sport and activities

Western Canada's great tracts of near-wilderness, sensational natural beauty, extreme topographical variety and sport-minded population combine to make this arguably the best destination in the world for outdoor pursuits. With very few exceptions, any such activity you could mention is pursued here to a world-class standard. Countless specialist tour operators are on hand to offer guidance up to any level (see page 37 and listings throughout the book). A great place to find out more about these activities is in British Columbia's extremely useful *Outdoor Adventure Guide*, available from any Visitor Information Centre. Most individual regions also put out their own Adventure Guides, and www.HelloBC.com, is very useful as it outlines what is available town by town.

Birdwatching

Western Canada is crossed by one of the most important migratory routes in the world, with thousands of geese, swans, ducks, waterfowl and other birds passing through each year. Major spots for seeing them are mentioned throughout the book.

★ **Head for …**
Courtenay ▸▸ *p131* **Parksville to Qualicum Beach** ▸▸ *p130* **Brackendale** ▸▸ *p150* **Vaseux Lake** ▸▸ *p194* **Creston** ▸▸ *p208* **Marsh Lake** ▸▸ *p331*
ⓘ www.sco-soc.ca; www.nmnh.si.edu/BIRDNET.

Canoeing

Northern BC and the Yukon are overflowing with world-class canoeing. A good guide for the latter is Ken Madsen's *Paddling in the Yukon*. Trips can be as easy or hard, remote or accessible as you wish. If going without a guide, always wear a lifejacket and carry a bailing bucket, throw-rope and whistle. Avoid paddling in the afternoon on larger lakes because of high winds.

★ **Head for …**
Powell Forest ▸▸*p 83* **Sayward Forest** ▸▸ *p 132* **Bowron Lakes** ▸▸ *p223* **Tweedsmuir Park** ▸▸ *p225* **Wells Gray Park** ▸▸ *p226* **Yukon River** ▸▸ *p327* **Teslin Lake** ▸▸ *p330*
ⓘ Recreational Canoeing Association of BC, T250-847 4349, www.bccanoe.com; www.canoebc.ca.

Caving

There are many cave systems in Western Canada, especially on Vancouver Island; the commercial to the totally unexplored.

★ **Head for …**
Horne Lake ▸▸ *p130* **Nootka Sound** ▸▸ *p134* **Nakimu Caves (Glacier National Park)** ▸▸ *p172* **Cody Caves** ▸▸ *p208*
ⓘ Caving Canada, www.cancaver.ca.

Climbing/mountaineering

Climbing is a major activity throughout the area, with thousands of routes in dozens of stunning locations. Mountaineers will find North America's highest peaks in the St Elias Range which runs through the Yukon and Alaska.

★ **Head for …**
Horne Lake ▸▸ *p130* **Strathcona Provincial Park** ▸▸ *p132* **Squamish** ▸▸ *p149* **Bugaboo Provincial Park** ▸▸ *p174* **Skaha Bluffs near Penticton** ▸▸ *p193* **Canmore** ▸▸ *p278*
ⓘ Alpine Club of Canada, www.alpineclubofcanada.ca; Association of Canadian Mountain Guides, T250-372 0118, www.acmg.ca; British Columbia Mountaineering Club, www.bcmc.ca.

Fishing

Freshwater
In Canada you're never far from a lake or river renowned for its fishing. A freshwater licence is required, with additional permits for national parks. Ask for the *Freshwater Fishing Regulations Synopsis*, which details possession

limits, and pick up a copy of the *BC Freshwater Fishing Guide* from Visitor Centres.

★ **Head for ...**
Campbell River ▶▶ *p132* **Fraser River** ▶▶ *p154* **Kamloops** ▶▶ *p170* **Princeton** ▶▶ *p174* **Kootenay Lake** ▶▶ *p207* **"The Fishing Highway" (Cariboo)** ▶▶ *p223* **Skeena River** ▶▶ *p229*
ⓘ BC Fishing Resorts and Outfitters Association, www.bcfroa.ca, www.bc fishing.com

Saltwater
The West Coast is famous for its year-round salmon fishing, and its giant halibut from Apr-Aug. A tidal waters sport fishing licence is required to fish in BC's waters, available at sports shops. Pick up the *BC Saltwater Fishing Planning Guide* at any Visitor Centre. Tour operators will take you to the best spots and supply all equipment.

★ **Head for ...**
Sunshine Coast ▶▶ *p79* **Barkley Sound** ▶▶ *p80* **Clayoquot Sound** ▶▶ *p115* **Campbell River** ▶▶ *p132* **Bella Coola and Stewart** ▶▶ *p225* **Prince Rupert** ▶▶ *p230* **Haida Gwaii** ▶▶ *p231*
ⓘ Fisheries and Oceans Canada, T604-666 2828, www.dfo-mpo.gc.ca, sets the fishing regulations; **Oak Bay Marine Group**, T1800-663 7090, www.obmg.com, has 7 destinations in key fishing areas and a lot of experience; **Sport Fishing Institute**, T604-270 3439, www.sportfishing.bc.ca.

Golf

Golf is Canada's most popular participation sport, played by 7.4% of the population. In April 2003, the US Masters was won by Mike Weir, the first Canadian to win a golf major.

★ **Head for ...**
Vancouver ▶▶ *p75* **Whistler** ▶▶ *p152* **Columbia Valley** ▶▶ *p185* **Kelowna** ▶▶ *p189*

Hiking

Western Canada has to be one of the world's best destinations for hiking and has some superlative walks. Most of these are to be found throughout the Rockies and the other

mountain parks. There are also a number of one-off trails offering a chance to encounter some of the remaining old-growth rainforest on the West Coast. For details of the very best hikes, we recommend *Gotta Hike BC* by Skye and Lake Nomad (Voice in the Wilderness Press, 2001). The TransCanada Trail is an ambitious attempt to build a single trail right across the country. When completed, it will be the longest recreational trail in the world, and is destined to be a classic trek or cycle. In the meantime, whole stretches of the trail are in place, offering many hiking possibilities.

★ **Head for ...**
Suncoaster Trail ▶▶ *p79* **West Coast Trail** ▶▶ *p81* **East Sooke Regional Park** ▶▶ *p83* **Juan de Fuca Marine Trail** ▶▶ *p94* **Cape Scott Provincial Park** ▶▶ *p136* **Garibaldi Provincial Park** ▶▶ *p150* **Tweedsmuir Provincial Park** ▶▶ *p225* **Banff National Park** ▶▶ *p273* **Jasper National Park** ▶▶ *p295* **Yoho National Park** ▶▶ *p307* **Kluane National Park** ▶▶ *p342* **Tombstone Mountains** ▶▶ *p354*
ⓘ www.trailpeak.com; www.clubtread.com.

Kayaking

Exceptional kayaking is available around the West Coast. A good place to learn is **Strathcona Park Lodge** on Vancouver Island (see page 133), but most tour operators are happy to instruct beginners.

★ **Head for ...**
Indian Arm or Bowen Island, Vancouver ▶▶ *p75* **Desolation Sound Marine Park** ▶▶ *p80* **Broken Group Islands** ▶▶ *p81* **Gulf Islands** ▶▶ *p81, p114* **Clayoquot Sound** ▶▶ *p115* **Nootka Sound** ▶▶ *p134* **Haida Gwaii** ▶▶ *p231* **Tatshenshini and Alsek rivers** ▶▶ *p344*
ⓘ Sea Kayak Association of BC, T604-290 9653, www.skabc.org; Whitewater Kayaking Association of BC, T604-515 6379, www.whitewater.org.

Mountain biking

BC's outdoor enthusiasts take their mountain biking very seriously and most ski hills in BC stay open in summer.

• Heli-skiing and cat-skiing

Skiers and snowboarders seeking the ultimate thrill will find heli- or cat-skiing in British Columbia to be the most exciting winter experience anywhere in the world. You are taken high into the backcountry, where vast tracts of terrain are available covered with abundant, powdery, untouched snow, offering spectacular landscapes and no other people. Of course, such an experience does not come cheap. Most packages start at around $750 per day, all inclusive.

Some specialize in daily heli-skiing from a ski resort, while others offer only week-long trips from a destination lodge.

For more information, visit www.helicatcanada.com or contact **BC Heli and Snowcat Skiing Operators Association**, T250-542 9020, www.bcadventure.com/ adventure/heliskiing/index.html. In summer, heli-mountain biking is popular and can be organized through **Ticket 2Ride** in Whistler, www.ticket2ridebc.com.

★ **Head for ...**
Vancouver's North Shore ⏵▶*p55*
Mt Washington Alpine Resort ⏵▶ *p131*
Whistler ⏵▶ *p152* Kicking Horse Ski Resort ⏵▶ *p173* Rossland ⏵▶ *p175*
Fernie ⏵▶ *p176* Nelson ⏵▶ *p207*
Kaslo ⏵▶ *p208* Williams Lake ⏵▶ *p223*
ⓘ www.cycling.bc.ca; www.canada trails.com.

Rafting

Some of the best rafting in the world is to be found in Western Canada, including anything from stomach-churning white-water to gentle floats that are suitable for any age group or ability. In some cases rafting is the only way to access the most stunning scenery.

★ **Head for ...**
Gold River ⏵▶ *p134* Fraser Canyon ⏵▶ *p170* Kicking Horse River ⏵▶ *p185*
Chilko-Chilcotin-Fraser River system ⏵▶ *p224* Tatshenshini and Alsek rivers ⏵▶ *p344*

Sailing

With its hundreds of small islands and extensive marine life, Canada's West Coast is a Mecca for sailors. Marinas and boat supply shops stock nautical charts, pilot guides, and tide and current tables. The **Canadian Hydrographic Service**, www.charts.gc.ca, sells charts and tide and current tables. Those sailing into Canadian waters must clear customs, or can obtain an advance CANPASS permit. The BC edition of the *Guide to Federal Small Craft Harbours* can be obtained from **Fisheries and Oceans Canada**, www.dfo-mpo.gc.ca.

★ **Head for ...**
Sunshine Coast ⏵▶ *p79* Desolation Sound Marine Park ⏵▶ *p80* Gulf Islands ⏵▶ *p81, p114* Inside Passage from Port Hardy to Prince Rupert ⏵▶ *p135*
ⓘ BC Sailing Association, T604-737 3126, www.bcsailing.bc.ca; **Canadian Coast Guard**, T1800-267 6687, www.ccg-gcc .gc.ca, information on boat regulations and safety practices; **Canadian Yachting Association**, www.sailing.ca.

Scuba-diving

Thanks to its cold, clear water and abundant marine life, the Georgia Strait between the mainland and Vancouver Island's east coast has been named by the Jacques Cousteau Society as one of the top ten regions for scuba-diving in the world. Visibility is best from Oct-Mar when it reaches up to 30 m.

★ **Head for ...**
Whytecliff Park and Porteau Cove near Vancouver ⏵▶ *p76* Sunshine Coast ⏵▶ *p80*
Barkley Sound ⏵▶ *p80* Nanaimo ⏵▶ *p112*
Clayoquot Sound ⏵▶ *p115* Discovery Passage around Quadra Island ⏵▶ *p132*

Essentials Planning your trip Sport & activities

Port Hardy ⏩ *p136*
ⓘ Underwater Council of BC, T604-675 6964, www.underwatercouncilbc.com.

Skiing

Backcountry skiing
Unless you're travelling with a snow mobile, getting into the backcountry will probably entail a tour operator. Experienced skiers can ski from the road at the Creston/Salmon Pass on Hwy 3, and Rogers Pass on Hwy 1.

★ **Head for ...**
Callaghan Valley ⏩ *p167* **Revelstoke**
⏩ *p172* **Golden** ⏩ *p173* **Nelson** ⏩ *p207*
Kaslo ⏩ *p208*

Downhill and snowboarding
Western Canada is laden with first-class ski hills that are far less busy and expensive than those in the European Alps. Many resorts are currently being expanded in anticipation of the 2010 Winter Olympics, which will be hosted by Vancouver and Whistler. A marvellous winter tour of Western Canada could be based on ski hill hopping and indeed, many visitors come here just to ski.

★ **Head for ...**
Mt Grouse ⏩ *p56* **Mt Seymour** ⏩ *p55*
Mt Cypress ⏩ *p57* **Mt Washington** ⏩ *p131*
Whistler/Blackcomb ⏩ *p157* **Sun Peaks**
⏩ *p172* **Kicking Horse Ski Resort**
⏩ *p173* **Red Mountain in Rossland**
⏩ *p175* **Fernie** ⏩ *p176* **Big White**
⏩ *p192* **Whitewater** ⏩ *p207* **Sunshine
Village** ⏩ *p279* **Lake Louise** ⏩ *p281*

Cross-country (or Nordic)
Most ski hills also have a cross-country area with trails that are usually groomed and track-set. The following are in addition to those mentioned above.

★ **Head for ...**
Manning Park ⏩ *p179* **Kootenay National
Park** ⏩ *p 207* **Silver Star near Vernon**
⏩ *p207* **Wells Gray Park/Clearwater**
⏩ *p226* **Canmore** ⏩ *p278* **100 Mile House,
Cariboo** ⏩ *p223*
ⓘ Cross-Country BC, T250-545 9600, www.crosscountrybc.ca.

Whale watching

In Mar and Apr, around 24,000 Pacific grey whales pass Vancouver Island's west coast. Pods of resident orca (killer whales) are easily seen from many locations, even from the shore or a ferry. Humpback whales can be seen around Feb from more northerly spots.

There are plenty of reputable operators running whale-watching tours. When choosing one, bear in mind that the most important decision is whether you want to ride in an inflatable Zodiac, which is a faster, wetter and more exciting trip, or a hard-shell boat, which is more sedate.

★ **Head for ...**
Victoria ⏩ *p42* **Ucluelet** ⏩ *p80*
Tofino ⏩ *p115* **Johnstone Strait**
⏩ *p134* **Prince Rupert** ⏩ *p230* **Haida
Gwaii** ⏩ *p231*
ⓘ Whale Watch Operators Association Northwest, www.nwwhalewatchers.org.

Getting there

Arriving by air
For visitors other than those from the United States, who have the option of driving or taking a train and bus from Seattle, the only feasible way of getting to Canada is by air. The best-served city in the west is Vancouver, though Calgary is a much more obvious starting point for those focusing on the Rockies. One-way and return flights are available to both destinations. Enquire also about 'open jaw' tickets (flying into one and out of the other). From the UK, **Zoom**, www.flyzoom.com, offers the most departure points, but Air Transat currently has the cheapest flights.

It is advisable to start looking for your ticket early, as some of the cheapest have to be bought months in advance and the most popular flights sell out quickly. On the other hand, those with the flexibility to leave at a moment's notice can sometimes snap up unbelievable last-minute bargains. The best way to find a good deal is on the internet, at www.ebookers.com, but note that the cheapest flights often limit your stay to two weeks. The prices below are for return fares, including all taxes fees and charges, and are for the high season. Typically, this means July and August only; the rest of the year – even June and September – is roughly 65% of this price, with a slight further drop in November and January.

From the UK

Flight time from the UK is roughly 10 hours direct. There are daily flights to **Vancouver** and **Calgary** from London Heathrow with **Air Canada**, www.aircanada.ca, and **British Airways**, www.britishairways.com, all starting around £770. Flights from other UK airports work out at about £850. **Zoom**, www.flyzoom.com, flies from London Gatwick, Cardiff, Manchester, Glasgow and Belfast, all for around £700. **Air Transat**, www.airtransat.com, flies from Gatwick and Glasgow to Vancouver and Calgary for £420-500. **Air Canada** also flies from Heathrow to Whitehorse for about £900

From the rest of Europe

The following are arranged in order of current price, from cheapest to most expensive. Those flying from European cities not mentioned here should seek out the cheapest flights to Heathrow or Frankfurt, and continue from there.

Air Condor www.condor.com flies from Frankfurt to Vancouver (€ 650-700) and Whitehorse (€600-750). **Air Transat** flies from Amsterdam, Frankfurt and Munich to Vancouver (€ 920-950) and Calgary (€ 1000-1050). **Belair**, www.flybelair.com, flies to Vancouver from Berlin (€840-900), Munich, Zurich, Vienna and most major German cities (€ 900-1000), and to Calgary from Zurich (€1000). **KLM**, www.klm.nl, flies from Amsterdam to Vancouver or Calgary (€ 1100). **Lufthansa**, www.lufthansa.com, flies from Frankfurt to Vancouver and Calgary (€ 1120).

From the USA and eastern Canada

Flights from the US are numerous and frequent. The following flights are to **Vancouver**. Most of these airlines also fly to Calgary. **Air Canada** has return flights to Las Vegas (US$430), Los Angeles (US$440), New York (US$600), and San Francisco (US$425). **United Airlines**, www.united.com, flies from Chicago (US$645), Denver (US$520), and San Francisco (US$550). **Alaska Airlines**, www.alaskaair.com, flies from Denver, San Francisco, Las Vegas and Los Angeles. **Philippine Air**, www.philippineairlines.com, and **America West**, www.americawest.com, fly from Las Vegas. **Cathay Pacific**, www.cathaypacific.com, flies from New York.

Air Canada, and **West Jet**, T1800-538 5696, www.westjet.ca, both fly from all Canadian cities, including Montreal (US$760), and Toronto (US$750).

Flights from Australia and New Zealand

To **Vancouver** there are flights from Auckland with **Air New Zealand/Air Canada**, www.airnz.com, via Los Angeles or Honolulu, for NZ$2040 return. From Sydney, **Air Canada** flights start at AU$2250 return, and are direct; **Qantas**, www.qantas.com, flies via Los Angeles, from AU$2800 return.

Discount travel agents

In the UK

STA Travel, have 47 branches including 33 Bedford St, London WC2E 9ED, 0871-468 0612; 11 Goodge St, London W1T 2PF, 0871-468 0623; 86 Old Brompton Rd, London SW7 3LH, T0870-160 0599, www.statravel.co.uk. Specialists in low-cost student/youth flights.

Trailfinders, 194 Kensington High St, London, W8 6FT, T020-7938 3939; 1 Threadneedle St, London, EC2R 8JX, 0207-628 7628,www.trailfinders.com.

Air Brokers International, 685 Market St, Suite 400, San Francisco, CA94105, T1800-883 3273, www.airbrokers.com. Specialist and consolidator in RTW tickets.
Discount Airfares Worldwide On-line, www.etn.nl/discount.htm. A hub of consolidator and discount agent links.
STA Travel, 5900 Wiltshire Blvd, Suite 2110, Los Angeles, CA 90036, T1800-781 4040, www.statravel.com. Discount student/ youth travel company with branches in New York, San Francisco, Boston, Miami, Chicago, Seattle and Washington DC.
Travelocity, www.travelocity.com. Online consolidator.

Australia and New Zealand

Flight Centre, www.flightcentre.com.au. Throughout Australasia.
STA Travel, 841 George St, Sydney 2000, T02-9212 1255; 10-243 Edward St, Brisbane 4000, T07-3221 3722; 5-240 Flinders St, Melbourne 3000, T03-9654 7266; and 267 Queen St, Auckland, T09-356 1550, www.statravel.com.au. Also in most major towns and university campuses.
Travel.com.au, 80 Clarence St, Sydney 2000, T1300-130482, www.travel.com.au.
Trailfinders, 8 Spring St, Sydney 2000; 372 Lonsdale St, Melbourne 3000, T1300-780212, www.trailfinders.com.au.

...and leaving again

All passengers departing from Vancouver Airport have to pay an **Air Improvement Fee**, which is $5 for BC/Yukon, $15 elsewhere. This is now included in the ticket price.

Getting around

Regional flights

The easiest way to cover Western Canada's vast distances is with internal flights, mostly operated by **Air Canada**, www.aircanada.com, its subsidiary **Jazz**, www.flyjazz.ca, and **West Jet**, www.westjet.ca. Their prices are usually identical these days. Many mid- sized towns such as Kelowna, Kamloops, Cranbrook, Castlegar, Prince George and Prince Rupert have an airport, and some communities in the north are only linked to the outside world by air. To give an idea of prices from Vancouver, one-way to Kelowna costs $120-30; one way to Calgary costs $180. Returns are double and advance booking secures a better deal. ▶▶ *For further details, see Ins and outs sections throughout the guide.*

Bicycle

Canada can be a wonderful country to explore by bicycle, but remember how vast the distances are, and try to stick to lesser-used roads. For information, ask at bike shops or visit www.cycling.bc.ca. See also Mountain biking, page 22.

Bus

Due to long distances and regular stops, travel by bus can be very slow and seriously limits your flexibility. The network operated by **Greyhound**, T1800-661 8747, www.greyhound.ca, concentrates on towns close to the TransCanada and Yellowhead highways. Getting from Greyhound depots to sights and accommodation can also be very difficult, and may mean shelling out for a taxi. If relying on public transport, it's best to keep your schedule simple and concentrate on one area, such as the Rockies or Vancouver Island.

An excellent and very economic way to get around BC and the Rockies is with **Moose Travel Network**, T604-777 9905, www.moosenetwork.com. They run at least 16 different well-planned routes – from 2 days/$62 to 19 days/$999 – usually starting and ending in Vancouver, covering most possible itineraries and all the best sights. Travel is in mini-coaches seating up to 24 people, with most routes covered three or four times a week. You can get on and off where and when you want,

⦂ Over the border

The main highways into Western Canada from the United States are Highway 5 from Seattle to Vancouver, a three-hour drive; Highway 395 from Spokane to Grand Forks; Highway 93 from Kalispell, Montana to Cranbrook; and Highway 15 from Great Falls, Montana to Lethbridge, Alberta. Traffic jams and long queues are not uncommon at the very busy Peace Arch Border Crossing on Highway 5, especially at weekends, in summer and on Canadian or US holidays.

with no time limits, allowing for maximum freedom and flexibility. They also schedule stops for sights such as hot springs, include numerous sporting activities like hiking and kayaking, and have negotiated a number of discounts for their customers. Similarly, **True North Tours**, T403-934 5972, www.back-packertour.com/truenorth tours, run 3- to 10-day tours of the Rockies in a 15-passenger van from Banff or Calgary, including accommodation in hostels, and most meals. The 6-day **Rocky Express** from Banff or Calgary to Jasper and back costs $550.

Car

The best way to explore Western Canada properly is by car, since many sights cannot be reached by public transport. If hiring a vehicle seems expensive, consider off-setting this cost against accommodation by camping; in summer, a car and a tent are all you need. Older travellers tend to favour **Recreational Vehicles** (RVs), but these can be prohibitively expensive. Before hiring a vehicle, be sure to check if there is a mileage limit, and whether the insurance covers forestry roads. All-wheel, 4WD or front-wheel drive vehicles are useful if you are planning to go off the beaten track. **Hitchhiking** is a way of life in some rural areas, but even in Canada this carries a certain risk, especially for lone women.

Rules and regulations   You must have a current driving licence to drive in Canada. Foreign licences are valid up to six months for visitors. If crossing the border in a vehicle, be sure to have your registration or ownership documents, and adequate insurance. Throughout Canada you drive on the right, and seat belts are compulsory. Speed limits are 90-110 kph on the open road, usually 50 kph in built-up areas. The police advise people to drive with lights on even during the day. Compared to most countries, driving is easy and relaxed, with wildlife representing the main hazard. In many towns, traffic lights are replaced by four-way stops: vehicles proceed according to the order in which they arrived. Turning right at traffic lights is legal if the way is clear.

Fuel costs   Fuel (called 'gas' here) is easy to come by anywhere but the far north. It's expensive (around 115 cents a litre), unless compared to British prices.

Maps   We recommend investing in Rand McNally's good-value *BC and Alberta Road Atlas*, which includes the whole region covered in this book, even the Yukon, and also has larger scale maps of key areas such as the southern interior and Rockies, and most towns and cities, with additional city centre maps for the biggest. Those who really want to get off the beaten track could invest in a *Backcountry Mapbook* (2001), Mussio Ventures, $16, which shows all the secondary and forestry roads, with full details on free and forestry campsites, hot springs and other useful features. For transport information throughout Canada, visit www.tc.gc.ca.

Vehicle hire   Details of rental agencies are given in the transport sections of Vancouver, Calgary and Whitehorse. Some companies have a one-way service, meaning you can rent a car in one place and drop it off elsewhere. Prices start at about $25 per day, $180 per week, $700 per month plus tax and insurance. Another option would be to rent something you could sleep in. A mini-van works out at about

$400 per week all-inclusive. RVs are the expensive but luxurious choice; prices start at about $175 per day for a small unit, $320 per day for a 24-footer, plus tax and insurance. All hire vehicles are registered with the **Canadian Automobile Association** (CAA); in case of breakdown, simply call their T1800 number and give directions to where you are, and a towing operator will take you to the nearest CAA mechanic.

Buying a car For long-term travellers, it would work out cheaper to buy a vehicle and sell it at the end of your trip. Bargains can be found in Vancouver. The classified section of the *Vancouver Sun* is a good place to start looking.

Ferry

On the West Coast, ferries are a way of life. The main routes, operated by **BC Ferries**, T1888-223 3779, www.bcferries.com, connect Vancouver with Victoria and Nanaimo on Vancouver Island, and with the Gulf Islands and the Sunshine Coast. Sailings on all these services are fairly regular (see specific locations for details, and pick up the latest timetable). Vehicles can be taken on all but a few minor crossings and bikes can be taken on all.

Two very popular long-distance routes from Port Hardy on Vancouver Island – the **Inside Passage** to Prince Rupert and the **Discovery Coast Passage** to Bella Coola (see page 135) – provide excellent means of accessing the north, and can be treated as cheap but beautifully scenic cruises in their own right. In addition, a number of free ferries provide essential links across lakes in BC's southern interior. The longest and most important of these are in the West Kootenays, crossing the Arrow Lakes near Nakusp, and Kootenay Lake near Nelson.

Two other services worth mentioning are privately run boats that provide a popular means of accessing some very remote coastal spots around Vancouver Island. The *MV Lady Rose* out of Port Alberni runs to Bamfield, Ucluelet and Barkley Sound. The *MV Uchuck III* out of Gold River runs to Nootka Sound, Tahsis and Yuquot. Both will take and launch kayaks.

Train

Only three **VIA Rail,** www.viarail.ca, services operate in this region: the Malahat between Victoria and Courtenay on Vancouver Island, the Prince Rupert-Jasper service and the Vancouver-Jasper line, which takes 16½ hours, with sleepers available.

Sleeping

Until you stray far from the beaten track, accommodation in Western Canada is plentiful and easily found across the price ranges. Mid-range, usually characterless, **hotels** and **motels** dominate the scene, especially in smaller towns. Rooms are typically clean but uninspiring, with generic decor, a TV, tub, small fridge and coffee maker. Facilities such as saunas, hot tubs, fitness rooms and indoor pools are often small and disappointing. Many of the most impressive hotels, operated by the Fairmont chain, were constructed by the Canadian Pacific Railway (CPR) at the turn of the last century, and resemble French chateaux. Motel rooms are usually side-by-side, with an exterior door and often a parking spot right outside.

For the same price as a mid-range motel, you can usually find an attractively furnished room in a small **B&B** or **guesthouse**, with a hearty breakfast included, representing much better value. Generally operated by friendly, helpful and knowledgeable hosts, these offer an excellent opportunity to meet Canadians on their own ground, but might deter those who value their privacy or can't shake off that feeling of staying with their auntie.

In a similar vein, many travellers have had wonderful experiences when staying in **lodges**. Often found in remote spots, sometimes associated with outdoor

⁞ Sleeping price codes

Accommodation price grades in this guide are based on the cost per night for two people sharing a double room in the high season, with breakfast, not including tax (see page 35). Many places offer discounts during low season or for long stays. **Prices are in Canadian dollars**.

LL over $300	**A** $180-220	**D** $70-100
L $220-260	**B** $140-180	**E** $40-70
AL $220-260	**C** $100-140	**F** under $40

Almost all the campsites listed in this guide are in the **F** price category.

activities, these usually consist of a large central building containing facilities and rooms, with cabins scattered around the extensive grounds. Some of the gorgeous log constructions, for which the West Coast is famous, are exceptional and well worth a splurge. For something more exotic, consider staying on a working **ranch** or **farm**, which abound in Alberta and the Cariboo. For more details contact the **BC Guest Ranchers' Association**, www.guestranches.com. **Resorts**, primarily found on the coast, tend to have cabins, huts or chalets of varying standards, along with their own restaurants, beaches and other facilities. There has not always been room to mention these, so seek them out in the excellent *BC Approved Accommodation Guide*, www.HelloBC.com.

Almost all Canadian towns have a **hostel**, many affiliated to **Hostelling International** (HI), with a reduced fee for members. For information and reservations contact www.hihostels.ca. There is no age limit. A typical hostel has dormitories with four or more beds, usually single sex, and a few private rooms for couples and families. Facilities include shared washrooms with showers, a common room with TV and sometimes games, and a library, a kitchen/dining room, and lockers. Many organize activities or tours. Almost all are clean, friendly, a bit noisy and great for gleaning information and meeting fellow travellers. In the Rockies, a string of rustic HI hostels enjoy locations second only to the campgrounds, making them a great budget option. For the latest non HI-affiliated hostels, and they have started proliferating of late, check www.backpackers.ca. A number of other low-cost options can be found at www.budgetbeds.com.

Camping is the cheapest option, and the best way to immerse yourself in Western Canada's magnificent countryside. Where the scenery is wildest, camping is often the only choice. The best campgrounds are those within provincial parks, which are not driven by profit margins and tend to have more spacious sites, with plenty of trees and privacy. The busier ones often have shower facilities and hot running water. Campsites in big towns tend to be far from the centre, expensive and ugly, making a hostel a better option. Those that cater to RVs, with pull-through sites and hook-ups, often resemble car parks, with few trees and no privacy.

Seekers of calm will gravitate towards the small campgrounds that have no facilities beyond an outhouse and a water pump. Even cheaper are forestry campgrounds, which are almost always situated in remote spots on logging roads (ask at local Visitor Centres). 'Guerilla camping' means finding out-of-the-way spots where you can pitch your tent for free, or sleep in the back of your van, without being bothered. Much of Western Canada (but not the Rockies) is remote enough to make this possible. Logging roads are always a good place to look (and you may stumble on a forestry site). Anyone interested in this approach might want to buy

⁞ Restaurant codes

The prices below refer to the cost of a main meal (often called an entrée) and an appetizer or dessert. **Prices are in Canadian dollars**.

♈♈♈ over $40   **♈♈** $20-40   **♈** under $20

Kathy and Craig Copeland's *Camp Free in BC* (Voice in the Wilderness Press). Volume one covers the south, volume two the north.

Eating and drinking

Food

Western Canada, unlike the country as a whole, has developed a strong culinary identity, focused on the gastronomic playground of Vancouver. **West Coast cuisine** combines Asian, Californian and European techniques with a strong emphasis on the use of very fresh, locally produced ingredients, a genuinely innovative, creative, eclectic philosophy, and the extensive use of seafood. Elements are also taken from traditional Native American cooking, such as the grilling of salmon on cedar or alder, and the use of wild game like caribou and buffalo. Many different ethnic cuisines are fused with the West Coast sensibility, and are usually healthier for it.

Not surprisingly, **vegetarians** are well catered for in Vancouver, and in bohemian areas like the Gulf Islands and West Kootenays. The more you move into the redneck communities further north and east, however, the harder it gets to avoid the meat-and-potatoes mentality. However, if you are a meat-eater, Alberta AAA beef is as good as it gets, so if you like steak this is the place to indulge.

In Canadian cities you can find any kind of food you want, until late at night. Most towns will have an expensive 'fine-dining' establishment, which usually means old-style European, predominantly French, with the emphasis on steak and seafood. In smaller communities, however, you're often stuck with unimaginative 'family' restaurants, Chinese restaurants of dubious authenticity, pizza, and early closing. Certain ubiquitous chains like **Earl's** and **Milestone's** cover most of the comfort-food bases, and really are fine, especially if you're travelling with kids. Equally ubiquitous are the family chains like **Denny's** and **Smitty's**, which are okay for big breakfasts, but the coffee leaves a lot to be desired. All the American fast-food outlets are here too, **Subway** is always a good bet for sandwiches.

Drink

While Vancouver has its share of sophisticated cafés, bistros and tapas bars, as well as the inevitable Irish pubs and phoney English boozers, the typical small-town Canadian pub has a pool table, a TV set screening sporting events, soft-rock or country music, a burger-dominated menu and a handful of locals propping up the bar playing keno (a lottery game). Chances are though, they'll be a friendly bunch.

Sadly, most of the **beer** sold here is tasteless, weak, watery lager, such as Molson, Kokanee and Canadian. Yet Western Canada has pioneered the concept of **microbreweries**, which produce small-batch, carefully crafted beers using natural ingredients. All styles of beer are available, served carbonated and chilled. Breweries to look out for are Big Rock (Calgary), Nelson (West Kootenays), Yukon (Whitehorse), Tree (Kelowna), and Phillips (Victoria). Very small but excellent breweries include Raven (Vancouver), Crannog (Shuswap), and Salt Spring (southern Gulf Islands). Unibroue, based in Québec, brew Canada's best beers.

While here, you should also make a point of trying some BC **wines**, the best of which are made in the Okanagan Valley. This region specializes in German-style whites, sparkling wines, pinot noir, and the sweet and sophisticated ice-wine. It's hard to recommend specific wineries, but Tinhorn Creek and Red Rooster never disappoint.

Canadians take their **coffee** pretty seriously. Locally brewed examples to look out for include Kicking Horse (Invermere, East Kootenays), Oso Negro (West Kootenays), and Salt Spring (southern Gulf Islands).

Shopping

Canada has its share of tacky souvenirs, usually featuring moose, grizzlies or maple leaves, but a bottle of authentic maple syrup makes a nice gift, or you can buy smoked salmon (which will keep) in a hand-crafted cedar box, decorated in native Northwest Coast-style. The most popular items among tourists are works by Canada's various First Nations, such as the Inuit or Haida. These include carvings in gold, silver, wood and argillite (a black slate-like rock), jewellery, masks, paintings and prints, clothing, mocassins, beadwork, dream-catchers and much more. Arts and crafts costs less in the places where they are made, such as Haida Gwaii (Queen Charlotte Islands). There is a lot of mass-produced rubbish sold to tourists, so be sure to shop around to get an idea of just how exquisite good native art can be.

Non-aboriginal arts and crafts are also exceptionally fine and often extremely good value given the workmanship involved. Regions such as the Gulf Islands and West Kootenays are overrun with artists, but Vancouver's Granville Island is the best place to see a wide range of works. Visitors to Alberta may want to buy some authentic cowboy boots, a stetson hat or a set of chaps. Music lovers will be pleased to hear that Canada is one of the cheapest places in the world for CDs. It could also be better for sports equipment than your home country. Note that most things are cheaper in Alberta where there is no provincial tax.

Entertainment and festivals

While the standard and choice of entertainment and nightlife is good in Vancouver and, to a lesser degree, Calgary and Victoria, most Western Canadian towns simply don't have the populations to support a thriving cultural scene comparable to European cities. Generally you will find a cinema or two, a theatre, a museum full of pioneer artefacts, gold-rush relics and stuffed animals, maybe an art gallery, a nightclub of dubious merit frequented by teenagers, and an arena for ice hockey, Canadian football, basketball, baseball or curling. On the other hand, summer in Western Canada is a time for non-stop festivals, and even the smallest towns hosts wonderful events that might focus on music (jazz, folk, blues), street entertainment, storytelling, food, or Native American culture (powwows).

Jan Brackendale Winter Eagles Festival, near Squamish, celebrates the world's biggest gathering of bald eagles ►► *p162*.
Feb Chinese New Year, Vancouver ►► *p70*. All Native Basketball Tournament, Prince Rupert, a massive and popular event that celebrates its 50th year in 2009 ►► *p243*.
Mar Pacific Rim Whale Festival, held around Tofino, to celebrate the migration of up to 24,000 grey whales ►► *p80*.

Apr Telus World Ski and Snowboard Festival, Whistler. The biggest winter sports event in North America, featuring the world snowboarding championship ►► *p163*.
May International Children's Festival in Vancouver. Spring Wine Festival, Okanagan ►► *p201*.
Jun Jazz festivals in Vancouver ►► *p70*. and Victoria ►► *p104*. Mid- to late Jun is the best time to see orca (killer whales) in the

Johnstone Strait off Vancouver Island, where they stay until Oct ▸▸ *p130*.

Jul Dancing on the Edge Festival, Vancouver, Canada's largest showcase of independent North American choreographers ▸▸ *p70*. **Vancouver Folk Music Festival. Celebration of Light**, late-Jul to early Aug, Vancouver, a 2-week international fireworks competition ▸▸ *p70*. The annual salmon migration occurs Jul-Sep, with peaks varying in different areas ▸▸ *p130*. **Merritt Mountain Music Festival** is a huge country music event. **Starbelly Jam Global Music Festival**, East Shore, West Kootenays. **Williams Lake Stampede**, weekend closest to 1 Jul, is one of the biggest and oldest of its kind in BC ▸▸ *p243*. **Calgary Stampede**, a 10-day cowboy extravaganza and **Calgary Folk Music Festival**, Calgary ▸▸ *p259*. **Banff Festival of the Arts**, throughout the summer, showcases young artists in various media,a nd includes a Jazz Festival ▸▸ *p290*. **Great Northern Arts Festival**, Inuvik, a 10-day bonanza featuring over 100 artists from north of the Arctic Circle ▸▸ *p358*. **Dawson City Music Festival**, one of the best ▸▸ *p358*.

Aug Vancouver's **Pride Season** the biggest Gay event in Western Canada culminates in the Gay Pride Parade ▸▸ *p71*. **Victoria Fringe Theatre Festival**, the most important festival of its kind in BC, and Victoria's major event ▸▸ *p104*. **Filberg Festival**, Comox, Vancouver Island. A massive 4-day expo of the best arts and crafts in BC ▸▸ *p143*. **Beach Festival**, Parksville, features the Canadian Open Sandsculpting Competition ▸▸ *p84*. **Squamish Days**, a loggers' sports festival ▸▸ *p162*. **Kamloops Powwow**, one of the best in the country ▸▸ *p183*. **Peach Festival**, Penticton, is a massive party ▸▸ *p201*. **Ironman Triathlon**, Penticton, a very serious event ▸▸ *p201*. **Jazzfest**, Kaslo, enjoys one of the most spectacular locations of any festival ▸▸ *p218*. **Shambhala**, a one of a kind rave in Salmo near Nelson ▸▸ *p218*. **Calgary Fringe Festival** ▸▸ *p270*. **Yukon International Storytelling Festival** in Whitehorse ▸▸ *p336*. **Discovery Days Celebrations** in Dawson City feature the **Yukon Riverside Arts Festival** ▸▸ *p358*.

Sep Vancouver Fringe Festival and **Vancouver International Film Festival** ▸▸ *p70*. **Sandcastle Festival**, Harrison Hot Springs ▸▸ *p169*. **Fall Wine Festival**, late Sep/early Oct throughout the Okanagan ▸▸ *p201*. **International Film Festival**in Calgary ▸▸ *p270*.

Oct Vancouver ComedyFest ▸▸ *p70*.

Dec Festival of Lights at Vancouver's VanDusen Gardens ▸▸ *p72*.

A to Z

Accident and emergency

Contact the emergency services on T911 and your embassy or consulate (see page 33). Remember to get police/medical records for insurance claims.

Children

Canada is generally a safe country that presents few worries for people travelling with kids. There are no poisonous animals, crime levels are low, the people tend to be relaxed and tolerant, and there's plenty of space and countryside to enjoy. The only potential problem is the huge distances that often have to be covered.

An excellent resource to explore, full of tips on kid-friendly accommodation, restaurants and attractions throughout BC is www.kidfriendly.org. A good site for resources aimed at Canadians but also useful for travellers is www.childrencanada.com.

Customs and duty free

The duty-free allowance for people over 19 (18 in Alberta) is 1.14 litres of spirits or wine, 8.5 litres or 24 bottles of beer, 200 cigarettes, 50 cigars and 200 grams of tobacco. UK travellers can take back 1 litre of spirits or 2 litres of wine, 200 cigarettes or 50 cigars, and £145 worth of goods, including gifts and souvenirs.

Disabled travellers

Disabled travellers should call ahead to make arrangements with hotels and restaurants, many of which will go out of their way to be helpful. Being such a young country, Canada has a relatively high proportion of modern buildings, which tend to be wheelchair friendly. Many national and provincial parks have wheelchair-accessible interpretive centres and trails. For more information, contact the **Canadian Paraplegic Association**, T604-324 3611, www.canparaplegic.org. Information on accessible transport around Canada can be found at www.access totravel.gc.ca. **Freedom Rentals**, 4996 Westminster Av, Delta, Vancouver, T604-952 4499, www.wheelchairvanrentals.com, rent out wheelchair-accessible vans for about $150 per day, $900 per week. *Abilities Magazine* is a cross-disability life-style magazine published by the **Canadian Abilities Foundation**, www.enablelink.org.

Drugs

All the usual drugs are illegal in Canada, and with the Conservatives in power, this is not likely to change. British Columbia is a large producer of high quality marijuana (BC bud), whose use is widespread.

Consequently, attitudes toward the drug are pretty relaxed, but it is still advisable to be very discrete if indulging, and obviously be careful if buying.

Electricity

Canada uses 110 V, 60 cycles, with a US-style plug, usually 2 flat pins, sometimes with a third earth pin which is round. UK appliances will not work in Canada without a heavy-duty invertor to up the voltage to 220 volts.

Embassies and consulates

Australia High Commission: Commonwealth Av, Canberra, ACT 2600, T02-6270 4000.
England High Commission: Macdonald House, 1 Grosvenor Sq, London, W1K 4AB, T020-7258 6600.
Ireland 7-8 Wilton Terrace, Dublin 2, T01-234 4000.

New Zealand High Commission: 11th floor, 125 The Terrace, Wellington, T04-473 9577
Northern Ireland Consulate: Unit 3, Ormeau Business Park, 8 Cromac Av, Belfast, BT7 2JA, T2891-272 0060.
Scotland Consulate: 50 Lothian Rd, Festival Sq, Edinburgh, EH3 9WJ, T131-473 6320
South Africa High Commission: 19th floor, Reserve Bank Building, 60 St George's Mall, Cape Town 8001, T21-423 5240.
USA 501 Pennsylvania Av NW, Washington DC 20001, T202-682 1740.
Wales Beignon Close, Ocean Way, Cardiff, CF24 5PB, T2920-449645.

Gay and lesbian

Canadians are generally tolerant of homosexuality although, as everywhere, exceptions exist. Be more wary in redneck communities, especially in Northern BC, Alberta, and logging and mining towns. The Gulf Islands and West Kootenays are especially tolerant, and Vancouver's West End has a flourishing gay scene.

For general information and links, check out www.gaycanada.com. An excellent site for listings of gay-friendly businesses across the country is www.purpleroofs.com. **The Centre**, 1170 Bute St, Vancouver, T604-684 5307 (programmes/services), has a library and clinic, and organizes discussion groups. **Vancouver Prideline**: T604-684 6869. **BC Prideline**: T1800-566 1170.

Health

Western Canada must be one of the safest places on earth: it has good medical facilities, and there are no prevalent diseases, so no vaccinations are required before entry. Tap **water** is safe to drink but drinking water from dubious sources, especially slow-moving streams, can lead to giardia, commonly known here as 'beaver fever'. The result is vomiting, diarrhoea and weakness.

Those hiking in the mountains should be aware of **altitude sickness**, which can begin at 3000 m. If you experience headaches, nausea, and shortness of breath, the best treatment is to descend. The best prevention is to ascend slowly.

To combat **hypothermia** and frost-bite, which may occur when your core temperature falls below 35°C, keep warm by wearing several layers of suitable clothing (see page 20). If you feel cold, move about rather than just standing still.

Sunburn also occurs easily in the mountains, so avoid extensive exposure, wear a hat and sunglasses, and use a high-protection sun cream.

The health service in Canada is maintained by provincial governments. Travellers should make sure their insurance covers all medical costs and visitors suffering from a condition that may need immediate care, such as those with serious allergies or diabetes, are advised to carry what they need in case of an emergency. Medical services are listed in each town's directory.

Pharmacies (chemists) are plentiful and stock all the usual provisions. They are often large retail outlets that stay open late, even 24 hrs in big cities. As elsewhere, many drugs are only available with a doctor's prescription.

Insurance

Travel insurance is highly recommended and should cover theft or loss of possessions including passport and money, the cost of medical and dental treatment, cancellation of flights, delays in travel arrangements, accidents, missed departures, personal liability and legal expenses. Keep any relevant medical bills and police reports to substantiate your claim. Note that many policies exclude 'dangerous activities' or charge a higher premium for them. This may include scuba-diving, skiing and even trekking. Some companies will not cover people over 65 years old, or may charge high premiums. **Age Concern**, T01883- 346964, www.ageconcern.org.uk, usually have the best deals for seniors. **Columbus Direct**, T0207-375 0011, www.columbus direct.com, is one of the most competitive British companies.

STA Travel and other reputable student travel organizations also offer good-value policies. Travellers from the US should check to see if their existing policies cover travel in Canada. Otherwise, try the **International Student Insurance Service** (ISIS), available through **STA Travel**, T1800- 777 0112, www.statravel.com, or **Travel Guard**, T1800-826 1300, www.travelguard.com;

Access America, T1800-284 8300, www.accessamerica.com; **Travel Insurance Services**, T1800-937138, www.travelinsure.com; and **Travel Assistance International**, T1800-821 2828, www.travelassistance.com.

Internet

All but the smallest Canadian towns will have a cyber-café, and free internet access is always available at public libraries, though you may have to register in advance to get a slot. Otherwise charges vary, averaging about $1 for every 15-20 mins, considerably cheaper in big cities. Look in each town's directory section for details of internet access.

Language

Canada has 2 official languages: English and French, or rather Québecois, which you may hear but will never need in Western Canada. First Nations groups still speak indigenous languages in remote areas of Northern BC and the Yukon.

Media

Newspapers and magazines

There are 2 national newspapers. *The Globe and Mail* is a broadsheet that appeals to a more intellectual and liberal-minded readership. The *National Post* has a more right-of-centre and populist approach, as do BC's *The Province* and *Vancouver Sun*. The bookshop **Chapters** is a good place to browse.

Foreign newspapers and magazines, available in larger newsagents in Vancouver and Calgary, include *USA Today*, the *International Herald Tribune* as well as weekend editions such as *The Observer*.

Radio and television

The best way to get an idea of the Canadian psyche is to tune in to *CBC Radio One*, where current issues and all manner of topics are discussed. The news is broadcast every 30 mins, with an extended national news at 1700, and world news at 1800. Shows in the morning are provincial, those in the afternoon are national. *Cross-country Check-up* (Sun 1300-1500) and the provincial *BC Almanac* (weekdays at noon) are phone-in shows where people talk about key current issues. BC's *Sad Goat* (Mon-Fri 1400-1600), is also a phone-in show, but more light-hearted and humorous. Other shows to listen out for are: *Definitely not the Opera* (Sat 1400-1700), usually good for new Canadian music; *Tapestries* (Sun 1500), which deals with spiritual and metaphysical matters; and *Quirks and Quarks* (Sat 1200), an intelligent show about science. *CBC Radio Two* has hitherto been dedicated to classical music, but this looks set to change.

Canadian television tells you very little about the country beyond its obvious proximity to the US. There are only 2 Canadian channels, one national (*CBC*), the other provincial (*BCTV* in BC, for example). Even these have ads and are dominated by US content.

Money

Prices throughout this book are in Canadian dollars. The Canadian currency is the dollar ($), divided into 100 cents (¢). Coins come in denominations of 1¢ (penny), 5¢ (nickel), 10¢ (dime), 25¢ (quarter), $1 (called a 'loonie' because it carries a picture of a loon, a common Canadian bird), and $2 (called a 'toonie'). Banknotes come in denominations of $5, $10, $20, $50 and $100. The loonie has been very strong lately, making Canada a more expensive place to travel, especially for those coming from the US, whose own currency has plummeted.

At the time of printing the exchange rate was: 1 Canadian dollar = US$1.00; €0.65; £0.50; AU$1.09; NZ$1.26.

What to take
As in most countries today, the easiest and safest way to travel in Canada is with a credit or debit card using ATMs, which are found in all but the smallest, remotest communities. The major credit cards are also accepted just about everywhere. Traveller's cheques (TCs) remain a safe way to carry money, but mean more hassle. **American Express (Amex)**, **Visa** and **Thomas Cook** cheques are the most widely accepted. You're never far from one of Canada's big banks: **Royal Bank**, **Bank of Montreal**, CIBC, **Scotiabank** and **TD Bank**. They all give reasonable rates

for TCs and cash. Minimum opening hours are Mon-Fri 1000-1500, but they're usually open until 1630. Bureaux de change, found in most city centres, airports and major train stations have longer hours but worse rates. Avoid changing money or TCs in hotels, the rates are usually poor. The quickest way to have money sent in an emergency is to have it wired to the nearest bank via **Western Union**, T0800-833833, www.west ernunion.com, or **Moneygram**, T0800-894887, www.moneygram.com.

Taxes
Almost everything in Canada is subject to the federal Goods and Services Tax (GST) of 5%. A rebate can no longer be claimed by visitors. In BC (but not Alberta, the Yukon or NWT) most goods and services also carry a Provincial Sales Tax (PST) of 7% (10% on liquor). In addition there is a hotel and motel tax of 8%, with an additional 2% tourism tax levied by municipal governments where approved. None of these taxes are included in the original price, meaning everything you buy ends up costing more than you expect (up to 23% more for accommodation).

Cost of travelling
The cost of living is considerably lower in Canada than in the UK. Things that will cost £1 in England will often cost $1 in Canada. Notable exceptions are luxuries like beer and cigarettes which are roughly on a par with the UK and therefore more expensive than they are in the US. Petrol (gas) is cheaper than in the UK but more expensive than the US.

Canada is not a budget destination, though it is still reasonably affordable for those coming from Britain. Apart from accommodation, the single biggest expense is travel, due to the vast distances that need to be covered. Petrol gets considerably more expensive the further north you go. Accommodation and restaurant prices tend to be higher in popular destinations such as Whistler and Banff, and during the summer months (or winter at ski resorts).

Budget
The minimum daily budget required per person for those staying in hostels or

camping, travelling by bus and hitching, and cooking their own meals, will be roughly $50-80 per day. If you stay in cheaper motels or B&Bs and eat out occasionally that will rise to $80-100 per day. Those staying in slightly more upmarket places, eating out daily and visiting attractions can expect to pay at least $120-150. The best way to budget is to move around less and camp a lot. In destinations like the Rockies, this is also about the best way to experience the country. Single travellers will have to pay more than half the cost of a double room in most places, and should budget on spending around 60% of what a couple would spend.

Opening hours

Shops tend to stay open 0900-1730. Bank hours vary, but typically they are open Mon-Fri or Tue-Sat 1000-1600. Visitor Centres are typically open 0900-1700, longer in summer. Some are only operat- ional May-Sep. All shops and businesses keep longer hours in cities, with everything shutting down earlier in smaller and more remote communities.

Post

Most towns have Canada Post offices, www.canadapost.ca, which are usually open Mon-Fri 0900-1700. It is often more convenient to send post from one of the major pharmacies. Costs for a standard letter are 52¢ within Canada, 96¢ to the US, and $1.60 anywhere else. Prices for packages depend on exact destination and weight. Within BC this is roughly $5 for 1 kg then 30¢ for every additional 500 g. It is consider-ably cheaper to send parcels abroad as 'small packages'. To the US this includes anything up to 1 kg. To Europe, a small package can be up to 2 kg.

Note that international mail can take up to 2 weeks to arrive. In smaller towns, regular post offices will hold general delivery (post restante). In big towns this should be addres-sed to the main post office, addresses will be given in the listings.

Public holidays

Most services, attractions, and many shops close on public holidays, or greatly reduce their opening hours. Accommodation and transport tends to be more heavily reserved, especially ferries between Vancouver and Vancouver Island.

National holidays
New Year's Day, 1 Jan; Good Friday; Easter Monday; Victoria Day, 3rd Mon in May; Canada Day, 1 Jul; Labour Day, 1st Mon in Sep; Thanksgiving, 2nd Mon in Oct; Remembrance Day, 11 Nov; Christmas Day; Boxing Day.

Provincial holidays
Alberta Family Day, 3rd Mon in Feb; Alberta Heritage Day, 1st Mon in Aug. BC British Columbia Day, 1st Mon in Aug. Yukon Discovery Day, 3rd Mon in Aug.

Safety

Few countries are as safe as Canada. Even here though, common sense should prevail in cities. Avoid walking alone in remote, unlit streets or parks after dark. Elsewhere the biggest danger is from wildlife, though there are no poisonous animals. Never approach wild animals, even the ones deemed safe. More people are injured annually by elk than by bears, see page 399.

Smoking

Smoking is not permitted in public places including restaurants, cafés or pubs where eating is a primary activity, or on any mode of public transport.

Student travellers

Most sights in Canada offer a discounted price for students. ISIC cards are widely accepted as proof of ID. Most of Canada's hostels are affiliated to Hostelling International (HI), and reductions are available for members.

Telephone

For international calls to Canada, dial your country's IDD access code (00 from the UK) +1, then the local code, then the number. Local codes are: 250 for all of BC, except Vancouver, the Sunshine Coast and Sea to

Sky Highway, which are **604**; most of Alberta is **403**, except the Edmonton region (including Jasper), which is **780**; the Yukon is **867**. These codes have been included throughout the guide.

Long-distance calls within North America must be preceded by **1**, then the 3-digit local code. Any long-distance numbers beginning with **1800**, **1888**, **1877**, or **1777** are free in North America. For long-distance and international calls it works out much cheaper to buy one of the cards available from newsagents and petrol stations. Those from **7-11** shops are reliable. For international calls, ask for one with no connection fee. To reach an operator, dial **0**. For directory enquiries, dial **411**. To dial out of Canada the IDD access code is **011**. For all emergency services, dial **911**.

In Canada as elsewhere, the advent of the mobile phone has led to a decrease in the number of public phones. Many take coins and credit cards, some take **Telus** phone-cards, available at **7-11** shops, petrol stations, or larger pharmacies. Local calls are free from personal phones, with a charge of 25¢ at pay phones for an unlimited amount of time.

Time

BC and the Yukon are 8 hrs behind GMT in summer, 7 hrs behind GMT in winter. BC and the Yukon operate on Pacific Time. Alberta is on Mountain Time, which is 1 hr ahead.

Tipping

Western Canadians take tipping very seriously and in restaurants the customary tip is 15%. Bars and pubs usually have waiter/ waitress service, and these too are tipped 10-15%. Even if you buy your drink at the bar you are expected to leave a tip, usually change up to around 10%. Taxi drivers and hairdressers should also be tipped 10-15%. Naturally, this all depends on service.

Tourist information

Visitor Information Centres can be found in almost every Canadian town and are listed in the relevant sections of this book. Many are only open mid-May to mid-Sep and tend to be well stocked with leaflets. In **British Columbia**, T1800-534 5622, www.hello bc.com, literature includes a *Vacation Planner*; the indispensable Approved Accommodation Guide, which also includes addresses and toll-free phone numbers for Visitor Centres; vacation guides for each region; the extremely informative *Outdoor Adventure Guide*; and other guides covering topics such as fishing and golf. **Alberta**, T1800-252 3782, www.travel alberta.com, produces an *Accommodation Guide* and a separate *Campground Guide*, a very useful *Vacation Guide* full of attractions, and some regional brochures. The **Yukon**, T1800-661 0494, www.touryukon.com, produces a helpful *Vacation Planner*. Look out also for *Welcome*, a visitor guide put out by the **Yukon First Nations Tourism Association**, T867-667 7698, www.yfnta.org.

Most Visitor Centres will provide infor-mation on local transport and attractions, and sell relevant books and souvenirs. Many also produce self-guiding walking-tour maps of their towns, and have illustrated directories of local B&Bs. **Parks Canada**, www.pc.gc.ca, operates its own offices, usually in conjunction with the local tourist board. These tend to be excellent facilities, especially in the Rockies. Their website has lots of information, but ferreting it out it can be frustrating.

Tour operators

In the UK
Canada Travel Specialists, Barrhead Travel, 190-194 Main St, Glasgow, G78 1SL 4PA. T0871-226 0474, www.canadatravel specialists.com. Ski packages, rail tours, motorhome holidays.
Connections Worldwide, HiTours House, Crossoak Lane, Redhill, Surrey, RH1 5EX, T0800-988 5847, www.connectionsworld wide.co.uk/canada-holidays.asp . All kinds of packages offered.
HF Holidays, Catalyst House, 720 Centennial Court, Centennial Park, Elstree, Herts, WD6 3SY, T208-732 1220, www.hfholidays.co.uk. Walking and cycling tours of Western Canada.

In North America
Adventure Link Tours, Suite 202, 298 Main St, McBride, BC, VOJ 2EO, T1888-229 4266.

www.adventurelinktours.com. Train tours, lodge holidays and ski vacations. Specialists in Rocky Mountain holidays.

Adventures Abroad, PMB 101, 1124 Fir Av, Blaine, Washington, 98230, USA, www.adv entures-abroad.com. All kinds of tours, including 2-week bus tours from Calgary to Vancouver Island.

Midnight Sun Adventure Travel, 1027 Pandora Av, Victoria, BC, V8V 3P6, T1800-255 5057, www.midnightsuntravel.com. Tours of Vancouver Island, the Rockies, the Yukon, and Haida Gwaii. Also kayaking, hiking and camping tours for small groups.

In Australia and New Zealand

Scenic Tours, PO Box 807, 11 Brown St, Newcastle, Australia, T1300-136001, www.scenictours.com. Tours of the Rockies.

Ski Tours Canada, T02-9499 9639, www.ski tourscanada.com. Ski tours around resorts from Big White to Fernie.

Talpacific Holidays, level 5, 11 Finchley St, Milton, Queensland, 4064, T07-3218 9900, www.talpacific.com. Rail tours.

Visas and immigration

Visa regulations are subject to change, so it is essential to check with your local Canadian embassy or consulate (see page 33) before leaving home, or at www.cic.gc.ca. Citizens of the EU, Scandinavia and most Common-wealth countries do not need an entry visa, just a full valid passport. Residents of South Africa, Hungary and Turkey do need a visa. US citizens require a US birth certificate or passport, or a green card, and are also advised to carry proof of residence such as a driver's licence. All visitors have to fill out a waiver form, which you will be given on the plane or at the border. If you don't know where you'll be staying just write 'touring', though immigration officers may then ask for an idea of your schedule. They will decide the length of stay permitted, usually the maximum of 6 months. You may have to show proof of sufficient funds, such as a credit card or $300 per week of your proposed stay. If you wish to extend your stay beyond the allotted time, send a written application to the nearest Canada immigration centre well before the end of your authorized time limit.

Weights and measures

The metric system is universally used, though many Canadians still talk about feet rather than metres. Hectares and acres are both used.

Women travellers

There are few, if any, regions in the world where women are as emancipated, and that are as safe for women travellers, as Western Canada. Naturally the usual precautions need to be taken in cities and larger towns, such as avoiding quiet unlit streets and parks at night. In more redneck logging and mining communities, or in sports-oriented places like Whistler, a surfeit of pumped-up males may result in more attention than most women would want, but even here the problem is more one of irritation than danger.

Gaia Adventures for Women, T604-875 0066, www.gaiaadventures.com. Organize a number of differing adventures for women throughout the year.

Wild Women Adventures, T1888-993 1222. An outdoor adventure company for women, organizing all sorts of activities and trips throughout Canada.

Working in Canada

Non-Canadian residents need a permit to work legally in Canada. To get one you must first have an offer of employment. **Human Resources and Development Canada**, T1800-6226232, www.hrdc-drhc.gc.ca, must confirm this. You then have to apply to **Citizenship and Immigration Canada**, www.cic.gc.ca, for the permit. Performing artists can sometimes work legally without the permit. People without permits tend to have the best luck waiting at tables in Vancouver or picking fruit in the Okanagan. Wages for the latter can be reasonable if you work fast. Another, legal, option is **WWOOF Canada (Willing Workers on Organic Farms)**, T250-3544417, www.ww oof.ca. The deal varies from place to place, but generally entails working 3 to 5 hours per day for room and board. A 48-page booklet listing 600 farms costs $40. Many farms expect a minimum commitment of 2 weeks.

Vancouver & around

⁞ Footprint features

Introduction

All the elements that have allowed Vancouver to top the list of the world's most liveable cities also make Western Canada's gateway a great place to visit. The beautiful Coast Mountains tower over the city, providing a breathtaking backdrop, as well as skiing, hiking and mountain biking of the highest calibre. The ocean is equally pervasive, offering a lively beach scene, a 28-km sea wall promenade and easy access to world-class kayaking, canoeing, sailing, scuba-diving and whale watching.

The population is young and vibrant, and Vancouver supports more restaurants per capita than any other Canadian city. Closer to Japan than it is to Britain, with 30% of its residents of Asian origin, this is also a meeting place of east and west, affectionately nicknamed 'lotus land'.

Vancouver's distinctive neighbourhoods, burgeoning culinary scene, delightfully eclectic architecture and numerous parks are major selling points, as is the close proximity to many other prime destinations. Vancouver Island and the Gulf Islands are a short ferry-ride away and the sporting Meccas of Squamish and Whistler are just to the north. Closer still are the outdoor pursuits and picturesque harbours of the Sunshine Coast.

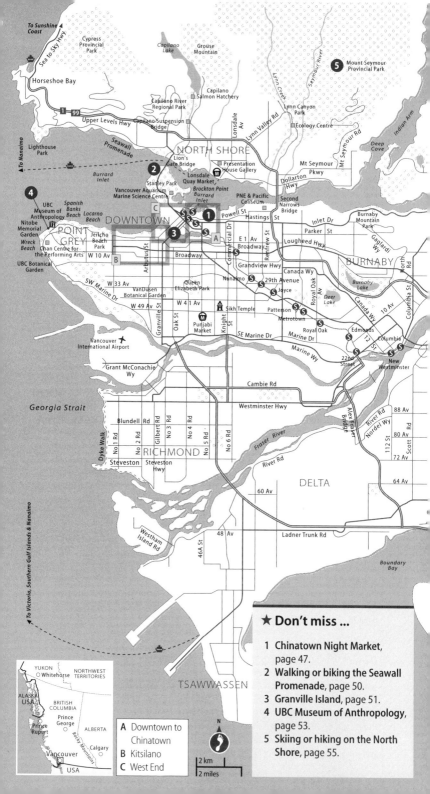

To Sunshine
Coast

Cypress
Provincial
Park

Grouse
Mountain

Capilano
Lake

Mount Seymour
Provincial Park

5

Sea to Sky Hwy

Horseshoe Bay

Capilano
Salmon Hatchery

Lynn Valley Rd

Lynn Creek

Seymour River

1 99

Upper Levels Hwy

Capilano River
Regional Park

Capilano Suspension
Bridge

Lynn Canyon
Park

Ecology Centre

Indian Arm

To Nanaimo

Lighthouse
Park

Seawall
Promenade

Lonsdale
Av

NORTH SHORE

Deep
Cove

Burrard Inlet

Lion's
Gate Bridge

Presentation
House Gallery

Mt Seymour

Mt Seymour Rd

2

Stanley Park

Vancouver Aquarium
Marine Science Centre

Lonsdale
Quay Market,
Brockton Point
Burrard Inlet

Dollarton
Hwy

Second
Narrows
Bridge

UBC
Museum of
Anthropology

4

Spanish
Banks Beach

Locarno
Beach

C

Powell St

PNE & Pacific
Coliseum

Inlet Dr

Burnaby
Mountain
Park

Nitobe
Memorial
Garden

**POINT
GREY**

DOWNTOWN

Jericho
Beach Park

1

Hastings St

E 1 Av

Parker St

Gaglardi Wy

Wreck
Beach

Chan Centre for
the Performing Arts

B

3

S

A

Commercial Dr

Renfrew St

Broadway

Lougheed Hwy

BURNABY

North Rd

UBC Botanical
Garden

Arbutus St

W 10 Av

Broadway

Grandview Hwy

Canada Wy

Burnaby
Lake

Columbia St

10 Av

SW Marine Dr

W 33 Av

VanDusen
Botanical Garden

Queen
Elizabeth Park

Nanaimo

29th Avenue

Joyce

Deer
Lake

Granville St

Oak St

W 49 Av

W 41 Av

Knight St

Patterson

S

Royal Oak

Metrotown

Edmonds

Columbia

12 St

Vancouver
International Airport

Grant McConachie
Wy

SE Marine Dr

Sikh Temple

M

Punjabi
Market

Marine Wy

Royal Oak

Marine Dr

22nd
Street

New
Westminster

Alex Fraser
Bridge

Georgia Strait

Cambie Rd

Westminster Hwy

88 Av

River Rd

Nordel Wy

80 Av

Scott Rd

112 St

Blundell Rd

Gilbert Rd

No 3 Rd

No 4 Rd

No 5 Rd

No 6 Rd

Fraser River

72 Av

Dyke Walk

No 1 Rd

No 2 Rd

RICHMOND

Steveston

Steveston
Hwy

River Rd

DELTA

64 Av

60 Av

Ladner Trunk Rd

Westham
Island Rd

46A St

48 Av

Boundary
Bay

To Victoria, Southern Gulf Islands & Nanaimo

★ Don't miss ...

1 Chinatown Night Market,
   page 47.

2 Walking or biking the Seawall
   Promenade, page 50.

3 Granville Island, page 51.

4 UBC Museum of Anthropology,
   page 53.

5 Skiing or hiking on the North
   Shore, page 55.

YUKON

NORTHWEST
TERRITORIES

Whitehorse

ALASKA
USA

BRITISH
COLUMBIA

Prince
Rupert

Prince
George

ALBERTA

Calgary

Vancouver

Rocky Mountains

USA

A Downtown to
      Chinatown

B Kitsilano

C West End

N

2 km
2 miles

TSAWWASSEN

Vancouver City

Vancouver's compact Downtown peninsula contains most of the city's sights, but none compares with the pleasure of discovering its many neighbourhoods and incredibly diverse architecture. Surrounded by water on all sides, and largely undeveloped, Stanely Park is a green oasis, containing some giant trees and possibly the peninsula's best sight, the Aquarium. South of False Creek, Granville Island is another must, combining a Covent Garden-style market, arts and craft studios and galleries, a marina, lots for the kids to do and a surprisingly good museum. More museums are nearby in Vanier Park, but the most remarkable of all is the anthropology museum in Point Grey. South and east Vancouver have some fascinating neighbourhoods, such as Commercial Drive and Main Street, and some beautiful parks and gardens but, if nature calls, the semi-wilderness parks that head up into the giant mountains on the North Shore are hard to resist. ▸▸ *For Sleeping, Eating and other listings, see pages 58-84.*

Ins and outs

Getting there

All international flights land at **Vancouver International Airport** (YVR), T604-207 7077, www.yvr.ca, 13 km south of Downtown. There is a **Visitor Information** desk on the arrivals floor (Level 2) and an airport information desk (which operates a lost-and-found service) in the departure lounge, along with most of the shops. There are also plenty of phones and ATMs, a children's play area and a nursery. Three forms of transport head Downtown from outside the international terminal: the **Airporter Shuttle Bus**, T604-946 8866, www.yvrairporter.com, leaves every 15 minutes from 0820-2135, running to Downtown hotels and Canada Place ($13.50 one-way, $21 return); **taxis** operate around the clock, charging $25-30 for the 25-minute trip downtown; a limousine from **Limojet Gold** ① *T1800-278 8742, www.limojetgold.com*, costs $45 for up to eight passengers. All the major car rental agencies are located on the ground floor of the indoor car park. **City bus** No 424 runs from the domestic terminal (follow the signs) to Airport Station, ask for a transfer. From there, buses No 98B and 496 run downtown (45 minutes in total). A new high speed light railway, the **Canada Line**, connecting Vancouver International Airport with Downtown, is due to open in November 2009 in time for the 2010 Olympics.

All long-distance buses and trains arrive at the **VIA Rail Pacific Central Station** ① *1150 Station St, T1888-842 7245*, a short **SkyTrain** ride from Downtown. **BC Ferries** arrive from Victoria and the southern Gulf Islands at Tsawwassen, about 30 km south of Vancouver. City buses run downtown from the ferry terminal ($5). Ferries from Nanaimo in central Vancouver Island arrive at Horseshoe Bay, 15 km northwest on Highway 99, with two direct buses Downtown ($3.75). ▸▸ *For further details, see Transport, page 76.*

Getting around

Many of Vancouver's attractions are concentrated within the Downtown peninsula, which is best explored on foot. The public transport system operated by **TransLink** consists of buses, an elevated rail system called the **SkyTrain**, and a passenger ferry called the **SeaBus**. The same tickets are valid for all three. The SkyTrain is the quickest, most efficient way to get around, but its route is of limited use to visitors. Buses run everywhere but can be slow, and information on routes is rarely displayed. If time is limited, think about taking taxis. A couple of private mini-ferries also ply the waters of False Creek. ▸▸ *For further details, see Transport, page 76.*

: Airport art

Vancouver International Airport is packed with some wonderful pieces of art. Before clearing the arrivals hall, have a look at the *Spindle Whorl*, a giant version of a traditional Coast Salish art form. Carved out of red cedar, it is suspended from a wall of granite shingles over which water flows, suggesting the rivers that are so integral to Salish life. On the arrivals level of the terminal building is a pair of 6-m high *Welcome Figures*, carved from the same red cedar log.

Don't even think about leaving this building without going upstairs to see Bill Reid's exquisite *Spirit of Haida Gwaii, the Jade Canoe*. This bronze casting with its distinctive green patina is considered his masterpiece and he is credited as the man who reintroduced North west Coast native carving to the world (see page 53). Behind it is *The Great Wave Wall*, a giant piece of glass art that changes with the light to suggest the ocean.

Best time to visit

As with most of Western Canada, there is little doubt that summer is the best time to visit Vancouver, unless you're looking for winter sports. Temperatures are high but not uncomfortably so (average 21.7°C), Vancouver's lively residents take to the beaches, parks and mountains, and a string of great festivals keep the party spirit flowing.

Climate

Vancouver is a rainy city, with an average of 170 days of precipitation per year. Since the local topography involves a jump from sea level to mountains within a few kilometres, plus close proximity to the Pacific Ocean, the Georgia Strait and the mountains of Vancouver Island and Washington's Olympia Range, it's not surprising that the weather here is unpredictable. Forecasts are definitely not to be trusted. Having said that, a warm Pacific Ocean current combined with a strong airflow originating near Hawaii help make Vancouver's climate the mildest in Canada. Spring flowers start blooming in early March, and winter snowfalls are rare enough to throw the city's motorists into confusion. For these reasons Vancouver has been called the Canadian city with the best climate and the worst weather.

Tourist information

Vancouver's main tourist office is the **Touristinfo Centre** ① *Plaza Level, Waterfront Centre, 200 Burrard St, T604-683 2000, www.tourismvancouver.com, daily 0830-1800*. Staff are friendly and extremely efficient, and the range of facilities is excellent. A broad range of literature is available on the city and province, as well as illustrated details of hotels and B&Bs, travel information, a reservation service, currency exchange and branches of **Ticketmaster** and **Tickets Tonight** (see page 68). For up-to-date listings and information, there are three magazines: *Official Visitors' Guide*, *Where Vancouver* and *Visitors' Choice Vancouver*. For nightlife and entertainment listings with a more streetwise angle, pick up a free copy of the *Georgia Straight*.

Downtown ⬤🎭🎵 ›› *pp58-84.*

In keeping with its status as the heart of one of the world's youngest cities, Vancouver's Downtown presents the visitor with a fine example of postmodern aesthetics; a constantly evolving hotchpotch of architecture, where sleek glass-and-chrome skyscrapers rub shoulders with Gothic churches, Victorian warehouses and a handful of curiosities. The best way to appreciate this jamboree bag is on foot, so the peninsula is presented here as a walk, starting at the **TouristinfoCentre**, following an anticlockwise circle around Downtown, Yaletown, Chinatown, East Side and Gastown, then shooting north through the West End to Stanley Park.

Canada Place and around

Built to resemble an ocean liner, with five giant white masts rising from its 'deck', Canada Place begs comparisons with Sydney's famous opera house. The main terminus for Vancouver's thriving cruise-ship business, it also has an **IMAX theatre** ⓘ T604-682 4629, www.imax.com/vancouver, $12, child $11, at the back. Opposite the **Touristinfo Centre** on Burrard is the magnificent **Marine Building**, the British Empire's tallest building for more than a decade after its completion in 1930, and described by Sir John Betjeman as "the best art-deco office building in the world". In keeping with the architects' vision of "some great crag rising from the sea", the relief frieze around its base and the brass surroundings of its double revolving doors are dotted with marine flora and fauna. The art deco façade is decorated with panels illustrating the history of transport. Over the main entrance, Captain Vancouver's ship *Discovery* is seen on the horizon, with Canada geese flying across the stylized sunrays. The lobby is designed to resemble a Mayan temple.

Up the road is the old **Canadian Pacific Railway (CPR) Station** ⓘ 601 West Cordova St. Built in 1914, this neoclassical beaux-arts-style building with its arches and white columned façade is now a terminus for the **SeaBus** and the **SkyTrain**. The 1978 restoration retained many features of the original interior such as the high ceilings, woodworking and tile floor. Almost opposite is the **Lookout! Harbour Centre Tower** ⓘ 555 West Hastings St, T604-6890421, www.vancouverlookout.com, mid-Oct to Apr daily 0900-2100, May to mid-Oct daily 0830-2230, $13, youth $9, child $6, hourly guided tours included, with its flying-saucer-shaped top level. No longer the tallest building in BC, the observation deck here still gives the best close-up 360° views of the city, particularly striking at sunset on a clear day. In 50 seconds, glass-walled elevators on the outside of the building whisk you up the 167 m. From there it is much easier to get a feeling for the layout and architecture of the city. The ticket is expensive but allows as many visits on the same day as you wish.

Vancouver Art Gallery and around

ⓘ 750 Hornby St, T604-662 4719, www.vanartgallery.bc.ca. Mon, Wed, Fri-Sun 1000-1730, Tue and Thu 1000-2100, $15, under 12 $6, under 4 free. Suggested donation of $5 on Tue evenings.

The Art Gallery occupies an imposing neoclassical marble building designed by Francis Rattenbury in 1910 as Vancouver's original courthouse, and renovated in 1983 by Arthur Erickson. Of the 9000 works in its collection, only the **Emily Carr Institute** is a permanent fixture, but this justifies a visit in itself. The world's largest collection of works by this prominent Victoria artist (see page 380) are accompanied by a video about her life. The four spacious floors are dedicated to temporary exhibitions, which tend to be contemporary and hit-and-miss, but potentially involve some top names. The gallery shop is a great place to buy original crafts and the café is worth a visit.

Hotel Vancouver across the road is one of the city's most distinctive landmarks. A typical example of the grand hotels erected across Canada by the Canadian Pacific Railway, this hulking Gothic castle sports a striking green copper roof, gargoyles, some fine relief sculpture and an admirably opulent interior. Dwarfed by the surrounding modern giants, **Christ Church Cathedral** (finished in 1889) is Vancouver's oldest surviving church. Built in Gothic Revival style, this buttressed sandstone building features a steep gabled roof, impressive pointed-arch, stained-glass windows and some splendid interior timber framework. **Cathedral Place**, next door, has a neo-Gothic lobby full of art deco features that leads to a lovely grassy courtyard. On the same block

⁝ Orientation

Unlike most North American cities, Vancouver's Downtown streets have names rather than numbers, making orientation more tricky. If in doubt, remember that the mountains are always north. Block numbering is divided into east and west by Ontario Street, which runs in a north-south direction just east of the Downtown core. So, the address 39 W Broadway is in the block immediately west of Ontario, whereas 297 W Fourth Avenue would be in the third block west.

Unlike most cities built on a grid, the numbers of avenues in Vancouver do not correspond directly to block numbers. To work out the block number from a numbered avenue, add 16. So numbers between Eighteenth and Nineteenth Avenue will start at 3400.

of Hornby Street is the **Bill Reid Gallery** ① *639 Hornby St, T604-682 3455, www.billreidgallery.ca*, due to open in May 2008. This important new gallery will feature many works by the master Haida artist, including the bronze killer whale and his largest stone carving, in onyx, *The Raven and the First Men*. The **Treasure Box Gallery** will contain case after case of his jewellery, while the **Audain Great Hall** will contain his monumental bronze frieze, *Mythic Messengers*, and a new pole carved for the gallery by Jim Hart. Opening in Spring 2009, the exhibition **Continuum** will aim to draw attention to the false dichotomy that places traditional or classical style in opposition to contemporary art, featuring commissioned works by 22 Aboriginal artists from along the Northwest Coast of BC, Alaska and Washington State. Opposite, the **HSBC Building** ① *Mon-Thu 0800-1630, Fri 0800-1700*, has a towering atrium lobby containing the world's largest pendulum, and one of Vancouver's best unofficial art galleries and cafés.

Robson Street is Vancouver's undisputed shopping focus, and Granville is the heart of the justly named **Entertainment District**. The junction of these two busy streets is the unofficial pivot of this bustling city, though Granville is temporarily disrupted by major construction of a new SkyTrain line.

Yaletown and the Public Library

A small triangle of land to the south, hemmed in by False Creek, and Homer and Nelson streets, and concentrated on Hamilton and Mainland, **Yaletown** was once Vancouver's rowdy warehouse district, with more saloons per kilometre than anywhere else in the world. Today, most of the massive old brick buildings have been converted into spacious apartments, trendy bars and upmarket restaurants which line the narrow streets whose atmosphere owes much to the raised brick walkways of former loading docks. Finally mellowing into a genuine sense of style, this is a fascinating and unique area to explore, especially at night.

The curving walls and tiered arches of nearby **Vancouver Public Library** bear a resemblance to the Roman colosseum, whatever architect Moshe Safdie might say, and this postmodern masterpiece, classical and futuristic in equal measure, contains a pleasant shop-filled atrium spanned by elegant bridges. Nearby is the Gothic Revival **Cathedral of our Lady of the Rosary**, built in the late 1880s with asymmetrical towers, a vaulted ceiling and some decent stained-glass windows.

BC Place and Science World

① *1455 Québec St. SkyTrain, bus No 3 or 8 on Granville or Hastings, or No 19 on Pender.*
Just east of Yaletown is the vast air-supported dome of **BC Place Stadium**. From behind here a ferry runs across, and the sea wall promenade runs around,

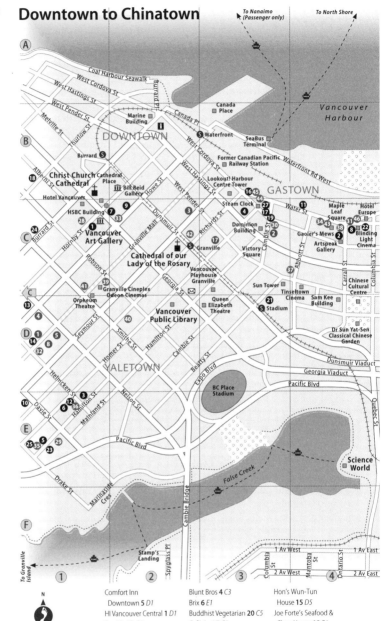

N

200 metres
200 yards

Sleeping 🛏
Bosman's Motor Hotel **4** *D1*
Cambie Hostel Gastown
 & Cambie Pub **2** *C3*
Cambie Hostel
 Seymour **3** *C2*

Comfort Inn
 Downtown **5** *D1*
HI Vancouver Central **1** *D1*
Patricia **13** *C6*
SameSun Backpacker
 Lodge **8** *D1*
Victorian **17** *C3*

Eating 🍴
Bamboo Café **19** *C3*
Blake's **2** *C4*
Blue Water Café & Raw
 Bar **3** *E1*

Blunt Bros **4** *C3*
Brix **6** *E1*
Buddhist Vegetarian **20** *C5*
Café Ami **7** *C2*
Café Dolcino **8** *C4*
Chambar **21** *D3*
Coast **5** *E1*
Cobre **22** *C4*
DIVA at the Met **9** *C2*
Elbow Room **10** *E1*
Gallery Café **1** *C1*
Ganache Patisserie **25** *E1*

Hon's Wun-Tun
 House **15** *D5*
Joe Forte's Seafood &
 Chop House **18** *B1*
Kitanoya Guu **16** *B3*
La Luna Café **11** *C4*
Le Crocodile **24** *C1*
Plan B **12** *E1*
Relish **13** *D1*
Rodney's Oyster
 House **23** *E1*
The Annex **17** *C3*
The Templeton **14** *D1*

Related maps
Kitislano, page 60
West End, page 62

False Creek to another of Vancouver's unusual structures, a giant silver golf ball that makes a suitably futuristic venue for **Science World** ① T604-443 7443, www.science world.bc.ca, Mon-Fri 1000- 1700, Sat-Sun 1000-1800, $16, youth $13, child $11, with Omnimax $21, youth $18, child $16. Educational, fascinating and entertaining in equal measures, this place is a delight for adults but particularly kids. You can investigate the wonders of your own body and mind in the **BodyWorks Gallery**, explore the mysteries of water, light, sound and motion in the **Eureka! Gallery** and have your mind bent and senses deceived by the **Illusion Gallery**. **The Kidspace Gallery** has lots of hands-on stuff for younger children, the **Sara Stern Search Gallery** encourages exploration of the natural world and the **Our World Gallery** does a good job of making environmental lessons fun. There are live demonstrations on the Centre Stage, free High Definition films in the science feature and an the **Alcan Omnimax** theatre whose 27-m diameter dome screen and 10,000-watt wrap-around speakers have the edge over the giant IMAX.

Chinatown

Main Street heads north to Vancouver's bustling Chinatown, which, in keeping with the city's east-meets-west persona, is the third biggest in North America after New York and San Francisco. The restaurants here are as authentic as you'll ever find outside China and the streets are lined with noisy shops selling the kind of weird and wonderful ingredients only the Chinese would know how to cook (look out for the geoducks). An experience not to be missed is the open-air **night market** ① Keefer and Main St, www.vcma.shawbiz.ca, May-Sep Fri-Sun 1830-2300, T604-682 8998. Ninety-minute tours of the district are offered by the **Chinese Cultural Centre** ① 50 E Pender, T604-658 8883, www.cccvan.com, Jun-Sep, $10 ($11 with Museum tour), child $7, $13 and $8 with a slide show, and inevitably include the disappointing **Sam Kee Building**, aka 'Slender on Pender'. The story goes that when the city appropriated most of Chang Toy's 30-ft lot for street widening, his neighbour expected to get the remaining 6 ft at a bargain price, but to frustrate him Toy built the world's skinniest building.

Water Street Café **27** C3

Bars & clubs ●
Alibi Room **26** C5
Bacchus **28** C1
Bar None **29** E1
Cambie **30** C3
Chill Winston **31** C4
Crush Champagne
 Lounge **32** D1
Element Sound
 Lounge **33** C2
Fabric **34** C4

Flight **35** E1
George Ultra Lounge **36** E1
Honey Lounge **37** C4
Irish Heather **38** C4
Lennox **39** C1
Lucy Mae Brown **40** D2
Plaza Club **41** C1
Railway Club **42** C2
Salt **43** C4
Shine **44** B3
Steamworks **45** B3
The Modern **46** C4

⦂ East meets West

The Oriental community of Lotus Land is in itself a rich multicultural mix, embracing immigrants from Hong Kong, Taiwan, China, the Philippines, Japan, South Korea, Malaysia and Singapore. Asians now account for nearly one-third of Vancouver's population – with 38% of BC's exports flowing into the Pacific Rim – but they have not always been made so welcome. The first Chinese settlers came up from San Francisco during the Fraser Valley Gold Rush of 1858. Queen Victoria gave assent in 1875 to an act passed in BC's legislature to deny Chinese and First Nations people the vote, a law that remained in effect for more than 70 years. During the 1880s, a great influx arrived to work on the Canadian Pacific Railway. They received half the wage of their white fellows and were often used as cannon fodder during dynamite blasting. It is estimated that three Chinese lives were lost for every kilometre of track laid in the almost impenet- rable Fraser Canyon. Over 24 items of anti-Chinese legislation such as head-taxes were passed in BC between 1878 and 1913 alone, and public hostility also included rallies, campaigns and rampaging mobs. During World War II, Japanese citizens were rounded up, robbed of all their possessions and removed to internment camps in BC's interior.

Infinitely more worthwhile is **Dr Sun Yat-Sen Classical Chinese Garden** ⓘ *578 Carrall St, T604-662 3207, www.vancouverchinesegarden.com, May to mid-Jun 1000-1800, mid-Jun to Aug 0930-1900, Sep 1000-1800, Oct-Apr 1000-1630, $10, child $7, under 5 free, bus No 19 or 22 east on Pender*, the first authentic Ming classical garden built since 1492, and the first ever outside China. Created by 52 experts from Suzhou, this is a carefully planned realm of symmetry, simplicity and symbolism, where buildings, rocks, water and plants recreate a microcosm of the world. There are walls within walls, courtyards within courtyards, pavilions, bridges and galleries. Hourly guided tours, included with admission, are recommended for an understanding of the Taoist principles at work. Music events and art exhibitions are hosted in summer.

East Side

Just a block north of Chinatown is Vancouver's seediest quarter, the East Side. Over a century ago, when the city's first trams connected Gastown to a newly emerging business district along Granville, Hastings Street entered a decline that has led to its current rating as Canada's lowest-income postal district. The corner with Main in particular has become notorious as a meeting place for Vancouver's homeless and drug addicts. Some of the last remaining examples of neon have survived here from an era when Vancouver had 18,000 such signs. There are also some interesting buildings. In 1910, the distinctive French classical-style **Dominion Building** ⓘ *207 West Hastings*, was the British Empire's tallest and most modern structure. Two years later, its record height was topped by the nearby **Sun Tower** ⓘ *100 West Pender*. Opposite the Dominion Building is **Victory Square**, now run-down and nicknamed 'Pigeon Park'. Just east of Main, on Cordova, is the **Firehall Arts Centre** and **St James Anglican Church**, which combines touches of the Romanesque, Gothic, Byzantine and modern.

Gastown

Keep walking north and you arrive in **Gastown**, site of Vancouver's first industry and, maybe more importantly, the saloon of 'Gassy' Jack Deighton, after whom the district

was named. One of Vancouver's favourite historic characters, he is remembered for
rowing across the Burrard Inlet and offering a bunch of thirsty workers at Stamp's Mill
all the whisky they could drink if they helped him build a bar. Within 24 hours the
Globe Saloon was finished. A statue of the legendary Yorkshireman standing on a
whisky barrel graces the quaint **Maple Leaf Square**. Behind him is the site of his
second saloon, along with **Gaoler's Mews**, an attractive little courtyard. Opposite is the
thin curved end of the wedge-shaped **Hotel Europe** (1909), the first reinforced-concrete
building in Vancouver and certainly one of its most charming constructions.

Just west of here is Gastown's main drag, Water Street, site of the much-touted
Steam Clock, which entertains tourists every 15 minutes by tooting and erupting in a
cloud of steam. Still overrun with souvenir shops, the street is finally becoming less
tacky and is positively gorgeous when illuminated at night. Many handsome old
red-brick buildings and cobbled streets redeem Gastown, which also holds some of
the city's best antique shops, commercial art galleries, bars and clubs.

West End to Stanley Park ⊜⊘⊘⊘ ›› pp59-68.

West End

The most interesting way to get to Stanley Park is via **Robson Street**, which is lined with
fashionable boutiques and restaurants, and perpetually thronged with trendsetters,
posers and Japanese students. It marks the northeast boundary of the **West End**,
Western Canada's most densely populated area, whose proximity keeps the Downtown
core perpetually buzzing through the night. The rectangle is completed by Denman and
Davie streets, both packed with restaurants and cafés, creating a neighbourhood vibe
that gains much of its character from the district's large gay community.

Most of the area's traditional buildings were replaced with high-rises during
the 1960s. The best surviving block is **Barclay Heritage Square**, where a park-like
setting contains nine historic houses built 1890-1908. One 1893 Queen Anne
Revival-style home, furnished in Edwardian style and attributed to architect Francis
Rattenbury, has been converted into the **Roedde House Museum** ① *1415 Barclay St,
T604- 684 7040, www.roeddehouse.org, guided tours only, mid-May to mid-Sep
Tue-Fri 1000-1600, $5, tea and tour Sun 1400-1600, $6, bus No 5 to Broughton*, and
provides an opportunity to see inside one of these buildings.

Stanley Park

① *T604-257 8400, www.vancouverparks.ca. Stanley Park never closes but isolated
trails should be avoided after dark. Bus No 135 Mon-Sat daytime , No 23 or 25 evening
or on Sun. Parking $2 hr or $7 day. From mid-Mar to end Oct, an Express Bus runs 5
times daily from Downtown hotels and Canada Place to Stanley Park, $3, redeemable
against horse-drawn tours or aquarium passes. A free shuttle bus runs round the park
every 15 mins mid-Jun to late Sep.*

The peninsula's northwestern tip is dedicated to the 450-ha Stanley Park.
Miraculously, this evergreen oasis has been allowed to remain undeveloped, most of
its space filled with second-growth but still giant cedar, hemlock and fir. Restorations
following a devastating storm in 2006 are due to end late 2008. At the park's entrance
is the extensive **Lost Lagoon**, a haven for swans, ducks, geese and the occasional
blue heron. The Ecology Society based in the newly renovated **Nature House**
① *T604-257 8544, www.stanleyparkecology.ca, mid-May to mid-Sep Tue-Sun
1000-1900, mid-Sep-mid-May Fri 1200-1600, Sat-Sun 0930-1630*, offers ecological
information and useful maps, and organizes two-hour Sunday **EcoWalks** ① *daily 1300,
$10, child $5*, birdwatching and other children's activities.

Particularly in summer, the action is focused around the 9-km sea wall, a
first-class walk, jog, rollerblade or bike ride, which follows the park's perimeter

The Seawall Promenade

The 9-km sea wall around Stanley Park has long been celebrated as one of Vancouver's highlights. An unbroken sea wall promenade now runs from the end of Burrard Place near Canada Place, along Coal Harbour, round Stanley Park, through Sunset Beach Park, round False Creek, past Science World, around Granville Island, through Vanier Park and Kits Beach, and all the way to Spanish Banks Beach in Point Gray, 28 km in all. This waterfront environment represents an integral facet of Vancouver's complex personality, as important as any of the city's neighbourhoods, and we strongly recommend getting at least a taste of it. Cycling is the ultimate way to explore, for details, see Activities and tours, page 75.

between a number of viewpoints, notably the popular **Prospect Point**. Equipment can be hired from shops at the north end of Denman Street, where cyclists and rollerbladers begin the anticlockwise circuit. A further 20-odd km of sea wall continues round False Creek, past Kitsilano and almost to UBC. A couple of decent beaches hug the west side, including **Second Beach**, where facilities include a heated ocean-side **swimming pool** ① T604-257 8370, $5, youth $3.70, child $2.50. Nearby, the **Rhododendron Garden** shelters a collection of ornamental trees, including azaleas, camellias and magnolia. The bulk of the park's interior is devoted to shady walking paths, which were once skid roads used by early loggers to drag mighty trees down to the water. Look for the stump of one such, now endangered, giant known as the **Hollow Tree**. Between here and Third Beach is a living cedar believed to be one of the largest trees and oldest cedars, it's almost 5 m across and roughly 1000 years old.

To protect this central area from overuse, most of the park's attractions are concentrated on the narrow spit that juts out north of the sheltered Coal Harbour. Next door to the Vancouver Rowing Club is an information booth, and base of the one-hour **horse-drawn tours** ① T604-681 5115, www.stanleyparktours.com, Mar and Oct 0940-1600, Apr-Jun and Sep 0940-1700, Jul-Sep 0940-1730, every 20-30 mins, $25, child $15. To the north are a **Rose Garden** and the **Malkin Bowl**, home to the **Theatre Under the Stars** ① T604-687 0174, www.tuts.bc.ca, Jul-Aug daily 2000. Nearby are the **Aquarium**, a **Water Park**, a **Miniature Railway** and the **Children's Farmyard** ① T604-257 8531, Apr-Sep daily 1100-1600, Oct-Mar weekends only, railway or farmyard $5.50, youth $4, child $2.75. Further round the shore of Coal Harbour, past the Royal Vancouver Yacht Club, is **Brockton Point**, which has a picturesque old lighthouse and a decent stand of Kwakiutl and Haida totem poles. At the eastern point is the **9 O'clock Gun**, a cannon that has been fired at that hour every evening since a century ago, when it signalled the end of the day's legal fishing.

Vancouver Aquarium Marine Science Centre ① T604-659 3474, www.vana qua.org, mid-May to mid-Sep daily 0930-1900, mid-Sep to mid-May 0930-1700, $20, youth $15, child $12, bus No 19 from Georgia, one of Vancouver's prime rainy-day activities, is even better when the sun shines since the most exciting animals – seals, dolphins and otters – live outside. Even these are utterly upstaged by a pair of giant and graceful white beluga whales that can be watched from an underwater viewing room downstairs, where a wealth of background information includes a video of the female giving birth. It's best to save the belugas until last though, as the other 60,000 creatures from the world's many seas tend to pale by comparison. Indoor highlights include the Treasures of the BC Coast gallery, with a giant Pacific octopus, coral, anemones and some eerily beautiful jellyfish; a large collection of handsome frogs; and the Tropic Zone and Amazon Rainforest galleries. There are several talks and

Outside, look out for Bill Reid's magnificent bronze sculpture of a killer whale, *The Chief of the Undersea World (1984).*

Granville Island to Point Grey 🍴🎭🎿 ⟫ *p 58-84.*

Granville Island

ⓘ *Although Granville Island is always open, many attractions are closed on Mon. Parking can be a nightmare, so avoid driving and take the ferry ($2.25, and the best way to arrive) from the Aquatic Centre next to Burrard Bridge, or Bus No 50 from Granville St and then walk.*

When Vancouver was first settled, the waterfront area of False Creek was five times the size it is today. Land has been reclaimed all around the inlet, much of it for Expo '86. Nowhere has this process been more successful than at Granville Island. Originally no more than a sandbar, the area was built up into an industrial zone, then transformed into an attractive yachting, shopping and arts district and has become a magnet for tourists and locals. The ambience is similar to London's Covent Garden and there are countless arts and crafts shops scattered around, or clustered together in the **Net Loft** ⓘ *daily 1000-1700,* or on Railspur Alley.

Though not strictly pedestrianized, the island is well geared to aimless strolling. Meander at will, but be sure not to miss the **Public Market** ⓘ *daily 0900-1900.* As well as a mouth-watering collection of international fast food stalls, the place is packed with tempting produce from gourmet breads to seafood and sausages. The building itself is a fine lesson in the renovation of industrial structures, making great use of the natural lighting, large windows and doors, heavy timber and steel. The courtyard outside and adjacent bars are good places to watch the aquatic world float by and nearby is Canada's first microbrewery, **Granville Island Brewing Company** ⓘ *1441 Cartwright St, T604-687 2739, www.gib.ca, tours run daily 1200, 1400 and 1600, $9.75, 40 mins, include tasters and a souvenir glass.*

Close to the road entrance is a **Visitor Information Centre** ⓘ *T604-666 5784, daily 0900-1800,* which provides a *Visitors' Guide* with discount vouchers and a very useful map. There are also a number of sights perfect for children, including the **Kids' Market**, the **Waterpark** – an aquatic play area with multiple slides and a playground, and the **Model Ships and Model Trains Museums** ⓘ *1502 Duranleau St, T604-683 1939, www.modelshipsmuseum.ca, www.modeltrainsmuseum.ca, Tue-Sun 1000-1730, $7.50, child $3.50.* Tucked away in the Maritime Market, these two museums rolled into one represent one of Vancouver's most unexpected delights. Even if you have just a passing interest in models, it's well worth a visit. It includes the world's largest collection of model toy trains and a fabulous O-scale working layout that took 20,000 hours to complete. The extensive collection of model ships and submarines includes several dozen, huge, one-off pieces that demonstrate an obsessive attention to detail.

Vanier Park

ⓘ *Bus No 2 or 22 from Burrard then walk or take the ferry from the Aquatic Centre. Contains 3 fairly important sights, which can all be seen with an Explore Pass, $30, under 18 $24.*

Part of the sea wall promenade leads west from Granville Island to Vanier Park, a small but pretty and popular summer hang-out. Housed in a building whose interesting shape was inspired by the hats of Haida natives, the **Vancouver Museum** ⓘ *T604-736 4431, www.vanmuseum.bc.ca, Fri-Wed 1000-1700, Thu 1000-2100, mid-Sep to mid-May closed Mon, $10, under 18 $6, under 5 free, with Space Centre $17, under 18 $11,* has a small collection of artefacts and recreated scenes that tell the story of the city's first explorers and settlers. Often of greater interest are temporary exhibits such as The Unnatural History of Stanley Park, starting September 2008.

Sharing the same building is the more upbeat **HR MacMillan Space Centre** ① *T604-738 7827, www.hrmacmillanspacecentre.com, mid-Jun to mid-Sep daily 1000-1700, mid-Sep to mid-Jun Tue-Sun 1000-1700, $15, under 18 $10.75, under 5 free, observatory open Fri-Sat sunset-2400, free*. Its collection of interactive exhibits in the Cosmic Courtyard talk you through the Earth's geological composition, the nature of life in space and the logistics of space travel. The Planetarium hosts a variety of 40-minute shows in the afternoon, and laser shows set to the music of bands like Radiohead and Pink Floyd on Thursday to Saturday evenings ($10.75). **Ground Station Canada Theatre** holds video-assisted lectures involving experiments designed to interest kids. Tickets include a 15-minute ride in the Virtual Voyages Simulator.

The front section of the nearby **Maritime Museum** ① *1905 Ogden Av, T604-257 8300, www.vancouvermaritimemuseum.com, mid-May to mid-Sep daily 1000-1700, mid-Sep to mid-May Tue-Sat 1000-1700, Sun 1200-1700, $10, under 18 $7.50, under 5 free*, has a distinctive, steep triangular shape because it was built around the RCMP vessel, *St Roch*, which has been lovingly restored to its original 1944 condition. Before exploring this hardy little ship, watch the video about all the firsts it achieved: first to travel the treacherous and long-sought Northwest Passage, a 27-month journey from Vancouver to Halifax; first to make the same trip back via the faster, more northerly route; and first to circumnavigate North America. This is the museum's highlight but there's much more to see, with lots of artefacts and stories, a fun exhibit on pirates, a hands-on area for children and some bigger pieces on the lawn outside. There is usually also an interesting guest exhibit.

Kitsilano
① *Bus No 2 or 22 south on Burrard to Cornwall then walk.*
Walking westwards on the well-used path, Vanier Park melds seamlessly into **Kitsilano** (or Kits) **Beach**, the most popular stretch of sand in the city, with great views of English Bay, Downtown and the Coast Mountains, and Canada's longest **Outdoor Pool** ① *T604-731 0011, 22 May-12 Sep Mon-Fri 1200-2045, Sat-Sun 1000-2045, $5, youth $3.70 , child $2.50*. In the 1960s, Kitsilano was the main focus of Vancouver's subculture. By the 1980s, many of the local hippies had got high-paying jobs, bought and restored their houses, and helped turn Kits into a Yuppie's dream. Many of the old wooden town houses have been replaced by condos, but plenty of character remains and the area's two main drags, **West Fourth between Burrard and Vine** ① *bus No 4 or 7*, and the less interesting **West Broadway between MacDonald and Waterloo** ① *bus No 10 or 16*, offer some of the city's best browsing strips, with plenty of interesting speciality shops, trendy hair studios, snowboard outlets and good restaurants. Weekend brunch here is a Vancouver institution, but parking can be a nightmare (try Fifth).

Point Grey
From Kitsilano, Fourth Avenue and the more scenic Point Grey Road lead west to the jutting nose of Point Grey, home to some of the city's best beaches, the University of British Columbia (UBC), some botanical gardens and Vancouver's best sight, the Museum of Anthropology. On the way is Vancouver's oldest building, **Hastings Mill Store** ① *1575 Alma St, T604-734 1212, mid-Jun to mid-Sep Tue-Sun 1100-1600, mid-Sep-mid-Jun Sat-Sun 1300-1600, entry by donation, bus No 9 Broadway or No 4, 7 or 44 to Alma and walk*. Transported from its original Gastown site in 1930, today it houses a small museum with displays of First Nations and pioneer artefacts.

From here, a clutch of beaches and parks run almost uninterrupted around the edge of Point Grey. First of these is Jericho Beach, set in a large, very scenic park with a fine youth hostel, a sailing school and a bird sanctuary. Three unbroken kilometres

⦂ Bill Reid

Born in Vancouver to a Haida mother and Scottish-American father, Bill Reid (1920-1998) was a teenager before he was told about his native heritage. Though he only began investigating Haida arts at the age of 31, he was clearly to the manner born, quickly gaining international recognition for his carvings and castings. In the words of Barry Mowatt, President of Vancouver's Inuit Gallery: "He is the pre-eminent West Coast native artist, who is responsible for re-creation of respect for the art of Northwest Coast people. He is probably the most important and significant native artist ever to have come to the world stage". Anthropologist Edmund Carpenter wrote: "I've followed Bill Reid's career for many years and come to believe that, in some strange way, the spirit of Haida art, once the lifeblood of an entire people, now survives within him, at a depth, and with an intensity, unrelated to any 'revival' or 'preservation', but deriving from primary sources and leading to daring innovations".

You can see Bill Reid's work in Vancouver at the airport, outside the aquarium and, above all, in the UBC Museum of Anthropology.

lead to **Locarno Beach**, a quiet area popular with families, and **Spanish Banks**, which has a beach café and warm, shallow water that's ideal for paddling. From UBC, roughly where Marine Drive meets University Boulevard, about 100 steps lead down through the forest to the 6-km strip of **Wreck Beach**. On a hot day as many as 10,000 sun-worshippers take advantage of its clothing-optional status, while wandering peddlers supply them with cold beers, food and the ubiquitous BC Bud.

UBC Museum of Anthropology

ⓘ *6393 NW Marine Dr, T604-822 5087, www.moa.ubc.ca. Mid-May to mid-Oct Wed-Sun 1000-1700, Tue 1000-2100, mid-Oct to mid-May Wed-Sun 1100-1700, Tue 1100-2100, $9, under 18 $7, under 6 free, Tue 1700-2100, $5. Bus No 4 or 10 south on Granville then walk, or change to No 42 at Alma. Avoid driving as parking is the most expensive in town and is limited to 2 hrs.*

Founded in 1949, and situated on native Musqueam land, the extraordinary UBC Museum of Anthropology is the only attraction in Vancouver that absolutely must be seen. By the end of 2009, $52 million worth of renewals are due to expand its size by 50%. Designed by Arthur Erickson to echo the post-and-beam structures of Northwest Coast First Nations, it contains the world's finest collection of carvings by master craftsmen from many of these Nations, most notably the Haida of Haida Gwaii (Queen Charlotte Islands) and the Gitxsan and Nisga'a from the Skeena River region of Northern BC. Be sure to pick up a *Gallery Guide* at the admissions desk ($1.50). As well as providing a commentary on the exhibits, it gives a brief but excellent introduction to First Nations cultures, the stylistic differences between them and an overview of their classic art forms.

Sculptures inside are grouped by cultural area and are informatively labelled. Most date from the early to mid-19th century, but an encouraging number are recent including several exceptional works by the late master Bill Reid, such as Bear (1963), *Sea Wolf with Killer Whales* (1962), a 7.5-m inshore cedar canoe (1985) and, housed in a natural light-filled rotunda, his most exquisite masterpiece, *The Raven and the First Men* (1980). Master carver Lyle Wilson can be seen at work in the Great Hall, and behind the Hall are a number of outdoor exhibits, including a large Haida family dwelling and a collection of 10 poles. The Visible Storage galleries make over

14,000 smaller carvings accessible to the public, about 40% of the museum's permanent collection. It's hard to do the museum justice in one visit, especially as a bit of energy should be reserved for the small gift shop in the lobby, which is packed with splendid books, carvings, jewellery and prints.

Nitobe and UBC Botanical Gardens

A short stroll from the museum is the **Nitobe Memorial Garden** ① *T604-822 9666, www.nitobe.org, mid-May to mid-Sep daily 1000-1700, mid-Sep to mid-May Mon-Fri 1000-1430, $5, $10 with UBC gardens, by donation in winter*. An authentic Japanese tea garden, this is a subtle experience, with every rock, tree and pool playing its part in the delicate harmony to create an ambience that encourages reflection and meditation. There are cherry blossoms in spring, Japanese irises in summer and Japanese maples in autumn. Moving anticlockwise, the garden represents the stages of a person's life.

A further 3 km south on Marine Drive are the much more extensive but equally delightful **UBC Botanical Gardens** ① *6804 SW Marine Dr, T604-822 3928, www.ubc botanicalgarden.org, mid-May to mid-Sep daily 1000-1800, mid-Sep to mid-May 1000-1630, $7 for botanical garden, $10 with Nitobe, free tours Wed and Sat 1300, bus No 4 or 10 south on Granville*, the oldest of their kind in Canada. Spread over 30 ha are a number of expertly maintained themed gardens, such as the Physick Garden, devoted to traditional medicinal plants from 16th-century Europe. The experience is as educational as it is aesthetic, with well-labelled exhibits and regular lectures.

South and east Vancouver 🖼️🚻🚶 ►*p58-84.*

Neighbourhoods

The broad swathe of Vancouver south of Burrard Inlet is dotted with small, interesting neighbourhoods each with its own particular atmosphere. The most worthwhile is **Commercial Drive** ① *bus No 20*. Once known as Little Italy, the area still has a number of Italian coffee shops but has become much more cosmopolitan, populated by artists, immigrants and all manner of alternative individuals. There are no 'sights' as such, but it's a fascinating place to wander, eat, drink and people-watch. Main Street from Seventh to Sixteenth Avenues, known as 'Uptown', is dominated by trendy, gritty cafés and restaurants, boutiques and galleries. **South Main** or 'SoMa' from Sixteenth to Thirtieth Avenues has lots of antique and second-hand shops, and more boutiques. Further south on Main between Forty-ninth and Fifty-first Avenues is Vancouver's Indiatown, the **Punjabi Market**. If in the area, pay a visit to the splendid **Sikh Temple** ① *8000 Ross St*, another Arthur Erickson special. **South Granville**, from the bridge to Sixteenth Avenue abounds with antiques shops, private art galleries, boutiques and cafés.

Queen Elizabeth Park and VanDusen Botanical Garden

① *For information on both parks, visit www.vancouver.ca/parks.*
Conveniently close together near Granville, Cambie and Thirty-third Avenues, South Vancouver's two main pieces of green are both worth a visit. The 53-ha **Queen Elizabeth Park** ① *33rd Av/Cambie, T604-257 8570, Apr-Sep Mon-Fri 0900-2000, Sat-Sun 1000-2100, Oct-Mar 1000-1730, $4.25, child $2, bus No 15 on Burrard or Robson*, is the former site of two basalt quarries, now converted into ornamental gardens, which make for very pleasant summer strolling. Along with an extensive rose garden, there is an arboretum said to contain a specimen of almost every tree found in Canada. Paths lead to Vancouver's highest point (150 m), the peak of an extinct volcano, with good if rather obstructed views of the city below and the wonderfully romantic **Seasons in the Park** restaurant (see Eating, page 65). Nearby is the beautiful

Bloedel Floral Conservatory ⓘ *daily 1000-1700, $4.60, youth $3.45, child $2.30,*
a giant triodetic dome that contains 500 varieties of exotic plants from tropical rainforest, subtropical and desert ecosystems, as well as floral displays that change with the seasons, koi carp and about 100 species of free-flying tropical birds.

The 22-ha **VanDusen Botanical Garden** ⓘ *5251 Oak St and 37th Av, T604- 878 9274, www.vandusengarden.org, opens daily Jun-Aug 1000-2100, May 1000-2000, Apr 1000-1800, Sep 1000-1900, Oct-Mar 1000-1600, $8.50, under 18 $6.50, under 12 $4.25, under 6 free, bus No 17 on Burrard or Pender*, contains over 7500 different plants from around the world, including some rare species. Set around lakes, ponds and waterfalls, and dotted with sculptures, the 40-odd themed gardens are considerably more romantic and contemplative than those at UBC, and they feel bigger. A favourite with children is the Elizabethan hedge maze. In December the gardens host the **Festival of Lights** (see Festivals, page 72).

North Shore 🏊🏃 ▶ *p58-84.*

The mountainous landscapes, tracts of semi-wilderness and potential for outdoor pursuits offered by Vancouver's North Shore represent for many people the city's finest feature, though it's not the place to stay or eat. The obvious way to get there is on the SeaBus, a lovely inexpensive chance to get out on the water. It leaves from behind the Waterfront SkyTrain in the old CPR building and docks at **Lonsdale Quay Market**, the North Shore's only real focal point. Local buses continue from here. The glazed and galleried interior of the market, a throwback to 19th-century industrial architecture, is well worth a look.

East from Lion's Gate Bridge

The other main route to the North Shore is from Stanley Park across the **Lion's Gate Bridge**, the British Empire's longest suspension bridge when it was built in 1938, inspired by San Francisco's Golden Gate. Roughly 8 km east of from here, Lynn Valley Road leads to **Lynn Canyon Park** ⓘ *www.britishcolumbia.com/parks, Apr-Jun and Sep-Oct daily 0700-1900, Jul-Aug 0700-2100, Nov-Mar 0700-dusk, exit 19 from Hwy 1, bus No 229 from Lonsdale Quay,* 250 ha of relatively unspoilt forest and home to the tallest tree ever measured on the planet, a 120-m Douglas fir. The **Ecology Centre** ⓘ *3663 Peters Road, T604-981 3103, www.dnv.com, Jun-Sept, daily 1000-1700, Oct-May Mon-Fri 1000-1700, Sat-Sun 1200-1600, guided walks Jul-Aug daily 1400,* has displays, films and information about the park, as well as a free map. The 68-m suspension bridge that hovers 50 m above the rushing waters of Lynn Creek is free to walk across. Many hiking trails of varying length begin on the other side, including a 15-minute stroll to a wooden footbridge that crosses the creek at Twin Falls.

At the eastern end of the North Shore, Mount Seymour Road climbs steeply up 1000 vertical metres to **Mount Seymour Provincial Park**, passing two stunning viewpoints, both worth a stop. Other than the commercial ski hill, Mount Seymour, the park's semi-wilderness old-growth forest and sub-alpine wild flower meadows make for some excellent hiking. **Flower Lake Loop**, a pleasant 1.5-km stroll through bog and ponds, is a good place for spotting birds. **Mount Seymour** ⓘ *T604-986 2261, www.mountseymour.com, Mon-Fri 0930-2200, Sat-Sun 0830-2200, day pass $40, under 18 $33, under 12 $20, under 5 free, family pass $100, reduced rates from 1300 and 1600, night skiing 1600-2200, $31, under 18 $27, under 12 $16, snowshoeing, $26, concessions $21 including rentals, snowphone, T604-718 7771,* is the most affordable Vancouver ski hill and is good for beginners, with over 20 runs and two snowboard terrain parks. Ski and snowboard rentals are available, as are lesson, ticket and rental packages. A **shuttle bus** ⓘ *every hour, Dec-Mar, $4 one-way,* runs from Parkgate Mall in the afternoon during the week and from the early morning at weekends.

At the North Shore's eastern extremity is **Deep Cove** ⓘ *SeaBus, then bus No 229 to Phibbs Exchange, then bus No 211 or 212*, a picturesque spot that has retained the unspoilt feel of a seaside village and enjoys great views across the bay to snowy hills beyond. As well as prime kayaking and biking, there's a nice green park by the water, a few good restaurants and the best neighbourhood pub in Vancouver. ▶▶ *For further details, see Activities and tours, page 74.*

Capilano Valley and Grouse Mountain

Almost due north from the Lion's Gate Bridge, Capilano Road runs parallel to the eponymous river, valley and regional park all the way to the dammed Capilano Lake and beyond to Grouse Mountain. **Capilano Suspension Bridge** ⓘ *3735 Capilano Rd, T604-985 7474, www.capbridge.com, daily 0830 or 0900, closing hours vary, $26.95, under 16 $15.65, under 12 $8.30, under 6 free, parking $3, bus No 246 from Georgia or No 236 from Lonsdale Quay*, is Vancouver's oldest and most excessively vaunted attraction. The current bridge is the fourth to span the 137 m across Capilano River 70 m below, making it the longest and highest suspended footbridge in the world, and very exciting to cross. On the other side, the new **Treetops Adventure** consists of a series of smaller suspension bridges strung between Douglas firs up to 30 m high, offering a unique perspective from which to appreciate the astounding beauty of the surrounding rainforest . There's also a small collection of totem poles, a diminutive First Nations carving shed, a few photos and artefacts, and the Living Forest interactive exhibition, aimed at children, with lots of displays of dead bugs.

For a free and more genuine taste of the valley's natural beauty, head up the road to the 160-ha Capilano River Regional Park, which protects the Capilano River as it heads south to Burrard Inlet, a journey followed by the 7.5-km one-way **Capilano Pacific Trail**, the longest of 10 trails through unmanicured forest. Trail maps are available at the car park or from information centres, and they outline a number of pools and other features. The park also contains the **Capilano Salmon Hatchery** ⓘ *T604-666 1790, free*, one of the best places to see the salmon run and learn the extraordinary story of their journey.

Grouse Mountain ⓘ *T604-980 9311, ww.grousemountain.com, general admission, covering all activities but skiing $33, under 18 $19, under 12 $12, under 4 free, ski pass $47, under 18 $37, under 12 $21, night skiing 1600-2200, $37, under 18 $31, under 12 $19, 5-day pass $185, under 18 $155, under 12 $95*, is the most popular and easily reached ski hill on the North Shore, its lights seeming to hang from Vancouver's night-time skyline like Christmas tree decorations. It has easy access, tremendous views and the best facilities. There are 26 runs, predominantly intermediate, with a vertical drop of 384 m. There's also ice-skating, snowshoeing and 5 km of cross-country trails that are lit at night. Skiers and sightseers are whisked up to 1100 m above sea level in about eight minutes by the **Skyride Gondola** ⓘ *T604-980 9311, www.grousemountain.com, daily 0900-2200, every 15 mins, $33, under 18 $19, under 12 $12, under 4 free, SeaBus then bus No 236 from Lonsdale Quay*. At the top are year-round panoramic views, 5-m chainsaw sculptures, a 30-minute multimedia action film in the **Theatre in the Sky** and all kinds of facilities, including a couple of fine restaurants. In summer there's hiking, mountain biking, paragliding and horse-drawn carriage rides (the horses also come up in the gondolas); in winter there's downhill and cross-country snowboarding, ice-skating, snowshoeing and sleigh rides. All activities except access to the slopes are included with the gondola ticket.

West from Lion's Gate Bridge

Some 7 km west the access road to **Cypress Provincial Park** ⓘ *T604-926 5612, www.cypressmountain.com*, can be seen ascending the mountainous terrain in wide, drunken zigzags. This has been a popular recreation site since the 1920s, and offers the same range of summer and winter activities as Grouse Mountain, though with less extensive facilities and thinner crowds. Some of the North Shore's best hikes are here (see Activities and tours, page 75), leading to panoramic views that take in the city, Howe Sound, Mount Baker to the southeast, and the Gulf Islands, Georgia Strait and Vancouver Island to the west. There's also a lift-assisted mountain bike park. **Cypress Mountain** ⓘ *T604-926 5612, snowphone T604-419 7669, www.cypressmountain.com, ski pass $50, child $26, daily 0900-2200, night skiing $17, child $10, T604-922 0825*, is geared towards more advanced skiers, with the largest vertical drop being 610 m. Terrain divides up 18% beginner, 27% intermediate, 45% advanced or expert, and 10% freestyle. Nine chair lifts lead to 51 runs on two mountains, with night skiing on all main runs. It also has a snowboard park with half-pipe and 10 km of snowshoeing trails. The SnowPlay area has tubing and tobogganing, and there's a café and a lounge. The new day lodge is due to be completed in late 2008. Also in the park at Hollyburn Ridge are 19 km of track-set cross-country trails including 7 km lit up at night. A winter-only **shuttle bus** ⓘ *T604-637 7669, www.cypresscoachlines.com, $18, child $13, up, $8, child $6, back*, runs here from numerous Vancouver locations.

Further west still, is the comparatively tiny **Lighthouse Park** ⓘ *free, bus No 250 from Downtown*, one of the most accessible parks and the best for strolling. It contains some of Vancouver's most rugged forest, including one of the last remaining stands of old-growth Douglas firs. A number of short trails lead to arbutus trees, cliffs and the (out of bounds) Point Atkinson Lighthouse, which has been staffed continuously since 1875.

Highway 1/99 swings north towards Squamish, passing Horseshoe Bay, terminal for ferries to Nanaimo, the Sunshine Coast and Bowen Island. A mere 20 minutes away, the latter offers visitors a quick and easy taste of the Gulf Islands' laid-back atmosphere, its population of 3500 characteristically including a large number of writers and artists. Ferries leave more or less hourly from 0605 until 2135, with a break for lunch. Just off the ferry landing is the island's main hub, **Snug Cove** where there's an **Information Kiosk** ⓘ *432 Cardena Rd, T604-947 9024, www.bowenisland.org*, and where you can pick up a free copy of the *Bowen Island Guide* (also available online), with maps, restaurant and accommodation listings, activities and everything else you may need. Many people come for the fine boating and kayaking in the sheltered bays that surround this 50-sq-km island. **Mount Gardner** is an excellent 16-km return day-hike that is possible almost year-round.

Hiking around Vancouver (east to west)

Mount Seymour ⓘ *9 km round trip, 440 m elevation gain. Trailhead: Mt Seymour Provincial Park National Park car park.* Providing one of the easiest routes to astonishing summit panoramas, this trail is understandably very popular. But it is certainly no pushover. The route can be confusing, and is dangerously exposed to bad weather. Views from the top are some of the most extensive around. The route is rarely snow-free before August.

Brothers and Lawson Creeks *10 km loop, 437 m elevation gain. Trailhead: From Hwy 1 or Marine Dr take Taylor Way north. Turn left onto Highland Dr and continue until you can turn left onto Eyremount Drive. Park where this road intersects Milstream Rd.* Walk west on gated road and look for signs for Brothers Creek Forest Heritage Walk. This short, undemanding hike takes in a gorge and some cascades, but is best recommended for the ease with which you can see some really big cedars in their natural environment.

Mount Strachan ⓘ *10 km round trip, 534 m elevation gain. Trailhead: by the ski area map next to the car park in Cypress Provincial Park.* A first-rate hike, this route follows the Howe Sound Crest Trail for a while before heading through Strachan

Meadows then steeply up the edge of a gorge, alongside precipitous cliffs and through a beautiful stretch of old-growth forest. The north summit offers the best views. This trail is rarely free of snow before mid-July.

Hollyburn Mountain ① *8 km round trip, 405 m elevation gain. Trailhead: by the ski area map next to the car park in Cypress Provincial Park.* This is one of the finest and easiest trails on the North Shore with panoramic views from the top. You also walk through what is probably the finest stand of ancient giant cedar, fir and hemlock within reach of the city. Snow-free from mid-June to mid-November.

Mount Gardner ① *16 km round trip, 750 m elevation gain. Trailhead: take the ferry from Horseshoe bay to Bowen Island.* Directions are complicated so ask at the information centre or consult *Don't Waste Your Time in the BC Coast Mountains*. This is a fairly demanding but highly rewarding hike that is possible almost year-round. Catch an early ferry to allow plenty of time. Panoramic views from the top are spectacular.

The Lions ① *15 km round trip, 1525 m elevation gain. Trailhead: at Lions Bay on Hwy 99, turn east onto Oceanview Rd then left onto Cross Creek Rd, right onto Centre Rd, left onto Bayview Rd, left onto Mountain Dr, left onto Sunset Dr and park at the gate.* This is a steep hike, but the views are great from the base of the Lions, especially if you can scramble down to the gap between them.

● Sleeping

Downtown *p43, map p46*
A Comfort Inn Downtown, 654 Nelson St, T604-605 4333, www.comfortinndowntown.com. Long-standing hotel in the heart of Downtown, with very clean rooms. Continental breakfast and fitness pass included.
C Bosman's Motor Hotel, 1060 Howe St, T604-682 3171, www.bosmanshotel.com. Very conveniently located, the rooms here are standard but pleasant enough and are a reasonable size. There's a heated outdoor pool and free parking.
C Victorian Hotel, 514 Homer St, T604-681 6369, www.victorianhotel.ca. A renovated 1898 house, with small but comfortable rooms tastefully decorated in pastel shades with hardwood floors. Can be noisy. Continental breakfast.
D Patricia Hotel, 403 E Hastings, T604-255 4301, www.budgetpathotel.bc.ca. Housed in a nicely renovated 1914 building enlivened with many plants, the **Patricia** is surprisingly classy given the seedy area, and certainly the best non-hostel budget option in town. Rooms are simple, clean and comfy, with en suite bathrooms. Some have fine views. There's a brewpub downstairs. Off-season weekly rates available. Staff on duty 24 hrs.

E Cambie Hostel Gastown, 300 Cambie St, T604-684 6466, www.cambiehostels.com. Well run and handily situated, the vibe of this busy backpacker hostel is somewhat influenced by the popular down-to-earth pub downstairs. Dorms and a few private rooms, all with shared bathroom. The common room (with TV) is a good place to meet travellers and pick up information. There's a small kitchen, and free coffee and muffin from the excellent bakery next door. Their smaller, sister hostel is nearby at 515 Seymour St, T604-684 7757.
E HI Vancouver Central, 1025 Granville St, T604-685 5335. Situated in the heart of Downtown, this modern and efficient hostel offers dorms and private rooms, as well as common room, express kitchen (microwaves, no cooker) and lockers. They also organize daily activities.
E SameSun Backpacker Lodge, 1018 Granville St, T604-682 8226, www.samesun.com. This centrally located, colourful hostel has everything you need. There are lots of dorms, double rooms with en suite bathroom, a huge kitchen, 2 large common rooms, a pool table, a TV room, a cheap bar-restaurant with nightly music, an outdoor patio, internet access, laundry,

lockers and a travel information desk. Also organizes activities around town.

West End to Stanley Park *p49, map p62*
AL English Bay Inn B&B, 1968 Comox St, T604-683 8002, www.englishbayinn.com. Hidden away close to Stanley Park, this friendly B&B in a pretty Tudor-style house offers 4 attractive and comfortable en suite rooms and 2 suites. Big breakfast.
AL The Listel, 1300 Robson St, T604-684 8461, www.thelistelhotel.com. Smaller than most high-end hotels, **The Listel** is beautiful and stylish throughout, with highly attentive staff. 'Museum suites' are decorated with First Nations art and exquisite hand-carved wood furnishings, while each 'Gallery suite' is dedicated to displaying original works by a different established artist. All are immaculately equipped, with big windows. Facilities include a fitness centre and hot tub, and there is live jazz in the restaurant.
A Blue Horizon Hotel, 1225 Robson St, T604-688 1411, www.bluehorizonhotel.com. The biggest and best of a cluster of mid-range hotels nicely situated on Robson. Rooms are large and plain but well appointed, with balconies and good views. Those with 2 beds ($10-20 more) sleep 4 and are much bigger. There's a small pool, hot tub, sauna, gym, bistro and café.
A Meridian at 910 Beach, 910 Beach Av, T604-609 5100, www.meridianhotel.org. Wide range of attractive, open-plan, fully-equipped suites, some with patio/balcony. All have floor-to-ceiling windows that take full advantage of the hotel's prime location on False Creek, with views of the water and Granville Market or the city. Continental breakfast included.
E HI Vancouver Downtown, 1114 Burnaby St, T604-684 4565, www.hihostels.ca. This clean and professional hostel on a central but quiet street has 4-bed dorms and simple private rooms with shared bath. Top-notch facilities include a large kitchen, TV room, library, games room with pool table, laundry, lockers and dining room. Many cheap activities can be arranged, free shuttle from bus/train station and a buffet breakfast.

Kitsilano *p52, map p60*
Kitsilano is taken as stretching east to Granville and south to 15th.

St T604-734 5082, www.betweenfriends-vancouver.com. 3 small but very nice and distinctive rooms, a small suite and an apartment in a classic Kitsilano home close to 4th Av. Guests share a pleasant sitting room and the friendly hostess serves up a big breakfast.
B Mickey's Kits Beach Chalet, 2142 W. 1st Av, T604-739 3342, www.mickeysbandb.com. 3 bright and pleasant rooms in a quiet spot close to **Kits Beach**, with a friendly and helpful host and a garden. Breakfast included.
C Graeme's House B&B, 2735 Waterloo St, T604-732 1488, www.graemewebster.com. 3 rooms in a pretty heritage house with lots of interesting features, and a deck and flower garden. Close to the most interesting section of Broadway.
E HI Jericho Beach Hostel, 1515 Discovery St, T604-224 3208, www.hihostels.ca. Built in the 1930s as barracks for Jericho Air Station, this vast and interesting building is the largest hostel in Canada. It has 288 dorm beds and 10 private rooms, all with shared bath. All the usual facilities are here: a massive kitchen and dining room, TV room, games room, library, laundry, lockers and bike rental. Free or cheap tours, hikes and activities. The main factor here is the location, it is in a beautiful and quiet spot right on the beach but is a long way from town. A free shuttle runs frequently to and from the **HI Vancouver Central hostel** (see above) and bus station. Take bus No 4 (UBC).

South and east Vancouver *p54*
B Delta Vancouver Airport, 3500 Cessna Dr, T604-278 1241, www.deltavancouverairport.com. The nicest place to stay close to the airport, thanks to a riverside location by a marina, a pub housed in a small pagoda and lovely gardens. There's also an outdoor pool, exercise room, restaurant and access to riverside trails.
B Douglas Guest House, 456 W 13th Av, T604-872 3060, www.dougwin.com. 6 fairly large rooms/suites in a restored Edwardian manor, with elegant decor, and en suite bath in all but 2. Breakfast served in a sunroom with patio. They also have a sister guesthouse, the 11-room **Windsor Guest House**.

60 **D-E City Center Motor Hotel**, 2111 Main St, T604-876 7166, www.citycentermotor hotel.com. Handy for transport connections and the interesting section of Main, this brightly coloured hotel has simple but clean rooms with TV and bath, and plenty of parking. A bargain.

Camping

Capilano RV Park, 295 Tomahawk Av, near Lion's Gate Bridge, T604-987 4722. Very much an RV park, but centrally located with great facilities including full hook-ups, tent sites, free showers, a swimming pool, jacuzzi, playground, laundromat and lounge area with TV and games.

🍴 Eating

Eating out is one of the highlights of a trip to Vancouver, the culinary scene is now as dynamic as anywhere in North America. Since the turnover of restaurants is exceptionally high, the listings concentrate largely on reliable, established favourites. Details of the latest exciting newcomers can be found in *Eat Magazine*, www.eatmagazine.ca, or at www.urbandiner.ca. Vancouver's chefs have pioneered a style of cooking known as West Coast cuisine (see page 30), emphasizing fresh, local produce and embracing an innovative, pan-global fusion mentality. Given the cosmopolitan population, it's no surprise that you can find whatever international cuisine you crave. We have favoured venues that offer a unique Vancouver experience.

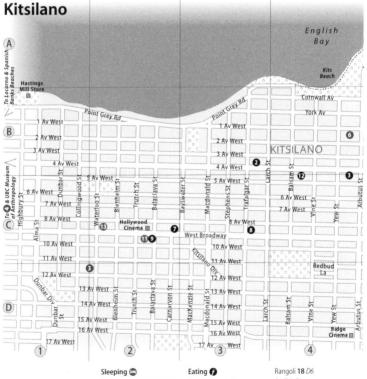

Kitsilano

English Bay

Kits Beach

Hastings Mill Store

To Locarno & Spanish Banks Beaches

To Jericho & UBC Museum of Anthropology

Point Grey Rd — Point Grey Rd

Cornwall Av
York Av

1 Av West
2 Av West
3 Av West
4 Av West
5 Av West
6 Av West
7 Av West
8 Av West
10 Av West
11 Av West
12 Av West
13 Av West
14 Av West
15 Av West
16 Av West
17 Av West

KITSILANO

West Broadway

Kitsilano Div

Dunbar Div

Hollywood Cinema

Redbud La

Ridge Cinema

Alma St, Highbury St, Dunbar St, Collingwood St, Waterloo St, Blenheim St, Trutch St, Balaclava St, Camarvon St, Bayswater St, Mackenzie St, Macdonald St, Stephens St, Trafalgar St, Larch St, Balsam St, Vine St, Yew St, Arbutus St

N

200 metres
200 yards

Sleeping 🛏
Between Friends B&B **1** *B5*
Graeme's House B&B **3** *D2*
HI Jericho Beach Hostel **4** *C1*
Mickey's Kits Beach
  Chalet **6** *B4*

Eating 🍴
49th Parallel **3** *B4*
Bin 942 **1** *C6*
Bishop's **2** *B3*
Calhoun's **7** *C2*
Fuel **5** *C5*
Lumière **8** *C3*

Rangoli **18** *D6*
Sai Z **9** *C2*
Sophie's Cosmic Café
  15 *B5*
Terra Breads **12** *C4*
Vij's **18** *D6*
Watermark **10** *A5*

Downtown *p43, map p46*

ŸŸŸ DIVA, at the Met, 645 Howe St, T604-602 7788. A contender for the best restaurant in town, the food here is classic nouveau French, prepared with flair, creativity and a West Coast sensibility. Decor is bright and elegant, sophisticated but not stuffy. An extensive wine list includes many offered by the glass.

ŸŸŸ Joe Forte's Seafood and Chop House, 777 Thurlow St, T604-669 1940. Dominated by a large horseshoe-shaped bar, this exceptionally opulent room makes for a special dining experience, though the food and service fail to justify the prices. Seafood is the speciality, with a broad choice of oysters. The selection of wines and beers is great and there's a roof garden and live piano music nightly.

West 4 *D6*

Bars & clubs ♦
Fringe Café **11** *C2*
Lou's Grill & Bistro **13** *C2*

ŸŸŸ Le Crocodile, 909 Burrard St, T604-669 4298. Classic French cuisine, whose sophistication lies in its simplicity. The ambience is upscale bistro and the prices reasonable for food of this calibre.

ŸŸ Chambar, 562 Beatty St, T604-879 7119. Small and crowded, yet relaxed and slow-paced, this hip and happening spot is great for drinks and skillfully crafted Belgian fare that focuses on seafood. Try the mussels.

ŸŸ Relish, 888 Nelson St, T604-669 1962. More consistently good than exceptional, this is a casual, unpretentious, friendly spot that's equally good for brunch, lunch, dinner or drinks in the lounge. The broad menu touches Asian, Mediterranean and West Coast bases.

ŸŸ The Templeton, 1087 Granville St, T604-685 4612. An authentic 1930s diner with jukeboxes and booths, offering typical diner comfort food but with a healthy and original twist. Try the ahi tuna.

Ÿ The Elbow Room, 560 Davie St, T604-685 3628. A popular breakfast spot that has become famous for its large portions and the abuse regularly dished out to customers, especially those who fail to polish off their plate.

Yaletown *p45*

ŸŸŸ Blue Water Café and Raw Bar, 1095 Hamilton St, T604-688 8078. Oozing genuine, unpretentious chic and upmarket class, this spacious venue features leather chairs and couches, soft lighting and jazzy music. The open kitchen is renowned for serving some of the best, freshest seafood in town, raw and cooked, and great steaks. There's a wide selection of wines and beers.

ŸŸŸ Brix 1138 Homer St, next door to **Plan B**, T604-9159463. Modern Canadian cuisine in stylish surroundings, with the bonus of a small enclosed courtyard.

ŸŸŸ Coast Restaurant, 1257 Hamilton St, T604-685 5010. Dominated by pale wood furnishings, high ceilings, a waterfall and a large 'community' table, this is a tranquil and elegant location to enjoy all manner of West Coast-style seafood creations, including multi-course tasting menus.

ŸŸŸ Plan B, 1144 Homer St, T604-915 9463. Tiny but exquisitely designed, prepared and presented tapas served in a dark, intimate, elegant space. Not for big eaters.

Vancouver & around Vancouver City Listings

West End

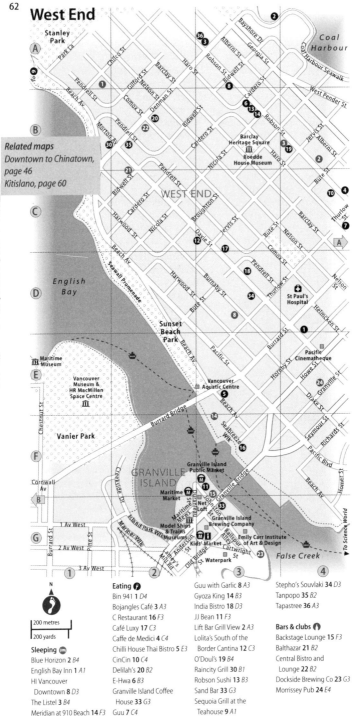

Related maps
Downtown to Chinatown, page 46
Kitislano, page 60

Eating 🍴
Bin 941 **1** D4
Bojangles Café **3** A3
C Restaurant **16** F3
Café Luxy **17** C3
Caffe de Medici **4** C4
Chilli House Thai Bistro **5** E3
CinCin **10** C4
Delilah's **20** B2
E-Hwa **6** B3
Granville Island Coffee
  House **33** G3
Guu **7** C4

Guu with Garlic **8** A3
Gyoza King **14** B3
India Bistro **18** D3
JJ Bean **11** F3
Lift Bar Grill View **2** A3
Lolita's South of the
  Border Cantina **12** C3
O'Doul's **19** B4
Raincity Grill **30** B1
Robson Sushi **13** B3
Sand Bar **33** G3
Sequoia Grill at the
  Teahouse **9** A1

Stepho's Souvlaki **34** D3
Tanpopo **35** B2
Tapastree **36** A3

Bars & clubs 🍷
Backstage Lounge **15** F3
Balthazar **21** B2
Central Bistro and
  Lounge **22** B2
Dockside Brewing Co **23** G3
Morrissey Pub **24** E4

Sleeping 🛏
Blue Horizon **2** B4
English Bay Inn **1** A1
HI Vancouver
  Downtown **8** D3
The Listel **3** B4
Meridian at 910 Beach **14** F3

N

200 metres
200 yards

Rodney's Oyster House, 1228 Hamilton St, T604-609 0080. Classic converted warehouse space with brick walls and huge wooden beams. Downstairs is casual with stools at
the bar, upstairs is a little smarter. Clientele is slightly older but the ambience is lively and crowded. Focusing on oysters, mussels and chowder, the food is excellent.

Chinatown *p47, map 46*
For a snack try one of the numerous local bakeries for a curry beef, BBQ pork or honey bun; they quickly become addictive.
Buddhist Vegetarian, 137 Pender St, T604-683 8816. Consistently tasty and healthy vegetarian Chinese food.
Hon's Wun-Tun House, 268 Keefer St, T604-688 0871; also at 1339 Robson, T604-685 0871. There are countless options in Chinatown and it's hard to go wrong, but this is the obvious choice, having for some time scooped up most awards for best Chinese and best restaurant under $10. The decor is cafeteria- style, the menu huge.

Gastown *p48*
Cobre, 52 Powell St, T604-669 2396. Sophisticated pan-Latin American cuisine in an interesting space, creatively wrought from brick, dark wood and installation art.
Kitanoya Guu, 375 Water St, T604-685 8682. Perhaps the all-round best of the **Guu** restaurants. Try the oyster gratin, deep fried brie and a cocktail or 2.
Water Street Café, 300 Water St, T604-689 2832. The menu seems unimaginative, mainly pasta, with some steak and seafood but it's always fresh and very reasonably priced. The interior is classically elegant and the massive windows and outdoor seating make the most of an excellent location.
The Annex, 307 W Cordova St, T604-669 4991. A funky, friendly, charmingly eclectic café with a broad menu that covers pizza, quesadilla and goulash. Big portions at reasonable prices.
Bambo Café, 301 W Cordova St, T604-681 4323. Great for breakfast or lunch, with superior focaccia sandwiches, home-made soups and unusually tasty omelettes.

Cafés
Blake's, 221 Carrall St, Gastown, T604-899

3354. Exceptional, downbeat, tasteful coffee house in a prime location, with good music, brick walls, beer on tap, a modest menu and internet access.
The Blunt Bros, 317 W Hastings St, East Side, T604-682 5868. Calling itself 'a respectable joint', this is the main bastion of attempts to sell Vancouver as the new Amsterdam. Toking is permitted and large amounts of pot paraphernalia sold, but there's no booze. The interior is spacious, with lots of couches for vegging out.
Café Ami, 885 W Georgia St, in the HSBC building, Downtown, T604-688 0103. A very relaxed and attractive spot for a coffee.
Café Dolcino, 12 Powell St, Gastown, T604-801 5118. Perfectly situated on picturesque Maple Leaf Sq, with a couple of tables outside to take in the scene.
Gallery Café, in the Art Gallery, 750 Hornby St, T604-688 2233. A hidden gem. The patio is a fantastic place for a coffee or glass of wine on a sunny day, the atmosphere is relaxed and the light food menu is impeccable.
Ganache Patisserie, 1262 Homer St, Yaletown, T604-899 1098. If you like cakes, this is the place. A bit pricey but worth it.
La Luna Café, 131 Water St, 604-687 5862. Well-situated and comfy. They roast their own beans, so the coffee is great.

West End to Stanley Park *p49, map p62*
The West End's large and lively population breathes constant life into the city's most competitive culinary district, with Robson, Denman and Davie representing the finest streets for restaurant window-shopping.
C Restaurant, 1600 Howe St, False Creek, T604-681 1164. The prototype for many of Vancouver's finest new West Coast venues, famous for its range of fresh local seafood, prepared in exciting and innovative ways. A great wine list that includes many sakes.
Caffe de Medici, 109-1025 Robson St, T604-6699 322. Consistently excellent and less busy and more affordable than **CinCin**.
CinCin, upstairs at 1154 Robson St, T604-688 7338. Often rated as the best Italian food in town, it has lots of awards, many for its wine list. The Mediterranean decor is warm, romantic, sophisticated and comfortable, with balcony seating for summer evenings.
Lift Bar Grill View, 333 Menchion's Mews, off Bayshore Dr, T604-689 5438.

On the water, with floor-to-ceiling windows offering views of Coal Harbour and Stanley Park. A modern, sophisticated interior and an upbeat West Coast menu that concentrates on seafood. Try their signature 'whet' plates.

O'Doul's, 1300 Robson St in the **Listel Hotel**, T604-661 1400. This long-standing survivor offers warmth, sophistication, class and impeccable service. Emphasizing freshness, the eclectic West Coast menu is reliable from breakfast to dinner. With a fine wine list and live jazz every night, it's also a great place for a drink.

Raincity Grill, 1193 Denman St, T604-685 7337. One of the original exponents of West Coast cuisine. Ingredients are fresh, locally produced, organic when possible, and used with subtlety and panache. The decor is simple and elegant. The award-winning wine list focuses on BC's finest and many are available by the glass.

Sequoia Grill at the Teahouse, Stanley Park at Ferguson Point, T604-669 3281. The nicer of the park's 2 restaurants, set in a bright and breezy summerhouse with lots of plants and big windows that offer fabulous views of English Bay. The menu has eclectic West Coast inclinations.

Bin 941, 943 Davie St, T604-683 1246. This small and intimate bistro combines quirky decor, a lively atmosphere, inspirational tapas and a well-stocked bar.

Chilli House Thai Bistro, 1018 Beach Av, T604-685 8989. Perfectly situated right on the water, spacious yet intimate and evocatively decorated. It's almost a bonus that the Thai food here is arguably the best in town.

Delilah's, 1789 Comox St, T604-687 3424. With its delightfully louche atmosphere, hand-painted ceiling, velvet drapes and nightly entertainment, this place provides an all-round enjoyable experience. Justly famous for its martinis, but the set menus are also fine and very reasonable.

E-Hwa, 1578 Robson St, T604-688 1322. The full Izakaya experience, Korean-style.

Guu, 838 Thurlow St, T604-685 8817. Izakaya joints, serving small tapas-sized Japanese dishes washed down with beer, sake or a martini, are all the rage in Vancouver these days. They tend to be dark, atmospheric, loud, social, lots of fun and open late. They are an all-round unique experience. The 3 **Guu** restaurants are among the best, with staff shouting back and forth, and food that is fresh, tasty and very authentic.

Guu with Garlic, 1698 Robson St, T604-6858678. The least hectic **Guu** restaurant. Daily specials are worth exploring.

Gyoza King, 1508 Robson St, T604-669 8278. This is an atmospheric and very popular spot for Japanese-style tapas and sake. It's calmer than the **Guu** restaurants and the food is possibly even better.

Lolita's South of the Border Cantina, 1326 Davie St, T604-696 9996. Highly inventive and original take on Mexican food, with a tapas sensibility and an emphasis on cocktails. Small, packed and noisy, the party continues until 0200.

Tanpopo, 1122 Denman St, T604-681 7777. Probably the best choice for all-you-can-eat sushi. An experience that we highly recommend.

Tapastree, 1829 Robson St, T604-606 4680. A large, casually elegant space with tasteful art, an open kitchen and a patio out the front. Possibly the largest selection of tapas in town. Great atmosphere.

Café Luxy, 1235 Davie St, T604-669 5899. Exceptionally well-priced and tasty Italian food, but often disappointingly empty.

India Bistro, 1157 Davie St, T604-684 6342. Dimly lit and very busy, a fine spot for everyone's favourite Indian classics. Lunch buffet for just $9.

Robson Sushi, 1542 Robson St, T604-688 4789, Cheaper than **Tanpopo** and almost as good.

Stepho's Souvlaki, 1124 Davie St, T604-683 2555. Don't be put off by the generic exterior, the food here is top-notch Greek. Generous portions and very low prices, the long queues pay testament to its legendary status.

Cafés

Bojangles Café, 785 Denman St, West End, T604687 3622. A long-running favourite in a prominent location.

Granville Island to Point Grey   p51, map p62

The Sand Bar, 1535 Johnston St, Granville Island, T604-669 9030. A beautifully renovated warehouse with high ceilings, industrial metal trimmings, vast windows overlooking False Creek and a heated roof patio. West Coast food, including tapas and seafood, and wood-grilled burgers and pizza can be washed down with a fine selection of ales and wines. Occasionally too busy, service can be poor.

¶ Granville Island Public Market. Countless excellent, cheap fast-food stalls selling all kinds of international cuisine, with seating outside by the water.

Cafés
Granville Island Coffee House, 1551 Johnston St, on the boardwalk behind the Sand Bar, T604-682 7865. Cosy little spot away from the hustle and bustle.

JJ Bean, 1689 Johnston St, T604-6850613. Great coffee.

Kitsilano *p52, map p60*
Kitsilano contains many of the city's most celebrated restaurants and also the best selection for vegetarians.

¶¶¶ Bishop's, 2549 W 4th Av, T604-738 2025. The quintessential West Coast eatery. Owner John Bishop is famous for his impeccable hospitality and for changing his menu frequently to highlight the best locally grown organic ingredients available. The extensive wine list favours BC's best.

¶¶¶ Fuel, 1944 W 4th Av, T604-288 7905. New and highly praised, **Fuel** specializes in West Coast fine dining, its many tasting menus changing with the seasons and availability of local produce. The uber-chic, minimalist interior focuses on the bar and open kitchen.

¶¶¶ Lumière, 2551 W Broadway, T604-739 8185. Though its famous 'Iron Chef' owner Rob Feenie has gone, word is that this remains one of the city's (if not country's) finest restaurants. There's no à la carte, just French-inspired tasting menus from $85-180 without wine, apparently worth every penny. The modern interior is stylish to the point of being intimidating.

¶¶¶ Vij's, 1480 11th Av, T604-736 6664. The only Indian restaurant that is regularly cited as one of the city's finest overall eateries. Skilful, innovative variations on old favourites. Reservations not accepted,

so queues are common. Dinner only.

¶¶¶ West, 2881 Granville St, T604-738 8938. Large and idiosyncratic, dominated by a library of wine bottles. Another superlative purveyor of imaginative, fresh and tasty West Coast cuisine, regularly cited as one of the city's best.

¶¶ Bin 942, 1521 W Broadway, T604-734 9421. A thin room stuffed with weird and wonderful pieces of art, trendy and lively with modern but mellow dance music. Reasonable beer selection and an incredible menu of involved, delicious tapas.

¶¶ Rangoli, 1488, 11th Av, next door to Vij's, T604-736 5711. A more casual and inexpensive version of **Vij's**, only open for lunch.

¶¶ Sai Z, 3116 W Broadway, T604-732 7249. Highly praised, imaginative Japanese fusion dishes with perfectly balanced flavours. The house-like interior is spacious and colourful, yet intimate, with live piano in the evening.

¶¶ Watermark, 1305 Arbutus St, T604-738 5487. Situated on Kits Beach, it has huge windows and the view could hardly be better. The interior is a little cafeteria-like, but the food and broad menu are better than regular tourist fare.

¶ Sophie's Cosmic Café, 2095 4th Av, T604-732 6810. An eccentric, diner-style Kitsilano institution that is legendary for its weekend brunches (hence the queues) and large portions. Almost too popular for its own good but a great spot to observe Vancouverites in their natural habitat.

Cafés
49th Parallel, 2152 W 4th Av, T604-420 4900. Roasted on site, the coffee here is just about perfect. The pastries are a revelation.

Calhoun's, 3035 W Broadway , T604-737 7062, open 24 hrs. A huge and lively coffee shop with a slightly rustic feel, serving coffee, juices, breakfasts and cakes.

Terra Breads, 2380 W 4th Av , T604-736 1838. The baking here is to die for. Breads, croissants, muffins, cakes and sandwiches to eat in or take away. Good coffee too.

South and east Vancouver *p54*
¶¶¶ Seasons in the Park, Queen Elizabeth

● *For an explanation of sleeping and eating price codes used in this guide, see inside*
● *the front cover. Other relevant information is found in Essentials, see pages 28-31.*

Park, T604-874 8008. One of the most
romantic, high-class choices in town, with
a sumptuous interior and exquisite views.
Fresh seafood and steak, good appetizers
and brunch.

¶¶¶ **Tojo's**, 777 W Broadway, T604- 872
8050. A favourite with visiting celebrities,
the undisputed best (and most expensive)
Japanese restaurant in Western Canada,
with the freshest fish, best sake and most
beautiful presentation. Recent renovations
have made the interior even more impressive.

¶¶ **Aurora Bistro**, 2420 Main St, T604-873
9944. Like the minimal wood decor, the
atmosphere here is modern and sophisticated but unpretentious. Focusing on
fresh ingredients and simplicity, the
West Coast cuisine is perfectly pitched.

¶¶ **Havana**, 1212 Commercial St, T604-253
9119. The food is nothing special and the
service poor, but the busy patio is still
the best place for soaking up the Drive's
unique atmosphere.

¶¶ **Latin Quarter**, 1305 Commercial St,
T604-251 1144. Tapas, paella and sangria
in a crowded, party atmosphere with live
music late at night.

¶ **Café Deux Soleils**, 2096 Commercial St,
T604-254 1195. Spacious, downbeat and
friendly, with a little play area. Frequently
packed with young couples and families.
Large portions of reasonably priced
vegetarian food, best for breakfast.

¶ **Slickity Jim's Chat 'n' Chew**, 2513 Main
St, T604-873 6760. Small and quirky, overflowing with weird and wonderful artefacts,
this is the breakfast place of choice for a
mixed, predominantly arty or bohemian
crowd. Variations on the eggs bennie
theme abound, with very silly names.
Portions tend to be on the small side.

Cafés

La Casa Gelato, 1033 Venables St, near
Commercial Dr. Tucked away in this unlikely
spot is Vancouver's finest ice cream emporium, with 218 wonderful (and often weird)
flavours to choose from and servers who are
pleased to let you taste before you buy.

Continental Coffee, 1806 Commercial
Dr, T604-255 0712. Large, busy and dimly
lit. Good prices for speciality coffees, beans
roasted on site.

JJ Bean, Main/14th Av. The nicest and

busiest café on Main these days. Elegant
but cosy inside, with armchairs by the wood
fire. Roasted on site, the coffee is fresh and
very tasty.

Turk's Coffee Exchange, 1276 Commercial
Dr. A long-running contender for the best
coffee in town. A small but elegant interior,
the outdoor seating area is great for
people-watching.

North Shore *p55*

¶¶ **Moustache Café**, 129 W. 2nd St, T604-987
8461. An ever-changing menu of taste-heavy
French and Mediterranean food prepared
with a West Coast sensibility and served in
a cosy, colourful 1920's house with an open
kitchen. With its friendly staff and fine wine
list, this is possibly the best all-round dining
experience on the North Shore.

¶ **The Raven**, 1052 Deep Cove Rd, T604-
929 4335. Superb neighbourhood pub
with enormous portions of superior pub-
style food.

⚡ Bars and clubs

Like most big cities, Vancouver offers something for everyone and has developed a
reputation for excellent microbrewed
beers and a panoply of funky, atmospheric
little bistros and tapas bars (see Eating).

For the short-term visitor there are more
than enough nightclubs to check out.
Those listed here tend to host DJs spinning
different music every night. Most charge
$5-10 for entry (cover), and drinks can be
on the pricey side. These days Granville from
Drake to Smithe is the place to be, its many
clubs packed, with long queues at the weekends. Gastown is more genuinely trendy and
Yaletown more sophisticated. Look out for
the quarterly magazine *Nitelife*. For more
specific night-to-night details consult the
indispensable *Georgia Straight* or the useful
www.clubvibes.com. Details of gay bars are
listed on page 69.

Downtown *p43, map p46*

Alibi Room, 157 Alexander St, Gastown,
T604-623 3383. Recently renovated, with
a warehouse look and long tables upstairs
and intimate vodka bar downstairs. This
long-standing favourite is as hip and
visually enticing as ever. The music is

skilfully selected, not too loud, and the small menu is exciting, innovative and reasonably priced.

Bacchus, 845 Hornby St, Downtown in the Wedgewood Hotel, T604-608 5319. The restaurant of this plush, romantic venue has faded but it's a lovely place for a cocktail. Weekend brunch and afternoon tea also retain a following.

Bar None, 1222 Hamilton St, Yaletown, T604-689 7000. Mon-Tue for live music, Fri-Sat for house and hip-hop. Housed in a minimalist industrial warehouse space, this uber-chic club has 3 bars, a decent dance floor and well-chosen music.

The Cambie, 300 Cambie St, Gastown, T604-684 6466. Gritty, down-to-earth and friendly, this huge, English-style boozer is understandably popular for its wide selection of cheap beer and food, pool tables and crowded summer patio.

Chill Winston, 3 Alexander St, Gastown, T604-288 9575. In a prime location and effectively illuminated at night, the red-brick building is gorgeous. Spacious, dimly lit and packed to the gills, this is the place to be in Gastown. The island kitchen puts out good food and there are plenty of well-priced wines and beers on tap.

Crush Champagne Lounge, 1180 Granville St, Downtown, T604-684 0355. Squarely aimed at a trendy and sophisticated 30-something clientele, with the cool atmosphere of a 1950s lounge and well-chosen jazz, soul and R&B music, this comfy, surprisingly unpretentious venue is more mellow than most. Smaller dance floor and tends to close a bit earlier.

Element Sound Lounge, 801 Georgia St, Downtown, T604-669 0806. Fancy club aimed at the upmarket martini set. Top DJs play funk, techno and house.

Fabric, 66 Water St, Gastown, T604-683 6695. A fantastic, recently renovated basement space with brick walls, wood floors and different areas for music, dancing and lounging. DJs play a variety of music ranging from house to hip-hop to reggae. One of the biggest and best clubs in town.

Flite, 1269 Hamilton St, Yaletown, T604-687 1269. Dark, atmospheric and trendy, with a good selection of small dishes and wine by the glass

George Ultra Lounge, 1137 Hamilton St,

Yaletown, T604-628 5555. Sophisticated and chilled, specializing in cocktails and wines by the glass. Music runs from jazz and motown to more modern beats.

Honey Lounge, 455 Abbott St, Gastown, T604-685 7777. This hip bar sucks you in with impossibly comfortable couches smothered in huge velvet cushions, and a good drinks menu. Dark, capacious and open-plan with loud, conversation-killing music that creates a club-like atmosphere without the dancing.

The Irish Heather, 217 Carrall St, Gastown, T604-68 89779. A small, upmarket, genuinely Irish pub with regular music and superior versions of comfort food.

The Lennox, 800 Granville St, at Robson, Downtown, T604-408 0881. Standard pub with some outstanding but overpriced beers. Located on Downtown's busiest corner, the small patio is an ideal spot for watching the city rush by.

Lucy Mae Brown, 862 Richards St, Downtown, T604-899 9199. Stylish and bordering on pretentious, this is a favourite with the young, trendy crowd. Downstairs is a modern martini bar playing trip hop-style music. Upstairs is an expensive, reservation-only restaurant with a Pacific Rim menu.

The Modern, 7 Alexander St, Gastown, T604-627 0124. A new club in a heritage building, fitted out with state-of-the-art sound and light systems, with music by top DJs. Great location next to Chill Winston.

Plaza Club, 881 Granville St, Downtown, T604-646 0064. One of the classiest of the DJ-led dance hot spots, with one of the best sound and lighting systems. Very popular on Sat and has a party atmosphere

The Railway Club, 579 Dunsmuir St, Downtown, T604-681 1625. Upstairs bar, cosy and atmospheric with lots of wood, knick-knacks and intimate corners. Varied live music every night, sometimes with cover charge.

Salt, 45 Blood Alley, T604-633 1912. In a scary dark alley, in a minimalist, rather loud, urban-warehouse space, this 'tasting room' is quite an experience. Artisan dried meats and cheeses are sampled with bread and condiments and can be washed down by 1 of the 40 wines available by the glass.

Shine, 364 Water St, Gastown, T604-408 4321. Smart, colourful and intimate club with varied DJ-led music, attracting a 20-30s crowd that's a bit more well-heeled than usual. One to dress up for.

Steamworks, 375 Water St, Gastown, T604- 689 2739. Different bar and restaurant spaces cater to different tastes, but the real draw here is the range of fine beers brewed on the premises.

West End to Stanley Park *p49, map p62*

Balthazar, 1215 Bidwell St, West End, T604-689 8822. A spacious and inviting restaurant/lounge/club that stays open and busy until late. DJs spin progressive house and more mainstream sounds.

Central Bistro and Lounge, 1072 Denman St, T604-689 4527. A chilled spot with a fine drinks list, including good value wines by the glass. The food is very good too, especially brunch.

Morrissey Pub, 1227 Granville St, T604-682 0909. Big and stylish with a river-stone fireplace and lots of dark wood and leather. Choice of beers on tap, decent cheap food, DJs and nightly drink specials.

Granville Island to Point Grey *p51*

Backstage Lounge, 1585 Johnston St, T604-687 1354, in the **Arts Club**. Great, airy spot with a lively patio, decent food and live music most nights.

Dockside Brewing Co, 1253 Johnston St in the **Granville Island Hotel**, T604-685 7070. Tucked away from the hordes, with comfy leather armchairs and fine in-house beers. The menu is mid-range with wood-oven pizza and seafood.

Kitsilano *p52, map p60*

The Fringe Café, 3124 W Broadway, T604-738 6977. Tiny, downbeat bar with a bohemian attitude.

Lou's Grill and Bistro, 3357 W Broadway, T604-736 9872. Large, trendy bar and restaurant with terracotta walls, interesting art and a patio. Dim lighting, jazzy music and a great selection of beer on tap.

South and east Vancouver *p54*

WaaZuBee Café, 1622 Commercial Dr, T604-253 5299. Comfortable, atmospheric space playing loud upbeat music. Good selection of beers and big portions of food. Best place for a drink on 'the Drive'.

North Shore *p55*

The Raven, 1052 Deep Cove Rd, T604-929 3834. English-style pub with the best selection of draught beers in town, including 19 microbrews and 6 imports. Lots of malt whiskies and the food comes in mammoth portions. Live music once or twice a week. Understandably popular.

The Rusty Gull, 175 E 1st St, T604-988 5585. Lively neighbourhood pub with good ales on tap, food and frequent live music. Magical views of the city from the patio, with shipyards and derelict warehouses in the foreground.

● Entertainment

The first place to look for weekly listings is the *Georgia Straight*, available free on most major streets. The Visitor Centre has a branch of **Ticketmaster**, T604-280 4444, www.ticket master.ca, through which tickets to most events are available, inlcuding sports; and **Tickets Tonight**, T604-280 4444, www.ticket stonight.ca, which has half-price same-day tickets for many events.

Art galleries

Apart from the major galleries already mentioned, Vancouver has a wealth of smaller spaces, usually highlighting the work of contemporary local artists. Details of commercial galleries, which are usually just as interesting, are included under Shopping (see page 72).

There are a few worthwhile artist-run galleries in Gastown, such as **Artspeak Gallery**, 233 Carrall St; and **Vancouver Access Artist Run Centre**, 206 Carrall St. Granville is good for commercial galleries and there is an active art scene on the North Shore. Elsewhere, the **Grunt Gallery**, 116-350 E 2nd Av, and **Or Gallery**, 208 Smithe St, usually have interesting displays **Charles H Scott Gallery**, in the **Emily Carr Institute**, entrance by donation. Always has interesting, sometimes controversial displays. **Contemporary Art Gallery**, 555 Nelson St, T604-681 2700, www.contemporaryart gallery.ca. Usually has 3 temporary exhibits. **Presentation House Gallery**, 333 Chester-field Av. One of Vancouver's oldest and has a good reputation for its photography and media arts exhibitions.

Western Front, 303 E 8th Av. Tends to exhibit video and performance art.

Cinemas

Fifth Avenue Cinemas, 2110 Burrard St, T604-734 7469. Most of the mainstream international films.

Granville 7 Cinemas, 855 Granville St, T604-684 4000. The most convenient downtown location, but small screens.

Hollywood, 3123 W Broadway, T604-738 3211, www.hollywoodtheatre.ca. The best repertory theatre in town, screening double-bills of well chosen films just off the first-run circuit. Less well known but worthwhile choices for $7.

Ridge, 3131 Arbutus St/16th Av, T604-738 6311, www.ridgetheatre.com. Built in 1950, the **Ridge** is a delightful building and the last venue to still offer a glassed-in 'crying room' for parents with babies or noisy children.

Pacific Cinematheque, 1131 Howe St, T604-688 3456, www.cinematheque.bc.ca. The main venue for rep, independent, art-house, foreign or just plain off-the-wall films.

Patricia Theatre, 5845 Ash Av, Historic Townsite, T604-483 9345. Built in 1928, this architectural gem, resembling a classic Hollywood fantasy movie palace, has just been restored and is once again showing well-chosen first-run and independent films on a daily basis. Also hosts the occasional concert and live theatre. There's a tea room and bistro, and tours by arrangement.

Tinseltown, 88 W Pender St, T604-806 0799. One of the best and most reasonably priced.

VanCity Theatre, 1181 Seymour St, T604-6833456, www.vancity.org. State-of-the-art, shows high calibre international films.

Comedy

New Revue Stage, 1601 Johnston St, Granville Island, T604-738 7013, Wed-Thu 1930, Fri-Sat 2000, 2200 and 2345. Host of **Vancouver Theatre Sports League**, world champions of comedy improvisation.

Yuk Yuk's, Century Plaza, 1015 Burrard St, T604-696 9857, Tue-Thu 2030, Fri-Sat 2000, 2230. The city's premier venue for stand-up comedy.

Gay and lesbian

The **West End**, and **Davie St** in particular, is the most gay-friendly part of a very gay-

friendly city and host of the summer **Gay Pride Celebration**. To find out what's going on pick up a copy of *XtraWest*, or check out www.gayvancouver.net. **Little Sister's Book and Art Emporium**, 1238 Davie St, is a gay and lesbian bookshop where you can get a free copy of the **Gay and Lesbian Business Association Directory**, www.glba.org.

1181, 1181 Davie St, T604-687 3991, www.tightlounge.com. An extremely hip and stylish lounge, with drink specials or events nightly.

Celebrities, 1022 Davie St, www.celebrities nightclub.com. A very busy club with a state-of-the-art light and sound system, a big dance floor, DJs, theme nights and speciality performers.

The Fountainhead Pub, 1025 Davie St, T604-687 2222. Gay-friendly neighbour-hood pub, with a heated and covered patio and weekend brunch.

Numbers, 1042 Davie St, T604-685 4077, www.numbers.ca. Vancouver's longest-running gay bar. Karaoke and a heaving dance floor entertain a very cruisy, older denim/leather-type crowd.

The Oasis Pub, 1240 Thurlow St, T604-686 1724, www.oasisvancouver.com. A gay-friendly upmarket piano bar, with a heated patio, decent food and 200 martinis.

Odyssey, 1251 Howe St, T604-689 5256, www.theodysseynightclub.com. The main surviving gay club, with high-energy dance music and nightly entertainment. Attracts a young, multicultural crowd, mostly men.

Live music

For information on jazz performances, www.vancouverjazz.com.

Backstage Lounge, Arts Club, Granville Island. A small but atmospheric venue for local and/or progressive acts.

Cellar Jazz, 3611 W Broadway, T604-738 1959. The principal jazz venue in town, with local or visiting musicians every night.

The Chan Centre for the Performing Arts, 6265 Crescent Rd, T604-822 2697, www.cha ncentre.com. Mostly dedicated to classical performances, this UBC venue has 3 stages in one complex; the main hall is one of the city's finest.

Commodore Ballroom, 868 Granville St, T604-739 4550. A wonderful old venue with a 1000-seat capacity and a massive dance floor built on rubber tyres. One of the best and most popular venues for international touring acts.

O'Doul's, 1300 Robson St, T604-661 1400. An upmarket restaurant and bar in the **Listel Hotel**, hosting live jazz every night.

Orpheum Theatre, 884 Granville St, T604-665 3050. Probably the best venue in town for highbrow acts of all types (no dancing allowed). When it was built as a part of the vaudeville circuit in 1927, this 2800-seat venue was the largest theatre in Canada. The elegant Spanish baroque-style interior with its arches, tiered columns and marble mouldings was almost converted into a cinematic multiplex before the city intervened. Home to the **Vancouver Symphony Orchestra**, it hosts most major classical events.

Queen Elizabeth Theatre, Hamilton and Georgia streets, T604-299 9000. This 1960s modernist building with almost 3000 seats is one of the main venues for classical music but also hosts ballet, musicals and major rock and pop acts.

The Yale Hotel, 1300 Granville St, T604-681 9253. A rough-looking bar that's the city's premier blues venue.

Spectator sports

General Motors Place, 800 Griffith Way. Home to the Canucks ice hockey team (www.canucks.nhl.com), a Vancouver obsession.

Nat Bailey Stadium, Queen Elizabeth Park, T604-872 5232. Home to the Canadians baseball team Jun-Sep (www.canadians baseball.com).

Pacific Coliseum, 100 Renfrew N/Hastings St E, at the **PNE**, T604-444 2687. Home to the Vancouver Giants junior hockey team (www.vancouvergiants.com).

Hastings Park Raceway, Renfrew N/Hastings St E, at the **PNE**, T604-254 8823, www.hastingspark.com. Has been hosting thoroughbred horse racing since 1889.

Theatre and performing arts

The main season for concerts, opera and ballet is Oct-Apr, but a number of festivals run continual shows throughout the summer (see opposite). As well as an active theatre world, Vancouver has achieved recognition for its dance scene. The 2 main areas for theatre are Granville Island (see page 51) and the Entertainment District of Downtown (see page 45).

Arts Club Granville Island Stage, 1585 Johnston St, T604-687 5315. Small venue for casual theatre such as musical comedies.

Centre in Vancouver for the Performing Arts, 777 Homer St, T604-602 0616. Opposite the main library, and designed by the same architect, this state-of-the-art theatre is Vancouver's main Broadway-type venue for large-scale and popular theatre, dance and musicals.

Firehall Arts Centre, 280 E Cordova St, T604-689 0926, www.firehallartscentre.ca. An operating fire hall from 1906-1975, the building now provides a small, intimate setting for quality dance and theatre.

Performance Works, 1218 Cartwright St, Granville Island, T604-689 0926. Small-scale contemporary works of a generally high standard.

Stanley Theatre, 2750 Granville St/12th Av, T604-687 1644. An elegantly restored 1931 cinema, now an arts club venue for drama, comedy or musicals.

Vancouver East Cultural Centre, 1895 Venables St, near Commercial Dr, T604-254 9578. This converted Methodist church is one of the best performance spaces in the city, thanks to great acoustics, sightlines and an intimate 350-seat capacity. It hosts a range of events including theatre, music and dance, with an emphasis on the modern and sometimes controversial.

Vancouver Playhouse, Hamilton St/Georgia St, T604-873 3311. Fairly intimate venue for mostly serious theatre, including many modern Canadian works.

⊛ Festivals and events

Jan Polar Bear Swim, T604-665 3424. Every year on 1 Jan, since 1819, lunatic locals have proven themselves by starting the New Year with an icy dip at English Bay Beach. **PuSh International Performing Arts Festival**, T604-6058284, www.pushfestival.ca. Takes place at numerous venues around town for 2 weeks at the end of Jan.

Feb Vancouver Storytelling Festival, www.vancouverstorytelling.org. Involves 3 days of great stories at the Heritage Hall, Main St at 15th. **Chinese New Year Festival,**

⁞ 2010 Winter Olympic and Paralympic Games

The 21st Winter Olympic Games will take place from 12 February to 28 February 2010, the 10th Paralympic Games from 12 March to 21 March 2010. Vancouver will host ice hockey, figure skating and speed skating, with freestyle skiing and snow- boarding events held at Cypress Mountain on the North Shore. The main Alpine and cross-country skiing, biathlon, ski jumping, bob- sleigh, luge and skeleton events will all take place around Whistler Mountain.

The 1.6 million tickets will be available from 11 October 2008, costing from $25 to $775 for events and $175 to $1100 for the opening and closing ceremonies, which will be held in BC Place Stadium. Half of all Games tickets will cost $100 or less. The biggest problem for spectators will be finding accommodation, so if you're planning on attending, make reservations as early as possible. Otherwise, avoid Vancouver during this time.

includes a massive parade in Chinatown, www.vancouverchinatown.ca, and numerous activities such as fortune telling, t'ai chi, music, crafts and demonstrations at the Dr Sun Yat-Sen Chinese Garden. **Vancouver Playhouse International Wine Festival**, T604-87 33311, www.playhouse winefest.com. Includes 60 events involving 1600 wines from 16 countries.
Mar Vancouver Celtic Festival, T604-683 8331, www.celticfestvancouver.com. A parade and 60 events for 4 days around St Patrick's Day.
May International Children's Festival, T604-708 5655, www.childrensfestival.ca. Runs for a week in mid-May and involves a host of shows, events and activities to delight the youngsters in Vanier Park. Cloverdale Rodeo, T604-576 9461, www.cloverdalerodeo.com. The 2nd biggest festival of its kind in the west after the Calgary Stampede (see page 259), attracting cowboys from all over the continent. **Eat! Vancouver's Everything Food and Cooking Festival**, www.eat-vancouver.com. Brings 3 days of culinary obsession to BC Place.
Jun Alcan Dragon Boat Festival, T604-688 2382, www.adbf.com. Takes place in mid-late Jun and is the a weekend of racing and cultural activities on False Creek. International Jazz Festival, T604-872 5200, www.coastaljazz.ca. A major festival, it involves 400 concerts on 40 stages around town over 10 days. Also includes free shows.

Jun-Aug Pride Season, T604-687 0955, www.vancouverpride.ca. Culminates in the Gay Pride parade in early Aug, a massive party that moves down Denman to Beach Av and on to the main party zone, Sunset Beach on English Bay.
Jun-Sep Bard on the Beach Skakespeare Festival, T604-739 0559, www.bardonthe beach.org. Four months of the master's plays under tents in Vanier Park.
Jul Dancing on the Edge Festival, Firehall Arts Centre, T604-689 0926, www.dancing ontheedge.org. Canada's largest showcase of independent choreographers runs for 10 days at the beginning of the month. **Vancouver Folk Music Festival**, T604-602 9798, www.thefestival.bc.ca. Has been going for over 30 years and involves 3 days of music and storytelling at Jericho Beach and other venues. **Theatre Under the Stars**, T604-6870714, www.tuts.bc.ca. A month of classic musicals in Stanley Park's Malkin Bowl. **Celebration of Light**, T604-738 4304, www.celebration-of-light.com. An inter-national fireworks competition. The most popular places to watch it from are the West End beaches and Vanier Park.
Aug Festival Vancouver, T604-688 1152, www.festivalvancouver.bc.ca. Fills the first fortnight of Aug with over 80 classical, jazz and world concerts around town. **Vancouver Chinatown Festival**, T604-632 3808, www.vancouver-chinatown.com. A free 2-day block-party featuring all manner of entertainment. **Powell Street Festival**,

T604-739 9388, www.powelstreet festival.com. A 2-day celebration of the city's Japanese community. **Abbotsford International Air Show**, T604-8528511. Held on the 2nd weekend in Aug, this is the 2nd-largest air show in North America. Aircraft from around the world compete and perform. **Vancouver Queer Film and Video Festival**, T604-844 1615, www.outon screen.com. For 2 weeks starting mid-month, 200 films are screened mainly at CinemarkTinseltown. **PNE Fair** at the Pacific National Exhibition, T604-253 2311, www.pne.bc.ca. Includes live entertainment, exhibits, livestock and the Playland Amusement Park.

Sep Vancouver Fringe Festival, T604-257 0350, www.vancouverfringe.com. Performances by 100 international companies in indoor and outdoor venues over 10 days.

Sep-Oct Vancouver International Film Festival, T604-685 0260, www.viff.org. Features some 300 films from 50 countries.

Oct Vancouver ComedyFest, T604-683 0881, www.vancouvercomedyfest.com. Features stand-up, improv shows and free street entertainment on Granville Island.

Dec Festival of Lights, T604-736 6754, www.vandusengarden.org. For most of Dec the VanDusen Gardens are illuminated with 20,000 lights and seasonal displays.

O Shopping

Antiques

Many antique, junk and consignment shops are clustered on stretches of South Main and South Granville. There are also many on Richards between Hastings and Pender.

Arts and crafts

Gastown has some interesting galleries but the best place for art-seeking is Granville Island. Cartwright St contains some of the key galleries and Net Loft, opposite the public market, also houses many fine shops. Railspur Alley is a nucleus for small and unique artists' studios. South Granville is the best place to pick up works by established artists.

Art Emporium, 2928 Granville St, T604-738 3510. Open since 1897, selling big-name domestic and international artists from the famous Group of Seven to Picasso.

Buschlen-Mowatt Fine Arts, 1445 W Georgia St, T604-682 1234. Knowledgeable staff and an extensive collection.

Crafthouse Gallery, No 1386 Cartwright St, T604-687 7270. Collection of quality work including pottery, textiles and jewellery.

Equinox, No. 2321 Granville St, T604-736 2405. Contemporary Canadian and international art, as equally revered as **Art Emporium**.

Federation Gallery, 1241 Cartwright St, T604-681 8534. Operated by members of the Federation of Canadian Artists.

Industrial Artifacts, 49 Powell St, T604-874 7797. A stunning collection of furniture and art, ingeniously fashioned from reclaimed pieces of old industrial machinery.

Monte Clark Gallery, 2339 Granville St, T604-730 5000. Specializes in avant-garde paintings, prints and photography.

Potters' Guild of BC, 1359 Cartwright St, T604-669 5645. Large selection of top-notch pottery that changes monthly.

Books

The best selection of new books can be found at **Chapters**, 2505 Granville St, T604-731 7822, and the more likeable **Duthie Books**, 2239 W 4th Av, T604-732 5344. For second-hand books try **Macleod's Books**, 455 W Pender St, T604-681 7654, and **Pulp Fiction Books**, 2422 Main St, T604-876 4311. **The Travel Bug**, 3065 W Broadway, T604-737 1122 or **Wanderlust**, 1929 W 4th Av, T604-739 2182 stock travel books and accessories and **Does Your Mother Know?**, 2139 W 4th Av, T604-730 1110, is the place for magazines and newspapers, they carry a wide range including some internationals. **Granville Book Co**, 850 Granville St, T604-687 2213. A wide selection of interesting books and magazines, great for browsing and open till midnight.

Little Sister's Book and Art Emporium, 1238 Davie St. A gay and lesbian bookshop where you can get a free copy of the **Gay and Lesbian Business Association Directory**. **Tanglewood Books**, 2932 W Broadway, T604-731 8870. A second-hand bookshop specializing in non-fiction.

Clothes and accessories

Most big name fashion and shoe boutiques are situated on Robson St between Burrard and Jervis, or nearby in the gigantic **Pacific Centre Mall** at Georgia St and Howe St. Granville St is good for off-the-wall new and used clothing and footwear shops. More exclusive designer labels are found in gorgeous heritage buildings on and around W Hastings St between Burrard St and Richards St. South Main is the area for more original boutiques, many showcasing local designers, such as **Eugene Choo**, No 3683, T604-873 8874; **Pleasant Girl/Motherland**, No 2539, T604-876 3426; and **Smoking Lily**, No 3634, T604-873 5459. There's also 4th Av west of Burrard in Kitsilano. For those interested in retro clothing, head to Gastown and the shops around W Cordova St including **Deluxe Junk Co** at No 310.

The Bay, 674 Robson St, T604-68 16211. Forever having sales, bargains can often be found.

Lulu Lemon, 2113 4th Av, T604-732 6111. Sells unique items designed for sports and yoga, but is phenomenally popular for fashion.

Pharsyde, 2100 4th Av, T604-739 6630. Stocks hip, casual clothing and shoes for men and women.

First Nations arts and crafts

The best place to start looking for native art is on Water St in Gastown.

Hill's Native Art, 165 Water St, T604-685 4249, www.hillsnativeart.com. Contains 3 floors of Northwest Coast arts and crafts, including some spectacular pieces.

Spirit Wrestler Gallery, 8 Water St, T604-669 8813. Works by major artists of various First Nations, with some very high-class pieces of sculpture.

Inuit Gallery, 206 Cambie St, T604-688 7323, www.inuit.com. North America's leading Inuit art gallery, with very beautiful modern and traditional sculpture and prints.

Gifts

For touristy souvenirs head to Water St in Gastown. For more unusual ideas check out the speciality shops on 4th Av in Kitsilano.

Obsessions, 595 Howe St, T604-684 0748; 387 Water, T604-622 7494; 1124 Denman, T604-6058890. A wide range of gift ideas.

The Postcard Place Net Loft, Granville Island, T604-684 6909. Has the city's best selection of postcards.

Salmagundi West, 321 W Cordova, T604-681 4648. For something more off the wall. This is a really fun shop, packed with eccentric oddities, toys and tit-bits.

Vancouver Art Gallery Shop, 750 Hornby St, T604-662 4706. Has lots of inspiringly beautiful items.

Kids

Kidsbooks, 3038 W Broadway, T604-738 5335; **The Games People**, 157 Water St, T604-685 5825; **It's all Fun and Games**, 1308 Commercial St, T604-253 6727; and **The Toybox**, 3002 W Broadway, T604-738 4322, are all shops dedicated to children.

Kid's Market, 1496 Cartwright St, Granville Island, T604-689 8447. Contains 25 shops just for children. Many of the toys and clothes here are one-offs, educational and handmade locally.

Markets

The best place for food shopping is the **Granville Island Public Market**, T604-666 6477, a mouth-watering high-end food hall and produce market open daily 0900-1900. **Lonsdale Quay Market**, T604-985 6261, www.lonsdalequay.com, where the SeaBus arrives at the North Shore, is a good second choice and is open daily 0900-1830.

Flea Market, Main St, in the block south of Terminal Av, Sat-Sun. For bargain-hunting.

Open-air night market, Keefer and Main, T604-682 8998, www.vcma.shawbiz.ca, May-Sep Fri-Sun 1830-2300. Great for browsing.

Music

A&B Sound, 556 Seymour St, T604-687 5837. Best deals on new music. Large selection and listen before you buy.

Zulu, 1972 W 4th Av, T604-738 3232. Good selection of new and used music of all kinds, with an emphasis on modern or alternative sounds.

Photography

Dunne & Rundle, 891 Granville St, T604-681 9254, and **Lens & Shutter**, 700 Dunsmuir St, T604-684 4422; 2912 W Broadway, T604-736 3461, carry new and used equipment.

Sports equipment

The biggest sports equipment shops are grouped together around W Broadway and Cambie and this is also the area for ski and snowboard shops, such as **Pacific Boarder**, 1793 W 4th Av, T604-734 0212. For a great selection of used equipment head for **Sports Junkies**, 600 W 6th Av, T604-879 0666, or **Cheapskates**, 3644 W 16th, T604-222 1125; and 3208, 3228 and 3496 Dunbar.

Coast Mountain Sports, 2201 W 4th, T604-731 6181. The other biggest and best all-round supplier.

Mountain Equipment Co-op, 130 W Broadway, T604-872 7858. Has the widest and best selection. Often has great deals but you'll have to buy a $5 membership first though.

Sigge's Sport Villa, 2077 W 4th Av, T604-731 8818. Has the biggest selection of cross-country equipment and offers lessons and rentals.

Sport Mart, 735 Thurlow St, T604-683 2433. For general supplies.

▲▲ Activities and tours

Adventure tours

For impartial, enthusiasts' information on just about any outdoor pursuit in BC, visit www.trailpeak.com.

Lotus Land Tours, T604-684 4922, www.lotuslandtours.com. Offers a broad range of activity-based tours including eagle watching, snowshoeing, whale watching, rafting, sea kayaking and hikes.

Moose Travel Network, T604-777 9905, www.moosenetwork.com. Runs a wide selection of 2- to 25-day tours around BC departing from hostels, aimed at young, independent travellers. The Whistler 'Sea to Sky Pass' is still $62, while trips around BC and the Rockies cost from $259 for 4 days to $729 for 13-14 days, including tax.

Outblaze Tours, 1829 Venables St, T604-710 1948, www.outblazetours.com. Runs hiking, biking, camping, surfing and ski tours for small groups (6-16).

Birdwatching

George C Reifel Migratory Bird Sanctuary, Westham Island, Richmond, T604-946 6980, www.ducks.ca/reifel. Daily 0900-1600, $4, child $2. A 360-ha sanctuary in the Fraser River for thousands of birds on their way from Mexico to Alaska. A good viewing tower close to the car park. Shore birds start arriving in mid-Aug, followed by mallard and pintail ducks. Numbers rise during Sep-Oct, and peak in early Nov, when about 20,000 snow geese noisily arrive. Many birds remain all winter. Nesting occurs Apr-May.

Boating/fishing

Granville Island has plenty of operators. Check the **Charter Information Centre** by the Maritime Market for information and **Granville Island Boat Rentals**, behind Bridges Restaurant, T604-682 6287.

Bites-on Salmon Charters, 200-1128 Hornby St, T604-688 2483, www.bites-on.com. 5- to 8-hr fishing tours from $450.

Coal Harbour Boat Rentals, 1525 Coal Harbour Quay, T604-682 6257. Speed-boat rentals.

Boat tours

Accent Cruises, 100-1676 Duranleau St, T604-688 6625, www.champagnecruises. com. Sunset dinner cruise, 1745-2015, $60.

False Creek Ferries 1804 Boatlift Lane, T604-684 7781, www.granvilleislandferries. bc.ca. Runs tours every 15 mins for $9, child $6. Tours can be joined at any stop en route.

Harbour Cruises, north tip of Denman St, T604-688 7246, www.boatcruises.com. Tours include the sunset dinner cruise, 2½ hrs, $70; Indian Arm luncheon cruise, 4 hrs, $62; and Vancouver harbour tour, 1 hr 15 mins, $25.

Bus tours

Grayline, T604-879 3363, www.grayline. com. Bus tours anywhere. Tour Vancouver in a double-decker bus.

Vancouver Trolley, 875 Terminal Av, T604-801 5515, www.vancouvertrolley.com, daily 0900-1430, $35, under 18 concessions. 2-hr trolleybus tours with 23 stops and on-off privileges. Starts in Gastown.

Climbing

Cliffhanger Indoor Rock Climbing Centre, 670 Industrial Av, T604-874 2400, www.cliff hangerclimbing.com. Over 4500 sq m of climbing terrain with views of the North Shore Mountains. Programs and courses for ages 6 and up. For the best climbing nearby, head to Squamish.

Cycling

Possibly the best way to discover Vancouver is by riding the 28-km Seawall Trail (see page 50). Almost all of it is on trails, with occasional well-marked stretches on public roads.

There are a lot of first-class, hard-core mountain bike trails around Vancouver, not for the inexperienced. The 3 main areas are Cypress, Seymour and Fromme Mountains. Seymour is probably the least difficult trail but Burnaby Mountain and Fisherman Trail are more appropriate rides for intermediates and beginners. Trail maps of these areas, along with some much-needed advice, are available at bike shops. See also *Mountain Biking BC* by Steve Dunn. For professional information or tours contact **Bush Pilot Biking**, www.bushpilotbiking.com. Note that by law you must wear a helmet.

There are a number of rental shops, such as **Simon's Bike Shop**, 608 Robson St, T604-602 1181, **Bicycle Sports Pacific**, 1380 Burrard St, T604-682 5437, and **On Top Bike Shop**, 3051 Lonsdale Av, T604-990 9550. **Bayshore**, 745 Denman St, T604-688 2453. For rollerblades and pushchairs. **Spokes Bicycle Rentals**, 1798 W Georgia St, T604-688 5141. Road bikes, tandems, child trailers and baby joggers.

Golf

There are some excellent golf courses in and around Vancouver, the best are situated outside the city and a handful are listed below. Those closer to town are **Fraserview**, 7800 Vivian Dr, T604-28 0181; **McCleery**, 7188 MacDonald St, T604-257 8191; and **University Club** at UBC, 5185 University Blvd, T604-2247799.
Meadow Gardens, Pitt Meadows to the east, T604-465 5474. Constructed by Les Furber and aimed at experienced players.
Morgan Creek, T604-531 4653. The par-73 home to BC's CPGA. Course designed by Arnold Palmer that includes a 14-ha wildlife refuge. Set in naturally attractive landscape.
Westwood Plateau, in Coquitlam, T604-694 1223. Famed for its spectacular natural features and mountain setting.

Hiking

For a short walk, it's hard to beat sections of the Seawall Trail especially around Stanley Park, or west from Vanier Park. For something longer, hiking in the Coast Mountains on the North Shore is prime (see page 57), but even better trails are found further north around Squamish, Whistler and Garibaldi.
Natural Trekking, T604-836 2321, www.naturaltrekking.com, www.eco trailescapes.com. Offers hikes and snowshoeing around Vancouver.

Kayaking

The best local kayaking is up Indian Arm, reached from Deep Cove. This 30-km fjord reaches deep into the Coast Mountains, passing old-growth forest and waterfalls, with ample chance to view wildlife.

The second-best local starting point is Bowen Island, from where the 8 Paisley Islands can be visited as a day trip. English Bay and False Creek offer mellow paddling in the heart of the city. For rapids, head for the Capilano and Seymour rivers. The following companies offer rentals and 3-hr lessons or tours for around $65:
Bowen Island Sea Kayaking, T604-947 9266, www.bowenisland kayaking.com;
Deep Cove Canoe and Kayak, 2156 Banbury Rd, North Vancouver, T604-929 2268, www.deepcovekayak.com; and **Ecomarine Ocean Kayak Centre**, 1668 Duranleau St, Granville Island; 1700 Beach Av, English Bay; 1500 Discovery, Jericho Beach; T604-689 7575, www.ecomarine.com.
Takaya Tours, 3093 Ghum-Lye Dr, North Vancouver, T604-904 7410, www.takaya tours.com. Runs trips up Indian Arm from Deep Cove with First Nations guides.

Sailing

The Yellow Pages is full of luxury yacht cruises. For something more authentic, **Cooper's Boating Centre**, 1620 Duranleau St, T604-687 4110, www.cooperboating. com; or just shop around in this part of Granville Island.
Jericho Sailing Centre, Jericho Beach, T604-224 4177, www.jsca.bc.ca. Arranges trips, lessons, and rentals.
Simplicity Sailing Charters, North end of Denman St, T604-765 0074, www.simp licitysailingcharters.com. Offers sailing tours from $320 for 3 hrs.

Scuba-diving

Whytecliffe Park at the western tip of the North Shore, Cates Park in Deep Cove and Porteau Cove on Hwy 99, are all renowned underwater reserves. **BC Dive and Kayak Adventures**, 1695 W 4th Av, T604-732 1344, www.bc dive.com, and **Rowand's Reef Dive Team**, 1512 Duranleau St, Granville Island, T604-669 3483, www.rowands reef.com, are recommended for courses, trips and rentals. **Diving Locker**, 2745 W 4th Av, T604-736 2681, www.vancouverdivinglocker.com. PADI diving instructors for 30 years. Offer beginners' course for $350 all inclusive. A wide range of advanced courses available, as well as 2- and 3-day dive trips. Sun Safari day trips for $100, all gear included.

Skiing

Cypress Mountain, see page 57; **Grouse Mountain**, see page 56; **Mount Seymour**, see page 55.

Swimming

The 2 best swimming spots in town are the large open-air pool at Kits Beach (see page 52) and the heated saltwater pool in the **Vancouver Aquatic Centre**, 1050 Beach Av, T604-665 3424. The latter also contains a fitness centre.

Walking tours

Architecture Institute of BC, 100-440 Cambie St, T604-683 8588 ext 333, www.aibc.ca. 6 different guided architectural tours, Jun-Aug, Tue-Sat: Gastown, Chinatown, Downtown, West End, False Creek North/Yaletown. Tours start 1300, $5 per person. **Vancouver Movie Tours**, www.vanmovie tours.com, $35, child $17. Conducts tours of sites used for Hollywood films and for the X-Files. **Walkabout Historic Vancouver**, 6038 Imperial St, T604-720 0006. Walking tour with costumed guides recounting stories and folklore.

⊖ Transport

TransLink, T604-953 3333, www.trans link.bc.ca, operates a reasonable network of city buses, a fast and generally efficient elevated rail system called the **SkyTrain** and a passenger ferry between Waterfront SkyTrain Station and North Vancouver's Lonsdale Quay called the **SeaBus**. Tickets bought on these are valid for any number of journeys in any direction on all 3 within a 90-min period. The system is divided into 3 fare zones, with Zone 1 covering almost everything of interest.

Fares are $2.50 for 1 zone, $3.75 for 2 and $5 for 3. Concession fares are $1.75, $2.50 and $3.50. Discount fares available for all zones after 1830 and at weekends and holidays. A day pass is $9, child $7. A book of 10 tickets is $19, child $16. Transit maps are posted on most bus shelters or are available at the Visitor Centre ($2), who also offer a free guide to reaching major attractions.

Air

For airport details, see page 42; for flight information see Essentials, page 25.

One-way fares from Vancouver in the summer are: $125 to **Kelowna** with West-Jet; $170 to **Castlegar** (for Nelson) with **Air Canada**; $179 to **Calgary** with Air Canada; $195 to **Whitehorse** with Air North; $100 to **Victoria** with Air Canada, West Coast Air and Pacific Coastal; $80 to **Powell River** (Sunshine Coast) with **Pacific Coastal**.

Airline offices Air Canada, 1030 W Georgia, T1888-247 2262; **American**, T1800-433 7300; **British Airways**, T1800-247 9297; **Continental**, T1800-2310856; **KLM**, T1800-225 2525; **Lufthansa**, T1800-563 5954; **Qantas**, T1800-227 4500; **WestJet**, T1800-538 5696.

In Canada, it is sometimes cheaper to book flights with a travel agent. **Flight Centre**, with many branches including 903 Denman St, T1866-246 6703, www.flight centre.ca, is cheap and useful, as is **Travel Cuts**, 1114 Burnaby St, HI Hostel, T604-6592845.

Floatplanes Fly to Victoria's Inner Harbour from Downtown (by Canada Place) or from the airport. The cost is about $130, saving at least an hour of bus time. **West Coast Air**, T604-606 6800, www.westcoast air.com and **Harbour Air**, T604-274 1277, www.harbour-air.com.

Bus

Local Vancouver's relatively narrow streets make bus travel slow and the system is not geared towards visitors, there are very few bus stops or vehicles carring information. Think about buying a transit map ($2) at the Visitor Centre, check online at www.bc transit.bc.ca, or ask the usually friendly and helpful drivers. The exact fare is dropped into a machine, which doesn't give change. If you have bought a ticket in the last 90 mins (time of expiry is on the ticket), feed it into the machine, which will give it back. Most routes run until 2400/0100.

There is also a transit service for the disabled called HandyDART. It mainly runs Mon-Fri 0630-1900, but for more information and booking call T604-430 2692. Additional information on all services, including maps and timetables for individual routes is available at the Visitor Centre, public libraries and SkyTrain ticket booths.

Long distance Buses and trains all leave from the VIA Rail Pacific Central Station, 1150 Station St, in a grim but handy part of town near the Main St/Terminal Av intersection and the Science World SkyTrain Station.

Greyhound, T604-482 8747, www.grey hound.ca, has connections to most Canadian towns and to Seattle. The following prices are one-way for adult/child and times are approx. Lower fares are sometimes available with 1 day advance purchase. There are 4 daily buses to **Banff** (13½ hrs, $119/$61); 4 to **Calgary** (15-18 hrs, $137/$70); 2 to **Jasper** (11 hrs, $119/$61); 5 to **Kamloops** (5 hrs, $58/$30); 6 to **Kelowna** (7 hrs, $65/$34); 3 to **Prince George** (12½ hrs, $116/$59); 3 to **Toronto** (70 hrs, $374/$188); 8 to **Whistler** (2½ hrs, $19/$9); and 8 to **Nanaimo** (3 hrs, $32/$25 including the ferry so no need to catch a city bus to Horseshoe Bay). Look out for special deals such as the 'Go Anywhere' fares, as little as $119 one-way or $189 return to anywhere in Canada if booked 14 days in advance.

Pacific Coach Lines, T604-662 8074, www.pacificcoach.com, runs to Victoria from the bus station or airport, $38/$20, including ferry (almost hourly); to **Whistler**, $61.50 one-way from the airport.

There are a few other choices to Whistler: The Snowbus, T604-685 7669, www.snow bus.ca, costs $43 return, $29 with ISIC. Perimeter Whistler Express, T604-266 5386, picks up at the airport and major hotels, $55 one-way. Malaspina Coach Line, T1877-227

8287, 2 buses daily to Powell River on the Sunshine Coast (6 hrs, $56).

Moose Travel Network, T604-7779905, www.moosenetwork.com, is the simplest way to get around BC and the Rockies. At least 16 different routes, mostly starting and ending in Vancouver, cover most itineraries. You can hop on and off and there are few time limits. Travel is in 11-24 seat mini-coaches, with lots of activities on the way.

To/from USA Greyhound, T1800-231 2222, runs 5 daily buses between **Seattle** and Vancouver (4 hrs, $25/15 one-way). The Quickshuttle, T1800-665 2122, www.quick coach.com, also connects Vancouver with Downtown **Seattle**, 5 services daily from the Holiday Inn at 1110 Howe St, stopping at the airport (4 hrs, $36/$23 one-way).

Car
For advice on travelling by car, including the cost of rental, see Essentials, page 27. All the major car hire agencies have offices Downtown and at the airport. **Avis**, T604-606 2869; **Budget**, T604-668 7000; **Hertz**, T604- 606 4711; and **Thrifty**, T604-606 1666, offer a one-way service. **Rent-a-wreck**, T604-688 0001, rents minivans which you can sleep in.

RV Rentals One-way RV rentals, often just to Calgary: **Candan**, T604-530 3645, www.ca ndan.com; **Cruise Canada**, T604-946 5775, www.cruise canada.com; and Go West, T604-528 3900, www.go-west. com.

Ferry
Local SeaBus ferries leave every 15 mins and take 12 mins to make the journey across Burrard Inlet from Waterfront Station to Lonsdale Market. They are wheelchair accessible and can carry bikes. On False Creek, the **Aquabus** T604-689 5858, www.theaquabus.com, runs from the south end of Hornby St to Science World, stopping at the Arts Club on Granville Island, the end of Davie St in Yaletown and behind Monk McQueens at Stamp's Landing, $2.50-$5 one-way. **False Creek Ferries**, www.granvilleislandferries.bc.ca, run from the Maritime Museum in Vanier Park to Science World, stopping at the Aquatic Centre on Beach Av, Granville Island Public Market, Stamp's Landing and BC Place. From $2.50-$5 one-way.

Long distance BC Ferries www.bc ferries.ca, run from Tsawwassen, about 30 km south of Vancouver, to **Victoria** (0700-2100, 95 mins), **the southern Gulf Islands** and **Nanaimo** (0630-2100, 95 mins). To get downtown from here take bus No 404 and transfer to No 98 at Airport Junction ($5). Horseshoe Bay, some 15 km northwest of the city on Hwy 99, is a far nicer terminal and much more convenient for Nanaimo, as well as **Bowen Island** and the **Sunshine Coast**. To get downtown take bus No 250 or No 257 ($3.75).

Train
Local The SkyTrain is a much better and faster service than the bus, but with only a few really useful stops: Waterfront in the old Canadian Pacific Station next to Canada Pl; Burrard at Burrard/Dunsmuir; Granville, beneath the Bay on Granville St; Science World-Main St; and Broadway at the Broadway/Commercial junction. The SkyTrain route to the airport is scheduled to be finished by the end of 2009.

Long distance Like buses, trains leave from the **VIA Rail Pacific Central Station**, 1150 Station St. VIA Rail's **The Canadian**, T1888-842 7245, www.viarail.ca, connects Vancouver and **Toronto** via **Kamloops** (8½ hrs, from $114) and **Jasper** (17½ hrs, from $238). Trains leaves Vancouver Fri, Sun and Tue. **Amtrak**, T1800-872 7245, www.amtrak.com, 5 daily trains to Seattle (4 hrs, $28).

Taxis
Taxis are well regulated and compare favourably with public transport prices. After midnight they are about the only way to get around. The main companies are **Black Top/Checker Cabs**, T604-731 1111, and **Yellow Cab Co**, T604-681 1111.

❶ Directory

Banks
Finding an ATM in Vancouver is never a problem. The main Canadian banks are clustered in a few blocks around Burrard St and Georgia St. **Currency exchange** Thomas Cook, 777 Dunsmuir St in the Pacific Centre Mall; Custom House 999 West Hastings St or 355 Burrard St.

Consulates
Australia, 1225-888 Dunsmuir St, T604-684 1177; **France**, 1100-1130 W Pender St, T604-681 4345; **Germany**, 704-999 Canada Pl, T604-684 8377; **Italy**, 1100-510 W Hastings St, T604-684 7288; **Japan**, 900-1177 W Hastings St, T604-684 5868; **Netherlands**, 883-595 Burrard St, T604-684 6448; **New Zealand**, 1200-888 Dunsmuir St, T604-684 7388; **Norway**, 1200-200 Burrard St, T604-682 7977; **Sweden**, 1100-1188 W Georgia St, T604-683 5838; **Switzerland**, 790-999 Canada Pl, T604-684 2231; **UK**, 800-1111 Melville St, T604-683 4421; **United States**, 2100-1095 W Pender St, T604-685 4311, 24-hr visa information for US citizens, T1900-451 2778.

Disabled access and facilities
With more than 14,000 sidewalk ramps, Vancouver claims to be one of the most wheelchair-accessible cities in the world. Half of the buses and all but the Granville St SkyTrain station are wheelchair accessible, and the **HandyDART** bus service is designed for wheelchair users, see page 77. Vancouver Airport was designed to accomodate those with hearing, visual and mobility difficulties. For accessible taxis call **Vancouver Taxi** at T604-255 5111. **Greyhound** has lift-equipped services to **Kelowna**, **Calgary** (via **Banff**) and **Prince George**, and the Pacific service to **Victoria** is also accessible.

Emergencies
24-hr Crisis Centre, T604-872 3311; **BC Women's Hospital and Health Centre**, T604-875 2424; **Fire and Rescue**, T604-665 6000; **Police**, 2120 Cambie St, T911, T604-717 3321 (non-emergency); **Women's Shelter**, T604-872 8212; **Rape Crisis Centre**, T604-255 6344.

Internet
Free in public libraries. Internet Cafés can be found at 616 Seymour St, T604-681 1088; 340 Robson St, T604-915 9327; 1690 Robson St, T604-68 54645; 1741 Robson St, T604-684 6004; 779 Denman St, T604-633 9389. All charge around $2/hr.

Laundry
Davie Laundromat, 1061 Davie St, T604-682 2717; Kitsilano Laundromat, 2208 W 4th Av,

T604-732 1320; **Swan's**, 1352 Burrard St, T604-684 0323.

Medical services
Acute Dental Centre, 2561 Commercial Dr, T604-877 0664; **Care-Point Medical Centres**, 1123 Davie, T604-915 9517; 1175 Denman St, T604-681 5338; 711 W Pender, T604-687 4858; 1623 Commercial St, T604-254 5554; 1861 W Broadway, T604-678 0598, www.carepoint.ca, 0900-2000 but hours vary. **St Paul's Hospital**, 1081 Burrard St, T604-682 2344; **Travel Clinic**, 1030 W Georgia, T604-6815656; **Vancouver**

General Hospital, 855 W 12th St, T604-875 4111.
Pharmacies London Drugs, 710 Granville St, 1187 Robson St, 665 Broadway and 1650 Davie St (24-hr); **Shoppers Drug Mart**, Pacific Centre at 700 Georgia St, 1006 Homer St, 1020 Denman St, 1125 Davie St, 2302 W 4th.

Post office
Canada Post The main post office with General Delivery (Poste Restante) is at 395 W Georgia. Others are at 595 Burrard St, 418 Main St, 732 Davie St. Letters can be posted at major pharmacies.

Sunshine Coast

Beginning at Langdale, a short ferry hop from Vancouver's Horseshoe Bay, the strip of Highway 101 optimistically known as the Sunshine Coast is the only major road on the Canadian mainland's Pacific coast. The pretty harbour town of Gibsons Landing, 10 minutes' drive from Langdale, makes a worthwhile day's excursion from the city. Otherwise, the area is mainly of interest to divers, boaters and kayakers. ➤➤ *For Sleeping, Eating and other listings, see pages 80-84.*

Gibsons Landing and the Sechelt Peninsula 🖪🚹
➤➤ *p80-84. Colour map 1, C3 and C4.*

Gibsons itself is nothing special, but the quarter clustered around the harbour, known as **Gibsons Landing**, is the prettiest community on the Sunshine Coast. Gathered around the **Visitor Info Centre** ⓘ *417 Marine Dr, T604-886 2374, www.gibsonsbc.ca*, are a number of worthwhile shops, art galleries, restaurants, an attractive boardwalk and the **Maritime Museum**, featuring paraphernalia from the long-running TV series *The Beachcombers*, which was set here. The marina is gorgeous, and there are plenty of beaches, parks and viewpoints to explore.

The quaint little community of **Roberts Creek**, 10 km further on, has a friendly and laid-back hippy vibe that would appeal to some, with lots of galleries, studios, children and dogs. There's also some good-value lodging, as well as beaches and forest.

Many hiking and biking trails criss-cross the **Sechelt Peninsula** to the west, including the 33-km **Suncoaster Trail**, whose foothills offer incredible views, and patches of old-growth forest. The shoreline has some pleasant bays and beaches, of which **Sargeant Bay** is maybe the most scenic, but few places to stay or camp.

Just before the second ferry crossing at Earl's Cove, a right turn leads to the pleasant village of Egmont, and **Skookumchuck Narrows Provincial Park**. The force of up to 200 billion gallons of water flowing through the narrows connecting the Sechelt and Jervis Inlets at a rate of up to 14 knots is dramatic indeed. Best viewing times are posted at the beginning of the trail, on BC Ferries and at local Visitor Info Centres. The phenomenon is greatly enhanced by the beautiful 4-km access trail through giant second-growth trees.

Powell River ⬛⚡🎵 ➠p80-84. Colour map 1, B3.

Powell River is the Sunshine Coast's most prominent town, with the majority of its facilities and the best Visitor Info Centre, **Powell River Visitor Center** ⓘ *4871 Joyce Ave, T604-485 4000, www.discoverpowellriver.com*. Buses from Vancouver terminate here, and Westview ferry terminal has departures to Comox on Vancouver Island, opening up the possibility of a pleasant circuit back to Vancouver via Nanaimo or Victoria. This is a useful base for outdoor pursuits, with lots of biking, hiking, fishing and kayaking, but particularly renowned for its scuba-diving. There is an interesting Historic Townsite and plenty of beaches, three of the best being **Palm Beach**, **Willingdon Beach** and **Mowat Bay**.

Lund and Desolation Sound Marine Park ⬛⚡

➠ *p80-84. Colour map 1, B3.*

Highway 101 ends at the village and marina of Lund, the closest inhabited point to **Desolation Sound Marine Park**. The largest water-access park in BC, with 5666 ha of high land, and 2570 ha of shoreline and water, this is a yachter's and kayaker's paradise, with countless places to dock and spend the night. As well as paddling, there is ample fishing, hiking and first-class scuba-diving. The park is famous for the size of the wolf eel and giant octopus. Petroglyphs can be seen at Walsh Cove.

Savary Island ⓘ *www.savary.ca, 8-km long crescent-shaped clay ridge reached from Lund by water taxi, T604-483 9749*, is about as remote as the accessible islands get. The north shore is one long white- and grey-sand beach and its calm, shallow water is the warmest in the Pacific Northwest. There is a restaurant, art galleries, campgrounds and the general store rents bicycles.

● Sleeping

Gibsons Landing and the Sechelt Peninsula *p79*
There are lots of very nice B&Bs in the picturesque harbour of Gibsons Landing, all good value compared to Vancouver prices, many with only 1 or 2 rooms. The Information Centre has listings, or visit www.bbsunshinecoast.com. **Roberts Creek** also has plenty of options, and is better value still.
AL-A Rockwater Secret Cove Resort, about 16 km beyond Sechelt on Secret Cove, T604-885 7038, www.rockwater secretcoveresort.com. One of the best of many resorts dotted along the beaches of the peninsula. Self-contained with a fine strip of private beach, a gorgeous pool/ patio area and a wide range of sleeping options, ranging from unique tent house suites to semi-rustic ocean-front cabins. There's a licensed restaurant, kayak rentals, a spa, volleyball and other games.

A A Woodland Garden Inn, 1214 Lysander Rd, Roberts Creek, T604-885 5730, www.a woodlandgardeninn.com. The ultimate venue for a romantic getaway. 3 suites with private hot tubs, in-room massage, a bottle of champagne, TV/DVD player, chocolates and flowers included in the price. The West Coast-style house is also magnificent, with an atrium with pool table, a living room and a sunroom.
A Bonniebrook Lodge B&B, 1532 Ocean Beach Esplanade, Gibsons Landing, T604-886 2887, www.bonniebrook.com. 7 suites in an immaculate ocean-front home offering a romantic treat close to Vancouver. Suites are exquisitely furnished with their own jacuzzi tubs, fireplace and sundecks, and are either on the beach or have views. A gourmet breakfast in the expensive, highly-praised restaurant is included.
A-B Maritimer B&B, 521 South Fletcher Rd, T604-886 0664, www.maritimerbb.com.

3 attractive rooms and a cottage, nicely situated right on the harbour in Gibsons Landing and surrounded by stunning landscaped gardens. Breakfast on the deck included.

B Secret Beach B&B, 999 Grandview Rd, Gibsons, T604-630 9313, www.secretbeach bandb.com. Set in extensive grounds that contain various theme gardens and a 2-person hot tub, this attractive home offers 3 varied rooms, a library, lounge, deck, spa services and ocean views. Breakfast is included.

C Ritz Inn, 505 Gower Point Rd, Gibsons Landing, T604-886 3343, www.ritzinn.com. Situated close to the harbour, this is the most appealing motel in town. Some rooms have ocean views and kitchenettes.

C-D Secret Garden Cottages B&B, 925 Byng Rd, Roberts Creek, T604-886 5999, www.secretgardencabins.com. A genuine slice of local character. 2 rustic heritage cabins with shower, TV, kitchen and wood stoves. Also offers 2 rooms in an extraordinary geodesic dome with guest lounge. All are set in 1 ha of gardens and orchards.

E Up the Creek Backpackers B&B, 1261 Roberts Creek Rd, Roberts Creek, T604-885 0384, www.upthecreek.ca. The best budget option around, with mostly dorms, kitchen, large sun deck with hammocks and BBQ, friendly social areas, a hot tub and a book swap. 10-min walk to the village, beach and forest.

Camping
Porpoise Bay Provincial Park, 4 km north of Sechelt up Sechelt Inlet Rd, T604-8983 678. A large and very popular campsite featuring 84 private leafy sites, showers and a large sandy beach.
Roberts Creek Provincial Park, on the highway in Roberts Creek. 21 primitive campsites in a beautiful old-growth forest with some walking trails. The day use area of the park, 1.5 km south, also has a beach.

Powell River p80
B Ocean Point B&B, 3344 Cortez Av, T604-485 5132, www.oceanpointbb.com. 2 large and luxurious suites in an impossibly grandiose mansion with a spiral staircase and antique furnishings. Near the beach and Westview ferry.

7074 Westminster Av, on the ocean, T604-485 6267, www.beachgardens.com. 2 big, fairly attractive ocean-front buildings. Dozens of simple but pleasant rooms with big windows and good views. The older building is more rustic, the newer rooms have private decks. New restaurant and lounge. Lots of activities available.

D Adventure B&B, 7439 Nootka St, 2 km south of Westview ferry, T604-485 7097, www.adventureb-b.com. 2 comfortable rooms with lofts and 1 suite, all in a grand, cottage-style wooden house surrounded by 2 ha of gardens. Sunroom, deck and sauna. Good value.

D The Old Courthouse Inn, 6243 Walnut St, T604-483 4000, www.oldcourthouseinn.ca. Situated by the water in the heart of the Historic Townsite, this Tudor-style 1939 building contains 8 rooms with plenty of character and charm. There's a TV, kitchen, laundry and patio with BBQ.

E Powell River Harbour Guesthouse, 4454 Willingdon Av, T604-485 9803, www.powell riverhostel.com. Dorms and private rooms in a conveniently central location, with a kitchen, internet, storage, laundry, parking, a café and an activity booking centre.

Camping
Haywire Bay Regional Park, 5776 Marine Av, 7 km north on Powell Lake via Manson Av, T604-483 3231. 45 sites, some with lake access, a playground, beaches, showers and access to the Lost Lake and Inland Lake hiking trails.
Saltery Bay Provincial Park, Mermaid Cove, 1 km north of Saltery Bay ferry. 42 attractive and private sites in a beautiful forest 200 m from the beach.

Lund and Desolation Sound Marine Park p80
LL-A Desolation Resort, signposted from Malaspina Rd, right 3 km before Lund, T604-483 3592, www.desolationresort. com. Beautifully crafted, luxurious chalets and apartments of various sizes, all fully equipped and tastefully decorated with wooden furnishings. The stunning 3-ha location, with views out onto the Okeover Inlet, can be appreciated from private decks. The use of kayaks and canoes is included in

the price and tours of the Marine Park can be arranged.

B Lund Hotel, on the marina, T604-414 0474, www.lundhotel.com. A quaint, picturesque hotel, built in 1905 and renovated in 2000. The 31 rooms are pleasant with interesting murals. Views can be enjoyed from the balcony and from the extensive deck of the pub/restaurant downstairs.

Camping

Okeover Arm Provincial Park, end of Malaspina Rd, T604-898 3678. The 14 vehicle-accesible sites are open seasonally and the 4 walk-in sites are open year-round. All very pleasant but basic, close to a rocky beach with oysters, mussels and clams.

🍴 Eating

Gibsons Landing and the Sechelt Peninsula *p79*

¶¶¶ Chez Philippe at the Bonniebrook Lodge (see Sleeping). The finest restaurant on the Sunshine Coast, with an excellent reputation for French fine dining in impeccable romantic surroundings. A great wine list.

¶¶ Leo's Tapas and Grill, 274 Gower Point Rd, T604-886 9414. Fine Greek dishes and ouzo specials.

¶ Backeddy Marine Pub, 16660 Backeddy Rd, Egmont, T604-883 2298. Good food and great views.

¶ Molly's Reach, on the boardwalk, T604-886 9710. Good, plentiful pub food, including a very cheap dinner special. The deck is the town's most obvious spot for enjoying wonderful ocean views.

Powell River *p80*

¶¶ Alchemist, 4680 Marine Av, T604-485 4141. High quality bistro-style French-Mediterranean dishes.

¶¶ Bemused Bistro, 4623 Marine Av, T604-485 4298. A varied, fairly ambitious and reassuringly small menu. Entertaining hosts, interesting art, great views. Fresh, mostly organic ingredients.

¶¶ La Casita, 4578 Marine Av, T604-485 7720. Funky blue adobe joint with authentic, consistently good and reasonably priced Mexican food.

¶¶ Shinglemill Pub and Bistro, on Powell Lake, north of town at 6233 Powell Pl,

T604-483 3545. An all-round wonderful eating experience, well worth the drive. Superb views, busy, friendly, good service and a fine menu that specializes in seafood.

¶ Flying Yellow Bread Bowl, 4722 Marine Av. A delightful spot with an arty, eccentric feel and good wholesome food.

¶ Local Loco's Music and Arts Café, 4692 Willingdon Av, T604-485 5626. Quirky and bohemian. A good range of mostly vegetarian food served in a downbeat atmosphere complete with resident dog and cat. Varied and exciting music and art.

Lund and Desolation Sound Marine Park *p80*

¶¶¶ Laughing Oyster, just beyond Okeover Arm Park, T604-483 9775. Exquisite West Coast cuisine and seafood which is served on a romantic patio, despite the plastic tables, with striking views. Almost an obligatory treat having come this far.

🎉 Festivals and events

Apr Sunshine Coast Festival of the Performing Arts, Sechelt, T604-885 7637, www.coastfestival.com. Running now for 35 years, involves almost a month of classical music performances.
Jun Jazz Festival, in Gibsons, www.coastjazz.com. The mostly outdoor festival occupies 3 days in mid-Jun.
Aug The Festival of the Written Arts, at the Rockwood Centre, Sechelt, T604-8859631, www.writersfestival.ca. The largest of its kind in the country. Blackberry Festival, Powell River, T604-485 2511. A week of various events at the end of the month.
Sep Sunshine Music Festival, T604-487 1906, www.sunshinemusicfest.com. Long-running event held on Labour Day weekend at Palm Beach Park, Powell River. A great musical event which attracts quality musicians of varied genres.

🚣 Activities and tours

Boat tours

Sunshine Coast Tours, T1800-870 9055, www.sunshinecoasttours.bc.ca. Tours to Chatterbox Falls on Princess Louisa Inlet and to Skookumchuck Narrows.

Canoeing and kayaking

Powell Forest Canoe Route is an excellent 5- to 7-day trip travelling through 12 lakes, as well as rivers and creeks, with a choice of 20 forestry campgrounds and a few B&Bs along the way. Open Apr-Nov, the route includes 80 km of canoeing, with 10 km of portage along good trails. Start at Lois Lake, 7 km down logging roads from a clearly marked turning 10 km past Saltery Bay.

Pedals and Paddles, Tillicum Bay Marina, Sechelt, T604-885 6440, www.pedals paddles.com. Rentals, lessons and 6-hr trips up Sechelt inlet for $75.

Porpoise Bay Charters, 5718 Anchor Rd, Sechelt, T604-885 5950, www.porpoisebay charters.com. Scuba-diving, kayak rentals and tours up Sechelt, Narrows and Salmon Inlets as far as the Skookumchuck Narrows.

Powell River Sea Kayak, Malaspina Rd, Powell River, T604-483 2160, www.bcsea kayak.com. Rentals, equipment, drop-off/ pick-up and all manner of highly rated tours (3 hrs to 6 days) around Malaspina Peninsula, Desolation Sound and beyond.

Rockfish Kayak, Lund Harbour, T604-414 9355. Rentals.

Sunshine Kayaking, Molly's Lane, Gibsons Landing, T604-886 9760, www.sunshine kayaking.com. Rentals, lessons and tours.

Scuba-diving

This area has some of the best diving in the world, with at least 20 sites, many accesible from the shore. Expect to see octopus, wrecks and at Saltery Bay, a 9-ft mermaid.

Alpha Dive Services, 6789 Wharf St, Powell River, T604-485 6969, www.dive powellriver.com. Equipment rentals, charters, instruction and information.

Pristine Charters, Lund Harbour, T604-483 1131, www.pristinecharters.com.

Hiking and cycling

The Sunshine Coast Trail stretches from Saltery Bay to the tip of the Malaspina Peninsula north of Lund, a total of 178 km. Pioneered by volunteer enthusiasts as a means of connecting the region's remaining sections of old-growth forest, this hike is still young and quite unknown, but destined to become a classic. Incorporating shorelines, lakes and views, it's accessed from several points along the highway, skirting close to campsites, B&Bs and hotels, and connecting with a canoe route. Look out for a number of interesting wooden bridges crossing creeks. The trail can also be used by mountain bikers, starting at Lund (take a water taxi). For details contact Powell River Information Centre or www.sunshine coast-trail.com. There are dozens of other hikes inland. A good but easy hike, with wheelchair access, is around Inland Lake.

Taw's Cycle and Sports, 4597 Marine Av, Powell River, T604-485 2555. Bike rentals.

Rock climbing

The Eldred River Valley has a number of challenging climbs of varying difficulty. Pick up the *Climbers Guide to Powell River* at the Visitor Centre.

☉ Transport

Air

Pacific Coastal, T604-482 2107, www.pacific-coastal.com, flies up to 5 times daily in summer between **Vancouver** and Powell River ($162 one-way, $100 with 14 days advance reservation).

Bus

Local Powell River is the only town too large to get around on foot. **Powell River Transit System**, T604-485 4287, runs the local service, including connections between the airport and Downtown. Bus No 1 runs hourly from the Mall to the Historic Townsite and Powell Lake. Route No 14 runs from the Mall to Lund at 1005 and 1605 (42 mins).

Long Distance Malaspina Coach Lines, 4675 Ontario St, T1877-227 8287, www.mala spinacoach.com, runs 1 daily bus between Powell River and **Vancouver** (5½ hrs, $56), with all stops along the way, leaving Vancouver's Pacific Central Station at 1400 and from behind Powell River's Town Center Hotel at 0815.

Car/Ferry

Driving from Vancouver to the Sunshine Coast involves 2 ferries. The first, from Horseshoe Bay to Langdale leaves every 2 hrs, 0720-2115 (0620-2020 return). The second, from Earls Cove to Saltery Bay, runs every 2 hrs, 0630-2210 (0540-2115 return), $10, vehicle $35 for return on either ferry.

Ferry/water taxi
BC Ferries, www.bcferries.bc.ca, run 4 times
daily between Powell River and Comox/
Courtenay on Vancouver Island, $9.20,
vehicle $37.20 (80 mins), 0810, 1200, 1715,
2045 from Powell River; 0630, 1010, 1515,
1915 from Comox. In summer, **Lund Water
Taxi**, T604-483 9749, www.lundwater
taxi.com, runs to **Savary Island** almost every
hour, 0900-1800, leaving Savary on the ½-hr,
always phone to reserve, $8.50 one-way,
they will transport bikes and kayaks.

❶ Directory

Powell River *p80*
Bank Royal Bank, 7035 Barnet St, T604-
485 7991. **Internet** Visitor Centre and
Public Library, 4411 Michigan Av, T604-
485 4796. **Laundry** Westview Dry
Cleaners, 4290 Joyce Av, T604-485 2616.
Medical services Powell River General
Hospital, 5000 Joyce Av, T604-485 3211.
Post Office 4812 Joyce Av, T604-485
5552.

Vancouver Island

Footprint features

Introduction

Dissected lengthwise by a central mountain range, Vancouver Island has two distinct faces. Most inhabitants live on the sheltered east coast, which enjoys Canada's mildest climate. Located on a picturesque natural harbour and known as the City of Gardens, Victoria is the province's capital and its most attractive town. Nearby in the Georgia Strait, the Gulf Islands are friendly and laid-back with plenty of walks, viewpoints and beaches. Halfway up the coast, the town of Courtenay offers skiing at Mount Washington and hiking in Strathcona Provincial Park, while further north there is increasing wilderness, outdoor pursuits and the chance to see orca whales. The scenic Inside Passage from Port Hardy to Prince Rupert, and the remote Cape Scott Trail also lie beyond the island's salmon capital, Campbell River.

Wild and weather-beaten, the West Coast has some of the world's biggest and oldest trees. Pacific Rim National Park contains the ever-popular West Coast Trail, the kayaker's paradise of Barkley Sound and the endless surf-beaten sands of Long Beach. The seaside village of Tofino is a fun base for numerous great excursions while, further up the coast, Gold River is the gateway to wild and pristine Nootka Sound, another magnet for kayakers and cavers.

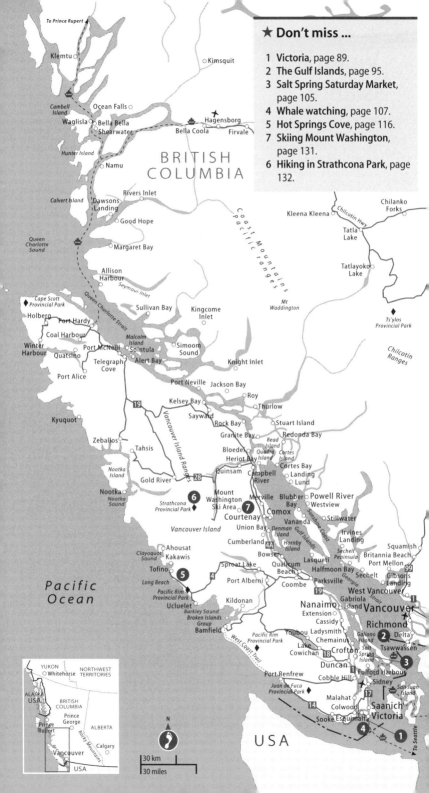

To Prince Rupert

Klemtu

Kimsquit

Cambell Island
Ocean Falls
Waglisla
Bella Bella
Shearwater

Hagensborg
Bella Coola   Firvale

Hunter Island
Namu

BRITISH COLUMBIA

Calvert Island

Rivers Inlet
Dawsons Landing

Good Hope

Queen Charlotte Sound

Margaret Bay

Allison Harbour
Seymour Inlet

Chilanko Forks

Kleena Kleena   Chilcotin Hwy
Tatla Lake
Tatlayoko Lake

Coast Mountains Pacific ranges

Mt Waddington

Ts'ylos Provincial Park

Chilcotin Ranges

Cape Scott Provincial Park
Holberg
Port Hardy
Coal Harbour
Winter Harbour
Quatsino
Port McNeill
Telegraph Cove
Port Alice

Sullivan Bay
Kingcome Inlet

Malcolm Island
Sointula
Alert Bay

Simoom Sound

Knight Inlet

Queen Charlotte Strait

Kyuquot

19

Zeballos

Tahsis

Nootka Island
Nootka
Nootka Sound

Gold River

Port Neville   Jackson Bay
Kelsey Bay   Roy
Sayward   Thurlow
Rock Bay
Granite Bay   Stuart Island
Bloedel   Read Island   Redonda Bay
Heriot Bay   Quadra Island   Cortes Island
Quinsam   Cortes Bay
    Campbell   Landing
    River   Lund

28

6
Strathcona Provincial Park

Mount Washington Ski Area
7
Courtenay
Comox

Merville   Blubber Bay   Powell River
    Vananda   Westview
    Stillwater

Vancouver Island

Union Bay   Denman Island   Irvines Landing
Cumberland   Hornby Island
4A
Bowser   Lasqueti

Sunshine Coast

Squamish
Britannia Beach
Port Mellon
99

Ahousat
Kakawis
Tofino
5
Clayoquot Sound
Long Beach

Sproat Lake
Qualicum Beach
Port Alberni
Coombe
Parksville

Halfmoon Bay   Sechelt Peninsula
Sechelt
Gibsons Landing
West Vancouver

Pacific Ocean

Pacific Rim Provincial Park
Ucluelet
Bamfield

Barkley Sound
Broken Islands Group
Kildonan

Pacific Rim Provincial Park

West Coast Trail

Youbou
Lake Cowichan
18

Nanaimo
Extension
Cassidy
Ladysmith
Chemainus
Crofton
Duncan
Cobble Hill

Gabriola Island
Strait of Georgia

Vancouver
Richmond
Delta
Tsawwassen

Galiano Island
2
Salt Spring Island
3

Port Renfrew

Juan de Fuca Provincial Park

14

Malahat
Colwood
Sooke Esquimalt

11
Cowichan

Fulford Harbour
Sidney
17

San Juan Island

4
Saanich
Victoria
1

To Seattle

USA

YUKON   NORTHWEST TERRITORIES
Whitehorse
ALASKA USA
BRITISH COLUMBIA
Prince George
ALBERTA
Prince Rupert
Rocky Mountains
Calgary
Vancouver
USA

N

30 km
30 miles

Victoria and the southern Gulf Islands

British Columbia's capital is arguably the most charming town in Western Canada. Surrounded by water on three sides, Victoria huddles around a picturesque harbour and seduces visitors with its pleasant ocean walks, fresh air and whale-watching trips. There's also a first-class museum and a fine selection of restaurants, pubs and bars. A liberal scattering of gardens, parks and flowers complements the grandiose architecture, adding to the natural beauty of the location, though the pervasive Englishness might make this an unwise first stop for visitors from the UK.

A short ferry ride away are Salt Spring and Galiano islands, the two most enticing southern Gulf Islands, where bucolic landscapes and a laid-back lifestyle are combined with a thriving arts and crafts scene, and plenty of hiking, cycling and kayaking opportunities. To the west of Victoria, the rugged coast leads to the attractive community of Sooke, with some decent beaches and a couple of great hikes, ending at Port Renfrew, southern terminus of the famous West Coast Trail. ▶▶ *For Sleeping, Eating and other listings, see pages 97-109.*

Ins and outs

Getting there and around

Victoria International Airport (YYJ) ① *www.victoriaairport.com*, is 20 km north of town on Highway 17. **Akal Airport Shuttle Bus** ① *T250-386 2525, www.victoriaairport shuttle.com, $15,* leaves from arrivals every 30 minutes 0700-2100, and takes one hour, stopping at the major Downtown hotels; taxis charge around $45. It's also possible to take a floatplane from Downtown Vancouver, which lands directly in Victoria's Inner Harbour, saving an hour of bus time. Ferries from Vancouver's Tsawwassen terminal arrive at Swartz Bay, 40 km north of Victoria, from where bus No 70 runs to Douglas Street in Downtown Victoria ($2.75); taxis are $55. Drivers are advised to book their ferry

Southern Gulf Islands

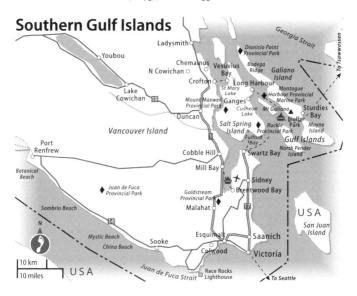

tickets well ahead in summer and during the holidays. There are also ferries to the Southern Gulf Islands (see page 95), which can be conveniently visited en route. The **bus terminal** is downtown ① *700 Douglas St*. The **VIA Rail station** ① *450 Pandora, T1888-842 7245, www.viarail.ca*, is on the waterfront downtown and connects with points north.

The majority of Victoria's sights can be easily reached on foot. Most buses run from the corner of Douglas and Yates, and there are numerous bicycle lanes. Driving in Victoria can be confusing and circuitous with many one-way streets, and parking can be tricky. ▸▸ *For further details, see Transport, page 108.*

Best time to visit
Protected from the harshest winds and chills of the Pacific by Washington's Olympic Peninsula, Victoria boasts the mildest climate in Canada but still tends to be rainy and windy in autumn and winter. January is the coldest month, with an average temperature of 6.5°C. Spring can begin as early as the end of February and is arguably the most beautiful season, when the cherry trees are in bloom. A holiday atmosphere reigns throughout the summer, when Victoria's many gardens erupt into colour, hanging baskets adorn the lamp posts, thousands of tourists mill around the Inner Harbour and a festival is usually underway. Autumn begins in late September, when the gardens take on a fresh set of colours and many of the tourists disappear.

Tourist information
Victoria has a very useful **Travel Information Centre** ① *812 Wharf St, Inner Harbour, T250-953 2033, www.tourismvictoria.com, mid-May to mid-Sep 0830-1830, mid-Sep to mid-May 0900-1700*. For information about the island and Gulf Islands try the **Tourism Association of Vancouver Island** ① *T250-754 3500, www.vancouverisland.travel or www.vancouverisland.com*. For ecotourism, visit www.ecoisland.ca. Note that accommodation can be heavily booked throughout the summer.

Victoria ⬛🚶🏃🎣❄🅾▲🚇🏃 ▸▸ *pp97-109. Colour map 1, C3.*

Downtown
Concentrated around Fisgard Street and the striking 'Gate of Harmonious Interest' is the oldest **Chinatown** in Canada, a bustling, fascinating quarter, with some unique buildings, eye-catching murals, plenty of restaurants and food shops, and a couple of fascinating alleys. Seek out the obscure Dragon Alley or Fan Tan Alley, the former red-light district and apparently the narrowest street in Canada. **Market Square**, to the south, is worth a quick look and the streets around Yates are the best for food and drink. You'll be drawn to Wharf Street just to be by the water, but many of Victoria's oldest and finest brick and stone buildings are on **Government Street**, disguised by the tacky ground-floor façades. Check out the art nouveau-style tobacconist at No 1116.

Bastion Square, site of the original Fort Victoria, is pleasant enough but there's little to see except the handsome former provincial courthouse, which today houses the **Maritime Museum** ① *28 Bastion Sq, T250-385 4222, www.mmbc.bc.ca, mid-May to mid-Sep daily 0930-1700, mid-Sep to mid-May daily 0930-1630, $8, child $3*. Artefacts and commentaries tell the story of the Pacific Northwest's explorers, pirates, early settlements, shipwrecks and whalers. The highlight is the *Tillikum*, a dugout canoe in which Captain John Voss successfully circumnavigated the globe, reaching London in 1904 after three years at sea.

Inner Harbour
Victoria's focal point is the picturesque Inner Harbour. A multitude of craft, from kayaks and ferries to yachts and floatplanes, ply these waters where passenger

steamships once unloaded their genteel cargo. The wide-open space and undeniable grandeur of the surrounding architecture create a magical atmosphere, especially at night or in summer when the harbour walkway is thronged with art peddlers,

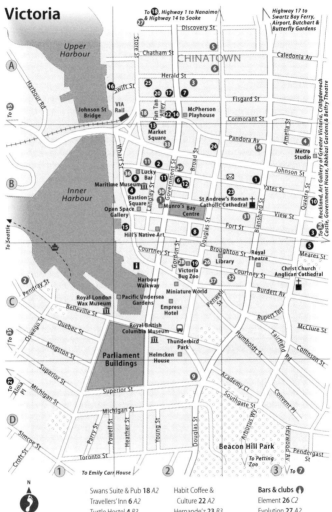

Sleeping 🛏
Admiral Inn **2** C1
Agra House **3** A2
Bedford Regency **1** B2
Dashwood Manor **7** D3
Helm's Inn **9** D2
HI Victoria **11** B2
Ocean Island Backpackers Inn **14** B3
Paul's Motor Inn **5** A2
Spinnakers **15** A1
Swans Suite & Pub **18** A2
Travellers' Inn **6** A2
Turtle Hostel **4** B3

Eating 🍴
2% Jazz **18** A2
Azuma Sushi **6** B2
Blue Fox Café **5** C3
Brasserie L'Ecole **7** A2
Café Brio **3** B3
Camille's **4** B2
Canoe Brew Pub **16** A1
Daidoco **19** C2
Demitasse Café **1** B3
Don Mee **20** A2
Ferris' Oyster Bar & Grill **2** B2
Fisherman's Wharf **21** D1
Habit Coffee & Culture **22** A2
Hernande'z **23** B3
Mint **24** B2
Molé **14** A2
Pagliacci's **8** B2
Re-bar **9** B2
Red Fish Blue Fish **15** B2
Reef **11** B2
Solstice Café **13** A2
Tapa Bar **12** B2
Union Pacific Coffee Company **25** A2
Victoria BBQ House & Bakery **17** A2
Zambri's **10** B3

Bars & clubs 🍸
Element **26** C2
Evolution **27** A2
Fernwood Inn **34** B3
Hugo's Grill & Brewhouse **28** C2
Hush **29** B2
Irish Times **30** B2
Red Jacket **31** B3
Smiths Pub **32** C3
Social Club **33** B2
Stage **34** B3
Sticky Wicket **26** C2
Superior **35** C1
Upstairs Cabaret **36** B2
Vista 18 **37** C2

buskers and tourists. The view landwards is dominated by Victoria's two grandest constructions, the Empress Hotel and the lavishly illuminated Parliament Buildings, both designed by architect Francis Rattenbury.

Built in 1908, the **Empress Hotel** retains the opulence of the Victorian era quite splendidly. While you may not want to splurge on a room, a self-guided tour is recommended to explore the many lounges, lobbies and dining halls, all dripping with colonial excess. Have a drink in the Crystal Lounge, or partake in the popular (but expensive) ritual of high tea in the Tea Lounge. Next door, **Miniature World** ① *649 Humboldt St, T250-385 9731, www.miniatureworld.com, Jul-Aug daily 0830-2100, Sep-Jun daily 0900-1900, Nov-Mar daily 0900-1700, $12, child $7*, features tiny reconstructions of various themes such as the World of Charles Dickens, Space 2201 or Fantasyland. The highlight is the scale model of the coast-to-coast Canadian Pacific Railway.

One block further north is **Victoria Bug Zoo** ① *631 Courtney St, T250-384 2847, www.bugzoo.bc.ca, mid-Jun to mid-Sep daily 0930-1900, mid-Sep to mid-Jun Mon-Sat 1000-1730, Sun 1100-1730, $8, child $5*, an offbeat but strangely compelling collection of weird and wonderful insects from around the world.

Royal British Columbia Museum

① *675 Belleville St, corner of Government St, T250-356 7226, www.royalbc museum.bc.ca, daily 0900-1700, $14, concessions $9.50, under 5 free.*

Housed in a modest building to the south of the **Empress Hotel,** this highly informative museum ranks as one of Canada's finest, and provides an excellent introduction to the fauna, landscapes and culture of this province. In the **Natural History Gallery**, a series of dioramas populated by realistic stuffed animals evoke BC's extraordinary landscapes; particularly popular is a life-sized example of the woolly mammoths that roamed these lands until 13,000 years ago. The **First Peoples Gallery** uses wooden masks, artefacts, audiovisual displays, some major carvings and a reproduction of a longhouse to recount the culture and history of BC's aboriginal population. The journey through time continues with an exploration of the white man's world in the **Modern History Gallery**, which contains displays on the gold rush and the early pioneers, as well as a recreation of turn-of-the-20th-century Victoria, complete with cobbled streets, buildings and a cinema showing silent films. There is always at least one excellent temporary exhibition, usually the highlight. Also located inside the museum is the **National Geographic IMAX Theatre** ① *T250-480 4887, www.imaxvictoria.com, daily 1000-2000, $11, youth $8.75, child $5, show and museum, $23, youth $18.25, child $5.*

Behind the museum on Elliot Street is **Thunderbird Park** ① *May-Oct daily 0900-1700, by donation*, where a small collection of modern totem poles complements the First Nations Gallery within. A carving-shed offers the chance to see native masters at work. Next door is **Helmcken House** ① *10 Elliot St*, the oldest surviving house in BC. Built in 1852 for a pioneer physician, it contains an intact set of frightening 19th-century medical implements.

Parliament Buildings and around

Built in 1897, the very British-looking **Parliament Buildings** ① *501 Belleville St, T250-387 3046, www.lwg.bc.ca, mid-May to mid-Sep daily 0900-1600, mid-Sep to mid-May Mon-Fri 0900-1600*, set the tone for the whole town, especially at night when they are atmospherically illuminated by 3333 tiny light bulbs. The interior can be visited on a free guided tour but, despite the anecdotes and efforts of the guides, and a few historical artefacts (such as the dagger that killed Captain Cook), it's really not as impressive as the outside.

In front of the Parliament Buildings are a number of attractions suitable for children. The **Royal London Wax Museum** ① *470 Belleville St, T250-388 4461, www.waxmuseum.bc.ca, mid-May to mid-Sep daily 0930-1900, mid-Sep to mid-May*

0900-1700, $12, child $5, also designed by the prolific Rattenbury, is in the same vein as London's Madame Tussaud's and just as inexplicably popular. Children inevitably favour the gory Chamber of Horrors. Jutting out into the harbour, the **Pacific Undersea Gardens** ⓘ *490 Belleville St, T250-382 5717, www.pacificunderseagardens.com, Apr-Jun daily 1000-1800, Sep-Mar daily 1000-1700, Jul-Aug daily 0900-2000, $9.50, under 18 $7.50, under 12 $5.50, under 5 free,* is a giant underwater aquarium full of octopuses, eels and various other cool marine animals. In a special theatre divers talk you through a 20-minute guided tour of the creatures they encounter.

Emily Carr House
ⓘ *207 Government St, T250-383 5843, www.emilycarr.com. Jun-Oct daily 1100-1600, Sep and May Tue-Sat 1100-1600, $6, child $5.*
Four blocks behind the Parliament Buildings is the house where this much-loved Canadian painter and writer was born and lived most of her twilight years, surrounded by animals. Built in 1864, the house features some of her paintings, which are important historically as well as artistically (see page 380). There is a small art gallery showing the work of other local artists.

Beacon Hill Park and the coast
Douglas Street leads south to the ocean and to beautiful **Beacon Hill Park**, where the bounty of Victoria's warm climate can be appreciated. Winding paths lead between all manner of different trees, from mighty old-growth giants to ornamental deciduous species, past duck ponds, swans and roaming peacocks, and through gardens where tens of thousands of flowers are lovingly tended. There are free tennis courts, lawn bowling, a football field, a cricket pitch, a great children's playground, summer waterpark and a **Petting Zoo** ⓘ *mid-Mar to mid-Oct, $2 donation.*

The park leads down to a cliff-front promenade popular with dog owners, para-gliders and winter storm-watchers. Occasionally, pods of orca can be seen from here. It's a lovely stroll along the shore, with access down to rock pools and the long breakwater. Those with a vehicle or bike can follow the coast east along Dallas Road, taking the scenic routes and admiring the grand houses, or take bus No 5 or 11 as far as the genteel community of **Oak Bay** with its picturesque marina.

Art Gallery and Craigdarroch Castle
A few sights are clustered together in an area called **Rockland**, east of Downtown along Fort Street. None necessarily justifies the trip on its own but together they make for a decent morning's diversion. **The Art Gallery of Greater Victoria** ⓘ *1040 Moss St, T250-384 4101, www.aggv.bc.ca, Fri-Wed 1000-1700, Thu 1000-2100, $12, child $2, bus No 11, 22 or 14 from Downtown,* has an extensive and varied permanent collection, including a massive store of Japanese art and quite a few less-distinguished works by Emily Carr. Usually the four or so temporary exhibitions provide the real interest, so check what's showing. A short walk away is **Craigdarroch Castle** ⓘ *1050 Joan Cres, off Fort St, T250-592 5323, www.craigdarrochcastle.com, mid-May to mid-Sep 0900-1900, mid-Sep to mid-May 1000-1630, $11.75, child $3.75, bus No 11 or 14,* built 1887-1889 by Robert Dunsmuir, a Scottish mining expert. He was drafted in to help exploit the black seams and ended up discovering the most productive coal mine in North America (see page 112), becoming BC's first millionaire in the process. Thanks to a shrewd business sense and utter lack of scruples, his net worth when he died – a mere six months before the castle's completion – was $20 million. The rooms are exquisitely decorated, with magnificent stained glass, immaculate Victorian furnishings and a few oddities like a 3D picture made of human hair. The first few rooms are the best.

While in the area you might also want to take a stroll around the 6 ha of ornamental gardens at **Government House** ⓘ *1401 Rockland Av, T250-387 2080, dawn till dusk, free, bus No 1,* where the British royal family stays when visiting.

Neighbourhoods, beaches, parks and trails

There's a lot more to Victoria beyond the touristy Inner Harbour. The best neighbourhood scenes to sample include Cook Street Village, between Dallas and Fairfield; Fairfield's Moss Street during the Saturday market; Fernwood around Pembroke; and Oak Bay Village on Oak Bay Avenue between Foul Bay Road and Hampshire Road.

Among the best beaches in town are Willows Beach in Oak Bay, which has an awesome view of the marina, Mount Baker and the Olympic Mountains in Washington state; Gonzales and Cadboro Bays further north, which also have nice beaches to explore; and the dog beach by Beacon Hill, which is good for watching the paragliding.

Our favourite parks not already mentioned include Mount Douglas, with trails and a road that lead to the summit for the best views; Playfair Park, near Quadra and Tattersall, which has a large stand of Garry Oaks, an extensive rhododendron garden and some immaculate flowerbeds; Beckwith Park on Beckwith off Quadra, which has the best summer water park; and Kinsmen Gorge Park at Tillicum and Gorge.

Butchart Gardens and Butterfly Gardens

If Beacon Hill has whetted your appetite, Victoria has plenty of other magnificent gardens to admire. The hype and price of the **Butchart Gardens** ⓘ *20 km north of Victoria, T250-652 5256, www.butchartgardens.com, Jun-Aug daily 0900-2200, closing times vary during the rest of the year, $26.50, under 18 $13.25, under 12 $3, follow red signs west onto Keating Rd from Hwy 17, or take Central Saanich bus No 75 from Douglas St*, are equally excessive, but its 22 ha of gardens – including Japanese, rose, Italian and sunken varieties – are beautifully executed, exceptional in any season and magical when illuminated at night. Firework displays set to music take place on Saturday evenings in July and August and live music or puppet shows are frequent. There's a gift shop, over-priced restaurant, coffee shop and a dining room serving the inevitable high tea. Having come this far, visit the nearby **Butterfly Gardens** ⓘ *1461 Benvenuto Rd, 3 mins' drive before Butchart Gardens, T250-6523822, www.butterfly gardens.com, May-Sep 0900-1730, Sep-Oct and Mar-Apr 0930-1630, $12, child $6.50*, an indoor conservatory turned into a tropical rainforest, complete with flowers, trees, waterfalls and packed with 50 species of butterfly from around the world.

An alternative to the above is the **Abkhazi Gardens** ⓘ *1964 Fairfield Rd, T250-598 8096, www.conservancy.bc.ca, Mar-Sep daily 1100-1700, $10, under 18 $7.50, under 12 free, bus No 7 from town*, an impressive landscape, skilfully forged from Victoria's characteristics rocky topography by Prince and Princess Abkhazi in the 1940s and saved from housing developers by the Land Conservancy. The upper garden affords great views of Victoria and the Juan de Fuca Strait.

West to Port Renfrew 🚌🚲⛰️🚏 ➤ *pp83-109. Colour map 1, C3.*

Hatley Castle

ⓘ *Just off Sooke Rd (Hwy 14), 8 km west of Victoria, T250-391 2666, www.hatleypark.ca. Bus No 50 to Western Exchange then Nos 39, 52 or 61, or Galloping Goose Trail by bike. Castle tours run 4 times daily, $15, youth $9, child $7 for 30 mins or $17, youth $11, child $9 for 1 hr, both include the gardens. Entry to gardens only $4.50, child $3.*
The castle was built in 1909 for James Dunsmuir, son of Robert, and is situated on the ocean front within the beautifully landscaped campus of Royal Roads University.

The setting is infinitely more conducive to grandeur than that of **Craigdarroch Castle**, and the ornamental gardens are the undeniable highlight. There is also a small museum, café and gift shop.

Fort Rudd National Historic Park
ⓘ *Fort Rodd Hill Rd, T250-478 5849, daily 1000-1730, $4, child $2. Bus No 50 to Western Exchange then No 39.*
A short drive away from **Hatley Castle** is this tranquil 45-ha park that contains some historic military installations and the **Fisgard Lighthouse**. Overlooking the harbour from the end of a causeway made out of scrap cars, this is the oldest lighthouse on the Pacific, having been in continuous operation since 1860.

Sooke → *Colour map 1, C3.*
A short 30-km hop west from Victoria, easily reached by bus No 61 or the Galloping Goose bicycle trail, Sooke has a great collection of B&Bs, a couple of excellent restaurants and a thriving artist community. For a full list of artists' studios, pick up the Art Map from the Visitor Information Centre, where there's also a small **museum** ⓘ *2070 Phillips Rd, T250-642 6351, www.sookeregionmuseum.com, www.sooke.org, mid-May to mid-Sep daily 0900-1700, mid-Sep to mid-May Tue-Sun 0900-1700.*

On a warm summer day, you'd be mad not to pay a visit to **Sooke Potholes Park**, north of town at the end of Sooke River Road. It's a magical spot with natural swimming pools carved out of rock and mellow waterfalls that have caves hidden behind them.

East of Sooke, Gillespie Road leads south from Highway 14 to a peninsula that contains the wonderful and surprisingly underused **East Sooke Regional Park**, a little pocket of wilderness full of hiking trails and viewpoints. The **Coast Trail** is an excellent one-day hike that stretches 10 km between trailheads at Pike Road and Aylard Farm. With jagged cliffs, windswept bluffs and beautiful, unspoilt rainforest, this trail is in good condition and compares favourably with the Juan de Fuca Marine Trail (see below). Allow at least six hours. Beechey Head is a favourite spot for spotting turkey vultures or watching the annual hawk migration at the end of September.

Juan de Fuca Provincial Park → *Colour map 1, C3.*
ⓘ *A guidebook is available from the Sooke Information Centre, $18. There are no fees or registration except for parking.*
Between Sooke and Port Renfrew the highway never strays far from the coast, which is dotted with a string of deserted, surf-beaten beaches looking out over the Juan de Fuca Strait. Just west of sleepy Jordan River, the trail and sand of **China Beach** mark the beginning of Juan de Fuca Provincial Park, which protects several long sandy beaches and a strip of coastal rainforest, all of it connected by the Juan de Fuca Marine Trail. This 47-km wilderness route opened in 1995 to provide an alternative to the over-burdened West Coast Trail. Four trailheads along the highway provide access: from east to west, China Beach, Sombrio Beach, Parkinson Creek and Botanical Beach. **Mystic Beach**, just west of China Beach, has a 45-minute hike through rainforest and over a suspension bridge to good sand, a waterfall and some shallow caves. **Sombrio Beach** is the place for surfing while **Botanical Beach** is the great for exploring tidal pools. Check the park noticeboards for low tide.

Port Renfrew → *Colour map 1, C3.*
There's little reason to visit this dispersed logging and fishing village other than to start or finish the Juan de Fuca Trail at Botanical Beach 6 km to the south, or the West Coast Trail. The latter starts across a narrow inlet at **Gordon River**, which also has an **Information Centre** ⓘ *daily 0900-1700*. Services are few, so hikers are

advised to stock up on supplies in Victoria. Forestry recreation sites and a few campgrounds are dotted along the logging roads to the north; ask at the Gordon River
Information Centre.

Southern Gulf Islands ⬤🚗🚲❄🅿▲🚌☕ ▸▸ pp83-109.

Ins and outs

Salt Spring Island and Galiano Island are reached by ferry from Vancouver's
Tsawwassen terminal and Victoria's Swartz Bay. **Harbour Air** ① *T1800-447 3247,
www.harbour-air.com*, operates two scheduled daily flights from Vancouver to Salt
Spring ($95 one-way). Salt Spring and Galiano have limited transportation, though
there are ferries between the islands. Cycling, driving and kayaking are great ways
to get around and hitchhiking is a way of life. Both islands have small Visitor
Information Centres. Pick up a copy of the *Gulf Islander,* available on the islands or
ferry, which has good hotel listings; or check www.gulfislands.net. ▸▸ *For further details,
see Transport, page 109.*

Salt Spring Island → *Colour map 1, C3.*

① *The websites www.saltspringtoday.com and www.saltspringmarket.com, are useful sources of information. Be sure to pick up a self-guided tour map of 32 nearby artist
and artisan studios, www.saltspringstudiotour.com.*

The southern Gulf Islands are an archipelago of odd-shaped landmasses huddled
together in the Georgia Strait, famous for their laid-back, bohemian atmosphere,
artist communities, natural beauty and outdoor pursuits. Salt Spring is the biggest,
most populated and developed island and the only one with any kind of urban focus,
the oddly named Ganges. The trade-off is a lesser degree of tranquillity and
quaintness, though these are easily found elsewhere on this sheep-dotted island.
There are plenty of eating and drinking options here and an unmissable **Saturday
Market**. There is also a small but eager-to-please **Visitor Information Centre** ① *by the
shopping centre car park, 121 Lower Ganges Rd, T250-537 5252, mid-May to mid-Sep
0900-1600, mid-Sep to mid-May 1100-1500.*

At the southern end of the island is **Ruckle Provincial Park** ① *9 km east of Fulford
Harbour at the end of Beaver Point Rd*, the largest and one of the nicest on
the Gulf Islands. Trails here incorporate forest, 7 km of shoreline, farmland and
historic buildings. There's a good chance of spotting marine life and birds, but the
park's outstanding feature is its campground (see Sleeping, page 99). For some
truly awe-inspiring views of the island-dotted Georgia Strait, head to the top of
Mount Maxwell Provincial Park ① *just south of Ganges take Cranberry Rd west to
Mt Maxwell Rd, then climb steeply for 8 km.* There are some trails through big old trees
but the temptation is just to sit and gawp. It's also a good place to experience the full
power of the winds whistling down the strait. West of Fulford Bay, some longer hikes
lead up Mount Tuam and Mount Bruce. Swimming is good at **Vesuvius Bay**, or at
St Mary Lake (north of Ganges) and **Cusheon Lake** (south) for fresh water.

Galiano Island → *Colour map 1, C3.*

Despite its rising and understandable popularity, Galiano Island strikes a balance
between adequate infrastructure (unlike many Gulf Islands) and scant development.
The closest thing to a village is the ferry terminal of **Sturdies Bay**, which has a small
Visitor Information Booth ① *2590 Sturdies Bay Rd, T250-539 2233.* Pick up the
all-important map here, on the ferry or at www.galianoisland.com. The main activity
is hiking through old-growth forest, much of which has been protected by the
determined efforts of locals. The longest hike covers the entire eastern coast
(about 25 km).

Salt Spring Island

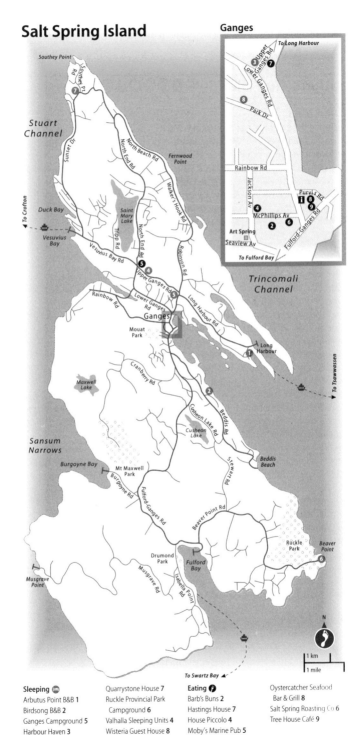

Sleeping
Arbutus Point B&B 1
Birdsong B&B 2
Ganges Campground 5
Harbour Haven 3
Quarrystone House 7
Ruckle Provincial Park
  Campground 6
Valhalla Sleeping Units 4
Wisteria Guest House 8

Eating
Barb's Buns 2
Hastings House 7
House Piccolo 4
Moby's Marine Pub 5
Oystercatcher Seafood
  Bar & Grill 8
Salt Spring Roasting Co 6
Tree House Café 9

The long, skinny finger of Galiano sits in the Georgia Strait pointing westwards away from Sturdies Bay in the east. Just after the ferry terminal, a left turn down Burrill takes you along Bluff Road and through **Bluffs Park**, a beautiful chunk of old-growth forest. Shortly after, a left fork leads to Active Pass Drive and the trailhead for ascending **Mount Galiano**, a satisfying hike leading to views of the Olympic Mountains, Navy Channel and, on a clear day, all of the southern Gulf Islands.

Take the right fork instead, then left down Montague Road, to connect back with Porlier Pass Road and reach **Montague Harbour Provincial Marine Park**. There are three white shell beaches here, a café, shop, great campground, cracking sunsets and a 3-km shoreline trail around Gray Peninsula. Two-thirds of the way along the island, Cottage Way gives access to **Bodega Ridge**, a 3-km walk with views all the way. **Dionisio Point Provincial Park** at the west end has camping but marine access only, many rare flowers, fine views and diving.

● Sleeping

Victoria *p89, map p90*

L-A Dashwood Manor, 1 Cook St, T250-385 5517, www.dashwoodmanor.com. A huge 1912 English Tudor mansion, sumptuous heritage rooms with wood-burning fireplace, balcony, jacuzzi and sea views. Location is hard to beat, right on the ocean near Beacon Hill Park. Full breakfast included.

L-A Spinnakers, 308 Catherine St, T250-384 2739, www.spinnakers.com. Tastefully furnished and spacious heritage rooms or stunning garden suites adjacent to the first-class pub-restaurant. All have en suite baths, private entrances, and decks or patios onto the lovely garden. The location on Victoria Harbour is attractive but it's a fair walk from Downtown. Breakfast included.

L-A Swans Suite Hotel, 506 Pandora Av, T250-361 3310, www.swanshotel.com. Exceptionally stylish rooms and huge suites, with high ceilings and lots of great art. Downstairs is a pub-restaurant with a wonderful collection of native art. Good value and great location.

A Admiral Inn, 257 Belleville St, T250-388 6267, www.admiral.bc.ca. The most reasonably priced hotel on the Inner Harbour, with simple but decent rooms, balconies/patios, a nice guest lounge and breakfast included.

B Helm's Inn, 600 Douglas St, T250-385 5767, www.helmsinn.com. Given its location between the Inner Harbour and Beacon Hill Park, this is a great deal. There's a variety of rather old-fashioned rooms and suites, most with kitchen and many with a balcony.

C Bedford Regency Hotel, 1140 Government St, T250-384 68357, www.bedford regency.com. Reasonable rooms in a very central, if somewhat noisy, location.

C-D Travellers' Inn, 1961 Douglas St, T250-953 1000; 1850 Douglas St, T250-381 1000, www.travellersinn.com. The rooms are pretty standard and not the amazing deal they would have you believe but you're almost guaranteed they'll have one available, a major bonus in the summer. There are also some handy extras, such as use of a pool and gym, and free parking.

C-E Ocean Island Backpackers Inn, 791 Pandora Av, T250-385 1788, www.ocean island.com. In a historic building Downtown, this is a very social and friendly hostel with plenty of facilities including a licensed bar hosting regular music events, a large and atmospheric dining room, a full communal kitchen, patio, laundry, internet access, storage and bike lock-up. Dorms or private rooms, some with bath and/or TV. Tours and activities. Also have 3 excellent value suites in a separate house.

D Agra House, 679 Herald St, T250-380 1099, www.agrahouse.com. Plain, pleasant, good-value rooms in a handy, central location. Parking and breakfast included.

D Paul's Motor Inn, 1900 Douglas St, T250-382 9231, www.paulsmotorinn.com. Fairly spacious rooms, a short walk from Downtown. Ask for a courtyard room.

E HI Victoria, 516 Yates St, T250-385 4511, www.hihostels.ca. This quiet, professionally-run hostel is conveniently located in the heart of Downtown. Spacious building with high ceilings. Facilities include a kitchen with microwaves, TV room, games room with pool table, a small library, laundry, bike rentals, storage, lockers and private rooms.

E Turtle Hostel, 1608 Quadra St, T250-381 3210, www.turtlehostel.ca. A funky little hostel with some interesting paintings scattered around, some in the guests' rooms. Dorms and private rooms, full kitchen, lockers and laundry.

Camping
Thetis Lake, 1938 W Park Lane, T250-478 3845. The closest campground to town (10 km away), with showers and laundry. The lake itself is somewhat removed, but has a great beach for swimming and some nice walks.

Sooke p94
Sooke is famous for its West Coast-style B&Bs, characterized by their wood-dominated decor, vaulted ceilings and big windows with ocean views. Those listed below are the best, but many more can be found at www.sookenet.com, www.sookebnb.com, and the Visitor Centre. Reservations are recommended.

AL-A Point No Point, 10829 West Coast Rd (23 km west), T250-646 2020, www.point nopoint.com. Attractive cabins and suites situated on a long private beach. Highly renowned restaurant serves lunch, English tea and dinner.

B Coopers Cove Guesthouse, 5301 Sooke Rd, T250-642 5727, www.cooperscove.com. 4 lovely, big, en suite rooms overlooking the ocean, with fireplaces and private decks. Guest lounge and dining room, lovely gardens and a big deck with hot tub. Connected to a prestigious cooking school (inclusive packages available).

B-C Arbutus Cove Guesthouse, 3018 Manzer Rd (6 km east), T250-642 6310, www.arbutuscoveguesthouse.com. 2 large, West Coast-style rooms with ocean views, and a cottage with kitchenette and hot tub on the private deck. Breakfast included.

Camping
French Beach Provincial Park, 20 km west. A great campground with private sites set in

the forest. Trails lead down to the mile-long sand and gravel beach, and a playground. Grey and orca whales can be spotted May-Oct.

Sooke Potholes Campground, T250-383 4627, www.secure1.conservancy.bc.ca/ PotholesCamping. Situated at the north end of the potholes, with private sites nestling beneath the giant Douglas fir. In summer, campers can arrive earlier and stay later at the potholes than other visitors, a huge bonus.

Sooke River Flats Campsite, T250-642 6076, by Visitor Centre. Basic but handy.

Juan de Fuca Provincial Park p94
Camping
Beach camping is available at China (78 drive-in sites), Mystic, Bear and Sombrio beaches. Forest camping at Kuitsche Creek and Payzant Creek, both near Parkinson Beach. A fee of $5 per person per night is payable at trailheads. Be aware that wood ticks exist in this region and are most prevalent Mar-Jun.

Port Renfrew p94
A-C Soule Creek Lodge, 2000 Powder Main Rd, T250-647 0009, www.soulecreek lodge.com. This wooden West Coast lodge is hands down the best place to stay, so book ahead. There are 4 comfy suites, a cabin and 2 surprisingly luxurious yurts to choose from. There's also a large deck with hot tub, views and 65 ha to explore. The food is exceptional, so stay for dinner. Can arrange shuttles from trailheads or town.

B Port Renrew Hotel, 17310 Parkinson Rd, T250-647 5541, www.portrenfrewhotel.ca. A good location, right on the waterfront overlooking Port San Juan on the way to Botanical Beach. There are simple but new motel-style rooms, 2-bedroom "duplexes" with kitchenettes (**AL**), and fancy log cabins (**L**). There's also a restaurant and bar.

Camping
Pacheedaht Campground, T250-647 0090. No reservations. Beach camping along a pristine 2-km long beach at the start of the West Coast Trail.

For an explanation of sleeping and eating price codes used in this guide, see inside the front cover. Other relevant information is found in Essentials, see pages 28-31.

Salt Spring Island *p95 map p96*

Apart from a couple of standard motels, Salt Spring's beds are mostly in B&Bs, of which there are over 100. The Visitor Centre has a picture book to help you choose, and will take reservations. Particularly in summer, booking ahead is recommended, using www.saltspring today.com, or www.salts pringmarket.com. Summer is the best time to find walk-in accommodation.

A Arbutus Point B&B, 215 Welbury Dr, 6 km from Ganges near Long Harbour Ferry, T250-633 9555, www.arbutus point.com. 3 bright and comfortable suites with private entrance and sun deck. Lovely garden and hot tub over-looking the ocean, use of rowboat or kayak.

B Birdsong B&B, 153 Rourke Rd, 5 mins south of Gange off Beddis, T250-537 4608, www.birdsongbedandbreakfast.com. A modern, open-plan home set in spacious grounds and gardens, with a library and hot tub with ocean views. Fully-equipped cottage and 2 large, homey and well-equipped rooms, each with private balcony and fireplace. Gourmet breakfast included.

B Harbour Haven, 121 Upper Ganges Rd, T250-537 5571, www.saltspringharbour house.com. A great location on the harbour in Ganges. Fairly standard but decent hotel rooms, many with ocean views.

B Quarrystone House, 1340 Sunset Dr, 6 km from Vesuvius Bay, T250-537 5980, www.quarrystone.com. 4 gorgeous en suite rooms with balconies, fireplaces, jacuzzis and private entrance. Beautiful ridge location with ocean views. Breakfast provided by the hospitable hosts.

B-C Wisteria Guest House, 268 Park Dr, 10 mins' walk from Ganges, T250-537 5899, www.wisteriaguesthouse.com. Very pleasant, bright and colourful rooms with private or shared bath, studios with kitchenette, and a cottage. A guest lounge and a full breakfast is included.

E Valhalla Sleeping Units, 601 Upper Ganges Rd, T250-538 1992, www.valhalla sleepingunits.com. 3 small cabins with shared outhouse, situated halfway between the 2 ferries.

Camping

Ganges Campground, 150 Leisure Lane, 1 km north of Ganges, T250-537 1210, www.gangescampground.com. 50 RV and tent sites on a large, flat field dotted with small trees. Privacy is minimal.

Ruckle Provincial Park, 9 km east of Fulford Harbour at the end of Beaver Point Rd, T250-391 2300. The 8 spots for RVs are nothing special, but those with a tent can walk in and claim one of the 70 sites dotted along the shore, with exquisite views of Swanson Channel. One of the best camping experiences in Western Canada.

Galiano Island *p95, map p100*

L-AL Galiano Inn, 134 Madrona Dr, T250-539 3388, www.galianoinn.com. One of the best lodges on the islands, set in lovely grounds overlooking the ocean. Spacious rooms with sumptuous decor, fireplaces, balconies and stunning views. Full spa on site, ask about packages. Breakfast included.

A Bodega Resort, 120 Monastee Rd, west end of island, T250-539 2677, www.bodega resort.com. Spacious and comfortable log cottages that sleep up to 6. Situated in beautiful, expansive grounds full of fruit trees and stone carvings, all with great views. All kinds of activities available.

C Driftwood Village Resort, 205 Bluff Rd E, T250-539 5457, www.driftwoodcott ages.com. In a nice setting near the ocean, these cottages are a bit old fashioned but good value. Ask about ferry pick-up.

C Moonshadows Guest House, 771 Georgeson Bay Rd, T250-539 5544, www.moonshadowsbb.com. 2 colourful, spacious en suite rooms with vaulted ceilings, and a suite. A gorgeous wood house with lots of light on a 40-ha farm between Sturdies Bay and Montague Harbour. Hot tub and full breakfast. Free shuttle bus.

C Rocky Ridge Bed and Breakfast, 55-90 Serenity Lane, 15 km north of ferry, T250-539 3387, www.cedarplace.com/rocky ridge. 3 lovely, big, modern rooms (2 with toilets but shared tub) in a gorgeous open-plan wooden house on a rocky bluff. Extensive ocean views, billiards, library, living room, sauna and hot tub. A great deal.

C Serenity by the Sea Retreat, 225 Serenity Lane, T250-539 2655, www.serenitybythe sea.com. 3 en suite rooms high above the ocean, with cosy homey decor, vaulted ceilings and a private deck. Breakfast and morning yoga included; bodywork and counselling available.

Camping

Montague Harbour Provincial Park, T250-539 2115. Wonderful walk-in sites overlooking the ocean, some nice vehicle sites too. Trails and beaches. Reservations crucial in summer.

❼ Eating

Victoria *p89, map p90*

Victoria has a very active culinary scene for a town its size, with a fairly rapid turnover. For the latest developments, check out www.eat magazine.ca. Fisherman's Wharf, at the north end of Superior or Michigan St, has a number of cheap stalls selling fish and chips and other dishes, with some outdoor tables. It's a great spot, there are seals in the harbour and you can buy raw fish to feed them.

Café Brio, 944 Fort St, T250-383 0009. European-style fine dining with a West Coast sensibility, using the freshest local ingredients, including homemade salamis and cheeses. The decor and ambience are perfectly pitched: colourful and lively, a fusion of class and casual, modern and traditional.

Camille's, 45 Bastion Sq, T250-381 3433. Fine dining in a classy but casual environment. The diverse menu couples international flavours with West Coast leanings, concentrating on fresh local seasonal produce. The well-chosen wine list features many of BC's finest.

Zambri's, 911 Yates St, T250-360 1171. The menu in this consistently impressive Italian-inspired favourite changes daily, incorporating fresh local produce and home-made sausages and salami.

Azuma Sushi, 615 Yates St, T250-382 8768. The liveliest and most attractive of several new sushi joints in town. Stylish and very Japanese, with extremely fresh, reliable food.

The Blue Fox Café, 919 Fort St, T250-380 1683. A breakfast/brunch institution. Small and atmospheric, always crowded, with queues out the door. Friendly service, great food, a prime people-watching spot.

Brasserie L'Ecole, 1715 Government St, T250-475 6260. Simple and stylish, romantic and intimate, with perfect service and a well-stocked bar. The menu is well-crafted, unpretentious and surprisingly reasonable. Try the duck confit or signature steak-frites.

Canoe Brew Pub, 450 Swift St, T250-361 1940. A wonderful reclaimed industrial warehouse with big wooden beams and a huge patio overlooking the ocean, the place to eat or drink on a sunny afternoon. The food is okay, stick to simple items like burgers. Also a brewpub, with arguably the best beer in town. There's live music at weekends.

Don Mee, 538 Fisgard St, T250-383 1032. One of Chinatown's finest, specializing in seafood and definitely the place to come for the unique dim sum experience.

Ferris' Oyster Bar and Grill, 536 Yates St, T250-360 1824. A personal favourite, small and perennially crowded. Lively atmosphere,

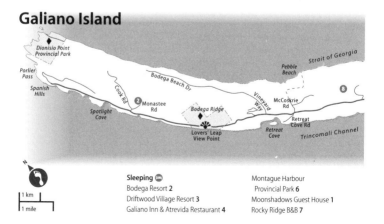

Galiano Island

Dionisio Point Provincial Park

Porlier Pass

Spanish Hills

Strait of Georgia

Pebble Beach

Bodega Beach Dr

Cook Rd

Monastee Rd

Spotlight Cove

Bodega Ridge

Lovers' Leap View Point

Vineyard Way

McCoskrie Rd

Retreat Cove Rd

Retreat Cove

Trincomali Channel

1 km
1 mile

Essentials Victoria & the southern Gulf Islands Listings

an excellent menu that concentrates on seafood and reasonable prices. Try the baked oyster platter. Upstairs has more of a wine bar atmosphere, very sophisticated, with a smaller and more interesting menu. Sit at the bar and watch the tiny kitchen space.

The Mint, downstairs at 1414 Douglas St, T250-386 6468. Hip and very busy. A great place for a drink and some tasty and filling Indian-Nepalese specialities like butter chicken. Broad drinks menu and surprisingly reasonable prices.

Molé, 554 Pandora Av, T250-385 6653. Occupying a beautiful room with good art on the brick walls, serving breakfast and lunch made from fresh, local, mostly organic ingredients. Many options for vegetarians and vegans. Gets packed with a mixed, savvie crowd.

Pagliacci's, 1011 Broad St, T250-386 1662. A locals' favourite. The interior is dark, full of theatrical detail, usually packed and noisy with nightly live music. Food is mainly Italian, with a good range of wines and spirits at reasonable prices. Many just drop in for drinks and dessert, their cheesecake and boozy coffees are legendary.

Re-bar, 50 Bastion Sq, T250-361 9223. A long-standing favourite for food that is vegetarian if not vegan, healthy, inter-national and varied. Menu includes curries, enchiladas, perogies, salads and brunch. The lively, colourful interior also features a fresh juice bar. A bit pricey for what you get.

The Tapa Bar, 620 Trounce Alley, T250-383 0013. A lively venue in a good location with a colourful, Mediterranean interior, lots of art and seating outside in the alley. There's a broad selection of tapas but the atmosphere and drinks are what keep people coming back.

Daidoco, inside the small arcade at 633 Courtney St and Douglas St, T250-388 7383, Mon-Fri 1100-1600. A tiny Japanese-style deli and café with delicious small dishes that go well beyond sushi. Reasonable prices.

Hernande'z, in the pedestrian mall between 735 Yates St and 736 View St. The secret's out! Despite it's obscure location, this cheap, cheerful and tastily authentic Salvadorean diner is always packed, but that's half the fun.

Red Fish Blue Fish, 1006 Wharf St, T250-298 6877. Housed in a recycled steel cargo container right by the floatplane terminal, with a garden on the roof and outdoor seating only. Incredible versions of fish and chips, fish tacones and other seafood favourites. A real experience.

The Reef, 533 Yates St, T250-388 5375. A vibrant, increasingly popular spot for good-value Caribbean favourites such as jerk chicken, fish tacos and spiced ribs.

Victoria BBQ House & Bakery, 1714 Government St, T250-382 8022. The best BBQ pork- or honey-buns in town and tasty BBQ or pork to go.

Cafés

2% Jazz, 2621a Douglas St, T250-384 5282. A bit out of the way, but if you take your coffee seriously this is the place to go.

Serenity by the Sea
Retreat **8**

Eating ⑦
Daystar Market **4**
Harbour Grill **5**
Hummingbird Pub **1**

La Bérengerie **2**
Max & Moritz Spicy
Island Food House **3**

Demitasse Café, 1320 Blanshard St, T250-386 4442. Great coffee in a tiny out-of-the-way spot, good inexpensive lunch menu too.

Habit Coffee and Culture, 552 Pandora Av, at Government St, T250-704 8304. Interesting art on the walls, a friendly, laid-back vibe, great coffee and magazines.

Solstice Café, 529 Pandora Av, T250-475 0477. Coffee and cakes in comfortable surroundings with a youthful, alternative vibe and a little patio at the back.

Union Pacific Coffee Company, 573 Herald St, T250-380 0005. Fine coffee, good baked goods and sandwiches, a selection of magazines to browse and a little courtyard at the back.

Sooke *p94*

Sooke Harbour House, 1528 Whiffen Spit Rd, T250-642 3421, www.sookeharbour house.com. A popular outing for Victorians and frequently voted one of the best restaurants in BC. Casually classy with ocean views, a sophisticated West Coast menu that changes daily and a great wine list. The emphasis is on the freshest ingredients, particularly seafood, with herbs, and vegetables from their own garden. They also have some excessively opulent and expensive rooms (**L**).

17 Mile Pub, 5126 Sooke Rd, 9 km east, T250-642 5942. English-style pub in a historic Tudor building, with a good selection of beer and food.

Point No Point, 10829 West Coast Rd, 20 km west of Sooke, T250-646 2020, open daily 1130-1530, 1730-2030, reservations recommended. Gorgeous views and a small, well-crafted menu that emphasizes the freshness of the ingredients.

The Fish Trap, 6688 Sooke Rd, T250-642 3474. The choice in town for fish and chips.

Mom's, 2036 Shields Rd, unmissable in the centre of town, T250-642 3314. The epitome of a diner, with grouchy waitresses, booths and cheap breakfast. A local institution.

Salt Spring Island *p95 map p96*

Hastings House, 160 Upper Ganges Rd, T250-537 2362, www.hastingshouse.com. Featuring locally raised lamb, fresh seafood and herbs from their own garden, this highly renowned restaurant, with its intimate atmosphere, is worth a little extra expense.

House Piccolo Restaurant, 108 Hereford Av, Ganges, T250-538 1844, www.house piccolo.com. Highly regarded gourmet European cuisine in casual but smart surroundings. Great wine list.

Moby's Marine Pub, 124 Upper Ganges Rd, T250-537 5559. As well as being perhaps the only place to experience locally brewed Gulf Island beers on tap (the Porter is excellent), this popular locals' hangout also serves up some decent food. Try the teriyaki salmon burger.

Oystercatcher Seafood Bar & Grill, Harbour Building, 104 Manson, Ganges, T250-537 5041. A casual seafood restaurant with a deck overlooking Ganges Harbour.

Tree House Café, 106 Purvis Lane, Ganges, T250-537 5379, live music every night May-Sep. This tiny outdoor venue is invariably packed, with quality live music making for a quintessential Salt Spring experience. The menu covers several bases, or there are baked goods and coffee in the morning.

Cafés

Barb's Buns, off McPhillips Av, Ganges. A popular bakery serving pizza, pastries and all sorts of delicious cakes.

Salt Spring Roasting Co, 109 McPhillips Av, Ganges, T250-653 2385. Renowned for their roasted java beans, this café is also the meeting place of choice for locals. Decent cakes and snacks, good art on the walls.

Galiano Island *p95 map p100*

Atrevida, Galiano Inn, 134 Madrona Dr, T250-539 3388. Delicious West Coast-style food in impeccable surroundings with ocean views.

La Bérengerie Restaurant, 2806 Montague Rd, close to the park, T250-539 5392. Authentic French dishes from a menu that changes daily and features the freshest local organic produce. A 4-course table d'hote with advanced reservation. Open-air seating in summer.

The Harbour Grill, at Montague Harbour Marina, T250-539 5733. The food is fairly predictable but the location is picturesque.

Hummingbird Pub, 47 Sturdies Bay Rd, T250-539 5472. This cosy pub is the best place to meet locals and it also serves some decent food. Their pub bus makes runs to and from the marina hourly, 1800-2300.

❦ **The Daystar Market**, 96 Georgeson Bay Rd, T250-539 2505. Coffee and baked goods.

❦ **Max & Moritz Spicy Island Food House**, T250-539 5888, by the ferry landing. Takeaway German and Indonesian food.

❶ Bars and clubs

Victoria *p89, map p90*

Most favourite places for a drink in Victoria, including **Ferris'**, **The Mint** and **Canoe**, are included under Eating. For clubs, visit www.clubvibes.com or pick up the free *Monday Magazine*. Victoria has an active but discreet gay scene, www.gayvictoria.ca.

Element, 919 Douglas St, T250-220 8587. One of the biggest, friendliest, more casual clubs. Recently refurbished it now has a loungey feel and music that ranges from chart music to hip-hop, house, alternative, retro and a variety of live acts.

Evolution, 502 Discovery St, T250-388 3000, no cover before 2200. This small, energetic, unpretentious club has different nightly music and is known for its cheap drinks.

The Fernwood Inn, 1302 Gladstone Av, T250-412 2001. Across the road from **Stage**, this is a great neighbourhood pub with regular live music.

Hugo's Grill and Brewhouse, 625 Courtney St, T250-920 4846, open till 0200. With its dark, industrial-style interior and well-chosen music, this is one of Victoria's hippest and most popular venues. There's a restaurant and martini-bar vibe in the evening. Live music until 2200, then DJs playing progressive tunes until the end of the night. Attracts a slightly older, more relaxed crowd. Their beers, brewed on the premises, are worth trying.

Hush, 1325 Government St, T250-385 0566. Different electronic music every night, with a good-natured party atmosphere. Rated by many as Victoria's best club, it certainly gets some top DJs.

Irish Times, 1200 Government St, T250-383 7775. A superior version of the Irish pub, this place is big, comfortable and popular. There are 20 different beers on draught and live Celtic music every night. The patio is the best people-watching spot in town.

The Red Jacket, 751 View St, T250-384 2582. Split between 2 rooms, there's a dance floor on one side and a lounge on the other. With cheap drinks and theme nights, it's especially popular Fri-Sat, and attracts a chart music or student crowd.

Smiths Pub, 777 Courtney St, T250-360 2544. A dark, atmospheric, alternative kind of pub with different nightly music themes: ska, psychedelic, soul, mod, Brit-pop, funk.

The Social Club, 560 Johnson St, T250-480 2874. One of Victoria's coolest and most stylish clubs. Recommended on Wed.

Spinnakers Brewpub, 308 Catherine St, cross Johnston St Bridge or take the harbour ferry, T250-386 2739. With its exceptional house-brewed beers and superb food prepared from scratch using local ingredients, this is a superior pub in every sense and a Victoria institution.

Stage, 1307 Gladstone Av, Fernwood, T250-388 4222. It's not exactly central, but this sophisticated little bistro and wine bar is the perfect spot for a snack and a glass of wine.

The Sticky Wicket, 919 Douglas St, T250-383 7137. On a sunny day it's hard to beat this long-running pub's rooftop patio.

The Superior, 106 Superior St, T250-380 9515. A unique, very Victorian venue. Large, open room with high ceilings and eccentric decor. Technically a restaurant but better for drinks, with live music every night, often jazz.

Upstairs Cabaret, above Darcy's Pub, 15 Bastion Sq, T250-385 5483. A friendly, un-pretentious, mid-sized club with live music or decent DJs.

Vista 18, 18th Floor, Chateau Victoria Hotel, 740 Burdett Av, T250-382 9258. With the best views in town, this is a lovely, sophis-ticated spot for a drink. Lots of wines by the glass and a surprisingly reasonable West Coast menu ideal for brunch, dinner or tapas.

❷ Entertainment

Victoria *pp89, map p90*
Galleries

There are plenty of galleries in town. For a list of what's going on, pick up the *Monday Mag*, www.mondaymag.com.

Alcheringa Gallery, 665 Fort St, T250-383 8224. The most impressive collection of First Nations art in town.

Gallery at the Mac, 3 Centennial Sq, T250-361 0800. Central, good temporary exhibits.
Legacy Art Gallery, 630 Yates St. Exhibits the collection of works by local artists donated by a recently deceased Victoria benefactor.
Open Space, 510 Fort St, T250-383 8833. Long-running, highly respected and operated by artists.
Studio 16 ½, in Fan Tan Alley, www.fantan studios.com. An interesting little space in a fascinating alley.

Live Music

Victoria has no shortage of large and small venues for live music, many of them the restaurants, pubs and clubs mentioned above. The place to look for full listings is the *Monday Magazine*.
Hermann's Jazz Bar and Grill, 753 View St, T250-388 9166. A bit run down and the service is terrible. The premier jazz venue.
Logan's Pub, 1821 Cook St, T250-360 2711. A key venue for alternative and/or local bands.
Lucky Bar, 517 Yates St, T250-382 5825. A trendy, wacky, colourful little bar with live music, usually alternative, or DJs every night. The sound system is great and the atmosphere high energy.
McPherson Playhouse, 3 Centennial Sq, Government/Victoria, T250-386 6121. Open since 1914, this is a delightful venue for films, dance and music
Royal Theatre, 805 Broughton St, T250-386 6121. With over 1400 seats, this attractive 1913 heritage building is a major music venue, hosting the Symphony Orchestra, Pacific Opera, major plays, dance and visiting names of all genres.
Save On Foods Memorial Centre, 1925 Blanshard St, T250-220 2600. Where the biggest names play.

Theatre

See also Live Music, above.
Belfry Theatre, 1291 Gladstone St, Fernwood, T250- 385 6815, www.belfry.bc.ca. In a former church, this venue is host to the island's largest professional theatre group, staging high-quality, serious drama.
Metro Studio, 1411 Quadra St, T250-412 0367. Another converted church, now a fantastic space for smaller, often more alternative or off-the-wall productions.

Salt Spring Island *p95 map p96*
There is plenty of art to be seen (see Shopping, page 105), so grab a map of galleries and studios from the Visitor Centre.
Art Spring, 100 Jackson Av, T250- 537 2102, www.artspring.ca. A vast timber space that hosts art exhibitions, events and shows in the 265-seat theatre throughout the year.
Tree House Café, 106 Purvis Lane, Ganges, T250-537 5379. Live music almost nightly.

❸ Festivals and events

Victoria *p89, map p90*
Feb Victoria Film Festival, T250-389 0444, www.victoriafilmfestival.com. For 10 days at the start of the month, some 190 films are shown at 6 venues around town.
May UNO Festival of Solo Performance, T250-383 2663, www.victoriafringe.com. For 10 days the Metro Theatre plays host to 14 one-person shows of a mixed nature and high calibre.
Jun JazzFest International, T250-388 4233, www.vicjazz.bc.ca. 10-days of jazz, blues and world beat on free and ticketed stages around town.
Jul Moss Street Paint-in, T250-381 4171. For one day in mid-July, the town's many local artists display and sell their work. A great, bustling event usually capped off by music at the Art Gallery. **Luminara**, T250-388 4728, www.luminaravictoria.com. A wonderfully evocative lantern festival held in Beacon Park. Walk round in the dark and witness gorgeous lantern creations, live music and acts. **Latin Caribbean Music Festival**, features live music and dancing in Market Square.
Aug Victoria Dragon Boat Festival, T250-472 2628, www.victoriadragonboat.com. Involves 90 boats in the Inner Harbour, with 24-crew paddlers, full dragon regalia, drums, food and crafts. **Victoria Fringe Theatre Festival**, T250-383 2663, www.victoria fringe.com. The event for which Victoria is most famous, countless venues staging all manner of shows.
Sep Classic Boat Festival, T250-385 7766, www.classicboatfestival.ca. Runs from Aug-Sept and is when the Inner Harbour is lined with restored boats. **Vancouver Island Blues Bash**, www.jazzvictoria.ca/bluesbash. Blues shows occupy various stages.

Salt Spring Island *p95 map p96*
Jun Salt Spring Jazz Festival, T250-537 1813, www.saltspringjazzfest.org. A modest gathering of jazz talent.
Sep Salt Spring Fall Fair, the biggest event of the year, featuring livestock, horsemanship, farm exhibits, games, music and food. Held at the fairgrounds, there are frequent free shuttles from Ganges.

○ Shopping

Victoria *p89, map p90*
Arts, crafts and gifts
Fort St between Douglas and Cook is known as 'Antique Row', and it is home to a number of art galleries and second-hand bookshops. For gift ideas, try the shop at the museum or the shops in and around Market Square between Johnston St and Pandora Av, Store St and Government St. Government is where you'll find the majority of the souvenir shops.
Capital Iron, 1900 Store St, T250-385 9703. A massive shop that sells just about everything. Makes for great browsing, and if you don't know where to get something useful, try here.
Chintz and Co., 1720 Store St, T250-381 2404, www.chintz.com. A big shop packed full of sinfully desirable home furnishings.
Hill's Native Art, 1008 Government St, T250-385 3911, www.hillsnativeart.com. The place for genuine First Nations arts and crafts, with a wide selection of masks, carvings and jewellery.

Books
There are lots of second-hand bookshops in town, mostly on Fort St.
Munro's, 1108 Government St, T250-382 2464. Arguably Canada's most beautiful bookshop. The 7.5-m coffered ceiling, stained-glass windows, wall hangings and well-chosen art create an environment perfect for browsing.

Clothes
Downtown is the place for shopping, with most of the key chain and fashion shops. Johnston St is the place for more up-to-the-minute clothing, Wharf St and Government St are great for boutiques and Government St to Blanshard St is where you'll find the second-hand shops.

Bay Centre, T250-385 1311, www.thebay centre.ca, 2 whole blocks between Government St and Douglas St, Fort St and View St. Surprisingly tasteful as malls go.
Footloose, 637 Fort St, T250-383 4040. Offers a good selection of funky and designer shoes.
Smoking Lily, 569a Johnson St, T250-389 5459. One of the best of many local designers.

Food and drink
The Wine Barrel, 644 Broughton St, T250-388 0606. Carries only BC wines and has a wealth of information on them.

Sports equipment
Mountain Equipment Co-op, 1450 Government St, T250-386 2667. Sporting and outdoor equipment.
Sports Traders, 508 Discovery St. A huge selection of used sporting equipment.

Salt Spring Island *p95 map p96*
Residents are very proud of their local currency, the Salt Spring Dollar. You can exchange Canadian dollars for Salt Spring Dollars and spend them in local shops. Any interest is spent on community projects.

Arts and crafts
Art galleries and studios are all over Ganges and most offer the chance to meet the artist, ask at the Visitor Centre for a full list.
Art Craft, Mahon Hall, 114 Rainbow Rd, Ganges T250-537 0899, www.artcraft gallery.com, Jun-Sep 0900-1700. This significant exhibition provides a great opportunity to see, and buy, the work of some 200 Gulf Island artists.
Coastal Currents Gallery, 133 Hereford Av, Ganges, T250-537 0070. A very tasteful selection of arts, crafts and gifts.
J. Mitchell Gallery, 3104 Grace Point Sq, Ganges, T250-537 8822. A fine collection of pieces in a variety of media, showcasing the work of many top Gulf Island artists.
Saturday Market, Centennial Park, Ganges, www.saltspringmarket.com, Apr-Oct 0830-1530. Excellent for local crafts. One of the highlights of Salt Spring, if not BC.
Waterfront Gallery, 107 Purvis Lane, T250-537 4525. Represents over 75 local artisans working in media from pottery to jewellery to painted silk.

▲▲ Activities and tours

Victoria *p89, map p90*
South and Central Vancouver Island Recreation Map, $5, published by Carmanah Forestry Society, covers biking, hiking, kayaking and camping in this region, and is well worth picking up.

For rentals of all sporting equipment, **Sports Rent**, 1950 Government St, T250-385 7368, including skis, bikes, tents, kayaks and surfboards.

Cycling

Victoria is famous for its biking, with plenty of trails and several off-road areas. Buses are bike equipped and a very good map can be bought at any bike shop for $6.50. The 60-km Galloping Goose Trail, T250-592 4753, www.outpostbc.ca, starts Downtown at Johnson Street Bridge, crosses the Gorge on the Selkirk Trestle and then hooks up with the scenic Lochside Trail enroute to such possible destinations as Swan and Blekinsop Lakes or Mt Douglas.
Cycle BC Rentals, 747 Douglas St; 950 Wharf St, T250-380 2453, www.cyclebc.ca. Rent cycles, scooters and motorbikes.
Cycle Treks, 450 Swift St, T250-386 2277, www.cycletreks.com. Tours of Victoria, the Gulf Islands and Vancouver Island.
Switch Bridge Tours, 800 Tyee Rd, T250-383 1466, www.switchbridgetours.com. Multi-day tours of Southern Vancouver Island and the Gulf Islands. Their shop near the Selkirk Trestle Bridge on the Galloping Goose is a handy place to rent bikes and kayaks. They also do repairs.

Fishing

Adam's Fishing Charters, 19 Lotus St, T250-370 2326, www.adamsfishing charters.com. Tours, sightseeing and fishing tours.

Golf

These courses are close to town and highly scenic: **Cedar Hill**, 1400 Derby, T250-475 7151, www.golfcedarhill.com; **Cordova Bay**, T250-658 4444, www.cordovabaygolf.com, 18 holes overlooking the ocean and the Gulf Islands; **Olympic View**, 643 Latoria Rd, T250-474 3673, 18 holes, 12 lakes, 2 waterfalls.

Hiking

Mt Douglas, 9 km north of Victoria at Cordova Bay, is a 10-ha park overlooking the Haro Strait and Washington's San Juan Islands. There are hiking trails leading up to a viewpoint and a decent beach, to get there take bus No 28 from Downtown. Elk Lake, north off Patricia Bay Hwy, and Thetis Lake, 15 mins' west off the Island Hwy, have mellow hikes around the lakes. Mt Finlayson in Goldstream Provincial Park is a fairly challenging half-day hike, and there are great views from the top.
Worlds of Wonder Excursions, T250-514 1086, www.wowe.ca. All manner of guided hikes in the Victoria area.

Kayaking and canoeing

Island Boat Rentals, 450 Swift St, below the Harbour Canoe Club, T250-995 1661. Rents kayaks, canoes or rowing boats for exploring the Inner Harbour and Gorge Harbour.
Ocean River Sports, 1824 Store St, T250-381 4233, www.oceanriver.com. Rents and sells paddling equipment and runs kayaking tours. Also a great source of information.
Pacifica Paddlesports, 575 Pembroke St, T250-361 9365, www.pacificapaddle.com. Canoe and kayak sales, rentals and 3- or 6-hr tours.

Paragliding

Vancouver Island Paragliding, T250-514 8595, www.viparagliding.com. Beginner courses from $300.

Sailing

A 3 Hour Sail, T250-885 2311, www.tallship adventure.ca. 3-hr tours on a sail boat for $60 per person.

Scuba-diving

Ogden Point Dive Centre, 199 Dallas Rd, T250-380 9119, www.divevictoria.com. The best of a few companies, offering everything from rentals to PADI courses to dive charters.

Swimming

For swimming the best and warmest water is at Thetis Lake, though it's often overrun with teenagers.
Crystal Pool, 2275 Quadra St, T250-361 0732. The handiest swimming pool, with sauna, hot tub and fitness centre.

Tour operators

For more information look up the very useful www.ec otoursvictoria.com.

Architectural Institute of BC, T1800-667 0753, www.aibc.ca. Guided walking tours of Victoria with an architectural slant. There are 5 tours, 2 of which are available on any given day. Jul-Aug Tue-Sat leaving 1300 from the Community Arts Council Office, G6, 1001 Douglas St. They last 1½-2 hrs, $5.

Discover the Past, T250-384 6698, www.discoverthepast.com. Historian and storyteller John Adams runs a number of walks (90 mins/$12). Chinatown tours run Jul-Aug, Tue, Thu and Sat at 1030 from the Bright Pearl sculpture at Government St and Fisgard St ($12), and the Ghostly Walks reveal the more sinister side of Victoria's history, departing nightly from the Visitor Centre at 1930 and 2130.

Gray Line West, 700 Douglas St, T250-388 6539, www.graylinewest.com. A range of narrated double-decker bus tours, from 1-hr tours of town to 4-hr Butchart Gardens trips.

Island Adventure Tours, 1032 Oliphant St, T250-812 7103, www.islandadventure tours.com. Hiking, kayaking, animal-watching and cultural tours with a First Nations perspective.

Royal Blue Line, Belleville St, in front of the Coho ferry terminal, T250-360 2249, www.royalbluelinetours.com. Uses open-top English double-deckers for its narrated tours of town. Hop on and off as you please. $25, child $15.

Travel with Taste Tours, 356 Simcoe St, T250-385 6052, www.travelwithtaste.com. 1-day to 1-week tours of town, local wineries, farms and restaurants.

Victoria Carriage Tours, Belleville and Menzies streets, T250-383 2207, www.vic toriacarriage.com. Horse and carriage tours from $90 for 30 mins.

Victoria Harbour Ferry, T250-708 0201, www.victoriaharbourferry.com. As well as their ferry service to 12 stops around Victoria Harbour ($4), they offer 45-min narrated harbour tours or 50-min narrated Gorge tours for $20, child $10.

Whale watching

There are at least 10 whale-watching operators on the Inner Harbour alone.

They all offer similar deals on 3 hr trips for about $100.

The real decision is whether you want to go in a Zodiac, hard-shell, sail boat or cruise ship. **Great Pacific Adventures**, T250- 386 2277, 811 Wharf St, www.great pacificadventures.com; **Naturally Salty Excursions**, T250-382 9599, 950 Wharf St, www.naturallysalty.com.

Wine tasting

The many wineries in the Cowichan Valley – the so-called Napa Valley of the North – can be toured independently or with a number of outfits based in Victoria, such as **Vancouver Island Wine Tours**, T250-661 8844, www.vancouverislandwinetours.com.

Sooke *p94*

Sooke Cycle, 6707 West Coast Rd, T250-642 3123. Bicycle rental.

Salt Spring Island *p95 map p96*

There's cheese tasting at **Salt Spring Island Cheese**, 285 Reynolds Rd, T250-653 2300 and **Moonstruck Organic Cheese**, 1306 Beddis Rd, 250-537 4987; and wine tasting at **Salt Spring Vineyards**, 151 Lee Rd/Fulford Ganges Rd, T250-653 9463 and **Garry Oaks Winery**, 1880 Fulford-Ganges Rd, T250-653 2687. For bike hire, see Kayaking below.

Kayaking

Salt Spring is a paddler's paradise and has destinations for all levels, but the inexperienced should go with a guide.

Saltspring Kayaking, 2923 Fulford-Ganges Rd, T250-653 4222, www.saltspringkayak ing.com. Rents kayaks and bikes, and offers tours and lessons. Will deliver your bike/ kayak from any ferry for $15.

Sea Otter Kayaking, 149 Lower Ganges Rd, on the dock, T250-537 5678, www.seaotter kayaking.com. Rentals and a range of tours.

Tour operators

Island Escapades, 163 Fulford-Ganges Rd, T250-537 2553, www.islandescapades.com. Highly respected company for sailing, kayaking, hiking and climbing. Offers rentals, lessons and tours.

Island Gourmet Safaris, T250-537 4118, www.islandgourmetsafaris.com. Culinary tours around the island stopping to taste local cheese, wine, coffee and seafood. Also runs art studio tours.

Lorenda Sailing, Moby's Pub, T250-538 0084. Offers 4-5 hr afternoon sails in a 40-ft yawl. A great way to see the islands.

Salt Spring Air, T250-537 9880, www.salt springair.com. Flight-seeing tours.

Salt Spring Guided Rides, 915 Mt Maxwell Rd, T250-537 5761. Horse riding.

Galiano Island *p95, map p100*

Galiano Adventures Company, 300 Sticks Allison Rd, T250-539 3443, www.galiano adventures.com. Rents mopeds and boats.

Galiano Bicycle, 36 Burrill Rd, T250-539 9906. Rents bicycles and does repairs.

Galiano Boat Rentals, Montague Harbour, T250-539 9828. Rents mopeds and boats.

Gulf Islands Kayaking, Montague Harbour, T250-539 2442, www.seakayak.ca. Offers kayak rentals, lessons and tours.

Sporades Tours Inc, T250-539 2278, www.cedarplace.com/fishing. Sightseeing tours on a 37-ft powered fishing vessel. The Captain has 40 years of experience and stories. $360 for 3 hrs, up to 10 people.

⊙ Transport

Victoria *p89, map p90*
Air

For airport details, see page 88.

Airline offices Air Canada, T1888-247 2262, www.aircanada.com; West Coast Air, T250-388 4521, www.westcoastair.com; Pacific Coastal, T250-655 6411, www.pacific-coastal.com. All have several daily flights to **Vancouver** for about $100 one-way.

Floatplanes Harbour Air Seaplanes, T250-385 9131, www.harbour-air.com, and West Coast Air, T604-606 6888, www.westcoastair.com. Both have regular daily flights between Canada Place in **Vancouver** and Victoria's Inner Harbour, $130 one-way.

Bus

Local BC Transit, T250-382 6161, www.bc transit.com, operates a comprehensive and efficient bus service throughout the city. Single-fare tickets cost $2.25 (child $1.40) or $3 (child $2.25) for 2 zones. If taking more than 1 bus in the same direction, ask for a transfer at no extra charge. It lasts for 90

mins. A sheet of 10 tickets costs $20.25 (child $12.60). A day pass is $7 (child $5). The low-floor buses are wheelchair access-ible, but only from designated stops.

Long distance All buses leave from 700 Douglas St, behind the Empress Hotel. Greyhound, T250-385 4411, www.grey hound.ca, runs 6 daily buses north to **Nanaimo** (2 hrs, $18), from where 1 service runs to **Tofino** (4 hrs) and 3 run to **Campbell River** (2½-3 hrs, $25). Pacific Coach Lines, T250-385 4411, operates a service to and from **Vancouver**, leaving Victoria bus station almost hourly in summer from 0600-2000, $38.50 one-way.

Ferry

BC Ferries, T250-386 3431, www.bcferries. com, run to **Tsawwassen** (for Vancouver) and the **southern Gulf Islands**. Ferries between Swartz Bay and Tsawwassen leave every 2 hrs, 0700-2100 or hourly at peak times, $12, child $5.50, vehicle $39. Several daily ferries run from Brentwood Bay on the Saanich Peninsula to **Mill Bay** across the inlet, $5, vehicle $11.60.

To the US Victoria Clipper, T250-382 8100, www.suffren.victoriaclipper.com, runs from the Inner Harbour to **Seattle**, US$81. Washington State Ferries, T250-464 6400, www.wsdot.wa.gov/ferries, Sidney to **Anacortes**, US$18, vehicle $55.

Taxi

AAA Airport Taxi, T250-727 8366; **Empress** Taxi, T250-381 2222.

Train

The **Malahat** service leaves from the Johnson St Bridge daily at 0800 (Sun 1000), and more frequently in summer, running as far north as **Courtenay** (4½ hrs, $30 if booked 5 days in advance) with several stops on the way including **Chemainus** and **Nanaimo**. You can make as as many stops as you like.

Vehicle hire

Airport, T250-657 2277, discount car and truck rentals; **Budget**, 757 Douglas, T250-953 5300, car hire; **Cycle BC Rentals**, 747 Douglas St, T250-885 2453, scooter and motorbike hire.

West to Port Renfrew p93

The **Juan de Fuca Trail Shuttle Bus**, T250-477 8700, www.trailbus.com, leaves Port Renfrew at 1645. Shuttles between trail-heads charge $20. Reservations advised.

Salt Spring Island p95 map p96
Air

Harbour Air Seaplanes, T250-537 5525, www.harbourair.com. At least 2 flights daily to and from downtown **Vancouver** and from the international airport, $95 one-way. **Salt Spring Air**, T250-537 9880, www.saltspringair.com, operates scheduled and chartered flights to and from **Vancouver** from $77 one-way.

Ferry

Ferries arrive at 3 different harbours on Salt Spring. Fulford Bay receives 8 ferries daily from **Swartz Bay** (Victoria), $8.35, child $4.65, vehicle $24, return; Long Harbour receives 2 ferries daily from **Tsawwassen** (Vancouver), $13.20, child $7.20, vehicle $49.40, one-way. Curiously, Long Harbour to Tsawwassen fares are almost half the price, $6.65, child $3.90, vehicle $27.50, $18 mid-week, one-way. Vesuvius Bay receives 14 sailings daily from **Crofton** in the Cowichan Valley, $8.35, child $4.65, vehicle $23.85, return. **Gulf Island Water Taxi**, T250-537 2510, www.saltspring. com/water taxi runs from the visitors' dock in Ganges to **Galiano Island** Wed and Sat, Jul-Aug, $25 return, $15 one-way. They will transport your kayak for $5.

Shuttle

Ganges is at the northern end of the island, some 15 km along the main Fulford-Ganges Rd from Fulford Bay, about 6 km from the other harbours. **Ganges Faerie Mini Shuttle**, T250-537 6758, www.gangesfaerie.com, runs shuttles 0700-1800 between all ferry landings and Ganges, Ruckle Park and Fernwood. Will drop off anywhere in-between. Best to book ahead. One-way from Fulford harbour to Ganges, $14.

Galiano Island p95 map p100

For rental of bicycles and boats, see Activities page 108.

Ferry

At least 3 daily sailings from **Swartz Bay** (Vancouver Island), $8.65, child $4.50, vehicle $26.65, return. 2 sailings daily to **Tsawwassen** (Vancouver), $13.20, child $7.20 vehicle $49.40, one-way; $5.60, child $3, vehicle $22.80 from Tsawwassen. 2 sailings daily to **Long Harbour** (Salt Spring Island) via Pender and Mayne Islands, $3.85, child $2.15 vehicle $8.90, one-way.

Shuttle

Go Galiano Island Shuttle, T250-539 0202, is a taxi and bus service, which meets every ferry Jun-Sep ($6 to Sturdies Bay).

Water taxi

Gulf Islands Water Taxi, T250-537 2510, connects with **Salt Spring** (see above).

❶ Directory

Victoria p89, map p90
Emergencies Ambulance, T911 or T250-727 2400; **Police**, T911 or T250-995 7654. **Internet** Stain Internet Café, 609 Yates St, T250-382 3352; any library. **Laundry** Maytag Homestyle Laundry, 1309 Cook St, T250-386 1799. **Library** Greater Victoria Public Library, 735 Broughton St, T250-382 7241. **Medical services** Mayfair Walk-In Clinic, 210-3214 Douglas St, T250-383 9898; Royal Jubilee Hospital, 1900 Fort St, T250-370 8000. **Post office** Canada Post 706 Yates St, T250-953 1352.

Salt Spring Island p95, map p96
Laundry Mrs Clean, 9-149 Fulford-Ganges Rd, behind the Petrocan in Ganges, T250-537 8844. **Medical services** Lady Minto Gulf Islands Hospitals, 135 Crofton Rd, T250-538 4800.

Tofino and the West Coast

Fringed with rocky bays, countless islands and dense rainforest that contains some of the world's biggest trees, Vancouver Island's ruggedly beautiful and relatively unspoilt West Coast is surely its most outstanding feature. The increasingly busy but still picturesque little resort town of Tofino makes a perfect base, with great facilities and several outstanding excursions. Whale watching is particularly prime, especially in spring, when some 22,000 grey whales are migrating through. Nearby Ucluelet is a more down-to-earth base, offering easy access to the Broken Islands Group, an archipelago of tiny islands in Barkley Sound that's a paradise for kayakers. Between Tofino and Ucluelet is Long Beach, a 20-km series of rain- and wind-lashed beaches ideal for surfing, storm watching and beachcombing, and lined with short trails through lush rainforest. Heading south from the boardwalk village of Bamfield, the West Coast Trail is one of the most challenging, rewarding and popular hikes in North America. The region's main gateway, Nanaimo, has an interesting, gritty downtown core, with Gabriola Island, well worth exploring, a short ferry ride away.
➤➤ *For Sleeping, Eating and other listings, see pages 118-129.*

Ins and outs

Getting there and around
Nanaimo Airport (YCD) ① *T250-245 4191, www.nanaimoairport.com*, 15 km south of the city on Highway 19, receives six daily flights from Vancouver. The **Nanaimo Airporter shuttle bus** ① *T1800-209 7792, www.nanaimoairporter.com, call to book, $19 and then further $5 per person*, runs to town. Nanaimo is also reached by ferry directly from Vancouver's Horseshoe Bay or Tsawwassen terminals, the former more direct and frequent. The **bus station** ① *1 Terminal Av, T250-754 6442*, is walking distance from Downtown. Nanaimo is served by several daily buses (one continuing to Tofino), or one train, from Victoria. The train station is on Selby Street, walking distance from Downtown. Getting around Tofino is possible on foot or bike, with a **Beach Bus** shuttling to Long Beach and Ucluelet. The *MV Lady Rose* from Port Alberni is a delightful way to reach Ucluelet, Bamfield and the Broken Islands. ➤➤ *For further details, see Transport, page 127.*

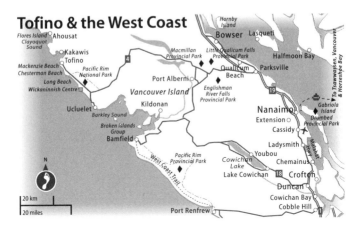

Tofino & the West Coast

⁝ Coastal rainforests

Temperate Coastal Rainforests have existed for some two million years, but are extremely rare, originally comprising just 0.2% of the earth's land surface. They are one of the most biologically productive ecosystems on earth, with a greater biomass per hectare than any other. Their estuaries, and inter-tidal and sub-tidal zones have also supported some of the world's most diverse marine life, plus the most complex human civilizations ever to emerge without the benefit of agriculture. Despite all that, these are among the least studied ecosystems on earth, and time is running out: about half of the original forests have already been cut down, including 95% of those that covered Washington, Oregon and California. Large tracts remain only in BC, Alaska and Chile.

British Columbia contains about a quarter of the world's remaining temperate rainforest, even though 53% has been axed. On Vancouver Island the figure is 74% and, although 13% of the island's area is protected by parks, only 5.7% of the temperate rainforest is protected. The single largest remaining tract is in Clayoquot Sound, 74% of whose productive ancient forests are still open to logging, with two companies retaining significant logging rights, despite massive protests. Many scientists support the protesters, including a government-appointed panel, which recommended that logging not compromise the integrity of the ecosystem, that community values be respected, and that watershed cutting be restricted to 1% per year.

For further information, contact **David Suzuki Foundation**, T604-732 4228, www.davidsuzuki.org or **The Friends of Clayoquot Sound**, 331 Neill St, Tofino, T250-725 4218, www.focs.ca.

Best time to visit

For most West Coast activities, summer is the obvious time. However, the great grey whale migration takes place mid-March to early April, beginning with the annual Pacific Rim Whale Festival. Winter would only really appeal to those interested in storm watching.

Tourist information

Tofino's **Visitor Information Centre** ① *1426 Pacific Rim Hwy, T250-725 3414, www.tourismtofino.com, mid-May to mid-Aug daily 1000-1800, mid-Aug to mid-May Tue-Sat 1000-1600*, is busy but helpful. Close to the Tofino-Ucluelet junction on Highway 4 as you approach Long Beach is the **Parks Information Centre** ① *T250-726 4600, mid-March to mid-Oct, fees are payable here and apply throughout the park, $6.80, under 16 $3.40, under 6 free, $17.10 for a family of up to 7 including up to 2 adults*. It provides all sorts of information including an indispensable map of Long Beach, which gives details of the hiking trails and includes smaller maps of Tofino and Ucluelet, as well as listings. Recommended books include the *Official Guidebook to Pacific Rim National Park Reserve* (MacFarlane et al, 1996), *The Pacific Rim Explorer* (Bruce Obee), and *Island Paddling* (MA Snowden). Nanaimo's **Visitor Information Centre** ① *2290 Bowen Rd, from Hwy 1 turn west onto Comox Rd then follow signs, T250-756 0106, www.tourismnanaimo.com, mid-May to mid-Sep daily 0700-1900, mid-Sep to mid-May Mon-Fri 0900-1700, Sat 1000-1600*, is well stocked but inconveniently situated far from Downtown.

Vancouver Island Tofino & the West Coast Ins & outs

Victoria to Nanaimo ⬤❷❼❹❀ ⇥ *pp118-128. Colour map 1, C3.*

Those travelling up from Victoria will find few reasons to stop along the busy Malahat Highway. **Goldstream Provincial Park** has some nice walks, including the Prospectors' Trail (details from the Freeman King Visitor Centre by the picnic area) and up to the viewpoint atop Mount Finlayson. From mid-October to December, salmon can be seen in the Goldstream River. Both of the viewpoints at the Malahat Pass are worth stopping for.

Those with their own vehicle and lots of time may wish to explore the broad **Cowichan Valley**, the winding country roads weave through fertile landscapes to pretty little villages such as Cowichan Bay where the waterfront buildings are all on stilts. A number of wineries clustered around Cobble Hill and a few local cheese producers are usually open for tasting. It's easy to get lost, so pick up a *Cowichan Tourism Association* map in Mill Bay or Victoria, or visit the helpful **Visitor Information Centre** ① *381A Hwy 1, T250-748 1111, www.duncancc.bc.ca,* in Duncan, the region's main town.

Duncan → *Colour map 1, C3.*

① *Free 45-min tours begin hourly, May-Sep daily 1000-1400, Jul-Aug extra tour 1500, from the train station at 130 Canada Av, T250-715 1700, www.downtownduncan.ca.*

While in Duncan, be sure to pick up a map of the 80-odd totem poles scattered around town and along the highway, which constitute the town's main draw. Enthusiasts can also buy a copy of *The Totem Walk of Duncan* ($5).

Those wishing to find out more about First Nations art, culture and history can visit **Quw'utsun Cultural Centre**, ① *200 Cowichan Way, Hwy 1 just south of town, T250-746 8119, www.quwutsum.ca, Mon-Sun 1000-1600, $7, student $5, under 12 $2, admission includes a 30-min interpretive tour (Jun-Sep only) and live demonstrations, songs and dances (Jul-Aug), there is also a 30-min multi-media presentation entitled 'Great Deeds',* housed in an impressive longhouse set in 2 ha of beautifully landscaped grounds beside the Cowichan River. From June to September the **Riverwalk Café** serves authentic Native dishes.

Chemainus → *Colour map 1, C3.*

Despite its excessive hype and popularity, Chemainus is the best stop on the road north thanks to a famous collection of 39 high-quality murals and 13 sculptures that depict the history of the town and area. The first was commissioned in 1982 as a brave attempt to attract tourism after the local sawmill went into decline and threatened to sink the town with it. The ploy worked, with tourists, murals and artisans continuing to arrive long after the mill ironically reopened. Such success owes much to the fact that Chemainus is a charming little village in its own right. You can pick up a useful mural map for $1 at the friendly **Visitor Information Centre** ① *9796 Willow St, T250-246 3944, www.chemainus.bc.ca, mid-May to mid-Sep daily 0900-1700, mid-Sep to mid-May Mon-Sat 0900-1700.* Just outside, you can take a 45-minute horse-drawn carriage tour of town ($10).

Nanaimo and around ⬤❷❶❹❀⬤▲⬤❶ ⇥ *pp119-128. Colour map 1, C3.*

After the urban sprawl of suburban Nanaimo, the small Downtown area comes as a pleasant surprise. It has a real sense of history and character. For a self-guided tour around some of the historic highlights of BC's third oldest town, pick up the Heritage Walking Tour brochure from the Visitor Centre. Alternatively, the warren of twisty streets around Church and Commercial make for interesting meandering. It's conveniently close to the ferry, train and the scenic harbour, and is packed with decent pubs, authentic diners, book and music shops, and art galleries. There are some nice beaches and sea walks in town and the usual water sports are available. **Newcastle Island** ① *a short ferry ride away, www.newcastleisland.ca*, is one big vehicle-free provincial park, good for hiking and biking. Ask for a map at the Visitor Centre.

In 1852, the local Salish natives made the mistake of showing samples of the 'black rock' that existed locally in staggering proportions to agents from Hudson's Bay Company (HBC). The white men came in droves to exploit one of the greatest coal mines of all time and a few of them became millionaires, notably Robert Dunsmuir.

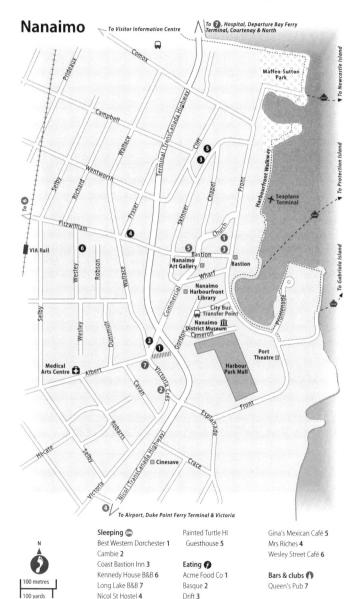

Nanaimo

To Visitor Information Centre

To ⑦, Hospital, Departure Bay Ferry
Terminal, Courtenay & North

To Newcastle Island

Maffeo-Sutton Park

Comox

Prideaux

Campbell

Wallace

Cliff ⑤ ③

Wentworth

Fraser

Skinner

Chapel

Front

Harbourfront Walkway

To Protection Island

Selby

Richard

Terminal (TransCanada Highway)

Seaplane Terminal

To ⑥

Fitzwilliam

④

Church

Bastion ⑤ ③ ①

VIA Rail ⑥

Robson

Wallace

Bastion

Nanaimo Art Gallery

Wharf

To Gabriola Island

Westley

Selby

Dunsmuir

Commercial

Nanaimo Harbourfront Library

City Bus Transfer Point

Promenade

Westley

Nanaimo District Museum

Gordon

Cameron

② ①

⑦

Medical Arts Centre

Albert

Victoria Cres

Port Theatre

Cavan

②

Harbour Park Mall

Front

Roberts

Esplanade

Hecate

Selby

Crace

Victoria

Nicol (TransCanada Highway)

Cinesave

④

To Airport, Duke Point Ferry Terminal & Victoria

N

100 metres

100 yards

Sleeping
Best Western Dorchester **1**
Cambie **2**
Coast Bastion Inn **3**
Kennedy House B&B **6**
Long Lake B&B **7**
Nicol St Hostel **4**

Painted Turtle HI
Guesthouse **5**

Eating
Acme Food Co **1**
Basque **2**
Drift **3**

Gina's Mexican Café **5**
Mrs Riches **4**
Wesley Street Café **6**

Bars & clubs
Queen's Pub **7**

The following year, in order to keep the natives under control while their land was plundered (or give themselves somewhere to hide), the HBC constructed the **Bastion** ① *63 Front St, a small museum of HBC memorabilia is open mid-May to Aug daily 1000-1600, $1, and a ceremonial cannon fires at noon Mon-Sat to the accompaniment of Scottish bagpipes and Highland dancing*, a squat, wood-plank building that's the oldest of its kind in the west.

The nearby **Nanaimo District Museum** ① *100 Cameron Rd, T250-753 1821, www.nanaimomuseum.ca, mid-May to mid-Sep daily 0900-1700, mid-Sep to mid-May Tue-Sat 0900-1700, $2, child $1.75*, is currently receiving a $2.3 million facelift. Due to open sometime in 2008, the new, larger space will include a First Nations exhibit, symbolic of the circle of life and featuring a diorama and a sunken display seen through a glass floor; a coal mine tunnel allowing visitors to experience as well as learn about the reality of Nanaimo's mining history; and more room for interactive temporary exhibits. The collection of petroglyph copies on the lawn at the back, which can be seen for free, are well worth a look. Close by is **Nanaimo Art Gallery** ① *150 Commercial St, T250-754 1750, www.nanaimogallery.ca, Tue-Sat 1000-1700, donation*, which has a strong permanent collection showcasing work by over 40 West Coast artists and carries two temporary exhibitions.

Gabriola Island → *Colour map 1, C3.*

Gabriola is one of the quickest Gulf Islands to get to and one of the most worthwhile. Straight ahead from the ferry on North Road, Folklife Village is a hub of local activity, with decent cafés, many of the island's galleries and the summer-only **Visitor Information Centre** ① *575 North Rd, T250-247 9332, www.gabriolaisland.org*. Try to come on a Saturday when the colourful farmers' market is held at the junction of North and South Roads.

Wonderful rock formations can be seen from the approaching ferry and in various parks throughout the island, but the best is the highly photogenic **Malaspina Gallery** ① *from the ferry, turn left onto Taylor Bay Rd and left again onto Malaspina Dr*, a collection of beautiful wave-shaped stone sculptures carved by the sea. **Drumbed Provincial Park** at the island's southeast corner has good swimming and an easy, pleasant walk leading to the island's best views, with a chance to see otters and eagles. **Gabriola Sands**, **Descanso Bay** and **Sandwell Parks** all have good beaches, the latter the quietest due to the short hike to get there. A number of petroglyphs are scattered around the island, many are inaccessible but you can see some on South Road, behind the United Church. *Gabriola: Petroglyph Island*, by M and T Bentley, is a valuable resource for those keen to seek them out. A collection of decent reproductions decorates the garden of the small **Gabriola Museum** ① *mid-May to mid-Sep Wed-Sun 1030-1600, mid-Sep to mid-May Sat-Sun 1300-1600, $2.*

West to Pacific Rim National Park 🍽🚲⛰ ›› *pp120-128.*

Travellers bound for Tofino might do best to bypass Nanaimo and dreary Parksville altogether, but for those with their own wheels there are a few places along Highway 4 to stop and enjoy a rare taste of Vancouver Island's forested interior. Before long, signs appear for **Englishman River Falls Provincial Park** to the south, where there's hiking, biking, fishing and a pleasant campground, as well as a waterfall. **Little Qualicum Falls Provincial Park** ① *Km 19*, has a more impressive waterfall, enticing swimming holes and a large, scenic campground. In summer the adjacent **Cameron Lake** with its splendid beach, is always popular.

Macmillan Park, opened by the eponymous logging giants, features Cathedral Grove, a tiny patch of old-growth spruce and cedar left behind almost as a sick joke to show tourists how the whole island once looked. A few points still exist around the island where the real thing can be seen, notably in Clayoquot Sound close to Tofino, but this spot is always worth a leg-stretch as the giant trees are magnificent.

Port Alberni is worth mentioning mainly as the place to catch the *MV Lady Rose* (see page 118), a fantastic way to access the Broken Islands or Bamfield. Boats leave from Harbour Quay, which is the nicest part of town. If you have time to waste, the best local diversion is the **McLean Mill National Historic Site** ① *west of town, 5633 Smith Rd, T250-723 1376, www.alberniheritage.com, Thu-Mon 1030-1715, $4,child $2, Shadow Tour $9.25, child $5*. This is Canada's only steam-operated mill and an interesting building in its own right, with various demonstrations and events. The way to get there is on the steam train, which leaves from the **E&N train station** ① *3100 Kingsway, daily 1000 and 1400*. Trains also now stop at the Chae and Warren Estate Winery for tastings and tours. For more information, contact the **Visitor Information Centre** ① *2533 Redford St, T250-724 6535, www.avcoc.com*.

Long Beach → *Colour map 1, C2.*

Frequent views of wild, rocky landscapes during the 130-km roller-coaster ride from Port Alberni provide a fitting introduction to the West Coast and Pacific Rim National Park. Unless you're heading to Ucluelet, the Pacific Rim Highway soon enters Long Beach, the collective name for a 20-km stretch of forest-fringed bays and beaches. Generally too rough for swimming and sunbathing, this is becoming a world-famous location for surfing. Storm watching is an increasingly popular winter activity and the very ruggedness of the scenery has a romantic quality conducive to long walks, with plenty of rock pools to explore. Almost immediately on the right is the **Parks Information Centre**. Pick up the free *Long Beach Map*, which describes nine well-tended trails, mostly short and sweet explorations of rainforest ecosystems with explanatory panels. The **Spruce Fringe Trail** is recommended. The highway runs parallel with the ocean, offering access to these trails and a number of beaches.

At the eastern end of Long Beach itself, the **Wickaninnish Centre**, ① *T250-726 7706*, has films and exhibits on the natural and cultural history of the Pacific Rim. These include some First Nations canoes and a wonderful new mural depicting large marine animals. It's also a useful place for information. There's a restaurant and a whale-watching telescope and it's a popular, safe spot for storm watching. Wickaninnish, meaning 'having no one in front of him in the canoe', is named after a powerful native chief, who gained much respect for his mediation between the white man and native fur trappers. Note that the rip tides here are particularly dangerous.

Shortly before **Cox Bay**, and **Chesterman** and **Mackenzie** beaches, a short drive and walk lead up to **Radar Hill**, with panoramic views of Clayoquot Sound.

Tofino ⬤🅟🏠❋⭕🔺🚌🅒 ⟩⟩ *pp118-128. Colour map 1, C2.*

The overwhelming popularity of this whaling-station-turned-surf-town is partly due to its idyllic location. Sitting at the end of a narrow peninsula in the middle of beautiful **Clayoquot Sound**, surrounded on all sides by ocean and islands, it is also the closest base for exploring the vast shoreline of Long Beach and visiting some of the destinations nearby. Many of the beaches are easily reached via a good bike path and local activities include whale watching, world-class sea kayaking, the country's best surfing, hiking, bear watching, beachcombing and storm watching.

Despite being packed to the gills in summer, Tofino itself almost manages to retain the feel of a scenic seaside village, but with the bonus of numerous fine restaurants, cafés, shops and sleeping options. For most people, the happy holiday atmosphere only adds to the experience anyway. However, if you want to avoid other tourists, think about going to Ucluelet instead. There are few indoor distractions, including the

Eagle Aerie Gallery ① *350 Campbell St, mid-May to mid-Sep daily 0900-2100, mid-Sep to mid-May daily 0930-1730*, which is housed in a splendid replica long-house with some beautiful carvings and a dugout canoe. The gallery highlights the work of highly respected native artist, Roy Henry Vickers. The **Rainforest Interpretive Centre** ① *451 Main St, T250-725 2560, by donation*, is a good place to find out about the remarkable ecosystems of temperate rainforests. For an equally educational taste of the real thing, head to the 5 ha of gardens, forest and shoreline at the **Tofino Botanical Gardens** ① *towards Long Beach at 1084 Pacific Rim Hwy, T250-725 1220, www.tbgf.org/gardens, daily 0900-dusk, $10, under 18 $6, under 12 free, valid for 3 consecutive days*. Linked by a network of paths and boardwalks, these gardens, some of which contain plants that once flourished in other temperate rainforests around the world, are designed to 'explore the relationship between culture and nature'.

Excursions from Tofino

There are plenty of things to do around Tofino. The most popular excursion is the 37-km boat trip to **Hot Springs Cove**. From the cove jetty, a 2-km boardwalk leads through rainforest to the gloriously romantic springs, where waters emerge at 43°C (108°F) before cascading down to the sea through a series of ever-cooler pools. Many operators combine this trip with whale watching but, if you want to avoid the summer crowds, it is also possible to travel independently and sleep at the springs.
➤ *For further information, see Activities and tours, page 126.*

The lush rainforest of **Meares Island**, closest of the local big islands, is just 10 minutes away from Tofino by water-taxi. This is one of the best places in Canada to go for a walk through giant ancient trees. On the 3-km loop of the **Big Cedar Trail** you'll gasp at trees that are more than 6 m across, and wonder why the logging companies are still intent on cutting them down. A shorter boardwalk stroll leads to the 2000-year-old **Hanging Garden Cedar**, the biggest tree in Clayoquot Sound at 18.3 m in circumference.

Vargas Island ① *5 km north of Tofino by water taxi*, is a beautiful and relaxing place. The 3-km **Telegraph Trail** that crosses the island passes some ancient crescent-shaped sand mounds, or 'berms', en route to the magnificent fine sand **Ahous Beach**, where you can camp. The island also has a high concentration of native heritage sites. **Flores Island** ① *20 km from Tofino by water taxi*, contains undisturbed watersheds with old-growth stands of Sitka spruce and is home to **Ahousat** village, one of the best places to encounter First Nations people and their culture. The 10-km **Walk the Wild Side Trail** follows a route used by natives for centuries, running from Ahousat to the wild west coast beaches via rainforest, beaches and the slopes of Mount Flores. The island is also one of the best places to watch the grey whale migration. Note that there are wolves on these islands, so all rubbish must be packed away.

Ucluelet 🖼️🕴️❄️⛺🚌 ➤ *pp122-127. Colour map 1, C2.*

Meaning 'people of the sheltered bay', Ucluelet is a major fishing port that has retained the feel of an ordinary village. This is the place from which to get to **Barkley Sound** and the Broken Islands Group, and there's just as good a chance of seeing whales here as in Tofino. The very helpful **Visitor Information Centre** ① *100 Main St, T250-726 4600, www.uclueletinfo.com, Mon-Fri 0900-1700*, can tell you more about B&Bs and the many operators for whale watching, fishing and kayaking. At the south end of town, the **Wild Pacific Trail** is a very pleasant 2.7-km loop that passes a lighthouse, with views of Barkley Sound and (sometimes) whales. Amphitrite Point on this trail is one of the best locations for storm watching.

Broken Islands Group

Pacific Rim National Park's central section consists of an archipelago of over 100 islands scattered throughout Barkley Sound, a dream location for sea-kayakers who come here in droves despite the difficult access. Coastal wilderness doesn't get much more remote than this, so the scenery is spectacular, with plenty of undisturbed temperate rainforest, lagoons, sandbars, blowholes and a good chance of seeing marine wildlife, including major colonies of sea lions. Archaeological digs have shown that native peoples also favoured the spot, with evidence of habitation on the islands dating back thousands of years, including ancient middens, village fortifications and stone fishtraps.

These days the Broken Islands are known internationally among kayaking and scuba-diving circles, and can be shockingly overrun, especially in July and August, with campsites regularly full. The waters are also notoriously treacherous, thanks to submerged rocks, reefs, sea caves, exposed channels, extreme and unpredictable weather and freezing water. Only the highly experienced should even think about paddling here without a guide, there are many in Tofino, Ucluelet and Bamfield.

Bamfield → *Colour map 1, C2.*

Bamfield is a tiny town on the edge of Barkley Sound, at the mouth of the Alberni Inlet. Unless arriving on the oft-vaunted *MV Lady Rose*, access is on a horrible 100-km logging road from Port Alberni. Nobody would bother, but this (or Pachena Bay, 5 km away) is the northern end of the formidable West Coast Trail. Having come so far, however, it's worth having a look round. There is a **Tourist Information Centre** ① *T250-728 3006, www.bamfieldcommunity.com, May-Aug only* and the main part of town is a somewhat drab, no-nonsense service centre for the forestry industry, but on the other side of a narrow inlet, accessible only by water taxi, is a boardwalk village. The very unlikelihood of its location has kept it much more unspoilt than others further north, and a community of artists has taken root. Wandering along board-walks from studio to studio is a delightful way to spend an afternoon. There's a café with a lovely deck where the ferry docks and a Tourist Information booth in the **Net Loft Gallery** to the north. **Brady's Beach**, a 20-minute walk west, is a fine and popular place to catch some rays: long, sandy and a little bit wild.

West Coast Trail ➡ *Colour map 1, C2 and C3.*

At least 66 ships at the bottom of the ocean bear witness to the treacherous nature of a strip of coast known as the 'graveyard of the Pacific'. Following the sinking of the *SS Valencia* in 1906, the decision was taken to convert an old 1890 telegraph trail between Port Renfrew and Bamfield into an escape route for survivors of shipwrecks, since this stretch of coast is practically uninhabited, covered in the densest forest and subject to appallingly heavy rainfall. From the 1960s, BC's trailblazing hiker community began to take the opportunity to experience some of the most pristine and spectacular wilderness imaginable. Today, it is recognized as one of North America's greatest hikes and quotas are in operation to limit numbers.

The trail runs 75 km from **Pachena Bay**, ① *5 km south of Bamfield*, to **Gordon River**, a ferry ride from Port Renfrew. It takes an average of six or seven days and is a commitment not to be entered into lightly. Over 60 hikers have to be evacuated each year, usually with strained knees and ankles. As the official blurb puts it: "You must be self-sufficient, prepared for foul weather, slippery terrain, creek fording, long days and heavy packs. You must be prepared to wait out storms and high water on creek crossings". If in doubt, it is possible to hike half of the trail, beginning at **Nitinat Lake**. Full camping equipment, plenty of food, good rain gear and boots, and a proper map and tide table are essential. Camping on the beach above the tideline

MV Lady Rose

Originally the sole function of this Scottish freighter was to transport mail and supplies from Port Alberni to isolated communities around Barkley Sound. However, passengers bound for difficult-to-access locations such as Bamfield and the Broken Islands Group began using the vessel as transportation, making the most of the meandering route to savour the dramatic scenery and spot wildlife. The journey became so popular that a second boat had to be added, the Norwegian *MV Frances Barkley*. Though the pioneering spirit has now been diluted by popularity, this is still a fantastic way to travel, though the boats were not built for comfort and still make frequent stops.

Reservations are essential and should be made in Port Alberni on Argyle Street, T250-723 8313, www.ladyrosemarine.com. There are year-round sailings on Tuesday, Thursday and Saturday from Port Alberni to Bamfield; additional sailings from June to September on Monday, Wednesday and Friday to Ucluelet and Sechart (Broken Group); and on Sunday to Bamfield and Sechart.

is recommended. Driftwood campfires are allowed on the beach only, but take a small stove and fuel for cooking. Avoid shellfish, which could be poisonous.

Trail logistics

ⓘ *Mandatory 1½-hr orientation sessions are held at the trailhead information centres, Pachena Bay, T250-728 3234 and Gordon River, T250-647 5434, both open daily 0900-1700.*

The trail is open 1 May to 30 September and gets heavily booked. Quotas limit the number of starters per day with five standby places available at each trailhead; get on the waiting list, and be prepared to wait for a few days. There is no hiker quota in the shoulder season (1 May to 14 June and 16 to 30 September) from Monday to Friday. **Reservations** ⓘ *T250-381 642, T1800-435 5622, cost $25*, and are taken up to three months in advance (eg hikes in July can be reserved from 1 April). Register at the trailhead by 1300 on your allotted day, or your spot may be taken. For year-round information, contact the **Park Administration office** ⓘ *Ucluelet, T250-726 7721, www.parkscanada.ca*. The trail user fee is $127.50. There are two ferries during the hike, at Gordon River and Nitinat Narrows, $15 each, payable when registering. In addition, those starting at Nitinat Lake have to take a water taxi costing $25. There is no bank or ATM at either Bamfield or Port Renfrew. The **West Coast Trail Shuttle Bus** ⓘ *T250-477 8700, www.trailbus.com*, runs daily from Victoria, Nanaimo and Port Alberni and between trailheads; there is also a service to Nitinat from Port Renfrew. Advance booking is recommended, see Port Renfrew and Bamfield for more details. If all this seems too complicated, crowded or expensive, or if you just plain can't get a place, consider doing the **Juan de Fuca** (see page 94) or the **Sunshine Coast Trail** instead.

● Sleeping

Victoria to Nanaimo *p112*
Chemainus is overflowing with 'quaint' B&Bs, ask at the Visitor Centre. Further out of town on Chemainus Rd are a number of old renovated mill houses, where you will find a couple of good-value places to stay.

A-B Fairburn Farm Country Manor, 3310 Jackson Rd, Duncan, T250-746 4637, www.fairburnfarm.bc.ca. A lovely 19th-century manor house set in 52 ha, with lots of trails and animals. There are 4 tasteful and comfy en suite rooms and a cottage, plus library, lounge and patio. Cooking lessons and dinner available.

B-C Olde Mill House, 9712 Chemainus Rd, Chemainus, T250-416 0049, www.olde millhouse.ca. 3 very nice, cosy rooms with great beds and en suite baths. Ask for the one with TV, private garden and deck.

D Iguana Ranch, 5070 Culverton Rd, Duncan, T250-709 9010, www.iguana ranch.com. 7 km out of town off Lake Cowichan Rd, take local transit No 7. Set in beautiful, wild surroundings, this is a gem of a place, especially if you're a mountain biker. Dorm beds and 2 private rooms, a hot tub, sauna, decks, a clubhouse, TV, a trampoline and weights room. Bike rental and activities are arranged, breakfast is included.

D Horseshoe Bay Inn, 9567 Chemainus Rd, T250-416 0411. The best place for a drink, this pub also has some surprisingly nice (and cheap) rooms, some with clawfoot bath and king-size bed.

Camping
Bald Eagle Riverside Campground, 8705 Chemainus Rd, T250-246 9457, Chemainus. Some 7 km from town, a quiet spot by the river with decent forested sites and plenty of activities.

Nanaimo and around *p112, map p113*
B Coast Bastion Inn, 11 Bastion St, T250-753 6601, www.coasthotels.com. It's a chain hotel and the rooms are clean, comfortable, but somewhat lacking in character. The central location and harbour views are hard to beat. Facilities include a sauna, exercise room, restaurant and lounge.

B Long Lake B&B, 240 Ferntree Pl, T250-758 5010, www.lodgingnanaimo.com. 3 en suite rooms with private entrances, situated on a private beach on the lake close to town. Canoes for guests to use.

C Best Western Dorchester, 70 Church St, T250-754 6835, www.dorchesternanaimo. com. The rooms and suites here are fairly plain and predictable but, again, the central location and harbour views make this a great option and good value.

C Kennedy House B&B, 305 Kennedy St, T250-754 3389. 2 lovely rooms in a beautifully restored heritage house a short walk from Downtown and ferries.

E The Cambie, 63 Victoria Cres, T250-754 5323. A more rough and ready backpacker hostel, with single-sex dorms and some en suite rooms. There's a small kitchen and common room, and a great café and pub downstairs. Breakfast and admission to weekend gigs included.

E Nicol St Hostel, 65 Nicol St, T250-753 1188, www.nanaimohostel.com. Out of the centre, but a first-class, friendly hostel with private rooms or dorms, and facilities including a common room, kitchen, TV room, laundry, parking and free internet.

E Painted Turtle HI Guesthouse, 121 Bastion St, T1866-309 4432, www.painted turtle.ca. Handily located downtown near the harbour, with small but stylish en suite rooms, family rooms and hostel-style bunks. Guests share a large kitchen, dining room and lounge.

Camping
Newcastle Island Marine Provincial Park, T250-754 7893, 10 min ferry ride (see Transport, page 127). Ideal for those who value their tranquillity and are not in a hurry. 18 beautiful walk-in sites, first-come first-served. Open year-round, with fees Apr-Sep only. Showers and flush toilets, but few other facilities.

Gabriola Island *p114*
AL The Melville Grant Inn, 2310 Windecker Dr, T250-247 9687, www.melvillegrant inn.com. Set on an ocean-front rocky bluff, surrounded by woods, beaches and gardens, this gorgeous home is opulently furnished. The 4 romantic en suite rooms each have jacuzzis and a couple have private verandas. Gourmet West Coast breakfast included.

AL-C Haven By the Sea, 240 Davis Rd, T250-247 9211, www.haven.ca. This centre for personal development courses is also open to casual guests who can enjoy the ocean-front location and the facilities, which include gym, sauna, hot tub and an outdoor swimming pool. The very broad range of rooms and cabins (some with kitchen) are a bit faded, but the restaurant serves wholesome buffet-style meals at reasonable prices.

C Hummingbird Lodge B&B, 1597 Starbuck Lane, T250-247 9300, www.hummingbird lodgebb.com. A giant, delightful West Coast lodge with high ceilings, lots of decks and windows and gardens. The 3 en suite rooms have bags of character.

C Surf Lodge & Sunset Lounge, 885 Berry Point Rd, T250-247 9231, www.surflodge. com. 7 rooms in an attractive wood lodge, and 8 cabins (**A**) in ample forested grounds with ocean views. There's also a pub and restaurant.

Camping

Descanso Bay Regional Park, 595 Taylor Bay Rd, near ferry terminal, T250-247 8255. 28 sites in a nice forest setting close to the water. Open year round.

West to Pacific Rim National Park *p114*

B Cedar Wood Lodge, 5895 River Rd, Hwy 4, Port Alberni, T250-724 6800, www.cedarwood.bc.ca. Nicely removed from Downtown, this attractive lodge has 8 lovely rooms and a comfortable lounge with pool table. Breakfast included.

E Fat Salmon Backpackers, 3250 3rd Av, Port Alberni, T250-723 6924, www.fat salmonbackpackers.com. A cosy, colourful and friendly hostel, with 6 dorms, a kitchen-dining room and a large lounge.

Camping

Sproat Lake Provincial Park, 13 km north-west of Port Alberni, off Hwy 4, T250-474 1336. This is a huge and attractive lake, good for warm swimming, watersports and fishing, and very popular in summer. All the lakeside sites are RV pull-through types, the nicest being on the north side.

Stamp River Provincial Park, off Beaver Creek Rd, 14 km northwest of Port Alberni on Hwy 4, T250-474 1336. A small, forested, attractive campground set on a river renowned for its fishing. From late Aug-Dec, half a million salmon travel up the falls via ladders, an incredible sight.

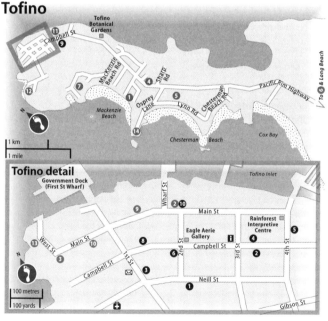

Sleeping
Bella Pacifica Campground 1
Cable Cove Inn 3
Dolphin Motel 4
Gull Cottage 5
Greenpoint Campground 6
Inn at Tough City 2
Middle Beach Lodge 7
Paddler's Inn 9
Tofino Trek Inn B&B 10
Water's Edge 12
Whalers On the Point Guesthouse 13
Wickaninnish Inn & Pointe Restaurant 14

Eating
Breaker's Fresh Food Café 4
Caffe Vincente 2
Common Loaf Bake Shop 3
Local Motion 8
Raincoast Café 5
Schooner 6
Shelter 9
Sobo 1
Tough City Sushi 10

Bars & clubs
Marine Pub 11

Tofino *p115, map p120*

Tofino's B&Bs represent a better deal than the motels, which are overpriced. For those with a vehicle, Mackenzie and Chesterman beaches, 7 km away, are ideal, quiet, waterside locations, with copious resorts and lodges offering anything from ugly old cabins to luxurious suites. Prices drop considerably after Labour Day in Sep. In summer, reservations are essential.

LL Wickaninnish Inn, 500 Osprey Lane, Chesterman Beach, T250-725 3100, www.wickinn.com. One of the most stylish places to stay in Western Canada, with rooms tastefully decorated in West Coast style and handmade driftwood furniture. There are fireplaces, CD players, shelves of books, binoculars, oversized tubs and huge TVs. Balconies and floor-to-ceiling windows make the most of the spectacular ocean views. There's a full spa, not included but ask about packages, and the **Pointe Restaurant** is highly renowned.

LL-B Middle Beach Lodge, 400 Mackenzie Beach, 3 km south, T250-725 2900, www.middlebeach.com. The best of many self-contained lodges on the beaches near Tofino. The beautiful, spacious timber lodge features hardwood floors, pine furnishings, stone fireplaces and sits in 16 ha of forested land which includes a mile-long private beach. Cosy lodge rooms, some with decks and views, and luxurious suites and ocean-front cabins. Continental breakfast included, West Coast dinners available in the restaurant. Adults only.

AL Cable Cove Inn, 201 Main St, T250-725 4236, www.cablecoveinn.com. 7 immaculately decorated, romantic rooms with fireplaces, huge beds and either in-room jacuzzi tubs or hot tubs on private decks. Ocean views, shared lounge with fireplace, full kitchen, direct beach access and breakfast included. There's also a gourmet West Coast restaurant and a full spa.

A The Inn At Tough City, 350 Main St, in town, T250-725 2021, www.toughcity.com. 8 vibrant and modern en suite rooms with balconies, hardwood floors and big windows in an attractive brick building. Sushi bar and lounge downstairs.

B Gull Cottage, 254 Lynn Rd, Chesterman Beach, T250-725 3177, www.gullcottage

tofino.com. 3 lovely, bright en suite rooms in a Victorian home set amongst the trees. Guest lounge and hot tub.

B Water's Edge, 331 Tonquin Park Rd, T250-725 1218, www.watersedgeinn.ca. The 3 rooms and 2 suites in this West Coast home are not as luxurious as some, but the views from the common room are about as good as it gets. There's a hot tub, a private staircase down to the tide pools and breakfast is included.

C Dolphin Motel, 1190 Pacific Rim Highway, T250-725 3377, www.dolphinmotel.ca. A pretty standard motel, but the grounds are brightened up by flowers and trees, and Chesterman Beach is 5 mins walk away.

D Paddler's Inn, 320 Main St, T250-725 4222. Simple but clean and pleasant rooms with views, shared baths and dining room/kitchen. Buffet breakfast included.

D-E Tofino Trek Inn B&B, 231 Main St, T250-725 2791, www.tofinotrekinn.com. 2 private rooms and 5 dorm beds only. Simple breakfast, use of kitchen, deck with ocean views and BBQ. Bike rentals.

D-E Whalers On the Point Guesthouse, 81 West St, T250-725 3443, www.tofino hostel.com. This very spacious, HI-affiliated hostel is one of the best in the West, with first-class facilities that include a solarium sitting-room with stunning harbour views, a kitchen, games room with pool table, TV room, library, patio with BBQ, laundry, sauna, lockers and discounts on tours. Mostly dorms, with some private and family rooms. Reservations essential.

Camping

Bella Pacifica Campground, 3 km south, T250-725 3400, www.bellapacifica.com. The best of a few places offering camping possibilities with access to Mackenzie Beach. Sites are small, but some are right on the beach. Coin showers and laundry.

Greenpoint Campground, 19 km south of Tofino, T1877-737 3783, www.pccamping.ca. The only campground on Long Beach and easily the best in the area, with small but densely forested and private sites, some overlooking the beach. Reservations through Parks Canada are almost essential. Fees, including $11 reservation fee, are payable when reserving.

AL Innchanter, Hot Springs Cove, T250-670 1149, www.innchanter.com. This 1920s arts and crafts-style coastal freighter, moored just off the dock, offers the cove's most intimate and stylish lodging. The 5 rooms are small but full of character, with shared bath. The living room has a fireplace, sofas and a splendid library. The price includes breakfast and dinner prepared by the excellent resident chef, with lots of local seafood on the menu, and use of canoes and dinghies.

C Hot Springs Lodge, T1888-781 9977. A motel-style set-up with kitchenettes in the en suite rooms and patios with BBQ. Situated across the water from the springs, free use of boats. Guests are advised to bring groceries. They also have a campground.

Ucluelet *p116*

LL-L Tauca Lea By the Sea, 1971 Harbour Cres, T250-726 4625, www.taucalea resort.com. This beautiful lodge is situated on a point out in the water. Luxurious, fully equipped waterfront suites come with kitchen, fireplace and jacuzzi. Full spa available. The expensive **Boat Basin Restaurant** serves gourmet cuisine in elegant surroundings with fantastic views.

A-B Reef Point Cottages, 1012 Peninsula Rd, T250-726 4425, www.reefpoint cottages.com. A broad range of small and simple, but very comfortable and attractive new 1- and 2-bedroom cottages with hardwood floors. Close to the beach.

A-C Canadian Princess Resort, 1943 Peninsula Rd, T250-5983366, www.canadian princess.com. The moored steam ship's onboard cabins make for rather basic but characterful private rooms with bunk beds. Shore rooms are a lot nicer.

C Pacific Rim Motel, 1755 Peninsula Rd, T250-726 7728, www.pacificrimmotel.com. One of a few fairly cheap motels on this road, unexciting but decent enough.

E C&N Backpackers Hostel, 2081 Peninsula Rd, T250-726 7416, www.cnnback packers.com. Private rooms and dorms in an attractive house surrounded by trees, on its own private beach. Facilities include a kitchen, lounge with TV, laundry, storage, internet access, and bike and kayak rental.

E Surfs Inn, 1874 Peninsula Rd, T250-726 4426, www.surfsinn.ca. Dorm beds and 1 private room in a colourful hostel in the centre of town. Full kitchen, TV and internet.

Broken Islands Group *p117*

Camping is in one of the 8 designated areas only, for which there is a charge of $5 per person per night. Maximum stay at each site is 4 days. Maximum stay on the islands is 14 days. There is very little drinking water available, so take all you will need with you.

A-B Sechart Lodge, T250-723 8313, www.ladyrosemarine.com. Operated by Alberni Marine Transport who run the *MV Lady Rose*, which will deliver you here. Otherwise, take a water taxi from Toquart Bay ($30). This gloriously remote 1905 whaling station makes a great base from which to explore the region. Kayaks and canoes are rented for $35 per day and for $30-45 the owners will provide transfers for you and your boat. Rooms are simple with shared bath. Price includes all meals, and the price drops if you stay for more than 1 night.

Bamfield *p117*

AL-B Woods End Landing Cottages, 380 Lombard St, T250-728 3383, www.wood send.travel.bc.ca. Fully equipped, 2-bedroom cottages with kitchens and private decks. Situated on the water amidst lovely secluded gardens. Free use of rowing boat.

C Bamfield Lodge, on the boardwalk side, T250-7283 419, www.bamfieldlodge.com. Rustic but pleasant cabins with kitchen, adjacent to a wood lodge with common room. They also run the Boardwalk Bistro. Will pick up.

Camping

Pachena Bay Campground, 5 km from Bamfield at the start of the West Coast Trail, T250-728 1287. On a very fine beach, this wonderful, native-run campground is a perfect place to relax before or after the hike. Reservations essential.

🍴 Eating

Victoria to Nanaimo *p112*

🍴 **Vinoteca**, at Vignetti Zanatta winery, 5039 Marshall Rd, Glenora, T250-748 2338, www.zanatta.ca. Apr-Oct Wed-Sun 1200-1430, Sat-Sun 1200-1600. One of the best wineries in this area, the beautiful, very popular (but expensive) restaurant has a lovely garden patio and a menu that focuses on local ingredients, simplicity and wine pairings. Reservations recommended.

Lizzy-Lou's Funky Fusion Café, 9893 Maple St, T250-246 1050. Just what you'd expect from the name.

Willow Street Café, 9749 Willow St. This beautiful big house is the best spot for coffee and snacks in the New Town.

Nanaimo and around *p112, map p113*

Drift, 77 Skinner St, T250-753 7438. An extremely modern and chic space, attracting a hip and sophisticated clientele. The small West Coast menu changes frequently, according to the availability of fresh local ingredients. There's a patio with views, and a decent drinks list.

Wesley Street Café, 321 Wesley St, T250-753 6057. Nanaimo's best fine dining, with an intimate, romantic interior, a small menu that changes frequently and a great wine list.

Acme Food Co, 14 Commercial St, T250-753 0042. Occupying an old building with bags of character and stylishly fitted out with antique wood tables, brick walls and high ceilings, this trendy eatery boasts an international menu with a West Coast accent and a sushi bar in the back. Also a good place for a drink, with frequent live music.

Basque Restaurant, 489 Wallace St, T250-754 7354. French and Spanish influenced cuisine, including paella and tapas, prepared with a West Coast emphasis on freshness and served in a sophisticated, upmarket environment.

Gina's Mexican Café, 47 Skinner St, T250-753 5411. A Nanaimo institution, authentic Mexican food served in bright and colourful surroundings. Friendly and very popular.

Mrs. Riches, 199 Fraser St, T250-7532977. Plays the diner card nicely, with eccentric decor, large portions and a wide range of comfort food that is surprisingly good. A local favourite and very busy.

The Cambie, 63 Victoria Cres. There are a couple of authentically seedy diners on Church St and Commercial St, but this bakery/café is a better choice for a cheap breakfast, as well as excellent cakes and pastries and cheap pints.

Gabriola Island *p114*

Raspberry's Jazz Café, Folklife Village Mall, T250-247 9959. A hip little licensed café with good coffee, some tasty lunch options and occasional live jazz.

Silva Bay Pub, at the island's eastern tip, T250-247 8662. Overlooking the marina and ocean, the busy patio here is a wonderful place for food or a drink.

Suzy's Restaurant, 560 North Rd in the village, T250-247 2010. A cosy little place with a predictable menu but some good daily specials. About the only central spot for dinner.

West to Pacific Rim National Park *p114*

The Clam Bucket, 4479 Victoria Quay, Port Alberni, T250-723 1315. Not the most central location, but this is the restaurant most consistently recommended by locals. Large portions of good seafood.

Swale Rock Café, 5328 Argyle St, Port Alberni, T250-723 0777. A central and reliable choice for varied dishes including seafood, curry and burgers. The atmosphere is down-to-earth, the portions large.

Blue Door Café, 5415 Argyle St, Port Alberni, T250-723 8811. Conveniently close to Harbour Quay, this is the place for cheap breakfasts and lunches. For coffee shops, head down to the quay.

Tofino *p115, map p120*

Fresh crab is widely available year-round for about $10-15 each (look for signs).

Pointe Restaurant, Wickaninnish Inn, T250-725 3100. As well as offering spectacular panoramic ocean views and sumptuous surroundings, this place has an excellent reputation for gourmet dining with a West Coast accent. If you're not up for a major splurge, a drink in the lounge is more affordable and almost as gratifying.

Schooner Restaurant, 331 Campbell St, T250-725 3444. This long-standing favourite has a conservative but romantic atmosphere and is still rated as the best place for traditional gourmet seafood. Menu also features some good salads

Raincoast Café, 4th/Campbell St, T250-725 2215. The fairly large but expertly crafted menu here combines pan-Asian influences with a West Coast fusion sensibility and changes often. The top notch food, combined with stylishly minimalist decor and surprisingly reasonable prices, have allowed this chic eatery to remain the place to eat in Tofino.

Shelter, 601 Campbell St, T250-725 3353. Housed in a large, open space dominated by the wood ceiling, stone fireplace and bar, this new contender for Tofino's finest offers a varied menu of West Coast-style dishes renowned for freshness and creativity. They also have a great heated patio.

Sobo, 311 Neill St, T250-725 2341. Fresh, nutritious, 'sophisticated street food' with an emphasis on salads and seafood. The new location has a bistro feel, with big windows giving views of Clayoquot Sound and an outdoor patio with a stone fireplace.

Tough City Sushi, 350 Main St, T250-725 2021. A unique and appealing spot for authentic sushi and other West Coast cuisine, with the bonus of a waterfront patio for harbour views.

Breaker's Fresh Food Café, 430 Campbell St, T250-725 2558. Healthy and wholesome lunches like burritos or pizza, all-day breakfast and good coffee.

Caffe Vincente, 441 Campbell St, T250-725 2599. Probably the best coffee in town, with baked goods and lunch items.

The Common Loaf Bake Shop, 180 1st St, T250-725 3915. A warm, friendly place for good coffee, fresh baking and light meals. Popular as a meeting-place, with a very useful bulletin board.

Local Motion, 230 Main St, T250-725 3669. Enjoy a coffee on the patio with ocean views. Has good light food options.

Ucluelet *p116*
Matterson House, 1682 Peninsula Rd, T250-726 2200. The local's choice. Home-cooked food in a relaxed environment.
Blueberries Restaurant and Bar, 1627 Peninsula Rd, T250-726 7707. A down-to-earth and licensed spot for home-cooked food. Views from the patio.

ⓕ Bars and clubs

Nanaimo and around *p112, map p113*
The Cambie, 63 Victoria Cres. Cheap, spit-

and-sawdust style boozer with live music at weekends.
Queen's Pub, 34 Victoria Cres. A dark and slightly dingy venue that's ideal for the nightly live music.

Tofino *p115, map p120*
The Marine Pub, Weigh West Resort, 634 Campbell St, T250-725 3277. The best choice in town, with good views and a few beers on tap.
On the Rocks Lounge, T250-725 3100, Wickaninnish Inn. Has the best views.

ⓔ Entertainment

Victoria to Nanaimo *p112*
Chemainus Theatre, 9737 Chemainus Rd, T250-246 9820, www.chemainustheatre festival.ca. Pretty serious theatre year-round.

Nanaimo and around *p112, map p113*
Nanaimo has a thriving art scene. The *Visitor Guide* contains a map of local galleries.
Art 10 Gallery, 650 Terminal Av, T250-753 4009. A cooperative of 28 local artists, one of whose work is highlighted each month.
Artisan's Studio, 70 Bastion St, T250-753 6151. An art and craft co-op displaying work by potters, weavers, painters, photographers, jewellers and more.
Gallery 223, 223 Commercial St, T250-741 1188. A large space in a renovated heritage house with regularly changing exhibits by local artists.
Port Theatre, 125 Front St, T250-754 4555, www.porttheatre.com. Outside Victoria, this is the best venue for plays and the performing arts on the island.

ⓕ Festivals and events

Victoria to Nanaimo *p112*
Jun Cowichan Bay Boat Festival, T250-746 4955, www.classicboats.org/festival. This visually delightful event is held for 1 day towards the end of Jun and has been running for over 20 years.
Jul Islands Folk Festival, T250-748 3975, www.folkfest.bc.ca. A long-running 3-day event toward the end of Jul, held at Providence Farm between Duncan and Cowichan Bay. Camping on-site.

Nanaimo and around *p112, map p113*
Jun The Cadillac Van Isle 360° Yacht Race, www.vanisle360.com. 2-week, 580-nautical mile race that begins and ends in Nanaimo. It happens every 2 years, next in 2009.
Jul Marine Festival, T250-7537223, www.bathtubbing.com. A 4-day festival on the 3rd weekend of the month, features music and fireworks on the harbour as well as the famed World Championship Bathtub Race, when hopefuls compete for the coveted silver plunger trophy.
Aug Summertime Blues!, T250-753 2522, www.nanaimoblues.com. 2 weekends of free, outdoor blues concerts held in the Harbourfront Plaza.

Gabriola Island *p114*
Aug Salmon BBQ, the island's major event, has taken place annually for over 50 years.
Oct Studio Tour, on thanksgiving weekend the island's many artist studios open their doors to the public for 3 days. Pick up the detailed brochure from the Visitor Centre.

Tofino *p115, map p120*
Mar The Pacific Rim Whale Festival, T250-725 4426, www.pacificrimwhale festival.org. A 2-week celebration, with various whale-related events to mark the beginning of the annual grey whale migration. Hosted by Tofino, Ucluelet and the Pacific Rim National Park Reserve.
Jun Tofino Food and Wine Festival, www.tofinofoodandwinefestival.com. 3 days at the start of Jun.
Jul Pacific Rim Summer Festival, T250-725 4271, www.pacificrimsummerfestival.ca. Kicking off summer, 2 weeks of music and dance of all genres in Tofino and Ucluelet.
Aug Tofino Lantern Festival. A magical event held at the Botanical Gardens.
Sep Tofino Art in the Gardens Festival, T250-726 7755. 2 days of visual and performing arts in the Botanical Gardens, near the start of Sep. West Coast Maritime Festival, T250-382 6613, www.tonquin foundation.org. Near month's end, featuring varied shows, demonstrations and events, many of them on Clayoquot Sound.
Oct Tofino Film Festival, www.tofinofilm festival.com. 4 days of films shown at Clayoquot Sound Community Theatre.

O Shopping

Nanaimo and around *p112, map p113*
Arts and crafts
Hill's Native Art, 76 Bastion St, T250-755 7873. One of the largest selections of glorious First Nations artwork on the West Coast, including jewellery, sculptures, masks, clothes, totem poles and paintings.
Nanaimo Art Gallery 150 Commercial St, T250-754 1750. A decent giftshop show-casing local artisans.

Books and maps
Bygone Books, 99 Commercial St, T250-741 1766. The best of many second-hand bookshops on this street, with a great selection including lots of Canadian fiction and non-fiction.
Nanaimo Maps and Charts, 8 Church St, T250-754 2513. A giant collection of nautical and topographical maps.

Music
Fascinating Rhythm, 51 Commercial St, T250-716 9997. One of the best new and used CD shops in the West. Huge selection.

Gabriola Island *p114*
Gabriola Artworks, 575 North Rd, T250-247 7412. Representing many of the 50 or more resident artists. Also has a café.

Tofino *p115, map p120*
Arts and crafts
House of Himwitsa, 300 Main St, T250-725 2017, www.himwitsa.com. Owned by First Nations people, one of the best among many galleries in town specializing in native art and crafts.
Shorewind Gallery, 4th/Campbell St, T250-725 1222, www.shorewindgallery. com. Another large collection of West Coast art.
The Village Gallery, 321 Main St, T250-725 4229. Selection of authentic First Nations art, including wooden masks and paintings.

Books
Wildside Booksellers, 320 Main St, T250-725 4222. A well-chosen selection of new fiction and books about the area, plus kites and an Espresso Bar.

Clothes
Plush, 381 Main St, T250-725 2730. Most
interesting, contemporary boutique in town.

Sports equipment
Tofino Fishing and Trading, 120 4th St,
T250-725 2622. Camping, hiking, sports gear.

▲ Activities and tours

Nanaimo and around *p112, map p113*
Cycling
Bikes can be hired from **Bastion Cycle & Ski** ,
4196 Departure Bay Rd, T250-758 2453.

Kayaking and sailing
The many little islands off the coast, with
resident sea-life such as octopus, seals and
otters, make this a prime location for sailing
and kayaking.
The Kayak Shack, just off the ferry at 1956
Zorkin Rd, T250-753 3234. Tours and lessons.
Seadog Kayaking & Sailing, T250- 468
5778, www.seadog.bc.ca. Lessons, tours,
rentals and skippered sailing charters.

Scuba-diving
Several places around Nanaimo are recom-
mended for diving, such as the sunken *HMCS
Saskatchewan*, an artificial reef teeming with
marine life. Contact **Nanaimo Diving
Association**, 1956 Zorkin Rd, T250-756
8871, for information.
Ocean Explorers Diving, 1690 Stewart Av,
T250-753 2055, www.oceanexplorersdiving.
com. Offers lessons, charters and dives.

Swimming
Nanaimo Leisure and Aquatic Centre,
741 3rd St, T250-756 5200, has a good
pool, sauna, hot tub and exercise room.

Gabriola Island *p114*
Cycling
CC Rentals, 1235 South Rd, T250-247 0247.
Rent bikes, scooters and equipment.

Kayaking
Jim's Kayaking, T250-247 8335, www.jims
kayaking.com. Tours, trips and equipment.

Scuba-diving
High Test Dive Charters, T250-247 9753,
www.hightestdive.com. Guided dives to a

number of sites around the island. Gear
rental and sales.

West to Pacific Rim National Park *p114*
Canoeing
Choo-Kwa Ventures, Victoria Quay,
Johnston Rd, Port Alberni, T250-724 4006,
www.chookwa.com. Guided cultural excursions in a replica native cedar canoe, with
wildlife spotting and storytelling.

Scuba-diving
Rendezvous Dive Adventures, Port
Alberni, T250-735 5050, www.rendezvous
diving.com. Accommodation and diving in
Barkley Sound. Packages include lodging,
meals and diving. Booking ahead is essential.

Tofino *p115, map p120*
Birdwatching
Adrian Dorst, T250-725 1243, www.adrian
dorst.com. Guided bird walks in the Meares
Island rainforest with a nature photographer.

Cycling
TOF Cycles, 660 Sharp Rd, T250-725 2453.
For bike hire, repairs and information.

Fishing
Clayoquot Ventures, 564 Campbell St,
T250-725 2700, www.tofinofishing.com.
Salmon and halibut fishing trips.

Floatplane
Tofino Air, T250-725 4454, www.tofino
air.ca. Chartered flights to Hot Springs
Cove, wildlife tours, glacier tours and
guided fishing by floatplane.

Kayaking and canoeing
Clayoquot Sound may well be the coast's
best overall location for kayaking. It's less
crowded than the Broken Islands Group but
more so than Nootka Sound and the beauty
of the scenery is almost unparalleled. Be
careful though, the currents and waves here
are dangerous, causing a few deaths every
year. If in doubt, go with a professional.
Rainforest Kayak, T250-725 3117, www.rain
forestkayak.com. Eco-friendly lessons, courses
and tours with very experienced guides.
Remote Passages Kayaking, T1800-666
9833, www.remotepassages.com. Day and
evening paddles and instruction.

Tla-ook Cultural Adventures, T250-725 2656, www.tlaook.com. Tours in traditional native dugout canoes, with local First Nations guides who focus on the culture, history and ecology of the area. From 2-hr harbour tours to all-day adventures with hiking and salmon BBQ.

Tofino Seakayaking, T250-725 4222, www.tofino-kayaking.com. Offers tours and lessons. Will rent to experienced kayakers.

Scuba-diving
Ocean Planet Adventures, 1180 Pacific Rim Hwy, T250-725 2221. Lessons, charters and trips for all levels.

Surfing
Tofino has become an internationally recognized surf destination. The following are recommended for gear, rentals, lessons (around $80 for 2 hrs, including board) and advice: **Live To Surf**, 1180 Pacific Rim Hwy, T250-725 4464, www.livetosurf.com; **Pacific Surf School**, 430 Campbell St, T250-725 2155, www.pacificsurfschool.com; **Surf Sister Surf School**, 625 Campbell St, T250-725 4456, www.surfsisterschool.com, an all-girl surf school; **Westside Surf School**, 1180 Pacific Rim HWY, T250-725 2404, www.westsidesurfschool.com.

Whale watching
The number one activity hereabouts. For excellent value, combine it with a trip to Hot Springs Cove. There are many decent operators in town, the 3 listed below all have good, long-standing reputations and offer similar packages and prices. A 2½ hr whale-watching trip costs about $80. A 6-8 hr trip including Hot Springs costs around $110-120. Ask if they will let you stay overnight and take the boat back the next day. You can also opt to fly back from the Hot Springs in a floatplane for $165 all-in. Before booking, decide if you want to travel in an inflatable Zodiac or a rigid-hull cruiser. The former tend to get thrown around a bit, making for an exciting and wet ride, the latter are a little calmer. These companies also offer black bear watching trips in Clayoquot Sound for around $80/2 hrs: **Jamie's Whaling Station**, 606 Campbell St, T250-725 3919, www.jamies.com; **Ocean Outfitters**, 421 Main St, T250-725 2866, www.oceanoutfitters.bc.ca.

Remote Passages, T250-725 3330, www.remotepassages.com. Also sea kayaking, $74 for 4 hrs, including a walk on Meares Island.

Yacht cruise
Browning Pass Charters, 890 Main St, T250-725 3435, www.browningpass.com. Sightseeing and bear watching trips.

Ucluelet *p116*
Jamie's Whaling Station, 168 Fraser Lane, T250-726 7444, www.jamies.com, offers the full range of activities.

Cycling
Ukee Bikes, Boards & Kites, 1559 Imperial Lane, T250-726 2453. Bike sales, rentals, and also repairs.

Bamfield *p117*
Broken Island Adventures, T250-728 3500, www.brokenislandadventures.com. Marine wildlife tours, $75/3 hrs; diving, $75 per person per dive; kayaking, $40/half day; sailing in a 33-ft Viking, $125/hr. Can also arrange a water taxi to anywhere in Barkley Sound and even accommodation (**D**).

Tyee Resort and Fishing Lodge, Michelsens Lane, T250-728 3296, www.tyeeresort.com. Fishing excursions, lodging (**B**), meals and any combination of the 3.

⊖ Transport

Nanaimo and around *p112, map p113*
Air
For airport details, see page 110.

Air Canada, T250-245 7123, www.air canada.com, has several flights daily to **Vancouver** ($100 one-way). Harbour Air Seaplanes, T250-537 5525, www.harbour-air.com, operate regular flights from the Seaplane Terminal behind the Bastion to Vancouver Harbour ($77, 15 mins).

Ferry
There are 5 separate terminals in Nanaimo. BC Ferries, T1888-223 3779, www.bcferries.com, operates the following services: Departure Bay, 2 km north of Downtown (Bus No 2) to Vancouver's **Horseshoe Bay**, every 2 hrs, 0630-2100, $12, child $6, vehicle $39, one-way, 95 mins; Nanaimo's Duke

Point (12 km south, with only taxis into town) to Vancouver's **Tsawwassen**, every 2½ hrs, 0515-2245, 0630-2100, $12, child $6, vehicle $39, one- way, 2 hrs; Gabriola Island to **Nanaimo Harbour** behind the Harbour Park Mall Downtown, hourly 0615- 2255, $7.55, child $4.25, vehicle $17.80, 20 mins. Smaller ferries leave from behind the Bastion for **Protection Island**, and from Maffeo-Sutton Park for **Newcastle Island**.

Bus
Local City buses, T250-390 4531, www.rdn. bc.ca, all meet downtown at Harbour Park Mall and go as far north as Qualicum Beach.
Long distance Greyhound, T1800-661 1725, www.greyhound.ca, run 6 buses daily to **Victoria** (2-2½ hrs, $18), 1 west to **Port Alberni** and **Tofino** (1030, 4 hrs, $38 to Tofino), 3 north to **Campbell River** (2½-3 hrs, $28), of which the 0830 continues to **Port Hardy** (7 hrs, $62) and 4 to **Departure Bay**. Tofino Bus operates services to **Tofino**, **Vancouver** and **Victoria** (see Tofino, below).

Taxis
AC Taxi, T250-753 1231; **Budget Car Rentals**, 17 Terminal Av, T250-754 7368.

Train
VIA Rail, www.viarail.ca runs 1 train daily each way between **Victoria** and **Courtenay**.

Gabriola Island *p114*
The easiest way to get around the island is by bike or kayak. Hitchhiking works well too, or you can use **Island Taxi**, T250-247 0049.

Air
Tofino Air, T250-2479 992, www.tofinoair.ca, runs a floatplane from Silva Bay at Gabriola's eastern tip to Vancouver's Air Seaplane Terminal in Richmond, $70 one-way for the 15-min flight.

Ferry
BC Ferries, T1888-223 3779, run hourly, 0615-2255 from Nanaimo Harbour.

Tofino *p115, map p120*
Everything in Tofino is close, clustered around Campbell St and Main St. Bikes are recommended for getting to the beaches. Beach Bus, T250-725 2871, www.tofino bus.com, runs shuttles between **Tofino**, **Long Beach** and **Ucluelet**. Tofino Water Taxi, T1877-726 5485, www.tofinowater taxi.com, charges about $20 return to Meares Island, $30 return to Vargas Island.

Air
Orca Air, T1888-359 6722, www.flyorca air.com. Mid-May to mid-Sep, up to 5 daily flights to and from Vancouver and a daily flight to Victoria. **Tofino Air**, T250-247 9992, www.tofinoair.ca, have daily flights mid-May to mid-Sep between Tofino and Vancouver ($180 one-way). **Sound Flight**, T1866-921 3474, www.soundflight.net, have daily mid-May to mid-Sep flights between Tofino and Seattle (US$390 one-way).

Bus
Tofino Bus, T1866-986 3466, www.tofino bus.com, runs 2 daily mid-May to mid-Sep services to Vancouver ($62 including ferry) and Victoria Greyhound station, 0815 (5 hrs, $64). Also services to Nanaimo ($38), Port Alberni ($23) and north to Port Hardy ($95). Greyhound , T1800- 6611725, operates 1 morning service to Victoria (7 hrs, $60) and Nanaimo (4 hrs, $38).

Water taxi
Tofino Water Taxi, T1877-726 5485, www.to finowatertaxi.com, **Meares Island**, $20 per person; **Vargas Island**, $30 per person.

Bamfield *p117*
Travellers to Bamfield or the Broken Islands Group should consider getting off the bus in Port Alberni and completing the trip aboard the MV Lady Rose (see page 118). Drivers taking the abominable 100-km logging road from Port Alberni to Bamfield should be very careful and carry at least one spare tyre.

Bus
The West Coast Trail Shuttle Bus, T250-723 3341, www.trailbus.com, leaves daily from 700 Douglas St for **Victoria** at 0630 stopping in **Nanaimo** and **Port Alberni** ($75 one-way). Another leaves **Port Renfrew** at 0830 and **Gordon River** at 0900 ($65), for hikers who need to get back to their vehicles. Both go to town and **Pachena Bay**, leaving again at 1300.

Water taxi
Juan de Fuca Express Water Taxi, T250-755 6578, operates between **Port Renfrew**, **Nitinat Narrows** and Bamfield. Nitinat Lake Water Taxi, T250-745 3509, crosses Nitinat Narrows to the village daily, 1700. **Bamfield Express Water Taxi**, T250-728 3001.

⊕ Directory

Nanaimo and around *p112, map p113*
Internet Library; Zombie's Internet Café, 2157 2nd Av, T250-668 6620. **Laundry** Boat Basin Laundry, 650 Terminal Av, T250-754 8654. **Library** Nanaimo Harbourfront Library, 90 Commercial St, T250-753 1154. **Medical services** Caledonia Walk-in

Medical Clinic, 340 Campbell St, T250-754 7777; **Nanaimo General Hospital**, 1200 Dufferin Cres, T250-775 42141.
Police 303 Prideaux St, T250-754 2345.
Post office Canada Post, Shoppers Drug Mart, 530 5th St, T250- 753 8234.

Tofino *p115, map p120*
Internet Whalers On the Point Guesthouse, 81 Wets St, T250-725 3443; Tofitian Café, 1180 Pacific Rim Hwy, T250-725 2631.
Medical services General Hospital 261 Neill St, T250-725 3212; Tonquin Medical Clinic, 220 First St, T250- 725 3282. **Post office** Canada Post 161 1st St/Campbell St, T250-725 3734.

Central and north Vancouver Island

The further north you go on Vancouver Island, the more remote and unexplored it becomes. Courtenay, a pleasant town in its own right, is handy for Mount Washington Ski Hill and the western section of Strathcona Provincial Park, with some great hiking among the island's highest peaks. The bulk of the park is reached from the salmon-fishing Mecca of Campbell River via Highway 28, which continues west to the largely undiscovered West Coast wilderness of Nootka Sound, a paradise for kayakers and cavers. A visit to at least one of the Gulf Islands is highly recommended, particularly Hornby or Cortes which, two steps removed from the main island, are even more relaxed, yet brimming with character.

There's little infrastructure beyond Campbell River, except the interesting native community of Alert Bay, the tiny village of Sointula with its fascinating history, and the phoney boardwalk village of Telegraph Cove, one of the world's top spots for seeing orcas. Most travellers this far north are heading to Port Hardy, to catch the Inside Passage ferry to Prince Rupert or the Discovery Coast Passage ferry to Bella Coola, two stunning journeys, or to hike in Cape Scott Provincial Park, as rugged, remote and notoriously wet a place as anyone could desire. ▸▸ *For further Sleeping, Eating and other listings, see pages 137-146.*

Ins and outs

Getting there and around
Greyhound runs three buses daily as far as Campbell River, one continues north to Port Hardy, and **VIA Rail** runs one train daily between Victoria and Courtenay. **BC Ferries** has four daily sailings from Powell River to just north of Comox/Courtenay and services to all the Gulf Islands, Alert Bay and Sointula, and to Port Hardy from Prince Rupert and Bella Coola. There are many sailings from Vancouver to Nanaimo, just to the south. There are flights from Vancouver to Courtenay, Nanaimo, Campbell River and Port Hardy. There is no public transport to Gold River and Nootka Sound, and getting around can be difficult without a car, especially as you go further north. ▸▸ *For further details, see Transport, page 145.*

Best time to visit

Mid- to late June is the best time to see orca whales in the Johnstone Strait, though many whales remain until mid-October. The salmon migration, so significant for Campbell River, peaks between July and September. Except for skiers, summer is best.

Courtenay and around ⊕⊘⊕⊕❀▲⊜⊜ ▸▸ pp137-146.

Colour map 1, B3.

North to Courtenay

A major parting of roads occurs north of Nanaimo. With its dearth of scenic interest, the Inland Island Highway (Highway 19) is only for drivers in a hurry or those wanting to branch west towards Pacific Rim National Park on Highway 4. The older and more scenic Coast Highway (Highway 19A), winds its way through Parksville, a drab town where the only attraction is **Rathtrevor Beach Provincial Park**, containing one of the coast's finest and busiest beaches. In July, the park attracts thousands of visitors for the **Beach Festival**, featuring the Canadian Open Sandsculpting Competition.

The stretch of coast to the north is a great birdwatching zone. The Coast Highway offers increasingly striking views of the island-dotted coastline and mainland Coast Mountains as it passes through a series of sleepy seaside villages and bays, of which **Qualicum Beach** is the nicest place to stay or grab a bite to eat on the waterfront. About 15 km further on, a gravel road leads 12 km to **Horne Lake** ⓘ *T250-248 7829, www.hornelake.com, helmets and lights can be hired from the park office, $8, tours 1½ to 5 hrs, $20-150*, where a set of caves can be explored either alone or on a tour. There's also a campground, lots of scope for paddling and some first-class rock-climbing, including the Horne Lake Amphitheatre, one of the toughest climbs of its kind in the country. Further north up the coast, huge piles of oyster shells define **Fanny Bay** as one of the world's most prolific suppliers of the fabled aphrodisiac.

Denman Island → *Colour map 1, C3.*

From Buckley Bay, ferries cross to super-mellow Denman Island, another magnet for all kinds of artists, whose work can be seen on display at the annual **Festival of the Arts** in early August. There are no information points on Denman or Hornby, so pick up a copy of the very useful *Denman & Hornby Islands Visitor's Guide* from information centres elsewhere, and visit www.denmanisland.com or www.hornbyisland.com. Both have useful maps.

Denman Village, walking distance from the ferry, is the island's focal point with bikes and scooters for rent at the local shop but no ATMs. **Fillongley Park**, 4 km away on the opposite (east) side, has a long pebble shoreline with great beachcombing, large stands of old-growth cedars and Douglas firs, views of the Coast Range and a number of trails, one of which is wheelchair-accessible. **Boyle Point Provincial Park** at the south end also offers trails through giant trees, great views and a good chance of seeing eagles and sea lions. Off the northwestern tip, only accessible by water, is **Sandy Island Provincial Park**, where camping is allowed. **Denman Hornby Canoes and Kayaks** (see Activities and tours, page 143) will help you get there.

Hornby Island → *Colour map 1, C3.*

From Gravelly Bay in the southeast of Denman, several daily ferries make the 10-minute journey to **Hornby Island**. From the dock at Shingle Spit, a single road (Central Road), leads most of the way round the island. One small hub of activity is around the bakery and Co-op roughly 4 km away, but the island's main centre is on the east side, clustered around the Ringside Market, a health-conscious grocery shop that doubles as post office and liquor outlet. Close by is an ATM machine and bike rentals. Within walking distance is **Tribune Bay Provincial Park**, with a beautiful long sandy beach, bike rentals and camping. St John's Road, north of the Co-op, leads down the island's south-eastern spit to **Helliwell Bay Provincial Park**, where a gorgeous 5-km circular walk takes in some amazing bluffs with great views and nesting eagles. Apart from the **Performing Arts Festival** another summer draw is scuba-diving and the rare chance to see six-gilled sharks. There's a scuba-diving base, marina and accommodation at **Ford's Cove**, though equipment has to be rented on Vancouver Island.

Courtenay → *Colour map 1, B3.*

Back on the mainland, Courtenay is the most prominent of three sister towns clustered within the farming landscape of the Comox Valley and, unpromising as its outskirts may be, must rank as Vancouver Island's most attractive settlement after Victoria and Tofino. A clutch of decent shops, restaurants, cafés and galleries make this a more alluring base than Campbell River to the north, and it's well placed for hiking the **Forbidden Plateau** section of Strathcona Park, skiing or mountain biking at Mount Washington or visiting Denman and Hornby islands. Since many of Vancouver Island's places of interest are either close to Courtenay or further south, it's worth taking the ferry from Courtenay to Powell River on the Sunshine Coast as part of a nice loop back to Vancouver (see Transport, page 145). Outdoor lovers might even consider basing themselves here instead of Victoria.

Highly significant for over-wintering waterfowl, this area is popular for birdwatching, and from October to March trumpeter swans can be seen from the Air Park Walkway, which makes for a pleasant stroll at any time. It's conveniently close to the helpful **Visitor Information Centre** ⓘ *2040 Cliffe Av, T250-334 3234, www.discovercomoxvalley.com, www.downtowncourtenay.com*, which can provide a bird checklist, a book of nature viewing sites and information about the many local outdoor pursuits.

The **Courtenay and District Museum and Palaeontology Centre** ⓘ *207 4th St, T250-334 0686, www.courtenaymuseum.ca, mid-May to mid-Sep daily 1000-1700, mid-Sep to mid-May Tue-Sat, by donation. Tours last 3 hrs and must be pre-booked, Jul-Aug daily and Jun Sat-Sun 0900 and 1300, Apr-May 1300, $25, child $15.* Fossil tours give you the chance to view and learn about findings from an 80-million-year-old sea bed at nearby **Puntledge River**, then drive to the site to hunt for fossils.

The outskirts of town merge seamlessly with the more genteel **Comox**, pleasantly situated on Comox Harbour and home to a significant airport and Canadian naval base, a marina, a few decent pubs and **Filberg Lodge and Park** ⓘ *61 Filberg Rd, Comox, T250-339 2715, www.filberg.com, daily 0800-dusk. Tours run daily 1100-1700, $4.* The 3 ha of meticulously landscaped grounds can be visited year-round.

Mount Washington Ski Resort

ⓘ *Day pass for alpine skiing $56, concessions $46, child $30; for cross-country $19, concessions $15, child $10. Some trails and a terrain park are lit up for night skiing, Fri and Sat 1630-2100, $25, $20, $15. Chairlift open Jun-Aug daily 1100-1900, Sep daily 1100-1600.*

Situated 25 km northwest of Comox, reached most easily on the Inland Island Highway, Mount Washington has been expanding steadily over the last few years and its reputation is also growing, thanks in part to the 10 metres of powder it receives annually. Still relatively small, unintimidating and with superb ocean views, it's great for beginners and intermediates. Eight lifts (including a six-person chairlift) lead to 60 alpine runs (20% beginner, 35% intermediate, 45% expert). There are also 55 km of track-set cross-country trails, 20 km of snowshoeing trails, and snow-tubing.

From June to September the chairlift opens for mountain biking and alpine hiking, with views of Comox Glacier, the Coast Mountains and the Georgia Strait. Bikes can be rented here but it's cheaper in town. Favourite downhills include the steep and scary **Monster Mile** and **Discovery Road**. There's also a nine-hole mini-golf course and disc-golf. All facilities are available on the hill, including lessons, rentals, plenty of restaurants and cafés and on Sundays the arts and crafts Mountain Market.

Strathcona Provincial Park: Forbidden Plateau → *Colour map 1, B2.*

Established in 1911, this is BC's oldest park and it contains the lion's share of Vancouver Island's most elevated peaks, including its highest point, **Golden Hinde** ① *2200 m.* It also provides one of the few chances to sample the beauty of the island's gloriously undeveloped interior. Hiking is the main activity, with most trails clustered in two areas: the Forbidden Plateau region, and Buttle Lake (see page 133). The more remote southern section of the park, including the famous **Della Falls**, is accessed, with difficulty, from Port Alberni and is not recommended. Seek trail information from the Visitor Information Centres in Courtenay or Campbell River, or at www.env.gov.bc.ca/bcparks/explore/parkpgs/strathco. Serious hikers might invest in the *National Topographic Series* maps, scale *1:50,000: -92 F/11 Forbidden Plateau*, and *-92 F/12 Buttle Lake.*

Jutting out from the park's eastern flank, the high altitude of the Forbidden Plateau means that hikers barely have to climb to reach alpine scenery and views. Paradise Meadows trailhead gives the easiest access to this formidable zone. Follow signs from Highway 19 to Mount Washington Ski Resort for 20 km, then turn left on Nordic Lodge Road for 1.5 km. A 4-km hike, with minimal elevation gain, leads to **Kwai Lake**, an excellent base with a backcountry campground and a network of trails radiating out like spokes in all directions.

Campbell River and around 🖴🍴🏠🚣❄️🔺🚌🛒

→ *pp137-146. Colour map 1, B3.*

Campbell River → *Colour map 1, B3.*

The strip of seafront houses and hotels emanating from Campbell River stretches so far south down the Coast Highway that the town itself, nicely placed around the water, comes as a pleasant relief, though Courtenay, Strathcona Park Lodge and the nearby Discovery Islands are all more enticing places to stay. There is some justification for Campbell River's claim to be the salmon capital of the world, and in winter there's halibut a-plenty to keep the angling industry going. **Discovery Pier** ① *open 24 hrs, 182 m long (46 m of it jutting out over the ocean) and illuminated at night,* is a popular and easy place to fish. Alternatively, you can go snorkelling to see the aquatic superstars up close or visit **Quinsam Salmon Hatchery** ① *5 km west on Hwy 28, T250-287 9564, daily 0800-1600, free,* to see them and learn all you want to know about their journey. The salmon spawning run peaks between July and September.

Campbell River Museum ① *470 Island Hwy, T250-287 3103, www.crmuseum.ca, mid-May to mid-Sep daily 1000-1700, mid-Sep to mid-May Tue-Sun 1200-1700, $6, child $4,* has exhibits on pioneers, salmon fishing, First Nations' history and a multimedia presentation of a mystical journey beneath the sea from a First Nations' perspective, based on traditional masks. **Wei Wai Kum House of Treasures** ① *Discovery Harbour Centre, 1370 Island Hwy, T250-286 1440,* sells and exhibits First Nations' arts and crafts. The **Visitor Information Centre** ① *1235 Shoppers Row (Ocean Hwy), T250-287 4636, www.visitorcentre.ca, www.campbellrivertourism.com, mid-May to mid-Sep daily 0900-1900, Sept-Apr Mon-Fri 0900-1700, Sat 1000-1600,* is next to the **Art Gallery** ① *Tue-Sat 1200-1700, free.*

Quadra Island → *Colour map 1, B3.*

At the northern end of the Georgia Strait is a complex cluster of large and tiny islands, known collectively as the Discovery Islands, through which are threaded numerous

Captain George Vancouver would have negotiated, let alone charted, this maze. The landscapes here are even more dramatic, best enjoyed from the only easily accessible islands, Quadra and Cortes. All these closely huddled, virtually uninhabited islands, along with the proximity of Desolation Sound Marine Park (see page 80) on the other side of the strait, make this an exciting playground for sailors and kayakers. A good source of information is www.discoveryislands.ca.

Quadra is the biggest of the Northern Gulf Islands and one of the most populated. The main hub is **Quathiaski Cove**, which hosts most shops and a popular Saturday Farmers' Market. A short drive or hitch across the island is the nicer village of **Heriot Bay**, which has a summer-only **Visitor Information Booth** ① *T250-285 2724, www.quadraisland.ca,* an adjacent Credit Union and bike/kayak rentals. Neither village is as good a place for soaking up the Gulf Island vibe as similar centres on Cortes, Hornby or Gabriola, though the usual plethora of galleries and studios is easily found and visited during the Studio Tour in June.

The island's main attraction for visitors is the native village of **Cape Mudge** at its southern tip. The **Carving and Artist Centre**, adjacent to the outstanding but currently closed Kwagiulth Museum, exhibits a number of old totem poles and craftsmen can be seen creating new works. A walk from here leads to a 100-year-old lighthouse and a beach with over 50 petroglyphs.

The vast bulk of the island is north of the two main communities, barely inhabited and criss-crossed with some very fine hiking and biking trails. The most popular hike is up **Chinese Mountain**, with splendid panoramas at the top. Nearby **Morte Lake** is also a worthwhile destination. The trail to **Nugedzi Lake** is a steady climb through old-growth forest also leading to excellent views. For mountain biking, Mount Seymour has most of the best descents, with some 400-m drops. For swimming and mainly rocky beaches head for **Village Bay Park** or **Rebecca Spit Provincial Park**, the latter also makes a nice stroll.

Cortes Island → *Colour map 1, B3.*

Cortes ① *www.cortesisland.com*, is in many respects the quintessential Gulf Island. As with Hornby, being two steps removed from Vancouver Island has ensured the laid-back and friendly spirit of the people. Manson's Landing, 15 km from the Whaletown ferry landing, is the best place to meet them and has a café, ATM, post office and launderette. The **Arts Festival** in mid-July is the best time to visit.

Manson's Landing Provincial Park has one of the better sand beaches around and a warm freshwater lagoon for swimming, with the chance to legally pick some of the clams and oysters that are all around the island. The adjacent **Hague Lake Provincial Park** is good for hiking and **Smelt Bay Provincial Park** ① *25 km south of the ferry*, has camping and a nice beach walk to **Sutil Point**. At Cortes Bay is the bizarre folly, **Wolf Bluff Castle**, an eccentric, five-storey structure, including a dungeon and three turrets. The island's most famous feature, worth the trip on its own, is the popular **Hollyhock Retreat Centre**, where you can follow courses on yoga and meditation, or simply enjoy the relaxing grounds, great vegetarian food and decent accommodation.

Strathcona Provincial Park: Buttle Lake

This second key section of the wonderful park begins 48 km from Campbell River on Highway 28. Just outside the park boundary is the superlative Strathcona Park Lodge, hands down the best base from which to explore the region and an excellent outdoor pursuits centre, especially for novices. All manner of rentals, lessons and tours are available and the staff tend to be friendly, young and enthusiastic.

From the nearby junction, Buttle Lake Road heads south along the edge of this long, skinny strip of water into the very heart of the park. It's a fantastic drive, lined with hiking trails of all lengths. **Lupin Falls**, near the north end, **Karst Creek**, two-thirds down, **Myra Falls** at the bottom and **Lady Falls**, off Highway 28, are all short and easy walks leading to gorgeous waterfalls, usually through lush rainforest.

Most of the longer hikes start at the lake's south end. **Flower Ridge**, at Km 29.6, is a steep and rough 14-km round trip (extendable to 24 km), gaining 1250 m elevation as it climbs to an open alpine ridge. **Bedwell Lake** ① *complicated access, see BC Parks map*, is a 12-km hike with 600-m gain, also leading to good mountain views and a campground on the lake. Accessible only by boat from the Auger Point day-use area is the **Marble Meadows Trail** ① *13 km return, 1250 m gain*. Many different peaks can be reached from here and the Golden Hinde is visible. From Highway 28 at the western edge of the park, the **Crest Mountain Trail** ① *10 km return with 1250-m gain*, gives quick access to the alpine scenery and views. South-facing, it's a good choice early in the season.

Nootka Sound and Gold River → *Colour map 1, B2.*

Nootka Sound is touted as the birthplace of BC, for it was here at **Yuquot** in 1778 that Captain James Cook made his first West Coast landing. When he asked the Mowachaht people, whose ancestors arrived at least 6000 years ago, the name of their land, they thought he wanted directions around a smaller island and replied 'Nutka, itchme' ('Go around that way'). Mistaking it for a place name, Cook dubbed the region Nootka, a name that was eventually extended to the people themselves. So warm was the welcome he received from Chief Maquinna, that he nicknamed the place 'Friendly Cove' and quickly entered into a burgeoning trade in sea otter fur that made Yuquot the busiest port north of Mexico for several years and almost wiped out Canada's sea otter population. Ironically, the last remaining survivors are found here in Zeballos.

Today, this wild and undeveloped portion of Vancouver Island's Northwest Coast is attracting a new breed of adventurer. It is quickly being discovered by BC's in-the-know outdoor community, who come to kayak around its hundreds of small islands, surf the Pacific breakers, dive the reefs and walls where gill shark roam, fish, explore the numerous local cave systems, rock climb, or hike a section of the West Coast that is guaranteed to be crowd-free. If all that sounds too hard-core, another option for seeing this rugged strip of coast is aboard the *MV Uchuck III,* which has become a popular way to take a cheap cruise (see page 146).

Many drivers and cyclists agree that the beautiful 91-km ride on Highway 28 from Campbell River to Gold River is one of the most gratifying in the province. Utterly dominated by logging until the pulp-mill closed in 1998, the inhabitants of this remote little town have increasingly looked towards tourism for their survival, though there's still very little infrastructure to encourage interest in the region beyond the summer-only **Visitor Information Centre** ① *Hwy 28/Scout Lake Rd, T250-283 2418, www.goldriver.ca*. Tahsis, an even smaller, more remote community at the end of a long inlet leading from Nootka Sound, has some of Canada's best caving, particularly at the 100-plus Upana Caves, 17 km west. There is a summer-only **Visitor Information Booth** ① *Rugged Mountain Rd, T250-934 6667*. Still more remote, Zeballos with a summer-only **Visitor Information Booth** ① *122 Maquinna Av, T250-761 4070* and Kyuquot are even tinier communities, accessible only with the *MV Uchuck III,* but perfectly placed for adventurous and experienced kayakers to push further into pristine territory. ▶▶ *For further information, see Activities and tours, page 143.*

North to Port Hardy and beyond ●✈▲⊖

▶▶ *pp137-146. Colour map 1, B1.*

North of Campbell River, the solitary highway heads inland through increasingly wild, uninhabited scenery, with no real reason to stop until the coast is regained. **Robson Bight Ecological Reserve** in **Johnstone Strait** is one of the most reliable

⁑ The Inside Passage

Most visitors to Port Hardy are there to embark on one of two spectacular ferry journeys up the coast: the Inside Passage to Prince Rupert, or the Discovery Coast Passage to wild and remote Bella Coola. Both routes lead through rugged and pristine stretches of wilderness coast, dissected by long fjords, dotted with tiny islands and lined with steep mountains, waterfalls and rainforest. There's a good chance of seeing whales, dolphins, sea lions and eagles.

These two popular northbound services are run by **BC Ferries**, T250-386 3779/T1888-223 3779 or T250-386 3779 (from outside North America), www.bcferries.com. The ferry dock is at Bear Cove, 10 km east, on the other side of Hardy Bay. The Inside Passage ferry to Prince Rupert runs during the day every other day from mid-May to the end of September (leaving at 0730, arriving at 2230, $141 one-way, child $79 child, vehicle $334). Check the website for times and prices in the low season.

Cabins are available (from $80 one-way) and kayaks/canoes can be taken ($17.50), as can bikes ($6.50). From early June to early September, The Discovery Coast Passage to Bella Coola leaves Port Hardy on Tuesday, Thursday (direct) and Saturday at 0930. The return leaves Bella Coola on Monday (direct) and Friday at 0800, and Wednesday at 0730. One-way fares are $133, child $81 and vehicle $289; kayak/canoe $12.75, bike $6.50. Direct ferries take 13 hours but most stop at McLoughlin Bay (Bella Bella), Namu, Shearwater, Klemtu and Ocean Falls, all utterly remote and ideal for experienced and adventurous sea-kayakers.

places in the world to see pods of orca, who like to rub their bellies on the gravel beaches. The best time is mid- to late June, though they stay until mid-October. Most people take tours from the picturesque boardwalk village of **Telegraph Cove** ① *11 km down a windy logging road, 8 km south of Port McNeill*. A short ferry ride from the latter, Alert Bay on Cormorant Island is a more interesting base for tours and one of the best places in BC to learn about First Nations' culture.

Alert Bay and Sointula → *Colour map 1, B2.*
Everything in Alert Bay is close and easy to find, including the **Visitor Information Centre** ① *116 Fir St, T250-9745024, www.alertbay.ca*. To the left when disembarking from the ferry is the **U'mista Cultural Centre** ① *T250-974 5403, www.umista.org, daily 0900-1700, $5.35*, one of the most culturally significant attractions in the province, which contains a large selection of wooden masks and other Potlatch items confiscated and dispersed by the government and now slowly being returned. The gift shop is an excellent place to buy a wide selection of authentic Kwakwaka'wakw fine art, crafts and souvenirs. Also nearby is **Culture Shock Interactive Gallery** ① *T250-974 2484, www.cultureshockgallery.ca*, with displays of native arts and crafts, films about culture and history, coffee, lessons in native skills, demonstrations and storytelling. The **World's Tallest Totem Pole** at 52.7 m, is just up the road, as are the **Namgis Burial Grounds**, which contain many more poles, though respect demands that these be viewed from the road. Ask for the totem poles brochure at the Visitor Information Centre. Though rebuilt in 1999, the **Traditional Big House** is still an impressive building. The inside can only be seen during traditional dance performances of the **T'sasala Cultural Group** ① *T250-974 5475, Jul-Aug Thu-Sat 1305, $15, child $6, 1 hr*.

Meaning 'harmony' in Finnish, the most compelling thing about nearby **Sointula** on **Malcolm Island** is its history. Much of the population today is descended from a group of Finnish coal miners from Nanaimo who attempted to establish their own Utopia here in 1900. Orcas can be seen from the 10 km of ocean trails at **Bere Point Regional Park**. A speciality of the island is sea-foam green rugs made of fishing nets.

Port Hardy → *Colour map 1, B1.*

Vancouver Island's northernmost community, 230 km from Campbell River, is a long way to go for what is essentially just another fishing village. Apart from the lure of the Inside Passage and Cape Scott Provincial Park, however, this is a fantastic location for scuba-diving, with excellent visibility and a good chance of seeing dolphins and wolf eels. Whale watching and kayaking are also prime, and the area possesses a great rugged beauty.

Most of the town is on Market Street, including the **Visitor Information Centre** ① *7250 Market St, T250-949 7622, www.ph-chamber.bc.ca, mid-May to mid-Sep Mon-Fri 0830-1800, Sat-Sun 0900-1700, mid-Sep to mid-May daily 0900-1700.* Otherwise, there is little reason to venture downtown. Hardy Bay Road, which shoots off to the right on the way in from the south, is a far nicer place to stay with the two best hotel-restaurants-bars around, both nicely situated on a marina. **Fort Rupert** ① *10 mins south of the ferry terminal*, contains the **First Nations Copper Maker Gallery** ① *114 Copper Way, T250-949 8491, www.calvinhunt.com, Mon-Sat 0900-1700*, a good place to see traditional artisans at work. Nearby is the long Stories Beach and the trailhead for the **Tex Lyon Trail** ① *9 hrs return*, which goes to **Dillon Point** along the shoreline. **Coal Harbour** to the southwest is a historic whaling station.

Cape Scott Provincial Park → *Colour map 1, B1.*

Situated at the island's northwestern tip, Cape Scott Provincial Park brings new meaning to words like rugged, wet and wild. Due to the remoteness and consistently appalling weather, a long hike here is a serious undertaking and the mosquitoes can be brutal. However, the forest is incredibly lush and beautiful and there are 23 km of deserted white-sand beaches from which grey whales, orcas, seals and otters are frequently seen.

Denman & Hornby Islands

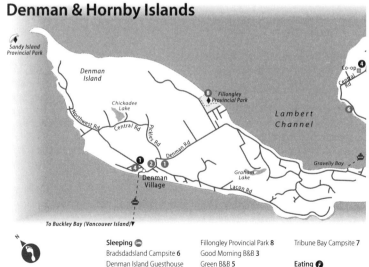

To Buckley Bay (Vancouver Island)▼

1 km
1 mile

Sleeping 🛏
Bradsdadsland Campsite **6**
Denman Island Guesthouse & International Hostel **2**
Devenish House **1**

Fillongley Provincial Park **8**
Good Morning B&B **3**
Green B&B **5**
Hawthorn House **4**
Sea Breeze Lodge **9**

Tribune Bay Campsite **7**

Eating 🍴
Cardboard House Bakery **4**

All trails start at the San Josef Bay trailhead, at the southeast corner of the park, a 67-km drive from Port Hardy on gravel logging roads past the small town of **Holberg**. The biggest hiking challenge is the tough 48-km return trip to **Cape Scott**, located at the end of a narrow spit that does a very convincing impression of the end of the world. Before embarking on this, get thoroughly briefed at the Port Hardy Visitor Information Centre. Maps can usually also be found at various information shelters. There are also some fine shorter trails. The **San Josef Bay Trail** is the most accessible, a 5-km return hike to some sandy beaches. The best beach is **Nels Bight**, a six-hour hike one-way. On a clear day climb to the top of **Mount St Patrick** for fantastic views. The trail then continues to **Sea Otter Cove**, a 10-km, five-hour hike one-way.

⊜ Sleeping

North to Courtenay p130
C **Qualicum College Inn**, 427 College Rd, Qualicum Beach, just off the highway, T250-752 9262. The most interesting of several options, this Tudor-style ex-college has an authentic historic interior and an extensive garden. Rooms have a fireplace and/or balcony and there's also a restaurant.

Denman Island p130, map p136
Accommodation on Denman is particularly scarce. There are a few B&Bs scattered around, but many require bookings for 2 nights or more. The best place to find details is at www.gulfislands-bc.com.
C **Devenish House**, call for directions, T250-335 9146, www.devenishhouse.com. 3 lovely rooms in a house with a splendid ridgetop location. Full, nutritious breakfast, solarium with hot tub and a living room with internet.
C **Hawthorn House**, 3375 Kirk Rd, just off Northwest Rd, T250-335 0905, www.haw thornhouse.ca. One of the few B&Bs in or near the village and ferry, this 1904 heritage home offers 3 attractive en suite rooms, a hot tub, garden, hearty breakfasts and views.
E-F **Denman Island Guesthouse & International Hostel**, 3806 Denman Rd, T250-335 2688, www.earthclubfactory.com. This lovely wooden home has 5 reasonable private rooms with shared bath, dorm beds, camping, an outdoor hot tub, internet, laundry and a bistro where they roast their own coffee.

Camping
Fillongley Provincial Park, T1800-689 9025. 10 drive-in campsites right on the beach. Be sure to reserve a spot.

Hornby Island p130, map p136
Hornby also has a shortage of beds, with most B&Bs now only renting rooms by the week in summer. Book as early as possible at www.hornbyisland.com.
B **Sea Breeze Lodge**, Fowler Rd, T250-335 2321, www.seabreezelodge.com. A wide range of unique cabins, some with kitchens, fireplaces or ocean views, with a cliff-side hot tub and licensed dining.
C-D **Good Morning B&B**, 7845 Central Rd, T250-335 1094. A charming West Coast home, though owned by hospitable Europeans, in gorgeous forested surround-ings with a guest living room. The 3 rooms have shared bath and there's also a guest cottage. A large breakfast is included.
D **Green B&B**, 5075 Kirk, T250-335 0920, www.hornbyislandgreenbandb.com. A Tudor house Hornby style, with 3 large, elegantly decorated rooms, a garden patio,

Denman Island Bakery **1**
Jan's Café **2**
Leticia's Café **1**
The Thatch **3**
V0R1Z0 Café **2**

gourmet breakfast and a guest living room with hardwood floors and vaulted ceilings.

Camping
Bradsdadsland Campsite, 3 km from the ferry on Central Rd, T250-335 0757. Situated on the bluffs, with a friendly, family atmosphere and good sunsets.
Tribune Bay Campsite, 5200 Shields Rd, T250-335 2359. 120 drive-in sites, some with hook-ups.

Courtenay *p131*
A number of resorts line the highway to the south, but if you're after an inexpensive motel there are many strung along Cliffe Av heading south from Downtown. There is also a good selection of B&Bs close to town, in addition to those listed below.
L-A Kingfisher Oceanside Resort, 4330 Island Hwy S, 7 km south, T250-338 1323, www.kingfisherspa.com. Ocean-view rooms and luxurious beach-front suites with balconies and fireplaces. Extensive facilities include hot tub, pool, sauna, fitness room, spa, restaurant and lounge.
C Copes' Islander B&B, 1484 Wilkinson Rd, T250-339 1038. Not as central as some, but convenient for taking the ferry to Powell River. Nice rooms with private entrance, views and easy access to the beach.
D Comox Valley Inn, 1190 Cliffe Av, T250-334 4476, www.comoxvalleyinn.com. One of the better motels, with reasonable rooms, an indoor pool, sauna, jacuzzi and internet.
D Greystone Manor, 4014 Haas Rd, 2 km south, T250-338 1422, www.greystone manorbb.com. This waterfront heritage home is surrounded by flower gardens and has 3 nice rooms with private bath.
E Courtenay Riverside Hostel, 1380 Cliffe Av, T250-334 1938. A friendly and helpful hostel handily situated Downtown in a lovely big old house. All the usual facilities are on offer, including a kitchen, lockers, laundry and internet.
E Estuary House B&B, 2810 Comox Rd, T250-890 0130, www.tartanweaving.com. About the best of the B&Bs in this price range, with good value en suite rooms. Also offers sailing trips and tartan weaving lessons. Home-cooked breakfast included.
E Shantz Hause Hostel, 520 5th St, T250-703 2060, www.shantzhostel.com.

Conveniently located, superior hostel with a fine interior. Dorms and private rooms with shared bath, an appealing common room, a full kitchen, patio, BBQ and storage.

Camping
Miracle Beach Provincial Park, 22 km north at 1812 Miracle Beach Dr, exit Hwy 19 at Hamm Rd, T250-337 2400. 200 sites close to a large sandy beach. Very popular in summer.

Mount Washington Ski Resort *p131*
Accommodation at the resort is generally expensive, with package deals sometimes offering the best value. Try **Central Reservations**, T250-338 1386, www.mtwashington.bc.ca, or **Peak Accommodations**, T250-8973851, www.peakaccom.com.

Campbell River and around *p132*
B-C Heron's Landing Oceanside Hotel, 492 S Island Hwy, T250-923 2848, www.heronslandinghotel.com. Not too central, but the best value and most attractive of many hotels stretching away to the south. There are tasteful rooms with balconies and larger suites with kitchens.
C-D Haig-Brown House, 2250 Campbell River Rd, T250-286 6646. About the nicest of the few B&Bs, this heritage house/museum has a very big garden on the river and 3 rooms with shared bath.
D Rustic Motel, 2140 N Island Hwy, T250-286 6295, www.rusticmotel.com. Our pick of the many cheaper motels in this area. Amenities such as laundry, sauna, hot tub and dry room are included, as is breakfast.
D Town Centre Inn, 1500 Dogwood St, T250-287 8866, www.towncentreinn.com. One of many cheaper options downtown. Breakfast included.

Camping
Elk Falls Provincial Park, 3 km NW on Hwy 28, T1800-689 9025, www.discover camping.ca. 122 very nice sites on the Quinsam River, with trails leading to the dramatic 24-m falls. It's also a very popular fishing spot.
Loveland Bay Provincial Park, NW on Hwy 28, 15 km on a gravel road, T250-956 4600. Further away and smaller than **Elk Falls Provincial Park** but very quiet and private.

Morton Lake Provincial Park, north on Island Hwy to Menzies Bay, then take a logging road west for 20 km, T1800-689 9025, www.discovercamping.ca. Small and remote, has sites on the lake.

Quadra Island *p132*

B Tsa-Kwa-Luten Lodge, 1 Lighthouse Rd, Cape Mudge, T250-285 2042, www.cape mudgeresort.bc.ca. This beautiful wooden-beam building, based on a traditional West Coast 'Big House', is owned and operated by the local Kwagiulth First Nation and is full of traditional and contemporary native art. The location is very peaceful, on bluffs right by the ocean surrounded by 450 ha of forest. Lodge rooms and 2- to 4-bedroom cabins with kitchen. Offer spa facilities, guided tours, activities and native cultural events. Also has RV sites.

C Heriot Bay Inn, T250-285 3322, www.heriotbayinn.com. Good mid-range option, offering 10 bright and surprisingly elegant rooms with private bath, 3 equally nice cottages and 60 tent sites with showers. Kayak, bike and canoe rentals are available and there's a pub and restaurant. Price includes breakfast.

D Coast Mountains Kayak Lodge, at the end of Surge Narrows Rd, T250-285 2823, www.seakayaking-bc.com. Single, double or family hostel-style rooms in a beautiful wood lodge on stilts. Full kitchen, spacious living room and wood-fired sauna. Particularly suitable for those wanting to try kayaking; there are lessons, tours and rentals available.

E Travellers' Rural Retreat, 10-15 mins' drive from Heriot Bay ferry on a logging road, T250-285 2477 for directions. A small and extremely remote guesthouse right on the water, favoured by artists or those seeking silence and solitude. Dorms and private rooms, with shared kitchen, living room with woodstove and access to beach and trails.

Cortes Island *p133*

L-B Hollyhock, T250-935 6576, www.holly hock.bc.ca. Essentially a retreat offering various workshops, this highly-respected institution can also be treated as a surprisingly affordable treat. Peaceful and beautiful surroundings. A number of sleeping options are available, including private rooms, dorm beds and camping. Prices include all meals, gourmet vegetarian with an excellent reputation, meditation, yoga, guided walks, ocean-view hot tubs, library and shuttle from the ferry. Reservations are recommended.

C Picard's B&B, Gorge Harbour, T250-935 6683. Surrounded on 3 sides by water, this splendid house has 3 en suite rooms with patios and ocean views, and the use of a rowing boat.

D Cortes Island Motel, close to Manson's Landing, T250-935 6363, ww.cortesisland motel.com. A standard motel in a pleasant, very convenient location.

E Gorge Harbour Marina Resort, 5 km from ferry at 1374 Hunt Rd, T250-935 6433. Has 5 reasonable rooms and a 36-site campground with hook-ups for RVs. Scooter, boat and kayak rentals.

Camping

Smelt Bay Provincial Park, 25 km south of the ferry, T250-474 1336. The best choice for tent camping, with attractive, private sites and a nice beach walk to Sutil Point.

Strathcona Provincial Park: Buttle Lake *p133*

LL-C Strathcona Park Lodge, just before the Buttle Lake junction, on Hwy 28, T250-286 3122, www.strathcona.bc.ca. Basic but pleasant rooms in the lodge, cottages of all sizes and comfort-levels. All-inclusive holiday packages, including meals and unlimited use of kayaks and canoes, run from $129 per person. Transport from Campbell River can be arranged through the lodge ($50, then $10 for each additional person). You don't have to be a guest to enjoy the healthy all-you-can-eat buffet meals.

Camping

Buttle Lake at the north end, and **Ralph River** at the south end are both vehicle-accessible campgrounds on Buttle Lake Rd. Spacious and private sites on the lake, out-houses but no showers, free after 30 Sep. Backcountry camping, including use of designated areas such as Kwai Lake, is $5 per person per night, self-registration, cash only. Many are accessible by boat only. For Forbidden Plateau day-hikers, lodging is available at Mt Washington Ski Area or Courtenay.

Nootka Sound and Gold River *p134*

C **Mason's Lodge**, 203 Pandora Av, Zeballos, T250-761 4044, www.masonslodge.zeballos. bc.ca. Fairly nice rooms, some with views of the Zeballos River, and a restaurant with a patio. Fishing or kayaking can be arranged.

C **Ridgeview Motor Inn**, 395 Donner Court, Gold River, T250-283 2277, www.ridgeview-inn.com. Reasonable rooms in an interesting building, with views over the village. On-site pub and restaurant.

C **Yuquot Cabins and Campground**, Yuquot, T250-283 2015, www.yuquot.ca. Run by the local mowachaht/muchalaht native people, these rustic but enchanting cedar cabins are all situated on the lake or ocean among the trees. There's a camp-style kitchen, cold showers and no drinking water (so bring your own).

C **Zeballos Inlet Lodge**, 167 Maquinna Av, Zeballos, T250-761 4294, www.masons lodge.zeballos.bc.ca. 5 fairly large rooms with private baths and TVs. There's also a patio with BBQ and laundry facilities.

D **Gold River Chalet**, 390 Nimpkish Dr, Gold River, T250-283 2688, www.goldriver chalet.com. Recently renovated rooms, some with kitchenette. Continental breakfast.

D **Peppercorn Trail Motel**,100 Muchalat Dr, Gold River, T250-283 2443. Fairly basic rooms on the edge of town. 75 tent sites.

D **Tahsis Motel**, Head Bay Rd, Tahsis, T250-934 6318. Basic rooms, pub and restaurant.

Alert Bay and Sointula *p135*

Almost all options in Sointula are cottages or single-room deals. Check www.sointula. com/accom for a full list.

C-D **Sea 4 Miles Cottages**, 145 Kaleva Rd, Sointula, 2 km from ferry, T250-973 6486, www.sointulacottages.com. 2 fully equipped 2-bedroom cottages nestled in the trees right next to the ocean.

D **The Nimpkish Hotel**, 318 Fir St, Alert Bay, T1888-646 75474, www.nimpkishhotel.com. Newly renovated rooms in a distinctive building right on the water in town, with a restaurant, pub and big wooden deck.

D-E **Alert Bay Lodge**, 549 Fir St, Alert Bay, about 2 km from the ferry, T250-480 9409, www.alertbaylodge.com. 5 pleasant rooms

in a fantastic lodge housed in a former church, with amenities including breakfast (if staying 2 nights), use of kitchen, a sun deck with ocean views, TV and internet.

E **Old Customs House**, 119 Fir St, Alert Bay, T250-974 2282, www.alert-bay.com/customs. 3 reasonable rooms in a striking blue 1918 house handily close to the ferry, which also has a restaurant and patio.

Camping

Alert Bay Campground, 101 Alder Rd, Alert Bay, T250-974 5024. Fairly basic, but quiet and private.

Port Hardy *p136*

Due to the popular ferry journeys, Port Hardy is a busy place in summer. It's best to have a reservation, especially if catching the day ferry from Prince Rupert, which arrives at 2230. Some of the best places are out of town on Hardy Bay Rd.

B-C **Quarterdeck Inn**, 6555 Hardy Bay Rd, T250-902 0455, www.quarterdeckresort.net. Another great option, luxurious and spacious rooms that all face the ocean. Breakfast, use of a hot tub and fitness room included. The restaurant/pub is also good, it's more attractive than the **Glen Lyon** next door but less popular.

C **Glen Lyon Inn & Suites**, 6435 Hardy Bay Rd, T250-949 7115, www.glenlyoninn.com. Fairly luxurious, recently renovated rooms with balconies and views, some suites have kitchenettes. The mid-range restaurant/pub is probably the best option for food and is very popular with locals.

C-D **Seagate Hotel**, 8600 Granville St, T250-949 6348, www.seagatehotel.ca. The best downtown option. The decent rooms have big windows and are priced according to views. Some have balconies or kitchenettes for a few dollars more.

D **The Green House**, 9470 Scott St, T250-949 2364. 2 decent rooms and a hot tub.

Camping

Quatse River Regional Park and Campground, 8400 Byng Rd, T250-949 2395. Quiet sites set among trees, with showers and laundry. Vehicle parking.

Wildwoods Campsite, 8000 Clyde Creek Rd, signposted 2 km from ferry, T250-949 6753, www.wildwoodscampsite.com. Closest to the harbour and consequently a bit crowded. Fairly private, with showers and laundry. Vehicle parking.

Cape Scott Provincial Park *p136*
There is only wilderness walk-in camping in the park, in designated sites or where you please. Locals recommend the beach, which is best for drainage, but check tidal charts at the information shelters first. $5 per person, pay at the trailhead or someone will come around to collect.

⊘ Eating

North to Courtenay *p130*
♉ **Beach House Cafe**, 2775 W Island Hwy, T250-752 9626. Qualicum Beach is an ideal spot to stop for lunch and enjoy the ocean views. Of several good restaurants concentrating on seafood, this is our favourite. The menu is eclectic and of a high calibre, the interior stylish, and the patio as popular in summer as it is inviting.
♉ **Fish Tales Café**, 3336 W Island Hwy, T250-752 6053. Good fish and chips in a Tudor-style house.

Denman Island *p130, map p136*
Choices on Denman are limited. In the village, **Denman Island Bakery** and **Leticia's Café** (♉) are good for fresh baked goods, pizza, soups, sandwiches, coffee and desserts. For more interesting fare, the **Denman Island Guesthouse Bistro** (see Sleeping) serves grilled focaccia sandwiches and daily specials.

Hornby Island *p130, map p136*
Hornby is similarly limited. The **Cardboard House Bakery**, 4 km from the ferry landing by the Co-op, T250-335 0733, has fresh baked goods, pizza and coffee.
♉ **The Thatch**, by the ferry dock, T250-335 0136. For a pint and food. Has a lovely deck and Fri night jazz.
♉ **Jan's Café**, Ringside Market, T250-335 1487. The clear choice for breakfast and coffee.
♉ **V0R1Z0 Café**, Ringside Market, T250-335 1010. Light meals but as varied, tasty and interesting as you'll find on the island.

Courtenay *p131*
♉♉♉ **The Old House**,1760 Riverside Lane, T250-338 5406. Set in an atmospheric

wooden house full of romantic nooks and crannies. With fireplaces, gables and a lovely patio, this is the clear choice for a romantic dinner and it's very popular. The menu is seafood and steak with an international touch and is a bit overpriced. If you're not hungry, at least go for a drink.
♉ **Atlas Café**, 250 6th St, T250-338 9838. A popular choice with locals, giving it a lively, friendly atmosphere. Large portions of reasonably priced and tasty vegetarian international dishes, from sushi to spanakopita to curries. Also has great breakfasts, salads, wraps and coffee. Doubles up in the evening as a lounge, good for BC wines, beer on tap and spirits.
♉ **Tita's Mexican Restaurant**, 536 6th St, T250-334 8033. Authentic Mexican dishes with an emphasis on freshness. Menu that changes seasonally and offers some choice for vegetarians.
♉ **Union Street Grill & Grotto**, 477 5th St, T250-897 0081. The wide range of dishes cover many bases, maybe too many, with lots of international flavours and a relaxed atmosphere. Their **Café Lounge Tapas Bar** next door has a range of small dishes, wraps, breakfast, and drinks in the evening.
♉ **Bar None Café**, 244 4th St, T250-334 3112. Excellent coffee, baked goods, vegetarian food and good breakfasts.
♉ **Mudsharks Café**, 384 5th St, T250-338 0939. Great coffee, cakes, lunches and a big outdoor patio for watching downtown Courtenay drift by.

Campbell River and around *p132*
♉♉♉-♉♉ **Harbour Grill**, 1334 Island Hwy, T250-287 4143. The town's best French-influenced fine dining, focusing on fresh seafood and with a good range of meat and fowl dishes.
♉♉ **Baan Thai Restaurant**, 1090B Shoppers Row, T250-286 4853. An extensive Thai menu, with the bonus of a rooftop patio.
♉♉ **Bee Hive Café**, 921 Island Hwy, T250-286 6812. On the sea walk, with great views of the ocean and discovery pier from the patio. Some of the most expertly prepared seafood in town. Try the paella.
♉♉ **The Lookout Seafood Bar and Grill**, 2158 Salmon Point Rd, T250-923 7272. Buckets of scallops or mussels, oysters a-plenty, beer on tap and great views from the patio.

Dick's Fish and Chips, 1003B Island Hwy, T250-287 3336. Offers fresh fish and home-made burgers.

Quadra Island *p132*
April Point Resort, 900 April Point Rd, T250-285 2222. Upmarket cuisine with a West Coast bias and a sushi bar. Large ocean-front sundeck. Also good for drinks.
Herons, Heriot Bay Inn, T250-285 3322 (see Sleeping). Another fantastic patio with views of Heriot Bay. Reasonable West Coast menu and a cocktail lounge. **Heriot Bay Inn** also has a pub with reasonable food. Try the red snapper burger.
Café Aroma, 685 Heriot Bay Rd, Quathiaski Cove, T250-285 2404. Great coffee, good breakfasts and light lunches.
Gateway Café, 1536 Heriot Bay Rd, Quathiaski Cove, T250-285 2600. Organic fairtrade espresso, brunch, baked goods, juices and booze.

Cortes Island *p133*
Cortes Café, Manson's Landing. Place of choice for most locals, with good food using local ingredients, coffee, smoothies and a popular summer deck.
Old Floathouse, Gorge Harbour, T250-935 6631. Fresh seafood and West Coast dining in a beautiful setting overlooking the Gorge.

Port Hardy *p136*
There are a few other cheap eating options downtown, but none are particularly enticing. Better are the 2 inns on Hardy Bay Rd, see Sleeping.
Captain Hardy's, 7145 Market St, T250-949 7133. Has character and serves cheap breakfasts, fish and chips and burgers.

Bars and clubs

Courtenay *p131*
Most of the best places for a drink are listed under Eating. The nicest pubs are in Comox.
Billy D's Pub and Bistro, 268 5th St, T250-334 8811. A fun place for a drink and food. Wide selection of spirits and beers on tap.
Edge Marine Pub, 1805 Beaufort Av. A deck onto the ocean and a bistro with good food.

Entertainment

Courtenay *p131*
Comox Valley Art Gallery, 580 Ducan Av, T250-338 6211, www.comoxvalleyartgallery. com. Usually has interesting contemporary exhibitions, at least 3 change regularly.
I-Hos Gallery, 3310 Comox Rd, T250-339 7702, www.ihosgallery.com. A gallery of First Nations arts and crafts housed in a beautiful, traditional cedar building overlooking Comox Bay.
The Potters Place, 180B 5th St, T250-334 4613, www.thepottersplace.com. A large and very fine collection of ceramics presented by a local collective of potters.
Sid Williams Theatre, 442 Cliffe Av, T250-338 2420, www.sidwilliamstheatre.com. A significant venue for music, dance and for live theatre.

Campbell River and around *p132*
Campbell River & District Public Art Gallery, across from the Visitor Centre, T250-287 2261; Capri Cineplex, 100-489 Dogwood St S, T250-287 3233; **Galaxy Cinema**, 250 10th Av, T250-286 1744; **Tidemark Theatre**, 1220 Shoppers Row, T250-287 7465, distinctive peppermint-pink venue for live theatre and music, with art displays in the lobby.

Festivals and events

North to Courtenay *p130*
Aug Beach Festival, T250-248 4819, www.parksvillebeachfest.ca. Rathtrevor Beach Provincial Park in Parksville attracts thousands of visitors for this annual event, the highlight of which is the **Canadian Open Sandsculpting Competition.** The spectacular creations remain on display for 3 weeks after the competition.

Hornby Island *p130, map p136*
Though smaller than Denman, and more remote, there is always lots going on here, especially in summer.
Aug Hornby Festival, T250-335 2734, www.hornbyfestival.bc.ca. A perfect time to visit is during this 10-day festival, a major event that has grown to include all genres of music, modern dance, theatre, children's shows and the spoken word.

Courtenay *p131*

Jul Vancouver Island Music Festival, www.islandmusicfest.com. 3 days of Canadian and world music.

Aug Filberg Festival, 61 Filberg Rd, Comox, T250-334 9242, www.fil berg.com, $10. On the 1st weekend, this takes over Filberg Lodge and Park. 4 days of the best arts and crafts in BC and great food and music.

Campbell River and around *p132.*

May Painters Celebration of Art, T250-286 1102. In 2008, many of BC's finest artists will gather for the 14th annual artfest.

Aug North Island Logger Sports, T250-287 2044, www.crsalmonfestival.com. A 3-day redneck extravaganza. $5, child $3 entrance.

▲▲ Activities and tours

Denman Island *p130, map p136*

Bikes and scooters can be rented at **Denman Island Guesthouse** or the **General Store**.

Denman Island is a great place for kayaking. Reached only by water, **Sandy Island Marine Provincial Park** is a wonderful destination, with white sand beaches, rare wildlife and plants, and old growth forest.

Denman Hornby Canoes and Kayaks, 4005 East Rd, T250-335 0079, www.denman paddling.ca. Tours, lessons and rentals.

Hornby Island *p130, map p136*

Hornby Island Outdoor Sports, 5875 Central Rd, T250-335 0448, www.hornby outdoors.com. Bike rentals and equipment. Their website describes all the local trails.

Hornby Island Diving, 10795 Central Rd, T250-335 2807, www.hornbyislanddiving. com. Boat diving for $120/day, packages for $210 that include accommodation and meals. There's a good chance of seeing large animals, such as 6-gilled sharks.

Hornby Ocean Kayaks, T250-335 2726, www.hornbyisland.com/Kayaking. Specialize in teaching sea kayaking. Also offer rentals and guided tours.

Courtenay *p131*

Comox Valley Kayaks, T250-334 2628, www.comoxvalleykayaks.com. Lessons, rentals, tours and packages.

Mountain Meadows, 368 5th St, T250-338 8999. Sports equipment, rentals, eco-tours.

One on One Trail Rides, 3425 Mounce Rd, T250-897 5403. Personalized horse riding, including lessons, trips and campfire dinners.

Pacific Pro Dive and Surf, T250-338 6829, www.scubashark.com. Chartered dives all around the Georgia Strait, rentals, tours, snorkelling and water taxi service.

Union Bay Dive and Kayak, 5559 S Island Hwy, T250-335 3483, www.seashelldiving .com. Diving gear, lessons, charters and rentals. Also rents kayaks.

Mountain biking

Mountain biking is huge in the Comox Valley, with 50 km of trails around Cumberland, and more at Mt Washington. Try Seal Bay Park for an easy scenic ride. Several races and mountain bike festivals are held each year. For rentals and trail information go to **Dodge City Cycle**, 2705 Dunsmuir Av, Cumberland, T250-336 2200, or **Simon's Cycles Ltd**, 1841 Comox Av, Comox, T250- 3396683.

Campbell River *p132*

Fishing rods can be rented, but you'll need a Sport Fishing Licence, $7/day, $20/3 days for non-residents.

Aboriginal Journeys, T250-850 1101, www.aboriginaljourneys.com. Whale- and bear-watching tours from a 25-ft covered boat. Some First Nations history and culture thrown in, and experienced local guides.

Campbell River Kayaks, 1620 Petersen Rd, T250-334 2628, www.comoxvalleykayaks. com. Rentals and tours.

Coastal Island Fishing Adventures, 457 Albatross Cres, T1888-225 9776, www.coast alislandfishing.com. A reliable choice among many operators, offers fishing charters and all-inclusive packages.

Eagle Eye Adventures, T250-286 0809, www.eagleeyeadventures.com. Specialize in whale, bear and ocean rapid tours, including trips to the Arron Rapids, the second fastest rapids in the world.

Paradise Found Adventure Tour Co, 165-1160 Shellbourne Dr, T250-923 0848, www.paradisefound.bc.ca. Snorkel beside the migrating and spawning salmon, early Jul-late Oct ($119 for 3-4 hours). Arranges climbing, hiking, whale watching, fishing, caving, snowshoeing or snorkelling with colonies of sea-lions at Mitlenach Island.

Maps can be found online at www.discovery islands.ca. **Discovery Charters**, T250- 285 3146. Whale-watching tours and hiking trips; **Island Cycle**, Heriot Bay, T250- 285 3627. Trail maps, tours, information and rentals.

Kayaking
Coastal Spirits Sea Kayak Tours, T250-285 2895, www.kayakbritishcolumbia.com. Day tours, camping or lodge tours, and packages involving meals and accommodation.
Coast Mountain Expeditions, T250-287 0635, www.coastmountain expeditions. com. Kayaking tours, rentals and packages. See **Discovery Lodge** under Sleeping.
Quadra Island Kayaks, Heriot Bay, T250-285 3400, www.quadraislandkayaks.com. Tours, lessons, rentals and a range of multi-day trips to various locations. No experience is required.

Scuba-diving
Abyssal Dive Charters & Lodge, T250-285 2427, www.abyssal.com. Diving here is excellent, with great visibility, a very knowledgeable guide and lots to see and photograph. The all-inclusive package ($175 per person per day) includes 2 dives, air, tanks, weights, meals and accommodation at their lodge (also open to non-divers, $95 for a room).

Cortes Island *p133*
Gorge Harbour Marina Resort, T250-935 6433. Rents scooters and kayaks.

Nootka Sound and Gold River *p134*
Caving
With over 1000 known caves, Vancouver Island is Canada's top caving destination and Nootka Sound is the epicentre and home to **BC Speleological Federation**, T250-283 2283. Upana Caves Recreation Area, 17 km northwest of Gold River on the road to Tahsis, is perhaps the country's most spectacular caving destination. With 15 known semi-developed caves, and 450 m of passages, the site takes about 1 hr to explore self-guided. Look out for Resurgence Cave, the walls have been transformed by heat and pressure into smooth, white marble. Bring warm, waterproof clothes, sturdy boots and at least 2 torches with

spare batteries. Further details can be found at www.goldriver.ca.

Climbing
Climbing is excellent at Crest Creek Crags on Hwy 28, 15 km east of Gold River, with 100 or more routes.

Fishing
Nootka Sound is renowned for its salmon fishing, with big chinook and coho. There are operators listed on www.goldriver.ca. **Critter Cove Marina**, 18 km by water from Gold River, T250-283 7364, www.critter cove.com. Cottages with use of a fishing boat included, and a restaurant for meals.

Hiking
A 35-km 3-day hike runs along the rocky shorelines of **Nootka Island**, passing old First Nations sites. The experience is comparable to the West Coast trail without the crowds, fee or reservations. Access is by floatplane or the *MV Uchuck III* (see Transport, page 146).

Kayaking
Nootka Sound cannot compare to Clayoquot Sound for scenery, but is just as outstanding for kayaking and far less crowded. There's plenty of wildlife to spot, including whales, sea lions, bears, cougars, sea otters and bald eagles. The best spots are Nuchatlitz Inlet and Marine Provincial Park to the west of Tahsis and further west still, Catala Island Provincial Marine Park. The former offers the best chance of spotting sea otters. Gold River has 3 different stretches popular with experienced whitewater kayakers, including a famous section known as the Big Drop. The *MV Uchuck III* offers canoe and kayak trips. There seem to be no local operators, but **Spirit of the West**, www.kayakingtours.com, and **Comox Valley Kayaks**, www.comox valleykayaks.com, organize tours here.

Mountain biking
Local biking enthusiasts have pioneered numerous trails in the mountains surrounding Gold River. You have to bring your own bike.

Surfing
There is great surfing here, particularly at Beano Creek. It's like Long Beach, but without the crowds.

Tatchu Adventures, Tahsis, T250-934 6600, www.tatchuadventures.com. Surfing instruction, tours and all-inclusive packages. Lodging is in treehouses, with an emphasis on healthy living and organic foods. They will even pick you up in Campbell River.

Alert Bay and Sointula *p135*
Seasmoke Whale Watching, T250-974 5225, www.seaorca.com. Tours in a whale-friendly yacht, $95/4-5 hrs, $180/8 hrs (including lunch); and 4-hr cruises in a motorboat, $89.

Port Hardy *p136*
There are excellent opportunities for out-door pursuits such as scuba-diving, whale watching, kayaking, fishing or hiking.
Catala Charters, 6170 Hardy Bay Rd, T250-949 7560, www.catalacharters.net. A reliable operation, offering a range of services, including diving trips (but no gear rental), whale, bear or general wildlife watching tours, First Nation cultural tours, kayak rental and transport, and water taxis to Cape Scott.
Great Bear Nature Tours, T250-949 9496, www.greatbeartours.com. Specialists in bear-viewing tours, includes accommo-dation at their remote lodge.
North Island Daytrippers, T250-956 2411, www.islanddaytrippers.com. Based in Port McNeill, offering 1-day hiking trips to Cape Scott among other places.
North Island Dive and Charters, Market/Hastings, T250-949 8006, www.north islanddiver.com. Diving gear, rentals, training and trips.
Odyssey Kayaking Ltd, T250-902 0565, www.odysseykayaking.com. Rentals, transport and tours.

◎ Transport

Denman Island *p130, map p136*
Several daily ferries, roughly hourly from 0700-2300, to and from Buckley Bay just north of Fanny Bay, $7 return, child $4, vehicle $15.60, 10-12 min.

Hornby Island *p130, map p136*
Several daily ferries, at sporadic times from 0715-1835, to and from **Gravelly Bay** in the southeast of Denman Island, $7 return, child $4, vehicle $15.60, 10-min.

Courtenay *p131*
Courtenay is small enough to get around on foot. Local buses are operated by Comox Valley Transit System, T250-334 6000, www.busonline.ca. Bus No 11 runs to the ferry and airport, stopping at 4th Av/Cliffe, where many other routes converge, $1.50. No service on Sun. For a taxi try **United Cabs**, T250-339 7955.

Air
Comox Valley Airport receives daily flights: **Pacific Coastal**, T250-890 0699, www.pacific coastal.com, from **Vancouver** ($105 one-way) and Victoria ($178); **Central Mountain Air**, T1888-865 8585, www.flycma.com, from Vancouver ($72); **West Jet**, T1888-937 8538, www.westjet.com, from **Calgary** ($215). Book these flights with **Uniglobe**, T250-3389877.

Bus
The station is downtown at 9-2663 Kilpatrick Av. **Greyhound**, www.greyhound.ca, has 3 daily buses to **Victoria** (4-5 hrs, $39).

Ferry
BC Ferries, T1888-223 3779, www.bcferries.com, runs 4 daily sailings from **Powell River** on the Sunshine Coast to Little River, 13 km north of Comox. $10.35, child $5.75, vehicle $32.55, 1½ hrs.

Train
The station is on McPhee Av, a short walk from Downtown. **VIA Rail**, T1800-561 8630, www.viarail.ca, currently runs 1 train daily to and from **Victoria**, $28 one-way with 5 days advance booking, 0805 from Victoria, 1300 from Courtenay.

Campbell River and around *p132*
Air
Daily flights arrive at Campbell River and District Regional Airport (YBL) from **Vancouver** ($105) and Victoria ($177) with **Pacific Coastal Airlines**, T1800-663 2872, www.pacific-coastal.com.

Bus
Greyhound, T250-385 4411, www.grey hound.ca, run 3 buses per day to **Nanaimo** (2½ hrs, $25), and Victoria (6 hrs $47). 1 daily bus continues north as far as Port Hardy.

Quadra Island *p132*
BC Ferries, T1888-223 3779, www.bc
ferries.com, leave **Campbell River** every
hour on the half hour, arriving at Quathiaski
Cove on Quadra, $7, child $4, vehicle $16,
return, 45 mins. There is no public transport
here but hitchhiking is easy.

Cortes Island *p133*
Ferries leave 6 times daily from Heriot Bay
on the east side of Quadra Island, arriving
at Whaletown, $8.10, child $4.50, vehicle
$18.70, 45 mins. **Cortes Connection**, T250-
935 6911, www.cortesconnection.com,
runs to and from the Greyhound depot in
Campbell River via Quadra Island, $16, child
$10, one-way, not including ferry fare. It also
covers scheduled routes on the island, one
end to the other is $10, child $5.

**Strathcona Provincial Park: Buttle
Lake** *p133*
Campbell River Airporter, T250-286 3000,
run a service to and from Campbell River
on request, $50 for 2. Strathcona Lodge will
also transport guests, $50, then $10 for each
additional person.

Nootka Sound and Gold River *p134*
There is no public transport to Gold River, or
Tahsis, another 70 km northwest on a rough
but scenic logging road. Once here, the 100-
passenger *MV Uchuck III*, T250-283 2325,
www.mvuchuck.com, a 1942 US minesweeper, is the ultimate way to get around.
One-way to **Tahsis** $35, to **Zeballos** $45.
Meals available on board. They also run
some day trips and will transport kayaks for
a fee. **Air Nootka**, T250-283 2255, www.air
nootka.com, runs chartered and flightseeing
trips and scheduled trips to Tahsis, Zeballos
and **Kyuquot**, but they don't fly to Gold
River from anywhere useful. There's also
Maxi's Water Taxi, T250-283 2282.

Alert Bay and Sointula *p135*
Alternate ferries from Port McNeill run to
Alert Bay on Cormorant Island, and Sointula
on Malcolm Island. There are several daily

sailings to each, but no direct transport
between the islands. Both are $8.10, child
$4.50, vehicle $18.70, return. There is no
transport on the islands.

Port Hardy *p136*
Air
Flights from Vancouver ($149 one-way)
and **Bella Coola** ($365) with **Pacific Coastal
Airlines**, T250-273 8666, www.pacific-
coastal.com.

Bus
Greyhound, T250-385 4411, operates 1
daily bus to and from **Nanaimo** (0830),
and **Campbell River** (1215), leaving Port
Hardy at 0900 (Sat 0945) and stopping at
the ferry.

Water taxi
Catala Charters, T250-949 7560, www.catala
charters.net, new operation that runs a water
taxi service to Cape Scott Park and numerous
remote fishing and diving lodges that are
otherwise inaccessible.

❶ Directory

Courtenay *p131*
Banks CIBC Bank 2785 Cliffe Av, T250-897
3370. **Internet** Library; Cardero Coffee &
Tea Co, 208 5th St, T250-338 2519. **Laundry**
Home Style Laundry, 2401 Cliffe Av, T250-
334 0875. **Medical services** Acreview
Dental Clinic, 750 Comox Rd, T250-338
9085; Courtenay Medical Clinic, 788 Grant
Av, T250-334 2445; St Joseph's General
Hospital, 2137 Comox Av, T250-339 1432.
Post office Canada Post 2401 Cliffe Av,
T250-334 0875.

Campbell River and around *p132*
Banks RBC Bank, 1290 Shoppers Row,
T250-286 5500. **Laundry** Campbell River
Laundromat, 1231 Shoppers Row, T250-
286 6562. **Medical services** Campbell
River Hospital, 375 2nd Av, T250-287 7111.
Post office Canada Post 1251 Shoppers
Row, T250-286 1813.

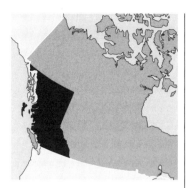

☘ Footprint features

Introduction

British Columbia's southern interior is criss-crossed with towering mountain ranges, broad river valleys and long skinny lakes. In two days you can drive through snowy peaks and glaciers in the Coast Mountains; arid, semi-desert hills covered with orchards and vineyards in the Okanagan; the forested slopes, pristine lakes and glaciers of the Columbia Mountains in the West Kootenays; moonscapes of muted colours in the Thompson Valley; and the sheer cliff walls of the Fraser Canyon.

All the outdoor pursuits you could want are here, too. The Sea to Sky Highway provides access to some of Canada's best skiing, climbing and biking. If you want to lie on a beach or tour a few wineries, head for the sun-baked Okanagan. The West Kootenays have charming former mining communities, a laid-back vibe and first-class hiking, biking and skiing.

North of the TransCanada Highway lies a vast under-populated hinterland of unimaginable proportions, where big animals and First Nations culture still thrive. Highlights include tours of abandoned ancient villages on Haida Gwaii, the Wild West ranching landscapes and gold-rush history of the Cariboo and Chilcotin, and a region of sublime scenery on the Cassiar Highway around Stewart.

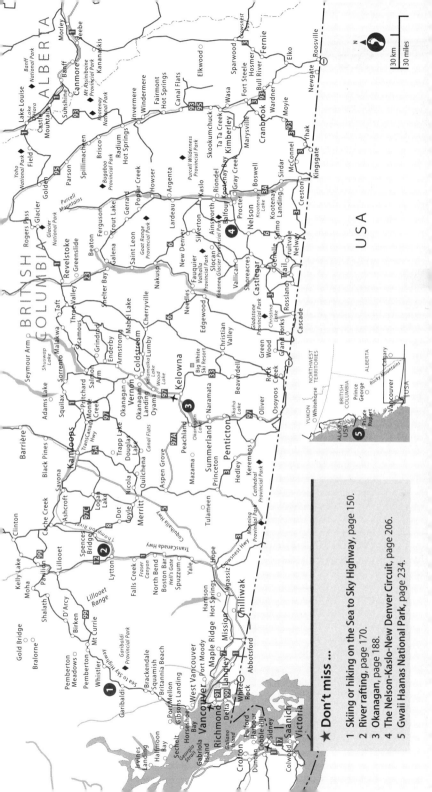

★ Don't miss ...

1 Skiing or hiking on the Sea to Sky Highway, page 150.
2 River rafting, page 170.
3 Okanagan, page 188.
4 The Nelson-Kaslo-New Denver Circuit, page 206.
5 Gwaii Haanas National Park, page 234.

Sea to Sky Highway

The Sea to Sky Highway (Highway 99) heads north from Vancouver to a treasure trove of activities. After Howe Sound, the road leaves the coast towards Canada's climbing, windsurfing and bald eagle capital, Squamish, before heading upwards through the gloriously scenic Coast Mountains to Garibaldi Provincial Park and the world famous ski resort of Whistler – co-host with Vancouver of the 2010 Winter Olympics. Almost every outdoor pursuit is available along this road, including hiking trails that rival the best in the Rockies. Beyond Whistler, the road gets rougher, passing the small villages of Pemberton and Lillooet, before emerging close to the TransCanada Highway.
▸▸ For Sleeping, Eating and other listings, see pages 158-169.

Ins and outs

Getting there and around
Buses from Vancouver run as far as Whistler, with **Greyhound** continuing to Pemberton. Major construction is underway along Highway 99, which gets absurdly busy on winter weekends. Taking your own car is unnecessary and inadvisable. All towns, except for Whistler's satellite suburbs, are small enough to get around on foot and Whistler has an efficient local bus network. ▸▸ *For further details, see Transport, page 167.*

Best time to visit
Summer is prime for most of the region's activities, while Whistler is at its busiest during the ski season (December to April). Roads are kept open throughout the winter as far as Whistler. Beyond Pemberton, snow chains are often required and road closures are common.

Tourist information
There are Visitor Information Centres in all towns, but the most useful are in Whistler and Squamish. *99 North*, a free and widely distributed magazine, is an extremely useful source of information about the Sea to Sky Highway. The *Visitor's Choice* brochures are also handy. For details on hiking, refer to Kathy and Craig Copeland's *Don't waste your time in the BC Coast Mountains* (Voice in the Wilderness Press).

North to Squamish ⊟🐟❄🅾▲🚌🛈 ▸▸ *pp158-169.*
Colour map 1, C4.

The opening stretch of Highway 99 is dramatic indeed, as the twisting road clings tenaciously to sheer cliffs, with views of Howe Sound and mountains on both sides swinging abruptly into view. It also contains no less than 10 important scuba-diving sites renowned for oversized sea life such as wolf eels and giant octopuses. **Whytecliff Park** at Horseshoe Bay is a famous marine reserve and **Porteau Cove Provincial Park** ① *Km 37*, is the Lower Mainland's most popular diving destination, with warm, shallow water and a series of artificial reefs created by sunken shipwrecks, including a Second World War minesweeper. There's a rocky beach here and a rather unattractive campground.

The first clear destination is the **Mining Museum** ① *Britannia Beach, 11 km south of Squamish, T1800-896 4044, www.bcmuseumofmining.org, May-Sep daily 0900-1630, Oct-Apr Mon-Fri 0900-1630, $17, under 18 $14, under 12 $12, under 5 free, all ages $7.50 in winter.* This was once the largest copper mine in the British Empire,

⦂ Whose name is it anyway?

Before the arrival of the Europeans, Squohomish natives came to the Squamish Valley to hunt and fish. Due to the frequent powerful air currents funnelled up Howe Sound from the Georgia Strait; the area became known as Squamish, meaning 'Mother of the Wind' in Coast Salish. Their first glimpse of white men was in 1792, when Captain Vancouver arrived and began trading. The settlers that eventually followed made a living from cattle raising and agriculture. Around 1912 some real-estate promoters decided a more civilized name than Squamish was needed, and chose the inspiring title Newport. Local people never liked this, so a few years later the railway invited school children to select a new name and win a $500 prize. The winning nomination was … Squamish.

with a population of 60,000, an output of £1.3 billion of copper in 70 years and a reputation for polluting the surrounding waters. As well as looking at educational displays, relics, videos, photos and a monster dump truck, you can pan for gold, have a glimpse inside the sadly but understandably renovated 'Concentrator' and, the highlight, take a train ride through an old mine tunnel.

Murrin Provincial Park ① *2 km north*, marks the beginning of hiking and climbing country. A hike to the Giuseppe Garibaldi Lookout gives a taste of the amazing views to come. **Shannon Falls** is the next obvious stop, an impressive 335-m waterfall visible from the road but worth the five-minute leg-stretch to see up close. From here, or from the campground 1 km down the road, you can watch climbers grappling with the granite walls of the sublime Stawamus Chief (see below).

Squamish and around → *Colour map 1, C4.*

Thanks to the 2010 Winter Olympics, Whistler's exorbitant real estate prices, closure of the local mill and a fairly justifiable claim to be 'the outdoor recreation capital of Canada', Squamish has finally started to embrace its identity as a tourist location. Hitherto very poor, its infrastructure is improving all the time. A major step forward was the construction of the excellent **Visitor Information Centre** ① *'Squamish Adventure Centre', on the highway, T1866-333 2010, www.tourismsquamish.com, www.squamish.ca, Jun-Sep daily 0900-1800, Dec-Feb daily 0900-1700, otherwise Mon-Fri 0900-1700, Sat-Sun 1000-1400.* Considerable potential remains unfulfilled, however and, despite its extraordinary mountain-ringed location, the sprawling town is not much to look at and offers little distraction for those not of a sporty persuasion.

Approaching from the south, you can't miss the 95-million-year-old **Stawamus Chief**, the second biggest granite monolith on Earth. The Chief is the centrepiece of Squamish's world-famous rock-climbing, attracting some 200,000 hopefuls every year. These massive rock walls that funnel the Howe Sound's strong ocean winds straight into Squamish, are also responsible for the town's name, 'Mother of the Wind' in Coast Salish and its recognition as the country's windsurfing capital.

A third local claim to fame is held by **Brackendale** ① *10 km north*, where more bald eagles have been counted than anywhere else in the world. Attracted by the spawning salmon, an estimated 10,000 of these magnificent birds stop by every winter and are now protected by the 550-ha **Brackendale Eagles Provincial Park**. The best places to see them and get more information are the **Brackendale Art Gallery** ① *Government Rd, north of Depot Rd, T604-898 3333, www.brackendale artgallery.com*, and the **Sunwolf Outdoor Centre** ① *70002 Squamish Valley Rd, 4 km off Hwy 99, T604-898 1537, www.sunwolf.net.*

Those with an interest in trains or locomotion will enjoy a visit to the **West Coast Railway Heritage Park** ⓘ *39645 Government Rd, T604-898 9336, www.wcra.org, open daily 1000-1600, $10, student $8.50*. It's packed full of vintage railway paraphernalia, including carriages, 50 locomotives, a restored executive business car and the celebrated *Royal Hudson*. A 3-km miniature steam train ride takes visitors around the park.

Hikes around Squamish (north to south)

Stawamus Chief ⓘ *6- to 11-km round trip; 612 m elevation gain. Trailhead: Shannon Falls Provincial Park or 1.2 km further north.* The mighty chief makes an excellent, not too difficult hike and is snow-free as early as March and as late as November. With fantastic views and close proximity to Vancouver, this is one of the busiest hikes around. Most people make for the first (south) of the three summits, so try heading for the second or third, or even hike to them all. Descending is more fun via the second summit than on the east trail.

Lake Lovely Water ⓘ *10 km round trip; 1128 m elevation gain. Trailhead: 10.6 km north of town, turn west onto Squamish Valley Rd. Turn left onto a dirt road at Km 6 and park by the BC Hydro right of way at Km 2.* You need to canoe across the river or arrange a ferry (roughly $20 per person) with **Kodiak Adventures**, T604-8983356. This is a very tough, demanding hike on a steep and narrow trail. However, the aptly named destination is possibly the most spectacular lake in the Coast Mountains. Consider packing a tent and spending an extra day or two exploring, or book a place in the **Alpine Club of Canada** hut, T604-687 2711.

High Falls Creek ⓘ *12 km round trip; 640 m elevation gain. Trailhead: Squamish Valley Rd, as above. At Km 24.2 stay right on Squamish River Rd. Park at Km 3.1 and look for sign 100 m further on the right.* As well as falls and gorges, this sometimes steep route offers views of the Tantalus Range. Continue up to the logging road and descend it in a loop.

Whistler and around ⊖⊘⋔⊛⊡⎐⊖❶ ➤ *pp159-169.*
Colour map 1, B4.

Garibaldi Provincial Park → *Colour map 1, B4.*
ⓘ *Walk-in campsites are primitive and tend to require self-registration, so take cash. There is also a $3 per vehicle per day charge for parking at some trailheads.*
Once you get beyond the Squamish sprawl, the journey to Whistler is a delight, giving an idea of the incredible scenery contained within Garibaldi Provincial Park to the east. This is the nearest thing to a wilderness park you'll find within such easy reach of a major city and two prime sporting centres. Too popular for some people's taste, it offers undeniably spine-tingling scenery packed with pristine lakes and rivers, alpine meadows, soaring peaks and huge glaciers. The hiking here is some of the best to be found outside the Rockies and the trails are clearly signposted and well maintained. For longer hikes, it is worth seeking further information from Visitor Information Centres or investing in a good hiking guide before setting out.

Hikes in Garibaldi Provincial Park

Elfin Lakes/Mamquam Lake ⓘ *22 km or 44 km; 915 m or 1555 m elevation gain. Trailhead: 3.1 km north of Squamish look for the Diamond Head sign, turn east (right) onto Mamquam Rd and continue for 15 km.* This trail leads quickly to outstanding views of the mighty snow-capped Tantalus Range, so it's no surprise that it gets irritatingly overcrowded at weekends. The walk to Elfin Lakes is along an ugly road also open to cyclists. In winter it becomes a popular Nordic skiing route. If possible, leave the crowd behind by continuing to Mamquam Lake. The campground here is in a wonderful setting (though you're unlikely to reach it in one day) and views from the ridge above are exceptional. The Elfin Lakes campground can be very busy. There is also a rudimentary overnight shelter with 34 bunk beds and a stove (a fee is collected). A number of side-trips fan out from here, the best leading to Little Diamond Head: take the Saddle trail to the Gargoyles then ascend 170 vertical metres.

Garibaldi Lake/Taylor Meadows ⓘ *35 km round trip; 2450 m elevation gain. Trailhead: Rubble Creek. 38 km north of Squamish or 20 km south of Whistler, turn east at the Black Tusk sign and proceed for 2.6 km.* This is one of the most rewarding areas for hiking in the park, with many options for making your own itinerary. Garibaldi Lake is huge, vividly coloured with glacial flour and surrounded by sights like Guard Mountain and the Sphinx Glacier. You can camp here or at the flower-strewn Taylor Meadows a few kilometres away. Both are wonderful locations, but don't expect to be alone and remember to bring cash for camping fees. Be sure to do at least one side trip. The most highly recommended is Panorama Ridge, which affords expansive views of ice and peaks, including Mount Garibaldi and the Warren Glacier. The second option is the distinctive volcanic peak known as the Black Tusk. The trail passes through expansive meadows and leads to awesome views, but the summit requires serious scrambling.

Brandywine Meadow ⓘ *13.6 km round trip; 600 m elevation gain. Trailhead: 15 km south of Whistler, 44 km north of Squamish, turn west onto Brandywine Forestry Rd. Park on the left at Km 4.4.* This is a popular, first-class hike to an alpine bowl full of wild flower meadows and set beneath towering cliffs. Early August is best for the flower show.

Cheakamus Lake ⓘ *6.4 km return; 12.8 km with a loop of the lake, mostly flat. Trailhead: 7.7 km south of Whistler, 51.3 km north of Squamish, turn east onto a logging road and continue 7.5 km to the end of the road.* This is an easy hike and negotiable from early June to late October. The trail leads through patches of old-growth forest and the big, beautiful turquoise lake itself is surrounded by ice-covered peaks that soar 1600 m over its shoreline. Bikes are allowed as far as the lake, where there is a campsite for those who wish to spend a bit of time at this stunning spot. The trout fishing is excellent.

Helm Creek ⓘ *16 km round trip; 717 m elevation gain. Trailhead: same as Garibaldi Lake, above.* This is an alternative route into the Garibaldi Lake area and the two hikes combine very well to make a 24-km one-way trip (though this requires a shuttle or hitching). Coming from the Helm Creek end is a longer and steeper route but consequently far less crowded and the campground at the creek is smaller and much nicer than the more popular ones mentioned above. Day hiking from there to Garibaldi Lake is a recommended option.

Musical Bumps ⓘ *19 km round trip to Singing Pass; 727 m elevation gain. Trailhead: at the top of Whistler Mountain gondola.* **Musical Bumps** is the nickname for Piccolo, Flute and Oboe summits. This is a ridge walk suitable for all levels. The gondola takes you up 1136 m, meaning almost anyone can enjoy the type of views usually only attained after hours of work. It's just a short ascent to the ridge, then the heart-stoppingly gorgeous views over a 360-degree panorama of peaks and glaciers are continuous. Cheakamus Lake and Glacier and Mount Davidson are the highlights, along with vast alpine meadows. For extra views of Brandywine Mountain, the glacier-clad Tantalus Range and the Pemberton Icefield, climb up Whistler

Whistler Village

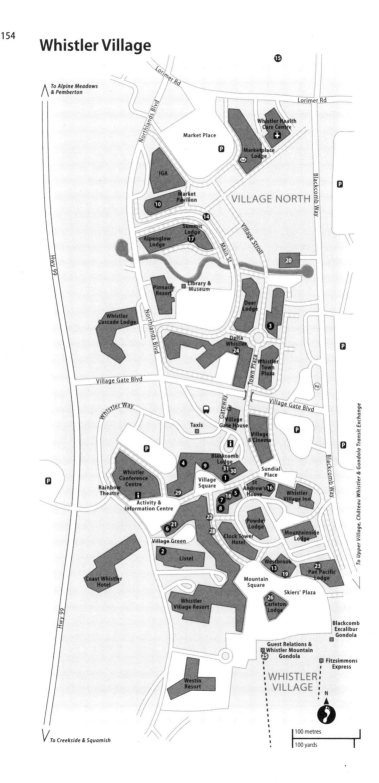

Orientation

To Pemberton ▲

Emerald Estates

Alpine Meadows

Green Lake

Meadow Park Recreation Centre

Nita Haus North

Château Whistler

Upper Village

Lost Lake

Village North

Alta Vista

Village

Whistler

Whistler Village

Alta Lake

99

To Function Junction & Squamish

To Alpha Lake

Whistler Creekside

To Function Junction & Squamish

1 km
1 mile

N

Sleeping 🛏
Brandywine Falls **2**
Brew Creek Lodge **12**
Cedar Springs B&B **4**
Chalet Luise B&B **5**
Edgewater Lodge **6**
Fireside Lodge **9**
Haus Heidi Pension B&B **7**
HI Whistler **8**
Renoir's Winter Garden
    B&B **10**
Riverside Resort **11**
Riverside RV Resort **14**
UBC Whistler Lodge **3**
Whistler Resort & Club **1**

Eating 🍴
21 Steps **16**
Araxi & Pub **1**
Bearfoot Bistro **2**
Caramba! **3**
Dups Burrito **14**
Elements **17**
Gone Bakery & Soup Co **4**
Ingrid's Village Café **5**
Kypriaki's **6**
La Bocca **7**
La Brasserie des Artistes **8**
Moguls Coffee Bean **9**
Pasta Lupino **10**
Rimrock Café **11**
South Side Diner **12**

Sushi Village **13**
Wild Wood **15**

Bars & clubs 🍸
Amsterdam Café **18**
Black's Pub **19**
Brewhouse Pub **20**
Buffalo Bill's **21**
Città **22**
Dubh Linn Gate **23**
Garfinkel's **24**
Garibaldi Lift Company **25**
Longhorn Saloon **26**
Mallard Lounge **27**
Mix **28**
Moe Joe's **29**
Savage Beagle **30**
Tommy Africa's **31**

Mountain first and descend on the Burnt Stew Trail rather than reaching the Musical Bumps via Harmony Lakes. Catch the earliest gondola possible (around 1000). Reaching Flute summit and returning in time for the last gondola should be possible, but getting to Oboe summit and back is tricky. Ideally, make it a 22-km one-way trip over the Bumps to Singing Pass then out via Fitzsimmons Creek Valley, though this means hitching or arranging a shuttle. Take plenty of water as the ridge is dry.

Blackcomb Peak ⓘ *9 km round trip; 355 m elevation gain. Trailhead: From Whistler Village car park take the Fitzsimmons Trail, then take the chairlift up 1174 m to Rendezvous Lodge.* The chairlift makes it easy to reach dizzying vistas. Almost immediately the Cheakamus and Overlord glaciers are visible and soon you're strolling through fields of wild flowers. Ascend on the Overlord Summit Trail to Decker Tarn and then descend on the Outback Trail, making a nice loop. Scrambling higher from the tarn will lead to even better views.

Fitzsimmons Creek/Russet Lake ⓘ *19 km round trip; 945 m elevation gain. Trailhead: From Blackcomb Way follow signs to Singing Pass Trailhead, 5 km up a dirt road. This hike can be done one-way as a second leg of the Musical Bumps Trail, above.* Or if you object to paying for the gondola, take this free route into the alpine. The path climbs at a reasonable grade, and takes you through some flower meadows, with views that include the stunning Cheakamus Lake. From an easily attained ridge, just above the dramatic setting of Russet Lake, an almost unparalleled array of ice is visible, including the Cheakamus and Overlord glaciers, and the Pemberton Icefield.

Cougar Mountain Cedar Grove ⓘ *5 km round trip; 150 m elevation gain. Trailhead: 5 km north of Whistler, turn west onto a dirt road signposted Cougar Mountain Ancient Cedar Trail.*

This is less a hike than an experience. The short walk is nothing special but the ancient cedars at the end are impressive and humbling.

Wedgemount Lake ⓘ *14 km, 1160 m elevation gain. Trailhead: 11.8 km north of Whistler, 20.6 km south of Pemberton, turn east at the Garibaldi/Wedgemount Lake sign and proceed 1.9 km up Wedge Creek Forestry Rd*. This steep, demanding climb leads to a beautiful lake in Garibaldi Provincial Park, passing a 300 m waterfall on the way. Take warm clothes as it tends to be chilly by the lake.

Whistler → *Colour map 1, B4.*

Whistler is the largest ski area in North America and is consistently voted the continent's number one ski resort by many respected publications. The terrain is vast, the facilities are constantly upgraded and the management bend over backwards to make sure the visitor's every need is anticipated. Other winter sports include endless cross-country ski trails, backcountry skiing, heliskiing, dogsledding, horse-drawn sleigh rides, snowmobiling, snowshoeing and many other possibilities. With Garibaldi Provincial Park right next door, this is also a hiking and biking haven in summer, when just about every kind of outdoor pursuit is available.

Due to considerable year-round prestige, and greatly exacerbated by the prospect of the 2010 Winter Olympics, Whistler has increasingly become the domain of the wealthy. Prices for everything, especially real estate, have risen astronomically and the atmosphere can be terribly posey and elitist. Young jocks are the second predominant social group and, with so many of them getting pumped-up on the slopes all day and drunk in the evening, the atmosphere can get a little boisterous. If you're looking for cheap, down-to-earth fun on the snow, consider heading to the Kootenays or Okanagan instead.

The purpose-built townsite centres on **Whistler Village**, where the ski lifts are located, with Village North and Upper Village both within walking distance. A toy-town maze of fancy hotels, bars, restaurants and sport shops, the resort has an unreal, Legoland appearance that might attract or repel, depending on your state of mind and predilections. The decision to keep all traffic out of the centre, leaving pedestrians to stroll around at leisure, reinforces the impression of being in a holiday camp and the perpetual party atmosphere is helped along by several major seasonal festivals (see Festivals, page 163), with smaller events taking place almost every weekend. On the outskirts are a few satellite suburbs, such as Function Junction and Creekside to the south, Alpine Meadows and Emerald Estates to the north; connected by the local bus service, they contain much of the more affordable lodging.

Whistler's helpful, well-stocked **Visitor Centre** ⓘ *handily located by the Bus Loop, 4230 Gateway Dr off Village Gate Blvd from Hwy 99, T604-935 3357, www.tourismwhistler.com, daily 0800-2000,* is the place to find and book accommodation, activities, get maps and buy bus tickets. Nearby in front of the Telus Whistler Conference Centre is the **Activity and Information Centre** ⓘ *4010 Whistler Way, T604-938 2769.* A wealth of information, including maps, can be gleaned from the seasonal publication *99 North*, which is free and widely distributed around town. The free *FAQ* gives a handy locals' perspective on what to do in town and the the free local *Pique* newspaper can also be helpful and interesting.

In being chosen as the alpine host of the **2010 Olympics** ⓘ *www.vancouver 2010.com,* Whistler has come full circle, as the whole town was forged out of the wilderness back in the early 1960's when a group of skiers, businessmen and dreamers had the crazy ambition to build a ski resort and host the Olympics. The town has a short but potentially fascinating modern history. To discover more, visit the **Whistler Museum and Archives** ⓘ *4329 Main, T604-932 2019, www.whistler museum.org.*

Skiing Whistler and Blackcomb

ⓘ *A day pass for all lifts is currently $83, under 6 free, book tickets online to save up to 20%. The slopes are open daily mid-Nov to late Apr; Nov-Jan 0830-1500, Feb 0830-1530, Mar-Apr 0830-1600, depending on conditions. One of the hills, Blackcomb in 2008, stays open until early Jun.*

In December 2008, Blackcomb and Whistler Mountains will be linked by a $53 million Peak to Peak Gondola, which will travel 4.4 km in just 11 minutes, offering skiers an intimidating amount of options. Between them, the two mountains cover 3300 ha of terrain, featuring 12 bowls, three glaciers, over 200 marked trails, six terrain parks and one superpipe for snowboarders, and 17 restaurants, all accessed by a network of 38 lifts with a capacity of over 61,000 skiers per hour. Each mountain has its own character, **Whistler** is a bit more laid-back, has a Family Zone and is suitable for beginners and intermediates. It has a breakdown of 20% beginner, 55% intermediate and 25% advanced. **Blackcomb**, with a breakdown of 15% beginner, 55% intermediate and 30% advanced, boasts the two longest lift-serviced vertical falls in North America, one of the biggest terrain parks in the world, a superpipe, tube park and an expert park (with a 148 m vertical drop), which you can only enter with a helmet and a special endorsement on your pass. Whistler-Blackcomb can an intimidating place with tough runs. Start modestly, choose your runs carefully, keep an eye on incoming weather and think about taking a refresher course.

Pemberton to Lillooet 🛏️🍴▲ ↠ *pp160-169. Colour map, B4, B5.*

Pemberton and beyond → *Colour map 1, B4.*

ⓘ *The summer-only Visitor Information Centre is on the way into town at 7374 Hwy 99, T604-894 6175, www.pembertonchamber.com.*

Beyond Whistler, the views open out as the highway approaches the steeper, more dramatic mountains to the north. Many people choose to stay in **Pemberton** and commute the half-hour to Whistler. The village is calmer, more picturesque and utterly free of the tourism-gone-mad that has blighted its popular sister to the south. Though there is little to Pemberton itself, the surrounding area is rich in possibilities for hiking, biking and fishing. There are also two fine hot springs within striking distance.

    Just east of Pemberton a rough road strikes north from the wonderfully scenic Mount Currie, passing through D'Arcy and eventually making its own tortuous way to Lillooet. At Devine, a gravel road heads 18 km west to **Birkenhead Lake Provincial Park**, a remote destination with 85 primitive campsites ideal for those seeking utter tranquillity. There's a good chance of spotting mountain goats, moose and blue herons and the 3.5-km lakeshore trail is pleasant enough. More impressive is **Place Creek Falls** ⓘ *at 21.4 km from Mt Currie take the dirt road right and proceed roughly 2 km*, a 3-km return hike.

    This is one of the best regions for hot springs, though they're characteristically hard to reach. **Meagre Creek Hot Springs** ⓘ *$5*, is the largest and one of the best in BC but is currently inaccessible. Also recommended are the free, clothing-optional **Skookumchuck Hot Springs** ⓘ *follow Highway 99 east to Mt Currie, take a very rough forestry road south along Lillooet River, passing various deserted homesteads and 2 native graveyards on the way; the 54-km drive takes about 1½ hrs.* For more information and directions to both, go to www.britishcolumbia.com/hotsprings.

Hikes around Pemberton (Accessible from Highway 99)

Stein Divide ⓘ *28.6 km; 1265 m elevation gain. Trailhead: 10.3 km north of Mt Currie turn southeast onto the In Shuk-ch Forestry Rd. At Km 16.6 turn left onto Lizzie Creek Branch Rd. Most vehicles will want you to stop at Km 8 and walk.* This is one of the most rewarding hikes, but it is also the longest and most difficult to access.

The trail through this region is extremely tough and demanding but it provides access to a vast unspoilt alpine wilderness with a generous smattering of lakes, mountains and glaciers. Highlights are the views from Tabletop Mountain and the eerily beautiful colour of Tundra Lake.

Joffre Lakes Trail ① *11 km; 370 m elevation gain. Trailhead: 30 km north of Pemberton, 69 km south of Lillooet at Joffre Lakes Recreation Area.* This excellent and relatively easy hike leads to three gorgeous teal lakes set in exquisite mountain scenery. The first lake would be a worthy reward for hours of hiking but is reached after just five minutes. Whatever your fitness, don't drive by without stopping to hike at least this far. The only downside is the trail's popularity.

Rohr Lake/Marriott Basin Trail ① *9-16 km; 430 m elevation gain. Trailhead: 3.7 km north from the above, then 1 km down Cayoosh Creek Forestry Rd.* This considerably less busy trail is tough, narrow, steep and sometimes obscure, so suitable only for experienced hikers. The reward is solitude, a pristine meadow and an amethyst lake set beneath Mount Rohr.

Cerise Creek Trail ① *8 km round trip; 305 m elevation gain. Trailhead: 12.5 km north of Joffre Lakes, then 6 km southwest on Cerise Creek Main Forestry Rd.* This short, fairly easy hike leads to great views of the Anniversary and Matier glaciers and the peaks to which they cling.

North to Lillooet
The journey to Lillooet is much more of a commitment than the easy jaunt to Pemberton, but well worth the effort. The road narrows and becomes more tortuous, with brake-destroying steep sections, narrow wooden bridges, the threat of landslides and ever more breathtaking mountain views. At Lillooet, Highway 99 meets the **Fraser River Valley**. As if in anticipation, the scenery changes about 20 km south of town with the arrival of a series of eye-catching bony rock faces, followed by an incredible downhill section, then the sudden appearance of **Seton Lake**, its water a striking milky aquamarine.

Lillooet → *Colour map 1, B5.*
After all the raw splendour of the journey, Lillooet comes as an inevitable disappointment, though its setting is spectacular. Should you feel like stopping, all the necessities are found on Main Street, including the **Visitor Information Centre** ① *790 Main St, T250-256 4308, www.lillooetbc.com, Jul-Aug daily 0900-1900, May-Jun and Sep-Oct Tue-Sat 1000-1600.*

Beyond Lillooet the scenery becomes even more extraordinary. The vast canyon, its cliffs dropping an impossible distance down to the Fraser River below, leads towards the harsh weather systems of the Cariboo and the Thompson Valley, both typified by vast, desert-dry landscapes in shades of yellow, red and ochre, dotted with lonely scraps of scrubby vegetation. Highway 99 intercepts Highway 97 just north of Cache Creek, from where the TransCanada heads east to Kamloops and beyond. Alternatively, Highway 12 follows the Fraser River south from Lillooet, picking up the TransCanada at Lytton and continuing south to Hope, from where you could head back to Vancouver to complete a very scenic loop.

⬤ Sleeping

Squamish and around *p151*
A number of B&Bs and a couple of decent restaurants are situated east of the Hwy,

4 km north of town, in an area called Garibaldi Heights.
C Glacier View B&B, 40531 Thunderbird Ridge, T604-898 1630. One of many large, attractive homes around, with amazing

views up in the Garibalda Highlands above town.

C Howe Sound Inn, 37801 Cleveland Av, T1800-919 2537, www.howesound.com. The best choice downtown, this beautiful wooden building contains large and stylish rooms, as well as a great pub and restaurant with views of the Stawamus Chief. Guests can use the sauna and climbing wall. Great value.

C-D Sunwolf Outdoor Centre, 70002 Squamish Valley Rd, Brackendale, 4 km off Hwy 99, 10 km north of town, T604-898 1537, www.sunwolf.net. Set on 2 ha at the confluence of the Cheakamus and Cheekeye rivers, this is the best place to see bald eagles. The owners organize eagle-spotting rafting trips, as well as whitewater rafting and kayaking, and offer good advice. Their 10 riverside cabins, some with kitchenette, are attractive and good value. There's a common room, café and volleyball court.

C-E Squamish Inn on the Water, Hwy 99 and Cleveland Av, T1800-449 8614, www.innonthewater.com. Nicely situated on Mamquam Blind Channel, this large, new hostel has 3- to 6-bed dorms, private en suite rooms and family suites. Facilities include a lounge with fireplace, a kitchen and dining room, a TV room, laundry, lockers, storage, a balcony with views of the Chief, internet access and BBQ.

Camping

Alice Lake Provincial Park, 13 km north on Hwy 99. Has 108 wooded private sites, none of them very close to the beach. Pretty lake with fishing and swimming, showers and a big grassy area.

Klahanie Campground, 5 mins' south of Squamish, T604-892 3435. Fairly private sites in a great location opposite Shannon Falls, with hot showers, plenty of trees and a restaurant.

Stawamus Chief Provincial Park, 5 mins' south. 45 walk-in sites and 15 ugly car park sites. No fires. Handy for hikers/climbers.

Whistler *p152, map p154*

Whistler Village is little more than a big hotel and condo complex, full of luxury choices that substitute comfort for character. You're well advised to book as far ahead as possible, especially during the ski season or Canadian or US holidays, using www.whistler chamber.com, www.tourismwhistler.com or www.whistler.com/accommodation, all of which have extensive listings. Or call the Reservation Centre, T1800-9447 8537. The few hostels catering to budget travellers fill up especially quickly, it's a challenge to find a bed for less than $120. The satellite suburbs, such as Creekside (within walking distance of the gondola), offer better value. Ski and accommodation packages can work out as the cheapest option. Rates are greatly reduced in summer and double at Christmas. If staying for a few days or more, you could rent a condo or holiday home, www.resort questwhistler.com or www.affordable whistler.com.

L-C Brew Creek Lodge, 1 Brew Creek Rd, 22 km south of Whistler, 37 km north of Squamish, T604-932 7210, www.brew creeklodge.com. A very private cluster of wood buildings nestled among the trees. Lodge rooms, suites, cabins and guest houses sleeping up to 8. There's an outdoor jacuzzi and a wonderful guest lounge.

L-C Whistler Resort and Club, 2129 Lake Placid Rd, 6 km south in Creekside, T604-932 5756, www.whistlerresortand club.com. The rooms here are nice enough, good value for the price and handily located. The more expensive rooms are suites. There's a hot tub, and canoes and bikes for rent.

A Edgewater Lodge, 8030 Alpine Way, 3 km north of Whistler Village, T604-932 0688, www.edgewater-lodge.com. This beautiful, quiet, seemingly remote lodge is situated on the shore of Green Lake, which can be admired from the 12 lodge rooms, the patio, outdoor jacuzzi or the highly esteemed restaurant.

A Riverside Resort, 8018 Mons Rd, 1.5 km from the village via Blackcomb Way, T604-905 5533, www.whistlercamping.com. Handsome, cosy log cabins set in a big campground, decked out in wood and equipped with kitchenettes and small patios. Other facilities include a games room, playground, volleyball court and putting greens. Bikes, skis and other gear for rent, tours arranged and free shuttles to the gondolas provided.

A-B Cedar Springs B&B, 8106 Cedar Springs Rd, Alpine Meadows, 4 km north of Whistler

Village, T604-938 8007, www.whistlerbb.
com. 8 attractive, varied rooms. Communal
lounge, buffet breakfast, afternoon tea
and free transport to the hill.
B Haus Heidi Pension B&B, 7115 Nesters
Rd, 15 mins walk from the Village, T604-
932 3113, www.hausheidi.com. Very
attractive and distinctive European-style
house, with 8 delightful en suite rooms,
an outdoor hot tub, sauna, lovely balcony
with views and big breakfasts.
B Renoir's Winter Garden B&B, 3137
Tyrol Cres, near Alta Lake, T604-938 0546,
www.renoirs.ca. One of the nicest and
most reasonable of Whistler's many B&Bs,
which is why you have to reserve so far
ahead. 3 en suite rooms, hot tub, views
and a gourmet breakfast.
C Chalet Luise B&B, 7461 Ambassador
Cres, T604-932 4187, www.chaletluise.
com. Swiss-style mansion, a short
walk from the Village. 8 large and bright
rooms, a fireside lounge, patio, garden,
jacuzzi, sauna and a good breakfast.
C-E Fireside Lodge, 2117 Nordic Dr,
3 km S of Village, T604-932 4545, www.
fire sidelodge.org. 4-bed dorms and
private rooms, with a fully equipped
kitchen, lounge with fireplace (no TV),
games room with pool table, internet,
storage and laundry.
D UBC Whistler Lodge, 2124 Nordic Dr,
3 km south of the Village, T604-822 5851,
www.ubcwhistlerlodge.com. A student
hostel with some beds available to the
public in dorms or private rooms. Full
kitchen facilities, common area with
wood fire, separate TV lounge, sauna
and hot tub, coin laundry, lockers, free
parking and lock-up shed. A great deal,
but book ahead.
E HI Whistler, 5678 Alta Lake Rd, opposite
side of lake, T604-932 5492, www.hihostels.
ca. Not as easy to get to but undoubtedly
the budget option of choice, so reserve early.
On the banks of the lake, it's very quiet and
scenic. Beds are mostly dorms, with a few
private rooms. There's a kitchen, living room
with fireplace, sauna, internet, canoes and
bikes. 5 daily buses run in town.

Camping
There are cheaper, more basic forestry
campgrounds further out at Calcheak
and Alexander Falls.
Brandywine Falls, 10 km south on Hwy 99.
A standard park campsite.
Riverside RV Resort, 8018 Mons Rd, T604-
905 5533, www.whistlercamping.com.
About the only real choice for campers
within Whistler itself and open all year.
Fairly private sites for tents, full service
for RVs. Facilities include hot showers
and laundry.

Pemberton and beyond *p157*
There are a couple of standard motels/hotels
in town but much better are the varied B&Bs,
many of which cluster around Pemberton
Meadows Rd.
B-C Log House B&B, 1357 Elmwood Dr,
follow signs in town, T604-894 6000,
www.loghouseinn.com. 7 attractive rooms
with en suite shower in a beautiful log home
with outdoor hot tub, a wrap-around deck
with good views, and a guest lounge. Full
breakfast included.
C Pemberton Valley Vineyard & Inn, 1427
Collins Rd, just off Pemberton Meadows Rd,
T604-894 5857, www.whistler wine.com.
3 large, light, airy and tastefully furnished
rooms with en suite clawfoot tubs. There's
a deck with mountain views, hot tub and
a gourmet vegetarian breakfast .
E C&N Backpackers Hostel, 1490 Harrow
Rd, T604-894 2442, www.cnnbackpackers.
com. Dorms and private rooms at a great
price. Few facilities.
E Holly Park Hostel, 7306 Clover Rd, 1 km
from town, T604-894 6670, www.hollypark
hostel.com. Kitchen, games room with pool
table, lockers, TV and a garden.

Camping
Nairn Falls Provincial Park, 3 km south,
T604-898 3678. Has 94 reasonable sites, with
hiking and fishing. 1.5-km walk to the falls.

Lillooet *p158*
D 4 Pines, 108 8th Av, T250-256 4247.
The most promising choice out of a
few motels downtown, with big rooms

*For an explanation of sleeping and eating price codes used in this guide, see inside
the front cover. Other relevant information is found in Essentials, see pages 28-31.*

and baths. It's worth paying the extra for the newer rooms which have kitchenettes.
D Reynolds Hotel, 1237 Main St, T250-256 4202, www.reynoldshotel.com. Great value with big bathrooms, mountain views and bags of character. The big wooden building resembles a Wild West saloon.

Camping
Cayoosh Creek, 1 km S on Hwy 99, T250-256 4180. A spacious and forested riverside setting, with hot showers and access to a walking trail.
Fraser Cove, 2 km N on Hwy 99, T250-256 0142, www.frasercove.com. Attractive location right by the river.

Eating

North to Squamish *p150*
♥ **Mountain WoMan Café**, Britannia Beach, by the museum. A longstanding kitchen-bus restaurant, good for fish 'n' chips and burgers.

Squamish and around *p151*
♥♥ **The Burrow Tapas Lounge**, 40437 Tanalus Rd, T604-898 2801. One of a few great new places in the Garibaldi Highlands area. Delicious titbits, wines and spirits in a refreshingly sophisticated atmosphere.
♥♥ **Essence of India**, 40367 Tantalus Rd, T604-898 1000. A humble, small, family-run place serving very tasty and authentic Indian food.
♥♥ **North Beach Lounge and Grill**, at the Howe Sound Inn, 37081 Cleveland Av, T604- 892 2603, www.howesound.com. A lively and very tastefully decked out pub and restaurant serving creative West Coast food, salads and pizza, as well as their own excellent beers. There are unbeatable views of the Stawamus Chief from the patio.
♥♥ **Sushi Sen**, 40382 Tantalus Way, T604-898 8235. Authentic sushi in elegant, unpretentious surroundings.
♥♥ **The Watershed Grill**, 41101 Government Rd, Brackendale, T604-898 6665. Wild salmon, seafood, pasta and burgers, with a fine patio overlooking the river. Open till midnight, it's also a good place for a drink.
♥♥ **Wild Wood**, Progress Way, in the Mountain Retreat Hotel, T604-815 4424. Sister to those in Whistler, but more needed in Squamish.

♥ **Sunflower Bakery Café**, 38086 Cleveland Av. Good coffee and freshly baked goods in bright, pleasant surroundings .

Whistler *p152, map p154*
Most of Whistler's restaurants and bars are in and around Village Sq, so it's easy to see where the action is.
♥♥♥ **Araxi Ristorante and Pub**, Village Sq, T604-932 4540. An excellent West Coast-influenced menu that concentrates on fresh, local meat, game, vegetables and fish. This is a contender for the best place to eat in town.
♥♥♥ **Bearfoot Bistro**, 4121 Village Green, T604-932 3433. Set in sumptuous surroundings, the emphasis here is on freshness of ingredients, with an à la carte menu featuring lots of game and some fine taster options. Their wine list is exemplary. The champagne bar next door is perfect for drinks, Asian-inspired snacks and live jazz.
♥♥♥ **Rimrock Café**, 2117 Whistler Rd in the **Highland Lodge**, Creekside, T604-932 5565. Probably the best in town and certainly the locals' choice, with a very comfortable, inviting interior that features a stone fire-place and small, intimate spaces. The up-market West Coast menu tends to focus on seafood, with some game, lamb and steaks.
♥♥ **21 Steps**, St Andrew's House, T604-966 2121. A stylish place equally suitable for food or drinks. The menu offers new twists on comfort foods, good portions at fair prices and a fine range of appetizers all made from scratch. There are cocktails, beer on tap and a good range of wines, many by the glass. The **Attic** upstairs is a lounge space set around a horseshoe bar.
♥♥ **Caramba!**, 4314 Main St, Village North, T604-938 1879. An incredibly popular venue thanks to its lively atmosphere and good, moderately priced Mediterr-anean dishes, such as calamari or the wood-oven pizzas.
♥♥ **Elements**, in the **Summit Lodge**, 4359 Main St, T604-932 5569. The best and swankiest place for West Coast-style tapas, many featuring seafood, and boutique wines and infused martinis. Also good for breakfast.
♥♥ **Kypriaki's**, opposite the **Telus Confer-ence Centre**, T604-9320600. Possibly the best Greek/Mediterranean food in town,

with great specials at reasonable prices. Laid-back and friendly ambience.

La Bocca, Village Sq, T604-932 2112. A funky, colourful interior dominated by a striking bar and a menu that focuses on eclectic West Coast fusion cuisine.

La Brasserie des Artistes, Village Sq, T604-932 3569. Stylish with a good atmosphere, reasonable prices and a great breakfast menu.

Pasta Lupino, 4368 Main St, Market Pavilion, Village North, T604-905 0400. Mix and match from a selection of fresh, home-made pastas and sauces in a tiny casual bistro setting. The prices are very reasonable prices.

Sushi Village, 2nd Floor, Sundial Hotel, T604-932 3330. A Whistler institution for over 20 years and understandably popular, with fresh fish, sake margaritas, top service and a casual, lively atmosphere.

Wild Wood, 4500 Northlands Blvd, Whistler Village North in the Tennis Club, T604-935 4077; 1085 Millar Creek Rd, Function Junction, T604-905 5066. Locally owned, these sophisticated bistro-bars feature broad menus of eclectic West Coast dishes, including seafood, steaks, lots of starters, sandwiches and very good breakfasts.

Dups Burrito, 4368 Main St, T604-905 0210. Big burritos made from fresh ingredients, all under $10. Great value.

Gone Bakery and Soup Co, behind Armchair Books, next to the liquor shop. Warm and cosy, a great spot for coffee, cakes, soups and salads.

Ingrid's Village Café, just off the Square, T604-932 7000. Cheap breakfasts and lunches, home-made bread and delicious sandwiches. Very popular.

Moguls Coffee Bean, Village Sq. Good for coffee or cheap food, including breakfasts, burritos, sandwiches and stir-fries.

South Side Diner, Whistler Creekside. Best for breakfast, but also an option for lunch and dinner. A local institution, with big portions.

Pemberton and beyond *p157*

Pony Espresso, 1426 Portage Rd, T604-894 5700. A popular hangout for locals, with good beer on tap, a deck on the roof and outdoor seating. The obvious choice

for coffee, breakfast and melts. Tasty dinner menu of salads, pasta and pizza.

Wicked Wheel Pizza Co, 2021 Portage Rd, Mt Currie, on the way to Lillooet, T604-894 6622. This is where locals go to treat themselves. Highly regarded and well worth the short drive from town.

Wild Wood, 101-1436 Portage Rd, T604-894 0114. Sister company to those in Squamish and Whistler.

Lillooet *p158*

Dina's, 690 Main St, T250-256 4264. Hands down the best choice in town. Popular and friendly, specializing in Greek cuisine.

⚘ Bars and clubs

Whistler *p152, map p154*

There are plenty of busy pubs around the village, most offering live music every weekend in the winter. For weekly listings pick up a free copy of *This Week*. Many of Whistler's best restaurants double up as wine bars and vice versa.

Amsterdam Café, Village Sq, T604-932 8334. Small, atmospheric and bursting with character.

Black's Pub, at the base of the Village gondola, T604-932 6408. With its prime location at the foot of Whistler Mountain, this place has fantastic views from the patio and the best selection of beers in town.

Brewhouse Pub, 4355 Blackcomb Way in Village North, T604-905 2739. A great place to relax and people watch. There's also a decent selection of microbrews, some pool tables and quite good food.

Buffalo Bill's, across from the Conference Centre, T604-932 6613, www.buffalobills.ca. With its huge dance floor, mainstream music, pool tables and TVs, this is the most party-oriented club in town.

Città, Village Sq, T604-932 4177. The patio here has the prime location on the square and is always packed with a lively crowd.

Dubh Linn Gate, 4320 Sundial Cres, T604-905 4047. A cosy and very popular Irish pub with a great selection of beers and decent food.

Garfinkel's, 4308 Main St, T604-932 2323. This underground club is Whistler's biggest, with an expansive sunken bar and a large stage. Attracts a lot of the major visiting acts.

Garibaldi Lift Company, 4165 Springs Lane, above the Whistler gondola loading area, T604-905 2220. A fun and happening spot in the thick of the action; bar by day, club by night.

Longhorn Saloon, Mountain Sq, T604-932 5999. Situated in the Skier's Plaza, with views of both gondolas, this is another easygoing spot to grab a beer and watch the crowds go by.

Mallard Lounge, in the Château Whistler, T604-938 8000. An upmarket, chic spot for cocktails made from fresh ingredients.

The Mix, 4237 Village Stroll, T604-932 6499. One of the best spots for a quiet drink.

Moe Joe's, Village Sq. A small but fun club playing funky dance tunes.

The Savage Beagle, Village Sq. Upstairs is a laid-back lounge and dining room, downstairs is a heaving dance floor. Both have an impressive selection of drinks.

Tommy Africa's, 4216 Gateway Dr, T604-932 6090. Attracts a younger crowd with hip-hop style sounds.

⊛ Festivals and events

Squamish and around *p151*
Jan Brackendale Winter Eagles Festival, will enjoy its 23rd year in 2009. Contact the Brackendale Art Gallery (see page 151) for details.

Jun Test of Metal Mountain Bike Race, T604-898 3519, www.testofmetal.com. One of the most exciting and prestigious mountain bike events in the world.

Aug Squamish Days Logger Sports, T604-892 9244, www.squamish days.org. This is the biggest chainsaw bonanza in Canada, with competitors from around the world, bed races, a parade, musical events, kids' activities and a pancake breakfast. It will celebrate its 50th birthday in 2008. Caribbean Summer Jam Festival, T604-892 8248. Plenty of lively music, food, dancing and entertainment mid-month.

Sep Cheakamus Challenge, www.cheak amuschallenge.ca. Toward month's end, this event closes the mountain bike season in style.

Whistler *p152, map p154*
Throughout the winter, Whistler plays host to a stream of ski and snowboard competitions. In summer, the spirit is kept alive with a number of mountain bike competitions and various smaller events. The best place to find out exactly what's going on is **Whistler-Blackcomb**, T604-932 3434, www.whistlerblack comb.com.

Jan Discover Whistler Days, gives guests 40% reductions on ski lessons for almost a month from mid-Jan. **Telus Winter Classic** is a weekend of skiing, food and entertainment at the end of the month.

Feb Peak to Valley Race, in early Feb and WinterPride, gay ski week. **Canadian Alpine Ski Championships**, follows shortly after. **FIS World Cup Alpine Ski Races**, runs for a week mid-month.

Apr Juvenile Ski Races, held in early Apr. **Telus World Ski and Snowboard Festival**, in mid-Apr. The biggest annual winter sports event in North America, a huge 10-day party featuring 50 free outdoor concerts, the world snowboarding championship and downhill skiing freestyle events.

Jul Children's Arts Festival , runs for 2 days in mid-Jul. **Crankworx**, www.crankworx.com. The most important mountain bike festival of the season.

Aug Whistler Music and Arts Festival, features 4 days of street entertainment, live music and interactive art activities.

Nov Cornucopia, T1888-999 4566, www. whistlercornucopia.com. A week-long food and wine festival. **Banff Mountain Film Festival**. Late in the month, the best of this festival is brought to Whistler for 2 days.

Dec Whistler Film Festival, T604-938 3200, www.whistlerfilmfestival.com. Starts in late Nov and gets everyone in the mood by showing mountain films, as well as other independent productions.

○ Shopping

Squamish and around *p151*
Vertical Reality, 37835 2nd Av, T604-892 8248. Biking, climbing, clothing and back-country gear.

Valhalla Pure Outfitters, Squamish Station Shopping Centre, 1200 Hunter Pl, T604-892 9092. The best place for camping gear, outdoor clothing and climbing equipment.

The market place in Village North has the most useful selection of shops, including an **IGA** supermarket. In Whistler Village, the grocery store, liquor store and **Armchair Books** are grouped together under one roof close to the square. **Franz's Trail Shopping Village** at Creekside contains a number of worthwhile speciality stores.

Arts and crafts

There are a number of art galleries in Whistler, many of them in hotels, such as **Mountain Galleries** in Chateau Whistler, T604-935 1862. **Black Tusk**, in the Hilton Hotel at 4293 Mountain Sq, T604-905 5540, www.black tusk.ca, has a wonderful collection of quality First Nations pieces worth seeing even if you're not looking to buy.

Clothing

Evolution, 4122 Village Green next to Buffalo Bills, 604-932 2967, and **Showcase Snowboards**, 4340 Sundial Cres, T604-938 7519, are 2 places to find some of the trendy clothes and accessories you see people modelling around town. **Open Country** in Chateau Whistler, T604-938 9268, carries some nice clothes and **Whistler Clearance Centre**, Village Sq, T604-932 6611, is where you can save up to 80% on gear, clothes and accessories.

▲▲ Activities and tours

For all types of activities along the Sea to Sky Highway, the free *99 North* magazine has excellent maps and listings.

North to Squamish *p150*
Golf

Furry Creek Golf and Country Club, just south of Britannia Beach, T604-896 2224. Great views, lots of water and a good (expensive) restaurant.

Scuba-diving

There are 10 dive sites accessible from the coast between Horseshoe Bay and Britannia Beach, the most celebrated being Whyte-cliff Park at Horseshoe Bay and Porteau Cove Provincial Park. See page 150 for more details and listings, page 76, for operators.

Squamish and around *p151*
Climbing

Almost 300 routes traverse the 625-m face of the Stawamus Chief, including the University Wall, considered Canada's most difficult climb. But the Chief is only one of many climbing venues around Squamish. The Smoke Bluffs, across from the entrance to town, is now a designated park, with developed pathways and over 300 routes of all levels that are better than ever. Murrin Provincial Park, 8 km south, has many more. *Squamish Select* by Marc Bourdon is a useful book with maps and descriptions of climbing and bouldering routes in the Squamish/Whistler area. A handy online guide is www.squamishclimbing.com. In winter, some challenging and excellent ice-climbing routes are to be found at Olesen Creek.

Squamish Rock Guides, T604-815 1750, www.squamishrockguides.com. Highly respected outfit offering anything from guiding to instruction to trips.
Vertical Reality Sports Store, 37835 2nd Av, T604-892 8248. A good source of information and also rents equipment.
Westcoast Mountain Guides, T604-892 4050, www.westcoastmountain guides. com. Rock- and ice-climbing guiding, instruction, mountaineering courses and backcountry ski touring offered by seasoned professionals.

Eagle spotting

Elaho Adventures, T1800-565 8735, www.elahoadventures.com. Whitewater rafting and eagle safaris.
Sunwolf Outdoor Centre, 70002 Squa mish Valley Rd in Brackendale, 4 km off Hwy 99, 10 km north of town, T604-898 1537, www.sunwolf.net. Watch the eagles from dry land or from the river. Whitewater rafting/kayaking also arranged.

Golf

Garibaldi Springs, just north of Squamish, T604-898 8356, www.garibaldisprings golfresort.com. Very scenic, incorporating salmon streams, waterfalls and rock faces.

Mountain biking

There are countless trails around Squamish, suitable for all levels up to the most extreme.

The majority are concentrated in the Smoke Bluffs and Crumpit Woods area east of town, or around Alice Lake and the Garibaldi Highlands further north.

Tantalus Bike Shop, 40194 Glenalder Pl, The Garibaldi Village Shopping Centre, T604-898 2588, www.tantalusbikeshop.com. The best place for bike equipment or rentals, can also offer good advice and information.

Vertical Reality, 37835 2nd Av, T604-892 8248. Rent and sell gear, and also organize bike touring.

Watersports

A popular spot for windsurfing, kiteboarding and whitewater kayaking is Squamish Spit just past the Railway Heritage Park about 3 km from town. It's maintained by the **Squamish Windsports Society**, T604-892 2235, www.squamishwindsurfing.org, who charge a small fee ($15). See their website for a map and Spit rules. On a good day, this makes for a great spectator sport.

Sea to Sky Ocean Sports, 37819 2nd Av, T604-892 3366, www.seatoskyocean sports.com. Kayak rentals, tours, sales and lessons. Also windsurfing, diving and snorkelling.

Whistler *p152, map p154*

Whistler is all about outdoor activities; the only difficulty is in choosing what to do. The website www.tourismwhistler.com, lists activities, tours operators and rental companies. Activities can be booked using www.whistler.com, T1800-944 78537.

Bungee Jumping

Whistler Bungee, T1877-938 9333, www.whistlerbungee.com. Free-fall from a 160-ft bridge towards a glacier-fed river.

Climbing

Nordic Rock, in Nordic Estates between the Village and Creekside and Cal-Cheak, 13 km south of Whistler, are the key sites for rock climbing. Ice climbing with **Whistler Alpine Guides Bureau** (see Tour operators, page 166) on a glacier is also available Jun-Oct.

The Core, located below Telus Conference Centre, T604-905 7625, www.whistler core.com, has 1670 sq m of indoor rock climbing for adults and kids, lessons, courses, equipment rental and a bouldering zone.

'Kids Climb and Dine' gives parents a night off by providing climbing instruction and dinner for $65 per child. They also organize outdoor guided climbs.

Dog-sledding

Blackcomb Sled Dogs, T604-932 8484, www.blackcombsnowmobile.com. 2½-hr tours leave 4 times daily and cost $160 per person. They also run snowmobile tours.

Fishing

99 North's summer edition lists 28 lakes and 11 rivers that are prime spots, mostly for trout and Dolly Varden. You need a non-tidal angling licence and should be aware of quotas, regulations and closures. Contact T604-666 0384, www.dfo-mpo.gc.ca, for further information.

Whistler Fishing Guides, T604-932 4267, www.whistlerriver.com. Organize river fishing and float trips all year round.

Golf

Whistler has a lot of courses, many of which are world class, as well as spectacular.

Chateau Whistler , T604-938 2095, www.fair mont.com/whistler. Beautifully merges with the surrounding countryside.

Nicklaus North, T604-938 9898. Designed by the pro; one of the best and most scenic.

Whistler Golf Club, T604-932 3280, www.whistlergolf.com. Designed by Arnold Palmer, it has 9 lakes and 2 creeks.

Helicopter tours

Blackcomb Helicopters, T604-938 1700, www.blackcombhelicopters.com. Glacier sightseeing tours start at $179 per person for 20 mins.

Hiking

Hiking around Whistler is prime and you don't have to be fit to hike in the alpine around here. Throughout the summer, the gondola whisks hikers up to breathtaking views of Black Tusk, Cheakamus Glacier and Cheakamus Lake and the start of numerous hikes. The Peak chair ($30/$24 with gondola) then ascends another 1000 m to the top of Whistler Mountain and 48 km of elevation trails. Blackcomb offer free guided tours daily at 1130. In 2009, sightseers will be able to take the Peak to Peak Gondola between Whistler and Blackcomb mountains, to witness undreamed-of vistas without having to hike at all.

Ice-skating

For those going it alone, Green Lake is a popular spot.

Whistler Outdoor Experience, T604-932 3389, www.whistleroutdoor.com. Organizes outdoor skating at Edgewater Outdoor Centre, 5km N of the Village. $5 per person or $10-12 for 1- or 2-day rentals.

Mountain biking

There are dozens of bike trails in the valley, particularly around Lost and Green Lakes, in Whistler North and the Whistler Interpretive Forest. Bikers can also carry their steeds on the lift ($47) up to Whistler Mountain Bike Zone, May-Sep daily 1000-1700, which consists of 200 km of single-track trails and 1450 m of vertical drop. They also offer lessons and tours, from $93/½-day, $118/ day, including lift.

Cross Country Connection, Lost Lake Park, just off Lorimer Rd, T604-905 0071, www.crosscountryconnection.bc.ca. Rentals, tours, instruction and information.

Ticket2RideBC, 7162 Nancy Greene Dr, Whistler, T604-938 6230, www.ticket2ride bc.com. Tailored mountain biking holidays for all levels, guided adventures including heli-drops, instruction and accommodation. Recommended.

Whistler Bike Company, 4050 Whistler Way. Bike rentals.

Rafting

Whistler River Adventures, Whistler Mountain gondola, T604-932 3532, www.whistlerriver.com. $75 for 2 hrs on the Cheakamus or Green Rivers for beginners, or longer trips on the Elaho-Squamish Rivers for thrill-seekers.

Sleigh Rides

Whistler Outdoor Experience, T604-932 3389, www.whistleroutdoor.com. Horse-drawn sleigh tours along the shores of Green lake, leave hourly and cost $55, child $27.50, for 30 mins.

Snowmobiling

Canadian Snowmobile Adventures , T604-938 1616, www.canadiansnowmobile. com. Offer anything from 2-hr cruises ($89 per person sharing) to 8-hr tours ($600 per single rider) to 4-hr fondue packages ($189 per person sharing).

Swimming

For indoor swimming, **Meadow Park Recreation Centre**, 6 km north on Hwy 99, T604-935 7529, has a pool, exercise room, skating rink, sauna and hot tub. For outdoor swimming, there are plenty of lakes, including Lost Lake.

Tour operators

Cougar Mountain, 18-4314 Main St, T604-932 4086, www.cougarmountain.ca. Wide range of backcountry adventures including snowmobile, Hummer or ATV tours, snowshoeing, dog sledding, zip-lining, fishing and horse riding.

Whistler Activity and Information Centre, 4010 Whistler Way off Hwy 99, T604-938 2769, daily 0900-1700. Can arrange any activity for you.

Whistler Activity Central, T604-935 4528, www.activitiescentral.com. A private company that also deals with all the activities listed here and claims to get the best rates. Shop around.

Whistler Alpine Guides Bureau, T604-938 3228, www.whistlerguides.com. Arranges tours and instruction for backcountry winter and summer touring; skiing, snowboarding, ice climbing and mountaineering.

Ziplining

Ziptrek Ecotours, inside Carleton Lodge across from Whistler Village Gondola, T604-935 0001, www.ziptrek.com. Careen down Fitzsimmons Creek attached to a zipline. The highest is 340 m up. Open year round, $98, child $78 for a 2½-hr tour. They also arrange treks through the tree tops along suspension bridges and boardwalks, $39, child $29 for a 1½-hr tour.

Skiing Whistler and Blackcomb *p157*
Alpine skiing

On a fresh powder day the **Fresh Tracks Breakfast** is highly recommended. Tickets, $17 on top of the regular lift pass, can be

reserved or bought at the lift. Turn up at 0700; you are taken up to the Roundhouse for a buffet breakfast then let out onto the fresh snow between 0730-0800, 1 hr or so before the regular crowds arrive. **Mountain Hosts**, run a free ski-guiding tour run daily at 1130, good for getting to know the mountains. Basic avalanche awareness courses are also available. For weather, snow and lift reports, and all current information, T604-932 3434, T1866-218 9684, www.whistlerblackcomb.com.
Affinity Sports, Clock Tower Inn, T604-938 8059; Blackcomb Lodge, T604-932 2141; Pinnacle Hotel, T604-932 6461; Cascade Lodge, T604-932 6770; Glacier Lodge, T604-938 3100; Chamois Hotel, T604-938 1743. Ski and snowboard gear, free shuttle and storage.
Whistler Ski School, T1866-218 9681. One of the best in North America. Learn to ski packages start at about $70 per day, $600 per day with a private instructor.

Backcountry skiing
Backcountry skiing is available all around Whistler, especially in Garibaldi Provincial Park (see page 152), but only for those with experience or with a guide.

Cat- and Heli-skiing
For real enthusiasts, Cats and helicopters get you higher, deeper into the backcountry with even more spectacular views and guaranteed fresh powder.
Powder Mountain Cat Skiing, T604-932 0169, www.powdermountaincatskiing. com. $480 for a full day.
Whistler Heli-Skiing, T1888-435 4754, www.whistlerheliskiing.com. Starts at about $730 per person for 3 runs.

Cross-country skiing, Nordic skiing and snowshoeing
Cross Country Connection, Lorimer Rd, T604-905 0071, www.crosscountryconn ection.bc.ca, oversees over 60 km of groomed cross-country trails, many of them around Lost Lake, connecting to Chateau Whistler and Nicklaus North golf courses, or at the brand new Whistler Olympic Park in the Callaghan Valley. Alternatively, the Valley Trail links the Village, Lost Lake, Alta Lake, Alpha Lake

and beyond. Hours are roughly 0900-2000 daily, with trails illuminated at night, $16, under 18 $10, under 12 $8, family $32. They also offer gear rentals ($24, under 18 $16, under 12 $12 per day), lessons, tours, snowshoeing and provide free trail maps.

Pemberton and beyond *p157*
Fishing
There are plenty of spots for fishing. Joffre Lake and Blackwater Lake (south of D'Arcy) contain rainbow trout.

Flightseeing
Pemberton Soaring Centre, Airport Rd, T1800-831 2611, www.pembertonsoaring. com. Customized glider flights over the Pemberton Valley, from $85 for 15 mins.

Golf
Pemberton Valley Golf and Country Club, off Hwy 99 N on the way to Mt Currie, T604-894 6197, www.pembertongolf.com.

Heli-skiing
Coast Range Heli-skiing, T1800-701 8744, www.coastrangeheliskiing.com. A 4-run package is $845.

Mountain biking
Pemberton Bike Co, 1392 Portage Rd, T604-894 6625, www.bikecowhistler.com. Rentals and trail information.

Lillooet *p158*
The local Native St'át'imc people offer a variety of cultural tours and experiences. Find out more at T250-256 0673, www. uslces.org.
Fishing
Seton Lake and the Fraser River are both good for rainbow trout and sturgeon.

● Transport

Squamish and around *p151*
Air
Sea to Sky Air, T604-898 1975, www.sea toskyair.ca. Daily scheduled flights to and from Squamish Airport from **Vancouver** ($130 one-way), Nanaimo ($100), Powell River ($160) and Campbell River ($180), plus a number of sightseeing tours.

Bus

All **Greyhound** buses (see Whistler, below) stop downtown and at Squamish bus station, 1 km north on Hwy 99 at Garibaldi Highlands (roughly $10 one-way from Vancouver or Whistler). All **Perimeter** buses stop at Squamish Adventure Centre.

Whistler *p152, map p154*
Bus
Local Whistler Village is small enough to get around on foot, but for the periphery there's an efficient local transit system, **The Wave**, T604-932 4020, www.bus online.ca, which links the many satellite suburbs, with all routes converging on Village Gate Blvd ($1.50). The free **Village Shuttle** runs around the village and to the gondolas all day. In Jul and Aug, a free shuttle (No 33) runs to Lost Lake from the Whistler gondolas.

   Long distance Whistler's buses stop at the Bus Loop, handily located next to Tourism Whistler, where outward tickets are sold. **Greyhound**, T1800-661 8747, www.greyhound.ca, runs 9 daily buses from **Vancouver** ($20 one-way), 8 stopping in Squamish, 6 continuing to Pemberton. Their non-stop Ski Express leaves Vancouver at 0630 arriving at the Village 0830. **Snow-bus**, T604-685 7669, www.snowbus.ca, leaves Burrard Skytrain Mon-Thu 0630, 1355, Fri 0630, 1355, 1820, Sat-Sun 0700, 1520, $24 one-way, $43 return. **Perimeter Whistler Express**, T1877-317 7788, www.perimeter bus.com, leaves 9 times daily (7 in summer) from the airport and major hotels, $67 one-way.

Car
The highway to Whistler is overcrowded and works will be in progress intermittently to widen the road in time for 2010. For up-to-the-minute information, T1877-472 3399, www.whistler.com/road_conditions. Parking in Whistler is about $10/night. **Avis Rent-a-car**, Whistler Cascade Lodge, 4315 Northlands Blvd, T604-9321236; **Budget Car Rental**, Coast Hotel, 4005 Whistler Way, T604-935 4122.

Taxi
Whistler Resort Cabs, T604-938 1515.

Train
Rocky Mountaineer, T604-606 7245, www.whistlermountaineer.com, is a picturesque 3-hr train journey to and from **North Vancouver**, with an open-air observation car at extra cost. Leaves Vancouver mid-Apr to mid-Oct daily 0730, $110, child $60, one-way, $199, child $109, return, including bus trans-port from Downtown to North Vancouver and into Whistler Village from the Whistler railway station.

Skiing Whistler and Blackcomb *p157*
The **Whistler Express, Fitzsimmons Express** and **Blackcomb Excalibur** gondolas leave from the south side of Whistler Village. The **Wizard Express** and **Magic Chair** lifts both head up to Blackcomb from the Upper Village. The **Creekside Gondola** heads up Whistler Mountain from Creekside, which has its own mini-village and infrastructure.

● Directory

Squamish and around *p151*
Internet Comfy's Internet Cafe 38201 Westway 1, T604-892 9870. **Laundry** Cascade Laundry, 38921 Progress Way, T604-892 9270. **Medical services** Sea to Sky Walk In Clinic, 1060 Edgewater Cres, T604-898 5555; Squamish General Hospital, 38140 Behrner, T604-892 5211. **Post office** Canada Post Cleveland Av/Victoria.

Whistler *p152, map p154*
Banks TD Bank, Market Pl, Village North, T604-905 5500; Thomas Cook, Market Pl, Village North, T604-938 0111. **Emergencies** 911; Police Village Gate Blvd/Blackcomb Way, T604-932 3044; Search and rescue, T604-932 2328. **Internet** Cyber Web Internet Café, 4340 Sundial Cres, T604-905 1280; Library; Whistler Java Boutique Café, in the Summit Lodge, 4359 Main St, T604-938 5924. **Laundry** Nesters Laundromat, 7009 Nesters, T604-932 2960. **Library** 4329 Main St, by the car park, Village North, T604-932 5564, currently under expansion and renovation. **Medical services** Aarm Dental Group, Timberline Lodge, above Buffalo Bill's, T604-966 0599; Town Plaza

Medical Clinic, 4314 Main St, T604-905 7089, open daily, no appointment necessary; **Whistler Health Care Centre**, 4380 Lorimer, T604-932 4911.

Photography Whistler One Hour Foto Source, in the Crystal Lodge, close to the Village Sq, T604-932 6676. **Post office** Canada Post Market Pl.

TransCanada and Crowsnest highways

Heading east from Vancouver, Highway 1 splits in three at Hope. Highway 5 (the Coquihalla Highway) is a high-speed, less attractive route to Kamloops (or Kelowna via Highway 97C) with a $10 toll. Highway 1 (the TransCanada Highway) is the most direct route to the Rockies; there are few reasons to stop but it's a beautiful drive through some wonderfully varied landscapes: the steep walls and thrashing water of the Fraser Canyon; the arid vistas of the Thompson Valley; weirdly-shaped expanses of water in the Shuswap; and increasingly sublime mountain scenery in the Columbia Mountains. Highway 3 – the Crowsnest Highway – is mostly scenic with some boring stretches. It skirts the US border, offering direct access to Nelson (West Kootenays) and Osoyoos (Okanagan), with a few highlights of its own, such as Manning Provincial Park and the ski villages of Rossland and Fernie. ▸▸ For Sleeping, Eating and other listings, see pages 176-188.

Ins and outs

Getting there and around

There are airports offering internal flights in Kamloops, **Kamloops Airport** ① *6 km northwest of town, T250-376 3613, www.kamloopsairport.com*, Castlegar and Cranbrook. **Greyhound** runs four buses daily between Vancouver and Calgary, serving most of the destinations in this chapter, as well as Banff; and two daily buses from Vancouver to the Alberta border, serving most of the Crowsnest Highway destinations in this chapter. The route is Vancouver to Hope (Highway 1) to Merritt (Highway 5) to Kelowna (Highway 97C) to Rock Creek (Highway 33) to the Alberta Border (Highway 3) via Nelson. **Via Rail** ① *T1800-5618630, www.viarail.ca*, runs trains from Vancouver to Jasper via Kamloops three times a week. ▸▸ *For further details, see Transport, page 187.*

Tourist information

All but the smallest towns on these routes have Visitor Information Centres. The most useful are in Hope, Kamloops, Revelstoke, Salmon Arm and Castlegar, and at the Highway 5/Highway 5A junction at Merritt.

TransCanada Highway ⊜🚗🛶🛷❄️⛰️🚌⛴️ ▸▸ *pp176-188.*

Vancouver to Hope → *Colour map 1, C4 and C5.*

The string of sprawling suburbs that line the TransCanada as it follows the Fraser River east from Vancouver barely lets up until you clear Chilliwack, some 120 km from Downtown. This suburban corridor is the main artery of the Lower Mainland, which contains most of BC's population. The first real diversion, north to **Harrison Hot Springs,** is only really worthwhile during the annual Festival of the Arts in July.

A quicker, easier diversion is to the spectacular **Bridal Veil Falls**, a 15-minute leg-stretch reached via exit 135.

Most people drive right past **Hope** on their way somewhere else, but there's some good hiking and biking around, including the **Othello Quintette Tunnels**, a 90-m-deep solid granite wall that was blasted through in 1911 as part of the Kettle Valley Railway (see page 193). Ask for details at the **Hope Visitor Information Centre and Museum Complex** ⓘ *919 Water Av, T604-869 2021, www.destinationhopeandbeyond.com.*

Fraser Canyon → *Colour map 1, C5.*

Between Hope and Lytton, the tumultuous Fraser River's massive volume of water is forced through a narrow channel between the sheer rock faces of the Cascade and Coast mountains, gouging out a steep, awe-inspiring canyon. Since the Fraser was the only river in southern BC to penetrate the mountain barrier, road and railway builders were obliged to follow this unlikely route. By either means, the journey is breathtaking.

The prettiest part of this spectacular drive is around tiny **Yale**, which is surrounded by sheer cliffs. It's hard to believe but, during the Fraser Valley Gold Rush, this sleepy village of less than 200 was a steamship navigation capital and one of North America's largest cities, with a population of over 20,000. You can find out all about it at the small **Yale Museum** ⓘ *31187 Douglas St, T250-863 2324, May-Sep daily 1000-1700, by donation*, on the highway. Also here is the summer-only Visitor Information Booth.

Fraser River reaches its awesome crescendo at **Hell's Gate**, where it is forced through a gorge 38 m wide and 180 m deep. The thrashing water reaches a depth of 60 m and thunders through with incredible power. The **Hell's Gate Airtram Gondola** ⓘ *T250-867 9277, www.hellsgateairtram.com, Apr-Oct daily 1000-1600, $16, under 18 $10, under 5 free*, carries up to 2500 people a day across the canyon for up-close views. Free canyon views can be had 8 km south at **Alexander Bridge Provincial Park**.

Heading north, the scenery remains spectacular, slowly taking on the dry, Wild West characteristics of the Thompson Valley, which the highway follows from Lytton. There's little to recommend the remaining towns, except as bases for some of the province's best rafting. There are excellent adrenaline-charged rapids just north of **Boston Bar** and further north between Spences Bridge and Lytton, with rapids such as the Jaws of Death.

At **Cache Creek**, Highway 1 veers eastwards. This funny little town, which has retained a distinctive 1950s feel, is surrounded by exceptional scenery, an arid, rocky moonscape of vast wrinkled mounds in shades of yellow and red, practically vegetation-free. The 'Painted Bluffs' between Savona and Ashcroft offer the best example of these colourful rock formations.

Kamloops → *Colour map 1, B6.*

The sublime Thompson Valley landscape between Cache Creek and Kamloops provides a magnificent setting for this bland city. The endless hills of semi-desert, with their subtle hues and weird shapes, are an unlikely location for the second largest city in BC's interior, but a chance meeting of valleys has made this an important transport hub ever since the days when the canoe was the vehicle of choice. The Shuswap name, Cumloops, means 'meeting of the waters'. Today the Canadian Pacific and Canadian National railways, as well as two major highways connecting Vancouver, the Rockies and points east, south and north all converge here. It's a tough place to avoid, but there's little reason to stop except in August when one of the best powwows in the country takes place (see Festivals, page 183).

⁞ Hell's Gate

Along the TransCanada Highway, you can find out the history of Simon Fraser, after whom the river is named. One of the greatest early explorers of North America, he was seeking a route to the Pacific, and followed the river along its whole 1300-km course thinking it was the Columbia. The hellish canyon section, driven today in a couple of hours, cost him 35 days of hard labour to cross.

For a long time it was believed that the canyon was impassable, and indeed it feels like a miracle of engineering and sheer audacity that the nation's major highway and railway go through it. In places the rock had to be blasted out. It has been estimated, for instance, that the Hell's Gate section of Fraser Canyon cost the lives of three Chinese workers for every kilometre of line that was laid.

Five minutes north on Highway 5, **Secwepemc Museum and Heritage Park** ① *T250-828 9749, www.secwepemc.org/museum, May-Sep daily 0800-1600, Oct-Apr Mon-Fri 0800-1600, $6, under 18 $3, under 5 free*, is an interesting place to learn more about the Secwepemc, or Shuswap, whose culture thrived here for thousands of years. As well as displays on hunting, fishing, clothing, games, food gathering and cooking, there are the archaeological remains of a 2000-year old Secwepemc winter village, four reconstructed winter pit houses, a summer village and a 5-ha park containing Ethnobotanical Gardens.

If you want to explore the surrounding area, a two-hour walk, starting 4 km west on Tranquille Road, leads to the **Hoodoos**, tall sandstone sculptures carved by wind and water. Alternatively, go hunting for semi-precious stones and fossils with a guided geological tour or visit **BC Wildlife Park**, ① *20 Km E on Hwy 1 at 9077 Dallas Dr, T250-573 3242, www.bczoo.org, Jul-Aug daily 0930-2000, May, June and Sep 0930-1700, Sep-May 0930-1600, $12, youth $11, child $9.* This 50-ha park contains over 60 species including cougars, grizzly bears, wolves, moose and mountain goats.

Nearby **Sun Peaks Ski Resort** ① *follow Hwy 5 north for 19 km to Heffley Creek, then right for 31 km at the Sun Peaks sign, www.sunpeaksresort.com, lift passes are $67, youth $54, child $34 per day, cross-country $12, child $9*, is one of the interior's best. With 122 runs up to 8 km long on 1500 ha of skiable terrain, which includes two vast alpine bowls and a 881-m vertical drop, **Sun Peaks** is BC's second largest ski area, serviced by 12 lifts capable of handling 12,000 skiers per hour. The breakdown favours experienced skiers and snowboarders, with 58% of runs intermediate and 32% expert. There's also a kids' terrain garden, 40 km of cross- country trails and the bonus of 2000 hours of sun per year (hence the name). The village has everything you could need, including cafés, restaurants, bars, clubs, lessons, rentals and plenty of places to stay. There's also lift-assisted mountain biking and hiking in the summer.

The Shuswap → *Colour map 2, B1.*

East of Kamloops, the arid vistas of the Thompson Valley give way to duller scenery and an abundance of water. The strangely shaped **Shuswap Lake** provides 1130 km of shoreline, beaches and waterways to explore. Of the many provincial parks in the Shuswap, the most popular and dramatic is **Cinnemousun Narrows**. The classic way to see the lake is in a houseboat from Sicamous (see Activities and tours, page 184) and the alternative is to rent a canoe and take a tent.

In summer, the Shuswap can get incredibly busy and booked up. The further you get from the highway, the smaller the hordes, but it is debatable whether the rewards justify the effort. One undeniable draw is **Roderick Haig-Brown Provincial Park** ⓘ *5 km north of an excellent hostel in Squilax*, on the north shore, which is the province's best place to witness the autumn return of migrating salmon, especially every fourth year when some 1.5 million fish turn the Adams River a brilliant red.

The Shuswap's rapidly expanding main resort town, **Salmon Arm**, is a disappointment, but there's a pleasant 9-km boardwalk trail along the lake in Waterfront Park, starting at the **Visitor Information Centre** ⓘ *200 Hwy 1, T250-832 2230, www.shuswap.bc.ca*. Pick up the very informative *Trail Guide* here. Between May and September you're likely to see one of the 250 pairs of endangered western grebe performing their extraordinary mating dance. Rock-climbing is big at nearby **Haines Creek** and there's a stunning historical suspension bridge at **Malakwa**, 17 km east of Sicamous.

Revelstoke → *Colour map 2, B2.*

As the TransCanada enters the lofty Columbia Mountains, the scenery takes a dramatic upswing with increasingly frequent glimpses of the majestic Rockies. Situated amidst giant trees halfway between Sicamous and Revelstoke, the **Enchanted Forest** ⓘ *T250-837 9477, www.enchantedforestbc.com, May-Sep 0900-2000, May, Jun and Sep 1000-1800, $8, child $7*, is a must for kids, featuring hundreds of fairy-tale settings and characters, some crazy giant tree houses, a long stretch of boardwalk and an 800 year-old cedar grove. **Revelstoke**, besides its splendid location, is a friendly, attractive town with top-notch outdoor pursuits and lots of heritage buildings sporting turrets and wrap-around balconies. A self-guided tour brochure is available from the two **Visitor Information Centres** ⓘ *204 Campbell Av, T250-8375345, www.seerevelstoke.com, open year-round; and corner of Hwys 1 and 23 N, T250- 837 3522, open summer only*. The town's only real sight is **Revelstoke Railway Museum** ⓘ *Victoria Rd, opposite the bears, T250-837 6060, www.railwaymuseum.com, Aug- May daily 0900-1700, Jun-Jul daily 0900-2000, $8, under 16 $4, under 6 free*, whose highlights include an entire passenger car, a locomotive and an interactive diesel simulator. Otherwise, Revelstoke is a major hub for outdoor activities. **Mount Revelstoke National Park** has some popular walking trails and fabulous wild flowers in July and August.

The recently developed **Revelstoke Mountain Ski Resort** ⓘ *4 km south of town, T1866-373 4754, www.revelstokemountainresort.com, lift passes $56, youth $42, child $32*, is now one of the province's finest. It has 27 runs and four alpine bowls, accessed by four lifts, including an eight-passenger high-speed gondola which will transport sightseers 900 vertical metres in seven minutes ($15). The 607 ha of terrain breaks down at 7% beginner, 37% intermediate and 55% advanced. A regular bus service runs from Downtown to the hill on weekends throughout the ski season ($2).

Glacier National Park → *Colour map 2, B2.*

ⓘ *For daily updated information about snow conditions call Backcountry Report, T250-837 6867.*

With the Rockies so close, not many people stop to admire this chunk of the **Selkirk Mountains**, yet the peaks here are just as impressive and even more snow-laden. As its name suggests, Glacier National Park's defining feature is the 422 fields of permanent ice that cloak an incredible 14% of its area year-round. Whereas most of the world's glaciers are rapidly retreating, the largest one here, **Illecillewaet Neve**, is still growing and some 70 new glaciers have been identified. The weather that fuels this ice-factory is wet and frequently abysmal.

Rogers Pass is recognized as one of the best backcountry skiing areas in the world, with some 1349 sq km of terrain featuring descents of up to 1500 m. For all but the most experienced, a professional guide is essential as avalanches are very common. Hikes in the park tend to be short and striking. Unfortunately, you're never very far from the highway. *Footloose in the Columbias* is a useful hiking guide to Glacier and Revelstoke national parks. There is a very helpful **Visitor Information Centre** ① *1 km west of Rogers Pass, T250-837 6274, www.pc.gc.ca/pn-np/bc/glacier, Jun-Sep 0730-2000, May and Nov 0830-1630, Dec-Apr 0700-1700*. As well as trail maps and information it has a number of impressive and entertaining hi-tech displays and guided walks are offered in the summer. There's a very helpful map of the park in *The Mountain Guide*, available throughout the Rockies at Visitor Information Centres.

Hikes in Glacier National Park

Glacier Crest ① *10.4 km return; 1005 m elevation gain. Trailhead: turn into Illecillewaet Campground and proceed just over 1 km to car park.* This glorious trail takes you up the ridge between the park's two major glacier-bearing valleys, Illecillewaet and Asulkan, with ample views of both. You start in an old-growth forest, follow a burbling stream, ascend a steep canyon wall into a land of icy peaks and top out at a viewpoint offering dramatic 360 degree views. The last stretch is dangerous when wet, so do not attempt after recent rain.

Perley Rock ① *11.4 km return; 1162 m elevation gain. Trailhead: as above.* This steep and challenging trail would be a torment without the well-built switchbacks. The Illecillewaet Glacier is again on full display, along with the polished bedrock beneath its receding tongue. The higher you go, the better the views get and on the way back they're even better.

Hermit Basin ① *5.6 km return; 770 m elevation gain. Trailhead: 1.4 km northeast of Rogers Pass Information Centre.* Even steeper than the above but well maintained, this trail leads to a tiny alpine shelf with great views of the peaks and glaciers on the park's south side. There are four tent pads for overnight stays.

Bald Mountain ① *35.2 km return; 1354 m elevation gain. Trailhead: 11 km northeast of Rogers Pass; or 11.5 km south of northeast park entrance, turn onto Beaver Valley/ Copperstain Rd. Go left after 1.2 km and proceed 200 m.* This long and little-used trail slogs through old-growth forest for most of the first day but then rewards you with an 8-km-long ridge covered in wild flower meadows (prime grizzly bear habitat). The scenery is gobsmacking, with the glacier-supporting massif in full view across the valley.

Golden → *Colour map 2, B2.*

Golden's location could hardly be more fortuitous: halfway between Glacier and Yoho national parks at the junction of the Columbia and Kicking Horse rivers, with the Selkirk and Purcell ranges to the west and the Rockies just to the east. Naturally enough, this is yet another magnet for adventure enthusiasts and, with the arrival of **Kicking Horse Ski Resort** ① *13 km from Golden, T250-439 5424, www.kickinghorse resort.com, mid-Dec to mid-Apr, $59, youth $49, child $27*, the area is booming. The Resort is the most recent large ski hill to be built in British Columbia, offering 1100 ha of award-winning powder, a pair of alpine bowls and a vertical rise of 1260 m. The eight-person Golden Eagle Express Gondola whisks skiers up 3413 m in 12 minutes to the highest peak, from where 106 runs (20% beginner, 20% intermediate, 45% advanced and 15% expert) fan out into the open spaces. In summer the lifts stay open for alpine hiking and diners. There is a **ski bus** ① *daily, 0600, 0705, 0815, 1010*, which runs during the season and leaves from various points in town.

Inevitably, the town fails to live up to its setting, though the ugly stretch of services on the highway bears no relation to the small, fairly pleasant centre.

The **Visitor Information Centre** ① *500 10th Av, T250-344 7125, www.goldenchamber. bc.ca*, is open year-round and is one of the pick-up points for the ski bus. From here it is about 60 km to Field in Yoho National Park (see page 308) and 11 km more to Lake Louise (see page 281), crossing the Alberta border (and putting clocks forward 1 hour) on the way.

Bugaboo Provincial Park

South of Golden, Highway 95 runs through the relatively disappointing Columbia Valley and a string of mediocre towns to join Highway 3 at dismal Cranbrook. Reached by a good 45-km gravel road from Spillimacheen, 65 km south of Golden, Bugaboo Provincial Park is famous in rock-climbing circles for its spectacular granite spires. Though the long access is off-putting, a couple of good trails allow hikers to enjoy the park's rugged beauty and extensive glaciers. Climbers should get the *Nat Topo Map 82K/10* and/or *82K/15* and might enjoy *Bugaboo Rock: A Climber's Guide* by R Green and J Benson.

Hikes in Bugaboo National Park

Bugaboo Spires ① *10 km return; 660 m elevation gain. Trailhead: parking lot at Km 43.3.* Leads to the base of the spires and Conrad Kain Hut, which sleeps 40 people and is equipped with propane stoves. Exploring beyond is recommended.

Cobalt Lake ① *17.4 km return; 930 m elevation gain. Trailhead: as above.* Involves a lot of hard work before mind-expanding views take over. A shorter trail (10 km return) leads from Bugaboo Lodge, which is operated by Canadian Mountain Holidays.

Crowsnest Highway ⬤🌊🚶❄️▲🚗🍷 ➤ *pp176-188.*

Manning Provincial Park

From Hope, Highway 3 climbs quite steeply into the Cascade Mountains, through a vast area of wilderness with no communities to speak of until Princeton, which is 126 km away. This area is liable to have snow most of the year and, in winter, is excellent for cross-country skiing, with some 130 km of ungroomed backcountry trails, a small ski hill and 30 km of groomed trails. Most of the hiking trails begin around the park's only accommodation, the Manning Park Resort (see Sleeping, page 179), also a good source of information. Some other good trails are accessed from Lightning Lake, including the hike to the east peak of **Frosty Mountain** ① *7 ½-hr return*, the park's highest point; it's a steep climb, rewarded by a ridge walk with fantastic views. **Princeton**, the first town east of the pass, is renowned in angling circles, boasting 48 trout-fishing lakes within 60 km, 15 of them clustered together about 37 km north on Highway 5A.

Hedley → *Colour map 1, C6.*

As the landscapes tend increasingly toward the arid, rolling hills of the Okanagan, the stretch east to Osoyoos is one of the most scenic sections of this highway. The tiny village of Hedley was once one of the most important gold-mining towns in BC. The museum, which doubles as a **Visitor Information Centre** ① *712 Daly St, signposted from the highway, T250-292 8422, www.hedleybc.ca, mid-May to mid-Sep daily 0900-1700, mid-Sep to mid-May Thu-Mon, by donation*, has photos, artefacts and information about the interesting remains and historic buildings around town. Borrow their binoculars to see from the porch the remains of **Mascot Gold** Mine ① *T250-292 8733, www.mascotmine.com, $37, child $29, shuttles leave the museum Jul-Aug daily 0900, 1400, May-Jun and Sep-Oct Sat-Sun 0900, 1400*, set amongst dramatic swirls of rock. The **Upper Similkameen Native Band** runs three-hour tours up to the mine including a 200 m underground tunnel, fabulous views of the valley and details about the history of mining in the area and the Similkameen people.

East to Christina Lake

East of Keremeos (see page 195) and Osoyoos (see page 194), the highway runs through some fascinating rocky landscapes, the scenery slowly shifting from the barrenness of the Okanagan to the densely forested mountains of the Kootenays. The best reasons to stop are the **Kettle River Museum** ① *T250-449 2614, $2*, in Midway, which celebrates the Kettle Valley Railway; and the quaint town of **Greenwood**, whose Wild West appearance is more natural than contrived.

The town of **Christina Lake** has few facilities and poor lake access. Fortunately over half of the beautiful, very warm lake is contained within **Gladstone Provincial Park** and easily accessed via the **Texas-Alpine turning** ① *5 km north on the highway; turn onto Alpine Rd and continue to the end for the campground*. A very satisfying hiking and biking trail begins here, hugging the lake to its northern tip. A right fork then continues deep into the park, the left leading to more private wilderness campsites, one close by on Christina Lake, another on Xenia Lake further west. You could also hire a canoe and cross the main lake to one of the remote wilderness campgrounds on the west shore. ▸▸ *For further details, see Sleeping page 179.*

East to Rossland → *Colour map 2, C2.*

At the junction with Highway 3B, **Nancy Greene Provincial Park** contains a lovely lake you can ski round, with a beach for summer swimming and fishing. Highway 3 carries on to Castlegar, but it's well worth making a diversion down Highway 3B to **Rossland**, one of the great unsung skiing Meccas and 'mountain bike capital of Canada'. Most people who live here are obsessed with one or both of these activities, so the atmosphere is saturated with an outdoor mentality. In winter the population doubles as the town fills up with ski-bums. Besides being young, lively and friendly, with a perpetual party atmosphere in winter, this is also an exceptionally picturesque little town with wide, impossibly steep streets, mountains all around and views above the clouds.

In the 1890s, Rossland was a booming gold-mining town, with 7000 people, 42 saloons and four local newspapers. The **Rossland Museum** ① *junction Hwys 22 and 3B, T1888-448 7444, www.rosslandmuseum.ca, mid-May to mid-Sep 0900-1700, $5, youth $3, child $1.50, tours leave every 30 mins Jul-Aug 0930-1530, 5 times daily May-Jun, with museum entry $10, youth $5, child $3*, documents this history and offers interesting 45-minute tours through the spooky (and chilly) turn-of-the-20th-century Le Roi Gold Mine, last operated in 1929 and filled with old equipment. The same building also houses the **Visitor Information Centre** ① *T250-362 7722, www.rossland.com*.

Red Mountain Ski Hill ① *3 km W on Hwy 3B, T250-362 7384, www.redresort.com, Nov-Apr, day pass $58, youth $46, child $29*, boasts 682 ha of terrain, two mountains, two basins and an additional 1012 ha of easily accessible backcountry. The vertical gain is an impressive 880 m, but a relatively low elevation makes the snow-pack less reliable here than at most hills. When conditions are good, experienced skiers rate this hill as one of the province's best. It's especially suited to experts, with 45% black diamond runs and lots of tree skiing. The Paradise Basin is good for beginners and very pretty, with lots of views and sunshine. There's a terrain park for snowboarders and plenty of places to sleep and eat. Further development is planned, including 1400 sleeping units and 21,300 sq m of commercial space plus new lifts.

Fort Steele Heritage Town → *Colour map 2, C3.*

① 9851 Hwy 93/95, 16km northeast of Cranbrook, T250-417 6000, www.fortsteele. bc.ca. Apr-Jun and Sep-Oct daily 0930-1700, Jul-Aug daily 0930-1800, Nov-Mar 1000-1600, $13, under 18 $4.25, under 12 $2, under 6 free. Steam train $6, under 18 $3, under 12 $2, live 1890s variety shows in the Wild Horse Theatre, 1400, $8, under 18 $3, under 12 $2, horse-drawn wagon rides $4, under 18 $2. All-inclusive pass for 2 days $23.25, under 18 $9, under 12 $5.75.

At dreary Castlegar, you're advised to take Highway 3A to Nelson (see page 207), then north through Nakusp to Highway 1. Highway 3 east via the Salmo-Creston pass is mostly a dull drive, as is Highway 93 north from dismal Cranbrook. If headed this way, however, it's worth stopping at the reconstructed late 19th century town of **Fort Steele**, one of the best 'living museums' in BC. There are over 50 buildings, some original, some replicas and some brought in from elsewhere. The overall effect is a convincing step back in time. All the requisite shops and services are represented, with costumed staff acting out their roles whilst also filling in historical details and anecdotes. The blacksmith shoes horses, the sweet shop and bakery sell wares made on the spot and the restaurant serves meals cooked in the wood-fired brick oven. There's a working printer, a tinsmith shop, general store, farm animals, street dramas and live shows in an old-time music hall. You can even be taken round in a steam train or horse-drawn wagon.

Fernie → *Colour map 2, C3.*

Towards Fernie, the Crowsnest finally rewards its faithful with titillating previews of the Rockies. Surrounded by the soaring, jagged mountains of the **Lizard Range**, Fernie doesn't exactly do the setting justice but it comes closer than most. Recent expansion of its excellent ski hill has resulted in a fair amount of development, as hotels have sprung up along the highway, but the pretty little Downtown has been almost entirely spared. Most buildings here were constructed in brick or stone after a fire in 1908 wiped out the whole town in 90 minutes. A historical walking tour highlights these heritage buildings, many of which are clustered around Sixth Street and Fourth Avenue. A map is available at the **Visitor Information Centre** *① 102 Commerce Rd, T250-423 6868, www.ferniechamber.com.*

Until quite recently the copious challenging runs and plentiful powder of **Fernie Alpine Resort** *① T250-423 4655, www.skifernie.com, 5 km from town, ski pass $72, youth $50, child $24, night skiing 1730-2100 on limited days, $11, child $8,* were a fairly well-kept secret, along the lines of Red Mountain in Rossland. Like Rossland, Fernie is equally fine for skiing and mountain biking, resulting in a dynamic energy that helps save it from the backwater red-neck ambience of most of the East Kootenays. It remains a great choice for those who know their skiing and would rather stay in a real town, with good restaurants and bars and excellent cheap accommodation, rather than a purpose-built resort. The hill features 107 trails and five alpine bowls on 1013 ha of terrain that breaks down as 30% beginner, 40% intermediate, 30% advanced, and is serviced by 10 lifts capable of carrying up to 13,700 skiers per hour. There are also 14 kms of groomed and track-set cross-country trails. The hill has restaurants, rentals, lessons and lots of accommodation, and the **Smokie Mountain Ski Shuttle** *① T250-423 8605, $3,* runs five times daily from Fernie.

● Sleeping

Fraser Canyon *p170*
C Chrysalis Retreat B&B, 31278 Douglas St, Yale, T250-863 0055. Offers 3 rooms in a beautiful cottage with lovely gardens,

hot tub and sauna. Also offers massage and hydro-therapy. Breakfast included.
C-D Bear's Claw Lodge, 1492 Hwy 97 N, Cache Creek, T250-457 9705. Far and away

the nicest place to stay and eat on this stretch. The striking log-built lodge has comfortable rooms, a spacious guest lounge and a decent restaurant.

D Teague House B&B,1 km west of Yale on Hwy 1, T250-363 7238, www.teague house.com. Built in 1864, this quaint little blue house has 3 bedrooms, a full kitchen and a comfortable sitting room, all furnished with historical artefacts. There's a covered deck from which to enjoy the views over a full breakfast.

Camping
Adventure Resort, 5 km north of Lytton. Has de luxe cabin tents, a campground, trails, various sporting facilities, a restaurant, fabulous bar, swimming pool and spa. All-inclusive packages available.

Skihist Provincial Park, 6 km north of Lytton. 58 decent sites, some dramatic views of the Thompson Valley, lots of Saskatoon berries and hiking trails on part of the Cariboo Wagon Rd.

Yale Campground, 28800 Hwy 1. Large sites, hot showers, laundry, playground and trails.

Kamloops *p170*
More upmarket accommodation is to be found near the junction of Rogers Way, on the highway above town. Columbia St, the road into town, has mid-range options.

B-C Sun Peaks Lodge, T250-578 7878, www.sunpeakslodge.com. One of several lodges at the Ski Hill, offering rooms with balconies, and a spa, sauna and hot tub.

C The Plaza, 405 Victoria St, Downtown, T250-377 8075, www.plazaheritagehotel. com. The most appealing Downtown choice. Rooms in this 1926 building are small, newly renovated and full of character.

D A Desert Inn, 775 Columbia St, T250-372 8235, www.adesertinn.kamloops.com. Good rooms with large beds, balconies and fairly new furnishings. There's an indoor pool and an on site restaurant. The views of the valley are the best feature.

E Joyce's B&B, 49 Nicola St W, T250-374 1417. The 3 pleasant rooms in this spacious

1911 Banker's House in a nice part of Downtown are a great deal.

E Sun Peaks Hostel, T250-763 0057, www.sunpeakshostel.com. The budget option at the Ski Hill. All the usual facilities, including a kitchen, common room with TV, internet, canoes, lockers and skiing. Phone ahead for transport from Kamloops.

Camping
Paul Lake Provincial Park, 17 km east off Hwy 5 N, T250-578 7376. There is no decent camping in town but you might find this secluded spot on a lovely lake worth the drive. There's good fishing and a steep hike to the top of Gibraltar for views.

The Shuswap *p171*
C Artist's House Heritage B&B, 20 Bruhn Rd, 1 km west of Sicamous, T250-836 3537, www.artistshouse.ca. A friendly, antique-filled B&B right on the lake, with 3 rooms, 1 with en suite shower. Library, living room, den, sun porch and a lovely big patio with views over the lake. Even has its own fallout shelter.

C-D Trickle Inn B&B, Tappen, T250-835 8835, www.trickleinn.com. 5 unique, sumptuously decorated rooms in a Victorian heritage home, overlooking the lake and surrounded by landscaped gardens. Superb restaurant, by prior reservation only.

D Alpiner Motel, 734 Hwy 1, Sicamous, T250-836 2290, www.alpinermotel.com. Fun little triangular cabins with large beds and kitchenette. Some very cheap tent sites. Great value.

D Villager Motor Inn, 61 10th St, Salmon Arm, T250-832 9793. One of a number of chain hotels and functional motels on the TransCanada in Salmon Arm. Handy for the bus station.

E Caboose Hostel, Squilax, T250-275 2977, www.hihostels.ca. Possibly the most interesting hostel in BC. The main building is a historic general store on the lake and the dorm beds are in 4 converted cabooses (railway cars), each with its own kitchen and bathroom. A common room, TV room,

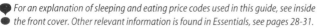
For an explanation of sleeping and eating price codes used in this guide, see inside the front cover. Other relevant information is found in Essentials, see pages 28-31.

sauna, library and laundry. Friendly staff rent out canoes and a self-guided hiking kit, and can set you up with all manner of local activities. The Greyhound stops here and there's a nearby beaver lodge to check out. Phone ahead to arrange pick-up.

Camping
There are remote campgrounds at **White Lake Provincial Park** and **Herald Provincial Park**, both T250-995 0861, which has a sandy beach and an easy trail to Margaret Falls.
Bush Creek Provincial Park, Adams Lake, 5.5 km up a rough logging road. One of the nicest, most peaceful and scenic places to camp in the area.
KOA, junction of Hwys 1 and 97B, T250-832 6489, ww.salmonarmkoa.com. A well-equipped campground with laundry, showers, hot tub, heated pool, cabins, TV and a games room.
Shuswap Lake Provincial Park, 1210 McGill Rd, east of Squilax at Scotch Creek. 270 nicely wooded, private and well-equipped sites, as well as a large beach.
Silver Beach Provincial Park, Seymour Arm. A remote but spectacular forested location at the northernmost extremity of the lake. Great for swimming, fishing, and ideal for peace and quiet.

Revelstoke *p172*
B Mulvehill Creek Wilderness Inn B&B, 4200 Hwy 23, 19 km south towards Shelter Bay ferry, T250-837 8649, www.mulvehill creek.com. A fabulous option for those with transport. This beautiful wood lodge stands on 40 ha of peaceful private land on the shore of Upper Arrow Lake. It has 9 rooms with en suite bath, a hot tub, games room and canoes. Friendly and interesting hosts, full breakfast included.
C Minto Manor B&B, 815 Mackenzie Av, T250-837 9337, www.mintomanor.com. 3 plush en suite rooms decked out with period furniture. The 1905 Edwardian mansion has a veranda, large gardens, a sitting room, music room and TV room.
C The Regent Inn, 112 1st St, T250-837 2107, www.regentinn.com. Large rooms with big beds and baths. Centrally located with an outdoor hot tub, sauna and gym access. The restaurant, lounge and pub downstairs are also appealing.

D Monashee Lodge, 1601 3rd St W, T250-837 6778, www.monasheelodge.com. A quiet, good-value motel, with hot tub and a light breakfast included.
E Samesun Backpacker Lodges, 400 2nd St W, T250-837 4050, www.samesun.com. One of the great hostels. 76 beds in clean, bright, wood-finished dorms of up to 4, or doubles at no extra charge. Huge kitchens, a common room with TV, free internet and laundry. Ask about their amazing skiing and cat-skiing packages.

Camping
Blanket Creek Provincial Park, 25 km S on Hwy 23, T250-825 4212. 63 sites on Arrow Lakes by Sutherland Falls.
Williamson Lake Campground, 1818 Williamson Lake Rd, 5 km south on 4th St/Airport Way, T250-837 5512, www.williams onlakecampground.com. Well located on a warm lake away from the highway, with plenty of trees and greenery. Playground, canoe and rowboat rentals, showers, and laundry facilities.

Glacier National Park *p172*
C Best Western Glacier Park Lodge, right on Rogers Pass, T250-837 2126, www.glacier parklodge.ca. The only beds in the park and a great location. Heated outdoor pool, sauna, restaurant, 24-hr café and service station. There are also a number of lodges on the way to Golden.

Camping
Illecillewaet, Loop Brook and **Mt Sir Donald** Campgrounds, 3, 5 and 6 km west of Rogers Pass respectively. Run by Parks Canada, non-reservable and rustic (especially the latter), these 3 sites give access to interpretive trails that pass through snow-sheds, bridges and other remains of the 1885 CPR railway line. The park also has backcountry campsites and cabins, or you can camp southeast of the park boundary where no fees or restrictions are in place.

Golden *p173*
Golden's mountain setting has led to a proliferation of log-built lodges, mainly west of the TransCanada, many of them accessed by helicopter only.

C **Ambler House B&B**, 815 12th St, T250-344 5001,www.amblerhouse.com. 3 lovely rooms in a heritage home. Living room, hot tub and full breakfast.

C **Kicking Horse River Lodge**, 801 9th St N, T250-439 1112, www.khrl.com. This spectacularly restored historic fir log building has a wrap-around balcony and views of the **Kicking Horse Ski Resort**. There are private rooms, loft rooms that sleep up to 9 (**A**), and dorm beds (**E**). Facilities include a 2-storey den with reading nooks and a stone fire- place, an entertainment area with TV, full kitchen, café and laundry.

C-E **Goldenwood Lodge**, 14 km west, then 6 km east on Blaeberry School Rd, T250-344 7685, www.goldenwoodlodge.com. This rustic but handsome wood lodge offers tranquillity, glorious surroundings and a variety of sleeping options, such as rooms, family lodges, cottages with or without kitchenette and tepees. Vegetarian meals and bikes available, canoeing and horse riding trips arranged.

D **Mary's Motel**, 603 8th Av, T250-344 7111, www.marysmotel.com. With so little accommodation in Golden, apart from the undesirable strip on the highway, this makes a good standby, with an indoor pool, sauna, hot tub and 81 rooms.

E **Kicking Horse Hostel**, 518 Station Av, take Hwy 95 exit off Hwy 1 then 1st left before the overpass, T250-344 5071, www.kickinghorse hostel.com. Dorms and camping. Kitchen, common room and sauna.

Camping

Waitabit Creek, 23 km to the west. Turn north onto Donald Rd for 500 m then left down Big Bend Rd for 2 km. A distance away, but the best camping that's right on the river.

Whispering Spruce Campground, 1430 Golden View Rd, off Highway 1 E, T250-344 6680, www.whisperingspruce.net. 135 sites overlooking the Kicking Horse canyon, with good facilities including hot showers, laundry and games room.

Manning Provincial Park p174

A-B **Manning Park Resort**, on the highway, T250-840 8822, www.manningpark.com. An impressive log building in a great location, decorated inside and out with

artfully crafted chainsaw carvings and with a good range of rooms and cabins. Has a 50-ft indoor pool, hot tub, sauna, steam room, fitness room, games room with billiards, a café, restaurant and lounge to warm up in. Bike, ski, canoe and kayak rental, an outdoor skating rink, volleyball, tennis, plenty of hiking and cross- country skiing trails.

Camping

Lightning Lake, 5 km from resort, T1800-689 9025. The most convenient of the park's 4 campgrounds, with 88 sites, canoeing and access to trails.

Hedley p174

C **Colonial Inn B&B**, Colonial Rd, T250-292 8131, www.colonialinnbb.ca. Bursting with character from the outside, this historic house is spectacular from the inside too. Antique furnishings, chandeliers and hardwood floors. 5 equally impressive rooms, 3 en suite, are a steal at this price.

D **Gold House B&B**, 644 Colonial Rd, T250-292 8418, www.thegoldhouse.com. A fabulous historic house occupying the mine's former office and storage room, which were built in 1904. The 4 lovely rooms, some sharing a bath, have access to the wrap-around balcony, with views of the mine and mountains. To the back are the scenic remains of a crushing plant, known as the Stamp Mill.

Camping

Stemwinder Provincial Park, just west of town. 27 nicely wooded and fairly private campsites on the river.

East to Christina Lake p175

C **Hummingbird Haven B&B**, 255 1st Av, T250-447 9293. Offers 3 very nice rooms in a spacious house. Peaceful location next to the golf course.

C **Sunflower Inn B&B**, Alpine Rd 159, T250-447 6201, www.sunflowerinnbb.com. Well situated next to the lake and park, with a private beach, canoes, deck with lake views and 3 pleasant rooms with shared bath.

D **Park Lane Resort & Motel**, 31 Kingsley Rd, T250-447 9385, www.parklane-resort. com. Bright, pleasant and away from the highway. Some rooms come with kitchen, patio and BBQ. Also have tent and RV camping available.

Camping
Gladstone Provincial Park, accessed via the Texas-Alpine turning, 5 km north on the highway, T250-548 0076. A large and extremely busy campground by the lake, with access to several beaches and hiking trails. Reserve early or else keep your fingers crossed.

East to Rossland *p175*
If you want to stay at the Red Mountain Ski Hill, a package is the best bet through Central Reservations, T1877-969 7669, www.redreservations.com.
B Angela's B&B, 1520 Spokane St, T250-362 7790, www.visitred.com. A classically-renovated 1920s house, with 2 suites that are geared to bigger groups but may suit a couple. Hot tub, fireplace, garden and a creek running through the property.
B Prestige Inn, 1919 Columbia Av, T250-362 7375, www.prestigeinn.com. A convenient downtown choice with a range of decent rooms and suites. Jacuzzi, fitness centre, restaurant, lounge and a noisy bar that's the best venue in town for live bands.
B Red Mountain Village, 3 km north on Hwy 3B at the base of the hill, T250-362 9000, www.redmountainvillage.com. A wide range of options, from luxury chalets to large cabins and motel rooms. Prices drop by 50% mid-May to mid-Sep.
C Rams Head Inn, Red Mountain Rd, 400 m before ski hill, T250-362 9577, www.rams head.bc.ca. By far the best option around. Beautiful, comfortable and homely rooms. Common room with a stone fireplace, sauna, outdoor hot tub with views, a games room, full breakfast and use of snowshoes. Prices drop considerably mid-May to mid-Sep.
E Mountain Shadow Hostel, 2125 Columbia Av, T250-362 7160. Dorms and private rooms, common room, kitchen and internet.

Camping
Rossland Lions Park, Red Mountain Rd, 1 km north on Highway 3B. 18 sites, some with hook-ups. Mid-May to mid-Sep only.

Fort Steele Heritage Town *p176*
Camping
Fort Steele Resort and RV Park, T250-489 4268, www.fortsteele.com. 200 sites right by the Village. Heated pool, hot showers, laundry, games room, playground and hook-ups.
The Original Fort Steele Campground, 2 km south on Kelly Rd, T250-426 5117, www.fortsteelecampground.com. This is a nicer, quieter spot with 60 wooded sites, heated pool, showers, RV hook-ups and lots of trails for biking and hiking.

Fernie *p176*
Fernie has lots of accommodation, look at www.fernie.com/lodging, for information. You can also book what you need through **Fernie Central Reservations**, T1800-622 5007, www.ferniecentralreservations.com. Note that these prices are for the peak ski season, with rates up to 50% less during the summer months.
B Park Place Lodge, 742 Hwy 3, T250-423 6871, www.parkplacelodge.com. Spacious and stylish rooms, some with balconies or kitchenettes. Indoor pool, hot tub, sauna, pub and bistro.
C Griz Inn, 5369 Ski Hill Rd, at the hill, T1800-661 0118, www.grizinn.com. One of several decent lodges at the ski hill, offering rooms, studios and suites. Indoor pool, 2 outdoor hot tubs and sauna.
D Snow Valley Motel, Hwy 3/10th St, T250- 423 4421, www.snowvalleymotel. com. One of many motels on the highway downtown, with suites and kitchenette rooms.
D-E Barbara Lynn's Country Inn, 691 7th Av, T250-423 6027, www.blci.ca. 10 small, slightly faded rooms just off the highway and close to town. Most with shared bath.
D-E Powder Mountain Lodge, Hwy 3, T250-423 4492, www.powdermountain lodge.com. One of the finest hostels you will ever see. A beautiful, spacious building with dorms and private rooms with en suite baths. All facilities including a games room, hot tub, sauna, pool table, reading area, laundry, storage, shuttle to the hill or bus station and even a piano.

 For an explanation of sleeping and eating price codes used in this guide, see inside the front cover. Other relevant information is found in Essentials, see pages 28-31.

D-E **Raging Elk Hostel**, 892 6th Av, T250-423 6811, www.ragingelk.com. An excellent hostel, with dorms, semi-private and private rooms. Common room, full kitchen, games room, movie room, sauna and storage. Free breakfast included.

Camping
Mount Fernie Provincial Park, 3 km SW on Hwy 3, T250-422 3003. Has 40 sites by the Elk River, wooded and private.

● Eating

Kamloops *p170*
Brownstone, 118 Victoria St, T250-851 9939. A heritage building with an intimate interior and a lovely courtyard patio. Offers an ambitious, broad, international fine dining menu with a West Coast emphasis on freshness.
Chapters Viewpoint, 610 W Columbia St, **Panorama Inn**, T250-374 3224. A long-term favourite, offering fantastic views, outdoor seating and a menu that ranges from steak and seafood to salads, pasta and Mexican. Has an equally wide price range.
326 Bistro, 326 Victoria St, T250-374 2913. A hip little eatery with steak, seafood, great salads and some refreshingly original menu items like sweet and sour halibut cheeks or lobster ravioli.
The Commodore Grand Café and Lounge, 369 Victoria, T250-851 3100. A great place for a drink but also good for food. A menu of interesting fusion dishes and tapas, as well as regular pub fare.
Hot House Bistro, 438 Victoria St, T250-374 4604. Vegetarian cuisine with a laid-back South American atmosphere and international food from Mexico to India.
Sanbiki, 476 Victoria, T250-377 8857. Great sushi and offers some good choices for vegetarians.
Cowboy Coffee, 229 Victoria St, T250-372 3565. The best coffee. Also try the cambozola panini.

The Shuswap *p171*
Mino's, 720 22nd St, Salmon Arm, T250-832 1038. Good, reliable Greek fare.
Moose Mulligans, 1122 Riverside Av, Sicamous. Decent enough pub food and draft beer, but the real draw here are the views of the marina.

Revelstoke *p172*
112 Restaurant, Regent Inn, 112 1st Av, T250-837 2107. The best choice for fine dining in romantic surroundings.
Bad Paul's Roadhouse Grill, 122 Mackenzie Av, T250-837 9575. One for the carnivores, specializes in prime rib.
Woolsey Creek, 600-2nd St, T250-837 5500. The best choice for food that is international, imaginative and well-executed. The interior is colourful and comfortable, with couches and good art on the walls. There's also a patio.
Conversations, 205 Mackenzie Av, T250-837 4772. The nicest spot for a coffee, but the coffee itself is disappointing.
The Ol' Frontier, corner Hwy 1 and Hwy 23 N, T250-837 5119. With its Wild West saloon theme this is a fun place to have a large breakfast.

Golden *p173*
Cedar House, about 4.5 km south at 735 Hefti Rd, T250-344 4679. Expertly crafted Pacific Rim-style fine dining in the beautiful surroundings of this stand-out cedar building, set in 4 ha of forest and organic gardens, with a lovely patio.
Eagle's Eye View, T1866-754 5425. At the very top of the ski hill, accessible via the gondola (free with reservation), this is the highest restaurant in Canada. Offers fine dining and even finer views from a timber-frame building with masses of glass.
Apostoles Restorante, 427 9th Av, T250-344 4906. Authentic Greek cuisine at very reasonable prices.
Eleven 22 Grill and Liquids, 1122 10th Av S, T250-344 2443. Hands down Golden's hippest spot. Warm, intimate and stylish, with a menu strong on interesting international appetizers. Good drinks list.
Kicking Horse Grill, 1105 9th St, T250-344 2330. International fusion cuisine in an authentic old log building on the banks of the river.
Bad Habit Bistro, 528 9th Av N, T250-439 1995. Wholesome lunches and breakfast served all day.
Bean Bag Coffee Roasters, 521 9th Av N, 250-344 6363. The best coffee in town.

Hedley *p174*

℣ **Gold Dust Pub**, 5625 Hwy 3, east of town, T250-292 8552. The best bet in town for food and drink.

East to Christina Lake *p175*

℣ **Jimmy Beans**, 9 Johnson Rd, T250-447 6610. Great coffee and light food, internet access and a pleasant garden and deck. A good place to stop for a break if you're driving through the area.

East to Rossland *p175*

℣℣ **Gypsy at Red**, 4430 Red Mountain Rd, at the ski hill, T250-362 3347. World cuisine with an emphasis on Asian and Mediterranean flavours with a West Coast edge. Warm and intimate setting.

℣℣ **Idgies**, Washington/2nd Av, T250-362 5333. A long-standing favourite with a mixed menu that covers seafood, curries, lamb, steaks and pasta dishes.

℣℣ **Mazatlan**, 111 Nancy Greene Hwy, T250-362 7385. Authentic Mexican food, a lively atmosphere and infamous margaritas.

℣℣ **The Old Fire Hall**, 2115 Queen St, T250-362 5802. A fantastic brick building that makes a perfect venue for a high-class restaurant, wine bar and live jazz venue. The menu focuses on meat dishes and tapas and there are 40 wines available by the glass.

℣ **Clansey's Capuccino**, 2042 Columbia Av, T250-362 5273. A great atmosphere, good for breakfast.

℣ **The Grind**, 2207 Columbia Av, T250-362 2280. Excellent home-made breakfast and lunches prepared by a top chef. Great coffee and views from the deck.

℣ **Sunshine Café**, 2116 Columbia Av, T250-362 7630, daily 0730-1500. Good for breakfast and paninis. The play area makes it a great choice for families.

Fernie *p176*

℣℣℣ **The Old Elevator**, 291 1st Av, T250-423 7115. Down-to-earth but excitingly original environment, housed in a 1908 grain elevator. The menu focuses on steak and game, cooked to perfection and artfully presented. There's also tapas in the lounge.

℣℣ **The Curry Bowl**, 931 7th Av, T250-423 2695. A cosy little place with a friendly atmosphere. The broad menu is pan-Asian,

the food fresh and tasty and there are 50 import beers to wash it down with. Try the panang curry.

℣ **Mug Shots Bistro**, 592 3rd Av, T250-423 8018. Good breakfast and coffee, fresh juices, second-hand books and internet access.

℣ **Rip'n Richards**, 301 Hwy 3, T250-423 3002. A good option to indulge your guilty pleasures with pizza, chicken wings, Mexican food, burgers, all done just as you like them.

♠ Bars and clubs

Kamloops *p170*

The Commodore Grand Café and Lounge, 369 Victoria, T250-851 3100. With brick walls, booths and relaxed music, this newly re-opened spot is perfect for a drink or 2.

The Shuswap *p171*

Hideaway Pub, 995 Lakeshore Dr, Salmon Arm, T250-832 9442. A nice spot where connoisseurs can sample excellent locally-brewed Crannog organic beers on tap.

Revelstoke *p172*

The 112 Lounge and **River City Pub & Patio**, in the Regent Inn, 112 1st St, T250-837 2107, are both good at what they do.
Big Eddy Inn, 2108 Big Eddy Rd, T250-837 9072. The best regular boozer in town.

East to Rossland *p175*

Flying Steamshovel Inn, Washington/2nd Av, T250-362 7373. An atmospheric pub with a lingering flavour of the Wild West saloon. Small, intimate and very light, with a pool table, a good selection of beer on tap, drink specials and good pub food.
Nowhere Special Social Lounge, Columbia Av/Queen St, T250-362 2190. Rossland's newest and hippest venue, with musical theme nights, DJs and live bands.
The Old Fire Hall, 2115 Queen St, T250-362 5804. See Eating.
Rock Cut Neighborhood Pub, 3052 Hwy 3B, T250-362 5814. Situated across from ski hill, there are great views from the patio of this popular pub. Decent après-ski munchies too.

Fernie *p176*

Eldorado Lounge, 701 2nd Av, T250-423 0009. A lively nightclub housed in a historic

⋮ Powwow

Derived from the Narragansett word for shaman, powwow traditionally refers to any gathering of native Americans. These days the word is usually used to denote a celebration, at which natives and non-natives meet in one particular area to dance, sing, socialize, and generally have a good time. Powwows can vary in length from a single session of about five or six hours to three days with one to three sessions a day. One of the best to visit is at Kamloops, see Festivals, below.

livery building, with live bands and DJs playing till late.

Grizzly Bar, above the **Daylodge** at the ski hill, T250-423 4655. This is the après-ski bar of choice.

The Pub Bar and Grill, in the **Park Place Lodge**, 742 Hwy 3, T250-423 6871. A great pub and a long-time favourite for locals and ski-bums alike. As pub-grub goes, the food is also very good.

⊕ Entertainment

Kamloops *p170*
For information and tickets, call **Kamloops Live!** on T250-374 5483 and to find out about all live music, visit www.kamloops music.com.

The Blue Grotto, 319 Victoria St, T250-372 9901, www.thebluegrotto.ca. Live, pre-dominantly rock, music on Thu-Sun.

Kamloops Art Gallery, 465 Victoria St, by the library, T250-377 2400, www.galleries. bc.ca/kamloops, Mon-Sat 1000-1700, Thur 1000-2100, Sun 1200-1600, $5, child $3. One of the town's finest features, with a collection of quality works by inspiring artists.

Paramount Twin Theatres, 503 Victoria St, T250-372 3911. The handiest cinema.

Sagebrush Theatre, 1300 9th St, T250-374 5483. Home of the Western Canada Theatre company and the Kamloops Symphony Orchestra. A major venue for visiting shows.

Revelstoke *p172*
The Roxy Theatre, 115 Mackenzie Av, T250-837 5540. Cinema.

Fernie *p176*
Vogue Theatre, 321 2nd Av, T250-423 3132. Cinema.

⊛ Festivals and events

Kamloops *p170*
Mar Kamloops Cowboy Festival, T1888-763 2223, www.bcchs.com/festival. A celebration of all things cowboy. One of the biggest and best of its kind in Canada.

Jul Merritt Mountain Music Festival, www.mountainfest.com. Held over 4 days in Merritt, 72 km South of Kamloops, one of Canada's most celebrated country music festivals.

Aug Kamloopa Powwow, T250-828 9700, www.kib.ca/powwow.htm. Held on the 3rd weekend of Aug at the Special Events Facility, this is one of the best powwows in the country. Everyone is welcome and it's the most enjoyable way to get an authentic taste of contemporary aboriginal culture. Brightly clad dancers from over 30 bands across Canada and the northern US perform to the rhythms of drumming and singing.

The Shuswap *p171*
Feb Shuswap International Film Festival, T250-832 2294, www.shuswapfilm.net. A week-long event held in late Feb at the unique **Salmar Classic Theatre**.

Jul Shuswap Lake Festival of the Arts, T250-955 6401, www.artsfestivalshuswap. com. A week-long judged exhibition of various art media held in Sorrento Memorial Hall, with demonstrations, workshops and an art walk. **Switzmalph Cultural Day & Powwow** , T250-803 0395, www.shuswap centre.com. The biggest of 3 local pow-wows, with numerous First Nations events and shows.

Aug Roots and Blues Festival, T250-833 4096, www.rootsandblues.ca. For 3 days in mid-Aug, this superb festival brings Salmon Arm to life with acts performing on 6 stages, $135 at gate, $50-60 per day. There is camping available.

Revelstoke *p172*

Jun Revelstoke Mountain Beats Festival, T250-837 5500, www.mountainbeats.com. Held for 3 days on the 3rd weekend, with various musical shows on 2 open-air stages.

Fernie *p176*

Mar Griz Days Winter Festival, T250-423 6868. A 4 day event in early March, featuring a parade, the Mardi Gras Cabaret, competitions, races and entertainment.

Apr Powder, Pedal, Paddle Relay Race, marks the closure of the ski hill and is an excuse for a big party, disguised as a fun variation on the gruelling triathlon.

Sep Taste of Fernie, T250-423 4842. The chance to sample the fare of local restaurants, with live entertainment throughout the day.

▲▲ Activities and tours

Fraser Canyon *p170*
Rafting

Fraser River Raft Expeditions, on the river-side at the south end of Yale, T1800-363 7238, www.fraserraft.com. A small, friendly company offering 1- to 7-day rafting tours on powerful rivers like the Fraser and Thompson, or calmer waters such as the Nahalatch and Coquihalla, starting at $130 a day.

Kumsheen Raft Adventures, T250-455 2296, www.kumsheen.com. The most professional operation around, offering 1- to 5-day rafting trips on all the local rivers, gear rental, kayaking, bike tours, fishing and rock climbing.

Kamloops *p170*
Fishing

This area is famous for its trout fishing, with over 200 nearby lakes. Among the closest and best are Paul Lake, 23 km northeast and Lac Le Jeune, 35 km south.

Fossil hunting

Earthfoot, T250-554 2401. A local expert leads geological and paleontologic tours in the mountains around Kamloops, searching for 36-60 million year-old fossils, minerals

and crystals. Suitable for all levels of rock-hound. Tools are supplied but your own vehicle is required. $60 per person per day, child $25.

Golf

There are 11 golf courses in the area, visit www.golfkamloops.com for more information. **Rivershore**, T250-573 4622, www.rivershoregolflinks.com; **The Dunes**, T250-579 3300, www.golfthedunes.com.

Mountain biking

There are a lot of good trails around Kamloops and it's a great way to explore the weird landscapes. The best places are Sun Peaks and Lac Dubois.

Full Boar Bike Store, 310 Victoria, T250-314 1888, www.fullboarbikes.com. Rents out bikes and can provide information.

Skiing

See Sun Peaks Ski Resort, page 171.

The Shuswap *p171*
Houseboats

All the rental companies are clustered together on the marina in Sicamous, so you can shop around and see what you're getting. Unfortunately, they're prohibitively expensive unless you're with a group and they can only be rented by the week.

Bluewater Houseboat Rentals, T250-836 2255, www.bluewaterhouseboats.ca. There are so many houseboat rental companies, but this outfit is as good as any. Best value is the 4-day sport cruiser mid-week rate of $1095 for up to 8 people.

Watersports

Adams River Rafting, 3993 Squilax-Anglemont Rd, Scotch Creek, T250-955 2447, www.adamsriverrafting.com. $62 for a 1-hr trip on the Adams River.

Get Wet Rentals Ltd, 1130 Riverside Av, Sicamous, T250-836 3517, www.getwet rentals.com. All kinds of water toys for rent, including fishing boats for $60/day and canoes for $40/day.

Sicamous Water Tours and Charters, T250-836 4318. Guided lake tours with narrative and petroglyph-viewing. Water taxi service.

Revelstoke *p172*
Hiking
A 10-km trail up Mt Revelstoke starts behind the Railway Museum. It can also be snowshoed in winter. Keystone and Standard Basins is a first-class 14.6- or 22-km hike with grand views of the Columbia Range, but the trailhead is 63 km away. Ask at the information centre if interested.

Arrow Adventure Tours, T250-837 6014, www.arrowadventuretours.com. Hiking and biking tours in the Selkirk and the Monashee Mountains.

Mountain biking
Revelstoke has some great trails. Get a map from the Information Centre.

High Country Cycle and Sports, 188 MacKenzie Av, T250-814 0090. Rentals, tours and advice.

Skiing
For years, Revelstoke has been revered for its ample powder and fabulous backcountry skiing and skiers have dreamed about the day when the local hill's potential will be realized. Well, it's finally happening with Revelstoke Mountain Ski Resort.

Most locals go backcountry skiing across the river on the Five Fingers of Mt McPherson. This is the best, most convenient spot, with northern exposure insuring good snow conditions. The Resort organizes cat-skiing in the Selkirk Mountains for $325/day.

Freespirit Sports, 203 1st St W, T250-837 9453. Backcountry and snowboard equipment and snowshoe rentals.

High Country Sports, 118 Mackenzie Av, T250-814 0090. Cross-country and backcountry gear rentals.

Revelstoke Nordic Ski Club, www.revel stokenordic.org. Maintains 24 km of groomed cross-country ski trails on Mt Macpherson, whose trailhead is 7 km S of Revelstoke on Hwy 23. Day fee $6, child $3.

Selkirk Tangiers , T250-837 5378, www.sel kirk-tangiers.com. Heli-skiing in 200,000 ha of terrain, from 1-day tasters ($689) to 7-day all-inclusive packages.

Golden *p173*
Hang-gliding
Mt Seven is considered Canada's premier site, hosting the annual Western Canadian Hang-gliding Championships and the Canadian National Paragliding Championships in Aug. Check www.flygolden.ca for more information.

Horse riding
Bear Corner Bed & Bale, 2054 Blaeberry Rd, 20 km W of Golden, T250-344 4785, www.bearcornerb-b.com. Horse riding trips from 1 hr ($40) to multi-day tours or packages that include accommodation and meals.

Ice-skating
There is an outdoor ice-rink in the Kicking Horse Ski Resort, with skate rentals on-site.

Mountain biking
Mountain biking is huge around Golden, with top trail networks at Mount 7, Moonraker and Dawn Mountain. Full details can be found at www.golden cyclingclub.com.

Selkirk Source for Sports, 504 9th Av, T250-344 2966. Mountain bike rentals, service and information on local trails.

Rafting
Between May and Sep the aquamarine untamed Kicking Horse River provides class III and IV rapids for exciting rafting and kayaking. Gentler trips explore the unique wetlands of the Columbia River.

Kootenay River Runners, T250-347 6595, www.raftingtherockies.com. Rafting the Kicking Horse from $83 and more gentle all-day trips on the Kootenay River for $90.

Wet'n'wild, 1509 Lafontaine Rd, T250-344 6546, www.wetnwild.bc.ca. Offers a range of different trips on the Kicking Horse, including the possibility of combining rafting with horse riding or a jet boat tour.

Skiing
Dawn Mountain Nordic Ski Trails, at the base of the Kicking Horse Ski Resort, www.goldennordicclub.ca, has 25 km of groomed and track-set cross-country skiing trails. There are more trails at the Golf Course. There is also a 4 km trail network for snowshoeing off Palliser Trail Rd. For rentals and trail maps, contact **Canyon Creek Outfitters** in the Glacier Lodge in the resort village.

To reach the Resort, there is a daily ski bus during the ski season which leaves from various points in town, including the Visitor Centre, daily at 0600, 0705, 0815, 1010. In summer the lifts stay open for alpine hiking and diners.

Purcell Helicopter Skiing, T250-344 5410, www.purcellhelicopterskiing.com. Heli-skiing from $669 for 3 runs.

Tour operators
Alpenglow Aviation Inc, 210 Fisher Rd, T250-344 7117. 45-min flightseeing tours over the Rockies.
Golden Mountain Adventures, T403-244 4795, www.adventurerockies.com. A big company covering many activities, including rafting, biking, hang-gliding, snow mobiling, birdwatching and skiing.

East to Christina Lake *p175*
Wild Ways Adventure Sports, 1925 Hwy 3, T250-447 6561, www.wildways.com. Bikes and general outdoor gear to buy or rent and mountain biking tours. Kayak rentals, tours, instruction and information.

East to Rossland *p175*
Mountain biking and hiking
Rossland is the self-styled 'Mountain bike capital of Canada', surrounded by a mountain network comprising over 100 km of progressive, well marked and maintained trails, many of them on old railway grades and logging skid roads. Visit www.rossland trails.ca, for up to date information and maps. There are also several good hiking and skiing trails from town, including Old Glory, a classic 8-hr return hike to 360° views of the mountain ranges. The trailhead is 11 km north of town on Highway 3B.
High Mountain Adventures, T250-362 5342, www.highmtntours.com. Biking, hiking and snowmobile tours.
Revolution Cycles and Service, 2044 Columbia Av, T250-362 5688, www.revolutioncycles.ca. Rentals, sales, shuttles and your best source of information.

Skiing
For cross-country skiing, Black Jack trails across from Red Mountain, T250-364 5445, www.skiblackjack.ca, day pass $10,

child $6. There are rentals available at the hill or at **Powder Hound**, 2040 Columbia Av, where bikes can also be rented.
Adrenaline Adventures, 1919 Columbia Av, T250-362 5005, www.adrenalinebc.com. Runs a daily shuttle to the hill ($2).
Red Express Shuttle, www.redreservations.com. Runs to the hill from International Airport, Castlegar, Trail, Kelowna and Spokane airports.
Rossland Mountain Adventures, T250-368 7375, www.rosslandmtadventures.com. Ski touring, hiking, backpacking and back- country equipment rentals.

Swimming
Trail Aquatic and Leisure Centre, 1875 Columbia Av, Trail, T250-368 6484. The best facilities in the Kootenays, including a large, unchlorinated pool, sauna, hot tub and fitness room.

Fernie *p176*
Mountain biking
Fernie is famed for its biking and hiking, much of it in Mt Fernie Provincial Park and at the ski hill. For full trail information, visit www.crankfernie.com, or www.bikefernie.ca.
Board Stiff, 542 2nd Av, T250-423 3473, www.boardstifftouring.com. Bike rentals, sales and parts; kayak rentals; ski and snowboard gear and rentals.
Ski Base, 432 2nd Av, T250-423 6464, www.skibase.com. Bike rentals and trail information. Ski and snowboard sales, gear, rentals and repairs.

Rafting
Mountain High, T1877-423 4555, www.raftfernie.com. Gentle or whitewater rafting and kayak trips on the Elk or Bull Rivers, from $93/day.

Skiing
Fernie Wilderness Adventures, T250-423 6704, www.fernieadventures.com. Cat-skiing, wildlife viewing, ice fishing and fly fishing.
Mountain Pursuits, T250-423 6739, www.mountainpursuits.com. Year-round guided hiking and backcountry skiing.

❂ Transport

TransCanada Highway p169
Bus

In summer, there are 7 daily Greyhound buses between **Vancouver** and **Kamloops** (4½ hrs, $55), travelling up the Coquihalla Hwy via **Hope** (2½ hrs, $24). The 0030, 0630, 1345, 1845 services continue east on the TransCanada, stopping at **Salmon Arm** (7 hrs, $69), **Revelstoke** (8½ hrs, $84) and **Golden** (11½ hrs, $105), continuing to Banff (14 hrs, $117) and Calgary (15-17 hrs, $135).

Fraser Canyon p170

Greyhound, www.greyhound.ca, runs 3 daily buses from **Vancouver** to **Cache Creek** (5½ hrs, $58), stopping at all towns along the way.

Kamloops p170
Air

Air Canada, www.aircanada.com, flies daily to **Vancouver** ($152) and **Calgary** ($187). Central Mountain Air, T1888-865 8585, www.flycma.com, flies daily to **Vancouver** ($117) and **Prince George** ($170).

BC Transit, T250-376 1216, runs a regular public bus service downtown. The **Airporter Shuttle**, T250-314 4803, charges about $12 for the same trip. Sun-Star Shuttle, T250-377 8481, www.sunstarshuttle.com, runs to and from Sun Peaks Ski Resort.

Bus

Local BC Transit bus No 1 (Tranquille) goes to the North Shore, airport and city park; bus No 6 (Cityloop) runs round town to the youth hostel and Greyhound station. **Long distance** The Greyhound station is at 725 Notredame Dr, T250-374 1212, with 7 daily buses to **Vancouver** (4½ hrs, $55), 4 to Calgary (9½ hrs, $91), 4 to **Prince George** (8 hrs, $81) and 4 to **Kelowna** (2 fast, 2 slow, $31).

Canada West Coach, T250-314 4256, www.canadawestcoach.com, runs a weekend shuttle bus to the hill leaving Kamloops 0740, $15 one-way, $25 same-day return.

Reservations must be made the day before by 1630.

Taxi
Kami Cabs, T250-554 1377; Yellow Cabs, T250-374 3333.

Train
Via Rail, T1800-561 8630, www.viarail.ca, runs west to **Vancouver** on Mon, Thu, Sat (9 hrs, from $86); and east to **Jasper** on Mon, Wed, Sat (7½ hrs, from $112).

The Shuswap p171
Bus

Salmon Arm receives 4 buses daily to and from **Kamloops** or **Kelowna** (2 hrs, $20) and several to and from **Vancouver** (7-9 hrs, $72).

Revelstoke p172
Bus

The Greyhound station, T250-837 5874, is on Fraser Dr, just off Hwy 1. There are 4 buses daily to **Vancouver** (8½ hr, $84) and 4 to **Calgary** (6 hr, $58) via **Banff** (4 hrs, $49).

Golden p173
Bus

The Greyhound station, 1050 Hwy 1, T250-344 2917, with 4 buses daily (1 via Vernon) to **Vancouver** (11½ hr, $105), 4 to **Calgary** (4 hrs, $49) and 1 to **Invermere** (1½ hr).

Crowsnest Highway p174
Bus

Greyhound runs 2 daily buses (0030, 0615) that follow Hwy 3 through Manning Park (3-4 hrs, $41) to Rock Creek and 2 (0645, 1800 fast service) that take Hwy 5 to Kelowna, then join Hwy 3 at Rock Creek and continue east along Hwy 3 to Fernie and beyond, via Nelson. The fastest times from Vancouver are: **Kelowna** (6 hrs, $65), **Rock Creek** (8 hrs, $81), **Midway** (8 hrs, $89), **Greenwood** (8 hrs 15m, $87), **Grand Forks** (9 hrs, $92), **Christina Lake** (9 hr 15 m, $92), **Castlegar** (10.5 hrs, $103), **Nelson** (11 hrs, $108), **Creston** (15 hrs, $117), **Cranbrook** (15 hrs, $129), **Fernie** (16½ hrs, $136).

Bus

The Greyhound station is in Trail at 1355 Bay Av, T250-368 8400. Local buses between Rossland and **Trail** leave every 1½ hrs from Cedar/Spokane in Trail and from Jubilee/St Paul in Rossland. The buses tend to be at inconvenient times, so you might need a taxi (T250-364 3344, $15).

Fernie *p176*

Bus

The Greyhound station is at Parks Place Lodge, 742 Hwy 3, T250-423 6871, with 2 buses daily in each direction. A shuttle to the ski hill leaves from several spots in town including the hostels. **Rocky Mountain Sky Shuttle**, www.rockymountainsky shuttle.com, runs a shuttle to Fernie from **Calgary** and **Cranbrook** airports.

---

❶ Directory

Kamloops *p170*

Internet Library (free); PC Doctors Digital Café, 350 Seymour St, T250-372 5723. **Laundry** McCleaners Drycleaning & Laundromats, 437 Seymour St, T250-372 9655. **Library** 465 Victoria St, T250-

374 7042. **Medical services** Royal Inland Hospital, 311 Columbia St, T250-374 5111. **Post office** Canada Post, 217 Seymour St, T250-374 2444.

Revelstoke *p172*

Internet Samesun Hostel, free for guests. **Laundry** Family Laundry, 409 W 1st St, T250-837 3938. **Medical services** Queen Victoria Hospital, 1200 Newlands Rd, T250-837 2131. **Post office** Canada Post, 301 W 3rd St, T250-837 3228.

East to Rossland *p175*

Internet Page One Used Books, 1703 2nd Av, Trail, T250-368 8004. **Laundry** on Washington St. **Medical services** Trail Regional Hospital, 1200 Hospital Bench, Trail, T250-368 3311. **Post office** Canada Post, 2096 Columbia Av, T250-362 7644.

Fernie *p176*

Internet Mug Shots Bistro, 592 3rd Av, T250-423 8018. **Library** 492 3rd Av, T250- 423 4458. **Medical services** Sparling East Medical Centre, 402 2nd Av T250-423 4442. **Post office** Canada Post, 491 3rd Av, T250-423 7555.

Okanagan

Sitting in the rain shadow of the Cascade and Coast Mountains, the Okanagan Valley receives the most sun and least rain in Canada. The barren hills, rocky bluffs and subdued but striking colours caused by such aridity possess an eerie beauty that intensifies towards the south, where Osoyoos contains Canada's only functioning desert ecosystem. The climate is ideal for beaches and water sports, as well as for orchards and vineyards, with plenty of great wineries to tour. The combination of sun, warm water and ample stretches of lakefront understandably transforms the region into one big holiday resort every summer and has attracted a sizeable retirement community. As ever, those who thrive on outdoor activities will find plenty on offer, including three major ski-hills. Kelowna is the main town and obvious destination, though sleepy Naramata might appeal to those who value tranquillity.
▶▶ *For Sleeping, Eating and other listings, see pages 196-205.*

Ins and outs

Getting there and around

Kelowna International Airport (YLW), ① *T250-765 5125, www.kelownaairport.com, 10 km north on Highway 97*, receives daily flights from Vancouver, Victoria, Calgary and Seattle. The **Airporter Shuttle** ① *T250-765 0182, www.kelownashuttle.com*, runs to Downtown from 0400. For Orchard Park or Downtown by city bus, take No 23, then transfer to No 8. Regular shuttles and city buses run to Downtown. The Big White Ski Resort runs daily shuttles every hour or so, to and from **Kelowna Airport** ① *T1800-663 2772, $43, child $30, one-way; $70, child $50, return*. On Saturday and Wednesday, a **shuttle bus** ① *T1800-663 2772, $68*, runs between Big White Ski Resort, Kelowna Airport and Silver Star Mountain Resort, and there is also a regular **shuttle** ① *T1877-777 2739, $29 one-way*, to Apex Ski Resort from Penticton. Osoyoos receives daily buses from Vancouver via Keremeos and Penticton.

Kelowna's Downtown is small enough to explore on foot, but some of the attractions require transport. A network of local buses operates from a depot on Queensway between Ellis and Pandosy, with a second useful exchange at Orchard Park mall just off Cooper and Harvey. All other towns are small enough to walk around. ▸▸ *For further details, see Transport, page 204.*

Best time to visit
Most people flock to the Okanagan's beaches in summer but spring and autumn are even better, not only to avoid the excessive summer crowds but also to catch blossom and harvest times. The former runs from roughly mid-April to mid-May, the latter continues as late as the end of October. Coinciding nicely with these periods are the **Spring Wine Festival** in early May and the **Fall Wine Festival** in late September. ▸▸ *For further details, see Festivals page 201.*

Climate
The Okanagan's tinder-dry conditions make this region particularly vulnerable to the numerous and devastating forest fires that plague BC every summer. In August 2003, the Okanagan Mountain forest fire reached the very edge of Kelowna, destroying many homes as well as 10 of the 16 historic Myra Canyon Tresles (see page 193). Efforts are now underway to rebuild some of them.

Tourist information
Each of the Okanagan towns has its own Visitor Information Centre, the biggest and best being the handily located **Tourism Kelowna** ① *544 Harvey Av, T250-861 1515, www.tourismkelowna.com, mid-May to mid-Sep Mon-Fri 0800-1800, Sat-Sun 0900-1800, mid-Sep to mid-May Mon-Fri 0800-1700, Sat-Sun 1000-1500*. A useful site for additional information is www.ilovekelowna.com. **Penticton's Visitor Centre** ① *553 Railway St, T250-493 4055, www.penticton.ca*, contains a wine centre. There are also a number of useful free magazines available, including the tourist board's guide and a *Where* guide.

Kelowna 🚌🚗🏠🚲❄🚻🏔🚍🛈 ▸▸ *pp196-205. Colour map 1, C6; colour map 2, C1.*

Blessed with a gorgeous location and climate, the Okanagan's biggest and most central town offers more recreational and cultural possibilities than any of its neighbours, but also more of the brash commercialism and urban sprawl that can detract from the region's natural charms. The key here is to stay away from the ugly highway (here called Harvey) and the characterless grid of malls and housing estates and concentrate on the town's assets. Pre-dating the town's unfortunately rapid expansion following the construction of the Coquihalla Highway, Kelowna's attractive little Downtown and adjacent Cultural District are worth exploring and there are plenty of wineries and orchards to visit, as well as beaches, hikes, golf courses and the nearby **Big White Ski Resort**.

Kelowna

British Columbia Okanagan Kelowna

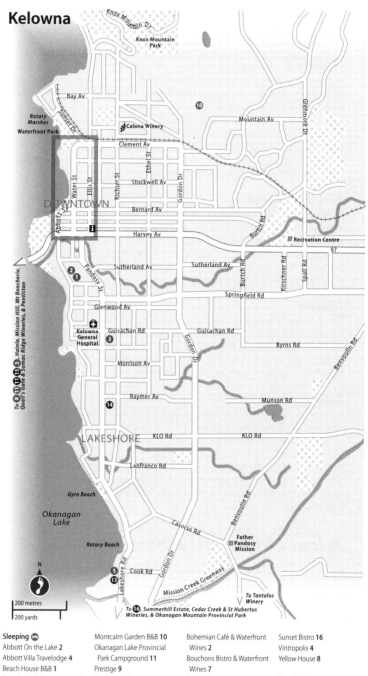

Sleeping

Abbott On the Lake 2
Abbott Villa Travelodge 4
Beach House B&B 1
Bear Creek & Fintry Provincial
  Park Campgrounds 8
Kelowna International Hostel 3
Manteo Resort & Wild Apple
  Restaurant 5
Montcalm Garden B&B 10
Okanagan Lake Provincial
  Park Campground 11
Prestige 9
Royal Anne 6
Same Sun International Hostel 7

Eating

Bean Scene Coffee House 1
Bohemian Café & Waterfront
  Wines 2
Bouchons Bistro & Waterfront
  Wines 7
Fresco 5
Hector's Casa 14
Lakeside Dining 13
Mission Hill Terrace 15
Old Vines 11
Sunset Bistro 16
Vintropolis 4
Yellow House 8

Bars & clubs

Gotchas 10
McCulloch Station 12
Pier Marine Pub 3
Rose's Waterfront Pub 6

Kelowna's Downtown, decorated in summer with hanging flower-baskets, is a pleasant place for a stroll. Most of the shops and restaurants cluster around Bernard Avenue, which heads west to meet the lake close to three of the city's landmarks: a white sculpture called *The Sails*, a model of the legendary lake monster, *Ogopogo* and the *MV Fintry Queen*, a 1948 paddle-wheeler. To the south is the lakefront **City Park**, a big green area fronted by a beach, perfect for enjoying the stunning views across the lake, with frequent events and live music.

North of Bernard, a waterfront walkway leads past the yachts and sailboats in the marina to an area roughly bounded by Water and Ellis streets and Queensway and Cawston Avenues, known as the **Cultural District**. Old packing houses and factories are being reclaimed as artistic venues or replaced by modern cultural institutions. Within a few blocks are the sedate (and free) Kasugai Gardens, behind the Bennett Clock on Queensway; the impressive Kelowna Library; the main sports and music venue, **Prospera Place**; the large **Rotary Centre for the Arts** and several museums, theatres and art galleries.

The **BC Orchard Industry Museums** ① *1304 Ellis, T250-763 0433, www.kelowna museum.ca, by donation* and **Wine Museum** ① *T250-868 0441*, are situated together in the restored brick Laurel Packinghouse, built 1917. The former has displays on the history of the fruit business and a model railway. The latter is the best place to find out about local wines and which wineries to visit. **Kelowna Art Gallery** ① *1315 Water St, T250-762 2226, www.kelowna artgallery.com, Tue-Sat 1000- 1700, Thu 1000-2100, Sun 1300-1600, $5, child $4*, is one of BC's finest, with a large permanent collection and two or three decent temporary exhibitions on show. The **Okanagan Heritage Museum** ① *470 Queensway, T250-763 2417, www.kelowna museum.ca, Mon-Fri 1000-1700, Sat 1000-1600, by donation*, provides an overview of the region's human and natural history. For a more concrete taste of Kelowna's beginnings, you can visit the **Father Pandosy Mission** ① *3685 Benvoulin Rd, Apr-Oct, by donation*, which preserves eight hand-hewn log buildings, four dating back to the original settlement.

The lakeside promenade runs without interruption from City Park north to **Waterfront**

Park, an area of lagoons, beaches, trails and lawns and an outdoor stage that is the main focus for live music and events during the summer. Further north at the end of Ellis Street, are the **Rotary Marshes**, a good place for birdwatching and the 235-ha **Knox Mountain Park**, with a trail that climbs high up to yield unbeatable views of the town, lake, floating bridge and valley. The **Myra Canyon** ① *take KLO Rd to McCulloch Rd, 2 km after the pavement ends, take Myra Forest Service Rd to the right and climb about 8 km uphill,* 12 km trail is a great hike or bike that takes you through tunnels and over bridges, affording magnificent views.

Lakeshore

South of Downtown, reached via a new bicycle path or Pandosy Street and Lakeshore Road, Kelowna's rapidly expanding Lakeshore district is set to become the town's most promising urban focus. There are shops and restaurants to explore between KLO and Lanfranco and nearby are the town's most popular beaches, **Gyro Beach** and **Rotary Beach**, both popular and crowded, noisy with sea-doos, motorboats, waterskiers and the like. For something more private, look out for the public beach access signs leading to tiny patches between the private beaches that have snapped up most of the sand.

Further south, past Cook, is one end of the **Mission Creek Greenway**, a lovely 18-km pathway that follows the course of the lake's main artery right through town. At the very end of Lakeshore Drive, past a few wineries, is the 10,500-ha **Okanagan Mountain Provincial Park**. Many trails lead through the semi-arid hillsides to some superb sub-alpine forests.

Big White Ski Resort → *Colour map 2, C1.*

① *T250-765 3101, www.bigwhite.com, late-Nov to Apr. Ski passes $68, concessions $56, child $33; night skiing Tue-Sat 1700-2000; cross-country skiing $20, youth $14, child $10; Tube Park $15, child $13, 2 hrs.*

One of BC's most significant ski resorts is 56 km from Kelowna via Highway 33. Its 1100 ha of patrolled skiable terrain get a lot of snow, particularly the light and fluffy powder most skiers dream about. The 118 runs are extremely varied, with a breakdown of 18% beginner, 54% intermediate and 28% expert. The resort has plenty of eating and sleeping options and all kinds of facilities, including three snowboard parks, 15 lifts, a high-speed gondola with a 28,000 person per hour capacity, North America's largest Tube Park, 25 km of groomed cross-country trails, snowmobiling, ice-skating, tobogganing, lessons and gear rental. It's especially well suited for families. The **Telus Park Express** ① *T250-765 3101, Fri-Sun and daily during Christmas and Spring breaks, $19 return,* runs from various downtown spots.

Vernon and around ⊜⊘⊕▲⊜⊕ ⇢ *pp196-205. Colour map 1, C6; colour map 2, C1.*

If moving north from Kelowna, Highway 97 is a pleasant-enough drive, half of it right alongside Wood and Kalamalka Lakes. However, for a real taste of the Okanagan, away from the hustle and bustle, a highly recommended route is the much slower road along the west bank of **Okanagan Lake** ① *cross the floating bridge then follow signs to Bear and Fintry provincial parks.* On this route, it might be tempting to bypass **Vernon** altogether as the oldest of the Okanagan towns is also the least interesting. Significantly, all the things worth noting in the vicinity are far from town. **Ellison Lake Provincial Park** ① *T250-492 2424,* has some of the least spoilt beaches around Okanagan Lake. The **Okanagan Highlands**, east of Oyama, offer a wealth of wilderness hiking and camping around small trout-filled lakes. And 12 km north on Highway 97 is the **O'Keefe Ranch** ① *T250-542 1415, www.okeeferanch.ca, May-Oct 0900-1800, $12, child $10, under 6 free,* a popular 20-ha site with original buildings

❖ Kettle Valley Railway

When silver was struck in the Kootenays, a railway was needed to help exploit the finds. The Kettle Valley Railway (KVR) became 'the most expensive railroad ever built' due to the virtually impenetrable terrain that had to be conquered, using tools no more sophisticated than hand-picks and shovels. This outstanding accomplishment, completed in 1916, was plagued by heavy snow and avalanches in winter, then washouts and rockslides in spring. Like most of Canada's great railway lines, the modern obsession with cars eventually left it redundant, with the last train running in 1989.

Today some 600 km of the KVR are suitable for hiking. The best sections are between Penticton and Kelowna, especially Myra Canyon Trestles just outside the latter. Also worthy of note are the Othello Tunnels just outside Hope. For more information, visit the **Kettle River Museum** in Midway, see page 175, or www.kettlevalleyrailway.org. Useful books include B Sanford's McCulloch's *Wonder* and D & S Langford's *Steel Rails and Iron Men*, and *Cycling the KVR*.

and furnishings from 1867, as well as animals, a restaurant and a decent gift shop. For more details on any of these, ask at the **Visitor Information Centre** ① *701 Highway 97, south of town, T250-5421415, www.vernontourism.com.* An additional summer-only information centre is north at 6326 Highway 97, T250-545 2959.

Silver Star Mountain Resort

① *T250-542 0224, www.skisilverstar.com. Fairly close to town, 22 km on Silver Star Rd from Hwy 97 North. Lift pass $68, youth $56, child $33 per day; night skiing $28, child $20, Thu-Sat 1530-2000; cross-country $20, youth $14, child $10.*

Silver Star is smaller, more relaxed and much prettier than most other resorts. The buildings are all painted bright, cheerful colours. Skiing here is good for beginners and intermediates, with 1240 ha of skiable terrain that breaks down as 20% beginner, 50% intermediate, 20% advanced and 10% expert. There are over 115 runs accessed by 12 lifts capable of handling 14,000 skiers per hour, and a snowboard park. There are also 100 km of cross-country ski trails in the area, as well as snowshoeing, skating, tubing, sleigh rides and snowmobile safaris. In summer the hill stays open for great biking and hiking. There is an **information kiosk** ① *T250-558 6092*, in the village centre and a free shuttle bus around the resort.

South of Kelowna ⬛🚲🏠🎠❄️🅿️⛰️🚌☕ ↦ *pp196-205.*

Penticton and around → *Colour map 1, C6.*

Every summer, the otherwise bland town of Penticton transforms into a hectic, throbbing beach-fest, attracting both families and a younger crowd, who come to party and show off their tans. Sandwiched between two lakes, the town has plenty of sand and water to go round and temperatures regularly exceed 35°C, sometimes reaching up to 45°C. Most of the action happens on **Okanagan Beach** around the Lakeshore Resort, where gear can be rented for a multitude of watersports. The beaches around **Skaha Lake** to the south are more family orientated and there's a nude beach at **3 Mile** towards Naramata.

Those bored of the beach scene will find plenty of other activities, including tubing down the channel between the two lakes, watching for birds, bighorn sheep and rattle-snakes at **Vaseux Lake Provincial Park** ⓘ *15 km south*, or rock-climbing at **Skaha Bluffs**. Seek advice at the helpful **Wine Country Visitor Centre** ⓘ *553 Railway St, T250-493 4055, www.tourismpenticton.com, mid-May to mid-Sep daily 0800-2000, mid-Sep to mid-May daily 0900-1700*. Knowledgeable staff can tell you all about the numerous local wineries. They also stock a broad range of Okanagan wines and organize daily tastings.

The only local sight is the **SS Sicamous** ⓘ *1099 Lakeshore Dr, on the beach, T250-492 0403, www.sssicamous.com, daily 1000-1600, mid-May to mid-Sep daily 0900-2100, $5, child $1*, a fully restored and decked out 1914 paddle-steamer. For railway buffs the highlight is a working model of the Kettle Valley Railway. The only section of that line still in use is 15 km north in Summerland. From late May to early October the **Kettle Valley Railway Steam Train** ⓘ *T250-494 8422, www.kettlevalley rail.org, May-Oct Sat-Mon 1030, 1330, also Thu-Fri in Jul-Aug, $20 return, youth $16, child $12*, leaves from Prairie Valley Station (take Prairie Valley Road from the highway) and covers just 10 km in two hours.

Naramata → *Colour map 1, C6.*

For those who understandably love the Okanagan's climate, scenery, orchards and vineyards, but feel that its towns are all a little brash and overcrowded, the answer is Naramata, a sleepy little village about 16 km north of Penticton on the east side of Okanagan Lake, away from the highway. With the highest concentration of wineries in the valley, this is the perfect place for a tour, which energetic visitors could even manage on foot. The trade-off, however, is that Naramat gets less sun and lacks a decent public beach. ►► *For further details, see Activities and tours, page 202.*

Apex Ski Resort

ⓘ *33 km west of Penticton, T1877-777 2739, www.apexresort.com. Day passes $55, youth $45, child $34, T250-292 8222; night skiing Fri-Sat 1600-2100, $12.*

With just 450 ha of skiable terrain, Apex village is dwarfed by Kelowna's Big White and even Vernon's Silver Star, but its small size is its strong point. The 67 runs, which break down as 16% beginner, 48% intermediate and 36% advanced, are serviced by four lifts. There's also night skiing, two terrain parks, snowshoeing and ice-skating. Equipment rentals and lessons are available at the hill. Carmi Road runs east of Penticton to the Carmi Cross Country Ski Trails, 17 km of well-marked but ungroomed trails.

Osoyoos → *Colour map 1, C6.*

As Highway 97 heads south through the copious wineries of Okanagan Falls and Oliver, the climate and scenery becomes increasingly arid. Osoyoos, a disappointingly ugly town set in a gloriously weird desert landscape of barren, scrub-covered hills, has Canada's lowest rainfall, highest temperatures and warmest water. Those entering from the Crowsnest Highway have to descend rapidly via a series of steep switchbacks to the bottom of the valley. Views from the top highlight the town's superb position on **Osoyoos Lake**.

Driving on Highway 97, it's hard not to be charmed by the endless parade of orchards and vineyards. Yet, before irrigation, most of this land was occupied by Canada's only living desert, an extension of the Great Basin Desert in the US and part of the Sonoran Desert ecosystem that runs right down into Mexico. The **Desert Centre** ⓘ *north of town, off Hwy 97, T250-495 2470, www.desert.org, mid-Apr to early Oct, 1000-1700, $6, child $3, tours run 1000, 1200, 1400, and the first of the day offers the best chance of seeing animals*, aims to protect the small, fragile pocket that remains, supporting over 100 rare plants and over 300 rare invertebrates, including about two dozen that are unique to the area. Fauna includes the great basin spadefoot toad, western rattlesnake and tiger salamander. The dominant flora are antelope brush and wild sage. There is over a mile of boardwalk from which to observe the desert's features but these are often so subtle that only the genuine enthusiasm of the guides brings the experience to life. Night tours and other occasional special events are listed on their website. The **Nk'mip Desert Cultural Centre** ① *1000 Rancher Creek Rd, T250-495 7901, www.nkmipdesert.com, mid-May to mid-Oct daily 0930-1630, mid-Oct to mid-May Mon-Sat 0930-1630, $12, child $8*, links this unique desert environment to the aboriginal culture that continues to flourish there. Inside and outside the extraordinary interpretive centre are interactive exhibits, walking trails through the fragile ecosystem, desert animals in 'critter corner', a reconstructed traditional Okanagan village, the multi-sensory 'Voices of the Past Pithouse' and the short film *Coyote Spirit*.

Some 11 km west of Osoyoos on Highway 3 is the highly photogenic **Spotted Lake**, where unusually high level of epsom salts, calcium and magnesium have resulted in large, almost circular blotches, which change colour dramatically according to weather conditions. Mud from the lake was used by natives to alleviate aches and pains and was believed to heal the spirit, bringing youth and wisdom. Warring enemies met here in peace to soothe battle wounds. For commanding views of the Okanagan Valley head 20 km up Kabau Forestry Road, just west of here, to the 1-km **Mount Kabau Lookout Trail** or the **Tuculnuit Trail**, a 4-km loop. For more information contact the helpful **Visitor Information Centre** ① *9912 Hwy 3, T250-495 5070, www.destinationosoyoos.com*.

Keremeos → *Colour map 1, C6.*

Set within the most stunning stretch of Highway 3, 46 km west of Osoyoos, Keremeos enjoys a classic Okanagan landscape, surrounded by orchards and is especially beautiful when the trees are in blossom. Justifiably dubbed the 'fruit stand capital of BC', the selection, quality and prices here are exceptional even by local standards. There is good golfing in the area and mountain biking at nearby Cawston but the major attraction in town is the **Keremeos Grist Mill and Gardens** ① *2 km north on Hwy 3A, T250-499 2888, www.keremeos.net, mid-May to mid-Oct 0930-1700, $5 including tour*. First built in 1877 to supply gold-rush pioneers travelling the Dewdney Trail, this mill has been lovingly restored as a very popular 'living museum'. Everything still functions as it did over a century ago: ancient strains of wheat grown on the premises are ground by the water-powered mill and baked into bread, which is sold in the café. People in costume do the work and give tours of the operation.

Cathedral Provincial Park

From the highway, 3 km west of Keremeos, Ashnola River Road leads over a historic red covered bridge and follows this pretty waterway 23 km to the **Lakeview trailhead** ① *a steep 6- or 7-hr hike, or $85 return transfer with Cathedral Lakes Lodge, with 1300 m elevation gain in 16 km*. This is the most direct of three routes into the spectacular 33,200-ha **Cathedral Provincial Park**. From the near desert of the Okanagan, the landscape changes to lush cedar and Douglas fir, then to pine, spruce, balsam fir and larch, finally climbing above the tree line to gain magnificent uninterrupted panoramas of the Cascade Mountains. It is well worth the effort for this is a chance to view paradise. Seven beautiful alpine lakes, their turquoise waters emphasized by the surrounding sharp granite peaks, are within easy walking distance. The trout fishing is excellent and there's a good chance of seeing mountain goats, bighorn sheep and marmots.

Around **Quiniscoe Lake** are the main wilderness campground, a ranger station and a private lodge. From here a network of trails leads to the other lakes; **Ladyslipper Lake**, the furthest and prettiest, is a mere 2.5 km away. Beyond are a number of strange rock formations that can all be seen on a 10-km round trip. The **Devil's Woodpile** is a series of upright jointed basalt columns. **Stone City** is a bizarre moonscape of eroded quartz monoliths. The **Giant Cleft** is a massive split in the granite mountain face. **Quiniscoe** and **Pyramid** mountains can both be reached via

British Columbia Okanagan South of Kelowna

Glacier Lake, each a 7-km round trip. A day's hike away is a wilderness campground at the **Haystack Lakes.** There is also a four-day hike to **Manning Park.**

● Sleeping

Kelowna p189, map p190

Kelowna has plenty of beds, though the mid-range choices and campgrounds are limited. Best of all are its 2 excellent hostels. If you're looking for a cheap motel, there are dozens stretching along the main drag on Harvey Av but none stand out.

L Manteo Resort, 3762 Lakeshore Rd, T250-860 1031, www.manteo.com. If you want to splurge, this is the place. It has incredible amenities, beautiful rooms and is in a perfect location.

A Abbott On The Lake, 1986 Abbott St, T250-762 0221, www.abbottonthelake.com. A heritage house right on the lake close to Downtown, offering 2 suites and 1 room tastefully decorated with antiques. Full breakfast, private beach and hot tub.

A Prestige Hotel, 1675 Abbott St, T250-860 7900, www.prestigehotelsandresorts.com. The rooms here are nicely kitted out, most have a glassed-in balcony and amenities include an indoor pool, hot tub and fitness room. The location across from City Park is the real attraction.

A-B Beach House B&B, 188 Beach Av, T250-763 2321, www.beach-house.ca. 2 luxurious rooms and 1 suite in a romantic historic house near Downtown. There's a lovely front veranda and a private beach.

B Abbott Villa Travelodge, 1627 Abbott St, T250-763 7771. The rooms are much plainer than those at the **Prestige** next door, but the plum location opposite City Park is the same and there's an outdoor heated pool.

B Royal Anne Hotel, 348 Bernard Av, T250-763 2277, www.royalannehotel.com. Big rooms with balconies (best on 2nd floor) and views, in a handy Downtown location. Exercise room and saunas.

D Montcalm Garden B&B, 951 Montcalm Dr, T250-762 0493, www.montcalmgarden.com. 3 reasonable rooms in a comfortable family home up above Downtown, with views from the patio and lovely gardens.

E Kelowna International Hostel, 2343 Pandosy St, T250-763 6024, www.kelownahostel.bc.ca. Well located close to Downtown, Lakeshore and beaches, this clean, friendly and helpful little hostel has dorms and private rooms with shared bath. There's a full kitchen, TV lounge, 2 outdoor decks with BBQ and hammocks, laundry, internet, lockers, free pick-up from the bus station and even a free coffee and a pancake breakfast.

E Same Sun International Hostel, 245 Harvey Av, T250-763 9814, www.samesun.com. This vast Mediterranean-style building downtown has 30 private rooms and 100 dorms. Top facilities, including a huge kitchen, common room with pool table, TV room, big patio with BBQ, lockers, internet, laundry and bike hire. Shuttles run daily to **Big White Ski Resort** during the ski season and they have a sister hostel in the Alpine Centre at the resort.

Camping

Okanagan Lake Provincial Park, 11 km north of Summerland, 45 km from Kelowna. North and south sites have different characters, but both are on the lake and have private pitches and showers. In the 1950s thousands of non-native trees were planted here, such as Russian olive, Chinese elm and Lombardy poplar.

Provincial Park Campgrounds, T250-548 0076. For the best camping, head to the north on the lake's west shore. Cross the bridge and follow signs. The 2 parks are open Apr-Oct and extremely busy. **Bear Creek** at Km 9, has 122 sites on the lake and showers. **Fintry**, at Km 32, has 100 sites amidst big trees and is right on the lake.

Big White Ski Resort p192

Big White can sleep an impressive 8900 people, mostly in quite expensive lodges, with ski packages often representing the best deal. Contact Central Reservations at T250-7658888 for details.

E Same Sun Ski-In Hostel, in the Alpine Centre, T250-765 7920, www.samesun.com. Has dorms and private doubles. There are hot tubs, internet, laundry, kitchen and a free pancake breakfast.

Vernon and around *p192*

C **Best Western Vernon Lodge**, 3914 32nd St, T250-545 3385, www.bestwestern vernon lodge.com. The best place to stay, thanks to a beautiful, tropical courtyard that has a creek running through the middle. There's also a restaurant, an indoor pool, hot tub and fitness room. Ask for a room with a balcony overlooking the creek.

C **Silver Lode Inn**, Silver Star Mountainside Resort, on the upper side, T250-549 5105, www.silverlode.com. Of the village's hand-ful of hostels, this is the best deal.

D **Richmond House 1894 B&B**, 4008 Pleasant Valley Rd, T250-549 1767, www. rich mondhousebandb.com. 3 pretty en suite rooms in an old house close to Downtown, with antique furnishings, veranda, hot tub and gourmet breakfast.

D **Schell Motel**, 2810 35th St, T250-545 1351, www.schellmotel.ca. Good-value rooms with balconies, some with kitchen-ettes. At the back is an outdoor heated pool with a natural creek running alongside, a hot tub and secluded BBQ area. Ask for a room overlooking the pool. Close to Downtown.

E **Same Sun Hostel**, Silver Star Mountainside Resort, the uppermost building, T250-545 8933, www.samesun.com. Dorms and private doubles with shared bath, kitchen, hot tub and a free pancake breakfast. Also an RV parking lot (**E**). The budget option.

Camping

Dutch's Campground, 15408 Kalamalka Lake Rd, T250-545 1023. Reasonable setting, conveniently close to the lake and Kal Beach. Open all year.

Ellison Provincial Park, 16 km southwest on Okanagan Lake. Take 25th Av west from Downtown and keep going straight. 71 private, wooded sites in a gorgeous park with hiking trails, great beaches, a playing field and even an underwater park for snorkelling and diving.

Penticton and around *p193*

Penticton has a lot of hotels and motels so, though most are pretty dreary, finding a room shouldn't be a problem except during the Ironman Triathlon in Aug.

A-B **Penticton Lakeside Resort**, 21 Lake-shore Dr, T250-493 8221, www.penticton lakeresort.com. Luxury option in the

best location, with pool, hot tub, fitness room, bar, casino and a first-class restaurant.

B **Sandman Hotel**, 939 Burnaby Av W, T250-493 7151, www.sandman.ca. Standard, reliable and well located, with kitchenettes, pool and hot tub.

B-C **Crown Motel**, 950 Lakeshore Dr, T250-492 4092, www.crownmotel.ca. Best value of the many motels rubbing shoulders opposite the main beach. Bright, reasonable-sized rooms with patios, BBQs and a heated outdoor pool.

E **Double Diamond Hostel**, Apex Ski Resort, T250-292 8256, www.doublediamond hostel.com. Dorms and private rooms, kitchen facilities, games room with pool table, ski lockers, internet, TV and laundry. There's also an RV parking lot (**F**).

E **Penticton HI Hostel**, 464 Ellis St, T250-492 3992, www.hihostels.ca. Friendly and well-run hostel in a Downtown building full of character. Dorms and private rooms with shared bath, kitchen, TV lounge, laundry, lockers and BBQ. Good for information.

Camping

Camp-Along RV Resort, 6 km south on Hwy 97, T250-497 5584, www.campalong. com. Set in an apricot orchard, with a pool and good views of Skaha Lake.

Vaseaux Lake Provincial Park, 25 km S on Hwy 97, T250-548 0076. Just 12 sites in a park. Great for swimming, hiking and wild-life spotting.

Wright's Beach Camp, 4071 Skaha Lake Rd, T250-492 7120, www.wrightbeachcamp. com. Quite ugly and cramped, despite trees and beach, but still about the best of the many in town around Skaha Lake.

Naramata *p194*

A-B **Naramata Heritage Inn and Spa**, T250-496 6808, www.naramatainn.com. Hands down the finest place to stay in the valley, this lovingly restored historic building has a gorgeous interior, featuring hardwood floors and period furnishings. The 12 classic rooms have clawfoot tubs and semi-private decks with wrought-iron furniture. Excellent on-site restaurant and wine bar. Breakfast and use of mountain bikes included.

B **Sandy Beach Lodge and Resort**, 4275 Mill Rd, T250-496 5765, www.sandybeach resort.com. 6 rooms with private verandas in a restored log lodge with original 1940s furnishings and attractive lounge and dining areas. Long private beach, heated outdoor pool, hot tub, tennis courts, canoes and games. Also log cottages rented by the week, sleeping up to 6.

C The Village Motel, 244 Robinson Av, T250-496 5535. Very pleasant and friendly.

D BC Motel, 365 Robinson Av, T250-496 5482. Another perfectly decent option.

Osoyoos *p194*

Osoyoos's rooms are greatly overpriced in summer and fill up quickly. The cheaper motels, mostly along the strip on Hwy 3, still sport 1970s decor and brown carpets.

C Avalon Inn, 9106 Main St, T250-495 6334, www.avaloninn.ca. Reasonable rooms with private balconies.

C Spanish Fiesta/Falcon Resorts, 7104-6 Main St, T250-495 6833/7544, www.falcon-spanish.com. Small, reasonable rooms with kitchenettes, right on the lake with private stretch of beach. 2 swimming pools, indoor hot tub, games room, playground, BBQ and laundry room.

D Villa Blanca B&B, 132 Deerfoot Rd, off Chapman, 10 km east on Hwy 3, T250-495 5334. Situated on the hilltop facing out over the valley, this is definitely the place to stay if you have transport and are happy to be out of town. The 3 rooms have private baths and great views. Gourmet breakfast.

D The White Horse B&B, 3800 Hwy 3 W, 1 Km E, T250-495 2887, www.thewhitehorse bb.com. Another great location, just out of town. 3 rooms with private bath and patio.

Camping

Brookvale Holiday Resort, 1219 Lakeshore Dr, T250-495 7514, www.brookvalecamp ground.com. The last of many RV parks along this road, also with simple cabañas, bedding not supplied.

Haynes Point Provincial Park, follow Hwy 97 S, then look for signs, T250-548 0076. Beautifully located on a sand spit reaching out into the lake. Showers and flush toilets, but sites are a bit too closely packed. The busiest provincial campground in BC, so reservations are essential.

Keremeos *p195*

D Pasta Trading Post, 629 7th Av, T250-499 2933. 3 quaint rooms in a centrally located historic building decorated with period furnishings. Natural stone hot tub and continental breakfast.

E Similkameen Motel, 3098 Hwy 3, T250-499 5984, A small, standard motel in an orchard setting that has 6 cheap and cheerful rooms.

Cathedral Provincial Park *p195*

LL Cathedral Lakes Lodge, T250-492 1606, www.cathedral-lakes-lodge.com, Jun to mid-Oct. Unless you're camping, this is the only place to stay in the park. Rooms are in the handsome log lodge, the adjacent bungalow, or one of 4 cabins. Price goes down the more nights you stay and includes all meals (all-you-can-eat). Campers can buy meals at the lodge. A jeep ride to the top is $120 return per person in high season, free if you get a room. Hot tub and use of canoes. Reservations required.

Camping

There is wilderness camping at Quiniscoe Lake. There are also campsites below the Lakeview trailhead at Buckhorn, 2 km further down Ashnola River Rd (vehicle accessible) and at Lake of the Woods. Visitors should be prepared to rough it.

⑦ Eating

Kelowna *p189, map p190*

Some of the best dining is at the winery bistros, which often have great views but usually only offer lunch (see Activities and tours, page 203).

ⵟⵟⵟ Fresco, 1560 Water St, T250-868 8805. Exquisite West Coast-style fine dining, consistently ranked as the town's finest.

ⵟⵟⵟ Old Vines, at Quails Gate Winery, 3303 Boucherie Rd, T250-769 4451. Beautifully nestled in the vineyard itself, the restaurant's small menu changes seasonally to reflect locally available produce and compliment the wines.

ⵟⵟⵟ-ⵟⵟ Bouchons Bistro, 1180 Sunset Dr, T250-763 6595. Classic, traditional French

For an explanation of sleeping and eating price codes used in this guide, see inside the front cover. Other relevant information is found in Essentials, see pages 28-31.

cuisine, specializing in bouillabaisse and seafood. Stylish but casual bistro setting.

Hector's Casa, 2911 Pandosy St, T250-860 3868. A lively little Mexican place that's a good bet for those exploring Lakeshore.

Lakeside Dining, 500 Cook Rd, at the Eldorado Hotel, T250-763 7500. A very satisfying eating experience in an intimate and atmospheric room with hardwood floors and an air of understated sophistication. Seafood and steaks, but also some very reasonably priced pasta dishes and salads. There are views of the lake, especially from the summer patio, which is right on the water.

Mission Hill Terrace, at Mission Hill Winery, 1730 Mission Hill Rd, T250-768 6448. A broad and sophisticated French-influenced lunch menu, daily 1130-1600, served on an exquisite terrace with views of Okanagan Lake behind the rolling vineyards.

Sunset Bistro, at Summerhill Winery, 4870 Chute Lake Rd, T250-764 8000, www.summerhill.bc.ca. Views over the lake from a covered patio and a menu that focuses on local produce, seafood, game, antipasti plates and artisan cheeses.

Vintropolis, 231 Bernard Av, T250-762 7682. A long, narrow space with tables as high as the elegant bar. The menu concentrates on tapas dishes, with a wide selection of wines by the bottle or glass.

Wild Apple, at the Manteo Resort, 3762 Lakeshore Rd, T250-860 4488. Elegant space in a perfect lakeside location, offering sophisticated West Coast and international dishes and tapas. Surprisingly reasonable prices.

The Yellow House, 526 Lawrence Av, T250-763 5136. Centrally located, with a lovely garden patio and a broad ambitious menu that stretches from goulash to ahi tuna to seafood linguine. Everything is made in-house and very fresh.

Bean Scene Coffee House, 274 Bernard Av, T250-763 1814. Casual, central and agreeably downbeat, the clear choice for coffee. Outside seating close to the beach.

Bohemian Café, 524 Bernard Av, T250-862 3517. Attractive and popular Downtown purveyor of good breakfasts and coffee.

Vernon and around p192

The Eclectic Med, 3117 32nd St, T250-558 4646. Lives up to its name. The menu is impressively broad and varied, and the decor is simple, tasteful and quite romantic. A little overpriced though.

Di Vinos Ristorante Italiano, 3224 30th Av, T250-549 3463. Fresh pasta and some exciting choices, such as sambuca prawns.

Mahoroba, 2921 30th Av, T250-558 0893. Lunch-only Japanese buffet that's a big hit with the locals.

Merona's, 2905 29th St, T250-260 4257. Intimidatingly large portions of good Greek food and cheap beer in surroundings that are nicer than the exterior suggests.

Bean Scene, 2923 30th Av, T250-558 1817. Casual Downtown spot for good coffee.

El Portillo, 2706 30th Av, T250-545 9599. Comfortable and attractive coffee shop slightly out of the centre. Good snacks and cakes. Nice views from the patio.

Little Tex, 3302 B 29th St, T250-558 1919, www.littletex.ca. A cute, colourful and very casual café-style joint for fajitas, quesadillas and pizza.

Penticton p193

Gunbarrel Saloon and Restaurant, Saddleback Lodge, 115 Clearview Cres, Apex Mountain Resort. A very popular no-smoking spot for grub and pints.

Magnum's, in the Lakeside Resort, 21 Lakeshore Dr, T250-493 8221. Good for breakfast or brunch on the outdoor patio overlooking the lake.

Salty's Beach House, 1000 Lakeshore Dr, T250-493 5001. An eccentric, pricey, but extremely popular spot resembling a beach shack. Serves tasty seafood specialities from Mexico to Thailand.

Theo's, 687 Main St, T250-492 4019, www.eatsquid.com. A Penticton institution, this place is vast and very popular, yet intimate and personal. Serves big portions of tasty, authentic Greek cuisine. An extensive wine list, good service and patio.

Elite, 340 Main St, T250-492 3051. An authentic diner, worth visiting for the atmosphere alone. The horseshoe booths and decor look as if they haven't changed since the place opened in 1927. Cheap breakfasts and other perennial favourites like grilled cheese sandwiches.

Green Beanz Café, 218 Martin St, T250-493 8085. The undisputed best choice for coffee, with an arty, downbeat atmosphere.

¶ **Tokyo Japanese**, 786 Westminster St, T250-492 6610. A tiny place with the best sushi and tempura in town. The lunch box is filling and tasty.

Naramata *p194*

¶¶¶ **Rock Oven Dining Room**, Naramata Heritage Inn, T250-496 6808. A very sophisticated location with a $70 taster menu, well-crafted West Coast dishes, a good wine list and live music on Fri evenings in the Cobblestone Winebar.
¶¶ **The Patio**, at Lake Breeze Vineyards, 930 Summit Rd, T250-496 5619, www.lakebreeze.ca, May-Sep 1200-1500. Mediterranean-inspired dishes served on a lovely patio.
¶ **Naramata Pub**, 986 Robinson Av. A local favourite, with a Kettle Valley Railway theme.

Osoyoos *p194*

¶¶¶ **The Sonora Room**, Burrowing Owl Winery, Oliver, T1877-498 0620, summer only. A setting to die for and a handsome room with vaulted wood ceiling. Serves gourmet food.
¶¶ **Campo Marina**, 5907 Main St, T250-495 7650, Tue-Sun from 1700. First rate, authentic Italian cuisine, and a good list of local wines.
¶¶ **Chalet Helvetia**, 8312 74th Av, T250-495 7552. Top notch authentically Swiss food and warm service in a European chalet ambience.
¶¶ **Wildfire Grill**, 8526 Main St, T250-495 2215. Global cuisine, with a coffee bar-bistro next door.

Keremeos *p195*

¶¶ **Pasta Trading Post**, 629 7th Av, T250-499 2933. Antique shop turned restaurant, specializing in steak and seafood, with a garden patio and B&B-style rooms (**C**).

⊙ Bars and clubs

Kelowna *p189, map p190*

Gotchas, 238 Leon Av, T250-860 0800, www.gotchaclub.com. 2 floors, 2 rooms and 2 DJs spinning hip-hop, R&B and chart music.
McCulloch Station, 2789 KLO Rd, T250-762 8882. Out of the way but pleasant and old-fashioned.

The Pier Marine Pub, cross the floating bridge, then take the first left, T250-769 4777. Appealing waterside location and patio. Good food, often involving great lobster, crab or steak deals.
Rose's Waterfront Pub, 1352 Water St, in the Grand Hotel,T250-860 1141. Perfect for summer drinking, with an attractive patio overlooking the lake and marina.
Waterfront Wines, 1180 Sunset Dr, T1866-979 1222. Set in a narrow room dominated by the bar, attached to a top wine store and equipped with a bistro serving delectable small dishes. This is the smart choice for a glass of wine or a martini.

Penticton *p193*

In summer, Penticton is a very lively town and it doesn't take long to find where the action is. The crowd's loyalties depend on variables like happy hours, drinks specials, favoured DJs and live music.
Barking Parrot Lounge, in the Lakeside Resort. Most evenings begin at this sophisticated but laid-back bar, which is certainly the town's nicest.
Blue Mule Country Club, 218 Martin St, T250-493 1819. A club usually specializing in country music, but the most happening spot in town nevertheless.
The Element, 535 Main St, T250-493 1023. A typical small-town club, with multiple bars, pool tables, booths and couches, mainly attracting a younger crowd.

Osoyoos *p194*

Sage and Sand Neighbourhood Pub, 6403 Cottonwood Dr, T250-495 2322. Reasonable food, good beer on tap and a pool table. The best place to meet locals.
Westridge Brew Pub, junction of Hwys 3 and 97, T250-495 7679. A nicer pub, which brews its own beers, but also further out and less popular.

⊙ Entertainment

Kelowna *p189, map p190*
Art
Kelowna has a lot of good pieces of art in public places. Pick up a Public Art brochure from the Visitor Centre, which also supplies

a handy map of the Cultural District, where most of the galleries are.

Art Ark Gallery, 135-1295 Cannery Lane, T250-862 5080, www.theartark.com. The best of the private galleries, with some exceptionally beautiful items.

Geert Maas Sculpture Gardens and Gallery, 250 Reynolds Rd via Hwy 97 N and Sexsmith Rd, T250-860 7012, www.geertmaas.org. Bronze sculptures and other unusual, impressive works by this well-known and respected artist. Phone to check hours.

Kelowna Art Gallery, 1315 Water St, T250-762 2226, Tue-Sat 1000-1700, Thu 1000-2100, Sun 1300-1600, $4. Excellent Canadian exhibits.

Rotary Centre for the Arts, 421 Cawston Av, T250-717 5304, www.rotarycentreforthearts.com, 0800-2300, free. A multipurpose venue with a wide array of cultural possibilities, including **Alternator Gallery**, T250-868 2298; **Gallery 421**, T250-448 8888; **Potters Addict**, T250-763 1875; **Mary Irwin Theatre**; and various working studios.

Turtle Island Gallery, 1295 Cannery Lane, T250-717 8235. A fine collection of First Nations art.

Cinema

Grand 10 Cinema, 948 McCurdy Rd, T250-491 4178. A long way down Harvey, but the multiplex with the best selection.

Paramount Theatre, 261 Bernard Av, T250-762 9066. A small cinema Downtown.

Music and theatre

Kelowna Community Theatre, 1375 Water St, T250-469 8506, ww.kelownacommunitytheatre.com; **Okanagan Symphony**, T250-763 7544, various venues; **Prospera Pl**, Water St, T250-979 0888, www.prosperaplace.com, the major arena for big-name concerts and sporting events; **Sunshine Theatre**, 1304 Ellis St, T250-717 5304, www.sunshinetheatre.org.

Vernon and around *p192*

Vernon and District Performing Arts Centre, 3800 33rd St, T250-542 9355, www.ticketseller.ca, one of the valley's best venues for live music, theatre and dance; **Vernon Cinema**, 2910 30th Av, T250-545 0352, www.vernoncinema.com; **Vernon Public Art Gallery**, 3228 31st Av, T250-545 3173, www.galleries.bc.ca/vernon.

Penticton *p193*

Art Gallery of the South Okanagan, 199 Marina Way, T250-493 2928, www.galleries.bc.ca/agso, Tue-Fri 1000-1700, $2, Sat-Sun 1200-1700, free, an attractive space, intelligently managed, with a good little gift shop; **Pen-Mar Cinema Centre**, 361 Martin St, T250-492 5974, www.cinemaclock.com.

✺ Festivals and events

Kelowna *p189, map p190*

Kelowna is the natural main focus of the valley-wide **Spring Wine Festival** in early May and the **Fall Wine Festival** in late-Sep/Oct. About 90,000 people attend over 100 events at various locations, including dinners, parades and grape stomps. For information on both festivals, T250-861 6654, www.owfs.com.

May Life and Arts Festival, T250-762 3991, www.lifeandarts.com. Held over 3 days in the Cultural District, music, theatre, street entertainers, visual arts and a lantern festival, all designed to be experiential and to draw audiences into the creative process.

Jun Fat Cat Children's Festival, www.fatcatfestival.ca. 2 days of activities and entertainment for kids in Waterfront Park.

Jul Cherry Fair, at the BC Orchard Industry Museum.

Sep The International Dragon Boat Festival, www.kelownadragonboatfestival.com. A 3-day event held in Waterfront Park in mid-Sep, featuring races, live entertainment and food.

Oct Apple Fair at the BC Orchard Industry Museum.

Vernon and around *p192*

Jul-Aug and **Dec** Caravan Farm Theatre, T250-546 8533, www.caravanfarmtheatre.com. For 3 weeks in summer and throughout Dec, this excellent 30 year-old company stages daily outdoor shows using varied and imaginative settings on their farm in Knob Hill, 11 km NW of Armstrong, sometimes moving from set to set or even transporting their audience in a wagon.

Penticton *p193*

The last weekend of Aug is the busiest in Penticton's calendar, with every room in

town reserved months ahead. Also takes part in the **Fall Wine Festival** in late-Sep/Oct.
May Okanagan International Children's Festival, T250-493 8825, www.okchildrens fest.org. 3 days of live entertainment, games, hands-on activities and workshops.
Jul Beach Blanket Film Festival, www.bea chblanketfilmfest.ca. Perhaps the most entertaining event of the year, films shown for 3 evenings on Okanagan Beach and are preceded by live entertainment.
Aug Peach Festival, T1800-663 5052, www.peachfest.com. A massive and long-running festival at the beginning of Aug.
Ironman Canada Triathlon, www.ironman. ca. Attracts 1000 iron men from over 30 countries, and requires 4000 volunteers.

♥ Shopping

Kelowna *p189, map p190*
The Cultural District is the best area for art and gifts, including the wonderful **Art Ark Gallery** (see Entertainment, above). The couple of Downtown blocks between Bernard and Lawrence, Water and Ellis are best for boutiques and window-shopping.
Blonde, 293 Bernard Av, T250-862 8778. A showcase for hip Canadian street-wear designers, including the owner.
Drydock & Lee Clothing Co, 1603 Pandosy St, T250-861 6770. Classic designer clothing.
Posh Gallery, 1579 Pandosy St, T250-862 9404. High-end designer jewellery and accessories, very trendy and desirable stuff.

Penticton *p193*
There are a string of craft stores along the very appealing but disappointingly short Front St, which is trying very hard to bring a bit of colour and culture to Downtown. The **Art Gallery** also has a good gift shop.
The Book Shop, 242 Main St, T250-492 6661. An excellent second-hand book-shop, arguably one of the best in the country for its breadth, organization of stock and knowledgeable staff.

▲ Activities and tours

Kelowna *p189, map p190*
Cheese tasting
Carmelis Goat Cheese Artisan, 170 Timberline Rd, T250-470 0341,

www.carmelisgoatcheese.com, May-Oct daily 1000-1800, Mar-Apr and Oct-Dec daily 1100-1700. Has 20 different goat's cheeses including blue cheese and brie. Book ahead for a tour ($4), which includes tasting. Combines well with a wine tour.

Golf
Predictably enough, the Okanagan has the longest, sunniest, driest golf season in the country. There are 15 courses in the Kelowna area alone.
Gallagher's Canyon, 4320 Gallagher's Dr W, T250-861 4240, www.golfbc.com. Narrow fairways run harrowingly close to a steep ravine.
Harvest Golf Club, 2725 Kelowna St, T250-862 3103, www.harvestgolf.com. Set among orchards, lake views.
Okanagan Golf Club, 3200 Via Centrale, T250-765 5955, www.golfbc.com. Boasts 2 championship courses.

Hiking
Mission Greenway in the town centre, makes for a pleasant stroll up to 18 km. Mission Creek Regional Park at Springfield and Leckie is particularly worth exploring. The trail up Knox Mountain is more demanding and satisfying. More difficult to reach, but the most recommended hike or bike in the area is the Myra Canyon Trestles section of the Kettle Valley Railway (see page 193). You can hike or bike the Kettle Valley Railway all the way to Naramata/Penticton via Chute Lake, where you can fish for rainbow trout and stay in a tent or rustic cabin. Okanagan Mountain Provincial Park also has some good longer trails. Mountain Goat Trail climbs through a granite obstacle course to Divide Lake and High Rim Trail is a 50-km wilderness route to Vernon, which offers a smorgasbord of the Okanagan's many diverse landscapes.

Orchards and Gardens
Elysium Garden Nursery, 2834 Belgo Rd, T250-491 1368, www.elysiumgardens.com, Apr-Sep daily 0900-1700. The 2 ha of peren-nial gardens are set in an old apple orchard, surrounded by mountain views.
Kelowna Land & Orchard Co., 3002 Dunster Rd, off KLO Rd, T250-763 1091, www.k-l-o.com,

Apr-Oct, $7.50, child $5. Call for opening times. Popular tours in a 50-seat covered hay wagon around this historic orchard that was one of Kelowna's first. Lunch is a special treat in the former home or on the patio of **Ridge Restaurant**.
Okanagan Lavender Herb Farm, 4380 Takla Rd, T250-764 7795, www.okanagan lavender.com. Self-guided tours around a lavender field and U-pick.

Skiing
See Big White Ski Resort, page 192.

Tour operators
Distinctly Kelowna Tours, T250-979 1211, www.wildflowersandwine.com, $73 for ½- day wine tour. Also offers hiking and walking tours, stopping at a couple of wineries.
Monashee Adventure Tours Inc, 470 Cawston Av, T250-762 9253, www.mona sheeadventuretours.com. Bike, hike, snow-shoe, winery, canoe and skiing tours. Their speciality is in combined bike and wine/food tours. They also operate a shuttle service around Myra Canyon.
Okanagan Wine Country Tours, www.ok winetours.com, ½-day tour for $75. Also offers full days and over-night stays.
Scenic Boat Tours of the Okanagan, T250-861 0691, www.okanaganboattours. com. A variety of tours, including 1-hr tours at $20 per person (time it for sunset).

Watersports
Lakefront Sports Centre, Grand Hotel, 1310 Water St, T250-862 2469, www.lake frontsports.com. Rental of everything from powerboats to baseball gloves.
Sports Rent, 3000 Pandosy St, T250-861 5699, www.sportsrentkelowna.com. Rents anything; bikes, skis and kayaks.

Wineries
For full information on Kelowna's dozens of wineries, visit the Visitor Centre or the BC Wine Museum.
Calona, 1125 Richter St, T250-762 9144, www.calonavineyards.ca. BC's oldest winery and the most central in Kelowna.
Cedar Creek Estate Winery, 5445 Lakeshore Rd, T250-764 8866. Lunch offered in their very pleasant terrace bistro.

Hainle, 5355 Trepanier Bench Rd, south on Hwy 97 near Peachland, T250-767 2525, www.hainle.com. One of the few organic wineries. Their **Amphora Bistro** is recommended for lunch (Tue-Sun).
Mission Hill, 1730 Mission Hill, T250-768 5125, www.missionhillwinery.com. A gorgeous property with views over the whole valley, newly expanded to include a bell tower that rings on the hour and a classic arched barrel room. Their **Terrace Restaurant** is a beautiful spot for lunch.
Quail's Gate, 3303 Boucherie Rd, T250-769 4451, www.quailsgate.com. A good selection of wines sampled in a turn-of-the-20th-century storehouse. Their **Old Vines Patio** is a nice spot for gourmet lunches and dinners.
Raven's Ridge Cidery, 3002 Dunster Rd, T250-763 1091. First in the province to make ice cider.
Sumac Ridge, Hwy 97, further south near Summerland, T250-494 0451, www.suma cridge.com. Experts in sparkling wines, with the **Cellar Door Bistro**, open daily in summer for lunch and dinner.
Summerhill Estate, 4870 Chute Lake Rd, T250-764 8000, www.summerhill.bc.ca. Possibly the most interesting and prog-ressive organic winery, where bottles are aged in a giant pyramid. There's a settlers' cabin to visit and the **Sunset Bistro**.

Vernon and around p192
Skiing
See Silver Star Mountain Resort, page 193.

Penticton p193
Birdwatching
Vaseux Lake Provincial Park, 25 km S on Hwy 97, T250-548 0076. Especially renowned for its birdwatching, but also has bighorn sheep, rattlesnakes and many other animals.

Hiking and biking
The total Kettle Valley route is 600 km. The most challenging section of the trail is north of Penticton, climbing 900 m through 2 tunnels and past Chute Lake on the way to the Myra Canyon on the edge of Kelowna. Access is where the rail crosses Naramata Rd, or right from this road to the top of Arawana or Smethurst roads. The lift

at Apex Mountain Resort is open Jul-Aug at weekends to access the Apex Moumtain Bike Park and a world of alpine meadows for hikers, $15, child $12. Campbell Mountain and Ellis Ridge Canyon are also recommended for hiking, while Munson Mountain is a nice walk and the place for views.

The Bike Barn, 300 Westminster Av W, T250-492 4140. Everything a cyclist could desire, including rental and trail information.

Rock-climbing

Skaha Bluffs has world-class rock-climbing, with 260 climbs and 400 bolted routes.
Skaha Rock Adventures, T250-493 1765 www.skaharockclimbing.com. Provides lessons and will take you out.

Skiing

See **Apex Ski Resort**, page 194.
Nickel Plate Nordic Centre, 6 km west of the resort, T250-292 8110, www.nickelplate nordic.org, has excellent cross-country skiing, with 65 km of groomed and track-set trails (70% beginner, 20% intermediate, 10% advanced), and 25 km of snowshoeing trails. Day passes are $14, youth $10, child $7; rentals are $16, youth $14, child $10. Snow-shoe trail fee and rental is $10. There's also a large day lodge with kitchen, lounge areas and showers.

Tour operators

Bacchus Tours, T250-770 8282. You drink, they drive. A tour of neighbouring wineries.

Tubing

In town, a path has been made along the 8 km river channel that connects the 2 lakes. Most people prefer to float down the channel on a giant inner tube.
Coyote Cruises, 215 Riverside Dr, T250-492 2115. Jun-Sep 0900-2000. For $10 they will rent you a tube and transport you back.

Naramata *p194*
Wineries

Hillside Estate, 1350 Naramata Rd, T250-493 6274, www.hillsideestate.com. Hourly tours 1215-1515. **Barrel Room Bistro** open for lunch, 1130-1500.
Lake Breeze, 930 Sammet Rd, T250-496 5659. Small winery with 2 self-catering cottages for rent.

Poplar Grove Winery, 1060 Poplar Grove Rd, T250-492 2352. Also makes some tasty cheeses.
Red Rooster Winery, 891 Naramata Rd, T250-492 2424, www.redroosterwinery. com. Some of the valley's finest reds.

Osoyoos *p194*
Golf

Osoyoos Golf and Country Club, 12300 Golf Course Dr, T250-495 7003.

Tour operators

Desert Country Wine Tours, T250-498 7316, www.desertcountrywinetours.com. 3-hr tours in an 11-person van, costing $73 per person.

Watersports

Wakepilot, T250-495 4195, www.wake pilot.com. Wakeboarding, waterskiing and tubing.

Wineries

Oliver, to the North of Osoyoos, has the valley's highest concentration of vineyards after Naramata.
Burrowing Owl Vineyards, T250-498 0620, Oliver, www.bovwine.com. Great wines, a lovely site and a fine restaurant.
Nk'mip Cellars, 1400 Rancher Creek Rd, T250-495 2985, www.nkmipcellars.com. The first aboriginal winery in North America, using grapes from their own vineyard. Stunning views, a desert cultural centre, campground, 9-hole golf course. The **Terrace Restaurant**, serves aboriginal-inspired cuisine, May-Oct.

Keremeos *p195*
Wineries

Crowsnest Vineyards, Surprise Dr, Cawston, T250-499 5129, www.crowsnestvineyards. com. Tours, tastings and a restaurant.

⊖ Transport

Kelowna *p189, map p190*
Air

Kelowna Airport has daily flights to **Vancouver** ($118 one-way), **Victoria** ($122) and **Calgary** ($132) with West Jet, T1800-538 5696, www.westjet.com; to **Vancouver** ($118) and **Calgary** ($132) with **Air Canada**,

T1888-247 2262, www.air canada.com; to
Seattle ($145) with Horizon Air, T1800-
547 9308, www.alaskaair.com.
  Airline offices Air Canada, T250-765
8777; WestJet, T250-4915600; Horizon Air,
T1800-547 9308.

Bus
Local BC Transit, T250-860 8121, www.bus
online.ca.
Long distance Greyhound, T250-860
3835, www.greyhound.ca, runs 7 daily
buses to **Vancouver** ($62, 6hrs), 3 to **Banff**
($75, 8 hrs) and **Calgary** ($87, 10 hrs), 4 to
Kamloops ($28, 3-4 hrs), 7 to **Vernon** ($13,
1 hr) and 2 to all points east on Hwy 3 via
Rock Creek, including **Nelson** ($55, 5-6 hrs).
The station is at 2366 Leckie Rd, off Hwy 97.
City bus No 8 runs to town.

Taxi
Kelowna Cabs, T250-762 2222.

Vernon and around *p192*
Bus
Local Vernon Regional Transit System,
T250-545 1361, www.busonline.ca.
Long distance The Greyhound station
is at 30th St/31st Av, T250-545 0527, with
7 buses daily to **Kelowna** ($13, 1 hr), 3 direct
to **Kamloops** ($21, 2 hrs) and 4 to **Salmon
Arm** ($13, 1 hr).

Penticton *p193*
Bus
Local Transit buses, T250-492 5602, run
from Downtown to Skaha Lake/Naramata.
  Long-distance The Greyhound station,
T250-493 4101, is just off Main at Nanaimo/
Ellis, with 5 buses daily to **Vancouver** ($62,
6-8 hrs), 3 to **Calgary** ($95, 12-14 hrs), 3 to
Kamloops ($40, 4½ hrs) and 2 to **Osoyoos**
($14, 1 hr).

Osoyoos *p194*
Bus
The Greyhound stop is at 9912 Hwy 3, T250-

495 7252, with 1 daily bus to **Vancouver**
($69, 9 hrs), 1 to **Kelowna** ($23, 3 hrs) and
1 to **Calgary** ($111, 16 hrs).

Keremeos *p195*
Bus
Greyhound buses stop in Downtown, with
1 service daily to **Vancouver** ($55, 6½ hrs)
and 2 to **Kelowna** ($21, 2 hrs).

❶ Directory

Kelowna *p189, map p190*
Banks HSBC Bank, 384 Bernard Av, T250-
763 3939. **Internet** Library; The Grand
Bay Café, 1310 Water St, T250-763 4500.
Laundry Cullen's Cleaning Carousel, 2660
Pandosy, T250-763 9992. **Library**, 1380 Ellis
St, T250-762 2800. **Medical services**
Kelowna General Hospital, 2268 Pandosy
St, T250-862 4000; Walk-in clinics 515
Harvey Av, T250- 862 3113; 3970 Lakeshore,
T250- 764 8878; 1990 Cooper Av, T250-861
3235. **Post office** Canada Post, 571 Bernard
Av, T250-868 8480; 3155 Lakeshore Rd,
T250-763 3939.

Vernon and around *p192*
Medical services Vernon Jubilee Hospital,
2101 32nd St, T250-545 2211. **Post office**
Canada Post, 3101 32nd Av/31St, T250-545
8239.

Penticton *p193*
Banks Around Main St and Nanaimo Av.
Internet Several cafés, such as the
Mousepad Café, 557 Main St, T250-493
2050. **Post office** Canada Post, 1160
Government St, T250-493 1737.

Osoyoos *p194*
Internet Library (free); Visitor Centre
(free). **Library** 8707 Main St, T250-495
7637. **Medical services** 7139 362nd Av,
Oliver, 20 km north, T250-498 5000. **Post
office** Canada Post, 8308 78th Av, T250-
495 6811.

West Kootenays

Hemmed in by the Selkirk and Purcell Mountains and the Kootenay and Lower Arrow Lakes, the West Kootenays comprises a ruggedly beautiful and undiscovered collection of small communities, connected by tortuous roads that wind through lake-filled valleys, jagged mountains, rocky bluffs and icy creeks. Their focal point, scenic and culturally vibrant Nelson, combines perfectly with Kaslo and New Denver to make a trio of pretty former mining towns that can be easily visited as a loop. Sporting activities are rewarding here, particularly skiing, mountain biking and hiking, and the crowds are relatively thin. There are also a few good, accessible hot springs and the odd atmospheric ghost town. As on the Gulf Islands, counter-culture thrives here, meaning plenty of arts and crafts, healthy living, organic farming (including less than legal crops), music, spirituality, colour and dogs. ▸▸ For Sleeping, Eating and other listings, see pages 213-221.

Ins and outs

Greyhound run two buses daily from Kelowna to Nelson via Castlegar. Getting around the Kootenays without your own vehicle is possible, but challenging. Nelson has the most useful Visitor Information Centre, but there are others in Kaslo, New Denver and Nakusp. Also check www.kootenays-bc.com, a very useful site. ▸▸ *For further details, see Transport, page 221.*

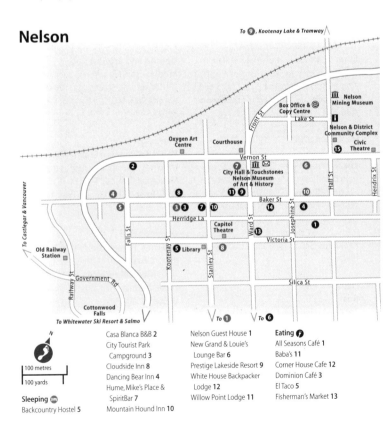

Nelson

To **9**, Kootenay Lake & Tramway

Nelson Mining Museum

Box Office & @ Copy Centre
Lake St

Nelson & District Community Complex

Oxygen Art Centre   Courthouse   Front St

Civic Theatre 15

Vernon St

2

City Hall & Touchstones Nelson Museum of Art & History **7**

6

11 9

10

4

8

Baker St

5   Herridge La   **3 3 7 10**   **14**   **4**

1

Capitol Theatre   Ward St   **13**   Josephine St

Falls St   Victoria St

5 Library   **8**   Kootenay St   Stanley St   Hall St   Hendrix St

To Castlegar & Vancouver

Old Railway Station

Railway   Government Rd

Silica St

Cottonwood Falls
To Whitewater Ski Resort & Salmo

To **1**   To **6**

N
100 metres
100 yards

Nelson 🔲🚲🏠🛏️❄️⛲⛰️🚌☕ ↠ pp213-221. Colour map 2, C2.

Beautifully situated on **Kootenay Lake** in a natural amphitheatre of rolling hills, Nelson is the obvious hub of the West Kootenays and arguably the most interesting small town in BC. The focal point for dozens of small communities scattered through the surrounding valleys, it caters to a large population without having to house or employ it, thus combining the positive facilities of a big town with the charm and friendliness of a small one. In particular, Nelson has a good range of quality restaurants, live music venues, cafés and craft shops. Benefiting from the creativity of the many satellite villages, it is one of the best small arts towns in the country.

Nelson developed following the discovery of large deposits of copper and silver ore in the surrounding mountains. Incorporated in 1896, with a population of 3000, a hydro-generating station, streetcars, a sewer system and police force, this is an old town by BC standards. Thanks to intelligent planning, it has managed to retain an overall appearance that has barely changed in 100 years, with over 350 well-looked-after heritage buildings, including the **Courthouse**, **City Hall**, the **Hume Hotel** and the old **Railway Station**. The **Visitor Information Centre** ① *225 Hall St, T250-352 3433, www.discovernelson.com*, can supply a *Heritage Walking Tour* pamphlet, which takes in the major sights. The town is a delight to explore, especially as everything is on or near Baker Street, where even the most pedestrian of businesses tends to be housed in a distinctive, historic building.

Those interested in the local history should talk to the curator of the **Nelson Mining Museum** ① *next to the Visitor Centre, T250-352 5242, daily 0900-1700, free.*

For accounts of the town's general history, visit the **Touchstones Nelson Museum of Art and History** ① *in City Hall, 502 Vernon St, T250-352 9813, www.touchstones nelson.ca, mid-May to mid-Sep Wed-Mon 1000-1800, Sun 1000-1600, mid-Sep to mid-May Tue-Sun 1000-1800, $10, under 18 $4, under 7 free.* Permanent exhibitions cover First Nations culture, European trade and travel, mining, paddlewheelers and past and present pictures of the town. Temporary exhibits celebrate contemporary creativity, through arts, crafts, architecture and design. The historic tramway, **Streetcar 23** ① *www.streetcar.kics.bc.ca, mid-May to mid-Sep 1110-1600; $3, child $2*, runs along the waterfront by the mall.

Nelson has many faces: arts town, cultural oasis, well-preserved historical relic. It's also a paradise for outdoor enthusiasts, with a ski hill down the road, backcountry skiing and hiking in the surrounding mountains, paddling and fishing in many local lakes and rivers, and a whole network of trails famous in mountain bike circles. This is also a magnet for all kinds of alternative types who hang out around the Kootenay Co-op and Oso Negro, playing drums and guitars.

Full Circle & Boomtown Emporium **10**
Fusion **8**
Kurama Sushi **14**
Main St Diner **4**
Oso Negro **6**
Outer Clove **7**
Preserved Seed Bakery & Maté Factor **2**
Redfish Grill **9**
Sage Tapas & Wine Bar **15**

Bars & clubs 🍸
Royal on Baker **3**

Whitewater Ski Resort

ⓘ *15 km south on Hwy 6, T250-354 4944, www.skiwhitewater.com. Lift pass $48, youth $38, child $30, or $20 if you're just going up once to ski the bowls.*

With a 1640-m base elevation, Whitewater regularly gets over 10 m of dry snowfall per season, making for powder aplenty without the crowds. The terrain breaks down as 20% beginner, 40% intermediate, 40% advanced, with lots of tree skiing. Ski Canada has rated Whitewater as having the Best Deeps, Best Bowls and Best Glades. There is no accommodation, but the lodge has a very good restaurant, a pub and ski rentals. For more information, visit their Nelson office, in the **Whitewater building** ⓘ *513 Victoria St, Mon-Fri until snow season, then Mon-Sun.*

East Shore 🏠🚹🟤🅾️🚻 ›› *pp213-221.*

From Nelson, Highway 3A follows a minor arm of Kootenay Lake towards Kaslo (an hour's drive), meeting the lake proper at **Balfour**, little more than a landing stage for the longest free ferry ride in the world, to Kootenay Bay on the East Shore. If travelling south to **Creston**, Highway 3A via the ferry at Balfour is a slower, but infinitely more enjoyable than the obvious route via Salmo. The road hugs Kootenay Lake tightly as it meanders through wonderfully dramatic scenery, passing a series of sleepy villages collectively known as the East Shore. On the road to Riondel, near the ferry-landing of **Kootenay Bay**, are the highly respected yoga retreat centre, **Yasodhara Ashram** ⓘ *T1800-661 8711, www.yasodhara.org,* and the **Tara Shanti Lodge retreat** ⓘ *T1800-811 3888, www.tarashanti.com.* If not Creston-bound, a good excuse to take the ferry is the artisan scene that is transforming **Crawford Bay** ⓘ *5 km south,* where the original blacksmith, glass blower and old-style broom maker are joined by more newcomers every year. There's a summer-only **Visitor Information Centre** ⓘ *just off the highway, T250-227 9267, www.kootenaylake.bc.ca.*

Further down the lake, near Boswell, is the clover-shaped **Glass House** ⓘ *T250-223 8372, May-Oct, $5.* Built entirely from 500,000 embalming fluid bottles assiduously collected from colleagues by a retired mortician, it's a truly fascinating oddity, all the more so as it was built as a home, not a tourist attraction. After a long descent, the highway enters a wide, flat valley, created by the flood plain of the Kootenay River.

Around Kaslo 🏠🚹🟡🟢🟤⛰️🅾️🅾️ ›› *pp213-221. Colour map 2, C2.*

Ainsworth Hot Springs

Highway 31 continues north from Balfour, shortly coming to **Ainsworth Hot Springs** ⓘ *T250-229 4212, www.hotnaturally.com, daily 1000-2130, day pass $11.50, child $8, free for guests at the resort pools and open from 0830,* the oldest village and first commercial hot springs in the mineral-rich Kootenay Arc. Today's resort features a horseshoe-shaped cave, the site of a mining shaft that had to be abandoned when miners struck hot water. There is also an icy-cold dipping-pool.

High in the Selkirk Mountains above Ainsworth, **Cody Caves Provincial Park** ⓘ *402 Anderson St, T250-353 7364, www.codycaves.ca, Jun-Aug daily 1000-1600, $2, child $1, 1-hr tours daily 1000-1600, $15 per person, 3-hr tours, daily 0900, $60 per person,* protects a natural limestone cave system sculpted by a glacier-fed stream that continues for over 1 km underground. Access is on a steep and rough 10 km gravel road, 2 km north of Ainsworth; or via a 15 minute walk on a clear trail.

Kaslo → *Colour map 2, C2.*

With an idyllic setting on Kootenay Lake, surrounded by parks and some of the highest mountains in the province, Kaslo is the quintessential small Kootenay town.

So pretty, in fact, that surely only its remoteness has protected the charming atmosphere of its wooden houses and friendly, laid-back inhabitants against rampant tourism. A perfect base from which to explore the great outdoors, there's little to do in town but the lake offers fishing, boating and waterskiing, and the views never disappoint.

Like so many of its neighbours, this formerly sawmill-driven town boomed with the discovery of silver in 1893. Originally called Kane's Landing, it was the region's first incorporated city with 27 saloons (now it has two pubs). It survived the bust when the ore ran out thanks to agriculture, steamships that served the mining industry and, one suspects, the determination of the inhabitants not to leave so idyllic a spot.

A fitting relic from the glory days, the **SS Moyie** ① *324 Front St, T250-353 2525, www.klhs.bc.ca, mid-May to mid-Oct daily 0900-1700, $5, youth $4, child $2*, built in 1890, is the oldest surviving paddle steamer in North America. Able to operate in extremely shallow waters, such vessels were vital for the economy of the Kootenays, carrying men, provisions and ore to and from the mines before the advent of roads. Retired in 1957, the *Moyie* was bought by the village of Kaslo from the Canadian Pacific Railway for $1. Now she is a designated National Historic Site and BC landmark, complete with artefacts, models and some eerie sound effects. Also here is the summer-only **Visitor Information Centre**.

Purcell Wilderness Provincial Park → *Colour map 2, C2.*
Much of Highway 31, which follows the west bank of Kootenay Lake north from Kaslo to Galena Bay, is a demanding dirt road whose rewards do not justify the effort. But the paved section to **Howser** makes a nice excursion from Kaslo, passing scattered no-nonsense farming communities that have retained a frontier homesteader feel. The snow around here is possibly the finest in the province, with unbeatable cat-skiing out of Meadow Creek and a planned ski hill, called Jumbo Ski Resort, that has come up against extensive local resistance.

About 35 km from Kaslo, a bridge crosses the Duncan River to access the small, idiosyncratic communities of **Argenta** and **Johnson's Landing**, and a number of excellent hikes in the vast and remote Purcell Wilderness Provincial Park.

Hikes in Purcell Wilderness Provincial Park
Fry Creek Canyon Trail ① *10- to 19-km return; 4-7 hrs. Trailhead: beyond Johnson's Landing.* This is a fairly easy, thoroughly rewarding hike. The canyon walls rise vertically over 1 km from the creek waters, an awesome spectacle.

Earl Grey Pass Trail (or Hamill Creek) ① *61-km one-way; 3-5 days. Trailhead: Argenta.* This is a tough but rewarding trek along the route by which Chief Kinbasket of the Shuswap natives led his people to their present home near Invermere. Though the path is distinct, it is full of obstacles and very demanding, so consult a hiking guide and get local information before attempting it. You're not likely to see another soul and the stands of ancient giant cedars are magnificent. It's worth doing the one-hour scramble up Slate Peak north of the pass for 360° views that rival anything in the Rocky or Coast mountains. From Duncan River Bridge, continue straight for the trailheads of three more highly recommended hikes.

Monica Meadows ① *8-km return; 5 hrs; 579 m elevation gain*. This beautiful alpine meadow, surrounded by glacier-clad mountains, is full of bright flowers at the height of summer. Access is difficult and a 4WD is needed.

Jumbo Pass Trail ① *8.4 km; 6-7 hrs; 686 m elevation gain. Hut for overnight stays, T250-342 4200 for reservations*. More challenging than Monica Meadows but easier to reach and preferable for views, the view from the pass is stunning.

British Columbia West Kootenays Around Kaslo

Macbeth Icefield Trail ① *12 km return; 9-10 hrs; 874 m elevation gain*. The final section could add an extra 3.6 km to the trip. Easy to reach but harder still, the views of the dual waterfalls cascading down from the glacier surrounded by a sea of ice are worthy rewards.

West of Kaslo → *Colour map 2, C2.*

From Kaslo, Highway 31A continues to New Denver in the Slocan Valley (see page 212). Clinging to the side of the fast-flowing Kaslo River as it winds its way through the steep cliffs of the Selkirk Mountains past a series of charming little lakes, this is one of the most scenic routes in the Kootenays. Halfway down is the abandoned mining townsite of **Retallack** and the **Retallack Ski Resort**. There is some exceptional summer hiking nearby in **Goat Range Provincial Park**.

Further down the highway, a signposted gravel road leads 13 km to the quintessential mining ghost town of **Sandon**. At its peak, Sandon had electricity (before Vancouver), an opera house, a red-light district, 24 hotels and 23 saloons. After a fire and two floods there is little left to evoke that heady history, but the location and dilapidated remains are worth the diversion, especially since some excellent hikes begin here. In addition, a steep but manageable gravel road leads 18 km to a car park from where it is just a 1.4-km walk to Idaho Peak, an easy way to reach stunning views.

Hikes West of Kaslo

Mount Brennan ① *14.6 km return; 7-10 hrs; 1463 m elevation gain. Trailhead: 5 km from Retallack*. This challenging trek leads to a jaw-dropping panorama that takes in glaciers, ice fields and countless peaks of a few ranges, including the Rockies.

White Canyon Trail ① *13.5 km return; 8-9 hrs, 893 m elevation gain. Trailhead: 2.7 km from Retallack.*

K&S Railway/Galena Hiking Trail ① *14.5 km one-way via Three Forks*. Follows the old ore-carrying railway line from Sandon to New Denver, passing old mine works and numerous artefacts and offering views of the Valhalla Range. The summer-only Visitor Information Centre in Sandon can provide you with a leaflet, describing the trail's highlights and the glory-days of 'Silvery Slocan', which on its way. If you parked in Sandon, there's little choice but to hitch back.

Kokanee Glacier Provincial Park

Established in 1922, this 32,000-ha park is one of BC's oldest. Radiating out from the eponymous glacier and **Mount Cond**, which at 2775 m is the park's highest peak, are a number of creeks whose deep valleys provide the park's access routes. Out of the drainage patterns has evolved a complete network of trails, most of them originally built to service the small mines whose remains are still visible. There are three glaciers, over 30 lakes and endless forested valleys to admire. The historic **Slocan Chief Cabin** now houses an interpretive centre, with displays on local geography, flora and fauna, which includes black and grizzly bears, mountain goats, marmots, pikas and ground squirrels. **Kokanee Glacier Alpine Cabin**, always full in winter, operates on a first-come first-served basis in summer. Many trails start here, including the popular hikes to Smuggler Ridge and Kokanee Glacier.

Access to Kokanee Glacier Provincial Park

Keen Creek ① *Trailhead: turn south off Highway 31A, 6.4 km northwest of Kaslo. This 24-km rough road requires 4WD in all but peak conditions, but gives deepest entry into the park.* Many trails lead from the car park at Joker Millsite, including a 4.8-km, three-hour hike to the Slocan Chief, or one of similar length to Joker Lakes.

Kokanee Creek ⓘ *8.8 km; 4½ hrs or 24 km; 10 hrs. Trailhead: turn north off*
*Highway 3A, 19.2 km east of Nelson. This easier 15.2-km road leads to a car park at
Gibson Lake.* There is a short loop round the lake. The 8.8-km hike to the Slocan Chief
passes four major lakes and gives easy access to extreme wilderness conditions.
The Glory Basin Circuit is a moderate 24-km hike taking in most of the park's
key sights. Can be done as a two-day trip camping at Kaslo Lake.

Woodbury Creek ⓘ *8 km; 4hrs. Trailhead: turn west off Highway 31, 6.4 km north
of Ainsworth. The parking area is at 13.2 km.* Two huts are accessible, Woodbury Hut
is a moderate hike and Silver Spray is shorter but harder. Above it is an old mine site
and some interesting relics.

Lemon Creek ⓘ *9.6 km; 5 hrs. Trailhead: turn east off Highway 6 at Lemon Creek,
14.4 km south of Slocan. Park off the road at a signposted trailhead after 16 km.*
A varied hike, not all of it well marked, leads to the beautiful Sapphire Lakes.

Slocan Valley ⊖❶❷❀❍▲❸❿ ⤏ *pp213-221. Colour map 2, C2.*

Running north to Nakusp from a point midway between Castlegar and Nelson, the
Slocan Valley remains one of the best-kept secrets of the Kootenays. Clinging to the
course of the enchanting Slocan River, sandwiched between Valhalla and Kokanee
Glacier provincial parks, the road weaves between undulating green hills, rugged
bluffs and icy creeks. Though there's not much to it, Winlaw is the heart of this area
and a good base for soaking up the valley vibe.

Slocan and around → *Colour map 2, C2.*
At **Slocan**, the winding river turns into a lake. There's a nice little beach in town
and across the bridge the lovely 8-km **Slocan Lake Trail** leads to Evans Creek and
the **Valhalla Retreat and Tipi Lodge** ⓘ *T250-365 3226,* also accessible by canoe
from Slocan. From here the **Cahill/Beatrice Lake Trail** ⓘ *12 km, 6 hrs,* offers relatively
easy access to the rugged Valhalla Provincial Park (see below), where there is
wilderness camping.
　　Above Slocan, the road climbs steeply towards a fine viewpoint. This stretch of
road is particularly dramatic, clinging to cliff faces, taking hairpin curves, crossing
rickety wooden bridges and losing sight of the lake until a bend is turned and it
suddenly fills the whole panorama. Almost 3 km north of here, a steep dirt road winds
down through a gravel pit, from where well-trodden paths lead to **Bannock Point**, a
beautiful, clothing-optional beach.

Valhalla Provincial Park
This 49,000-ha park was designated in 1983 after years of campaigning and protest
on the part of locals who sought to protect such an extraordinary area from the
whims of logging companies. It is easy to see how the jagged, snow-capped peaks
inspired association with the dwelling place of the nordic pantheon. There is
plenty here to satisfy professional adventurers and climbers, but from June to October
beginners can also gain easy access to areas of extreme wilderness. The routes are long
and confusing, so make sure you seek thorough instructions before setting out.

Hikes in Valhalla Provincial Park
Gwillim Lakes via Drinnon Pass. ⓘ *11.6 km return; 10 hrs; 701 m elevation gain.
Trailhead: signed access from Hwy 6 is at Passmore, south of Winlaw, or from
Slocan City. From the former, turn left at Km 25.3; from the latter turn right at Km 20.3,
onto Hodder Creek Forestry Rd. Follow for 18.8 km and turn right for the last 2.4 km.*

It's possible to stay at the lovely meadow campground, giving time to explore Lucifer Pass, a further 3-km, three-hour hike with a scramble at the end and even better views.

Mulvey Basin ① *9.7 km; 5-6 hrs; 765 m elevation gain. Trailhead: from Slocan, follow signs down the Little Slocan Lakes Forestry Rd for 10.9 km, then turn right onto Bannock Burn and follow for 12.9 km*. This is most people's second choice. It is more difficult but the rewards are incredible, glacial sculptures and world-class mountaineering.

Silverton and New Denver → Colour map 2, C2.

Soon enough, the highway rejoins the lake and passes through a duo of picturesque old mining towns, settled when silver and lead were found in nearby Idaho Mountain. **Silverton** contains a surprising number of artists' galleries and studios, and a museum with displays of old mining equipment.

New Denver is the valley's most worthwhile stop and similar in many ways to Kaslo. It's a pretty little lakeside town of quaint wooden houses that still resembles the mining boomtown it once was. To learn more about this rich history, take a hike along the old mining railway to **Sandon** (see page 210), with historical details supplied along the way, or visit the **Silvery Slocan Museum** ① *1202 6th Av, T250-358 2201, www.newdenver.ca/museum, Jul-Aug daily 1000-1600, $2*.

Another slice of local history is explored at the **Nikkei Memorial Internment Centre** ① *306 Josephine St, T250-358 7288, www.newdenver.ca/nikkei, May-Sep daily 0930-1700, $6, child $4*. In early 1942, in the wake of the Japanese bombing of Pearl Harbour, Japanese-Canadians, most of them living in Vancouver, were dispossessed of their belongings and herded into internment camps. This interesting museum is housed in one such camp and contains a lovely formal Japanese garden. There's another Japanese garden, the **Kohan Reflection Garden** ① *on the lake at the end of 1st Av, www.newdenver.ca/kohan, $1 donation for map and plant key*.

Almost everything else of interest is located on Sixth Avenue, which leads to **Greer Park**, with a shady picnic area, lakeside trail and beaches. On Fridays there's a splendid market selling local crafts and produce. There's also a summer-only **Visitor Information Centre** ① *101 Eldorado Av, T250-358 2719, www.slocanlake.com*.

Nakusp → Colour map 2, C2.

Attractive enough in its lakeside setting, Nakusp cannot rival some of the other Kootenay towns for picturesque qualities, but the many local hot springs make this a good stopover for those heading from the Okanagan or Nelson to the TransCanada Highway. In town, the biggest attraction is the lake itself, best admired from a pleasant promenade which takes in a small but pretty **Japanese Garden**. Almost everything of importance is found on or near the main street, Broadway, including the **Visitor Information Centre** ① *92 6th Av, T250-265 4234, www.nakusp arrow lakes.com*, which is disguised as a paddle steamer.

By car it is 49 km north (past the hot springs) to the free ferry at Galena Bay and a further 49 km to Revelstoke and the TransCanada Highway (see page 172). Highway 6 heads west from Nakusp towards Vernon (page 192) and the Okanagan, via the free ferry at **Fauquier** ① *every ½-hr 0500-2200*. The 135-km road to Vernon is a lonely, tortuous drive with few buildings or services and lots of deer on the road at night. ►► *For further details, see Transport, page 221.*

⊜ Sleeping

Nelson *p207, map p206*

A Prestige Lakeside Resort, 701 Lakeside Dr, T250-352 7222, www.prestigeinn.com. The only lodging right on the lake. Rooms have lake view balconies and kitchenettes. There's an indoor pool, hot tub, fitness centre and patio. Breakfast is included.

B Willow Point Lodge, 2211 Taylor Dr, 6.5 km north on Hwy 3A, T250-825 9411 www.willowpointlodge.com. Ideal for those with a car who want to be close to town but immersed in the glorious countryside. Attractive 1920s lodge nestled in mountainside forest, surrounded by flower-filled gardens featuring creeks, waterfalls and a gazebo. The 4 unique en suite rooms and 2 honeymoon suites are furnished with antiques. There's a hot tub, and breakfast is included.

C Casa Blanca B&B, 724 2nd St, T250-354 4431, www.casablancanelson.com. 3 rooms in an elegant, wood-finished art-deco home in a quiet area close to Downtown, over looking the lake. Guests have their own living room.

C Cloudside Inn, 408 Victoria St, T250-352 3226, www.cloudside.ca. Thanks to its handy location, the 6 pleasant rooms in this Victorian home get heavily booked-up, so reserve ahead. There is also a 3-bedroom guesthouse.

C Hume Hotel, 422 Vernon St, T250-352 5331, www.humehotel.com. This good-value centrally located hotel has bags of character, with a pub and restaurant downstairs. Rooms are spacious and comfortable, with antique furniture and feather duvets. Breakfast included.

C Nelson Guest House, 2109 Fort Sheppard Dr, T250-354 7885, www.nelsonguesthouse. com. This beautiful, handcrafted cedar West Coast-style home is a little removed from Downtown but has tasteful, wood-finished bedrooms, a spacious living room, shared kitchen, a back garden with fruit trees, wonderful views from the balconies and an outdoor hot tub.

C New Grand Hotel, 616 Vernon St, T250-352 7211, www.newgrandhotel.ca. Dating back to 1913, this bright and classic Downtown boutique hotel has 30 tasteful rooms with 1940s-style decor and hardwood floors.

There are also 15 private hostel-style rooms for 2 to 3 people (**E-F**), with shared bath, a common room and basic kitchen. There's a steakhouse and lounge downstairs and breakfast is included.

D Mountain Hound Inn, 621 Baker St, T1866-452 6490, www.mountainhound. com. Clean, modern and very comfortable private rooms with TV. Continental breakfast included.

E The Backcountry Hostel, 198 Baker St, T250-352 2151, www.thebackcountry hostel.com. Colourful, funky, friendly and recently renovated. Dorms and rooms all have private bathrooms and there's a large kitchen, common room, TV room, laundry, lockers and internet access.

E Dancing Bear Inn, 171 Baker St, T250-352 7573, www.dancingbearinn.com. A superior hostel, very clean, bright and comfortable, with hardwood floors throughout. There are 2-bed dorms, private rooms with shared bathrooms, a full kitchen, lounge area with wood fire, laundry, storage and lockers.

E White House Backpacker Lodge, 816 Vernon St, T250-352 0505, www.whitehouse.ca. A small hostel in a distinctive restored heritage house, elegant and artistic. Private rooms and dorms, spacious lounge, kitchen, garden, internet, veranda and free pancakes in the morning.

Camping

City Tourist Park Campground, High St, T250-352 7618. Small and not very private, but wooded and handy. Has showers and a laundry.

East Shore *p208*

B Kootenay Lake Lodge, Hwy 3A, 30 km south of Crawford Bay in Boswell, T250-223 8181, www.kootenaylakelodge.com. A beautiful log house on 3 ha with antique furniture, balconies, views, friendly owners and various animals. 5 spacious and attractive rooms, a suite, chalets and RV sites. Breakfast and use of boat and bikes included in the price. Canoes and kayaks for rent.

C Wedgwood Manor, 16002 Crawford Creek Rd, T250-227 9233, www.wedgwood countryinn.com. This exquisite heritage house, built for Wedgwood's daughter, is set on 20 ha of landscaped grounds. The 6 rooms are very tasteful, with hardwood floors, en suite baths and antique furnishings. Guests can enjoy the library, parlour, dining room and a self-guided historical tour of the grounds.

D Kokanee Chalets, 15981 Hwy 3A Crawford Bay, T250-227 9292, www.kokanee chalets.com. 1-bedroom motel-style rooms and nice 3-bedroom chalets. Campsite with hot showers, a hot tub and hook-ups.

Camping

Lockhart Creek Provincial Park, 13 km south of Gray Creek, T250-422 3003, May-Sep only. 18 basic but wooded and private sites, with a beach and trail.

Ainsworth Hot Springs *p208*

B Ainsworth Hot Springs Resort, T250-229 4212, www.hotnaturally.com. Decent rooms and a fairly expensive restaurant overlooking the pools. Price includes free multiple entry to the pools.

D Ainsworth Motel, Hwy 31, T250-229 4711, www.ainsworthmotel.com. A nice, economical alternative, with lake views.

Camping

Kokanee Creek Provincial Park, 20 km east of Nelson on Hwy 3A, T250-825 3500. A beautiful campground with lots of trees, sandy beaches and hiking trails.

Kaslo *p208*

C Dayspring Lodge B&B, 4736 Twin Bays Rd, 10 km south of Kaslo, T250-353 2810, www.dayspringlodge.com. A Southwestern-style building in striking waterfront surroundings, with 3 large and stylish suites.

C Lakewood Inn, 6 km north on Hwy 31, T250-353 2395, www.lakewoodinn.com. One of a long string of cabins and camping spots on Kootenay Lake, north of Kaslo. Cabins of varied age and size right on the lake, among trees and gardens. Kitchenettes and patio, use of sauna, marina and beach. Steep access.

D Edge of the Woods B&B, 116 C-Av, T250-353 2600, www.edgewoods.com. A lovely handmade wooden house brimming with character, in a peaceful spot just outside

Kaslo. 2 pleasant rooms and use of living area and deck. A bargain.

E Kaslo Motel, 330 D Av, T250-353 2431, www.kaslomotel.ca. Fairly standard but decent rooms and little cabins in a handy location, very cheap.

E Kootenay Lake Hostel, 232 Av B, T250-353 7427. Dorms and 4 private rooms in a large, wooden, barn-like house. Friendly and homely, with shared baths, kitchen, lounge, library and sauna . Bikes, canoes and kayaks for rent and the owner can advise on local activities.

Camping

Kaslo Municipal Campground, A Av & 2nd St, T250-353 2662. Basic but handy.

Mirror Lake Campground, 5777 Arcola Rd, 5 km south on Hwy 31, T250-353 7102, www.mirrorlake.kaslobc.com. Not particularly attractive but a nice location with a beach. Good for kids. Showers and boat rentals. 5 mins' drive further south are the very attractive Fletcher Falls, where a Forestry Site has free wilderness camping.

Purcell Wilderness Provincial Park *p209*

The first stretch of Hwy 31 north is thick with cabins, B&Bs and campgrounds.

Camping

Kootenay Lake Provincial Park has 2 sites. **Lost Ledge**, Km 25, 12 sites on the lake, calm, private and with a large beach; **Davis Creek**, at Km 28, 12 even more private and primitive sites, a rockier beach and no drinking water.

Howser Campsite, 8 km beyond Meadow Creek. A pretty, forested spot on Duncan Lake with drive-in and walk-in sites and a big sandy beach.

Slocan Valley *p211*

C Arica Gardens B&B, 6307 Youngs Rd, Winlaw, T250-226 7688, www.aricagard ens .com. An exquisite straw bale and timber-frame house with 2 spacious, luxurious rooms and a self-contained suite with sauna – a steal at this price. Hosts can also arrange activities to help get the most out of the area. Book early.

D Lemon Creek Lodge, 7680 Kennedy Rd, Lemon Creek, T250-355 2403, www.lemon creeklodge.com. Lodge rooms with shared bath, or fully-equipped cabins that are great value, especially for families. Sauna and breakfast included. There's also a good restaurant and some poor camping sites.

D-E The Artful Lodger, 6676 Appledale West Rd, Winlaw, T250-226 7972, www.artfullodger.ca. 2 enchanting straw bale cottages on 2 ha of land bordering the Slocan River, surrounded by organic gardens, flowers, fruit trees, decks and art created by the very interesting owner. Peaceful, warm and very inspiring. A perfect taste of valley life.

Camping
Springer Creek Campground, 1020 Giffin Rd, Slocan, T250-355 2226, May-Sep only. Certainly the valley's best campground, featuring 24 surprisingly private sites in a heavily wooded area right in town. Hookups, showers and information.

Silverton and New Denver *p212*
C William Hunter Cabins, 303 Lake Av, Silverton, T250-358 2844, www.williamhuntercabins.com. 6 suites with decks and kitchenettes, in 3 handsome, handcrafted log cabins on the lake. Canoe rental.

C-D Villa Dome Quixote, 602 6th Av, T250-358 7242, www.domequixote.com. These eccentric wood-shingled dome buildings are surprisingly stylish inside, with slate or beechwood floors. Lovely rooms or cottages with kitchenettes, a cedar sauna, outdoor spa and 2 balconies with views.

D Glacier View Cabins, 426 8th Av, New Denver, T250-358 7277, www.glaciercabins.com. Not the most attractive cabins, but clean with full kitchens. Near the lake and certainly good value.

D Mistaya Country Inn B&B, 10 km south of Silverton, signposted from highway, T250-358 7787, www.mistayaresort.com. Nice rooms with shared bath in a gorgeous, very remote spot by the lake. Hot tub and breakfast included.

D Sweet Dreams Guesthouse, 702 Eldorado Av, New Denver, T250-358 2415, www.newdenverbc.com. 5 comfortable rooms in an attractive heritage house near the lake,

with reservations-only restaurant. Offers kayak rentals and breakfast is included. 3-night minimum.

Camping
New Denver Municipal Campground, 3rd Av on S side of village, T250-358 2316. Right on the beach but pretty dingy.

Rosebery Provincial Park, 5 km N of New Denver, May-Sep only. 33 very nice, private sites on the banks of a creek.

Silverton Municipal Campground, Leadville St. A primitive but attractively wooded location on the lake, with a beach and a boat dock.

Nakusp *p212*
B-C Halcyon Hot Springs Resort, 34 north on Hwy 23, T250-265 3554, www.halcyonhotsprings.com. A great place to stay with a wide range of options, all wooden, cosy and comfortable. Cabins, various cottages, suites (**A**) and chalets (**AL**), with full kitchens, living area with TV and covered sundecks. There's a restaurant and spa on site and passes to the hot springs are included. There are also unattractive RV and tent sites, the latter overlooking the lake. All kinds of rentals and tours are available.

B-C O'Brien's, 2.5 km west on Hwy 6, T250-265 4575, www.obriens.kootenays.com. 3 fully-equipped, handcrafted log cabins. One of many resorts and camp- grounds on Hwy 6 heading west. Quiet and scenic choice if you have your own transport.

D Huckleberry Inn, 1050 Hot Springs Rd, T250-265 4544, www.huckinn.com. 4 comfortable theme rooms in a log cabin decorated with tasteful kitsch, showers not baths. Good value.

D Kuskanax Lodge, 515 Broadway St, T250-265 3618, www.kuskanax.kootenays.com. The best option in town, with decent, spacious rooms, a fireside lounge, games room and a good restaurant and bar.

D-E Selkirk Inn, 210 6th Av W, T250-265 3666, www.selkirkinn-nakusp.com. Standard rooms with kitchenettes, spacious and clean. Also has a sauna.

E Windsor Hotel, Trout Lake near Galena Bay, T250-369 2244. A bit off the beaten

---

 For an explanation of sleeping and eating price codes used in this guide, see inside ● *the front cover. Other relevant information is found in Essentials, see pages 28-31.*

track, but those with a taste for the quirky will relish this wonderfully eccentric establishment. It looks just as it must have when built in 1892.

Camping

McDonald Creek Provincial Park, 10 km SW on Hwy 6, T250-825 4212, Apr-Sep only. 42 wooded and private sites close to the beach. No showers or hook-ups.

Nakusp Village Campground, 381 8th St northwest. Wooded sites in a quiet part of town with fire pits and showers.

Summit Lake Provincial Park, 18 km SE on Hwy 6, May-Sep. 35 sites with toilets and water taps but no hook-ups (there's a private RV park next door). With fine views of the Selkirk Mountains, good fishing, sightings of mountain goats and an agreeable climate, this is a popular spot. At the end of the summer, thousands of migrating toads flood from the lake.

⊘ Eating

Nelson *p207, map p206*
Nelson has a surprising number of restaurants and also quite a turnover. Those listed are tried and tested survivors, but it's always worth strolling along Baker St to check out the latest contenders.

₩₩₩ All Seasons Café, 620 Herridge Lane, T250-352 0101. A long-term favourite with locals when it's time to celebrate or splash out. The menu is small and intelligently conceived; the food is influenced by European and West Coast cuisine and beautifully prepared and presented. There's a small courtyard for romantic summer evenings and an impressive selection of wines and malt whiskies. Servings are on the small side and the tables a little cramped.

₩₩ Baba's, 445 Baker St, T250-352 0077. Delicious, very authentic Indian food. Mon night is the very popular buffet.

₩₩ El Taco, 306 Victoria St, T250-352 2060. Tasty and very fresh Mexican favourites, with home-made salsa.

₩₩ Fusion, 301 Baker St, T250-352 0933. Pan-Asian fusion dishes, oriental tapas and cocktails.

₩₩ Kurama Sushi, 546 Baker St, T250-352 5353. Authentic dishes prepared by a master of the art.

₩₩ Outer Clove, 536 Stanley St, T250-354 1667. Everything on the menu, even the ice cream, revolves around garlic at this long-standing favourite, which has stood the test of time simply because the food never disappoints.

₩₩ Redfish Grill, 479 Baker St, T250-352 3456. A broad, international menu specializing in vegetarian and vegan dishes. Also offers breakfast and tapas.

₩₩ Sage Tapas and Wine Bar, 705 Vernon St, T250-352 5121. A large and ambitious international menu of tapas, with wine by the glass.

₩ The Corner House Cafe, 318 Anderson Av, T250-352 3773. A delightfully quaint spot for breakfast and coffee.

₩ The Fisherman's Market, 577 Ward St, T250-505 5501. Fish and chips in the fish market, so you know it's fresh.

₩ The Full Circle, 401 Baker St, T250-354 4458. Recommended for breakfast and the lunch specials are often the best deal in town. Impeccable service and a good spot for people-watching.

₩ Main St Diner, 616 Baker St, T250-354 4848. The best place to go for burgers, calamari and Greek entrées. Good portions and prices, fine beers on tap and a great summer patio.

Cafés

Dominion Café, 334 Baker St. An elegant New York-style coffee shop, with wooden interior and an attractive patio.

Oso Negro, 512 Latimer St, T250-352 7661. This famous coffee-roasting company had to move to larger premises to keep up with demand. The new wood-dominated building has an upbeat West Coast vibe and a nice patio. Needless to say, the coffee is excellent and there's good light food, such as bagels and muffins.

Preserved Seed Bakery and Maté Factor, 202 Vernon St, T250-352 0325. This relaxing, small, health-conscious bakery-café is a lovely spot for delicious cakes and cookies, salads and wraps.

East Shore *p208*

₩ Abracajava Café, 16072 Highway 3a, Apr-Oct Thu-Sun. Healthy, tasty dishes and good coffee in a colourful little room full of decent art, with a small patio.

Kaslo *p208*

Rosewood Café, 213 5th St, T250-353 7673. Amazing European-style fine-dining, always very fresh. Intimate seating in a pretty old house packed with antiques, or on the garden patio.

Meteor Pizza, 302 4th St, T250-353 7361. A warm and friendly spot, boasting a wide range of quality pizzas and a good French onion soup. There's live entertainment on the licensed patio most summer nights, making this about the nicest place in town for a drink.

Silver Spoon Bakery, 301 Front St, T250-353 2898. Good coffee and sandwiches, fresh bread, croissants and breakfasts, in a summer house-style room.

The Treehouse, 419 Front St, T250-353 2955. A popular meeting place for locals, serving a variety of good value, home-cooking-style food, very tasty and plenty of it. Especially good for breakfast.

Slocan Valley *p211*

Lemon Creek Lodge, 7680 Kennedy Rd, Lemon Creek, T250-355 2403. This place has long been considered the best eating option for miles around, especially for something a bit special or romantic.

Cedar Creek Café, 5709 Hwy 6, Winlaw, T250-226 7355. The usual range of comfort food, prepared with a little extra thought. Open from breakfast to dinner, with beer on tap, wine by the glass and occasional live music.

Herald Street Café, Herald St, Slocan. Burgers, breakfasts, pizza and grilled cheese sandwiches. Pictures of logging trucks on the walls.

Sleep is for Sissies, 5686 Hwy 6, T250-226 7663. The liveliest of a number of coffee shops. Also does some light food.

Silverton and New Denver *p212*

Wild Rose Mexican Restaurant, Rosebery, 5 mins' north of New Denver, T250-358 7744, mid-May to mid-Sep daily 1700-2100. First-class Mexican food, attractive surroundings and good service. The best choice for dinner.

Apple Tree Sandwich Shop, 210 6th Av, New Denver, T250-358 2691, closes at 1600. A long-standing favourite on the strength of its varied menu of creative sandwiches.

There's some seating in the secluded little garden at the side.

Panini Bistro & Delicatessen, 306 6th Av, New Denver, T250-358 2381. An appealingly bright and comfortable spot, offering the town's best coffee, breakfast, lunches and some creative paninis. It's also one of the few places selling wine and beer.

Nakusp *p212*

Kuskanax Lodge Restaurant, 515 Broadway St, T250-265 3618. The usual range of burgers and pasta, but also some more exciting main courses which are very well presented. The menu is also available in the lounge, which is a nicer environment, with a good selection of beers on tap.

Picardo's, 401 Broadway St, T250-265 3331. Menu concentrates on southern favourites like ribs and lots of appetizers.

Wylie's Pub, 401 Broadway St, T250-265 4944. Shares its location and menu with Picardo's. Favoured by a younger crowd, a preferable location if only for the fish tank.

Broadway Deli Bistro, 408 Broadway St, T250-265 3767. The best bet for breakfast.

What's Brewing on Broadway, 420 Broadway St, T250-265 4655. Serving Kicking Horse coffee, the best in town.

Bars and clubs

Nelson *p207, map p206*

Louie's Lounge, in the New Grand Hotel, 616 Vernon, T250-352 7211. An elegant, sophisticated interior that's your best bet for a quiet drink, with 28 martinis to choose from, an extensive wine list and Nelson Brewery beers on tap.

Mike's Place, in the Hume Hotel, 422 Vernon St, T250-352 5331. Nelson's most popular boozer, its 3 levels usually packed solid. Nelson Brewery beers on tap, reasonable pub food, big screens for sports fans and 3 pool tables.

Royal on Baker, 330 Baker St, T250-352 1269. A straight-ahead gritty pub that has live music most nights, traditionally of a bluesy nature.

SpiritBar, downstairs in the Hume Hotel at 422 Vernon St, T250-352 5331, www.my space.com/humehotel. A very stylish, trendy space that is Nelson's latest club of choice, with live music or top DJs every night.

British Columbia West Kootenays Listings

Fisherman's Tale Pub, 551 Rainbow Dr, across the bay on the marina (Hwy 31). Much better than the pub in town, it's quieter and there's outdoor seating by the water. Great views.

⊕ Entertainment

Nelson *p207, map p206*
The Capitol, 421 Victoria St, T250-352 6363, www.capitoltheatre.bc.ca. Opened in 1927 and one of the finest in the country at the time, this attractive little venue is still going strong with regular plays and live music.
Civic Theatre, 104-719 Vernon St, T250-352 5833. Mostly first-run films, often with more interesting choices on Thu night.
Oxygen Art Centre, 320 Vernon St, T250-352 6322, www.oxygenartcentre.org. A multi-disciplinary arts centre that hosts exhibitions (Wed-Sat 1300-1700), literary events, classes and performances.

Kaslo *p208*
Langham Cultural Society, 447 Av A, opposite the post office, T250-353 2661, www.thelangham.ca. An arts centre housed in a restored 1896 building, that contains a gallery, Thu-Sun 1300-1600, with consistently fine displays, as well as the Japanese Canadian Museum, daily 0900-1600, whose array of historic photos and artefacts document the local WWII internment camps. Also hosts live theatre.

⊛ Festivals and events

Nelson *p207, map p206*
Jul Procter Storytelling Festival,T250-505 1205, www.kootenaystory.org. Hosted by a small community 34 km east of Nelson, across the water from Balfour. 5 hrs of stories in each of the 4 venues over 2 days, $25, child $12 per day.
Jul-Sep Artwalk, T250-352 2402. On one day each in Jul and Aug, some 50 local artists display their works in 12-15 restaurants, shops, galleries and workshops around town. There's an auction of these works in Sep. Pick up a brochure at the Visitor Centre.

Aug Shambhala, T250-352 7623, www.shambhalamusicfestival.com. Held close to Salmo, 41 km south of Nelson, this has become the most important annual festival in the Kootenays. The non-stop 4- day orgy of music and mayhem gets bigger and more ambitious each year. All kinds of techno and live music takes place on unique and imaginatively conceived stages and dance areas dotted around in the forest.

East Shore *p208*
Jul Starbelly Jam Global Music Festival, T250-225 3333, www.starbellyjam.org. Held in Crawford Bay over a weekend in mid-Jul, this 2-day open-air bonanza of major and minor world, folk and roots bands, plus an assortment of other acts, is always lots of fun and very kid-friendly. Most of the serious action is rumoured to happen at the after-party, usually at the beach.

Kaslo *p208*
Aug Kaslo Jazz Fest, T250-353 7538, www.kaslojazzfest.com. This sleepy town bursts into life early in Aug with a fabulous 3-day event that attracts some major acts to play on a floating stage on Kootenay Lake.

Silverton and New Denver *p212*
Jul-Aug Slocan Lake Art Walk. The small communities around New Denver host this event. Maps are available from the local Visitor Centres.
Sep Hills Garlic Festival. On the 2nd Sun, New Denver (not Hills) hosts this celebrated 1-day outdoor event. Very popular and really all about the food.

Nakusp *p212*
Jul Nakusp Music Fest, T1877-265 5565, www.nakuspmusicfest.ca. A massive 3-day outdoor event held mid-month, with varied acts including some semi-big names.

⊖ Shopping

Nelson *p207, map p206*
Arts and crafts
The Craft Connection, 378 Baker St, T250-352 3006, www.craftconnection.org. An impressive collection of arts and crafts from a large co-operative of the region's most

talented artists. Their brand new location features a high-end gallery downstairs. **Ourglass Studio & Gallery**, 568 Ward St, T250-505 5595. Owned by a collective of glass artists, who can normally be seen at work.

Books and music
Pack Rat Annie's, 411 Kootenay St. A wide range of second-hand books, as well as new and used CDs. There's also a good café/ restaurant, the home-made spatzle is one of the best and most filling lunch options.

Camping equipment
Snowpack Outdoor Experience, 333 Baker St, a Patagonia outlet; **Valhalla Pure Out-fitters**, 626 Baker St.

Clothes
Lilikoi Clothing, 358 Baker St, T250-352 3382. A boutique selling lovely, nature inspired screen printed designs on soft jersey fabrics.
Very Hush Hush, next to **The All Seasons**, Herridge Lane, T250-359 8115. A very cool boutique located in a 1964 Airstream Trailer.

Food
Kootenay Co-op, 295 Baker St. The best place for healthy, organic local produce and for people-watching.
The Rising Sun French Artisan Bakery, 281 Herridge Lane, behind the **Bank of Montreal**. Has caused quite a stir among locals with the quality of its breads.
The Tree of Life Market, held on Sat in Cottonwood Falls Park, near the old railway station. Locally grown produce, music and more good people watching.

Sports
Boomtown Emporium, 104-402 Baker St, T250-505 5055, the only place for used equipment; **Gerick Cycle and Sports**, 702 Baker St, T250-354 4622; **Kootenay Experience**, 306 Victoria St, T250-354 4441, skiing equipment; **The Sacred Ride**, 213 Baker St, T250-3543831, mountain bike and snowboard equip-ment; **Village Ski Hut**, 367 Baker St, T250-352 6326.

East Shore *p208*

Crawford Bay's vibrant artisan scene curr-ently includes a blacksmith and an artist working with copper and glass at **Kootenay Forge**, T250-227 9467, www.kootenay forge.com; a glass blower at **Breathless Glass**, T250-227 9598; a traditional broom maker at **North Woven Broom**, T250-227 9245, www.northwovenbroom.com; traditional weavers at **Barefoot Hand-weaving**, T250-227 9655, www.barefoot hand weaving.com; and hand milled soaps at **The Soapstone**, just up from the ferry, T250-227 8905.

Slocan Valley *p211*

Arts and crafts can be bought directly from several artists and artisans in Silverton or at the Fri market in New Denver.

Books
Earth Spirit, almost next door to **Jennie's Book Garden**, T250-226 7265. Metaphysical books, artefacts and New Age music.
Jennie's Book Garden, 5729 Hwy 6, Winlaw, T250-226 7066. A small shop packed with an intelligently selected range of desirable fiction and non-fiction.

Clothing
Valhalla Pure Outfitters, 101 Eldorado/ 6th Av, New Denver. Outdoor clothing, equipment and information.

▲▲ Activities and tours

Nelson *p207, map p206*
Nelson and District Community Complex, 305 Hall St, T250-354 4386. A brand new facility with a good swimming pool, fitness centre and ice rink.

Climbing
Gravity Climbing Centre, 513 Victoria St, T250-352 6125, www.gravityadventures. net, Mon-Fri 1500-2200, Sat-Sun 1200-1900. Best place for information, equipment and practice on an indoor climbing wall. Also give lessons, run trips and operate a shuttle service for mountain bikers.
Summit Reflections Hiking & Climbing Adventures, 414 Beasley St, T250-354 4884, www.summitreflections.com.

Granite Pointe, 1133 Richards St W, T1877-677 6077, www.granitepointe.ca.

Kayaking

Kootenay Kayak Co, based in Balfour, T250-505 4549, www.kootenaykayak.com. Rentals, lessons and tours that range from 3 hrs to multi-day trips combined with other activities.

Mountain biking

Nelson is a Mecca for this sport, with dozens of trails. A useful map put together by the Nelson Cycling Club is for sale at bike shops. For information, follow links from www.disc overnelson.com and/or pick up the excellent *Kootenay Rockies Bike Vacations* brochure from the Visitor Centre.

The Sacred Ride, 213 Baker St, T250-354 3831, www.sacredride.ca. Rents top bikes, sells equipment and has all the information you need on trails and events.

Wright Wheels, T250-352 9236, www.bike toursbc.ca. Road bike tours such as the Silvery Slocan Loop, or the longer International Selkirk Loop.

Skiing

See Whitewater Ski Resort, page 208. Across the highway there's 20 km of cross-country skiing on 11 beautiful groomed trails in the Nordic Ski Club.

Baldface, T250-352 0006, www.baldface.net, 5 mins in a helicopter from Nelson. An increasingly revered cat-skiing operation that has 14,500 ha of perfect snow, luxurious lodging and gourmet food. $650 per person per day all-inclusive.

Wildhorse, T1888-488 4327, www.skiwild horse.com More affordable cat-skiing, with 1-day packages from $395, or $275 standby

Village Ski Hut, 367 Baker St, T250-352 6326, rents equipment.

Kaslo *p208*
Hiking and biking

Kaslo is the best base for trips into Kokanee Glacier Provincial Park, via Keen Creek. For a short walk to 360° panoramas of lake and mountain ranges, do the 2-km loop to Buchanan Lookout. Follow Hwy 31A west for 9.2 km then take the rough Buchanan Forest Service Rd to the right for 11 km. An extreme mountain bike trail heads straight

down 1220 m from here. Landmark Bakery, 416 Front St, T250-353 2250, rents bikes.

Kayaking

Kaslo Kayaking, T250-353 9649, www.kaslo kayaking.ca. Rentals, lessons and tours. They also rent out bikes.

Purcell Wilderness Provincial Park
p209
Cat-skiing

Selkirk Wilderness Skiing, Meadow Creek, www.selkirkwilderness.com. Week-long packages only, based out of their fantastic lodge, a 30-min cat-ride into backcountry.

White Grizzly, Meadow Creek, T250-366 4306, www.whitegrizzly.com. First class cat-skiing operation, accessing arguably the best powder in the province. All-inclusive packages involve accommodation in their lodge and all-you-can-eat gourmet meals.

West of Kaslo *p210*
Skiing

Retallack Ski Resort, T250-226 7784, www.retallack.com. One of the best and easiest bases for cat-skiing, with 5000 ha of terrain including 600 m runs and some of BC's steepest tree skiing. The cost is $825 per day, including luxury accommodation and gourmet meals. Standby rate of $315 for skiing and lunch only.

Slocan Valley *p211*

There's a 50-km trail for mountain biking or cross-country skiing along the old rail bed, following the river all the way up the valley. For rock climbing, there are some good cliff faces just past the mill in Slocan.

Paddling

Slocan River is mostly leisurely but there are some rapids around Lemon Creek. Most people put in at the Winlaw Bridge and take out at South Slocan.

Race Track Gas Station, Slocan Park. Rents inner tubes for floating down the river, a popular summer activity.

Smiling Otter, 8846 Slocan West Rd, Slocan, T250-355 2373, www.smiling otter.com. Kayak and canoe rentals, tours and lessons. Also offers climbing lessons and guided mountain tours.

Nakusp *p212*
Hot springs
There are a few small, free hot springs reached by logging roads about 24 km north of Nakusp on Highway 23. **Saint Leon** seems to be closed now but **Halfway**, situated amidst giant old-growth trees, is still accessible. It's not easy to find, so ask for directions. Nudity is common at this spring. **Halcyon Hot Springs**, 34 km north on Hwy 23, T250-265 3554, www.halcyon-hotsprings .com, 0800-2200. $9, youth $8, child $6.50 for a dip, or $124.50, youth $13.50, child $9.50 for a day pass. The best private resort in the area, with sulphur-free and lithium-rich water. The three pools, hot (40°C), warm (38°C) and cold (12°C), and the swimming pool (32°C) overlook Arrows Lake. **Nakusp Hot Springs**, 92-6th Av NW, T250-265 4528, daily 0930-2130, $7.50 for a dip, $11 for a day pass, $3 on Wed in winter. Cheaper and closer than Halcyon, but not as appealing. A simple, round pool is divided in 2, with temperatures of 38°C and 41°C in winter, 36°C and 38°C in summer. A bus to the springs leaves from the Seniors' Lodge Mon at 1000; from Overwaitea Wed at 1100.

● Transport

Nelson *p207, map p206*
Bus
Local Nelson is small enough to explore on foot. All bus routes, T250-352 8201, www.bu sonline.ca, converge at the junction of Baker and Ward Streets. Buses go as far as Balfour. Local shuttles go from the Chahko Mika mall to: **Salmo** (Thu 0800, 1250, 1630); **Kaslo** (Wed 1515); **Nakusp** (Tue, Thu 1530); **Slocan** (Mon-Fri 0905, 1537, 1715, every other Tue 0700, 1330); **Playmor** at the south end of the Slocan Valley (Mon- Fri 0635); **Passmore** near Winlaw (Mon-Fri 1645). Some services need to be reserved, T1877-843 2877.
Long distance Greyhound, T250-352 3939, has 2 daily buses west to **Kelowna** (5½ hrs, $55) for connections to **Vancouver** and **Kamloops** and east to **Cranbrook** (4 hrs, $38) for connections to **Banff** and **Calgary**. The station is in Chahko Mika mall.

East Shore *p208*
Ferry
The 9-km ferry from **Balfour** to **Kootenay**

Bay, leaves every 50 mins (summer), every 2 hrs (winter), 40 mins, free. An absolute must.

Kaslo *p208*
Kaslo is difficult to reach without your own transport. A single shuttle for **Nelson** leaves Wed morning, 0720, returns 1515.

Slocan Valley *p211*
For shuttle information, see Nelson. Buses from **Nakusp** pass through Slocan on Tue and Thu and can be flagged down. Otherwise, hitchhiking is a way of life.

Nakusp *p212*
Bus
The shuttle to **Nelson** leaves Tue and Thu 0815, returns 1530.

Ferry
Ferries from Galena Bay to **Shelter Bay** leave hourly 0530-0030, return hourly 0500-2400.

● Directory

Nelson *p207, map p206*
Banks Royal Bank, 401 Baker St, T250-354 4111. **Internet** Library. **Laundry** Plaza, 616 Front St, T250-352 3534. **Library** Nelson Municipal Library, 602 Stanley St, T250-352 6333. **Medical services** Kootenay Lake Hospital, 3 View St, T250- 352 3111. **Dentist** Dr L. Bickerton, 108 Baker St, T250-352 2281. **Pharmacy** Pharmasave Drugs, 685 Baker St, T250-352 2316. **Post office** Canada Post, 514 Vernon St, T250-352 3538.

Kaslo *p208*
Medical services Victorian Community Health Centre, 673 A Av, T250-353 2211. **Post office** Canada Post, 312 5th St, T250-353 2611.

Slocan Valley *p211*
Medical services Arrow Lakes Hospital, 97 1st Av, Nakusp, T250-265 3622; **Slocan Community Health Care Centre**, 401 Galena St, New Denver, T250-358 7911. **Post office** Canada Post, 5722 Hwy 6, Winlaw, T250-226 7522; 804 Harold St, Slocan, T250-355 2311; 219 6th Av, New Denver, T250-358 2611 and 605 Broadway St, Nakusp, T250-265 3337.

British Columbia West Kootenays Listings

Northern BC

Heading north, your chances of encountering wildlife, First Nations culture and solitude increase, but so do the distances, while good food, sights, sleeping options and the scenery-to-distance ratio all decrease. The Wild West-style Cariboo offers ranches, gold rush history, excellent canoeing on Bowron Lakes and the ultimate living museum of Barkerville. The Chilcotin includes the beautiful but remote town of Bella Coola and the vast wilderness of Tweedsmuir Provincial Park. Nisga'a Memorial Lava Bed Park is the highlight of a mostly dull drive west from Prince George to Prince Rupert, the north's most interesting town, with many worthwhile excursions. Haida Gwaii – the Galápagos of the North – is an extraordinary set of rugged islands, containing several abandoned Haida villages. The Cassiar Highway heading north passes through magnificent scenery, with a short diversion via the stunning blue Bear Glacier to Stewart and Hyder, where you can watch grizzlies fishing for salmon. ▸▸ For Sleeping, Eating and other listings, see pages 236-250.*

Ins and outs

Getting there and around

Given the vast distances involved, unless you have a vehicle it's definitely worth considering a flight north, which is a lot faster than the bus and not necessarily more expensive. **Pacific Coastal Airlines** flies to Bella Coola and Williams Lake from Vancouver, Victoria, Powell River and Port Hardy. **WestJet** flies to Prince George and Prince Rupert from Vancouver, Kelowna and Calgary. **Air Canada** flies to Prince George, Prince Rupert and Haida Gwaii from Vancouver. **Hawk Air** flies to Prince Rupert from Vancouver. **Prince George's Airport** ① *4141 Airport Rd, T250-963 2400, www.pgairport.ca*, is 10 km east of town, off Hwy 16 on the Old Cariboo Highway. The **Airporter shuttle** ① *T250-563 2220, www.pgairporter.ca, $8, child $2.50*, stops anywhere in town. Prince Rupert's airport is located on Digby Island. A **bus/ferry service** ① *T250-624 3355*, meets scheduled flights and the price is included in airline tickets. The return service leaves from Rupert Square Mall.

An even better idea is to take one of the sailings from Port Hardy (see page 135), such as the Inside Passage to Prince Rupert, or the Discovery Passage to Bella Coola. These are tantamount to a cheap cruise through spectacular scenery and take you straight to the most worthwhile destinations. **BC Ferries** ① *www.bcferries.com*, also operates a service from Prince Rupert to Haida Gwaii.

Greyhound operates three daily buses from Vancouver and four from Kamloops to Prince George via the Cariboo. There are two daily buses between Prince George and Prince Rupert and between Prince George and Dawson Creek; and three weekly buses up the Alaska Highway from Dawson Creek to Whitehorse, Yukon. There is no public transport on the Chilcotin or Cassiar Highways. **Seaport Limousine** ① *T250-636 2622*, runs a daily bus from Terrace to Stewart.

VIA Rail ① *T1800-561 8630, www.viarail.ca*, runs three weekly daylight-only trains from Prince Rupert to Jasper, with an overnight stop in Prince George. ▸▸ *For further details, see Transport, page 247.*

Best time to visit

The best time to visit is in summer as the winters can get pretty cold. Grizzly bears are best seen between April and September. May to July is the best time for orcas. The **Williams Lake Stampede** is held around 1 July (see page 243). August to October is the best time for humpback and grey whales. September to early October is best for those elusive white Kermode Spirit bears.

The Cariboo ⊜🚗❄️⛰️🚌 ➠ pp236-250. Colour map 1, A6.

The most obvious road to Northern BC follows the historic route of the Cariboo Wagon Road through the middle of a vast plateau between the Coast and Cariboo mountain ranges. This is dry ranching country, where the broad horizons are laden with endless pine forests and literally thousands of lakes. Apart from anglers, for whom this is a paradise, most people find that its scenic appeal runs thin fairly quickly and, without a single town of any interest, the monotony is only broken by constant reminders of the area's gold-mining past. The region's most useful base is Williams Lake, but the only real attraction is Barkerville, an extensive reconstruction of that Gold Rush town. Nearby are **Bowron Lakes**, which have been voted one of the world's top ten canoeing destinations.

Clinton and around
Today's **Cariboo Highway** (Highway 97) begins at Cache Creek, whose dry bluffs and colourful rock formations set the tone for the drive to come. **Clinton** ① 40 km north, is one of the better places for anyone who would like to experience the cowboy lifestyle first-hand by staying on a working **guest ranch** ① T250-459 2640 for information on Dude Ranches. ➠ For further details, see Sleeping, page 236.

A good map will show that a vast area west and north of here is covered with provincial parks and a network of dirt roads that connect isolated villages, ranches and remnants of mining communities. There are endless possibilities for exploring if you have a reliable vehicle and a passion for this kind of scenery and history.

Lined with over 100 well-stocked lakes of various sizes, the so-called Interlakes Highway (Highway 24) which runs east to Little Fort from just south of 100 Mile House is understandably renowned for its fishing.

Williams Lake and around
Williams Lake is an uninspiring town but a useful springboard to many activities, with the area's best year-round **Visitor Information Centre** ① 1600 S Broadway St, T250-392 5025, www.landwithoutlimits.com, www.williamslake.ca. Ask about the excellent local mountain biking, or hiking in the Williams Lake Valley. Rafting and whitewater kayaking trips are operated down the Farwell Canyon to the west. Williams Lake is also the place to pick up supplies if tackling the 456 km drive west to Tweedsmuir Provincial Park and Bella Coola (see page 225).

East of Williams Lake, a little circuit could be made along dirt roads to the small, pretty towns of Likely and Horsefly, both close to lakes and full of Gold Rush artefacts. The former in particular is the main base for exploring old mining sites and ghost towns such as Bullion Pit and Quesnel Forks. Likely also gives access to Quesnel Lake, which keen paddlers could follow east to the remote and beautiful Cariboo Mountains Provincial Park.

Xats'ull Heritage Village ① 3405 Mountain House Rd, T250-297 6502, www.xatsull.com, full day $38, child $25 or ½-day $17, child $11 programs involving ceremonies, songs, dances, arts and crafts, and plant and wildlife exploration, 1- to 12-day cultural programmes with food and lodging provided, $150 per day, is situated on a plateau overlooking the Fraser River, 37 km north of Williams Lake in Soda Creek. The first of its kind in North America, it features pit houses, petroglyphs, tepees and native artefacts.

Continuing north, the Fraser River breathes fresh life into the scenery, but the forests in these parts have been horribly decimated, so it comes as no surprise that **Quesnel** is just another ugly logging town. Gold Rush enthusiasts might enjoy the four-day **Billy Barker Days Festival** held in the third week of July and a visit to the **Quesnel Museum and Archives** ① *705 Carson Av, T250-992 9580, www.quesnelmuseum.ca, mid-May to mid-Sep Mon, Wed, Sun 0900-1800, Tue, Thu, Sat 0900-2100, mid-Sep to mid-May Tue-Sat 0830-1630, $3, youth $1.50, children free*, the best museum in the Cariboo, with a lot of Gold Rush and First Nations artefacts and many items from China. It's located on Hwy 97 in LeBourdais Park along with the **Visitor Information Centre** ① *T250-9928716, www.northcariboo.com.*

Barkerville and Bowron Lakes

The main reason to stop anywhere in the Cariboo is **Barkerville Provincial Historic Park** ① *82 km east of Quesnal, T1888-994 3332, www.barkerville.ca, May-Sep 0800-2000, $13.50, youth $8, child $4, under 6 free, $2 per person for second day; stagecoach ride $9, youth $6, theatre $13.75, child $7*. The most impressive monument to local history, it's set in the refreshingly beautiful scenery of the Cariboo Mountains. Billy Barker struck it lucky here in 1862 and, for the next 10 years, Barkerville became the biggest town north of San Francisco and west of Chicago. Today, it is the biggest and best of many reconstructed heritage towns scattered around the country, with historic displays and demonstrations and 125 restored buildings full of costumed, role-playing staff. The Theatre Royal features live vaudeville shows, old-style shops sell authentic wares and there are plenty of restaurants to visit. You can pan for gold, be photographed in period costume, tour the cemetery and ride in a stagecoach.

Barkerville provides the easiest access to **Bowron Lakes Provincial Park**, 24 km further east. This mountain wilderness, the top of a protected belt that runs north from Wells Gray Provincial Park, offers swimming, hiking and camping, but is especially renowned as one of the ten best canoe routes in the world. ▸▸ *For further details, see Activities and tours, page 244.*

The Chilcotin ⊜⊘⊙⊙❀▲⊜ ▸▸ *pp236-250.*

One of Canada's most unlikely roads, the **Chilcotin Highway** (Highway 20) heads 456 km west from Williams Lake to Bella Coola, one of the last great wilderness settlements, whose only other access is by ferry from Port Hardy at the northern tip of Vancouver Island. The first 350 km passes through the remote but flat, monotonous scenery of the Chilcotin Plateau. **Heckman Pass** ① *1524 m*, marks the end of the plateau and start of a 30-km section of narrow, winding, unpaved road, culminating in 'The Hill', 10 km of steep, brake-grinding switchbacks with up to 18% grades. The highlight along the way is the exceptional **Tweedsmuir Provincial Park**, which has some of the most remote trails in the Coast Mountains.

Chilcotin Plateau

As in the Cariboo, those excited by this kind of country will find much to explore on the back roads mostly to the south. **Bull Canyon Park** ① *10 km west of Alexis Creek*, is a good spot to admire the glacial blue water of the Chilcotin River and some fine rock walls. A little further west, a rough road leads to **Nazko Lakes Provincial Park**, where a 20-km canoe trip can be made between six lakes with easy portages. At Chilanko Forks, a fair 12-km road leads to scenic **Puntzi Lake**, with good fishing, visiting pelicans and trumpeter swans and 360° views.

From **Tatla Lake**, helicopter companies whisk hardcore enthusiasts to the Coast Mountains' highest peak, **Mount Waddington** ① *4016 m*, or its largest body of water, **Chilko Lake**, contained by the vast wilderness of **Ts'ylos Provincial Park**, which can also be reached via 60 km of rough roads. The **Chilko River**'s Lava Canyon is well known for its river rafting with a drop of 19 m/km over a 24-km stretch, including the infamous 'White Mile'.

⚡ Go north, white man

Major finds around Yale in the lower Fraser Valley encouraged prospectors to spread north, their path soon facilitated by the building of the Cariboo Wagon Road in 1861. Starting in Lillooet, this stagecoach route eventually led to Barkerville, where the ultimate lucky strike occurred in 1862, drawing some 100,000 hopefuls up the road by the end of the decade.

Today's Cariboo Highway (Highway 97) follows most of that original route, passing former resting and provision stops with names like 100 Mile House, spelling out (incorrectly, as it turned out) the distances from Lillooet. Mining for gold and other metals, along with the more recent interest in vast regions of standing lumber, has been the main reason for the white man's gradual colonization of the northern wildernesses. For millennia before his arrival, some of the most advanced pre-industrial civilizations in the history of the planet inhabited the Northwest Coast, most notably the Haida of Haida Gwaii, whose artworks, past and present represent one of Western Canada's cultural highlights (see page 235).

Tweedsmuir Provincial Park

British Columbia's largest park, Tweedsmuir contains 8967 sq km of breathtaking wilderness, spanning the full gamut of peaks, glaciers, wild flower meadows, waterfalls, forests and lakes, and is home to thriving populations of black and grizzly bears, moose and caribou. For more information on the park, visit www.env.gov.bc.ca/bcparks/explore/parkpgs/tweedsmu or www.bcadventure.com/adventure/explore/cariboo/parks/tweeds. On its eastern edge, near Heckman Pass, the plateau gives way to the **Rainbow Range**, named for the wonderful spectrum of reds, oranges, yellows and purples in the fragmented layers of rock and eroded lava. A number of hiking trails lead from the trailhead here.

On the highway, midway through the park at Atnarko River, is the main campsite, with water, toilets and wood. Nearby, an old tote road, suitable only for high-clearance vehicles, leads 12 km to the **Hunlen Falls/Turner Lake Trailhead**. The spectacular **Hunlen Falls** ① *the trail to get there is a difficult 16.4-km hike with a 800 m elevation gain*, is a major draw, plummeting 260 m and disappearing in a cloud of spray. Just to the south is **Turner Lake**, starting point of an excellent 19-km canoe route whose chain of seven lakes is connected by easy portages, with six campsites and great fishing for cutthroat trout; rentals are available at the lake. Further west, towered over by a wall of giant granite Coast Mountain peaks that mark the park's western boundary, is **Stuie**, the only village in the park. Nearby is the Fisheries Pool campground and the best of the park's short hikes, the two-hour **Burnt Bridge Loop**.

Bella Coola → *Colour map 1, A2.*

Sitting at the end of a long, saltwater fjord, Bella Coola's chief asset has to be its stunning scenery. Surrounded by utter wilderness and home to some of the healthiest animal life in the country, the town is the sole remaining dwelling of the Nuxalk or Bella Coola people, who have lived for 10,000 years along the rivers and coastline of this region. Their most ancient remnants are the **Thorsen Creek Petroglyphs**, forty or so rock carvings depicting human faces, frogs, fish and geometric patterns. To arrange a hike through the magical forest to visit them with a Nuxalk guide, ask at the **Visitor Booth** ① *Mackenzie St, Jun-Sep, T250-799 5202, www.bellacoola.ca, www.centralcoastbc.com*, or contact the **Nuxalk Nation** ① *T250-*

799 5959, www.nuxalknation.org. The descendants of a people who depended for thousands of years on the abundance of salmon in their rivers can still be seen catching and smoking fish in the age-old way. Rafting, kayaking or canoeing down the river are all great ways to appreciate the surroundings and the salmon fishing is still particularly good. Otherwise, there's plenty of hiking and wildlife watching and skilled native carvers can be seen at work in numerous small galleries and studios.

About half of today's non-aboriginal population can trace their heritage back to the first white settlers, a group of 120 Norwegians who were led here from Minnesota by Pastor Christian Saugstad in 1894, in order to found a Utopian society. Unlike many similar attempts, the hard-working Scandinavians managed to survive the challenge. **Bella Coola Museum** ① *269 Hwy 20, T250-799 5767, www.bella coolamuseum.ca, Jun-Sep Wed-Mon 0900-1200, 1300-1700, $2.50*, is housed in an 1892 Norwegian schoolhouse and contains many settler relics, as well as aboriginal and Hudson's Bay Company artefacts. Guided tours, historic videos and a Historic Walking Tour brochure are all available. In Hagensborg, 16 km east, there are more signs of the Norwegian past at the **Sons of Norway Heritage House** ① *$2*, on the highway and the 1904 Augsburg United Church. A short boat ride from Bella Coola leads to the relic of the **Talheo Cannery**, which capitalized on the Norwegians' commercial fishing expertise.

Highway 5 to Prince George ▣🚲❄🎣🛶⛰🏛☕

▶▶ *pp236-250.*

Highway 5 from Kamloops is a longer route north than the Cariboo Highway. Passing between the Cariboo and Rocky mountains, its scenery is stimulating enough, but none of the towns offer much of interest. **Wells Gray Provincial Park**, however, is one of the most rewarding parks in BC and relatively underused thanks to the proximity of the high-profile Rockies. **Valemount** is a good base for the classic Mount Robson/Berg Lake hike (see page 301), with plenty of places to stay; ask at the **Visitor Information Centre** ① *685 Cranberry Lake Rd, T250-566 4846*. At Tête Jaune Cache, Highway 5 meets the Yellowhead Highway, which heads east to Jasper and northwest through duller scenery to Prince George.

Wells Gray Provincial Park

Thanks to its location in the Cariboo Mountains, the scenery in Wells Gray is extremely varied, including large lakes and river systems, some impressive waterfalls, extinct volcanoes, lava beds and mineral springs. Deer, caribou, moose and bears are frequently seen and there's good fishing in most of the lakes and rivers. The south of the park has alpine meadows, while the inaccessible north and east edges are lined with peaks and glaciers. As in the Rockies, summers can be quite wet, the driest month being April. While there are many first-class hiking and canoeing trails, you don't have to walk far to see some of the most impressive natural phenomena.

The park entrance is at **Hemp Creek**, 40 km from Clearwater on the mainly paved Clearwater Valley Road. There's no public transport to the park. At the junction with Highway 5 is the very helpful **Visitor Centre** ① *T250-674 2646, www.clearwater bcchamber.com*, which can put you in touch with operators for horse riding, floatplanes, canoeing and whitewater rafting. On the way to the park is **Spahats Creek/Falls,** where the creek has carved a 122-m-deep canyon through layers of lava. There's a campground here and a viewpoint of the canyon and 61-m falls.

Beyond Hemp Creek, a side road leads to Green Mountain Viewing Tower and a chance to take in the full extent of the surrounding wilderness. Further along, the wide and powerful Murtle River crashes down **Dawson Falls**, which can be observed from vantage points along a short trail. Where the road crosses the river, the

King of the fish

All five species of Pacific salmon are born in gravel beds in streams. Laid in the autumn, their eggs are incubated through the winter by ice and snow up to several metres deep. In spring, they emerge as inch-long fry and then spend up to a year or more in a nearby river or lake before heading downstream to the ocean. One early summer day, after about three to five years, an unknown impulse compels them to return to their birthplace. Some species cover distances of up to 1600 km, at speeds of more than 50 km per day. For weeks the salmon struggle upstream, jumping up steep waterfalls and negotiating fierce rapids. What's more, the entire journey is undertaken without food. On the way, they change colour from their normal blue-tinged silver to varying shades of red. By late summer they reach the exact place of their birth and, after enacting the reproductive stage of the life cycle, promptly die.

The best places to see the salmon run are on the Adams River in the Shuswap (page 172), the Campbell River on Vancouver Island (page 132), or around the Skeena River between Prince George and Prince Rupert in Northern BC (page 230).

Devil's Punch Bowl (or Mush Bowl) is the dramatic result of fierce water cutting its way through a narrow gorge. A little further on, a 10-km side road heads left to the most impressive sight of all, the 137-m **Helmcken Falls**.

The main road continues for 23 km, passing three more vehicle-accessible campsites and the homestead remains of **Ray Farm** on the way to **Clearwater Lake**. Linked by a short portage to Azure Lake, this is ideal canoeing country, with a possible 102-km round-trip that has fishing and campsites all the way. A 2-km trail leads from Clearwater Lake campground to the **Dragon's Tongue** lava flow, while the 12-km Chain Meadow Loop has numerous viewpoints.

Prince George → Colour map 3, C6.

Situated at the crossroads of the only highways heading north (Highway 97 and Highway 16), Prince George is the main service centre and transport hub for an incredibly vast region and almost impossible to avoid. It is also the focus for some of the most heavily logged land in Canada and no place to linger. There's a **Visitor Information Centre** ① *1300 1st Av, T1800-668 7646, www.tourismpg.com, Mon-Sat 0900-1600, longer in summer.*

If you have time to kill, the best place to head is **Fort George Park**, on the Fraser River about 10 minutes' walk southeast of Downtown. As well as a miniature railway, water park and native cemetery, it contains the museum and science centre of **Exploration Place** ① *333 Becott Pl, end of 20th Av, T250-562 1612, www.theexplorationplace.com, mid-May to mid-Sep daily 1000-1700, mid-Sep to mid-May Wed-Sun, $11, child $9*, which includes seven different galleries devoted to themes as diverse as palaeontology, children and First Nations.

From here, the pleasant Heritage River Trail, an 8-km loop that connects a number of parks, follows the Fraser 2 km to **Cottonwood Island Nature Park**, which contains several interpretive trails and the **Railway and Forestry Museum** ① *take River Rd from 1st Av, T250-563 7351, www.pgrfm.bc.ca, May-Oct daily 0900-1730, suggested donation $4*, where a collection of steam engines, assorted railway relics and forestry artefacts are presented mostly in the open air.

Prince George to Prince Rupert ⊟🏃▲ ⇥ *pp236-250.*

West to Smithers → *Colour map 3, B4.*

The eastern section of the Yellowhead Highway is a monotonous drive with few reasons to stop, but the Lakes District, west of Prince George between Fraser Lake and Houston, has good wilderness fishing in over 300 lakes and there's prime birdwatching at the **Nechako Bird Sanctuary** in Vanderhoof, which is on the Pacific Flyway. The best viewing area is in Riverside Park, 1 km north on Burrard.

There's plenty of hiking, biking and skiing close to **Smithers** in the Babine Mountains Recreation Area, 15 km east and at **Hudson Bay Mountain** ⓘ *T250-847 2058, www.skismithers.com, lift passes $45, youth $35, child $25,* where there's 120 ha of skiable terrain, 34 runs (25% beginner, 55% intermediate, 20% advanced), a vertical drop of 500 m, four lifts, lodging, food, lessons, rentals and a freestyle park. Ask at the **Visitor Information Centre** ⓘ *1411 Court St, T250-847 5072, www.tourism smithers.com.* There are also fossil beds to explore at **Driftwood Canyon Provincial Park** ⓘ *11 km northeast.* The Babine and Bulkley rivers are good for canoeing, kayaking or river rafting. Just west of Smithers, **Telkwa**, is a pretty riverfront village full of heritage buildings, with a charming pioneer museum.

Hazeltons → *Colour map 3, B4.*

For 4000 years, the region has been home to the Gitxsan Wet'suwet'an people, the most easterly of the West Coast First Nations. Like all Native American groups, their way of life was irrevocably disrupted by the white man's arrival, but a decision by the tribe's elders in the 1950s to preserve what remained of their legacy has made this one of the best places in Western Canada to encounter aboriginal culture. At the summer-only **Visitor Information Centre** ⓘ *on the highway, New Hazelton, T250-842 6071,* you can pick up a copy of the *Hands of History* self-guided driving circuit, which covers many First Nations villages. Among the most interesting are **Kispiox**, **Gitwangak** (Kitwanga) and **Gitanyow** (Kitwancool).

Old Hazelton ⓘ *8 km north of Hwy 16 on a secondary road that crosses a single-lane suspension bridge 76 m above the Bulkley River,* is a well restored 19th- century sternwheeler terminus full of heritage buildings. A pair of totems mark the entrance to the regional highlight, **'Ksan Historical Village** ⓘ *T250-842 5544, www.ksan.org, $2 museum, $10, child $8.50 with tour, mid-May to mid-Sep daily 0900-1700, mid-Sep*

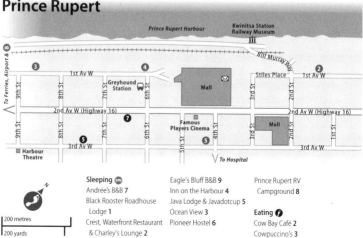

Prince Rupert

Sleeping 🛌
Andrée's B&B **7**
Black Rooster Roadhouse
  Lodge **1**
Crest, Waterfront Restaurant
  & Charley's Lounge **2**

Eagle's Bluff B&B **9**
Inn on the Harbour **4**
Java Lodge & Javadotcup **5**
Ocean View **3**
Pioneer Hostel **6**

Prince Rupert RV
  Campground **8**

Eating 🍴
Cow Bay Café **2**
Cowpuccino's **3**

200 metres
200 yards

to mid-May Mon-Fri 0930-1630, gift shop and museum. This 1970 reconstruction of a settlement that had stood on the site for centuries until 1870, was the main focus of attempts to resurrect the dying culture. The grounds contain seven colourful longhouses: the museum, a gift shop, the House of Carving, a silkscreen studio (closed to the public) and three that can only be visited on the very worthwhile guided tour, the Fireweed, Wolf and Frog Houses. There are also many significant totem poles. The museum contains about 600 artefacts including boxes, masks, robes, headdresses and shaman's regalia. There are also performances by the fabulous **'Ksan Performing Arts Group** ① *4 Jul-8 Aug every Fri 1900, $8, child $5.*

Terrace and the Nisga'a Memorial Lava Bed Park → *Colour map 3, B3.*

With the entrance of the **Skeena**, a river capable of rising 5 m in a day and fluctuating 18 m between low and high tide, the scenery suddenly comes alive and remains riveting most of the way to Prince Rupert. The broad valley is framed within magnificent mountain peaks such as the photogenic **Seven Sisters**, which dominate the southern skyline west of Kitwanga. While **Terrace** is another uninspiring logging centre, its surroundings are quite the opposite.

Salmon fishing in the Skeena and its many tributaries is a major obsession and this is one of the best places to see the creeks turn red in spawning season. It's also a good region for thermal waters, such as the easily reached **Mount Layton Hot Springs** ① *16 km south on Hwy 37 to Kitimat, T250-798 2214, www.mountlayton.com, Mon, Tue 1400-2200, Wed-Sun 1200-2200, $6.75.* They also have rooms, a restaurant and a lounge. **Shames Mountain** ① *35 km west of Terrace, T250-638 8754, www.shamesmountain.com, daily 0900-1530, $41.50, youth $32, child $23,* is a modest ski hill with 28 trails on 57 ha (21% beginner, 60% intermediate, 19% advanced), 45 ha of natural glades, 3 lifts, a small day lodge and lots of powder. In autumn, this area is unparalleled for wild mushroom picking. The helpful **Visitor Information Centre** ① *4511 Keith Av, T250-635 2063, www.kermodeitourism.ca,* can provide a list of local hikes.

Just west of town, the Nisga'a Highway heads north to pretty **Kitsumkalum Lake** and the remarkable **Nisga'a Memorial Lava Bed Park**, hands down the area's top attraction. In the mid-18th century, the most recent of several volcanic eruptions wreaked havoc here, burying several villages and killing some 2000 Nisga'a. The whole area is now a fascinatingly eerie lunar landscape, with exquisite blue-green ponds and streams, good for spotting salmon in season. There is the **Nisga'a Park Visitor Centre** *T250-798 2466, www.nwesc apes.ca, Mon-Fri 1100-1800, Sat-Sun 2000, 4-hr hikes to visit the volcano leave from here mid-May to mid-Sep Sat 1000, 6 km round trip, $25, youth $20, child $15, led by Nisga'a guides,* which is housed in a striking longhouse at Vetter Creek. Alternatively, pick up one of the self-guided auto tour brochures ($1.50). In 1999 the Nisga'a made history as the first Native band to negotiate legal ownership of their traditional land in the Nass Valley.

Prince Rupert ⬤🅿🏍🛈🏧✳🅾🔺📧ℹ ⤷ *pp236-250. Colour map 3, B3.*

Most travellers will be passing through Prince Rupert on their way somewhere else, but this picturesque fishing town, at the mouth of the Skeena River, is worth a stop. First Nations history, art and culture are integral to this region and the town contains one of the largest collections of totem poles in the north. **Cow Bay**, a pretty little harbour area dotted with gift shops and restaurants, is the place to relax. A high number of Chinese and Vietnamese descendants lend the town a cosmopolitan flavour that is unusual in the north. Plenty of tours and excursions run to abandoned native villages, or to see whales or grizzlies. Sport fishing is also a big draw. For further details, contact the helpful **Visitor Information Centre** ℹ *215 Cow Bay Rd, T1800-667 1994, www.tourismprincerupert.com, www.rupert.bc.ca, mid-May to mid-Sep Mon-Sat 0900-2000, Sun 0900-1700, mid-Sep to mid-May Mon-Sat 0900-1700.* ⤷ *For further details, see Activities and tours, page 244.*

Museum of Northern BC and around

ℹ *100 1st Av W, T250-624 3207, www.museumofnorthernbc.com, mid-May to mid-Sep Mon-Sat 0900-2000, Sun 0900-1700, mid-Sep to mid-May Mon-Sat 0900-1700, $5, youth $2, child $1. Mid-May to mid-Sep there are 1-hr tours of the museum at 1400, free, as well as the Heritage Walking Tour, $2, child $1 and Totem Pole Walking Tour, $2, child $1, both around town. The Prince Rupert Story is a 1-hr dramatization and slide show presented 3 nights weekly, free.*

This is hands down Prince Rupert's major attraction, illustrating the history and culture of the Northwest Coast back to the end of the last ice age, through exhibits and ancient artefacts housed in a replica native longhouse. The museum showcases the superb artworks for which the local aboriginal peoples are famous, as well as the cultures of other First Nations. The gift shop is stocked with locally made articles such as carved masks, silver Haida jewellery and books on art and culture. The museum also hosts diverse temporary exhibitions.

One block away at Market Place is the **Museum Carving Shed** ℹ *T250-624 2421*, where Haida, Nisga'a and Tlingit artists can be seen at work from June to August. Nearby, the new longhouse hosts drama, dance and song performances by the Gwisamiikgigot Dancers. The **Prince Rupert Archives** ℹ *100 1st Av East*, houses 20,000 historic photos. Another important part of Prince Rupert's past is the story of the railway, thoroughly explored in the **Kwinitsa Railway Station Museum** ℹ *Bill Murray Way, T250-624 5637, Jun-Aug daily 0900-1700, by donation*, which is housed in the original 1911 station in Waterfront Park.

Excursions from Prince Rupert

Several operators run boat tours to nearby Kaien Island, a good excuse to get out on the water and visit such local attractions as Prince Edward, Seal Cove and the Butzke Rapids a set of dramatic reversing tidal rapids with waves up to 6 m high. The following are longer trips.

Laxspa'aws (**Pike Island**), whose lush rainforest contains three abandoned Tsimshian villages dating back as far as 1800 years. Whale watching is big business here, with high concentrations of humpback whales to the north, as well as grey whales and orcas. The best time is August to October, or May to July for orcas. You're also likely to see bald eagles and sea lions. **Khutzeymateen Grizzly Bear Sanctuary**, the only protected grizzly habitat in Canada, is 45 km to the northeast and only accessed by water. The best time to visit is late April to September. People get very excited about the possibility of seeing one of the rare and elusive white Kermode (Spirit) bears. While the chances are slim, the best place to catch a

North Pacific Cannery and Fishing Village ① *20 km south of Prince Rupert in Port Edward, T250-628 3538, www.cannery.ca; May-Sep Tue-Sun 0900-1800, Jul to mid-Aug daily 1000-1930, $12, youth $10, child $8, including tours and shows,* is very popular. The cannery was operational from 1889 to 1981. Now the whole village has been restored and opened as a living museum with three different hourly tours, exhibits, live performances twice daily of the 35-min "River Skeena Story", a restaurant and a hostel in the atmospheric old bunkhouse. In summer, **Prince Rupert Transit buses** ① *T250-624 3343,* run all the way here.

Haida Gwaii: Queen Charlotte Islands

🖥️🚗🍴🏕️⛰️📷ℹ️ ⇥ *pp236-250. Colour map 3, B1, B2, C1, C2*

This 300-km long, horn-shaped archipelago 150 km west of Prince Rupert consists of two big islands and the 200 or so islets that surround them. One of only two places in Western Canada to have avoided glaciation during the last ice age, Haida Gwaii (also known as the Queen Charlotte Islands) harbours many species of flora and fauna not found anywhere else, prompting associations with the Galápagos. The world's largest black bears live here, as well as its greatest populations of Peale's peregrine falcons and black-footed albatross. Marine life is equally abundant, making for excellent fishing and whale watching. Fin, sperm, right, humpback and grey whales migrate through and resident pods of orca can be seen almost anywhere, even coming right up to the shores of Queen Charlotte City.

Another reason to visit is the Haida themselves, who have thrived on these islands for over 10,000 years. Widely recognized as being one of the most sophisticated aboriginal peoples on the continent, they are consummate artists and craftsmen. Like few other spots in Canada, this still feels like native land, inhabited by a mere 6000 predominantly aboriginal souls.

A fault line stretching from California to Alaska passes close to the west coast of Haida Gwaii, adding occasional earthquakes to the most wind- and tide-lashed coastline on the Pacific. **Cape St James** at the southern tip is the best place for storm watching, with an average wind-speed of 34 kph. It is little wonder that the communities cling to the protected east coast with its fine beaches. The warm streams of the so-called Japanese Current keep temperatures surprisingly mild here, even in winter. Combined with the copious amounts of rain that perpetually shroud the islands, this has resulted in a lush covering of ancient rainforest.

Ferries arrive at Skidegate on the more populated **Graham Island**, from where it's 4 km to Queen Charlotte City, the main base on the island with the most useful Visitor Centre. South of the Skidegate Narrows, connected by ferry, is the long, tapering **Moresby Island**, whose name also embraces the myriad tiny islets that surround it. Barely populated, it is an almost inaccessible wilderness, the whole southern half of which is now protected as Gwaii Haanas National Park, whose abandoned Haida villages are one of the main highlights of the islands. For additional information, visit www.qcinfo.ca or www.haidagwaiitourism.ca.

Graham Island → *Colour map 3, B1, B2, C1, C2.*

Graham Island contains almost all of Haida Gwaii's inhabitants in a few communities connected by a single paved road. Ferries arrive at Skidegate Landing. **Haida Heritage Centre at Qay'llnagaay** ① *Second Beach Rd, T250-559 7885, www.haidaheritage centre.com, mid-May to mid-Sep Mon-Fri 1000-1800, Sat-Sun 1000-1700, mid-Sep to mid-May Tue-Sat 1000-1800; $12, youth $9, child $6,* is a brand new 16,000 m

Haida Gwaii

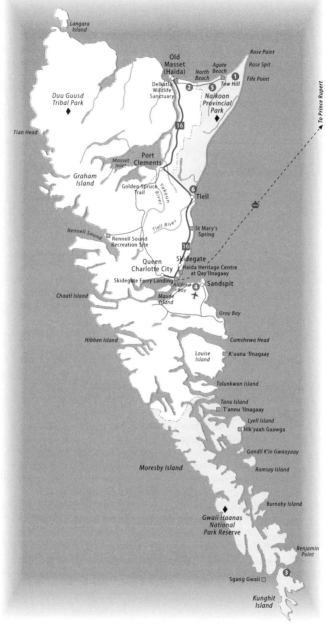

N

10 km
10 miles

Sleeping
Agate Beach Campground **1**
Alaska View Lodge **2**
Gwaii Haanas Guest House **3**
Misty Meadows
  Campground **6**

Moresby Island
  Guesthouse **4**
Rapid Richie's Rustic
  Rentals **5**

complex consisting of five contemporary monumental cedar longhouses and five replica longhouses. One of them contains the new, expanded **Haida Gwaii Museum**, whose many exhibits provide a fine introduction to the human, natural and cultural history of the islands, with a number of fine historic and contemporary artworks, including an excellent assortment of argillite carvings, monumental totem poles from the Haida villages of Tanu and Skedans and an extensive photographic archive of Haida Gwaii people and places from the 1870s to the present. Temporary exhibits are housed in an adjacent classroom. The centre also includes a Greeting House with gift shop; an Eating House, offering salmon BBQ and other native dishes; a Performance House, for theatre, music, presentations, films and lectures; the Canoe House, which includes Bill Reid's magnificent 50-ft cedar canoe, *Loo Taas*; and a carving House, where craftsmen can be observed and guided tours begin. Outside the complex are six totem poles. Also here is the Parks Canada Office, a must for those wanting to visit the **Gwaii Haanas Park**. Nearby in **Skidegate Village** ⓘ *www.skidegate.ca*, is the revered, gravity-defying Balance Rock, Bill Reid's dogfish totem pole and the interesting circular 3-km Spirit Lake Trail.

The picturesque fishing village of **Queen Charlotte City** ⓘ *4 km west of the ferry*, is centred around a pretty harbour and marina. The excellent **Visitor Information Centre** ⓘ *3220 Wharf St, T250-559 8316, www.queencharlotte.ca, May-Sep daily 1000-1900, Oct-Apr Thu-Sat 1000-1600*, contains a 3-D scale map of the islands, a 130-ft frieze depicting the Islands' history, wildlife and legends, various interactive and cultural displays, and local artisans demonstrating their work. They can arrange tours and permits to the abandoned villages on Moresby Island (the only way to get there is on a tour). Ask them about getting to **Rennell Sound Recreation Site**, the best place to experience the wild west coast, with wilderness campgrounds and paths through rainforest to sandy beaches.

Highway 16, the island's only paved road, runs north through Skidegate to Tl'ell, Port Clements and Masset. Halfway to Tl'ell a wooden carving marks the site of **St Mary's Spring**. According to legend, those who drink from here are destined to return. **Tl'ell** itself is a tiny artist community and home to the Naikoon Park Headquarters and interpretive centre. Trails along the Tl'ell River lead to endless beaches and dunes and the shipwreck of the Pesuta. At **Port Clements** ⓘ *www.portclements.com*, the eponymous, small **Port Clements Museum** ⓘ *T250-557 4576, www.portclements museum.org*, explores the pioneer history of the islands, including some massive logging equipment. A trail leads through temperate rainforest to the erstwhile site of the **Golden Spruce**, sadly chopped down by a crazed logger in 1997. A few kilometres further is the site of the partially carved **Haida Canoe**.

The island's most populated town, **Masset** is an ex-military base that lacks QCC's picturesque qualities, but its summer-only **Visitor Information Centre** ⓘ *1455 Old Beach Rd, T250-626 3995, www.massetbc.com*, can point you towards the local attractions. **Dixon Entrance Maritime Museum** ⓘ *2182 Collinson Ave, T250-626 6066, mid-May to mid-Sep daily 1000-1700, mid-Sep to mid-May open less frequently, $2*, celebrates Greater Massett's maritime and settlement history. To the north is the 230-ha **Delkatla Wildlife Sanctuary** ⓘ *T250-626 5015*, the best place for birdwatching on Haida Gwaii, with more than 140 visiting species and a new interpretive centre. **Old Masset**, or Haida, 2 km to the west, contains old totem poles and also the island's largest collection of new poles, plus many small carving sheds, studios and galleries, a café and a few B&Bs.

From Masset, the road leads 26 km east to the **Naikoon Provincial Park** ⓘ *trailhead at Tow Hill, base reached by a 1-km trail one-way*, a 130-m volcanic cliff with amazing rock formations created by lava flows. These are best appreciated at its base, where a blowhole springs into action when the tide comes in. Two other beautiful paths lead to the top of Tow Hill. From here you can take in the full extent of North Beach, which follows the whole strip of coast from Old Masset to Rose Spit.

This is a good place to collect razor clams, scallops and crabs (a saltwater fishing licence is needed for the latter). Just west of Tow Hill is Agate Beach with great camping and beachcombing. Just past Tow Hill is the start of the Cape Fife trail, which crosses the Argonaut Plain, spectacular bog environments and sections of boardwalk en route to a shelter on **East Beach** ① *10 km one-way*. To make this a 35 km, two to three day loop, follow East Beach northwards to **Rose Spit**, a sacred Haida site and ecological reserve, then follow North Beach back to Tow Hill. It's a good idea to get a tide chart before setting off.

Gwaii Haanas National Park → *Colour map 3, C2.*
① *Park fees $20, youth $17, child $10 per person per day. There is a compulsory orientation session.*
Half of Moresby Island is protected by the extraordinary **Gwaii Haanas National Park Reserve**, which includes 1600 km of coastline and 138 islands and was rated the No 1 Park Destination in North America by a panel of experts polled by *National Geographic Traveler magazine*. There are no hiking trails and entry is by boat or floatplane only, with kayak the best way to get around. If you are an extremely experienced kayaker or adventurer and want to travel independently, visit www.pc.gc.ca/gwaiihaanas for the very complex logistical instructions. Otherwise, you have little choice but to visit the park with a tour operator. This will not be cheap, but it will be one of the highlights of your time in Canada, if not your life.

Even more than its unblemished natural beauty and the prolific wealth of marine and terrestrial fauna and flora it supports, the park's main draw is a collection of abandoned Haida villages and over 500 important archaeological features that are evidence of 10,000 years of occupation. Today, these are co-managed by Parks Canada and the Haida Nation. The five most culturally significant sites are manned by Watchmen, traditional lookout guards sometimes depicted at the top of totem poles wearing distinctive tall hats. They live at the sites in the summer and are very liberal with information.

K'uuna 'Ilnagaay (**Skedans**) on Louise Island, the easiest village to access, was painted by Emily Carr (see page 380) in 1907 before most of the buildings and totems returned to the earth. A trail meanders through the eerie but beautiful remains of the ancient village and cemetery. Look out for abandoned logging equipment now covered with moss. **T'annu 'Ilnagaay** (**Tanu**) on Tanu Island is a beautiful spot facing two beaches. **Hlk'yaah Gaawga** (**Windy Bay**) on the eastern shore of Lyell Island is where the Haida blocked the road in 1985, bringing an end to logging in South Moresby, hopefully forever. A longhouse where the Watchmen now live was built in commemoration. There are trails here through 1000-year-old trees that are 70 m tall. **Gandll K'in Gwaayaay** (**Hot Spring Island**) is a gorgeous place with a dozen hot pools. A bathhouse is provided for rinsing off before dipping in. **Sgang Gwaay** (**Ninstits**), off the west coast of Kunghit Island, is a UNESCO World Heritage Site and the only village that has been preserved. Facing the beach is a magnificent display of over two dozen Haida mortuary totem poles.

Those wanting a taste of the island without visiting the park can take a ferry from Skidegate to **Alliford Bay**. The island's only village, **Sandspit**, is 15 km east and little more than an airport with a **Visitor Information Centre** ① *T250-637 5362, May-Sep daily 0900-1800*. To the south is **Gray Bay**, a large sandy beach with a great forestry campsite. A four-day trek leads south to Cumshewa Head, with beautiful beaches on the way.

Cassiar Highway ⬤ ⇥ *pp236-250.*

Back on the mainland, joining the Yellowhead Highway at Kitwanga 91 km east of Terrace and running to just west of Watson Lake in the Yukon, Highway 37 is one of

The Haida

The art of the Haida is utterly distinctive due to their particular style of representing animals and mythical creatures, often in red and black. Prolific carvers of totem poles, they also used the giant red cedars that once flourished on the islands to make huge dug-out canoes and ornately decorated houses. For many, the highlight of a visit to Haida Gwaii is the opportunity to buy authentic Haida art such as beautiful masks and jewellery, or delicate carvings in argillite; a black, slate-like rock only found on these islands.

As well as being artists, the Haida had a reputation as fearful warriors; their unsurpassed sea-faring skills gained them the label 'Vikings of the Pacific Northwest'. Up around Masset, where many pure-blood Haida still live, you get a feel for the sheer size often attained by this warrior race. More recently, they have proven themselves powerful negotiators in their dealings with logging companies and politicians. All this despite the decimation of their population by smallpox and other epidemics brought by the first Europeans: estimated at around 8000 in 1835, their number had dropped to 588 by 1915. This tragedy forced the Haida to abandon almost all of their villages, especially on the southern island, and today many of these can be visited on tours, the houses and totems slowly returning to the earth. Only one, Sgan Gwaii (Ninstints) at the southern tip of Moresby Island, has been preserved and declared a UNESCO World Heritage Site.

the West's last great frontier roads. The section between Meziadin Junction and Iskut has some of the best scenery in BC, with the sharp peaks and vast glaciers of the Coast Mountains almost tapping on your windshield. Outside the tourist season, you're almost as likely to see a black bear as another car. There are few towns or services and on either side of the road nothing but wilderness for hundreds of kilometres. A full list of facilities is available from Visitor Information Centres in Prince Rupert, Terrace and Meziadin Junction. This windy, often narrow road is now mostly paved but some portions are gravel and others are pot-holed. It's advisable to carry two good spare tyres. Snow can occur at almost any time of the year; for up-to-date road conditions visit www.drivebc.ca. It is important for drivers to fill up with petrol when they get the chance, especially as prices rise quite steeply the further you go. If doing a circuit, it's better to drive this road from north to south.

Stewart, Hyder and the Bear Glacier → Colour map 3, B3.

Just north of the Yellowhead-Cassiar junction, the villages of **Gitwangak** (**Kitwanga**) and **Gitanyow** (**Kitwancool**) have some interesting old and new totem poles; and Meziadin Junction, 90 km further on, has a pleasant lake and campsite, good fishing and a small summer-only Visitor Information Centre. Only here, however, does the Cassiar start to show its worth, with some of the province's most awe-inspiring scenery opening up both north and on Highway 37A, which runs 65 km west to Stewart and its Alaskan twin, Hyder. You'd be mad to come this far and not at least detour 28 km west to the famous **Bear Glacier**, an eerie blue sheet of ice that comes right down to the road, glows in the dark and cracks and groans like a living thing.

The ramshackle, photogenic town of **Stewart** is another slice of Wild West life. At the **Stewart Historical Museum** ① *603 Columbia and 6th Av, T250-636 2568, mid-May to mid-Sep 1100-1900, $3*, you can learn all about the twists of fortune that

⁞ Mould rush

If driving the Cassiar Highway in September or October, look out for **The Zoo**, about 70 km from Kitwanga.

In season, this shanty town of makeshift tarpaulin huts houses hundreds of mushroom-pickers, along with shops, restaurants, buyers and even a bar. The whole unofficial industry that surrounds the harvesting of wild and valuable Pine Mushrooms (*masutake*) is the closest modern equivalent to the Gold Rush, with some people making a small fortune, others barely scraping together the bus fare home, and everyone hoping to stumble upon the mother lode.

The Zoo could be seen as the Dawson City of its day, as raw and authentic a slice of life as you could ever hope to encounter. Don't expect anyone to tell you where the mushrooms are though!

constitute the town's interesting history, including a spell as North America's largest gold mine town. Film-makers (*Insomnia*, *The Thing* and *Leaving Normal* are among those films shot here) agree that Stewart's most reliable natural resource is its incredible setting at the heart of an amphitheatre of mountains, whose steep rocky peaks rise almost vertically from the Portland Canal, one of the world's longest fjords.

There's not much to do, but the summer-only **Visitor Information Centre** ① *222 5th Av, T250-636 9224, www.stewart-hyder.com*, can recommend local hikes and provide pamphlets for the Heritage Walking Tour around town and the Salmon Glacier Auto Tour. The latter follows the Salmon River past several old gold mines in BC and Alaska to viewpoints above the massive **Salmon Glacier** and **Summit Lake**. In mid-summer, this entire lake drains under the glacier leaving behind a weird landscape of scattered icebergs.

On the other side of the fjord, **Hyder** draws a lot of tourists just by being such an easily accessible part of Alaska. A surprisingly popular ceremony has built up here. It's almost compulsory to get 'Hyderized', which entails downing a shot of incredibly hard liquor in one of the town's two almost permanently open bars. A much more legitimate draw is the viewing platform at **Fish Creek**, about 5 km away, possibly the best and most reliable place to safely enjoy the awesome spectacle of grizzly and black bears, and bald eagles fishing for the chum and pink salmon that return here to spawn (July-September). You'll see grizzly mothers showing their cubs the ropes and observe the different strategies these fascinating animals adopt according to their personalities.

● Sleeping

Clinton and around *p223*
There are a few Guest and Dude Ranches around Clinton, offering a genuine Wild West experience, guided horse riding and often gourmet food or spa/health packages. Follow links from www.hellobc.com, or visit www.bcguestranches.com, for a selection.
LL Big Bar Guest Ranch, 9 km north of Clinton, turn west on Big Bar Rd for 45 km, T250-459 2333, www.bigbarranch.com. One of the best and most affordable ranches, with highly rated riding, lodge

rooms, cabins, tepees and RV sites. Rooms start at $184 per person, including all meals but not riding.
LL Moondance Guest Ranch, Isadore Rd, 20 km off Hwy 97 9 km N of Clinton, T250-459 7775, www.moondanceguestranch. com. 3-day packages for $699 per person, including a room in the beautiful log lodge, all meals, guided horse riding, sauna, hot tub and games room.
C Spring Lake Ranch, 15 km N of 100 Mile House, then 16 km E on Spring Lake Rd, T250-791 5776, www.springlakeranch.com. A more affordable way to stay on a working

ranch, this hand-built log cabin is set by a lake in extensive grounds. There are suites, a chalet and 4 cabins, all with kitchen facilities, though very good meals are also available. There's horse riding ($25/hr), a games room, canoes and plenty of scope for activities in the area.
D Red Coach Inn, 170 Hwy 97 N, 100 Mile House, T250-395 2266. There are plenty of cheaper motels in this rather dull town, but it's worth paying a little extra to stay here, with its indoor pool and hot tub.

Camping
Clinton Pines, 1204 Cariboo Av, Clinton, T250-459 0030. Decent sites, hot showers and walking trails.
Green Lake Provincial Park, 16 Km NE of 70 Mile House along N Bonaparte Rd. The nicest spot for miles around. 3 pleasant campgrounds around the lake, with walking trails and good fishing.

Williams Lake and around *p223*
C Drummond Lodge and Motel, 1 km south at 1405 Hwy 97, T250-392 5334, www.drummondlodge.com. Decent rooms with decks in a lakeside setting.
C Neilsen's Lakeshore Cabins, 6071 Cedar Creek Rd, 5 km from Likely, T250-790 2258. Cabins on Quesnel Lake and RV sites.
D Rowat's Waterside B&B, 1397 Borland Rd, T250-392 7395. A pleasant house on the lake, with 5 rooms, guest lounge, decks and en suite bathrooms. Full breakfast included.
D-E Morehead Lake Resort, Likely Rd, 15 km from Likely, T250-790 2323. Basic cabins with kitchenettes and 8 camping sites. Rowing boat, canoe and kayak rentals.

Camping
Wildwood Campsite, 13 km north on the highway, T250-989 4711. Much nicer sites.
Williams Lake Stampede Campground, 850 S Mackenzie St, T250-398 6718. A handy choice for town.

Barkerville and Bowron Lakes *p223*
A Becker's Lodge , Bowron Lake Rd, T250-992 8864, www.beckerslodge.ca. This is the ideal place to relax at the start and end of the Bowron Lakes circuit. It has a range of attractive log chalets and cabins right on the lake, camping, a great restaurant, a

shop, a very broad range of kayaks and canoes for rent and organizes full tours and packages.
C St George Hotel, 4 Main St, in Barkerville Heritage Park, T250-994 0008, www.stgeorgehotel.bc.ca. 7 rooms in a restored 1890s house with antique decor, some with en suite. Gourmet breakfast and a balcony from which you can watch the action.
C-D King and Kelly House B&Bs, Hwy 26, Barkerville, T250-994 3328, www.kellyhouse.ca. Sister B&Bs with 6 fairly nice rooms, shared or private bath and antique furniture. Full breakfast included.
D Bowron Lake Lodge, Bowron Lakes, T250-992 2733, www.bowronlakelodge.com. The cabins here aren't nearly as nice as the **Becker's Lodge** , but they're also on the lake and have camping, rentals and a restaurant.
D The Wells Hotel, 2341 Pooley St, Wells, T250-994 3427, www.wellshotel.com. Set in a charming, picturesque little town 8 km west of Barkerville, this homely heritage inn has comfy rooms, a pub and restaurant. Breakfast is included.

Camping
Barkerville Provincial Park, 3 km east, T250-398 4414. 168 sites in 3 campgrounds, reservations recommended in summer. Showers and hiking trails.

Chilcotin Plateau *p224*
D Puntzi Lake Resort, T250-481 1176, www.puntzilake.com. 1 of 5 such resorts on the lake, with rustic lakeside cabins, canoe and boat rentals, and a campsite with hook-ups, showers and laundry facilities.

Tweedsmuir Provincial Park *p225*
A-B Tweedsmuir Lodge, Stuie, T250-982 2402, www.tweedsmuirparklodge.com. Situated in the park and focused on a fantastic lodge. The giant, stylish living room has hardwood floors and a stone fireplace. A variety of lovely log cabins and more basic chalets, some with kitchenettes, in forested surroundings. Buffet-style meals available for $70 per person per day. Also has a games room with billiards table, spa with outdoor hot tub, and camping.

Bella Coola *p225*

C **Bella Coola Motel**, 1224 Clayton St, T250-799 5323, www.bellacoolavalley. com. Handily situated in town by the river, it offers reasonable rooms with kitchens. Scooters, bikes and canoes for rent. Also has 50 camping sites.

C **Bella Coola Valley Inn**, Mackenzie St, T250-799 5316, www.bellacoolavalley inn.com. The most upmarket choice and handy for the ferry, with an atmospheric lobby and lounge, a restaurant, patio, a nice pub and some fairly attractive rooms.

C **Tallheo Cannery Inn**, 10 mins' from the wharf in a water taxi which is free for guests, T250-982 2344. The most interesting choice by far. 15 rooms with shared bath in a restored 1920 bunkhouse that was part of a cannery village. Meals and canoe or kayak tours are available and there's lots of hiking on and beyond the 68-ha grounds. Also has a stream with salmon and trout and a 1.5-ha private beach.

C-D **The Cumbrian Inn**, 619 Cliff St, T250-799 5731, www.cumbrianinn.com. A brand new, attractive wood building with tasteful rooms, garden patio and front deck.

D **Sinclair House**, 10 km east of Hagensborg, T1888-867 6668. 3 lovely rooms in a house surrounded by flowers and gardens. Private baths, library and jacuzzi. Breakfast included and dinners by arrangement.

Camping

Bailey Bridge Campsite, off Hwy 20, Sallompt Rd, Hagensborg, T250-982 2342, www.baileybridge.ca. The nicest camping option, located on the river, with showers and 6 basic cabins with kitchenettes (**E**).

Rip Rap Campsite, 1854 Hwy 20 in Hagensborg, T250-982 2752. Situated on the Bella Coola River by an observation deck, with views, decent sites and hot showers.

Wells Gray Provincial Park *p226*

B **Helmcken Falls Lodge**, 6664 Clearwater Valley Rd, by the park entrance, T250-674 3657, www.helmckenfalls.com. Decent rooms in a rustic old lodge, some camping and a restaurant. Run trail rides, guided hiking and canoe trips.

C **Clearwater Lodge**, 331 Eden Rd, Clearwater, T250-674 3080. The nicest of many hotels and motels in Clearwater. Large rooms, an indoor pool, hot tub, sauna, laundry and restaurant.

C **Wells Gray Guest Ranch**, 9 km before entrance, T250-674 2792, www.wellsgray ranch.com. A range of sleeping options on an authentic working ranch, mostly in log cabin rooms. Also has bunks (**F**) and camping. Meals are available and they lead horseback riding, canoeing, hiking and wildlife viewing trips.

D **Trophy Mountain Buffalo Ranch**, 4373 Clearwater Valley Rd, 20 km N of Clearwater, T250-674 3095, www.buffaloranch.ca. Working buffalo ranch with friendly owners and nice rooms in a rustic log house built in the 1920s. There's a restaurant, camping and they run horse riding trips.

Camping

North Thompson River Provincial Park, T250-674 2194, west of the park entrance. The nicest and closest of several provincial park and private campgrounds in the area.

Park Campgrounds, T250-851 3000. There are a few vehicle-accessible campgrounds in the park but they all fill up in summer, so it's a good idea to reserve in advance. A small fee is charged for wilderness camping.

Prince George *p227*

A **Coast Inn of the North**, 770 Brunswick St, T250-563 0121, www.coasthotels.com. The nicest hotel in town, with a pool, sauna, gym, lounge, pub and 3 restaurants.

D **Bedford Place B&B**, 135 Patricia Blvd, T250-562 3269, www.bedford.bcbnb.ca The nicest and most convenient of many 2-room B&Bs, in a handsome 1940s house.

D **Esther's Inn**, 1151 Commercial Cres, T250-562 4131, www.esthersinn.com. All rooms in this interesting hotel are arranged around a central plant-filled atrium, which also contains a swimming pool, 4 hot tubs, a steam room and water slides in the summer. There's also a restaurant and lounge.

E **College of New Caledonia Student Residences**, 3330 22nd Av, T250-561 5849, mid-May to mid-Sep only. Hostel-

● *For an explanation of sleeping and eating price codes used in this guide, see inside*
● *the front cover. Other relevant information is found in Essentials, see pages 28-31.*

style accommodation in small dorms or private rooms.

E Downtown Motel, 650 Dominion St, T250-563 9241, www.downtownmotel.ca. About the nicest of many conveniently central budget options.

E National Hotel, 1201 1st Av, T250-564 7010. A hostel-type joint but private rooms only, with shared bath and kitchen.

Camping
Blue Spruce RV Park, 5 km west on Hwy 16 from Hwy 97 junction at 4433 Kimball Rd, T250-964 7272. Pool, laundry, showers and a playground.

West to Smithers *p228*
A-B Hudson Bay Lodge, 3251 Hwy 16 E, Smithers, T250-847 4581, www.hudson baylodge.com. The nicest option, this attractive hotel has a broad range of rooms and suites as well as a restaurant, pub and café.

C Douglas Motel, Hwy 16 W, Telkwa, T250- 846 5679. Log cabins with fireplaces, kitchens and views of the Bulkley River rapids from the balconies and patios. Sauna and hot tub.

C Two Rivers Lodge, 1400 Hwy 16, Telkwa, T250-846 6000, www.tworiverslodge.ca. Suites and log cabins, some with kitchen, in an amazing location on the Bulkley River.

D Stork Nest Inn, 1485 Main St Smithers, T250-847 3831, www.storknestinn.com. There are plenty of fairly characterless motels in town. This one is clean, handy and good value, with breakfast included.

D-E Smithers Guesthouse & Hostel, 1766 Main St Smithers, T250-847 4862, www.smithershostel.com. 5 private rooms and a common room, kitchen, internet access, laundry, storage and a deck.

Camping
Tyhee Lake Provincial Park, Telkwa, T250-847 7320. 59 forested sites, trails and beach.

Hazeltons *p228*
E Robber's Roost Motel, 3476 Laurier St, New Hazelton, T250-842 6916, www.rob bersroost.ca. A standard motel, but newly renovated and very comfortable.

Camping
Ksan Campground, River Rd, T250-842 5940. A pretty site on the banks of the river, handy for visiting the main sites of interest. Showers and hook-ups.

Terrace and the Nisga'a Memorial Lava Bed Park *p229*
C Coast Inn of the West, 4620 Lakelse Av, T250-638 8141, www.coasthotels.com. The most comfortable option.

D Costa-Lessa Motel, 3867 Hwy 16 E, T250-638 1885. Best value of many budget motels that line Hwy 16 on both sides of town.

Camping
Ferry Island Campground, in Terrace, follow signs from Hwy 16, T250-635 4244, May-Sep only. Nice location with wooded sites, hiking trails, coin-operated showers.

Kleanza Creek, 15 km E on Hwy 16, T250- 638 8490, May-Sep only. A small campground beautifully located on a creek cascading through a canyon.

Nisga'a Park Visitor Centre, T250-638 9589, see page 229. There's a simple but attractive campground here and it's also the place to ask about B&Bs in local Nisga'a homes, such as in New Aiyansh.

Prince Rupert *p230, map p228*
B Crest Hotel, 222 1st Av W, T250-624 6771, www.cresthotel.bc.ca. The rooms here are nothing special, but the location is great and facilities include harbour views, hot tub, gym, sauna, sundeck, restaurant and lounge.

C Inn on the Harbour, 720 1st Av W, T250-624 9107, www.innontheharbour.com. Another great location, boasting recently renovated and unusually tasteful rooms. Ask for one with a harbour view.

D Andrée's B&B, 315 4th Av E, T250-624 3666, www.andreesbb.com. 3 very attractive rooms with hardwood floors and harbour views. Guests can enjoy the living room, library, garden and deck.

D Eagle's Bluff B&B, 201 Cow Bay Rd, in Cow Bay, T250-627 4955, www.citytel.net/ eaglebluff. 7 rooms with lots of character, mostly en suite, in a historic house located right on the harbour with great views.

D Java Lodge, 516 3rd Av, T250-622 2833, www.citytel.net/javalodge. 4 stylish and large rooms above an internet café in central

Downtown, with TVs, internet access, deck, laundry and shared bath. Great value.

D-E Ocean View Hotel, 950 W 1st Av, T250-624 6117, www.oceanviewhotel.ca. A pretty, newly renovated small hotel overlooking the water downtown. Cheaper rooms have shared bath. There's a restaurant downstairs.

E Black Rooster Roadhouse Lodge, 501 6th Av, T250-627 5337, www.blackrooster.ca. A colourful little building offering dorm beds and private rooms with en suite or shared bath. Also has a common room with TV and a kitchen, internet access and a great café.

E Pioneer Hostel, 167 3rd Av E, T250-624 2334, www.pioneerhostel.com. Well situated in an idiosyncratic clapboard house close to town and Cow Bay, this friendly little hostel has dorms and private rooms, shared baths and kitchen facilities, internet access, bikes, laundry and a backyard with BBQ.

E The Waterfront Inn, North Pacific Cannery, T250-628 3538, www.cannery.ca. A hostel in the atmospheric old bunkhouse.

Camping

Prince Rupert RV Campground, 1750 Park Av, T250-627 1000, www.princerupertrv.com. A big, ugly parking lot, but close to the ferry terminal.

Prudhomme Lake Provincial Park, 16 km east on Hwy 16, T250-798 2277. Has 24 wooded sites by the lake.

Graham Island p231

C Alaska View Lodge, No 12291, 11 km from Masset, Tow Hill Rd, T250-626 3333, www.langara.com. 4 rooms on the ocean in a gorgeous, very remote setting in Naikoon Park. Shared or private bath, hot tub, large sun deck and breakfast.

C Gracie's Place, 3113 3rd Av, Queen Charlotte City, T250-559 4262, www.graciesplace.ca. 5 units ranging from a 2-bedroom suite with kitchen and bathroom to a closet-like room. Antiques and patio. Airport pick-up.

D Dorothy & Mike's Guesthouse, 3127 2nd Av, QCC, T250-559 8439, www.qcislands.net/doromike. 4 beautiful suites with kitchens and living rooms, and a couple of cheaper rooms all in a gorgeous house. Use of living room, library, decks and patio with views of the water. Breakfast included.

D Riverside B&B, Richardson Rd, Tl'ell, T250-557 4418, www.qcislands.net/ margaret. 4 spacious rooms in an attractive wooden building, with balconies offering views of the river.

D Sea Raven Motel & Restaurant, 3301 3rd Av, QCC, T250-559 4423, www.searaven.com. Regular motel room with balcony. Good for breakfast.

D Spruce Point Lodge, west end of town, near the school, QCC, T250-559 8234, www.qcislands.net/ sprpoint. A striking wood lodge in a dramatic, very peaceful waterfront setting on a point. Decent but plain rooms.

D-E Premier Creek Hostel and Lodging, 3101 3rd Av, T250-559 8415, QCC, www.qcislands.net/premier. A very interesting, restored 1910 building fronted with long balconies and surrounded by gardens. Spacious rooms have large windows with great views of the harbour. There's also a separate hostel with common room and cooking facilities.

E Rapid Richie's Rustic Rentals, No 15900, 16 km from Masset, Tow Hill Rd, T250-626 5472, www.beachcabins.com. Sweet cedar-shake cabins on the beach, with lots of windows facing the sea and a very relaxed vibe. Definitely a place to kick back and unwind, very comfy. Wood stove, cooking facilities but no flush toilet (private outhouse). Useful website.

Camping

Agate Beach Campground, Tow Hill Rd, 26 km east of Massett in Naikoon Provincial Park, T250-626 5115. A fantastic location, right on the beach.

The Bunkhouse Campground Resort, 921 3rd Av, QCC, T250-559 8383, www.islandsretreat.com. A lovely forested location with tent sites and dorm beds, showers and a playground.

Misty Meadows Campground, 0.5 km north of Tl'ell in Naikoon Provincial Park, T250-626 5115. Close to the Park HQ, offering 64 km of beach to explore.

Gwaii Haanas National Park p234

AL Gwaii Haanas Guest House, Rose Harbour, T250-559 8638, www.gwaiihaanas.com. Expensive and remote, accessible only by floatplane or boat. Check the website and consider the package with a visit to Hot Spring Island. The setting is spectacular, if rustic, and the price includes 3 organic meals a day. They also arrange kayak and floatplane tours of the park.

E Moresby Island Guesthouse, 385 Alliford Bay Rd, 1 km from airport, T250-637 5300, www.moresbyisland-bnb.com. 10 rooms with shared bath, kitchen and 2 lounge areas. Laundry and bike rentals, basic breakfast included.

Stewart, Hyder and the Bear Glacier *p235*
D Grand View Inn, Hyder Av, Hyder, T250-636 9174, www.grandviewinn.net. The more modern of Hyder's hotels.
D King Edward Hotel/Motel, 405 5th Av, Stewart, T250-636 2244, www.kingedwardhotel.com. The motel rooms are slightly nicer and have kitchenettes. The hotel contains almost the only restaurant, pub and coffee shop in town.
D Ripley Creek Inn, 306 5th Av, Stewart T250-636 2344, www.ripleycreekinn.com. Reasonable rooms in a number of interesting historic houses, one of which was the home of legendary Klondike Kate. Sauna, common room, bikes and the best restaurant in town.
E Sea Alaska Inn, Hyder Dock Rd, Hyder, T250-636 9006, www.sealaskainn.com. Several types of room in a rustic building and a campsite (**Camp Run-a-muck**) and one of the town's 2 restaurants. The bar is the place to get yourself 'Hyderized'.

Camping
Rainey Creek Campground, 8th Av, Stewart, T250-636 2537. Nicely placed on a salmon stream at the edge of town and the starting point for a few local trails.

⊘ Eating

You're often left with slim pickings for food in the north. The official brochures and websites tend to ignore the question altogether and hope you won't notice. If nothing is listed here, it means there was nothing recommended. Try restaurants in the hotels (see Sleeping).

Williams Lake and around *p223*
Ψ Laughing Loon Neighbourhood Pub, 1730 Broadway Av S, T250-398 5666. The nicest place to eat, with a warm, friendly atmosphere and great views over the lake from the patio in summer.

Bella Coola *p225*
Most of Bella Coola's limited eating options are in hotels and B&Bs. **Tallheo Cannery Inn** is probably the pick of the bunch.
Ψ Cooks Cuisine Artisan Bakery, Cliff St/Burke Av. A pleasant spot for coffee, pastries and cakes.

Prince George *p227*
Ψ Cimo Mediterranean Grill, 601 Victoria St, T250-564 7975. Pasta, seafood and desserts are all made from scratch at this central, Mediterranean-inspired eatery. Great food and service.
Ψ Log House, 11075 Hedlund Rd, T250-963 9515. Fine, European-style cuisine in a very romantic location right on Tabor Lake. Lots of big windows to admire the view from.
Ψ North 54, 1493 3rd Av, T250-564 5400. A European-inspired fine dining menu that changes daily according to available ingredients and inspiration. Has a good wine list, attentive service and a warm atmosphere. The No 1 choice.
Ψ Amigo's Taco Shop, 229 Brunswick St, T250-562 8226. Great Mexican food made from fresh ingredients at very reasonable prices. Friendly atmosphere, great service.

West to Smithers *p228*
Ψ Mountainside Café, 3763 4th Av, T250-847 3455. Wholesome and tasty food in a friendly atmosphere.
Ψ Mountain Eagle Books and Cappuccino, 3775 3rd Av, T250-847 5245. The best bet for coffee.

Terrace and the Nisga'a Memorial Lava Bed Park *p229*
Ψ Don Diegos, 3212 Kalum St, T250-635 2307, open till 2100. The best place in town by a long way. An excellent, reasonably priced menu that's more international than Mexican. Colourful, very popular, quite romantic, with decent portions, sangria and a good wine list.

Prince Rupert *p230, map p228*

The Waterfront, in the Crest Hotel, 222 1st Av W, T250-624 6771. The obvious romantic fine-dining option, with hardwood floors, ocean views and live piano. A vast steak and seafood menu and good wine list.

Cow Bay Café, 205 Cow Bay Rd, T250-627 1212. Don't be fooled by the casual café-style appearance, this place serves creative seafood dishes with an international edge and Pacific Rim leanings. The menu changes twice a day, the food is that fresh, and there are fine harbour views and a good wine list. It's very popular, so be sure to book.

Opa Japanese Sushi Story, 34 Cow Bay Rd, T250-627 4560. Sushi and other Japanese dishes made from the freshest fish imaginable and served in a newly refurbished turn-of-the-century fish net loft with wooden beams and a little deck out back. Good for sake and spirits too.

Rain Dining Lounge, 727 2nd Av W, T250-627 8272. A very modern and trendy but welcoming spot for fresh seafood, including crab, mussels and oysters. There are also steaks, venison and pasta dishes on offer. Open late, it's also an obvious choice for a drink.

The Salmon House, at the North Pacific Cannery, T250-628 3273.

Smile's Seafood Cafe, 113 Cow Bay Rd, T250-624 3072. A 1930s diner-style joint with a good reputation for its seafood dishes and a deck overlooking the marina. Try the halibut cheeks.

Cowpuccino's, 25 Cow Bay Rd, T250-627 1395. Funky café with bohemian atmosphere, good coffee, soups, bagels and fabulous baked goods.

Galaxy Gardens, 844 3rd Av, T250-624 3122. Possibly the best of Prince Rupert's many Chinese restaurants. Incredibly tasty and very authentic Cantonese cuisine.

Green Apple, 301 McBride St, T250-627 1666. A local institution for cheap, tasty fish and chips.

Javadotcup, 516 3rd Av, T250-622 2822. Stylish, trendy and spacious café, with baked goods, speciality coffees and internet access.

Graham Island *p231*

Dave's in the Village, 112 Front St, Queen Charlotte City, T250-559 8782. A local's favourite from breakfast to dinner.

Dress For Les, Tl'ell, on the highway, T250-557 2023. A funky café with good coffee, second-hand clothes, local news and art.

Golden Spruce Motel, 2 Grouse St, Port Clements, T250-557 4325. A good place for breakfast.

Howler's Bistro and Pub, 2600 3rd Av, Queen Charlotte City, T250-559 8600. Great views of the ocean, good selection of beer on tap, pool tables and a menu of burgers, steaks and seafood.

Marj's Cafe, 1645 Main St, Masset, T250-626 9344. Big portions of honest comfort food and the best place to go to meet the locals. Try the French toast.

Myles from Nowhere Gallery, 76 Bayview Dr, Port Clements, T250-557 4773. Coffee shop with great books and crafts.

Queen B, 3211A Wharf St, Queen Charlotte City, T250-559 4463. The best coffee in town and light home-made dishes.

Stewart, Hyder and the Bear Glacier *p235*

Bitter Creek Café, Ripley Creek Inn, 311 5th Av, Stewart, T250-636 2166. By far the best place to eat, with a broad menu covering pizza, burgers, Mexican dishes, steaks, fish and some more unusual possibilities.

King Edward Hotel, Columbia St/5th Av, T250-636 2244, Stewart. This is where the locals usually go. Specializes in fish and chips and king crab.

Bars and clubs

Prince Rupert *p230, map p228*
Breaker's Pub, 117 George Hills Way, Cow Bay. A friendly, popular place, with huge windows and harbour views. Good food, especially the fish and chips.
Charley's Lounge, Crest Hotel (see Sleeping). A comfy spot for martinis, cocktails and a good range of draft beers.
Rain Dining Lounge, 727 2nd Av W, T250- 627 8272. See Eating.

Entertainment

Williams Lake and around *p223*
Paradise Theatres, 78 3rd Av S, T250-392 4722. Cinema.

Station House Gallery, 1 MacKenzie Av N, 250-392 6113, www.stationhousegallery. com. Housed in a 1919 Railway Station, one of the town's oldest buildings, the gallery exhibits a variety of contemporary works by local, regional and touring artists.
Williams Lake Studio Theatre, 4100 Mackenzie Av N, T250-392 4383, www.thea trebc.org. A good local theatre for serious productions.

Bella Coola *p225*
Barb's Pottery, across from the Eagle's Lodge on Hwy 20, T250-799 5380. Fine pieces displayed in a Norwegian log house.
Petroglyph Gallery, T250-799 5673, www.petroglyphgallery.ca. The town's best collection of Northwest Coast art, particularly Nuxalk Native, including masks, carvings and jewellery.
Silyas Gallery, at the Four Mile Reserve, T250-799 5564, www.silyasgallery.com. A collection of masks and carvings by talented local artist, Silyas Saunders.

Prince George *p227*
Two Rivers Gallery, 725 Civic Plaza, T250-614 7800, www.tworiversartgallery.com, May-Sep Mon-Sat 1000-1700, Sun 1200-1700, Oct-Apr Tue-Sat 1000-1700, Sun 1200-1700, $4, child $3. Has consistently impressive exhibitions.

Prince Rupert *p230, map p228*
Artists' Co-op Gallery, 190-215 Cow Bay Rd, T250-624 4546; **Harbour Theatre**, 341 Prince Rupert Blvd, T250-624 3626; **Lester Centre of the Arts**, 1100 McBride St, T250-627 8888, www.lestercentre.ca, an up-to-date, 700-seat venue, which hosts more than 120 varied performances a year, predominantly dance and musicals; **Prince Rupert Cinemas**, 525 2nd Av W, T250-624 6770.

Graham Island *p231*
There are many great artists on Haida Gwaii, ask at local Visitor Centres about which studios can be visited to see them at work. **Eagle's Nest Gallery**, Main St, Masset, T250-626 3233; **Myles from Nowhere Gallery**, Port Clements, T250-557 4773.
Crystal Cabin Gallery , 778a Richardson Rd, Tlell, T250-557 4383, www.crystalcabin

gallery.com. High quality Haida art, especially jewellery and carvings. Checkout the outdoor 'Tlell Stone Circle' show- casing local minerals and fossils.
Rainbows Gallery , 3201 3rd Av, Queen Charlotte City, T250-559 8420. Haida art, clothing and books.
Raven Gallery, 1530 Old Beach Rd, Masset, T250-626 3979. Masks, prints and argillite.
Sarah's Haida Arts and Jewellery, 387 Eagle Rd, Old Masset, T250-626 5560. Carvings, jewellery and more.

✸ Festivals and events

Williams Lake and around *p223*
Jul Williams Lake Stampede, T250-392 6585, www.williamslakestampede.com. Held the weekend closest to 1 Jul, this major event was first held in 1919 and is one of the biggest and oldest of its kind in BC, with over 13,000 spectators for events like steer wrestling and chuck wagon racing. Xats'ull Traditional Powwow, T250-989 2323, www.xatsull.com. Held over 3 days at the start of Jul at Whispering Willow Campground. Billy Barker Days Festival, T250-992 1234, www.quesnelbc.com/ billybarkerdays. Held in Le Bourdais Park, Quesnel, with parades, live entertainment, sporting events, a barn dance and a large amateur rodeo.

Bella Coola *p225*
Jun Bella Coola Valley Rodeo, T250-799 5410. Held over 3 days at the end of Jun.
Jul Discovery Coast Music Festival, T250-799 5618, www.bellacoolamusic.org. For 3 days in mid-Jul, all types of music represented on a small open-air stage.

Prince George *p227*
Jul Folkfest, www.pgfolkfest.com. 2 days of music in Fort George Park.

Prince Rupert *p230, map p228*
Feb The All Native Basketball Tournament, T250-627 8997, www.allnativetournament. ca. A massive event, attracting over 10,000 spectators who watch basketball all day every day for a week.
May BC Annual Dance Competition, www.bdadc.com. Attracts plenty of

competitors with big cash prizes in categories such as jazz, tap, modern, ballet and hip hop.

Jun Seafest, T250-624 9118, www.tourism princerupert.com/seafest. Involves 4 days of various small events.

O Shopping

Prince George *p227*
Centre City Surplus, 1222 4th Av, T250-564 2400. A very impressive range of outdoor equipment, clothing and camping supplies.
Native Art Gallery, 1600 3rd Av, T250-614 7726. Has a good collection of quality local and national native works for sale.

Prince Rupert *p230, map p228*
Cow Bay is the place to go for interesting boutiques and gift shops. For aboriginal art head to the museum. **Dolly's Fish Market**, 7 Cow Bay Rd, T250-624 6090, sells locally smoked salmon, fresh and frozen seafood, and has a small restaurant.

Arts and crafts
Blue Heron Gallery, 123 Cow Bay Rd, T250-624 5700. First Nations art as well as gifts and souvenirs.
Cook's Jewellers, 527 3rd Av W, T250-624 5231. A fine collection of Native hand-carved jewellery.
Harris & Wick Goldsmiths, 421 3rd Av W, T250-627 7000. Designer jewellery and local fine art.
Ice House Gallery, 215 Cow Bay Rd in Atlin Terminal on the harbour in Cow Bay, T250-624 4546. A co-op of North Coast Artists.
Studio 9 Gallery, 515 3rd Av W, T250-624 2366. Pottery, glassware, wood carvings and assorted native art.

▲▲ Activities and tours

Clinton and around *p223*
Horse riding is popular in the area; follow links from www.landwithoutlimits.com, to find out about guest and working ranches, or see Sleeping.
Stillwater Angling Adventures, 4 Eagle Creek, Canim-Hendrix Lake north, T250-397 4121, www.stillwateradventures.com. All-inclusive guided fly fishing packages, including hiking and horse riding packages.

XH Buffalo Ranch, 938 S Green Rd, 70 Mile House, T250-456 2319, www.xhbuffalo ranch.com. Buffalo viewing from atop a hay wagon on an 324-ha ranch.

Williams Lake and around *p223*
Big Canyon Rafting, 120 Lindsay St, Quesnel, T250-992 7238, www.bcraft. bc.ca. A variety of whitewater rafting trips from $120 for 4 hrs.
Cariboo Mountain Charters, Quesnel, T250-991 0847, www.cariboomountain. com. Fishing and hunting in the Cariboo Mountains, based in a log lodge.
Cariboo Wilderness Adventures, 150 Mile House, T250-296 4216, www.cariboowild ernessadventures.com. Canoe and kayak tours on Cariboo lakes ($85, ½-day), hiking or backpacking tours ($50, ½-day), fishing with 57 lakes and 9 streams to choose from, and wildlife viewing.
Chilko River Rafting Co, 1118 Lakeview Cres, T250-267 5258, www.chilkoriver.com. Day and multi-day rafting trips on the Chilcotin, Quesnel and Chilko Rivers.

Mountain biking
There are over 50 established mountain biking trails in the area of all levels and lengths. Pick up a copy of the excellent *Bike Trails* map for full details, or visit www.puddlebike.com.
Red Shreds Bike Store, 95 1st Av, Williams Lake, T250-398 7873, www.redshreds.com. A bike and board shop for gear, rentals and information.

Barkerville and Bowron Lakes *p223*
Canoeing
The 116-km Bowron Lakes canoe circuit consists of 10 lakes with 8 portages and takes 6-10 days. You can also tour the lakes on the park's west side, which takes 2-4 days. As the number of daily departures is limited, reservations must be made up to 4 days before the start date by calling T1800-435 5622 or T250-387 1642 (if outside North America). There is a reservation fee of $18 per canoe and a circuit fee of $60 per person is also payable at this time. Paddlers must report to the Registration Centre (2 km beyond the boat launch at the lake's north-east corner) at a specified time to undergo an obligatory orientation session.

Check www.env.gov.bc.ca/bcparks/explore/parkpgs/bowrn_lk/can_broch.pdf for more details, including the necessary equipment and regulations.

Beckers Lodge Resort, Bowron Lake Rd, T250-992 8864, www.beckerslodge.ca. The best place to get kitted out.

Chilcotin Plateau *p224*
Hyak Wilderness Adventures, T1800-663 7238, www.hyak.com. River rafting in the Chilko River's Lava Canyon.
White Saddle Air, T250-476 1182. Helicopter trips from Tatla Lake to Mt Waddington.

Tweedsmuir Provincial Park *p225*
Rainbow Mountain Outfitting, Anahim Lake, T250-742 3539, www.rainbowadventuresbc.com. Horseback pack trips and horse-supported hiking tours in the Rainbow Moutains.
Stuie Guide Services, 732 Corboould Rd, Hwy 20, Stuie, T250-982 2477. Drifting trips down the Atnarko and Bella Coola Rivers in motorless boats with a knowledgeable guide. Perfect for wildlife viewing.

Hiking
From the Rainbow Range trailhead, the Rainbow trail offers the shortest route to the alpine (7 km one-way), from where almost unlimited terrain can be explored. Octopus Lake Trail is an easy 14-km hike (one-way) to a campsite by the lake.

Crystal Lake Trail is a difficult 20-km hike with a 1000 m elevation gain, leading to the Mackenzie Valley close to the Rainbow Cabin. These latter 2 hikes can be extended to a cabin and campsite at Tanya Lakes, 25 km further on.

Bella Coola *p225*
Bella Coola Air, Hagensborg, T250-982 2545, www.bellacoolaair.com. Flight-seeing tours in small Cessna planes, from 30 mins.
Bella Coola Grizzly Tours, T250-982 0098, www.bcgrizzlytours.com. Offers a range of activities, including wildlife viewing, ocean and freshwater fishing, hikes, petroglyph trips, canoe and kayak adventures, river rafting, heli-hiking and salmon barbecues.
Chris and Lance Nelson, T250-799 5190, xawisus@mailcity.com. 2-3 hr tours to the

petroglyphs led by 2 Nuxalk brothers, with drumming, chanting and explanations of the carvings' cultural and spiritual significance.
Heritage River Rafting, Fishing Bailey Bridge, T250-982 2972, www.centralcoastbc.com/rafting. Gentle 3-8 hr floats down the river in a 4-passenger raft. A great way to enjoy the awesome scenery.
Kynoch West Coast Adventures, at Brockton Inn, 1900 Hwy 20, Hagensborg, T250-982 2298, www.brocktonplace.com. All kinds of trips are run or arranged by these guys, including wildlife and bear watching, snorkelling with the salmon in the Atnarko River, rafting trips with an ecological emphasis, ½- to multi-day interpretive hikes in the area or Tweedsmuir Park and 3-hr estuary tours in a Zodiak.
Northern Natural Tours, Hagensborg, T250-982 2326. Plant identification and wildlife-habitat viewing tours.
Rick's Re-Cycling, Hwy 20, T250-982 2722. Bike rentals, sales and repairs.
West Coast Helicopters, Hagensborg, T250-982 2183, www.westcoasthelicopters.com. Heli-hiking and glacier tours, heli-fishing, heli-skiing and sightseeing tours.

Hiking
The Clayton Falls logging road, heading southwest from the Marina, leads to the 2.7 km MGurr Lake Trail, a good place to view local fjords and the Coast Mountains. Further on, a trail leads to Blue Jay Lake, with a campground and a boardwalk trail around peat bogs and on to Gray Jay Lake. A further drive leads to the Big Cedar, which at 4.6 m across, is one of BC's biggest trees. From Hagensborg, Nusatsum Valley leads 25 km south to a trail and campsite at Odegaard Fallsand 34 km to the longer Hammer Lake/ Ape Lake Trail.
Bailey Bridge, Hagensborg, T250-982 2342, www.baileybridge.ca. Fishing and hiking trips.
Doug on the Trail, T250-982 2537. Personalized hiking trips with an experienced guide who can explain all about local flora, fauna, geology, weather and landscapes.

Wells Gray Provincial Park *p226*
Clearwater Visitor Information Centre, T250-674 2646, www.clearwaterbcchamber.com. Well informed and can hook you up

with operators for horse riding, floatplanes, guided canoeing, whitewater rafting and other activities.

Helmcken Falls Lodge, by the park entrance, T250-674 3657, www.helmcken falls.com. Also arranges most activities.

Prince George *p227*
McBike, 2095 5th Av, T250-563 2453, www.mcbike.bc.ca. Tours, sales, rentals and information.

West to Smithers *p228*
For skiing, see Hudson Bay Mountain, page 228.
Bear Mountaineering, Smithers, T250-847 3351, www.bearmountaineering.ca. Mountaineering, rock climbing, hikes and retreats in summer, backcountry skiing and ice climbing in winter. All based at their Burnie Glacier Chalet.
McBike & Sport, 1191 Main St, T250-847 5009, www.mcbike.bc.ca. Bike sales, repairs, tours and rentals. Their website has lots of useful information.
Suskwa Adventure Outfitters, T250-847 2885, www.suskwa.bc.ca. Rafting day trips on the Bulkley River, featuring over 30 rapids and canoeing or kayaking trips on the Stikine or Babine Rivers.

Hiking
There are 2 great options for hiking the Hudson Bay Mountain, a very steep 4-km route via Glacier Gulch with 927 m elevation gain or the much gentler 9-km hike via Crater Lake, much of it through meadows, with 1076 m gain.

Hazeltons *p228*
Skeena Eco-Expeditions, T250-842 5249, www.kispioxadventures.com. Guided hiking and cultural tours with Gitxsan guides, as well as canoe rentals, fishing trips and ½- or full-day rafting trips on the Skeena and Kispiox Rivers.

Prince Rupert *p230, map p228*
Most local activities are offered by the two biggest operators **Seashore Charters**, T250-624 5645, www.seashorecharters.com, see Laxspa'aws (Pike Island) tours; **West Coast Launch** T250-627 9166, www.westcoast launch.com, see bear watching, below.

Bear watching
Ecosummer Expeditions, T1800-465 8884, www.ecosummer.com. Ecologically friendly trips using flota-planes, sailing ships and kayaks to access these remote parks. 5-day grizzly trips to Khutzeymateen Grizzly Bear Sanctuary ($1650) and 8-day Kermode trips to Princess Royal Island ($3300).
Palmerville Lodge, T250-624 8243, www.palmerville.bc.ca. Flights to the bear sanctuary in a helicopter or sea-plane, starting at $425 per person for 3 hrs, including 1 hr of flying and 2 hrs watching the bears graze on freshwater sedge from a Zodiac. 3-day tours for $1590 per person. In 2007, 97% of tours saw bears.
West Coast Launch, T250-627 9166, www.westcoastlaunch.com. 6-hr tours to the bear sanctuary in a hard-shell boat ($160 per person). They also offer 4-hr humpback whale watching tours ($99) and 1½-hr Kaien Island tours that take in various sights such as Prince Edward, Seal Cove and Butzke Rapids ($55).

Fishing
A long list of charter companies is available from the Visitor Centre. All 5 species of salmon, as well as halibut and lingcod, are plentiful in local hot spots such as Chatham Sound and Work Channel. The season for salmon is May-Sep, peaking in Jul-Aug. Halibut is May-Sep. There's freshwater trout fishing in the rivers May-Oct and steelhead Mar-Apr. **Fish-on Charters**, T250-624 9506, www.prince rupertcharters.com; **Rave- On-Charters**, 655 4th Av E, T250-624 9842, fishing and sightseeing on a 48-ft yacht; **Something Fishy Charters**, T250-624 4499, www.some thingfishycharters.ca; **Trayling's Tackle Shop**, 635 2nd Av, T250-624 9874, for all supplies.

Flightseeing
North Pacific Seaplanes, T250-624 1341, www.northpacificseaplanes.com. A variety of set tours are available.

Hiking and biking
Mt Oldfield is a challenging 8.4-km return hike with good views, it's a continuation of the shorter Mt Oldfield Meadows boardwalk trail. Another 5-km hike leads through old-

growth forest to Butze Rapids, 6 km east of town. Maps and information are available at the Visitor Centre.
Farwest Sport and Cycle, 125 1st Av W, T250-624 2568. Rentals, sales, sports gear.

Kayaking
Butze Rapids are reversing tidal rapids excellent for whitewater kayak surfing, though the 4.5-6 m tides are for the experienced only.
Skeena Kayaking, T250-624 5246, www.skeenakayaking.ca. Rentals, lessons, Kutzmateen or Skeena River trips and longer tours. They also run a B&B.

Excursions from Prince Rupert *p230*
Seashore Charters, T250-624 5645, www.seashorecharters.com. The main operator for tours to Laxspa'aws (Pike Island), occupied by the Tsimshian people for up to 10,000 years. Led by native guides, this 3½-hr tour includes 1½ hrs of hiking through rainforest, visiting ancient village sites, spotting petroglyphs and ending at their traditional cedar longhouse. They also do whale watching, sightseeing tours, bear viewing, Tsimshian cultural kayak and traditional canoe trips, cultural evenings, fishing charters, and Kaien Island tours.

Graham Island *p231*
Cycling
Eagles Nest Gallery, Main St, Masset, T250-626 3233; **Premier Creek Lodging**, 3101 3rd Av, Queen Charlotte City, T250-559 8415.

Gwaii Haanas National Park *p234*
Kayaking
This the obvious activity, with plenty of islands to explore and a good chance of seeing whales (including orcas), sea lions and otters. Stay away from the west coast and remember that sea lions can be dangerous. It's also the best way to visit the abandoned Haida villages of Gwaii Haanas Park. Experience, or a guide, is necessary. Peter McGee's *Kayak Routes of the Pacific North West* is recommended by BC Parks.
Anvil Cove Charters, T250-559 8207, www.queencharlottekayaking.com. 6-day ($2200) to 10-day ($3000) kayak tours in small groups, using a 53-ft schooner as a mother ship. Gives you the chance to paddle

only as much as you want and reach spots difficult to access by kayak alone.
Butterfly Tours, T604-740 7018, www. butter flytours.bc.ca. A variety of trips, mostly 8 days ($2360-3360), suitable for novice and experienced kayakers alike, with the choice of just kayaking and camping, or using a mother ship or lodge as a base.
Ecosummer Expeditions, T1800-465 8884, www.ecosummer.com. 10-day kayak trips ($2300), with one of the companies who pioneered ethical, ecologically friendly touring of the park.
Moresby Explorers, Sandspit, T250-637 2215, www.moresbyexplorers.com. Scheduled and custom boat and kayak tours, rental and transportation of kayaks.

Tour operators
Blue Water Adventures, T250-980 3800, www.bluewateradventures.com. 8- to 9-day trips in a 64-ft yacht, with a crew of trained naturalists (from $3775).
Delkatla Bay Birding Tours, Masset, T250-626 5015, delkatla@island.net. Birdwatching.
Gwaii Eco tours, Queen Charlotte City, T1877-559 8333, www.gwaiiecotours.com. From 1- to several days, these ecologically friendly tours can be done by bike, canoe, kayak or on foot. All have a First Nations spiritual flavour.
Haida Soul Fishing Charters, Skidegate, T250-559 8397, www.qcislands.net/chinihar.
QCI Ocean Charters, Port Clements, T250-557 4541. Diving in Rennell Sound on the West Coast.

⊖ Transport

Cariboo *p223*
Taxi
Caribou Taxi, T250-991 0007.

Williams Lake and around *p223*
Air
Pacific Coastal Airlines, T250-982 2225, www.pacific-coastal.com, has regular scheduled flights to **Vancouver** ($138), **Victoria** ($211), **Powell River** ($217), **Bella Coola** ($355) and **Port Hardy** ($291). **Central Mountain Air**, www.flycma.com, also has regular flights to **Vancouver** ($148).

Greyhound station is at 215 Donald Rd, T250-398 7733, www.greyhound.ca. There are up to 3 daily buses from **Vancouver** to **Williams Lake** (8½ hrs, $87) via the Fraser Valley and **Cache Creek**, continuing to **Quesnel** (10½ hrs, $103)and **Prince George** (12½ hrs, $117).

Bella Coola *p225*
Air

The airport is 20 km east in Hagensborg. Pacific Coastal Airlines, T250-982 2225, www.pacific-coastal.com, has regular flights to **Vancouver** ($233), **Victoria**, **Powell River**, **Williams Lake** ($355) and **Port Hardy**.

Ferry

BC Ferries, T250-386 3779 or T1888-223 3779, www.bcferries.com, operates the Discovery Coast Passage between **Port Hardy** and **Bella Coola**, with some services also stopping at the tiny coastal communities of **McLoughlin Bay** (**Bella Bella**), **Namu**, **Shearwater**, **Klemtu** and **Ocean Falls**. Summer only, reservations are essential.

Prince George *p227*
Air

WestJet, T250-963 8123, www.westjet.ca, has 5 daily flights to **Calgary** ($245), 3 to **Vancouver** ($200) and 3 to **Kelowna** ($235). Air Canada , www.aircanada.ca, has several daily flights to **Vancouver** ($189).

Bus

For regional transit information, T250-563 0011. The Greyhound station is at 1566 12th Av, about 5 blocks from Downtown, T250-564 5454, www.greyhound.ca. To get there, take buses No 3 or No 4 from Victoria St. There are 3 daily buses to **Vancouver** (12½ hrs, $117), 5 to **Kamloops** (7½ hrs, $80), 2 to **Jasper** (5 hrs, $65) and 1 to **Prince Rupert** (10½ hrs, $108).

Taxi

Emerald Taxi, T250-563 3333.

Train

VIA Rail, T1800-561 8630, www.viarail.ca, runs 3 trains weekly to and from **Jasper** (7½ hrs, $53 if booked 7 days ahead) and

Prince Rupert (12½ hrs, $69 if booked 7 days ahead). The station is Downtown on 1st Av (Hwy 16), reached by buses No 1 and No 3.

Prince Rupert *p230, map p228*
Air

Air Canada, www.aircanada.ca, has 3 flights daily to **Vancouver** ($285). Hawk Air, T1800-487 1216, www.hawkair.ca, also flies to **Vancouver** ($207).

Bus

Local buses are operated by **Prince Rupert** Transit System, 225 2nd Av W, T250-624 3343. The Greyhound station is at 112 6th St, T250-624 5090, www.greyhound.ca, with 1 daily bus to **Prince George** (10½ hrs, $108).

Ferry

2 companies operate a water taxi service to places like the native village of **Metlakatla** across the harbour: **West Coast Launch**, T250-627 9166, www.westcoastlaunch.com, and **Metlakatla Ferry Service**, T250-628 3201. Local ferries go 3 times weekly to **Port Simpson**, T250-624 5411, and twice weekly to **Kincolith**, halfway up Portland Inlet, T250-624 6116 (6½ hrs).

BC Ferries, www.bcferries.ca, operates the Inside Passage to **Port Hardy** on Vancouver Island (see page 135 for details) and a daily service to **Haida Gwaii** ($33, child $18.50, vehicle $122, one-way) . Alaska Marine Highway, T1800-642 0066, www.dot. state.ak.us/amhs, have at least 4 weekly sailings most of the year to Skagway, **Alaska**, with daily sailings in peak season (US$372, vehicle $498). They stop in some or all of: **Keichikan**, **Wrangell**, **Petersburg**, **Sitka**, **Hyder**, **Stewart**, **Juneau**, **Haines** and **Hollis**.

Train

VIA Rail, T1800-561 8630, www.viarail.ca, runs 3 weekly trains to **Jasper** with an overnight stop in **Prince George**.

Haida Gwaii: Queen Charlotte Islands *p231, map p232*
Air

Air Canada , T1888-247 2262, www.air canada.ca, has 2 flights daily to **Vancouver** ($256). A **shuttle**, T1877-747 4461, meets flights and charges $14 to Queen Charlotte.

North Pacific Seaplanes, T1800-689 4234, www.northpacificseaplanes.com, runs a floatplane service to Masset from **Prince Rupert** and 3 times weekly to Sandspit and Queen Charlotte City. **Pacific Coastal Airlines**, www.pacific-coastal.com, flies to Masset daily during the summer, 3 times weekly in winter from Vancouver ($257).

Ferry

BC Ferries, T250-386 3431, www.bcferries .com runs between **Skidegate** (Graham Island) and **Alliford Bay** (Moresby Island), 12 times daily each way, $7 return, child $4, vehicle $16.

BC Ferries operates a service from Prince Rupert to Skidegate (usually 6½ hrs). Reservations recommended. Mid-May to mid-Sep, departs Prince Rupert Thu-Sun 1100, Mon 2100, Wed 1300; $26 per person, vehicle $98. Mid-Sep to mid-May, departs Prince Rupert Sun-Mon 2300, Thu 1430, $33, child $18.50, vehicle $122, one-way. Kayak or canoe $7, bike $6. Cabins available.

Bus

Eagle Transit, T250-559 4461, www.qc islands.net/eagle, operates 1 shuttle Mon-Fri between **Queen Charlotte City, Skidegate** and **Sandspit Airport,** and another between **Queen Charlotte City** and **Masset**. They also run a charter service and an airport shuttle.

Car

Other than the paved road from Queen Charlotte City to Masset, all driving is on logging roads, which require much care. Give way to logging trucks and ask at the Visitor Centre which roads are active. **Budget**, Sandspit, T250-637 5688; **Thrifty**, Sandspit, T250-637 2299; **Charlotte Island Tires**, 605 Hwy 33, Skidegate, T250-559 4641.

Taxi

Eagle Cabs, QCC, T250-559 4461; Pete's Taxi, Skidegate, T250-559 8622; Sandspit Taxi, Sandspit, T250-637 5655; Tiiyaan taxi Service, Old Masset, T250-626 3535.

SMC Water Taxi and Sea Bus, T250-559 8383; T&S Water Taxi, Skidegate, T250-637 2299.

Stewart, Hyder and the Bear Glacier *p235*

Seaport Limousine, 5th & Columbia, T250-636 2622, www.seaportnorthwest.com, runs a bus from Stewart to **Terrace**, Mon-Fri, $51, child $26, one-way. Leaves at 1210 (4 hrs).

---

❶ Directory

Williams Lake and around *p223*

Banks CIBC, 220 Oliver St, T250-392 2351. **Laundry** Cariboo Quality Cleaners, 397 Oliver St, T250-398 7768. **Library** 180 3rd Av N, T250-392 3351. **Medical services** Cariboo Memorial Hospital & Health Centre, 517 6th Av N T250-392 4411. **Post office** Canada Post, 48 2nd Av S, T250-392 7543.

Prince George *p227*

Banks Royal Bank, 50 Victoria, T250-562 9822. **Internet** Library, 409 George St. **Laundry** White Wash, 1-231 George St, T250-563 2300. **Library** 887 Dominion St, T250-563 1338. **Medical services** Prince George Regional Hospital, 2000 15th Av, T250-565 2000. **Post office** Canada Post, 1323 5th Av, T250-561 2568.

Prince Rupert *p230, map p228*

Bank Royal Bank, 301-500 2nd Av, T250-627 1684. **Internet** Library; Javadotcup, 516 3rd Av W, T250-622 2822. **Laundry** King Koin, 745 2nd Av W, T250-624 2667. **Library** 101 6th Av W, T250-627 1345. **Medical services** Prince Rupert Community Health, 300 3rd Av W T250-624 7475. **Post office** Canada Post, 365-500 2nd Av W, T250-624 2353.

Haida Gwaii: Queen Charlotte Islands *p231, map p232*

Banks Northern Savings Credit Union, 106 Causeway, QCC, T250-559 4407; 1663 Main St, Masset, T250-626 5231. **Internet** At libraries and Northwest Community Colleges in Queen Charlotte City and Masset. **Laundry** Masset Laundromat,

Masset, T250-626 3195. **Library** 138 Bay St, Queen Charlotte City, T250-559 4518; 35 Cedar Av W, Port Clements, T250-557 4402; 2123 Collison, Masset, T250-626 3663; Alliford Bay Rd, Sandspit, T250-637 2247. **Medical services** Masset Medical Clinic, 1760 Hodges, T250-626 4702; Port Clements Medical Clinic, 12 Park St, T250-557 4478; Queen Charlotte Islands General Hospital, 3209 3rd Av, Queen Charlotte City, T250-559 4300. **Post office** Canada Post, 117 3rd Av, Queen Charlotte City, T250-559 8349; 1633 Main St, Masset, T250-626 5155.

Canadian Rockies

⁑ Footprint features

Introduction

The Canadian Rockies are like the Egyptian Pyramids: it's hard to imagine why anyone would visit the country without seeing them. If you go feeling that the reality will never live up to the hype, you'll be proved wrong, as the Rockies deserve their reputation as Canada's premier attraction and one of the natural wonders of the world. You can make a trip here whatever you want: there are luxury resorts and the option of viewing heavenly scenery without straying from your vehicle, or remote campsites beside waterfalls and emerald lakes that can only be reached through days of trekking across the mountain wilderness. Hiking is the obvious activity in the parks and the best way to commune with the exceptional scenery and wildlife, but every other major outdoor activity is pursued here: canoeing, whitewater rafting, mountain biking, climbing, fishing, caving, skiing, skating, golf and soaking in hot springs.

Calgary is the most convenient entry point for visiting the parks. Most people concentrate on Banff, which contains the lion's share of scenery and hikes; Jasper is further away, less busy, much bigger and wilder; between the two is the astonishing Columbia Icefield; Yoho, a compact jewel, combines with Kootenay to make a nice loop back to Banff.

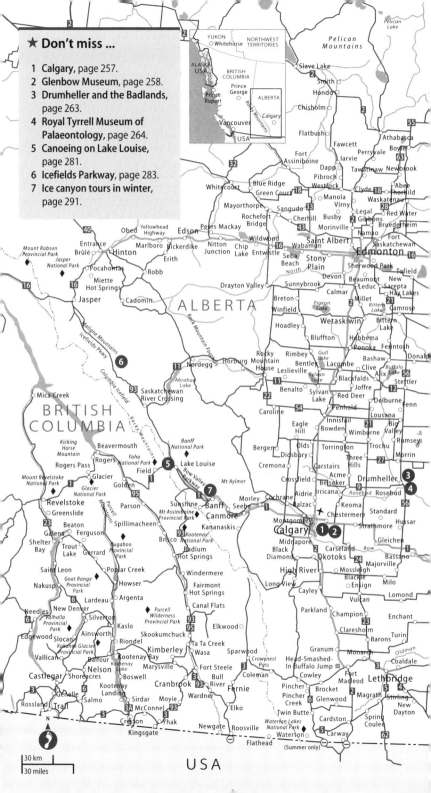

Ins and outs

Getting there and around

Calgary has the closest major airport to the Rockies, a mere 128 km east of Banff, receiving international and domestic flights. Several shuttle services run directly from Calgary Airport to Banff, Canmore and Lake Louise. **Greyhound** runs daily buses to Banff from Vancouver and Calgary and to Jasper from Prince George. **VIA Rail** operates three weekly trains to Jasper from Vancouver and Kamloops and three more from Prince Rupert and Prince George.

The best way to get around the Rockies is with your own vehicle or bike (starting at Jasper is easier for cyclists). Be aware that some people are prone to slam on their brakes in the middle of the road if they spot a sheep or deer so drive defensively. **Greyhound** buses connect Banff with Lake Louise, Field and Jasper.

▶▶ *For details of flights from Calgary Airport, see Essentials, page 25 and Transport, page 271.*

Visitor information

There are first-class **Visitor Centres/Park Offices** in Banff, Lake Louise Village, Field (Yoho) and Jasper. Staff here are excellent sources of information about hikes and all other park activities and usually keep a small library of key hiking guides. They hand out very useful maps with trail descriptions and backcountry guides, and issue compulsory wilderness passes for backcountry camping. They also organize guided hikes and other activities, and operate a voluntary safety registration programme for those engaging in potentially hazardous activities.

Friends of the Parks ① *www.friendsofbanff.com, www.friendsofjasper.com, www.friendsofyoho.ca, www.friendsrevglacier.com*, sell an assortment of guidebooks and maps. The *DEMR 1:50,000* topographic maps are expensive and tend to cover a limited area; the *Gem Trek* maps cover more terrain and so can be more useful. Most hikes are clearly marked, well maintained and much trodden, so finding your way is rarely an issue. **Parks Canada** ① *T1888-773 8888, www.pc.gc.ca*, produces two 1:200,000 maps—one for Banff, Yoho and Kootenay; one for Jasper – which are recommended as an overview.

Visitor centres keep track of local accommodation vacancies. If turning up without a reservation, their assistance can save a lot of time and hassle. They even have a courtesy phone. For a useful overview of all the parks, including maps that show the major trails, campgrounds and hostels, be sure to pick up the invaluable *Mountain Guide* from any Visitor Centre. Weather information is available at T403-762 2088 for Banff, Yoho and Kootenay national parks and T780-852 3185 for Jasper.

Best time to visit

Summer is best for most people, specifically July and August, when the days are warm and long and the trails most likely to be dry. Naturally, this is also when the trails and towns are at their busiest, which can be horrifying if you've come to get away from it all. Spring and autumn are much calmer and certain trails can be hiked as early as mid-May and as late as October. The majority, however, are snow-bound until July and in autumn the weather can be dangerously unpredictable. September is a favourite month for many people, as all the larches turn a glorious gold. Even at the height of summer, the Rockies receive a lot of rain, especially on the west of the divide. You could have clear blue skies every day for a week, or just as easily endure three weeks of solid downpours. At high altitude anything can happen any time and snow is never out of the question. The winter ski season generally runs from mid-December to the end of May, but conditions are best in March when days are warmer and longer and the powder is most plentiful.

Hiking in the Rockies

There are over 3400 km of trails in the Rockies from the very short to the absurdly long. As a rule we have only mentioned the best, chosen from personal experience with the help of two excellent trail guides. *The Canadian Rockies Trail Guide*, by Brian Patton and Bart Robinson is the standard choice, providing a great deal of useful information and a comprehensive overview. *Don't Waste Your Time in the Canadian Rockies*, by Kathy and Craig Copeland is less detailed but straightforward and really helps you choose from the daunting range of options. Brochures issued by parks offices are useful but devoid of opinion, though staff members are usually knowledgeable enthusiasts. They often have reference libraries for detailed research. The trail descriptions in this book are not intended to be sufficient to guide you through the hikes.

Top tips

It is important not to overstretch yourself, start with gentle hikes and build up from there. If you're not used to hiking, an 11-km day-hike can be very tiring. Even experienced backpackers tend to stick to about 16 km per day. The best clothing is several thin layers that can then be added or taken away at will. Synthetic fabrics are the best as they absorb moisture away from the skin, insulate when wet, and dry rapidly. Wool and fleece are also good. Avoid jeans and anything else made of cotton. Always take a waterproof jacket and trousers (preferably something that breathes, like Goretex) and a hat and gloves.

If backpacking, travel light and shed unnecessary items. Photocopy the pages of your guidebook or take notes, and keep everything in a plastic bag: most backpacks are not waterproof and rain is practically guaranteed. Good boots that fit well are essential for anything more than a stroll.

Take plenty of water, and only fill up from sources that are clearly safe, like glaciers or springs. All other water should be boiled, filtered or treated, since giardia lamblia (beaver fever) is widespread. Take more food than you think you'll need. Hunger adds to fatigue, clumsiness and risk of injury, and the risk of hypothermia should you get a soaking. During a six-hour hike, count on burning 1800-3000 calories. Food heavy with complex carbohydrates and relatively low in fat and protein is best. Take a few energy bars as a backup. Since campfires are usually prohibited, think about taking pre-cooked or raw foods instead of lugging a stove and pans. Pitta bread and tortillas, pre-cooked rice and pasta, granola, nuts, seeds, fruits and vegetables are all recommended.

A small first-aid kit should be taken, including anti-bacterial ointment, pain killers, bandages, sterile gauze and absorbent pads, adhesive tape, fold-up scissors, and maybe a compact manual. Always take matches in a plastic bag, and toilet paper! Consider taking a torch/flashlight, a compass, bug repellent, sunglasses, sunscreen and a hat with a brim.

Check the weather forecasts at a Visitor Centre (or T403-762 2088), but do not trust it. Always be ready for the worst.

Canadian Rockies Ins & outs

Park fees

Banff and Jasper have booths on the main access roads collecting park fees. **Day passes** ① *$8.80, senior $7.55, under 16 $4.40, under 6 free, family $17.60,* are valid for all the parks up to 1600 the following day. No fee is charged for through traffic. An **annual pass** ① *$61.80, senior $53, youth $31.40, family $122.60*, is valid for entry to 28 national parks in Western Canada. If staying for a week or more, it is well worth getting one of these, as they also entitle you to discounts at a number of sights and on certain tours. The annual **Discovery Package** ① *$76.50, senior 65.70, youth $38.20, family $154*, pass will get you into these 28 national parks and 77 national historic sites. You can buy passes at information centres and some campgrounds, or by credit card at T1800-748 7275. Day passes can be bought at 24-hour automatic pass machines.

Mandatory Wilderness Passes ① *$9.80 per person per night*, are for backcountry camping. An **annual pass** ① *$68.70*, is good for unlimited wilderness camping in all Western Canada national parks. If you buy one, you still have to register. You can trade seven day pass receipts for one of these. The fee for backcountry reservation (which is not mandatory, but necessary for Yoho) is $12. Front country campgrounds range from $35.30 with sewer and electrical, to $9.80 for overflow. A campsite day use permit is $7.80. A fire permit is $7.80 per day, including firewood. **Reservations** ① *T1877-737 3783, T1905-426 4648 (for outside North America), www.pccamping.ca*, can now be made. Fishing permits are $9.80 per day or $34.30 annually.

Flora and fauna in the Rockies

Flora From mid-July to mid-August, the Rockies' many meadows come alive with an exciting display of multicoloured wild flowers, including Indian paintbrush of all shades, alpine forget-me-nots, lousewort, western anemone, buttercups, daisies, alpine fleabane, false azalea, arnica, columbine, spring beauty, pearly everlasting and many more. Several types of orchid bloom about a month earlier. Red and white heather, mosses and multicoloured lichens are present throughout the temperate months. In autumn, larches and deciduous trees brighten the predominantly evergreen forests with their spectacular golden hues. Other vegetation includes a host of berry bushes, rhododendrons, red elder, cinquefoil and several species of saxifrage.

Fauna You are almost guaranteed a sighting of elk, deer and bighorn sheep, often on the roads or at campgrounds, causing a degree of excitement that after a while seems excessive. There's also a chance of seeing moose, black or grizzly bears, mountain goats and coyotes, as well as a host of smaller animals like otters, beavers, pikas and porcupines. Hoary marmots inhabit rocky slopes and make a distinctive whistling sound to warn each other of your presence. On rare occasions you'll catch a glimpse of a wolf, badger, wolverine, marten, cougar, caribou or lynx. Some first-class birdwatching spots attract of waterfowl and there's a good chance of seeing jays, ptarmigans, finches, chickadees, ospreys, various eagles and many other species.

There are only a couple of hundred grizzly bears left in the Rockies and the same number of black bears. As well as being much bigger, grizzlies have a dished face, a big, muscular shoulder hump and long, curved front claws. You are more likely to see one by the side of the road than in the bush, but to minimize the chances of a scary encounter, take a few simple precautions (see Wildlife, page 399). Any animal can be unpredictable and dangerous if scared, so keep a respectful distance. More people are attacked by elk than by bears. Female elk are most aggressive during the May to June calving season; males are especially dangerous during the September to October rutting season. According to a po-faced notice spotted at Lake Louise ski hill, the greatest number of injuries in Banff National Park result from people getting too close to squirrels.

Small creatures are indeed the ones most likely to prove a nuisance. At lower elevations, especially on dry overcast days, mosquitoes are sure to bug you. From early

❊ Suggested day hikes in the Rockies

Valley of the Ten Peaks/Sentinel Pass, Banff National Park, see page 283
Cirque Peak, Icefields Parkway, Banff National Park, see page 284
Wilcox Pass, Jasper National Park, see page 285
Apline Circuit, Yoho National Park, see page 310
Iceline, Yoho National Park, see page 310

to mid-June ticks are prevalent, especially on sunny, grassy slopes. Check vigilantly for them at the end of the day and ideally remove them using fine-pointed tweezers: grab hold of the mouth without squeezing the body and gently pull back until the tick lets go. Pull out any remaining parts like a splinter. Then there are black flies, deer and horse flies, and no-see-ums, so named because they're too small to see.

Calgary

One of North America's youngest and most modern cities, Calgary possesses a youthful brand of energy and optimism. The Downtown area is a grid of sleek glass, chrome and granite skyscrapers, the result of an oil boom that began in the 1970s. Despite a lingering redneck turned oil baron attitude, three decades of affluence have made the town increasingly cosmopolitan and sophisticated, resulting in a wealth of interesting restaurants, bars, clubs and art galleries. Still nick-named Cow-Town, however, Calgary is overtly proud of its cattle-ranching heritage and everyone from bank managers to ski guides dons their ten-gallon hats, leather boots and chaps to embrace their inner cowboy during the famous Stampede. Symbolically, two of the best Westerns of modern times, Brokeback Mountain and The Assassination of Jesse James, were shot here. The obvious starting point for those whose primary focus is the Rockies, Calgary merits a day of discovery. Most of what's worth seeing, including the excellent Glenbow Museum, is handily concentrated around the lively, pedestrianized Stephen Avenue Walk. With a day to spare, the fascinating Badlands and Dinosaur Museum of Drumheller, 148 km to the northeast, make a recommended day trip.
▸▸ For Sleeping, Eating and other listings, see pages 265-272.

Canadian Rockies Calgary Ins & outs

Ins and outs

Getting there
Calgary International Airport (YCC) ① *T403-735 1200, www.calgaryairport.com,* is 10 km northeast of Downtown. **Calgary Transit** bus No 57 runs to Whitehorn C-train station for connections into town. **Sun Dog Tours** ① *T403-291 9617, www.sundog tours.com, 0530-2130, $15, child $8, one-way,* operate a shuttle to Downtown hotels, leaving every hour on the half hour. Tickets can be bought from their counter at International Arrivals Area C. The **Greyhound** station is at 877 Greyhound Way SW. A free shuttle runs to the Seventh Avenue and Tenth Street C-train from Gate 4.
▸▸ *For further details, see Transport, page 271.*

Getting around
Greater Calgary is a vast ever-expanding metropolis that is difficult to negotiate, but the Downtown area is small enough to tackle on foot. The **Plus 15 Walking System** is

a 16 km maze of walkways connecting offices, shopping centres, restaurants and boutiques, designed to avoid the cold outside in winter. **Calgary Transit** ① *www.calgarytransit.com*, runs a cheap and efficient system of buses and the electric C-train. The grid of streets is divided into quadrants, with Centre Street dividing east from west and the river dividing south from north. In a three-digit street number, the first digit refers to the block, so 130 9th Av SE means that the building is No 30 on 9th Av in the block between Central and 1st streets southeast.

Driving in Calgary is difficult and parking is always a problem. Drivers should be aware that the **TransCanada Highway** runs north of Downtown as Sixteenth Avenue Northeast. Highway 2, the major north-south artery, splits the town in two. **Macleod Trail** is Highway 2 heading south, **Deerfoot Trail** is Highway 2 heading north. Signs often refer to the highway's name and not its number.

Best time to visit

With an average low of -15.7°C in January, Calgary is too cold to visit in the winter. The best month is July, which has the Stampede, a microbrewery festival, the folk festival and Shakespeare in the Park. September, which is also a great time to visit the nearby Rockies, has Art Week and the International Film Festival and enjoys a climate that is midway between the too-cold winter and too-hot summer.

Tourist information

Calgary's main **Visitor Centre** ① *101 9th Av SW, T403-263 8510, www.tourism calgary.com*, is at the base of the Calgary Tower. There is also a desk on the Arrivals level at the airport. Be sure to pick up their excellent *Destination Planning Guide* and also *Where Calgary*, www.where.ca/calgary, which is a useful bi-monthly magazine usually found at the Visitor Centres or high-end hotels. It's also worth checking www.downtowncalgary.com, and www.calgaryattractions.com.

Downtown Calgary ◉◉◉◉◉◉◉▲◉◉ ⇥ *pp265-272.*
Colour map 2, B4.

Calgary Tower

① *9th Av/Centre St, T403-266 7171, www.calgarytower.com. Mid-May to mid-Sep daily 0700-2300, mid-Sep to mid-May daily 0900-2130, $13, youth $10, under 5 $5.*
Since it contains the Visitor Centre, **Calgary Tower** is a good place to begin a tour of Calgary. This has been the city's most distinctive landmark since it was built in 1968, when its 190-m height was unchallenged by the surrounding structures. Even today, great views of the city, with the Rockies as a backdrop, can be enjoyed from the Observation Terrace where the glass walls are complemented by glass floors and give the novel sensation of being suspended in space. Next door is one of Calgary's oldest, most impressive buildings, the **Fairmont Palliser Hotel**, whose opulent interior, featuring marble columns and floors, handmade rugs and public art, is worth a quick look.

Glenbow Museum

① *130 9th Av SE, T403-268 4100, www.glenbow.org, daily 0900-1700, Thu 0900-2100, $14, youth $9.*
Spread over three floors, the large and varied collection of the Glenbow Museum represents Calgary's most compelling attraction. Besides **Many Faces, Many Paths: Art of Asia**, an impressive collection of Asian religious sculptures, the second floor is mostly devoted to two or three temporary exhibitions. These vary considerably, but are always fascinating and educational. Their theme is taken up in the **Discovery Room**, where children are encouraged to explore the subjects through

⠿ The Calgary Stampede

In early July, the whole city goes cowboy crazy for 10 days during the Calgary Stampede. Locals don ten-gallon hats, leather boots and Wrangler jeans, and start affecting a John Wayne drawl. Shop windows are covered with cowboy cartoons, free breakfasts are offered throughout Downtown every morning, and the streets are choked with parties and drunken revellers. It's even said that marital infidelity sky- rockets as a permissive, Vegas-style what happens at the Stampede stays at the Stampede attitude prevails.

Festivities begin with the Stampede Parade along Sixth and Ninth Avenues. Thereafter, the action takes place at the Stampede Grounds, on Macleod Trail Southeast and Forteenth Avenue. The major events are the Rodeo and the Chuckwagon races, involving nine days of heats building up to a final on the tenth day. Participants come from all over the world to compete for the $1.75 million of prize money. There is plenty of other entertainment put on during the stampede, including some big-name musical acts at three major venues (eg Bon Jovi and The Tragically Hip in 2008). Visitors are welcomed wholeheartedly.

Admission to the Stampede Grounds is $12. Basic tickets to the Rodeo range from $23-115 per day; and Chuckwagon races are $34-89, from the box office, T403-269 9822. For general information, T403-269 9022, www.calgarystampede.com. To get there, take the C-train to Victoria Park or Erlton Stampede stations; bus No 10 or 433.

interaction and reveal their artistic side. The third floor presents an intense introduction to native Canadian culture. **Niitsitapiisinni: Our Way of Life** uses interactive displays, artefacts and a circular narrative path to explore the history and culture of the Blackfoot. **We Are Still Here: First Peoples of the Four Directions** features artworks by various First Nations of the northwest. There are some fine examples of carving, beadwork, textiles and even music, such as the eerie throat music of the Inuit. The new exhibition **Mavericks: An Incorrigible History of Alberta** recounts the history of Southern Alberta through the stories of 48 spirited and adventurous individuals, using interactive technology to present this instructive material in a fresh, dynamic way. On the fourth floor is a section on minerals; a gallery exploring the cultures of West Africa; and a display that traces the history of warfare across different cultures. The ground floor contains a gift shop and a café.

Around Stephen Avenue Walk

After the museum, the obvious thing to do is wander down the pedestrianized section of Eighth Avenue between Macleod Trail and Barclay Mall. Known as **Stephen Avenue Walk** this is the most intact turn-of-the-century downtown street in Western Canada, with many of Calgary's finest and oldest buildings rubbing shoulders with the brand new. Those hungry for more culture could check out the nearby **Art Gallery of Calgary** ① *117 8th Av, T403-770 1350, www.artgallerycalgary.org, Tue-Sat 1000-1700, $5, youth $2.50, lunch-hour programmes Tue-Fri 1200-1300, $2*, which hosts 15 to 20 exhibitions each year, showcasing the works of 35 to 40 Calgary and Canadian artists. Across the road is **Art Central** ① *100 7th Av SW/Centre St, T403-543 9600, www.artcentral.ca, daily 0700-1900, free*, which contains 57 individual spaces dedicated to artist studios, galleries, cafés, arty boutiques and a restaurant. Also nearby are the **EPCOR Centre for the Performing Arts** and the **Cathedral Church of the Redeemer** ① *9th Av and 1st St SE*, one of Calgary's most attractive buildings.

Calgary

While Stephen Avenue Walk's ground level is lined with pubs, restaurants, street vendors, buskers and some funky shops, just above (connected by the Plus 15 walking system) is a world of cinemas, offices and nine department stores, such as the massive **Toronto Dominion Square** between Second and Third streets. This block is now dominated by a set of odd 20-25 m white steel sculptures called *The Trees*. Each 'tree' holds a large light that projects dozens of colour combinations at timed intervals, providing a weird atmosphere. Equally strange, spanning three floors of TD Square are some real full-sized trees, as well as 20,000 varieties of plants, fountains, waterfalls, ponds, bridges, pathways and art exhibitions. Known as the **Devonian Gardens** ① *317 7th Av, T403-268 2489, Sat-Wed 0930-1800, Thu-Fri 0930-2000, free*, this is a perfect place to escape the Calgary weather. Those craving yet more art are about four blocks from **Artists of the World** ① *514 11th Av SW, T403-244 8123, www.artevo.com, Mon-Fri 1000-1800, Sat 1000-1700, Sun 1200-1700, free*. This huge, restored historic building contains an eclectic collection of pieces, beautifully presented, as well as private lounge areas, interactive screens for finding out more about artists, theatre rooms and even a dance floor. The venue also hosts events such as live music, art demonstrations and wine tasting.

Seventeenth Avenue and Fourth Street

Seventeenth Avenue Southwest ① *just south of Downtown between 2nd and 10th Streets* and **Fourth Street** are hands-down Calgary's most interesting night-time areas, with lots of good restaurants and pubs and the highest concentration of clubs. While here, check out the nearby **St Mary's Cathedral** ① *1st St and 18th Av*, one of the latest Gothic-revival churches in Western Canada, with an incredibly striking symmetrical brick tower which is best appreciated at night. **Mission District** ① *4th St, southwest from 12th Av going south*, was originally settled by French Canadian priests and now has some classy restaurants and art galleries.

Wildwood Grill &
  Brewing Co 23 *F3*

Bars & clubs ()
Auburn Saloon **28** *C4*
Barley Mill **29** *A4*
Cherry Lounge **30** *D4*
Detour **31** *E3*
Don Quijote **32** *B4*
Ming **33** *E3*
Molly Malone's **34** *B1*
Muse Restaurant &
  Lounge **35** *A1*

Palace **36** *C4*
Ship & Anchor **37** *E3*
Tantra Nightclub
  & Lounge **38** *D3*
Tequila Nightclub **39** *E4*
Vicious Circle **40** *D4*
Warehouse **41** *D2*

Canadian Rockies Calgary Downtown Calgary

Along the Bow River 🍽️🎭🎵 ⟫ pp265-272.

Apart from the sights concentrated in the Downtown core, most places of interest are to the north, scattered along the banks of the Bow River. It makes most sense to wander down the pedestrianized **Barclay Mall** ① *3rd St SW,* to Eau Claire Market, then venture east or west to whatever appeals.

Eau Claire Market and Prince's Island Park
Pleasantly situated on the Bow River between 2nd and 3rd streets **Eau Claire Market** brings together fruit and vegetable stalls, a food hall of fast-food joints, a few cinemas and some tacky craft shops. Though this doesn't compare with Vancouver's Granville Market, it is worth a wander. Outside is an open area surrounded by pubs, which offers a welcome respite from Downtown Calgary's teeming streets, as well as acting as a meeting place and venue for cultural events. Across a pedestrian bridge is **Prince's Island Park**, a nice place for a stroll, with a wonderful café.

Kensington
Situated on the north bank, reached via a footbridge from Prince's Island Park or more directly from the **Louise Bridge** ① *4th Av SW,* the colourful and culturally stimulating neighbourhood of Kensington is as close as Calgary gets to a bohemian, alternative scene, with lots of pubs, tasteful restaurants and interesting shops. Those who dislike cities but are obliged to spend a day in Calgary should head straight here.

Telus World of Science
① *701 11th St SW, T403-268 8300, www.calgaryscience.ca. Mon-Thu 0945-1600, Fri 0945-1700, Sat-Sun 1000-1700, $13.50, child $9.50. Discovery Dome show $3. C-train to 10th St station.*
Predictably enough, this place is aimed predominantly at kids. Through hands-on mini experiments and intriguing snippets of information, they're taught about the human brain, the five senses, engineering, design, farming, ecology, the universe and much more. The **Discovery Dome** shows 40-minute IMAX-style films. The so-called Amazement Park is, however, half-hearted and the whole affair falls short of many similar venues elsewhere. In recognition of this fact, a new, bigger and better Science Centre is planned for about 2010.

In the same building is the **Creative Kids Museum** ① *www.creativekids museum.com, Mon-Thu 0945-1600, Fri-Sun 1000-1700, $15, child $12.* Kids are given the chance to let rip, dramatize, make art and music and get messy. There's a playground made to resemble the caves, rocks and hoodoos of Alberta's landscapes, surrounded by murals, and there's another fun exhibit based on sensory illusions. The **Shaw Millennium Park** next door is a giant purpose-built skateboard park which also has some volleyball courts.

Chinatown
A few blocks east of the market, Calgary's Chinatown is small but clean and packed with cheap bakeries and restaurants offering dim sum. The **Chinese Cultural Centre and Museum** ① *197 1st St SW, T403-262 5071, www.culturalcentre.ca, daily 1100-1700, $2, child $1 for museum, dome interior daily 0900-2100, bus No 31,* is its main attraction, featuring a magnificent dome copied from the c1420 Temple of Heaven in Beijing. Its interior features 561 individually crafted gold dragons and 40 phoenixes. There are temporary art galleries on the second and third floors (free entry) and a very worthwhile museum downstairs with a number of fascinating exhibits, such as a big picture of tigers made entirely of feathers, a 'transparent' bronze mirror and a bronze bowl which spurts water when it's rubbed.

Fort Calgary and Inglewood

Fort Calgary ① *750 9th Av SE, T403-290 1875, www.fortcalgary.com, daily 0900-1700, $10.75, under 18 $9.75, under 12 $6.75, under 3 free, bus No 1, 75 or 41 from Downtown*, is a reconstruction of the 1875 North West Mounted Police fort built to control the trouble caused by rogue whisky traders. It's staffed by costumed guides, whose stories about Calgary's roots supplement the exhibits. Just to the east, on Ninth Avenue Southeast between Tenth and Twelfth streets, is Inglewood which is Calgary's oldest district. This is where some of the city's grandest houses and cottages can be found, as well as a concentration of antiques shops. Still further east is **Inglewood Bird Sanctuary** ① *2425 9th Av SE, T403-221 4500, May-Sep daily 1000-1700, Oct-Apr Tue-Sun 1000-1600, paths open year-round till dusk, by donation, bus No 411 from Downtown, No 1 back*, with 32 ha of paths, 250 bird species, 300 plant species and an interpretive centre.

Calgary Zoo

① *1300 Zoo Rd NE, via Memorial Dr, T403-232 9300, www.calgaryzoo.com. Daily 0900-1700, $16, under 18 $10, under 12 $8, under 3 free. Train tours for children, $2.25. Take the C-train.*

Across from the fort, situated on St George's Island between two branches of the Bow River, are the **Botanical Gardens**, **Prehistoric Park** and **Calgary Zoo**. With over 1000 animals from all over the world, including the usual favourites, this is a good place to spend the day, with lots of facts about the animals dotted around to make it an educational experience. The Prehistoric Park, entered via a suspension bridge across the river, has plastic life-sized dinosaurs in rather unconvincing settings. The botanical gardens are 2 ha of colour. The conservatory, containing tropical, arid and butterfly gardens, is well worth a visit. There's also a great playground and tours on a little train for children under 12.

Drumheller and the Badlands ●❼▲● ⇥ *pp265-272.*
Colour map 2, B5.

Apart from the Rockies, the most worthwhile destination in Alberta is centred on the small, unexceptional town of Drumheller, an easy day excursion from Calgary. The Badlands scenery here is truly exceptional, easily enjoyed thanks to a circular driving route that connects some great vantage points and takes in one of the world's finest palaeontology museums.

On the way to Drumheller, you'll pass **Horseshoe Canyon**, one of the most dramatic viewpoints for admiring the Badlands. Just before you reach town, **Reptile World** ① *95 3rd Av E, T403-823 8623, www.reptileworld.net, May to Aug 0900-2200, Sep-Oct, Mar-Apr 1000-1700, Nov-Feb 1200-1700 Thu-Mon, $7, under 18 $5, under 5 free*, cashes in on the dominant theme, with a collection of 200 reptiles and amphibians, including cobras, anacondas, snakes and toads that can be handled, and Fred the 600-lb alligator. **Drumheller** itself remains hidden in the canyon until the last moment, which is no bad thing as it's a fairly drab place. The nicest part of town is on its north side just over the bridge. As well as a wading pool, which offers some relief from the intense summer heat and the **World's Biggest Dinosaur** ① *26 m high, $3 to climb up and stand in its mouth*, this is where you'll find the **Visitor Information Centre** ① *60 1st Av West, T403-823 8100, www.travel drumheller.com, mid-Sep to mid-May daily 0900-2100, Sep-Jun 1000-1730*. If here in July, ask about the celebrated **Passion Play** ① *17th St SW/Dinosaur Trail, T403-823 2001, www.canadianpassionplay.com*, staged for six days in a dramatic natural amphitheatre.

The Great Canadian Dinosaur Rush

Geological evidence suggests that 75 million years ago, at the time of the dinosaurs, this area was a lush coastal plain, supporting a wealth of plant and animal life. At the end of the last ice age, melting glaciers scraped away the upper layers of rock, gouging out a crazy jumble of odd sculptures and steep coulées (deep, narrow ravines).

As the erosion continues, fossils are revealed in the Cretaceous layers beneath. So it is that JB Tyrrell, looking for the coal deposits, stumbled across the skull of an Albertasaurus, thus sparking off the 'Great Canadian Dinosaur Rush'. More than 20 species of dinosaur, including many complete skeletons, have since been unearthed in one of the most fruitful beds of dinosaur remains in the world. Though these have found their way to museums around the globe, a large number are housed in the excellent Royal Tyrrell Museum just outside Drumheller.

Royal Tyrrell Museum of Palaeontology

ⓘ *6 km northwest of Drumheller on Hwy 838 (North Dinosaur Trail), T403-823 7707, www.tyrrellmuseum.com. Mid-May to mid-Sep daily 0900-2100, Sep daily 1000-1700, Oct-May Tue-Sun 1000-1700, $10, under 18 $6, under 6 free. There are 2 trails, a 1-hr and a 2½-hr loop, that lead from the museum through the Badlands in Midland Provincial Park. It's difficult to reach the museum without your own transport, so it makes good sense and is good value to go with a tour company.*

Half a million visitors a year flock to the Royal Tyrrell Museum to see the world's largest collection of complete dinosaur skeletons, almost 40 in all, including the ever-popular Tyrannosaurus rex. With this many people you can expect it to be very crowded in summer, so think about arriving early or late. State-of-the-art technology is used to talk visitors through the Earth's history, from the primordial soup to the present. Displays explain matters such as evolution, plate tectonics and geology, how fossils are created and how they are found and prepared. One engrossing exhibit deals with the findings at **Burgess Shale** in Yoho National Park, using a stunning display set in a dark tunnel to represent an ocean bed from 500 million years ago, with the bizarre prehistoric creatures blown up to 12 times their original size and floating around in a surreal, illuminated landscape. In the Cretaceous Alberta gallery, you can wander through a recreated 70 million year-old riverbed amidst a pack of Albertosaurus. The new Lords of the Land gallery showcases some of the Museum's rarest, most fragile and scientifically significant pieces.

The whole experience builds you up to the almost overwhelming climax of the **Dinosaur Hall,** where a mind-blowing collection of skeletons is exhibited in front of artistic backdrops evoking the deltas, swamps and lush vegetation that would have constituted this valley's scenery 75 million years ago. The story is completed with a series of displays that deal with the extinction of the dinosaurs, the dawn of the Age of Mammals and the occurrence of ice ages. As well as a museum, this is one of the world's premier palaeontological research facilities and runs many educational programmes. In the summer, you can assist the experts (for a fee) on one of their Day Digs.

Dinosaur Trail and Hoodoo Trail

A perfect complement to the museum is the well-signed 48-km road circuit known as the **Dinosaur Trail,** an excellent way to see the stunning Badlands. Highway 838 is the North Dinosaur Trail, Highway 837 the South Trail. They join at the Bleriot Ferry. Which way you drive the loop depends on whether you want to visit the museum at the beginning or end, it's the first stop if you follow Highway 838. The next key attraction is **Horsethief Canyon**, which has superb views. Thereafter the road drops down to cross the river, with a lovely campground on the south bank. Views from this side have a different quality, so be sure to stop at the **Orkney Hill Viewpoint** on the way back to town.

The less essential **Hoodoo Trail** runs 25 km southeast along Highway 10 to a minor collection of hoodoos, mushroom-shaped sandstone pillars that would have appealed to Dr Seuss. On the way, you pass yellow canola fields dotted with nodding donkeys, a suspension bridge and the **Atlas Coal Mine** ① *T403-822 2220, Jul-Aug daily 0930-2030, May-Jun daily 0930-1730, Sep daily 1000-1700, $6*, one of many remnants of the once-booming local mining industry. You can take a guided tour of Canada's last-standing wooden tipple mine, eight stories high amongst the giant machinery and miles of conveyor belts. A detour to the ghost town of **Wayne** is a pretty drive, with 11 bridges along the way, and highly recommended in September when the Wayne Music Festival takes place.

Cowboy Trail

① *For more information pick up a brochure, call T1866-627 3051 or visit www.thecow boytrail.com.*

Southern Alberta's tourist board has put together a number of self-guided tours for visitors. The most tempting is the **Cowboy Trail**, most of which follows Highway 22, which can be picked up just west of Calgary. It runs south from Rocky Mountain House National Historic Site, some 385 km north, to Cardston near Waterton Lakes (see page 317), via a number of ranches and heritage sites, including Longview's Bar U Ranch, Head-Smashed-In-Buffalo-Jump (see page 320) and the Kootenai Brown Heritage Village in Pincher Creek.

⊜ Sleeping

Downtown Calgary *p258, map p260*
There are disappointingly few mid-range options in Downtown Calgary. The major routes into town are lined with cheap chain motels, especially Banff Trail NW, which is known as Motel Village. Note that rates go up by at least 50% during the stampede (see Festivals), when reservations are essential.
B 5 Calgary Downtown Suites, 618 5th Av, T403-451 5551, www.5calgary.com. A pretty good deal considering the handy downtown location. A range of reasonable suites with outdoor swimming pool, hot tub, fitness room and internet access.
B Sandman, 888 7th Av SW, Downtown, T403-237 8626, www.sandmanhotels.com. The best centrally located mid-range hotel, offering comfortable rooms, an indoor pool, hot tub and fitness room.
D Calgary City View, 2300 6th St SE, T403-870 5640, www.calgarycityview.com. 2 fairly faded but good value rooms and a studio near the Stampede Grounds. Great views.

D-E Regis Plaza, 124 7th Av SE, T403-262 4641, www.regisplazahotel.com. About the cheapest option downtown, offering a variety of plain but reasonable rooms, some with shared bath.
E Auberge Chez Nous Hostel, 149 5th Av SE, T403-232 5475, www.auberge-cheznous. com. Very central, featuring bright and clean French-style decor. Dorm rooms each have 5-6 beds (not bunks) separated by lockers to afford some privacy. Communal living room and kitchenette.
E Calgary International Hostel, 520 7th Av SE, T403-283 6503, www.hihostels.ca. Conveniently close to Downtown, with newly decorated dorms and private rooms. Great facilities, including common room, a fully-equipped kitchen, lockers, laundry facilities and free internet.

Seventeenth Avenue and Fourth Street *p261*
B-C The Foxwood B&B, 1725 12th St SW, T403-244 6693, www.thefoxwood.com.

A beautiful Edwardian house furnished with antiques, close to the lively 17th Av district. 2 plush rooms and a suite with private bath and its own balcony. A living room, cosy den, hot tub, big veranda at the front and garden with a deck at the back.

Along the Bow River p262
B-C Inglewood B&B, 1006 8th Av SE, Inglewood, T403-262 6570, www.inglewoodbed andbreakfast.com. 3 pleasant rooms in a Victorian-style house near the river.
C A Good Knight B&B, 1728 7th Av NW, T403-270 7628, www.agoodknight.com. 2 attractive themed rooms with private bath and an apartment in an attractive Victorian-style house close to Kensington.
C River Wynde Executive B&B, 220 10A St NW, Kensington, T403-270 8448, www.riv erwynde.com. Lovely heritage home, with 4 unique themed rooms, with features such as hardwood floors, private balconies and wood-burning fireplace. There's also a sunny patio, a garden, library and use of bikes.

Drumheller and the Badlands p263
B Best Western Jurassic Inn, 1103 Hwy 9 S, T403-823 7700, www.bestwestern.com. The most reliable hotel in town, with an indoor pool, hot tub and exercise room.
C McDougall Lane B&B, 71 McDougall Lane, T403-823 5379, www.bbalberta.com/ mc dougall. A large house with 2 plush rooms and 1 suite, a very nice living room, hot tub and a fabulous sunken flower garden featuring fountains, ponds and decks. Full breakfast included.
C Taste the Past, 281 2nd St, T403-823 5889. A nicely restored turn-of-the-century home, with 3 reasonable rooms. Antique decor, a billiards table and a garden veranda. Full breakfast included.
C-D Newcastle Country Inn, 1130 Newcastle Trail, T403-823 8356, www.virtuallydrum heller.com/nci. 11 pleasant rooms in a rather plain house. Continental breakfast.
D Badlands Motel, Hwy 838, on way to museum, T403-823 5155. About the cheapest of the standard motels in town.

Camping
Bleriot Ferry Provincial Rec Area, 23 km west on the south side of the ferry crossing, on the Dinosaur Trail, T403-823 1749.

A pleasant little site right on the river, good for swimming. Great views of the landscape.
Dinosaur Trail RV Resort, 11 km west on Hwy 838 (Dinosaur Trail North), T403-823 9333. A nice spot with a swimming pool and canoe rentals. Reservations necessary in summer.
Little Fish Lake Provincial Park, T403-823 1749, 25 km east of the Hoodoos off Hwy 10 on Hwy 573. A great campground down a dirt road, with a lake setting.
River Grove Campground and Cabins, 25 Poplar St, off Hwy on north side of bridge, T403-823 6655. The best of a few campsites around town, with semi-private pitches on the river. The also have 7 rustic log cabins and some tepees (D).

🍴 Eating

Downtown Calgary p258, map p260
🍴 The Belvedere, 107 8th Av SW, T403-265 9595, Mon-Sat. One of Calgary's longest-running and most respected restaurants, this New York-style dining room has a romantic atmosphere and an international menu.
🍴 Buchanan's, 738 3rd Av, T403-261 4646. Dominated by a huge, well-stocked bar, this old-fashioned San Francisco-style chop house is renowned for its steaks and burgers. Also has a broad range of wines by the glass and 146 malt whiskies.
🍴 Catch Oyster Bar and Seafood, 100 8th Av SE, T403-206 0000. With its hardwood floors, chandeliers and classic furnishings, this long, elegant room is a beautiful place to enjoy international dishes prepared with French flair. There's also a handsome dark wood oyster bar, serving San Francisco-style seafood and draught beer.
🍴 Divino Wine and Cheese Bistro, 113 8th Av SW, T403-410 5555. With its red-brick walls, wood floor and open kitchen, this is a gorgeous, intimate little space. Broad menu of international, California-style cuisine, including gourmet applewood-fired pizzas and plenty of wines and cheeses.
🍴 River Café, Prince's Island Park, T403-261 7670. The best location in town, with views of the river and the Downtown skyline. A wonderful interior reminiscent of an upmarket mountain fishing lodge, with an open fireplace. The menu is broad and very sophisticated, with plenty of fish and a West

Coast-style emphasis on freshness and locality of ingredients.

Teatro, 200 8th Av, T403-290 1012. Set in an elegant vintage bank building with sumptuous decor. With attentive service and a lively but romantic ambience, this long-standing favourite serves up Italian-style cuisine with international influences. Uses only the freshest ingredients.

Bistro Piq Niq, 811 1st St SW, T403-263 1650. Gourmet food in an intimate setting genuinely reminiscent of a French bistro. Downstairs is a small venue for live jazz, Thu-Sat.

Catch Oyster Bar, 100 8th Av SE, T403-206 0000. Attached to a very beautiful but expensive restaurant, this stylish but casual San Francisco-style seafood joint is great for atmosphere and food.

MT Tuckers, 345 10th Av SW, T403-262 5541. Popular with big eaters, this rustic, Western-style eatery specializes in prime rib but is most renowned for its buffet lunches, Sunday brunch and 60-item salad bar.

Silver Dragon, 106 3rd Av SE, T403-264 5326. The place to go for the full dim sum experience or for very authentic Cantonese dishes. A locals' favourite for 40 years. Try the pan-fried prawns.

Thai Sa-On, 351 10th Av SW, T403-264 3526. Rated the best Thai food in town for 15 years.

Galaxie Diner, 1413 11th St SW, T403-228 0001. Great breakfasts in an old-style diner, complete with booths and bar stools.

Good Earth Café, Eau Claire Market; 119 8th Av SW; 602 1st St SW; and 333 5th Av SW. Casual atmosphere, speciality coffees, baked goods and vegetarian snacks.

Jing Jang Bakery, downstairs at 100 3rd Av SE, T250-205 4330. Delicious Chinese buns, like the BBQ pork, curried beef or honey.

Seventeenth Avenue and Fourth Street *p261*

Cilantro, 338 17th Av, T403-229 1177. A long-standing favourite, serving California-fusion eclectic cuisine in a setting dominated by dark wood and wrought iron. Has an open kitchen and an inviting outdoor patio.

La Chaumière, 139 17th Av SW, T403-228 5690. French-style haute cuisine with an emphasis on game and seafood, served in almost excessively opulent surroundings.

Brava Bistro, 723 17th Av SW, T403-228 1854. A warm, intimate, stylish setting for French/Canadian cuisine focussing on organic and vegetarian dishes. Excellent wine list and a nice patio.

The Living Room, 514 17th Av, T403-228 9830. The decor here is modern, sophisticated, minimalist and sleek. The food puts a contemporary twist on French and Italian cuisine, with fondues, shared meals and encouraged wine pairings. There's also an outdoor patio.

The Metropolitan Grill, 880 16th Av SW, T403-802 2393; TD Sq, 317 8th Av SW, T403- 263 5432. Open from breakfast to dinner, serving New World cuisine such as wild mushroom veal scallopini, and steak and lamb. Equally effective as a lounge with a good wine list, or as a club with live jazz and blues on a Thu, and DJs and dancing on Fri and Sat nights.

Wildwood Grill and Brewing Co, 2417 4th St SW, T403-228 0100. Downstairs is a pub that brews its own great beers, upstairs is a stylish restaurant with an eclectic West Coast fusion menu that concentrates on local ingredients including buffalo, caribou and rabbit. Good wine list.

Caffe Beano, 1613 9th St, T403-229 1232. A quaint, cosy café that's favoured by artists and intellectuals.

Eiffel Tower Bakery, 1013 17th Av SW. French-style breads, pastries and quiches.

Kensington *p262*

The Verve Restaurant and Martini Bar, 102 10th St NW, T403-2832009; 237 8th Av SE, T403-264 9494. Sleek, trendy and dimly lit. The menu features a broad variety of appetizers, some pasta dishes and sea- food, and a lot of Alberta beef. Equally recommended just for a drink. Live music of a jazzy nature on Fri and Sat nights.

Marathon, 130 10th St NW, T403-283 6796. Delicious Ethiopian curries. Popular and intimate. Lunch buffet.

Sultan's Tent, 4 14th St NW, T403-244 2333. Delicious authentic Moroccan dishes such as tajines and couscous. Decor made to resemble a Berber tent, with floor seating.

Heartland Café, 940 2nd Av NW, T403-270 4541. Pleasant local hang-out with a wholefood attitude.

¶ **The Roasterie Too**, 227 10th St NW, T403-283 8131. Fresh roasted coffee, in a comfy spot with outdoor seating.

Drumheller and the Badlands *p263*
Eating choices in Drumheller are mostly family-dining joints catering to tour buses.
¶ **Bernie and the Boys Bistro**, 305 4th St W, T403-823 3318. A classic diner serving superior burgers, shakes and ostrich egg omelettes.
¶ **Molly Brown's**, 233 Centre St, T403-823 7481. Cosy café serving home-made lunches and good desserts.
¶ **Sizzling House**, 160 Centre St, T403-823 8098. Excellent, cheap Szechuan and Thai food without the MSG or the sugar. Great value and a good veggie selection.
¶ **Whif's Flapjack House**, 801 North Dinosaur Trail, in the **Badlands Motel**, T403- 823 7595. Mostly breakfast but also serves lunch specials.

⚡ Bars and clubs

Downtown Calgary *p258, map p260*
Auburn Saloon, 115 9th Av SE, T403-266 6628. An arty Downtown spot with a theatrical, loungey vibe and martinis and cocktails on cosy couches.
Barley Mill, 201 Barclay Parade, T403-290 1500 The most tempting choice of the many pubs around the courtyard outside **Eau Claire Market**, whose inviting summer patios offer a reprieve from the Downtown traffic. A range of beers on tap.
The Cherry Lounge, 1219 1st St SW, T403-266 2540. A chilled and trendy club with a minimalist interior and a cosy martini lounge upstairs. There are different DJs every night, playing anything from underground funk to hip hop to electronica.
Detour, 318 17th Av, T403-244 8537. A throbbing club in a historic dairy building, popular with Calgary's gay scene but a great night for all-comers .
Don Quijote, 309 2nd Av SW, T403-205 4144. A Spanish restaurant and tapas bar that turns into a Latin dance club with dancing till 2am Fri and Sat.

The Palace, 219 8th Av SW, T403-263 9980. This big, plush, high-class club has a serious sound and laser system, 2 main dance floors, interesting, eclectic decor and an intimate atmosphere. Music is hip hop, R'n'B and house.
Tantra Nightclub and Lounge, 355 10th Av SW, T403-000 0000. As the name suggests, this is a trendy, sexy lounge/club. The ultra-sleek modern decor is interspersed with Asian sculptures.
Vicious Circle, 1011 1st St SW, T403-269 3951. A cosy café/lounge with couches, candlelight, good art, varied music, an appealing menu of small dishes and 140 different martinis. Attracts a mixed but sophisticated crowd.
The Warehouse, 733 10th Av SW, entrance down a back alley, T403-264 0535. A long-lasting yet progressive rave-culture favourite, attracting a mixed, down to earth crowd who are there to chill and dance to trance, jungle and house. Open till 0600 at weekends.

Seventeenth Avenue and Fourth Street *p261*
Ming, 520 17th Av SW, T403-229 1986. A very enticing, trendy martini lounge with dim lighting and an atmosphere of casual sophistication without a hint of pretence. Good food.
Ship and Anchor, 534 17th Av SW. Very popular with the locals and arguably the best pub in town. Outside seating that's perfect for people watching and an unbeatable selection of draught beers, including the whole range by excellent local brewers Big Rock.
Tequila Nightclub, 219 17th Av, T403-209 2215. With cheap drinks and DJs on Tue, Fri and Sat, this is a place to dance and party.

Kensington *p262*
There are far too many British-style pubs here, all with very slight variations, so just walk (or crawl) around. You can't knock their vast selections of quality draught beers. Happy hour is 1600-1900.
Molly Malone's, 1153 Kensington Cres, T403-296 3220. A little Irish-style pub with seating on the roof and live music.

● *For an explanation of sleeping and eating price codes used in this guide, see inside*
● *the front cover. Other relevant information is found in Essentials, see pages 28-31.*

Muse Restaurant and Lounge, 107 10A St NW, T403-670 6873. An expensive restaurant upstairs, serving West Coast-style dishes and a casual, chic lounge downstairs.

☻ Entertainment

Downtown Calgary *p258, map p260*
Check the listings in Calgary's free listings magazine, *FFWD*, www.ffwdweekly.com, free from cafés and elsewhere.

Art galleries
Calgary has many galleries besides the **Art Gallery of Calgary**, **Art Central** and **Artists of the World**, which are all described in the text.
Artspace Gallery, 1235 26th Av SE, www.artspace.ca. Galleries, gift shops, a café and a lounge. 10,670 sq m of exhibition space.
The New Gallery, 516 9th Av SW, T403-233 2399, www.thenewgallery.org. An artist-run, non-profit gallery exhibiting local, national and international contemporary artists.
TRUCK Contemporary Art, 815 1st St SW, T403-261 7702,www.truck.ca. Contemporary art with focus on hybrid and emerging work.

Cinema
Globe, 617 8th Av SW, T403-262 3308; **Plaza**, 1133 Kensington Rd NW, T403-283 2222; and **Uptown**, 612 8th Av SW, T403-265 0120, show mainly first-run indie, foreign and art-house films. **IMAX**, at 200 Barclay Parade SW, T403-974 4629, shows new releases.

Live music
Beat Niq Jazz and Social Club, downstairs from **Bistro Piq Niq** , 811 1st St SW, T403-263 1650. Live music Thu-Sat 2130, generally small, vocal-led acts, with a cover charge.
Bookers BBQ Grill, 316 3rd St SE, T403-264 6419. This is a great place to eat, with a rustic warehouse interior and cajun dishes like jambalaya or catfish po'boy. There's live blues and jazz on Fri and Sat nights.
Broken City Social Club, 613 11th Av SW, T403-262 9976, www.brokencity.ca. A great little gritty venue for local bands, with live music most nights, decent pub-style food, cheap drinks and a rooftop patio.
EPCOR Centre for the Performing Arts, 205 8th Av SE, T403-294 7455. Calgary's

most important performance venue, it includes a 1800-seat concert hall that is renowned for its beauty and fine acoustics, and which hosts all genres of music from classical to rock, as well as live theatre and dance. There are also 4 theatres, some galleries, workshops and a café.
Jubilee Auditorium, 1415 14th Av, T403-297 8000, www.jubileeauditorium .com. Home of the Calgary Opera and a major venue for all kinds of touring acts.
Ranchman's, 9615 Macleod Trail S, T403-253 1100. An authentic cowboy saloon with live country bands Mon-Sat and a big dance floor for all that two-stepping.
Rose and Crown Pub, 1503 4th St SW, T403-244 7757. A lively pub that's a great venue for live music on Fri and Sat nights.

Spectator sports
Baseball The Calgary Cannons play at **Burns Stadium**, across Crowchild Trail from the NW Banff Trail C-train.
Canadian football McMahon **Stadium**, across from the NW Banff Trail C-train, T403-289 0258. Where the Calgary Stampeders, www.stampeders.com, play.
Horse racing Takes place at **Stampede Park**, 17th Av/2nd St SE, T403-261 0214.
Ice hockey Pengrowth **Saddledome**, 555 Saddledome Rise SE, T403-777 2177. Where Calgary Flames, www.flames.nhl. com, play.
Show-jumping Takes place at **Spruce Meadows**, 3 km west of Macleod Trail on Hwy 22X, T403-974 4200.

Theatre
EPCOR Centre for the Performing Arts, see above, is home to Theatre Calgary and other major companies.
Pumphouse Theatre, T403-263 0079, www.pumphousetheatre.ca. Numerous small theatre groups produce plays throughout the year.
Theatre Junction at The Grand, 608 1st St SW, T403-205 2922, www.theatre junction.com. Recently renovated, **The Grand** is Western Canada's oldest theatre, now hosting small contemporary plays, as well as music and dance.
Vertigo Theatre, 115 9th Av SE, T403-221 3708. Mystery plays.

⊛ **Festivals and events**

Downtown Calgary *p258, map p260*
Calgary is famous far and wide for its sensational **Stampede** (see page 259), but there are plenty of other events scattered throughout the year.
Feb Calgary Winterfest, T403-543 5480, www.calgarywinterfest.com. A 10-day celebration of the cold.
Mar $100 Film Festival, www.csif.org. A 3-day festival that showcases work from local, national and international filmmakers working with Super 8 and 16 mm film.
May FunnyFest Comedy Festival, www.funnyfest.com. 11 days and nights of live comedy performances. **International Children's Festival**, T403-294 7414, www.calgarychildfest.org. Takes place at the EPCOR Centre.
Jul Calgary Stampede in early Jul. **Micro-brewery Stampede**, at Telus Convention Centre, T403-254 9204. During the Calgary Stampede, this 3-day festival adds to the revelry with samples of countless brews from across North America. **Calgary Folk Music Festival**, T403-233 0904, www.calgary folkfest.com. Held later in the month at Prince's Island Park, lasts for 4 days.
Jul-Aug Shakespeare in the Park, T403-440 6374, www.mtroyal.ab.ca/shakespeare-in-the-park. Free performances of the Bard's plays at Mt. Royal College in Jul, then on Prince's Island Park in Aug.
Aug Calgary Bluesfest, www.calgaryblues fest.com. A 4-day open-air blues bonanza. Calgary Fringe Festival, T403-265 3378, www.calgaryfringe.ca. 10 days of small shows at various venues. A couple of good music events also take place in nearby towns: **Big Valley Country Music Jamboree** in Camrose, T403-672 0224 www.bigvalley jamboree.com, and the **Shady Grove Blue-grass Music Festival** in High River, T403-652 5550, www.melmusic.com/sgrove.
Sep International Film Festival, www.cal garyfilm.com. 9 days in late Sep.

⦿ Shopping

Downtown Calgary *p258, map p260*
Antiques
There are several antiques shops in Ingle-wood, 9th Av SE between 11th and 13th St.

Arts and Crafts
Fosbrooke Fine Arts, 2nd floor, Penny Lane, 513 8th Av, T403-294 1362. Display a rotating selection showcasing 15-20 artists.
Galleria, 1141 Kensington Rd, NW, T403-270 3612. Handmade works in a variety of media from over 500 Canadian artists and potters.
Masters Gallery, 2115 4th St, T403-245 2064. More classic, high brow pieces.

Books and music
HMV, TD Sq, 8th Av SW, T403-233 0121; **McNally Robinson**, 120 8th Av SW, T403-538 1797, set in an attractive historic building, with 3 floors of books, including a good range of Prairie authors; **Pages Books on Kensington**, 1135 Kensington Rd, T403-283 6655.

Clothes and accessories
Alberta Boot, 614 10th Av SW, T403-263 4623. One of the best things to buy in town is an authentic, handmade pair of cowboy boots.
Boutik, in Hotel Arts, 119 12th Av SW. Trendy fashions and accessories from several cutting-edge designers.
Eye on Design, 1219 9th Av, T403-266 4750. A funky little store in Inglewood, carrying unique items by smaller designers, including lots of jewellery.
Lammle's Western Wear, 11 shops including 209 8th Av SW, T403-266 5226. The place for all your cowboy needs.
The Pendulum, 1222 9th Av SE, T403-266 6369. Carries a selection of brand name consignment clothing.
Riley and McCormack, 220 8th Av SW, airport, or Eau Claire market. Another fine purveyor of all things cowboy, as well as native crafts, gifts and souvenirs.
Shisomiso, 100 7th Av SW, T403-266 4211. Showcasing the clothes of 2 local designer-owners and that of other local designers.

Sporting and outdoor equipment
Coast Mountain Sports, 817 10th Av SW, T403-264 2444. A wide selection of high-end sports and mountain clothing and footwear.
Mountain Equipment Co-op, 830 10th Av SW, T403-269 2420. A massive store with all the sport and camping equipment you could need.

Patagonia, 135 8th Av, T403-266 6463. Outdoor clothing and accessories.
Ski West, 300 14th St NW, Kensington, T403-270 3800. Skis, snowboards and accessories from many leading brands.

▲▲ Activities and tours

Downtown Calgary *p258, map p260*
Golf
Calgary has many fine courses and 2 of the most handy are **RCGA Golf Centre**, 7100 15th St SE, T403-640 3555, www.rcgagolf centre.org; **McKenzie Meadows**, 17215 McKenzie Meadows Dr SE, T403-253 7473, www.mckenziemeadows.com.

Tour operators
Big Rock Brewery, 5555 76th Av SE, T403-720 3239, www.bigrockbeer.com. Calgary's formidable brewery offers tours and tastings, Tue-Thu 1330.
Chinook River Sports, T403-263 7238, www.chinookraft.com. Whitewater rafting on the Kicking Horse and Kananaskis rivers, through the Horseshoe Canyon and a ½-day float down the Bow River in Calgary ($45, child $30).
Creative Journeys, T403-272 5653, www.creativejourneys.com. A variety of 1-day tours, including 2-3 hr walking tours of Calgary ($30), 3-4 hr bus tours of town ($40) and longer trips to Banff ($80), Jasper ($100), Waterton ($100) and the Prairies and Badlands. Also offer day trips to Drumheller ($70), Footlands and Ranchlands, including Head-Smashed-In-Buffalo-Jump ($70).
Hammerhead Scenic Tours, T403-590 6930, www.hammerheadtours.com. 1-day tours to the Badlands, Banff, Waterton and Head-Smashed-In-Buffalo-Jump. Tours tend to be a bit more expensive than **Creative Journeys**, but also a couple of hours longer.
Home On The Range, T403-229 9090, www.homeontherange.ca. Cowboy tours geared to individual needs, including authentic western experiences like cattle drives, ranch stays, historic sites, powwows, rodeos and horseback tours of the Rockies.
Inside Out Experience Inc, T403-949 3305, www.insideoutexperience.com. A broad range of adventure tours, including white-water rafting, hiking, mountain biking, snowshoeing and cross-country skiing.

Legendary Tours, T403-285 8376, www.legendarytravels.net. 1-day tours to Banff, Drumheller, Blackfoot Crossing, Head-Smashed-In-Buffalo-Jump and a mixed Western Adventures trip (all $99).
University of Calgary Outdoor Centre, T403-220 5038, www.calgaryoutdoorcentre. ca. Whether you want instruction, tours or gear rental, they have it all. Climbing, canoe trips, biking, kayaking, caving, hanggliding, skiing, you name it they do it.

Drumheller and the Badlands *p263*
Dinosaur Trail Golf Club, across from the museum, T403-823 5622, www.dinosaur trailgolf.com. One of the most interesting settings imaginable.
Wild West Badlands Tours, T1888-823 3118, www.wildwestbadlandstours.com. A variety of tours of the Badlands in an 8-passenger van, $38 for 2½-3 hrs.

⊙ Transport

Calgary *p258, map p260*
Air
For airport details, see page 257. Calgary has flights to and from all major cities within Canada with **Air Canada**, T1888-247 2262, www.aircanada.com, and **West Jet**, T1800-538 5696, www.westjet.com. Example one-way fares are $149 to **Vancouver**, $145 to **Kelowna** and $190 to **Kamloops**.
   Travel agents   Travel Cuts, 815 10th Av SW, T403-686 7633, 109 10th St NW, Kensington, T403-270 3640, www.travel cuts.com. Offering student discounts.

Bus
Local   Calgary Transit has its own information centre at 224 7th Av SW, T403-262 1000, www.calgarytransit.com, Mon-Fri 0600-2100, Sat-Sun 0800-1800. They can provide very helpful maps. Tickets costing $2.50, youth $1.50, under 6 free, can be bought here from machines on C-train platforms or from shops with the **Calgary Transit** sticker. Bus drivers require the exact fare. Day passes cost $6.75, child $4.50. If you need to take more than one bus or C-train to complete a journey, ask the driver for a transfer (valid for 90 mins). The C-train is free Downtown on 7th Av between Macleod Trail and 8 St SW.

Long distance Greyhound, T1800-661 8747, www.greyhound.ca, runs 5 daily buses to **Banff** (1½-2 hrs, $24); 4 to **Vancouver** (15-17 hrs, $85 if purchased 1 day in advance); and 2 direct to **Kamloops** (9 hrs, $88 or $73 if purchased 1 day in advance). Banff Airporter, T403-762 3330, www.banff airporter.com, and Sun Dog Tours, T1888-786 3641, www.sundogtours .com, both run regular shuttles from the airport to **Banff** and **Canmore** (both $52, child $29 one-way), the latter continuing to **Lake Louise** ($65, child $39) and **Jasper** ($105, child $65). Brewster, T1800-760 6934, www.brewster. ca, run 2 daily buses from Downtown Calgary and 6 from Calgary Airport to Canmore and Banff ($55) and from Banff to Lake Louise ($73) and Jasper ($132).

Taxis
Associated Taxi, T403-299 1111; Calgary Cab Co, T403-777 2222.

Vehicle rental
Car hire All Season Rentals, 1510 10th Av SW, T403-204 1771, www.allseason motorsports.ca, offers motorbike hire; Budget, 140 6th Av SE, T403-226 1550, www.budget .ca; Thrifty, 123 5th Av SE, T403-262 4400, www.thrifty.com. **RVs** Canadream Campers, 2510 27th Av NE, T403-291 1000, www.canadream.com; Cruise Canada, 2980 26th St NE, T403-291 4963, www.cruisecanada.com. About $1100-1300 for 7 nights, plus 32c/km

Drumheller and the Badlands *p263*
Roughly 150 km northeast from Calgary, Drumheller is reached on Hwy 9 north from the TransCanada Hwy. Greyhound have made it impossible to do this as a day trip.

Bus
Daily buses leave Drumheller for **Calgary** at 0355 ($3 one-way).

Taxi
JB Taxi Services, T403-823 7433.

❶ Directory

Calgary *p258, map p260*
Banks National Bank of Canada, 2700-530 8th Av SW, T403-294 4946; Bank of Montreal, 222 5th Av SW, T403-234 1810. **Currency exchange** Citizens Bank of Canada, 150-505 3rd St SW, T403-266 7321; Olympia Trust Foreign Exchange, 100-237 8th Av, T403-266 7321. **Embassies and consulates** US Consulate, 615 MacLeod Trail SE, T403-266 8962. **Internet** Library; Wired Cyber Café, 1032 17th Av SW, T403-244 7070. **Laundry** Avenue Coin Laundry, 325B 17th Av SW, T403-262 8777. **Library** 616 Macleod Trail SE, T403-260 2600; 1904 14th Av NW, T403-260 2600, www.calgary publiclibrary.com. **Medical services** Foothills Medical Centre, 1403 29th St NW, T403-944 1110; Health Resource Centre, 1402 8th Av NW, T403-2200410; Rockyview General Hospital, 7007 14th St SW, T403-943 3000. **Post office** Canada Post 135-315 8th Av SW, T403-233 2400; 224-205 5th Av SW, T403-266 4304; 1702 4th St SW, T403-228 3788.

Banff National Park

Banff National Park, the oldest and most famous in the Canadian Rockies and Canada's number one tourist attraction, receives some 4.7 million visitors per year. This is partly due to its 6641 sq km of jaw-dropping scenery, including 25 peaks over 3000 m and 1500 km of trails, many of which are accessed from the highway and gentle enough for almost anyone. Of equal significance is its location on the country's main highway, a mere 128 km from Calgary. The park's popularity is its only drawback.

Banff Townsite is the park's main hub, a pleasant but absurdly busy place with services catering to every budget. A short hop north is Lake Louise, the single most famous location in the Rockies. From here, a nice loop leads through Yoho and Kootenay National Parks, while the incredible Icefields Parkway runs north to Jasper, lined with the most drool-inducing scenery of all, peaking around the extraordinary Columbia Icefields. ▸▸ *For Sleeping, Eating and other listings, see pages 285-294.*

Ins and outs

Getting there and around
At least three companies run regular shuttles from Calgary Airport to Banff (see page 271) and there are shuttles to Lake Louise. **Greyhound** ① *100 Gopher St*, also run numerous daily buses to Lake Louise. The TransCanada Highway connects Banff with Vancouver and all points east.

Banff Townsite can be easily explored on foot, as almost everything is on or near Banff Avenue. **Banff Transit** ① *T403-762 1215*, operates two shuttles that cover the whole town ($2). ▸▸ *For further details, see Transport, page 294.*

Tourist information
The **Banff Information Centre** ① *224 Banff Av, Jul-Aug daily 0800-2000, May-Jun daily 0900-1900, Sep-May daily 0900-1700*, comprises the **Parks Canada Office** ① *T403-762 1550, www.pc.gc.ca/banff*, and the **Banff Lake Louise Tourism Bureau** ① *T403-762 8421, www.banfflakelouise.com*. The former is an excellent source of information about hikes and all other park activities. It issues very useful maps for day-hikes and cycling, and one showing longer trails and backcountry campgrounds. To stay at one of the latter you must register here and buy a **Wilderness Pass** ① *$9 per person per night*. The Tourism Bureau can help out with sleeping arrangements. It keeps track of which hotels, B&Bs and campsites still have spaces and provides a courtesy phone. It can also provide brochures for the *Banff Historical Walking Tour.* The **Friends of Banff National Park** ① *T403-762 8918, www.friendsofbanff.com*, sells maps and all kinds of books on hiking and other activities as well as natural and cultural history. It also runs free guided walks throughout the summer. For park radio, tune in to 101.1 FM

Banff Townsite ⊖⊘⊕⊕✿⊙▲⊖⊕ ▸▸ *pp285-294.*
Colour map 2, B3.

Banff enjoys a stunning location and was once a pretty little village. Today, however, the 50,000 visitors it receives daily throughout the summer have taken their toll. The streets are perpetually heaving, the roads choked with tour buses. The relentless commercialism soon becomes tiresome and there is little to do but shop, eat and party.

Those craving creature comforts will find them here in abundance, but if you are camping or staying in hostels there are nicer places to be. The main reason to visit the Townsite is for its excellent Information Centre to help plan your excursion, then for a little R&R when you get back. The nicest part of Banff lies at its west end, where a picturesque bridge over the Bow River gives an idea of how the village might have looked before its popularity got out of hand.

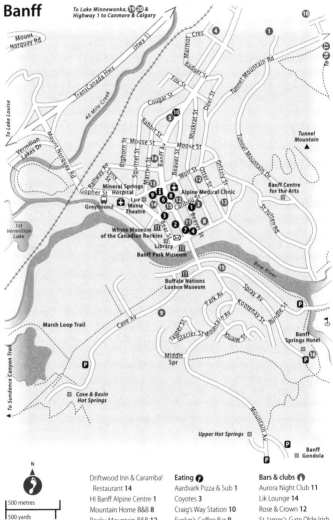

Banff

Sleeping
A Banff Boutique Inn **9**
Banff Y Mountain Lodge
  & Sundance Bistro **15**
Blue Mountain Lodge **3**
Bumpers Inn **4**

Driftwood Inn & Caramba!
  Restaurant **14**
HI Banff Alpine Centre **1**
Mountain Home B&B **8**
Rocky Mountain B&B **12**
Same Sun Banff Lodge **5**
Tan-Y-Bryn **13**
Tunnel Mountain I **17**
Tunnel Mountain II **18**
Tunnel Mt Trailer Court **16**
Two Jack Lakeside **19**
Two Jack Main **20**

Eating
Aardvark Pizza & Sub **1**
Coyotes **3**
Craig's Way Station **10**
Evelyn's Coffee Bar **9**
Fuze Finer Dining **7**
Grizzly House **8**
Le Beaujolais **4**
Maple Leaf Grille & Hoodoo
  Lounge **2**
Sukiyaki House **6**

Bars & clubs
Aurora Night Club **11**
Lik Lounge **14**
Rose & Crown **12**
St James's Gate Olde Irish
  Pub **13**
Waldhaus Pub **16**
Wild Bill's Legendary
  Saloon **15**

Whyte Museum of the Canadian Rockies

ⓘ *111 Bear St, T403-762 2291, www.whyte.org, daily 1000-1700, $6, under 18 $3.50, under 6 free. 90-min Historic Banff walking tour leaves once a day, $7.*

Created by artists Peter and Catherine Whyte, Banff's most worthwhile sight includes thousands of volumes of archives and Alpine Club records of early expeditions. Of greater significance to visitors is the fine collection of mountain-related art, much of it by the founders and a half dozen temporary exhibitions by local and international contemporary artists, usually of a documentary or educational nature. Most fascinating of all is an excellent collection of photos that vividly documents the early days of the park and the changing attitudes that have prevailed regarding its wildlife. Countless black and white pictures depict fancily dressed Edwardian tourists standing next to their vintage cars, grinning stupidly as they feed a bear by hand; or a self-satisfied ranger standing smugly over some poor dead beast. The museum presents lectures and various tours.

Banff Park Museum and around

ⓘ *91 Banff Av, T403-762 1558, mid-May to mid-Sep daily 1000-1800, mid-Sep to mid-May daily 1300-1700, $4, child $2.*

The Banff Park Museum is housed in a splendid wood cabin built in 1895, its age explaining all the skylights, which compensated for the lack of electric light. Like the building itself, the interior is more a relic from the past than a place where the past is documented. A large collection of dusty, old stuffed animals pay their politically incorrect tribute to a time when people's idea of wildlife watching was taking high tea in a room lined with animal heads, and even the official park approach to wildlife preservation was to shoot all predators like cougars, lynx and eagles so that innocents such as elk, deer and sheep could multiply unhampered.

Across the river, the **Buffalo Nations Luxton Museum** ⓘ *1 Birch Av, T403-762 2388, www.buffalonationsmuseum.ca, May-Sep daily 100-1800, Oct-Apr daily 1300-1700, $8, child $2.50*, has a small collection of First Nations artefacts such as beadwork, costumes, headdresses, a decorated tepee and a number of poorly executed tableaux. The gift shop is its best feature.

Cave and Basin Hot Springs

ⓘ *311 Cave Av, T403-762 1566, mid-May to mid-Sep daily 0900-1800, mid-Sep to mid-May Mon-Fri 1100-1600, Sat-Sun 0930-1700, Tours mid-May to mid-Sep daily 1100, 1400, 1600, mid-Sep to mid-May Sat-Sun 1100, $4, child $2.*

A couple of kilometres southwest of Banff centre is the site of the thermal waters whose discovery prompted the park's formation. Upon seeing them for the first time, Canadian Pacific Railway builder William Van Horne exclaimed, "These springs are worth a million dollars", and how right he was. The story is told through a collection of exhibits on the second floor and the film *Steam, Schemes and National Dreams*. The cavernous, atmospheric setting of that first pool is the highlight, making you wish it were still open for bathing. The outdoor 'basin' pool is only slightly less enticing.

The grounds are also attractive and contain a couple of short and popular walks. The interpretive **Marsh Loop Trail** ⓘ *2.7 km*, leads on boardwalks around a wetland area whose warm microclimate has made it unusually lush and flower-filled and a rewarding spot for birdwatchers. The easy and popular **Sundance Canyon Trail** ⓘ *3.7 km, one-way*, follows a paved path to the canyon mouth.

Banff Springs Hotel

ⓘ *It's a boring walk up Spray Av from the centre, so take the No 1 local transit.*

After the discovery of the springs, the Canadian Pacific Railway quickly saw tourism as a means to pay for its expensive line and went about building a series of luxurious hotels. First of these was the **Banff Springs Hotel**, the largest in the world when finished

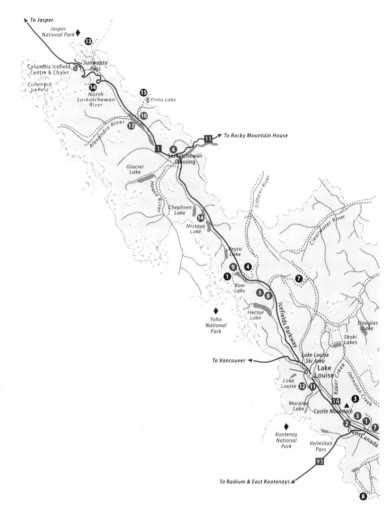

Sleeping 🛏

Castle Mountain Campground **1**

Castle Mountain Chalets **2**

Crossing **4**

HI Castle Mountain Wilderness Hostel **3**

Johnston Canyon Campground **6**

Johnston Canyon Resort **7**

Lake Louise Tent **11**

Lake Louise Trailer **12**

Mosquito Creek Campground **5**

Mosquito Creek Hostel **8**

Rampart Creek Campground **13**

Rampart Creek Hostel **10**

Simpson's Num-Ti-Jah Lodge **9**

Waterfowl Lake Campground **14**

Trails ⛰

Bow Glacier Falls & Bow Hut **1**

Castle Crags **3**

Cirque Peak/Helen Lake **4**

Citadel Pass & Mount Assiniboine **5**

Fish Lakes/Pipestone Pass/Devon Lakes **7**

Healy Pass & Egypt Lake **8**

Johnston Canyon **9**

Lake Minnewanka **10**

Mount Assiniboine (via Bryant Creek) **11**

Nigel Pass, Jonas Pass & Poboktan Pass **13**

Parker Ridge **14**

Sunset Pass **15**

N

10 km
10 miles

in 1888. Unfortunately, the Gothic giant was constructed back to front, with wonderful views from the kitchens and none at all from the guest rooms. Since then it has been rebuilt and developed, its 250 rooms expanded to 770, all of which are full in summer, mostly with Japanese tour groups. Known as the 'Castle in the Rockies', it is now more village than hotel, a vast, confusing labyrinth of restaurants, lounges, shops and other facilities. Utterly over-the-top, its sheer excessiveness makes it the only unmissable sight in Banff. Be sure to pick up a map from reception before exploring.

Upper Hot Springs

ⓘ *End of Mountain Av, T403-762 1515, www.hotsprings.ca, mid-May to mid-Sep Sun-Thu 1000-2200, Fri-Sat 1000-2300, mid-Sep to mid-May daily 0900-2300, $7.30, child $6.30. Reduced rates in the evenings and in winter.*

If the Cave Springs have put you in the mood, head here, an outdoor thermal swimming pool with great views where the very sulphurous water is cooled to 37-40°C. The **Hot Springs Spa** offers massage, aroma-therapy and a steam room.

Banff Gondola

ⓘ *End of Mountain Av, T403-762 2523, www.banffgondola.com, Jun-Aug daily 0730-2100, Dec-Jan 1000-1600, $26, under 15 $13, under 6 free. Bus No 1 to Fairmont then walk.*

Just down the road is the **Banff Gondola**. This eight minute ride takes you up 700 m at a 51° angle to the top of Sulphur Mountain, where there is a restaurant, observation decks for taking in the exceptional panoramic views and a couple of short trails leading to even more vistas. From Sanson's Peak, the South East Ridge trail runs along the mountain's ridge to its true summit.

Vermilion Lakes and Lake Minnewanka

The **Vermilion Lakes**, just west of town off Mount Norquay Road, are easily explored by bike or car. The marshes around them are home to a wide range of birds, such as ospreys and bald eagles, as well as like muskrat, beaver, elk and coyote. **Lake Minnewanka**, north of the eastern highway junction, is a focus for hiking, biking, fishing and boating.

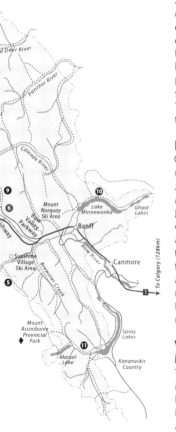

Red Deer River

Panther River

Cascade River

Mount Norquay Ski Area

Lake Minnewanka

Ghost Lakes

Bow Valley Parkway

Highway

Banff

Sunshine Village Ski Area

Brewster Creek

Bow River

Canmore

To Calgary (128km)

Mount Assiniboine Provincial Park

Spray Lakes

Marvel Lake

Kananaskis Country

Canadian Rockies Banff National Park Banff Townsite

Fenland Trail ① *1.5 km. Trailhead: Mt Norquay Rd*. A loop through the wetlands near the first Vermilion Lake, a haven for birds and other wildlife.

Marsh Loop ① *2 km. Trailhead: the Cave and Basin hot springs*. This trail explores a similarly rich area for flora and fauna.

Tunnel Mountain ① *3.6 km return; 200 m elevation gain. Trailhead: St Julien Rd*. This short, steep but easily attainable hike leads to fine views of Banff Village.

C-level Cirque ① *8 km return; 455 m elevation gain. Trailhead: 3.5 km north on Lake Minnewanka Rd*. This is a short, easy hike leading to some heart-warming mountain scenery. You'll also see mining remains and wild flowers.

Lake Minnewanka ① *6-60 km return with little elevation gain*. This trail is suitable for anyone and is open even in April and November when most others are closed. You can also go as far as you like. The **Ghost Lakes** are at Km 24, with frequent campgrounds along the way. At Km 7.8, you can turn left for the steep climb to **Mount Aylmer Lookout/Pass**, 23.6 or 27 km, 615 or 845 m elevation gain. This route also enjoys a longer season than most. From the lookout are great views of the lake and mountains towering above the opposite shore. From the pass the views are bigger but mostly limited to vast expanses of desolate grey rock.

Cory and Edith passes ① *13-km circuit; 960 m elevation gain. Trailhead: 0.5 km on Bow Valley Parkway after it leaves Hwy 1, turn right and continue 1 km*. Cory Pass can usually be hiked by late June. An extremely tough trail involving steep sections and some scree slope scrambling, this is only for the fit and reasonably experienced but if you can manage it, the rewards are an adrenaline-pumping quest and some exhilarating views. Edith is less exciting but makes for an easier descent and a neat loop.

Around Banff ●❷❶❺❀❸▲❸❸ ➠ *pp285-294.*

Canmore → *Colour map 2, B3.*

Though the highway around Canmore is now entirely engulfed by satellite suburbs of hotels and condos, its Downtown core, centred on Main (8th) Street, just about manages to retain the comfortable feel of an authentic small town, making this an attractive and cheaper alternative to the insanely busy and commercially-oriented Banff, just 21 km to the west. There are some decent, down-to-earth pubs, fine restaurants and as many sports equipment shops as anyone could desire. Moreover, many fine hikes into Banff and Mount Assiniboine Parks are most easily accessed from Canmore, a number of tour operators are based here and all kinds of outdoor activities are seriously pursued in the region, particularly climbing, Nordic skiing and mountain biking. ➠ *For further details, see Activities and tours, page 291.*

Across the bridge from town, past the Nordic Centre, a steep, rough road leads to the **Spray Lakes**, a nice quiet spot to camp. On the way, this road passes Canmore's most worthwhile attraction, **Grassi Lakes**. The unreal aquamarine/lime green colour of these lakes is extraordinary, even by local standards, and the whole area is a lovely, relaxing place. North of the lakes is a very popular spot for rock climbing; there's always plenty of action to watch for those who do not partake. Those who do will find lava cliff faces riddled with holes and all levels of climb with routes already anchored by locals.

For maps and trail information, call in at **Tourism Canmore** ① *907 7th Av, T403-678 1295, www.tourismcanmore.com*. They can provide a brochure for the self-guided

Historic Walking Tour of the town. More useful for general enquiries is **Travel Alberta**
ⓘ *at the south side of Hwy 1 on west end of Canmore service road, T403-678 5277,
www.travelalberta.com, May-Oct daily 0800-2000, Nov-Apr daily 0900-1800.* The
national HQ of the **Alpine Club of Canada** ⓘ *Indian Flats Rd, T403-678 3200,* a short
drive from town, are very helpful and knowledgeable about climbs and hikes, and sell
a good selection of maps and guidebooks. They also have a hostel and backcountry
huts dotted throughout the parks. For locations visit www.alpineclubofcanada.ca/
facility/info.

Mount Assiniboine Provincial Park → *Colour map 2, B3.*
Canmore is the main jumping-off point for hikes into the south of Banff National Park.
These are reached on the Smith-Dorrien Highway (No 742) beyond Spray Lakes. Just
past the south end of Spray Lakes reservoir, turn right onto Watridge logging road and
drive 5.3 km for Mount Shark trailhead, one of the starting points for hikes into Mount
Assiniboine Provincial Park in BC. Mount Assiniboine is one of the most recognizable
and visually gratifying peaks in the Rockies, a pyramid-shaped icon that has been
compared to the Matterhorn in the Swiss Alps. The rest of the park is equally
sensational and certainly one of the top backpacking destinations in the range.

From Mount Shark, the easiest route is via **Bryant Creek** ⓘ *27.5 km one-way, with
a 480 m elevation gain*, and the Assiniboine Pass. A strong hiker can do it in a day.
Otherwise there is a campground at Km 9.7 and a warden hut, campground and
shelter at Km 13.6. To stay at either, make arrangements with the Banff Visitor Centre.
The easiest route back to Mount Shark, making a nice loop, is over **Wonder Pass**
ⓘ *27.5 km, 230 m elevation gain and then a lot of downhill*, and by Marvel Lake.
A second access route and probably the best, is over **Citadel Pass** ⓘ *29 km, 450 m
elevation gain*, from Sunshine Village. This is a delightful, slightly easier hike. The
ultimate trip would be to enter this way and exit via Wonder Pass, but arranging a
shuttle would be tricky. None of this should be done without a map and a more
detailed trail description.

The core area of this triangular park is its southeast corner, which contains
Mount Assiniboine, eight other peaks over 3000 m and several beautiful lakes. The
main focus and campground is at **Lake Magog**. There is also a Park Headquarters/
warden's cabin. Some excellent one-day hikes from here give the chance to see some
of the park and recover from the trek in. **Nub Peak** ⓘ *a moderate 11.6-km round-trip,
from Magog*, offers excellent views of the surroundings. **Windy Ridge** ⓘ *a moderate
17.4-km round-trip*, is one of the highest trail-accessible points in the Rockies, with
even better views and wild flower meadows on the way. An easier excursion is the
8-km loop to **Sunburst**, **Cerulean** and **Elizabeth Lakes**, which can be extended to
18.6 km to take in the views from **Ferro Pass**. Whatever the skies are doing and the
forecasts say, always come prepared for the worst the weather can throw at you.

Sunshine Village Ski Area → *Colour map 2, B3.*
ⓘ *T403-277 7669, www.skibanff.com. Sat-Thu daily 0800-1730, Fri 0800-2230. Lift
pass $78, under 18 $55, under 12 $26. Shuttles from Downtown Banff and the major
hotels are free for pass holders, or $15, child $10 return.*
Bow Valley Parkway is the scenic route east from Banff to Lake Louise and beyond.
Highway 1 is still a beautiful drive, but much faster with less chances to stop and hike.
After 8 km, a road heads from the latter to **Sunshine Village Ski Area**. Twelve lifts,
including a high-speed gondola, provide access to 107 uncrowded runs on 1330 ha of
skiable terrain on three mountains (20% beginner, 55% intermediate, 25% expert).
Situated right on the Great Divide, these receive a much higher calibre of snow
than nearby Mount Norquay, with 10 m per year of first-class powder, Canada's
biggest snow-pack. The area also has one of the longest seasons, running from
mid-November until late May. The highest elevation is 2730 m, with a vertical drop of

1070 m. As well as rentals and lessons, the hill has restaurants and accommodation. Note that it's very cold up here.

Mount Norquay Ski Area

ⓘ *T403-762 4421, www.banffnorquay.com. Lift pass $49, under 18 $39, under 12 $17; night skiing Fri 1700-2200, $24. There are 3 shuttles from major Banff hotels, $15 return.*

Just 6 km to the north of Banff, Mount Norquay Ski Area receives 300 cm of snow per year and employs a snow-maker. Five lifts access terrain that is 20% beginner, 36% intermediate, 28% advanced and 16% expert. This has long been considered the domain of experienced skiers, with plenty of steep, deep runs and the only night skiing in the Rockies. The highest elevation is 2133 m, with a vertical drop of 503 m. The lodge has a restaurant, café, rentals and lessons. The season runs from early December to mid-April.

Hikes from Sunshine Village

The beauty of ski hills is the speed with which you can be whisked to elevations that would take hours of hard walking to reach otherwise. Then you can maximise your time and effort because the views are already fantastic. Unfortunately, the Sunshine gondola no longer runs in summer, though there is a shuttle bus run by **White Mountain Adventures**ⓘ *T403-678 4099, from the Sunshine parking lot, hourly from 0900, $25, child $14 return, or from Banff Townsite 0830 only, $50, child $30.*

Sunshine Meadows At the top of the gondola the meadows stretch for 15 km along the Great Divide, receiving copious amounts of rain and snow that feed one of the most glorious midsummer wild flower displays you'll ever see. Naturally, such an easily accessible Eden draws crowds of visitors. Most go only as far as **Rock Isle Lake**, an easy 1.6-km trail to a beautiful viewpoint. To avoid the crowds set a brisker pace towards **Citadel Pass** ⓘ *18.6 km return, 343 m elevation gain*. On a clear day many of BC's mighty and rugged peaks are visible, including Mount Assiniboine. Continue a little further towards Fatique Pass, 2.5 km away, for even better views. This is a popular way to begin a multi-day backpacking trip into Mount Assiniboine Provincial Park in BC.

Healy Pass ⓘ *18.4 km return; 360 m or 655 m elevation gain. Trailhead: there are 2 ways to reach Healy Pass, from Sunshine Village via the shuttle and Simpson Pass or from the Sunshine parking lot via Healy Creek.* The distance is the same but starting from the Sunshine parking lot involves a lot more climbing, though at a gentle pace. If you are fit and don't want to pay the shuttle fare, go via Healy Creek. Either way, the flowers are wonderful. The pass itself is unexceptional but offers good views of Egypt and Scarab Lakes and the Pharaoh Peaks. You could also explore the Monarch Ramparts south of the pass. **Egypt Lake** campground and a basic, cheerless hut is 3 km further on. To stay here book at the **Banff Visitor Centre** ⓘ *T403-762 1550, $17 per person (including Wilderness pass)*. There are some worthwhile side-trips if you do. **Whistling Pass** is a fine 6.6-km round-trip, which could be extended to **Shadow Lake** beneath the lofty Mount Ball (26 km return from Egypt Lake).

Bow Valley Parkway → *Colour map 2, B3.*

The Bow Valley Parkway leaves Highway 1 just west of Banff. Its speed limit is a sometimes-frustrating 60 kph but when drivers are liable to hit the breaks at any moment if a sheep appears, this is a good thing. Along the road are three campgrounds, a hostel, a few lodges and numerous hikes and viewpoints. At Km 16 is **Johnston Canyon** and its eponymous trail of the same name ⓘ *11.6 km return, 215 m elevation gain*, which is the most worthwhile hike along the parkway. The chasms and waterfalls of this canyon are famous and perpetually flooded with tourists, but it's a lovely walk. The canyon is at its most beautiful in winter, when the waterfalls are frozen (see Activities and tours, page 291). You can continue beyond the falls to the multicoloured cold-water springs of the **Inkpots** and views of Johnston Creek Valley.

Castle Mountain, 30 km from Banff, marks the junction with Highway 93, which heads south through Kootenay National Park to Radium Hot Springs. The mountain itself is a magnificent and aptly named sight, worth pulling over to admire. The nearby **Rockbound Lake Trail** is more trouble than it's worth but **Silverton Falls** from the same trailhead is a nice 1.6-km jaunt. About 5 km to the west is the **Castle Crags Trail** ① *7 km return, 520 m elevation gain*. This short but steep hike leads to an old fire lookout and an outstanding panorama of the Bow Valley from Banff to Lake Louise. It is also free of snow earlier and later than most trails. On the way up you'll pass wild flower gardens and a dilapidated old cabin.

Lake Louise ⊜🏊🌀⛰️🎭🌀 ▸▸ *pp285-294. Colour map 2, B3.*

Magnificent Lake Louise is the single most famous icon in the Rockies and consequently receives far more visitors than any place of natural beauty should have to endure. This is the only focus in the park other than Banff Townsite, with a better assortment of trails and things to see but far fewer facilities. There are actually four components to Lake Louise: the Village, the Lake, Moraine Lake and the Ski Hill.

The Village

You'll come to the village first, close to the important junction where Highway 1 veers west through Yoho towards Golden and Revelstoke. Highway 93 then becomes the sole route north, henceforth known as the **Icefields Parkway**. This 'village' is little more than the ugly, overpriced Samson Mall, though it does contain most of the limited local accommodation, including one of the best hostels in the country and the excellent **Lake Louise Visitor Centre** ① *T403-522 3833, Jun-Sep daily 0900-2000, Oct-May daily 0900-1600 or 1700*. The Parks Office and Information Centre helps out with hikes and accommodation, handing out brochures and maps and issuing backcountry permits. A number of interesting natural history exhibits explain some of the local geographical features, including displays on the Burgess Shale in Field (see page 308).

The Lake

① *4.5 km from the Village up a steep hill, 2.7 km on foot.*
There are many lakes in the Rockies with water that has an opaque, milky quality due to the presence of glacial silt known as 'rock flour'; mineral deposits that glaciers have scraped from the mountain rock. These particles absorb all colours of the light spectrum except green and blue. Far and away the most famous is **Lake Louise**, where the water is of the most exquisite aquamarine colour, or colours as the hue changes dramatically according to the time of year and angle of the sun. Add to this the lake's sheer size and dramatic location at the foot of an incredibly powerful, towering rock rampart and it is not difficult to understand why this is the definitive picture-postcard image of the Rockies and the single most popular sight in the range.

Around 10,000 people come here every day in peak season, so if you want to see its shores crowd-free, arrive at sunrise. It comes as little surprise that this was the spot chosen by the CPR for the second of their giant hotels, the **Château**, originally built in 1890. Many visitors are shocked by this behemoth and consider its monstrous presence on the shores of the heavenly water an outrage that would never be allowed today. The best thing is to ignore it and go for a walk, or hire a canoe and go for a paddle. **Lake Agnes Tea House** and **Plain of the Six Glaciers Tea House** are each situated on popular trails about one or two hours' hike above the lake.

Moraine Lake

ⓘ *Expensive canoes can be rented at the Lodge for a paddle, T403-522 3733. Note that parking is often a problem here.*

Halfway to Lake Louise, a left fork leads 12.5 km to Moraine Lake, another striking emerald product of rock flour. Half the size of its sister, it's equally beautiful and almost as popular, and the location might even be more dramatic. Stretching away from its shores is the **Valley of the Ten Peaks**, a wonderfully scenic cluster of mighty mountains, also known as the **Wenkchemna**, the Stoney word for ten. Some excellent trails lead into the valley and up to viewpoints.

Lake Louise Ski Area

ⓘ *T403-522 3555, www.skilouise.com. Day pass is $72, under 18 $50, under 12 $24, under 6 free. The turning is just before the Bow Valley Parkway crosses Hwy 1 on its way to Lake Louise. The gondola, T403-522 3555, www.lakelouisegondola.com, May-Sep daily 0900-1830, $24, child $12, $2 extra for breakfast buffet, $6 extra for lunch buffet. The Interpretive Centre gives presentations and runs 45-min guided nature walks daily 1030, 1230, 1530, $5.*

This is the biggest ski hill in Canada, 40 sq km of terrain featuring vast open bowls. With excellent powder and stupendous views, it ranks for almost all ski aficionados as one of the best hills in North America. A high-speed gondola and eight lifts service 139 runs that break down as 25% beginner, 45% intermediate and 30% expert. The top elevation is 2637 m, with a vertical drop of 911 m. The only drawbacks are the low snowfall of 360 m and the fact that it is bitterly cold, not helped by the fact that most runs are above the tree-line. The lodges at the bottom are open year-round, with restaurants, pubs, lounges, a cappuccino bar, equipment rentals and lessons.

In summer, the **Lake Louise Sightseeing Gondola** runs people to the top of the hill to enjoy the views, though there's not much else to do up there. A free shuttle bus to the hill leaves the Village every hour on the hour (0800-1700), leaving the Château 30 minutes earlier.

Hikes from the Lake

Saddleback/Fairview Mountain ⓘ *7.4-10.6 km return; 600-1014 m elevation gain. Trailhead: by the canoe rental at northeast end of lake.* The hike to Saddleback, despite its steepness, is very popular, especially in September when the larches turn to gold. This is a great viewpoint; even better is Saddle Mountain, 90 m straight up above it. Best of all is Fairview Mountain, a further steep 1.6-km climb. The panorama from here is to die for, with gargantuan peaks all around Lake Louise 1000 m below.

Plain of the Six Glaciers ⓘ *13.8 km; 380 m elevation gain.* This popular trail takes you up to the Teahouse and is perpetually crowded. Go anyway, because the views are astounding, embracing the giant peaks of mounts Lefroy and Victoria and their extensive glaciers and icefalls. Try starting after 1600 to minimize the company.

Hikes from Moraine Lake Road

Paradise Valley/Lake Annette ⓘ *18.2-km circuit/11.4 km return; 400 m/250 m elevation gain. Trailhead: 2.5 km from junction with Lake Louise Dr, 10 km before Moraine Lake.* Though this is a valley hike, the views it offers are as good or better than most ridge walks, with plenty of peaks and sheer rock faces. A return hike to Lake Annette is phenomenal in itself, but the longer circuit is recommended and best done in a clockwise direction. Horseshoe Meadow has a backcountry campground for those who want to take their time and extend it into a two-day trip. A possible enormous slabs of quartzite. The paths there are confusing.

Hikes from Moraine Lake

Valley of the Ten Peaks/Sentinel Pass ⓘ *11.6 km return; 725 m elevation gain. Trailhead: past the lodge.* This wonderful, exhilarating trail leads through Larch Valley, a particularly popular spot in the autumn when the trees turn to gold. It is a fairly gentle hike most of the way until the final switchback ascent to the pass, which is not as hard as it looks. The view from the top is spectacular, taking in most of the ten peaks and looking down on the other side into Paradise Valley. This hike can be combined with the Paradise Valley one to make a 17-km one-way trip ending 10 km down Moraine Lake Road. The best bet is to leave a vehicle here and hitch or take the shuttle up to Moraine Lake. This is a very popular trail but only takes four or five hours so think about starting early or late.

Consolation Lakes ⓘ *6 km return; 60 m elevation gain.* Though no substitute for the above, this is a short and easy walk and the cliffs that tower over the lakes are undeniably impressive. The rough trail beyond the first lake means that the second is always less busy.

Hikes from the Ski Area

Skoki Valley ⓘ *31.6 km, 785 m elevation gain. Trailhead: follow Whitehorn Rd towards the Ski Area, turn right at Km 2 onto Fish Creek Rd and follow for 1.1 km.* The high point of this hike are the alpine meadows and numerous lakes surrounded by rugged mountains with a romantically desolate air. The downside is that many hikers come this way, meaning trails are muddy if it's been raining. At least the first 4 km are on a boring fire-road. Think of doing it as a day trip and cycle that section. If camping, Merlin Meadows and Baker Lake are the best options, or you could stay at the **Skoki Lodge**, see page 287. A fine day-hike from here is the 6.2-km round-trip to the beautiful Merlin Lake. A 1.6-km scramble up Skoki Mountain leads to 360° views. This is also a very popular area for cross-country skiing.

Icefields Parkway 🚌🚶 ▸ *pp285-294.*

The 230-km road between Lake Louise and Jasper runs through some of the Rockies' most spectacular scenery, bridging the two major parks and must qualify as one of the most exciting drives in the world. In fact, the endless parade of lofty snow-capped peaks and vast glaciers is likely to push you towards sensory overload. The climax comes just beyond the Sunwapta Pass that separates Banff and Jasper National Parks. This is the Columbia Icefield, the single largest and most accessible area of ice and snow in the Rockies.

Distances given below are from Lake Louise. Dotted along the road at fairly regular intervals are youth hostels, campgrounds and a host of long and short trails. Pick up the Icefields Parkway map and guide from the Visitor Centre in Banff, Lake Louise or Jasper.

Lake Louise to the Columbia Icefield → *Colour map 2, B2.*

Bow Lake ⓘ *Km 37,* is a beautiful lake whose turquoise hue seems almost preternaturally vivid. **Bow Summit** ⓘ *2069 m, 3 km further north,* is the highest pass in the Rockies and the highest highway crossing in Canada. Just beyond, a short side road leads to the exceptional but very busy viewpoint above **Peyto Lake**, another of those Rocky Mountain icons whose undeniable beauty can get lost among the throngs and clamour. It's named after Bill Peyto, a legendary Rocky pioneer who was as famous for his exploits around town as for his wilderness exploration.

Saskatchewan Crossing ① *Km 78*, is a grim crossroads with Highway 11 but a useful service centre offering a rare chance to get gas and essential supplies. At 114 km the road enters a dramatic giant switchback known as the 'Big Bend'. At the top are the impressive **Panther Falls** and a couple of viewpoints where you can stop and enjoy the sweep of mountains back to the south. Look out also for the **Weeping Wall**, where water plunges down from a series of cracks in the apparently solid rock face.

Just beyond **Sunwapta Pass** ① *2023 m*, which marks the border between the national parks, comes the highlight of the drive. For further information on the Columbia Icefield and the surrounding area, visit the **Icefield Centre**, see page 297.

Hikes around Columbia Icefield

Fish Lakes/Pipestone Pass/Devon Lakes Trail ① *29.6-62.8 km; 762 m-1116 m elevation gain. Trailhead: park at Mosquito Creek, at Km 28, then walk across the road and over the bridge.* This trail leads through mostly open terrain with scenery that is consistently wonderful. There are a few possible itineraries. North Molar Pass makes a good 23-km day-hike. On this route, a scramble east of the pass gives views of the Fish Lakes and Pipestone River valley. Upper Fish Lake is reached at Km 14.8, a day trip for fast hikers. The campground, right on the lake beneath a towering rock wall, is a fine spot. To make it a four-day trip, continue to Pipestone Pass, with extensive views that include 19 km of the Siffleur River Valley, through the Clearwater Pass and on to the quiet and remote Devon Lakes at Km 31.4.

Cirque Peak/Helen Lake Trail ① *15 km return; 1043 m elevation gain. Trailhead: Crowfoot Glacier viewpoint, at Km 34.* One of the best hikes in the Rockies, leading quickly to open sub-alpine meadows covered with heather and wild flowers, offering views of the impressive mountains. The marmots at Helen Lake are daring and entertaining. It's a long, slow scramble up a scree slope from here to Cirque Peak, but easier than you'd think and amply rewarded by 360° views of the Dolomite Valley, Bow and Peyto Lakes and Crowfoot and Bow Glaciers.

Bow Glacier Falls ① *9 km return; 148 m elevation gain. Trailhead: Bow Lake at Km 37.* Stroll along the shore of this striking lake and witness the birthplace of the Bow River.

Bow Hut Trail ① *14.8 km return; 500 m elevation gain.* This follows the same trail as Bow Glacier, above, almost to the falls, then heads uphill through a canyon to a mountaineering hut close to the edge of the vast Wapta Icefield. The rock and ice views are wonderful but those scared of heights might baulk at the final ascent.

Bow Lookout Trail ① *6 km return; 260 m elevation gain. Trailhead: Peyto Lake at Km 40.* Leads up to a former fire lookout and gets you away from the crowds below. Commanding views take in the many lofty peaks and offer another perspective on the fabulous Bow Lake.

Sunset Pass Trail ① *16.4 km return; 725 m elevation gain. Trailhead: just north of Rampart Creek at Km 89.* This long expanse of meadows is usually snow-free by late June but can be very wet and is prime grizzly habitat. The landscape climaxes at the north end with views of the deep-blue Lake Pinto.

Nigel Pass Trail ① *14.4 km return; 365 m elevation gain. Trailhead: Km 113.* A gentle hike offering constant expansive views. At the pass, look beyond to the more starkly beautiful, formidable peaks of the upper Brazeau Valley. This is the opening section of a multi-day trek to Jonas Pass and Poboktan Pass (80 km return, 1913 m elevation gain).

Among the best long hikes in the range, this network of trails presents many options and factors that require thought and research. The highlight of the trip is Jonas Pass, an 11-km high meadow valley with pristine mountain scenery. Poboktan Pass is also a delight to explore but both the loop via Brazeau Lake and the one-way exit along Poboktan Creek have major drawbacks. Better is to camp at Jonas Cutoff, day-hike to Poboktan Pass, pass another night at the Cutoff, then hike out the same way. The lack of camping throughout Jonas Pass means either hiking 33 km to the Cutoff campground, then 33km out on the third day, or breaking the journey by camping at Four Point (14 km), making it a five-day trip.

Parker Ridge Trail ① *4.8 km return; 270 m elevation gain. Trailhead: Km 117*. A hike whose rewards far outweigh the effort expended. Breathtaking views take in the awesome expanse of the 9 km-long Saskatchewan Glacier, the longest tongue of the Columbia Icefield.

Wilcox Pass Trail ① *8 km return; 335 m elevation gain. Trailhead: just south of Wilcox Creek campground*. A short and easy hike that everybody should do, quickly leading to views that many longer hikes fail to equal. After a brief ascent through mature forest, the Columbia Icefield is suddenly visible in all its glory. Wild flower meadows and resident bighorn sheep complete the idyllic picture. With so much to be gained from so little effort, don't expect to be alone.

● Sleeping

Banff Townsite *p273, map p274*
Accommodation in Banff is overpriced and heavily booked. On midsummer weekends, every single bed and vehicle-accessible campsite in the park will often be full, so reservations are strongly recommended. You can book through **Banff Accommodation**, T1877-226 3348, www.banffinfo.com. If you turn up without a reservation, head straight for the Visitor Centre; they know exactly what is left. To plan ahead, check www.banfflakelouise.com, which has full details and links for just about everywhere in town.
AL-B Banff Boutique Inn, 121 Cave Av, T403-762 4636, www.banffboutiqueinn.com. A very beautiful house with hardwood floors. Most of the 10 rooms have an en suite bath, half have mountain views and some have fireplaces, prices vary accordingly. Guests enjoy a common room and a front terrace with a fireplace. Breakfast included.
B The Driftwood Inn, 337 Banff Av, T403-762 4496, www.bestofbanff.com. Reasonable, fairly spacious rooms with pine furnishings. Guests are allowed to use the spa and fitness room of the **Ptarmigan Inn**.
B Mountain Home B&B, 129 Muskrat St, T403-762 3889, www.mountainhomebb.com. 3 nice en suite rooms and a common room in a renovated 1940's home with antique furnishings.
B-C Blue Mountain Lodge, 137 Muskrat St, T403-762 5134, www.bluemtnlodge.com. 10 small but attractive en suite rooms in a centrally located turn-of-the-20th-century building with period decor and a shared lounge and kitchen.
C Bumpers Inn, 603 Banff Av/Marmot Cres, T403-762 3386, www.bumpersinn.com. Fairly nice, spacious rooms. Situated on the edge of town and quiet as a result, with forest at the back which can be enjoyed from the courtyard deck or 2nd floor balconies.
C Rocky Mountain B&B, 223 Otter St, T403-762 4811, www.rockymtnbb.com. 9 decent rooms and a large suite in a 1918 house. Shared common room has a historic feel.
D Tan-Y-Bryn, 118 Otter St, T403-762 3696, www.tan-y-bryn.zip411.net. 8 no-frills rooms at a great price.
D-E Banff Y Mountain Lodge, 102 Spray Av, T403-762 3560, www.ymountainlodge.com. A cheap, reliable option by the river at the pretty end of town. They have dorms and private rooms, a pleasant common room, kitchen, laundry, internet access and a bistro with an outdoor patio.
D-E HI Banff Alpine Centre, 801 Coyote Dr, Tunnel Mountain Rd, T403-762 4122,

www.hihostels.ca. 3 km from town but
the Transit Bus passes by. The best budget
option, with excellent facilities and plenty
of choice. En suite rooms with a lounge area,
private rooms with shared bath, cabins that
sleep up to 5 or dorm rooms, some with en
suite. 2 kitchens, a common room, deck,
laundry, internet access, lockers, a pub,
gamehouse with a pool table, and a cheap
restaurant with good food and big portions.
They also have a 10 mice-climbing wall and
can organize activities. Be sure to book ahead.
D-E SameSun Banff Lodge, 449 Banff Av,
T403-762 5521, www.samesun.com.
Situated downtown, has more of a party
atmosphere than the HI. All beds are in
pleasant dorm rooms and there's a kitchen,
TV room, games room, internet, courtyard
with BBQ, hot tub, lockers, and activities
can be arranged.

Camping
There are 5 campgrounds around Banff
Townsite and sites can be reserved,
T1877-737 3783, www.pccamping.ca.
Tunnel Mountain I and **Tunnel
Mountain II**, Tunnel Mt Rd. Big and ugly
with 618 and 188 crowded sites respectively.
The latter is the only one open year-round.
Tunnel Mountain Trailer Court, Tunnel
Mt Rd. A big parking lot with full hook-ups
for RVs.
Two Jack Lakeside, 12 km northeast of
Banff, Lake Minnewaka Rd. The nicest by
far, with 74 sites including some tent-only
spots on the lake and showers.
Two Jack Main, across the road from **Two
Jack Lakeside**. Has 380 fairly nice sites.

Canmore *p278*
Canmore has a dearth of decent hotels but
there are dozens of nice, reasonably priced
B&Bs. Many are close to Downtown on 1st
and 2nd St. Call the **B&B Hotline**, T403-609
7224, www.bbcanmore.com, or check the
Information Centre website.
A-B The Georgetown Inn, 1101 Bow Valley
Trail, T403-678 3439, www.georgetowninn.
net. 20 lovely rooms in a wonderful tudor-
style inn with patios and gardens. Guest
lounge and an English-style restaurant/pub.
B By the Brook, 4 Birchwood Pl, T403-688
0031, www.bythebrookbandb.com. 2 big
en suite rooms in a beautiful house with

vaulted ceilings and big windows. 2 guest
lounges with TV, a sauna, hot tub and sundecks. Full breakfast included. Good value.
B Hogs & Quiches, 506 2nd St, T403-678
5091, www.canmorebedandbreakfast.com.
2 tastefully decorated rooms in a handsome
wood house on a residential street. Gourmet
breakfast included.
C Drake Inn, 909 Railway Av, T403-678 5131,
www.drakeinn.com. The best downtown
option by far. Rooms are above average,
with large windows. Those overlooking the
creek have private balconies. Downstairs is
a popular pub.
C Riverview & Main, 918-8 St, T403-678
9777, www.riverviewandmain.ca. 3 bright
and pleasant rooms with decks and mountain views. Very nice private sitting room.
D Bow Valley Motel, 610 Main St, T403-
678 5085, www.bowvalleymotel.com. A
very central location and reasonable rooms,
some with balconies. Outdoor hot tub.
E HI-Canmore Hostel, in the **Alpine Club** on
Indian Flats Rd, a short drive east, no public
transport, T403-678 3200, www.hihostels.ca.
Made up of 2 buildings, each one has its own
fully equipped kitchen, living room, fireplace,
deck and BBQ. Sauna, library and laundry
available in the main building.

Camping
Spray Lakes Campground, T1866-366
2267. 16 km south on a rough and sometimes steep dirt road, with no public
transport. A wonderful campground that
hugs the lakeside for 6 km, making for
private sites right on the crystal-clear lake
and surrounded by mountains.

Mount Assiniboine Provincial
Park *p279*
E Naiset Huts, Lake Magog, T403-678
2883. Bunk beds in this basic cabin can
be booked and you're advised to do so.
Despite the long walk, don't expect to
have the place to yourself.

Camping
Lake Magog Campground. The park's main
campground. There's a quieter one 6 km
north at Og Lake. $5 per night, cash only.

Bow Valley Parkway *p280*
L Castle Mountain Chalets, T403-522 2783,

www.castlemountain.com. Attractive pine or cedar chalets that could sleep 4, with kitchens, bathroom and wood-burning fireplaces. There's also an exercise room, steam room, library and laundry on site.
B Johnston Canyon Resort, T403-762 2971, www.johnstoncanyon.com. A good alternative to staying in Banff. Attractive, semi-rustic cabins and bungalows with showers and fireplaces, but they're far too close together. Large 2-bedroom cabins (**L**) are a good deal for 2 couples sharing, they're modern and fully equipped with kitchen, clawfoot tub, TV, porch and fireplace. On site dining room, coffee shop, BBQ area and tennis court.
E HI Castle Mountain Wilderness Hostel, T403-670 7580, www.hihostels.ca. A fairly basic but picturesque little hostel with 28 dorm beds, laundry, kitchen and a cosy common room with a wood-burning fireplace and bay windows.

Camping
Castle Mountain Campground. With just 43 sites, this is one of the smaller, nicer sites in the park. No showers.
Johnston Canyon Campground , has showers and 140 not very private sites, but it's a great location.

Lake Louise *p281*
LL Skoki Lodge, T1800-258 7669, www.skoki.com. The only way to the lodge is by skiing or hiking an 11 km trail that starts behind the ski resort. The lodge has rooms and cabins but no electricity or running water. The price ($159 per person in winter, $194 per person in summer) includes a buffet-style breakfast and dinner. Sitting at 2000 m, surrounded by mountains, this is an excellent base for getting into the backcountry and has been used as such since the 1930s when it put Lake Louise on the Nordic ski map.
AL Mountaineer Lodge, 101 Village Rd, The Village, T403-522 3844, www.mountaineerlodge.com. The most reasonable of a hideously overpriced collection of hotels in the village. Spacious but fairly standard rooms, many with views. Also has hot tub and steam room.
AL-A Deer Lodge, 109 Lake Louise Dr, The Lake, T403-522 3747, www.crmr.com. Built in 'vintage national-park Gothic' style with

antique furnishings, this hotel has plenty of **287** character but its rooms are very small and rather ordinary. There's a rooftop hot tub and a decent but expensive restaurant with a patio.
C-D HI Lake Louise Alpine Centre, Village Rd, The Village T403-670 7580, www.hihostels.ca. A spacious, attractive, well-equipped hostel, with dorms and private double rooms, some with en suite bath. Facilities include 2 kitchens, laundry, library, lots of common places to relax, a sunny outdoor patio, fireplaces, internet, access to maps, storage and an excellent cheap restaurant. Some guided tours. Open year-round. Reservations well in advance are essential.

Camping
Lake Louise Tent, The Village, T403-522 3833, May-Sep. 220 not especially nice sites and showers.
Lake Louise Trailer, The Village, T403-522 3833, open year-round. 189 less pleasant sites designed for RVs, with hook-ups.

Icefields Parkway *p283*
L-AL Simpson's Num-Ti-Jah Lodge, T403-522 2167, www.num-ti-jah.com. In a prime location on the shore of Bow Lake, this octagonal construction was built in 1920 by Jimmy Simpson, a legendary pioneering guide. Age has lent a lot of charm to the rooms, which include some cheaper options with shared bath. There is a fine restaurant, a library with fireplace, and a lounge with pool table. Its popularity is a little off-putting and makes advance booking a necessity.
B The Crossing, Saskatchewan Crossing, T403-761 7000, www.thecrossingresort.com. An overpriced but heavily booked motel with an exercise room, hot tub, laundry and internet access. There's also a fast-food cafeteria, restaurant, grocery store and a tacky gift shop.
E Mosquito Creek Hostel, Km 28, T403-670 7580, www.hihostels.ca. 20 dorm beds and a few private rooms in 4 log cabins nicely situated by the creek. Rustic, with no electricity or running water but with a kitchen, a cosy common room and sauna.
E Rampart Creek Hostel, Km 89, T403-670 6580, www.hihostels.ca. 24 beds in 2 cabins. Rustic, with no running water or electricity

but a small kitchen, common room and sauna. Popular in winter, with over 150 ice climbs within 30 mins drive.

Camping
Mosquito Creek Campground, at Km 28. A small, basic year-round campground with 38 sites, of which 20 are walk-in only.
Rampart Creek Campground, at Km 89. Basic but pleasant, with 50 sites by the river.
Waterfowl Lake Campground, at Km 57. 116 nice sites close to the lake.

❼ Eating

Banff Townsite *p273, map p274*
Banff's expensive restaurants often have 'tasting menus' which are 4- to 8-course meals for around $90 per person.
Le Beaujolais, 212 Buffalo St, T403-762 2712. Very upmarket, with a dress code and an extensive wine list. The small French-inspired menu features game and seafood with delicious sauces, as well as favourites like stroganoff or steak-frites. 3-course 'prix fixe' menu for $72.
Fuze Finer Dining, 2nd Floor, 110 Banff Av, T403-760 0853. A dimly lit, warm, sophisticated and romantic venue for Banff's most exciting food. Fine dining with a pan-global approach. A very intelligent wine list.
Grizzly House, 207 Banff Av, T403-762 4055. A good choice for something fun and highly unusual. An absurd selection of meats is offered, mostly game, with even more exotic choices like rattlesnake, alligator and shark, cooked at your table in fondues or on hot rocks. Great service, but small portions and very expensive.
Caramba!, 337 Banff Av, T403-762 3667. Home-made pasta with innovative toppings, wood oven pizza, free range chicken. Nice patio, but the lounge is more intimate.
Coyotes, 206 Caribou St, T403-762 3963. Sophisticated southwest-style food such as orange chipotle prawns, nicely spicy and very tasty. Subtle decor with an open kitchen. A great breakfast option, too.
Maple Leaf Grille,137 Banff Av, T403-760 7680. The inviting lodge-style interior concentrates on Canadiana, with lots of wood and leather, and a genuine birch-bark canoe. The menu features lots of seafood, game, steak, pasta and other

favourites, while the comfy lounge is a good spot for a quiet drink. Great views from the dining room and a neat little coffee corner.
Sukiyaki House, 2nd floor, 211 Banff Av, T403-762 2002. Sushi, hot pot and other Japanese favourites, including all-you-can-eat options. Classic decor, including intimate tatami rooms.
Aardvark Pizza & Sub, 304 Caribou St, open till 0400. Take-out menu, good pizzas.
Craig's Way Station, 461 Banff Av, T403-762 4660. A great breakfast choice. Big portions of home-cooked food at reasonable prices. Friendly and popular with locals.
Evelyn's Coffee Bar, 201 Banff Av, T403-762 0352. Good coffee and great light food, from sandwiches to rhubarb pie.
Sundance Bistro, at the Banff Y Mountain Lodge. A charming bistro with an outdoor patio, serving wraps and salads and the best value breakfast in town.

Canmore *p278*
Murrieta's Bar & Grill, 737 Main St, T403- 609 9500. With its hardwood floors, big windows and elegant long bar, the atmosphere is sophisticated and the menu features seafood, pasta and European-style fine dining choices. A locals' favourite for years, it's also a great place for a drink with a good selection of wines and cocktails.
Tapas Restaurant, 633 10th St, T403-609 0583. With much more than just tapas on the menu, this is the real deal. Impressively broad menu of very authentic Spanish and Portuguese dishes, exquisitely prepared and presented. Live flamenco Thu and Fri nights.
Chez Francois, 1604 Bow Valley Trail, T403-678 6111. Consistently excellent French cuisine with an emphasis on fresh ingredients, served in elegant surroundings with an inviting mahogany wine bar. Try the duck.
Crazy Weed Kitchen, 626 Main St, T403- 609 2530. This tiny place has a surprisingly eclectic international menu, from curries to tenderloin or scallops, all done to perfection. Everybody loves it, so reservations are recommended. Top notch espresso too.
Grizzly Paw Brewing Co, 622 Main St, T403-678 9983. Fine ales brewed on the premises, superior versions of casual pub

food like fish and chips, and burgers. A fantastic, busy patio in summer.

Quarry Bistro and Wine Bar, 718 Main St, T403-678 6088. Bright, airy, sophisticated and modern, with an open beams and a long bar. The menu focuses on French and Italian bistro cuisine, with an emphasis on the freshness of ingredients.

Sunfood Café Vegetarian food, 743 Railway Av, T403-609 2613. A friendly, relaxed spot for tasty and varied vegetarian dishes ranging from stir fries to Thai curry to stroganoff.

The Trough Dining Co, 725B 9th St, T403-678 2820. A small house with an elegant, intimate interior and a contemporary West Coast menu that is innovative, ambitious and cosmopolitan.

Zona's Late Night Bistro, 7109th St, T403-609 2000. Situated in a cosy house decorated with eccentric pieces of art and with a garden courtyard, this is our favourite and is understandably very popular. The food is international, creative and perfectly executed. Try the Moroccan lamb and molasses curry. After the kitchen closes, drinks and tapas are available till late.

The Coffee Mine, 802 Main St, T403-678 2241. Coffee, snacks and outdoor seating.

The Summit Café, 1001 Cougar Creek Dr. Great Canadian and Mexican breakfasts. Organic coffee.

Bow Valley Parkway *p280*
Baker Creek Bistro, at the Baker Creek Chalets, T403-522 2182. Very good food, with a pleasant patio and a licensed lounge.

Lake Louise *p281*
Deer Lodge, Upper Lake Louise, T403-522 3747. 'Rocky Mountain Cuisine' such as elk and wild mushrooms. Great patio.
Lake Louise Station, 200 Sentinel Rd in the Village, T403-522 2600. The interior is very nice, with lots of wood, high ceilings and big windows, and there's a lovely garden patio with BBQ in the summer. In a good location and is a fine spot for a drink. The menu is fairly small but varied, ranging from gourmet burger to the duck confit.

Bill Peyto's Café, at the HI Alpine Centre. Cafeteria-style, good-value large portions, with great breakfasts, pasta and salads.
Laggan's Bakery, in Samson Mall, T403-522 3791. Good bakery items and cheap sandwiches to go.
Village Grill and Bar, in Samson Mall, T403-522 3879. Family-style joint with all-day breakfast, sandwiches, burgers, BBQ, Chinese food and some more expensive options.

Icefields Parkway *p283*
Num-Ti-Jah Lodge (see Sleeping). The famous lodge has a good fine dining restaurant and a lounge.
The Crossing, at Saskatchewan Crossing (see 284). Contains a fast-food cafeteria and a second-rate restaurant.
Icefield Centre (see page 297). An over-priced Chinese restaurant and a hamburger/hotdog cafeteria.

Bars and clubs

Banff Townsite *p273, map p274*
Aurora Night Club, 110 Banff Av, T403-760 5300. Combines heaving DJ-led dance floor action with an elegant martini bar. The best place for dancing.
Hoodoo Lounge, 137 Banff Av. An energetic, somewhat youthful spot for DJs, live music or drink specials every night.
The Lik Lounge, 221 Bear St, T403-762 2467. A lounge-style joint with cheap martinis after 2130, bands on Thu and DJs on Sun.
Rose & Crown, upstairs at 202 Banff Av, T403-762 2121. Varied live bands every night, a good atmosphere, decent pub food.
St James's Gate Olde Irish Pub, 207 Wolf St, T403-762 9355. Banff's most appealing pub, with 33 beers on tap, 30 malt whiskeys and upscale pub food. Really does feel like an Irish pub.
Waldhaus Pub, downstairs behind the Banff Springs Hotel, T403-762 6860. An authentic German-style boozer with low ceilings and Becks on tap. A good pub menu that features fondues from the more highbrow restaurant upstairs.

For an explanation of sleeping and eating price codes used in this guide, see inside the front cover. Other relevant information is found in Essentials, see pages 28-31.

Wild Bill's Legendary Saloon, 2nd floor, 201 Banff Av, www.wbsaloon.com. An attractive saloon-style setting, with different live music almost every night, that doesn't necessarily entail line dancing. Large portions of Western and Tex-Mex and an inviting a patio.

Canmore *p278*
Bandoleer's, Deadman's Flats, 5 mins east of Canmore, T403-609 3006. A Tex-Mex restaurant with live jazz and blues on Fri and Sat nights.
The Drake Inn, 909 Railway Av, T403-678 5131. Canmore's most popular night spot, with live bands on weekends and generous portions of pub fare.
Grizzly Paw Brewing Co, 622 Main St, T403-678 9983. The obvious pub of choice, with beers brewed on the premises and a summer patio.
Rose and Crown, 749 Railway Av, T403-678 5168. 14 beers on tap and a patio. Popular with locals, offers decent pub grub.

😃 Entertainment

Banff Townsite *p273, map p274*
Banff Centre for the Arts, 107 Tunnel Mountain Dr, T403-762 6281, www.banff centre.ca. One of the most highly respected art schools in North America, organizing all sorts of cultural events, including art exhibitions, theatre, dance, cabaret and regular music of all genres, including some big names. Their **Walter Phillips Gallery**, is open Wed-Sun daily 1200-1700, free.
Canada House Gallery, 201 Bear St, T403-762 3757, www.canadahouse.com, Sun-Thu daily 0930-1800, Fri-Sat daily 0930-2100. One of Alberta's most important private galleries, representing dozens of Canadian artists and sculptors for over 30 years.
Lux Cinema Theatre, 229 Bear St, T403-762 8595.

😃 Festivals and events

Banff Townsite *p273, map p274*
Jan Winter Festival, 6 days in late Jan, featuring the Mountain Madness Relay race and numerous winter-related events.
Jan-Mar Banff Winter Arts Festival, this is organized by the Banff Centre,

www.banffcentre.ca. Lots of music, exhibitions and events.
May Rocky Mountain Wine and Food Festival, www.rockymountainwine.com/ banff. For one day at the end of May, hosted by the Banff Springs Hotel.
May-Aug Banff Summer Arts Festival, organized and partly hosted by the Banff Centre, www.banffcentre.ca. Includes the Jazz Festival, cabarets, dance, opera, literary events, lots of music, art walks, exhibitions and lectures. Much of it is free and many events take place at the Central Park Gazebo, downtown.
May-Jun Art Banff Jazz Festival, attracts some big names, with Dave Douglas a regular contributor.
Oct-Nov Banff Mountain Film and Book Festival, showcases the best 50-60 films worldwide in mountain subjects, including alpinism, culture, environment and sport. The top 20 will then tour the rest of Canada and abroad.

Canmore *p278*
Jun ArtsPeak Arts Festival, www.artspeak canmore.com. 3 days in mid-June, featuring an Art Walk, street performers, films, art sales, competitions and musical events
Aug Canmore Folk Music Festival, T403-6782524, www.canmorefolkfestival.com. Held on the first weekend of the month, this is the town's main annual event, with lots of acts outside in Centennial Park. A 3-day pass $66 in advance, $80 at the gate.

🛍 Shopping

Banff Townsite *p273, map p274*
All along Banff Av are the often tacky gift shops offering souvenirs such as smoked salmon (which keeps well), maple syrup and copies of Aboriginal art.
Banff Book and Art Den, 94 Banff Av, T403-762 3919, in the Banff Springs. Big selection of outdoor recreation guides.
Friends of Banff, 224 Banff Av, T403-762 8918. Educational books and maps. All profits go to Banff Park.
The Glacier Shop, 317 Banff Av, T403-760 5130. Outdoor clothing, sports gear and ski equipment.
Mountain Magic Equipment, 224 Bear St, T403-762 2591. Massive selection of

outdoor gear. Rentals for camping, climbing and biking.

Standish Home Hardware, 223 Bear St, T403-762 2080. Good for camping gear.

Weeds and Seeds, 211 Bear St, T403-760 5060. A health food shop offering bulk organic goodies.

Canmore *p278*

The Second Story Used Books, 713 Main St, T403-609 2368. Stock up here because second-hand bookshops in the Rockies are a rarity.

Sobeys, 950 Railway Av, in front of the IGA supermarket, T403-678 6326. The perfect place to stock up on healthy camping food.

Sports Consignment, 718 – 10th St, T403-678 1992. Good deals on used sports or camping equipment.

Valhalla Pure, 726 Main St, T403-678 5610. Camping gear and sports equipment.

Lake Louise *p281*

Village Grocery, Samson Mall. Overpriced, but essential for stocking up on food for your trip.

Wilson Mountain Sports Ltd, in the Village, T403-522 3636, www.lakelouisewilsons.com. Bike rental for $39 per day. Climbing equipment, camping and fishing gear to buy or rent.

▲ Activities and tours

Banff Townsite *p273, map p274*
Boat tours

Lake Minnewanka Boat Tours, T403-762 3473, www.minnewankaboattours.com. Glass enclosed boat tours, $40, $20 child,for 1½- hrs. May-Oct 5 tours a day from 1000. Also boat rentals ($100/half day, $120/day) and fishing charters ($500/day for 1 or 2).

Canoeing and kayaking

Blue Canoe Rentals, at Bow River Canoe Docks, end of Wolf St. Canoe or kayak rentals, including all equipment, basic instruction, safety tips and a route map. Paddling is also possible on Two Jack Lake, Vermilion Lakes, Echo Creek and 40 Mile Creek.

Climbing and ice climbing

Yamnuska Mountain Adventures, T403-678 4164, www.yamnuska.com. A range

of guided mountain trips with experienced experts: climbing, mountaineering, ice climbing, hiking and backcountry skiing.

Dog sled tours

Howling Dog Tours, T403-678 9588, www.howlingdogtours.com.

Snowy Owl Sled Dog Tours, T403-678 4369, www.snowyowltours.com.

Fishing

Banff Fishing Unlimited, T403-762 4936, www.banff-fishing.com. The largest guiding and outfitting company in the region. Lake Minnewanka and the Upper Bow River are obvious local sites. They also do ice fishing. Gear and licences can be obtained from **Lake Minnewanka Boat Tours** (see above).

Helicopter tours

Icefield Helicopter Tours, T403-721 2100, www.icefieldheli.com. Sightseeing tours of the icefields and glaciers, from $155 per person for 20 mins.

Hiking and Ice Canyon tours

Great Divide Nature Interpretation, T403-522 2735, www.greatdivide.ca. Daily inter- pretive hikes and walks led by naturalists.

White Mountain Adventures, T403-678 4099, www.whitemountainadventures.com. Tours through thefrozen waterfalls of Johnston Canyon, highly recommended ($330 for up to 6 people). They also give skiing lessons, run wildlife walks in snowshoes and heritage tours of the Townsite.

Willow Root Nature Tours, T403-762 4335. Walks and hikes with full interpretation from a professional naturalist.

Horse riding

Trail Rider Store, 132 Banff Av, T403-762 4551, www.horseback.com. Arrange horse riding from their two local stables, 1-3 hr trips or multi-day rides using their lodges as bases, or sleeping in tents. Also covered wagon rides or horse-drawn sleigh rides in winter.

Ice-skating

Outdoor skating is possible on **Bow River**, end of Wolf St; **Banff High School**, Banff Av and Wolf St; and **Banff Springs Hotel**.

There's an indoor rink at **Banff Recreation Centre**, Mt Norquay Rd, T403-762 1235.

Mountain biking

Mountain biking is possible on many of the local trails, though **Lake Louise** is better and **Canmore** is better still. Highest calibre is the **Brewster Creek Trail** which extends the Sundance/Healy Creek trails from Cave and Basin Hot Springs to a possible 37-km one-way ride to Allenby Pass. An exciting 5.2-km downhill run is the **Lower Stoney Squaw** at Mt Norquay Ski Area. The **Rundle Riverside** is a 14-km rollercoaster ride to Canmore Nordic Centre and more trails. Good gentle cycling can be had at Lake Minnewanka, Vermilion Lakes or Sundance Canyon.
Bactrax, 225 Bear St, T403-762 8177, www.snowtips-bactrax.com. Offers bike rentals and 1- or 2-hr tours ($20/40). They also provide shuttles to and from trailheads.
The Ski Stop, 203A Bear St, T403-760 1650, www.theskistop.com. Run a number of bike tours, easy or hard, including a backcountry shuttle and ride package. Also rent bikes, skis, snowboards and winter equipment.

Rafting

Hydra River Guides, T403-762 4554, www.raftbanff.com. Whitewater rafting trips on the Kicking Horse River; gentle (75 mins, $69/44), medium (2-2½ hrs, $105) and intense (3½ hrs, $149). Also packages combining rafting with other activities.

Rentals

Whatever you need – skis, snowboards, ice skates, snowshoes, sleds, hiking boots, tents, sleeping bags, mopeds, rafts, climbing or fishing gear – you're likely to find it at **Bactrax**, 225 Bear St, T403-762 8177, www.snowtips-bactrax.com or the following:
Monod Sports, 129 Banff Av, T403-762 4571, www.monodsports.com Also sell men's and women's outdoor clothing.
Mountain Magic Equipment, 224 Bear St, T403-762 2591, www.mountainmagic.com.
Performance Sports, 1st Floor, 208 Bear St, T403-762 8222.

Skiing

Banff is very much a year-round resort, with 2 ski hills right on its doorstep. As well as the excellent Sunshine Village Ski Area, 18 km southwest of Banff off Hwy 1 (see page 279), there's Mt Norquay Ski Area, just 6 km to the north (see page 280).

Many local trails are groomed in winter for cross-country skiing. Pick up the *Nordic Trails* pamphlet from the Visitor Centre.

Tour operators

Banff Adventures Unlimited, 211 Bear St, T403-762 4554, www.banffadventures.com and **Discover Banff Tours Ltd**, T403-760 1299, www.banfftours.com. These 2 giants can set you up with any of the activities available within the park, including ATV tours, boat cruises, cave tours on Grotto Mountain, helicopter tours, hiking, horse-back riding, kayaking, rock climbing, sightseeing, wildlife viewing, skiing, dogsledding, heli- skiing, ice-climbing, sleighing, snowmobiling, snowshoeing and the list goes on.
Brewster, 100 Gopher St, T403-760 6934, www.sightseeingtourscanada.com. Sightseeing tours in a motorcoach to just about every destination in the Rockies.
Moose Travel Network , www.moosenetwork.com As well as arranging budget hop-on hop-off trips from Vancouver, they run a few trips from Banf, including a 2-day ($139) and 4-day ($250) trip to Jasper and a 2-day tour to Calgary, Drumheller and Head-Smashed-In-Buffalo Jump ($139).
True North Tours, T403-934 5972, www.back-packertour.com/truenorthtours. In association with HI, they offer 3- to 10-day tours of the Rockies in a 15-passenger van from Banff or Calgary, including accommodation in hostels and most meals. Usually they head up to Jasper and/or down to Waterton. The 6-day Rocky Express costs $550. A great way to go.

Canmore *p278*
Birdwatching
Halfway to Heaven Bird-Watching, T403-673 2542.

Caving

Canmore Caverns, T403-678 8819, www.canadianrockies.net/wildcave tours. Caving tours of Rat's Nest Cave under Grotto Mountain. Trips last 4½-6 hrs, no experience necessary.

Climbing

This is Canmore's local speciality. There are climbs at Grassi Lakes, Yamanuska, on Hwy 1A E and Cougar Canyon for a more challenging climb.

Alpine Club, T403-678 3200, www.alpine clubofcanada.ca. The best place for advice and to find out about mountain huts.

Yamnuska Mountain Adventures, T403-678 4164, www.yamnuska.com. Ice and rock climbing, backcountry skiing, mountaineering lessons and tours.

Cross-country skiing

Canmore Nordic Centre, off Spray Lakes Rd, well signposted from town, T403-678 2400, has some of the best trails in the Rockies and hosts various events.

Trail Sports, within the centre, www.trail sports.ab.ca. Rentals, lessons, tours and trail information.

Hiking

Access to excellent long-distance hikes, mostly in the south of Banff Park, is via Spray Lakes Rd and its extension, the Smith-Dorrien Hwy, a distance of some 40 km. Follow signs to the Nordic Centre and keep going up the steep, rough road, ignoring the right turn to Spray Lakes camp-ground. Local hikes include the Three Sisters area and Ha Ling Peak, across from the Goat Creek parking lot, both on Spray Lakes Rd; Grotto Mountain is accessed from the Alpine Club.

Horse riding

Cross Zee Ranch, T403-678 4171, www.cana dianrockies.net/crosszeeranch. Day horse riding trips.

Mountain biking

There are excellent networks of trails at Mt Shark and Mud Lake, both on the Smith-Dorrien Hwy and much closer at Canmore Nordic Centre.

Rebound Cycle, 902 Main St, T403-678 3668, www.reboundcycle.com. Bike rentals from $30-70 and the best place for local trail information.

Rafting

Canadian Rockies Rafting Co, T403- 678 6535; www.rafting.ca. Whitewater rafting for all ages and abilities on the Bow, Kananaskis and Kicking Horse Rivers.

Canmore Rafting Centre, 20 Lincoln Park, T403-678 4919, www.canmoreraftingcentre .com. 1½-hr floats down the Bow ($49), 3-hr trips on the gentle Kananaskis ($75) or more thrilling Lower Bow ($85) and longer trips down the Kicking Horse or Red Deer. Also canoe and kayak rentals and hiking and sightseeing trips.

Rentals

Gear Up, 1302 Bow Valley Trail, T403-678 1636, www.gearupsport.com. Your best bet for all rentals, including bikes, canoes, kayaks, climbing and camping gear, skis, snowboards, skates and snowshoes.

Lake Louise p281
Horse riding

Timberline Tours, T403-522 3743, www.tim berlinetours.ca. Horse riding trips starting from the corral behind Deer Lodge. 10 mins for $12, 3 hrs for $75, 1 day for $130), then anything up to 10 days. They will drop off or pick up at Skoki Lodge ($130 per person).

Lake sports

Canoes can be rented at both lakes. When the lake gets cold enough it provides an idyllic location for skating.

Brewsters, T403-522 3522, www.brewster. ca. Organizes sleigh rides on the lake when it is adequately frozen.

Monod Sports, in Château Lake Louise, T403-522 3628, www.monodsports.com, daily 0800-2100. Rents skates and skis.

Mountain biking

Some local trails are ideal for riding. The 14.6-km return Ross Lake Trail starts behind the Château and leads through forest to a small lake beneath a steep rockwall. The more demanding 10-km Moraine Lake High-line leads from the Paradise Valley trailhead to the scenic lake; sometimes closed due to grizzly activity. The 13.4-km Pipestone Trail starts off Slate Rd just west of the Village and follows the Pipestone River to the valley. The 7-km Bow River Loop is a gentle trail on both sides of the river. The 10.5-km one-way Great Divide Path is a paved but traffic-free route starting at Km 3.6 on Lake Louise Dr and ending at Hwy 1 in Yoho.

Rentals

Wilson Mountain Sports , in the Village, T403-522 3636, www.lakelouisewilsons. com. Rents bikes, fishing rods, climbing, mountaineering and camping gear, skis, snowboards, skates and snowshoes.

Skiing

As well as top notch downhill skiing at Lake Louise Ski Area, there is fine cross-country skiing in the Skoki Valley, around the picturesque log Skoki Lodge.

◉ Transport

Banff Townsite *p273, map p274*
Bus
Banff Transit, T403-762 1200, runs 2 bus routes. One connects the Banff Springs Hotel with the Tunnel Mountain Trailer Court; another connects the Luxton Museum with the campgrounds on Tunnel Mountain Rd. Both run along Banff Av, $2, child $1.

Greyhound, T1800-661 8747, www.grey hound.ca, runs 5 daily buses to **Calgary** via the airport (1½ -2½ hrs, $24), 4 to Canmore (25 mins, $9), 4 to Lake Louise (45 mins, $14), 3 to Jasper (12½-14½ hrs, $106), 3 to Field (75 mins, $18), 2 direct to Kamloops (7½ hrs, $76) and 4 direct to Vancouver (13- 15 hrs, $117). Brewster, T1800-760 6934, www.brewster.ca, runs daily buses from Banff to Lake Louise ($18) and Jasper ($77).

Rail
Rocky Mountain Rail Tours, T1877-460 3200, www.rockymountaineer.com. Prohibitively expensive, though admittedly spectacular, rail trips from **Vancouver** to **Banff** or **Jasper**, with an option to continue on to **Calgary**. High season prices start at $809 one-way for 2 days and 1 night.

Taxi
Banff Taxi, 103 Owl St, T403-762 4444.

Vehicle rental
Budget Car & Truck Rental, 202 Bear St, T403-762 4565, www.budget.com.

Canmore *p278*
Bus
The **Greyhound** station is at 701 Bow Valley Trail, T403-678 0832, www.greyhound.ca, with 4 daily buses to **Calgary** and **Banff**. All 3 shuttle services stop here on the way from Banff to Calgary. Sun Dog Tours, T1888-786 3641, www.sundogtours.com, run regular shuttles from Calgary Airport to Canmore, continuing to Lake Louise ($65, child $39) and Jasper ($105, child $65).

Taxi
VIP Taxi, T403-678 5811.

Lake Louise *p281*
Taxi
Lake Louise taxi and Tours, in the Samson Mall, T403-522 2020.

❶ Directory

Banff Townsite *p273, map p274*
Banks Bank of Montreal, 107 Banff Av, T403-762 2275. **Emergencies** Banff Warden Office T403-762 4506; Police, T403-762 2226; Medical and Fire T403-762 2000. **Internet** Cyberweb Internet Café, 215 Banff Av, T403-762 9226; Library is cheaper. **Laundry** Cascade Coin Laundry, 317 Banff Av, T403-762 3444. **Library** 101 Bear St, T403-762 2661. **Medical services** Alpine Medical Clinic, 211 Bear St, T403-762 3155; Mineral Springs Hospital, 305 Lynx St, T403-762 2222. **Post office** Canada Post, 204 Buffalo St, T403-762 2586.

Canmore *p278*
Bank Bank of Montreal, 701 8th St, T403-678 5568; Royal Bank, 1000 Railway Av, T403-678 3180. **Internet** Free at the library. Two Moose Internet Cafe, 717 10th St, T403-609 2678. **Library** 950 8th Av, T403-678 2468. **Medical services** Canmore General Hospital, 1100 Hospital Pl, T403-678 7200. **Post office** Canada Post, 801 Main St, T403-678 4377.

Lake Louise *p281*
Internet Samson Mall has internet and ATMs. **Medical services** Lake Louise Medical Clinic, 200 Hector St, T403-522 2184.

Jasper National Park and around

Jasper National Park feels much closer to wilderness than Banff. Neither as famous nor as convenient to reach, it receives far fewer visitors and has 10,878 sq km over which to spread them, an area bigger than Banff, Yoho and Kootenay National Parks combined. Vast tracts of this land are extremely remote and practically inaccessible, the overall emphasis being less on instant gratification, more on the long backcountry hikes that account for much of Jasper's 1000 km of trails. Apart from those on the Icefields Parkway, most of these are close to the pleasant town of Jasper, or around the attractive Maligne Lake, 48 km away. ▸▸ *For Sleeping, Eating and other listings, see pages 302-307.*

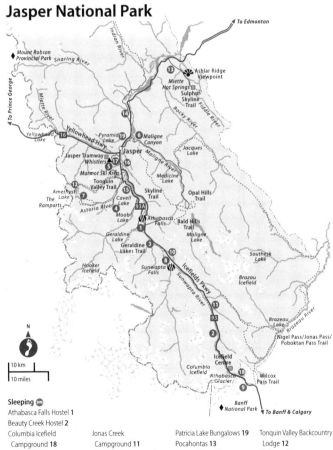

Jasper National Park

Sleeping 🛏

Athabasca Falls Hostel 1	Jonas Creek	Patricia Lake Bungalows 19	Tonquin Valley Backcountry
Beauty Creek Hostel 2	Campground 11	Pocahontas 13	Lodge 12
Columbia Icefield	Maligne Canyon Hostel 6	Snaring River 14	Wabasso 15
Campground 18	Mount Edith Cavell	Sunwapta Falls Resort 8	Wapiti 16
Columbia Icefield Chalet 9	Hostel 4	Tonquin Amethyst Lake	Whistlers 17
Honeymoon Lake	Mount Kerkeslin	Lodge 7	Wilcox Creek
Campground 10	Campground 3		Campground 18
Jasper International			
Hostel 5			

Canadian Rockies Jasper National Park & around

Ins and outs

Getting there and around

The airport closest to Jasper is in **Edmonton (YEG)** ① *www.edmontonairports.com*, 370 km to the west, about four hours' drive. The **Sky Shuttle** ① *T780-465 8515*, *www.edmontonskyshuttle.com*, *$15*, runs from the airport to the **Greyhound station** ① *10324 103rd St, T780-413 8747*, from where there are four buses daily to Jasper (five hours, $61). Trains run from the **Via Rail station** ① *12360 121st St*, to Jasper three times a week (five hours, $127); to get there take a taxi.

Note that **Calgary Airport** (see page 257) is not much further, just 412 km south of Jasper and the journey is infinitely more exciting. **Sun Dog Tours** and **Brewster** run shuttles from the airport, also picking up at Banff and Lake Louise, December to April only. The 281-km journey from Banff to Jasper is spectacular and for the best views, sit on the left-hand side. There are few services along what remains a region of extreme wilderness. Road closures are common from October to April after heavy snow. If cycling, note that Jasper is 500 m higher than Banff, so the journey is better made from north to south. Bikes can be rented in Jasper for one-way trips.

Jasper's train and bus stations are in the same attractive building, downtown at 607 Connaught Street. **Greyhound** ① *T780-852 3926, www.greyhound.ca*, runs regular daily buses from Edmonton, Vancouver via Kamloops and Prince George. **VIA Rail** operates three trains per week from Edmonton and Vancouver and Prince Rupert via Prince George. **The Rocky Mountaineer train** ① *T604-606 7245*, takes two days from Vancouver with a night in Kamloops, a beautiful journey. ➤ *For further details, see Transport, page 306.*

Tourist information

The **Visitor Information Centre** ① *T780-852 6176, T780-852 6177 for trail information, www.jaspercanadianrockies.com, Apr-Jun daily 0900-1700, Jun-Sep daily 0830-1900, Oct daily 0900-1700, Nov-Mar daily 0900-1600* and **Parks Canada** ① *T708-852 6288, www.pc.gc.ca/jasper, Jul-Sep daily 0830-1700, Apr-Jun daily 0900-1700, Sep-Oct daily 0900-1800, Nov-Mar daily 0900-1600*, offices are situated in an attractive 1914 stone building in the city park at 500 Connaught Drive. They have information on accommodation and trails, issue Park and Wilderness passes and hand out a number of useful maps such as the *Backcountry Visitors' Guide*, the *Day-hiker's Guide* and a *Cycling Guide*. They also operate a voluntary safety registration system at 1000 and 1400. **Friends of Jasper National Park** ① *T780-852 4767, www.friendsofjasper.com*, run free guided walks around the townsite nightly during the summer and sell books and maps. There is also a Jasper National Park desk in the Icefield Centre (see page 297).

Columbia Icefield 🖥 ➤ *pp302-307. Colour map 2, B2.*

The northern hemisphere's most extensive glacial area south of the Arctic Circle, the Columbia Icefield provides a dramatic introduction to Jasper National Park. As well as feeding three giant watersheds, its melt waters are the source of some of the continent's mightiest rivers, including the Columbia, Saskatchewan and Athabasca and drain into three oceans, the Atlantic, Pacific and Arctic. The only other icefield of equal scope and importance in the world is in Siberia. Most of the icefield's staggering 325 sq km terrain is high in the mountains out of view, but three of the six major glaciers are clearly visible from the road, including the huge **Athabasca Glacier** ① *6 km long, 1 km wide and 100 m thick*, which you can walk or even be driven on.

The ultimate way to see this spectacle is from the **Wilcox Pass Trail** ① *8 km return, 335 m elevation gain*, that starts just south of Wilcox Creek Campground. This is one hike that everybody should do. Short and easy, it quickly whisks you to views that many longer hikes fail to equal. After a brief ascent through mature forest, the Columbia Icefield is suddenly visible in all its glory and from an angle far more gratifying than you'll get taking the Snocoach. Wild flower meadows and resident bighorn sheep complete the idyllic picture. With so much to be gained from so little effort, don't expect to be alone.

A joint venture by Brewster and Parks Canada, the **Icefield Centre** ① *T780-852 6288, www.columbiaicefield.com, Apr-Oct daily 0900-2100*, resembles an airport and totally takes the edge off the wondrous surroundings, although it is a fine vantage point from which to ogle the Athabasca Glacier. The Glacier Gallery contains well-mounted informative displays, explaining glaciation, the icefield and the stories behind it. The **Parks Canada desk** ① *May to mid-Oct daily 0900-1700, mid-Jun to Aug daily 0900-1800*, is helpful and can provide maps and leaflets for whichever park you are entering. **Brewster's Icefield Glacier Experience** tours take you onto the glacier in a specially built bus (see page 305). Don't be tempted to walk on the glacier alone: people are killed and injured every year. Either they fall into one of its many crevasses, or injure themselves on the sharp sediment embedded in the ice.

North to Jasper → *Colour map 2, A2.*

Distances below are from the Columbia Icefield, where many people choose to turn round anyway: understandable, as it is the high point of the drive. After so much rich fare, the easy **Beauty Creek Trail** ① *3.6-km*, which starts 15.5 km to the north, provides a nice change. This tiny chasm and its chain of pretty scaled-down waterfalls can be an uplifting sight. The mountains along this stretch of highway are striated at a 45° angle and resemble cresting waves.

At 53 km, a side road leads to **Sunwapta Falls**, which are mostly interesting for the canyon they have carved through the valley. **Athabasca Falls**, some 25 km further, are less worth a stop. At this point Highway 93A, the old Parkway, branches off from Highway 93 and runs parallel for 30 km, providing access to a campground, a hostel, Marmot Basin ski hill and a number of hikes.

Marmot Basin Ski Hill

① *T780-852 3816, www.skimarmot.com, late-Nov to late-Apr. Lift tickets are $66, under 18 $53, under 12 $24. A shuttle runs daily from Jasper hotels at 0800, 0930 and 1145.* Has a reputation for being one of the most spacious, friendly and uncrowded ski hills in the country. It receives 400 cm of powder per year, with no need for snow-makers. Nine lifts service 84 trails on 678 ha of skiable terrain, which breaks up into 30% beginner, 30% intermediate, 20% advanced and 20% expert. The top elevation is 2612 m, with a vertical drop of 914 m and a longest run of 5.6 km. There are three lodges, one at the base and two mid-mountain, with lounges, dining rooms, rentals and lessons.

Hikes from Highway 93A

Tonquin Valley ① *43-km loop; 920 m elevation gain.* The Tonquin Valley is one of Jasper's most popular backpack trips, leading to the beautiful Amethyst Lakes and an incredible 1000-m rock wall known as The Ramparts that shoots straight up from their shores. Before considering this hike, be aware that it could easily turn into a nightmare. There are two possible routes to the valley and both of them are used by operators whose horses churn up the trails. If it rains, or has done so in the last few days, the hike in is likely to be a long, frustrating trudge through ankle-deep mud. To do the trip by horse, see Activities and tours, page 305. If it's not raining, the mosquitoes and other biting insects are ferocious.

Astoria River Trail ① *7.2 km south on Parkway, turn west onto Highway 93A, continue 5.3 km south, then right onto Mt Edith Cavell Rd and 12.2 km to parking area just past the hostel, known as the Tonquin Expressway*. This is an easier, flatter route into the Valley.

Portal Creek Trail ① *2.5 km south on Highway 93A, right onto Marmot Basin Rd, 6.5 km to car park over Maccarib Pass (which is steeper but consequently offers better views and is a more staisfying route)*. Ideally, hike in on one and out the other, arranging a shuttle or hitching between trailheads. There are plenty of campsites to choose from, Surprise Point being a good choice. Reserve sites well in advance. Nearby is the Wates-Gibson Hut, reserved through the **Alpine Club of Canada** ① *T403-678 3200, www.alpineclubofcanada.ca*.

Eremite Valley, is the best day-hike side-trip, leading to more glacier-bearing peaks. In winter, you can ski 23 km into the valley and stay at the Tonquin Valley Backcountry Lodge or Tonquin Amethyst Lake Lodge.

Geraldine Lakes ① *10.5 km return to second lake, 13 km return to fourth lake; 407-497 m elevation gain. Trailhead: 1 km north of Athabasca Falls on Highway 93A, then 5.5 km up Geraldine Fire Rd*. The first lake is an easy hike to an unremarkable destination, but after that, things get more difficult and more rewarding. It's a fairly tough climb to the second and biggest lake with ridge top views and a waterfall as compensation. Beyond there is no trail and much bushwhacking to reach pristine pools set in wild, alpine meadows.

Cavell Meadows ① *8-km loop, 370 m elevation gain. Trailhead: 13 km south on Highway 93A, 14 km on Cavell Rd*. This easy hike leads to spectacular views of the giant Angel Glacier. In mid-summer, these are also some of the finest wild flower meadows in the Rockies. The pay-off is marching along with crowds of people.

Jasper Townsite ⊟𝟬𝟬𝟬⊛𝗢▲⊟𝟬 ➠ *pp302-307.*
Colour map 1, A2.

Jasper is a far more relaxed base than Banff, having managed to hold on to its small-town charm despite a turnover of some three million visitors per year. There is little in the way of out-of-control commercialism and not much to do. Almost everything is on Connaught Drive, the road in and out of town, or Patricia Drive, which runs parallel to it. The only possible 'sight' in town is the **Yellowhead Museum and Archives** ① *400 Pyramid Lake Rd, T780-852 3013, www.jaspermuseum.org, mid-May to mid-Sep daily 1000-1700, mid-Sep to mid-May Thu-Sun, $4, child $3*, with a number of predictable displays exploring the town's fur trade and railway and a temporary exhibition in the Showcase Gallery.

Around Jasper Townsite
There are many loop day-hikes around the Pyramid Bench area, some leading to Pyramid Lake. Start at the **Activity Centre** ① *401 Pyramid Lake Rd*, and climb up to the bench. The Old Fort Point is a 3.5-km return trail leading to marvellous views of Athabasca River and Jasper. Take Highway 93A from town to the Old Fort Point access road. Turn left and cross the iron bridge. You can continue from here on signposted No 7 trail to **Maligne Canyon** ① *9.5 km one-way*, and return along the river for an easy 20.7-km loop.

Just 5 km east of town on Lodge Road are **Annette Lake** and **Edith Lake**, whose shallow waters are the warmest around in summer, making their beaches very

popular for swimming and sunbathing. There is a wheelchair-accessible path around **299**
the former. The winding Pyramid Lake Road leads 8 km northwest of town to **Pyramid Lake** and **Patricia Lake**. Apart from good views of Pyramid Mountain, this duo offers a couple of alternatives to sleeping in Jasper, and fishing, boating and horse riding.

The longest and highest of its kind in Canada, **Jasper Tramway** ⓘ *3 km south on Hwy 93, then 4 km west on Whistler Mountain Rd, T780-852 3093, www.jasper tramway.com, Apr-May daily 1000-1700, May-Jun daily 0930-1830, Jul-Aug daily 0900-2000, Sep-Oct daily 1000-1700, $25, child $13, Sun Dog Tours run a shuttle $27, child $11,* takes seven minutes to climb 1000 m in 2.5 km. At the top are an expensive restaurant, an interpretive centre and excellent views. Expect queues in summer. A steep trail gains another 600 m to reach **Whistlers Summit** ⓘ *2470 m,* and even more awe-inspiring vistas as far as Mount Robson, 80 km away. There's a cafeteria at the top.

Maligne Lake

The busy Maligne (pronounced 'maleen') Lake Road branches off Highway 16 east of town, leading 48 km to the most popular attraction in the park, with a few major sights on the way. In summer it is perpetually crowded with a stream of vehicles. The Maligne Lake Shuttle makes the journey several times daily. **Maligne Canyon**, 11.5 km from Jasper, is a spectacular gorge, 55 m deep and almost narrow enough to jump across. A number of short walking trails and footbridges lead to viewpoints. Unfortunately, the area is far too busy and taking on the unpleasant feel of a tourist trap. The canyon is at its best in winter, when the water freezes into an ice palace with 30-m icefalls and incredible, blue-ice caves. In winter a few operators run three-hour tours, with crampons, head lamps and other equipment provided. There is a hostel here and the northern terminus of the famous Skyline Trail.

A further 21 km is **Medicine Lake**, whose water level fluctuates dramatically with the seasons because it fills and empties through sink-holes into an elaborate

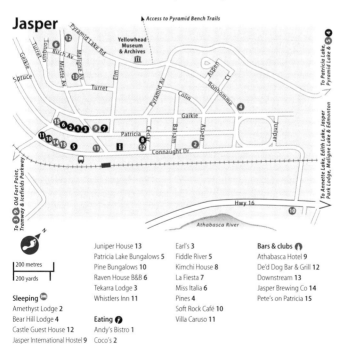

Jasper

Juniper House **13**
Patricia Lake Bungalows **5**
Pine Bungalows **10**
Raven House B&B **6**
Tekarra Lodge **3**
Whistlers Inn **11**

Sleeping 🛏
Amethyst Lodge **2**
Bear Hill Lodge **4**
Castle Guest House **12**
Jasper International Hostel **9**

Eating 🍴
Andy's Bistro **1**
Coco's **2**
Earl's **3**
Fiddle River **5**
Kimchi House **8**
La Fiesta **7**
Miss Italia **6**
Pines **4**
Soft Rock Café **10**
Villa Caruso **11**

Bars & clubs 🍸
Athabasca Hotel **9**
De'd Dog Bar & Grill **12**
Downstream **13**
Jasper Brewing Co **14**
Pete's on Patricia **15**

network of underground limestone caves. In summer the water is high, but in winter it sometimes disappears altogether. While such temporal variations fascinated Native Americans, the one-time visitor will see nothing but another lake.

At 22 km long, beautiful **Maligne Lake** is the largest lake in the Rockies and the second largest glacier-fed lake in the world. Surrounded by white-peaked mountains, it is a sight to behold, though not as overwhelming as Lake Louise. The best views open up from the middle of the lake, accessible on cruises and boat tours. Lots of hikes begin here, including the excellent Skyline Trail. For something shorter, the 3.2-km Schäffer Viewpoint loop leads along the east shore from Car Park 2. There is no accommodation at the lake apart from two backcountry campgrounds on the lakeshore that can only be reached by canoe (a four-hour trip) and must be booked at Jasper Information Centre. ➤➤ *For further details, see Activities and tours, page 305.*

Hikes from Maligne Lake

Skyline ① *44.5 km; 820 m elevation gain.* This is one of the all-time great backpack trips, offering everything you come to the Rockies for: drool-inducing views of lofty peaks, including some of the range's highest and sweeping meadows full of wild flowers. Fast hikers can do it in two days, but three is more realistic. It is a one-way hike best started at Maligne Lake. If driving, leave your vehicle at the Maligne Canyon terminus and hitch or take a bus to the lake. Book sites in the backcountry campgrounds well ahead, because this is one hike that is almost impossible to get onto at short notice. Plan your trip for after late-July, when the steepest section of the trail, known as 'the Notch', should be snow-free. This is the only steep section of a hike that is surprisingly level, considering that almost all of it is above the treeline. This last fact means you're particularly at the mercy of the weather, so go prepared for anything.

Bald Hills ① *12.6 km return; 610 m elevation gain.* The Bald Hills are actually a 7 km-long ridge. The lack of trees that gave them their name makes for excellent views of the surroundings, including Maligne Lake and the Queen Elizabeth Ranges, with razorback ridges, gleaming glaciers, rugged rock faces, green forests, alpine meadows and extraordinary rock formations. After about 45 minutes, take the cut-off trail through the trees and look out for wild flowers. Most people stop at the old fire lookout but you can continue for greater panoramas and less company.

Opal Hills ① *8.2 km; 460 m elevation gain.* This trail is short but very steep. The rewards are gorgeous views of mountains and the lake and a host of tiny wild flowers.

Miette Hot Springs

① *T780-866 3939, mid-May to mid-Oct daily 0830-2230, mid-May-Jun and Sep to mid-Oct daily 1030-2100, $6.25, child $5.25, road closed in winter.*
A favourite excursion from Jasper is to **Miette Hot Springs**, 60 km east on Highway 16, then 17 km south on Miette Road. Near the junction of these roads is an interpretive trail to the abandoned mining town of Pocahontas, a plesant wander through a forest that has grown around the ruins. **Ashlar Ridge Viewpoint** ① *8.5 km Miette Rd*, offers great views of this impressive rock wall, which can also be appreciated from the newly renovated springs themselves, which are the hottest in the Rockies. Cooled from 54°C to 40°C, the water is chlorinated and runs into two large outdoor pools. Interpretive displays explain the local geology and an interpretive trail leads to the source of the springs.

If you've driven this far, hike the short but steep **Sulphur Skyline** ① *8 km return, 700 m elevation gain*, offering views out of all proportion to the energy expended. It's also a good early-season hike.

Mount Robson Provincial Park ⊕▲⊕ ⇢ pp302-307.

Colour map 2, A2.

ⓘ The only public transport into the park is the Greyhound. Ask to be dropped at the Mt Robson viewpoint, also site of the Visitor Information Centre, T250-566 9174, May-Sep daily 0800-1700, mid-Jun to early Sep daily 0800-1900. The nearby café/garage is about the only place to get food. The reservation fee for hiking Berg Lake, $6 per night up to $18 for 3 or more nights, is paid at the time of booking T1800-689 9025, a credit card is essential. The camping fee, $5 per person per night, is paid at the time of registration at the Visitor Centre, which also retains a few first-come, first-served sites: be there before it opens to get one.

The Yellowhead Highway (Highway 16) accompanies the railway west from Jasper to the Yellowhead Pass ⓘ 1131 m, which has been used as a route across the Continental (or Great) Divide by fur-traders and gold-seekers for over 150 years. This is the border between Alberta and British Columbia, Mountain and Pacific time zones (BC is one hour behind) and Jasper and Mount Robson parks. There are few facilities in the latter, so if planning to do the overnight hike discussed below, stock up in Jasper. The next closest town is **Tête Jaune Cache** ⓘ 16 km beyond the park's western boundary, though Valemount to the south is more substantial.

More than any other of the Rocky Mountain parks, this one is utterly dominated by its crowning feature. At 3954 m, **Mount Robson** is the highest peak in the Canadian Rockies and possibly the most spectacular. It was one of the last mountains in the Rockies to be climbed and even today represents a difficult challenge. Whether you're approaching on Highway 16 or from Kamloops on Highway 5, the first sight of this colossal rock pyramid is likely to take your breath away: the perfection of its shape, highlighted by the pointed triangle of ice at its apex and the distinct layering of rock which inspired the native name Yuh-hai-has-hun, 'Mountain of the Spiral Road'. The only way to fully appreciate the peak's awesome beauty is by doing the hike, which reveals the incredible vast glaciers that cover its north side.

Hikes in Mount Robson Provincial Park

Mount Robson/Berg Lake ⓘ 39.2 km return; 786 m elevation gain. Trailhead: 2 km north of the Visitor Centre on a side road. This is the most popular and one of the very best backpacking trips in the range and can be attempted as early as mid-June. Most people reach Berg Lake in a day, spend a day exploring, then hike out on the third. The trail is extraordinary and varied, leading through lush, flower-dotted rainforest, past open gravel flats, over suspension bridges in a rugged river gorge, through the Valley of a Thousand Faces and past three powerful waterfalls, including the 60-m Emperor Falls. At Berg Lake, Mount Robson rises 2316 m directly from the shore, its cliffs wrapped in the vast ice-cloaks of Mist and Berg Glaciers. Huge chunks of ice regularly crash from the latter into the lake. There is a campground right here, a more private one 0.6 km further and another 1.4 km further still. A recommended 9-km day-hike is to Snowbird Pass. The path leads to the toe of Robson Glacier and for the next 3 km the views of the glacier are stupendous.

Yellowhead Mountain ⓘ 9 km return; 715 m elevation gain. Trailhead: 8.5 km west of the pass on Hwy 16, 1 km on a gravel road across Yellowhead Lake on an isthmus. Park below the railway where road splits. Passing through meadows and aspen forest, this trail is particularly attractive in autumn. The best day-hike in the park, it offers wonderful views of Yellowhead Pass.

Canadian Rockies Jasper National Park & around Mount Robson Provincial Park

Columbia Icefield *p296*

AL Columbia Icefield Chalet, T1877-423 7433, www.columbiaicefield.com/hotel.asp. Spacious, comfy rooms with high ceilings, some with glacier views and some with lofts. Book ahead.

A Tonquin Amethyst Lake Lodge, T180-852 1188, www.tonquinadventures.com. Private, heated cabins with log beds and warm blankets. Price includes meals. Access is only possible on foot or on horseback along a 18.6 km trail.

A Tonquin Valley Backcountry Lodge, Eremite Valley, T780-852 3909, www.tonquin valley.com. Comfortable Canadian Rockies chalets. Price includes meals. Access is only possible on foot or on horseback.

Camping

Wilcox Creek and **Columbia Icefield** campgrounds, right next to each other on the Jasper side and 5 mins walk from the Icefields Centre, enjoy one of the prime locations in the Rockies and are both predictably very crowded. The latter is for tents only and has very nice walk-in sites.

North to Jasper *p297*

A Sunwapta Falls Resort, T1888-828 5777, www.sunwapta.com. Small but very nice, cosy en suite rooms, some with sun decks and some with fireplaces. There's a reasonable restaurant and bikes for rent.

E Athabasca Falls Hostel, T1877-852 0781, www.hihostels.ca. 20 beds in 3 rustic cabins with no running water, showers or flush toilets. The location is fantastic.

E Beauty Creek Hostel, 14 km N of the Icefield Centre, T1877-852 0781, www.hi hostels.ca. A very basic, summer-only hostel with 24 beds in 2 cabins, no flush toilets or running water but sun showers and a small propane-fuelled kitchen. Situated right next to the creek, which through 8 sets of waterfalls along a limestone gorge.

E Mount Edith Cavell Hostel, 5.3 km S on Hwy 93A, then 12 km on Mount Edith Cavell Rd, T1877-852 0781, www.hihostels.ca. 32 beds in 2 cabins with views of the Angel Glacier and the 3363-m peak. Popular, as it's the perfect base to start backcountry hikes into the Tonquin Valley. Book ahead.

Camping

Jonas Creek Campground, 9 km beyond Beauty Creek. 25 sites by the creek, some walk-in only.

Honeymoon Lake Campground, just past Sunwapta Falls. One of the nicer places to camp with 35 spacious sites, some right on the lake.

Mount Kerkeslin Campground, 10 km further. 42 attractive sites.

Jasper Townsite *p298, map p299*

Jasper's hotels are not much better value than Banff's and are just as likely to be full in summer. There are, however, plenty of private homes close to town with reasonably priced rooms (**C-D**). Ask at the Information Centre, or visit www.stayinjasper.com, for a detailed list of over 120. Make hostel reservations online at www.hihostels.ca, or call T1877-852 0781.

AL-B Patricia Lake Bungalows, 6 km north towards Pyramid Lake at Patricia Lake, T780-852 3560, www.patricialake bungalows.com. Lots of options in a quiet spot by the lake, including luxury suites (**AL**), attractive, spacious cottages or cabins with kitchens (**A**) and good value motel rooms (**B**). Facilities include hot tub, laundry and canoe rentals.

A Amethyst Lodge, 200 Connaught Dr, T780-852 3394, www.mpljasper.com. Central location with big rooms, balconies, 2 outdoor hot tubs, restaurant and lounge.

A Bear Hill Lodge, 100 Bonhomme St, T780-852 3209, www.BearHillLodge.com. A wide range of cabins, lodge rooms and duplexes with full bath, some with kitchenettes or gas fireplace. Situated on a forested 1-ha lot on the edge of town, with hot tub, sauna, internet and laundry facilities.

A Tekarra Lodge, 1 km south off Hwy 93A, T780-852 3058, www.tekarralodge.com. In a quiet spot in the trees by the confluence of the Athabasca and Miette rivers. Tasteful cabins with hardwood floors, stone fireplaces, balconies and kitchens, or plain B&B lodge rooms. Common area with fireplace, good restaurant, continental breakfast, bike rentals and hiking trails nearby.

A Whistlers Inn,105 Miette Av, T780-852 3361, www.whistlersinn.com. Standard rooms and much nicer suites in a very central property with an outdoor rooftop hot tub, a steam room, 2 restaurants and a nice pub.

B Pine Bungalows, 2 km E at 2 Cottonwood Creek Rd, T780-852 3491, www.pinebungal ows.com. Situated in a forest setting on the banks of the Athabasca River, with 72 very nice, cosy, modern cabins, all with tubs, most with kitchenettes and many with stone fireplaces. The 2-bedroom cabins for 4 people are quite a bit nicer.

B Raven House B&B, 801 Miette Av, T780-852 4011, www.ravenbb.com. 2 pleasant rooms in a private house in town.

C Castle Guest House, 814 Miette Av, T780-852 5768, www.bbcanada.com/ 1688. 2 comfortable rooms in a splendid modern wood house with a garden patio.

C Juniper House, 713 Maligne Av, T780-852 3664, www.visit-jasper.com/juniper house. 2 very tasteful suites in a newly renovated heritage home, that's also very central. Good value.

E Jasper International Hostel, 7 km SW, near gondola on Whistlers Mountain Rd, T1877-852 0781, www.hihostels.ca. A chalet-style hostel with 84 beds, full kitchen, showers, laundry and bike rentals. Shuttles from Downtown

E Maligne Canyon Hostel, 11 km east on Maligne Lake Rd, T780-852 3215, T1877-852 0781, www.hihostels.ca. 24 beds in 2 cabins near the canyon. Open year-round (closed Wed in winter). Rustic, with no running water or flush toilets but a small propane kitchen.

Camping

Campgrounds close to town fill up very fast in summer, with queues starting about 1100, but **Pocahontas**, **Whistlers**, **Wapiti** and **Wabasso** can all be reserved ahead by calling T1877-737 3783, or on-line at www.pc camping.ca. When all the camp-grounds are full, overflow sites are put into effect (cheaper, but not very nice). Jasper has over 100 backcountry sites. Wilderness Passes cost $9 per person per night, refundable till 1000 on proposed date of departure. Reservation (with $12 fee) at Information Centre or T780-852 6177, up to 3 months before departure. Campsite Day use permit $7.

Pocahontas, 45 km east then 1 km on Miette Hot Springs Rd. 140 reasonable sites.
Snaring River, 15 km north off Hwy 16 on the road towards Celestine Lake. This is the nicest campground, with 66 sites. When all others are full, there is overflow camping here with space for 500.
Wabasso, 15 km south on Hwy 93A. 228 sites. The inconvenient location tends to mean it's the last one to fill up.
Wapiti, 4 km south on Hwy 93. Has 362 sites, some with hook-ups. Showers available. The only campsite open year-round, although less sites are available in winter and cannot be reserved. Ok for being so close to town.
Whistlers, 3 km south off Hwy 93. There are 781 sites, including some with full hook-ups. Campers should try to get a walk-in site.

Mount Robson Provincial Park *p301*
B-C Mount Robson Lodge, 4 km W of the Visitor Centre on Hwy 16, T250-566 9899, www.mtrobson.com. Situated close to the trail (phone for directions), offering a couple of lovely log cabins with kitchens and 4 rooms in the splendid wood lodge, with breakfast included. Spectacular location and views, with a lovely deck to enjoy them from.
C Mount Robson Guest Ranch, 2 km from the Hwy on Hargreaves Rd, T250-566 4654, www.mountrobsonranch.com. 7 rather plain rustic cabins, some with kitchenettes, in a very quiet, private spot near the Berg Lake Trail. Also has RV sites and a restaurant offering all meals.

Camping
Emperor Ridge Campground, within walking distance of the **Visitor Centre** on Kinney Lake Rd, T250-566 8438. Offers 37 decent sites and hot showers.
Robson Meadows and the much smaller **Robson River** Provincial Park campgrounds, are both close to the Visitor Centre on the park's west side. 144 sites between them, showers and lovely riverside locations.
Robson Shadows Campground, 5 km west of the park boundary on Hwy 16, T1888-566 4821. Nice sites on the Fraser River, with showers available. Panoramic views of Mt Robson.

🍴 Eating

Jasper Townsite *p298, map p299*

The Pines at Pyramid Lake, T780-852 4900. Sumptuous dishes like smoked trout chowder and seafood pasta flavoured with black sambuca, served in a comfortable interior or on a patio overlooking the lake.

Andy's Bistro, 606 Patricia St, T780-852 4559. European-influenced cuisine in an intimate setting, with a frequently changing menu that focuses on meat dishes and fondue. Chef Andy is undoubtedly one of the best in town.

Earl's, 600 Patricia St, T780-852 2393. The standard broad menu covering many popular bases, but they do it well and there are good views from the 2nd-floor balcony. One of the nicest locations in town.

Fiddle River, 1st Floor, 620 Connaught Dr, T780-852 3032. A cosy, pine finished loft that's casual but stylish. The place to go for seafood, immaculately cooked in a variety of imaginative or tried and tested ways. Also has a big wine list.

Kimchi House, 407 Patricia St, T780-852 5022. A real cultural experience, serving authentic Korean BBQ dishes that are big enough for 2. Choose between the cosy interior or outdoor patio.

La Fiesta, 504 Patricia St, T780-852 0404. One of the nicest interiors in town, with exposed wooden beams and hardwood floors, it's simple, elegant and romantic. The Spanish menu has lots of choice, but paella and tapas are their speciality.

Miss Italia, upstairs at 610 Patricia St, T780-852 4002. A sweet spot with little tables on the balcony, lots of plants and a great atmosphere, but many people find the pasta dishes bland.

Villa Caruso, 640 Connaught Dr, T780-852 3920. A classic steak- and seafood-style menu, in a downtown location dominated by lots of wood. Good atmosphere with 2 fireplaces and 3 outdoor patios. The bar is also a nice place for a drink.

Coco's, 608 Patricia St, T708-852 4550. A good place to hang out, with coffee, music, breakfast, scones, magazines and some vegetarian food.

Soft Rock Café, 632 Connaught Dr, T708-852 5850. Tasty breakfast and grilled sandwiches, internet access.

🍸 Bars and clubs

Jasper Townsite *p298, map p299*

Most of Jasper's hotels have lounges for a quiet drink, but with big screen TVs.

Athabasca Hotel, 510 Patricia St, T708-852 3386. Sleazy nightclub with DJs and live music.

De'd Dog Bar and Grill, Astoria Hotel, 404 Connaught Dr, T708-852 3351. Fairly good ale on tap, pool table and darts.

The Downstream Bar, 620 Connaught Dr, T708-852 9449. A cosy spot for a glass of wine. Live R'n'B on Sat night.

Jasper Brewing Co, 624 Connaught Dr, T708-852 4111. A decent pub that brews its own beers. Serves contemporary pub food.

Pete's on Patricia, 2nd Floor, 614 Patricia St, T708-852 6262. Dancing, drink specials and occasional live music.

✦ Festivals and events

Jasper Townsite *p298, map p299*

Aug Heritage Folk Festival, T780-852 3615, www.jasperfolkfestival.com. A major folk music festival held biennially (next in 2009). Jasper Heritage Pro Rodeo, www.jasper heritagerodeo.com. For 4 days in mid-Aug the rodeo attracts top cowboys and stock from around the world, with events like bull riding, bareback and saddle bronco riding, steer wrestling, calf roping, barrel racing and more. Dances on Fri and Sat nights featuring top Country entertainers.

🛍 Shopping

Jasper Townsite *p298, map p299*

Everest Outdoor Stores, 414 Connaught Dr, T708-852 5902. Maps and outdoor clothing and sports equipment to buy or rent.

Friends of Jasper National Park, opposite the **Visitor Centre** on Connaught Rd, T780-852 4767, www.friendsofjasper.com. Profits go to the park.

Gravity Gear, 618 Patricia St, T708-852 3155. The place for climbing gear.

Jasper Source for Sports, 406 Patricia St, T708-852 3654. Fishing equipment, boat rentals, bike and camping gear rentals.

Nutters Bulk Food, 622 Patricia St, T708-852 5844. Health food and hiking snacks, good salamis and cheeses.

Canadian Rockies Jasper National Park & around Listings

▲ Activities and tours

Jasper Townsite *p298, map p299*
Biking
Pick up the *Jasper Cycling Guide* at the Visitor Centre. There are several good trails starting from town. Experienced bikers will enjoy the Saturday Night Lake Loop, 27 km, starting at the Cabin Lake Rd parking lot, west end of town, with views of Miette and Athabasca Valley. There is some good riding across the river at Old Fort Point, which is also the start of the 23-km Trail No 7, a good all-level ride passing through Maligne Canyon.
Freewheel Cycle, 618 Patricia St, T780-852 3898, www.freewheeljasper.com. Trail-maps, rentals and information. Also rent skis and snowboards.

Climbing
Gravity Gear, 618 Patricia St, T780-852 3155, www.gravitygearjasper.com. Ask them about climbing at Maligne Canyon, Rock Gardens and Boulder Garden. Hidden Valley, 30 km east, is good for the experienced.
Jasper Activity Centre, 303 Pyramid Av, T708-852 3381. Has an indoor climbing wall.

Dog sledding
Cold Fire Creek,T780-968 6808, www.dog sleddinginjasper.com. Dog-sledding trips, 1-hr ($105), 2½-3 hrs ($165) and longer.

Fishing
Currie's Guiding & Tackle, T780-852 5650, www.curriesguidingjasper.com. Full and ½-day fishing trips, mostly on Maligne Lake, in a 21-foot cedar strip freighter canoe. They can obtain your permit for you.

Hiking, walking and ice canyon tours
Beyond the Beaten Path, T780-852 4292, www.jasperbeyondthebeatenpath.com. Maligne Canyon ice walks, as well as snow-shoe or cross-country ski tours and dog-sledding. Also offer wildlife safaris and van tours with interpretive talks and/or hikes in Maligne Canyon, Icefields Parkway and Mt Edith Cavell.
Overlander Trekking and Tours, T780-852 4056, www.overlandertrekking.com. Backcountry hikes in and around the park. Ski and snowshoe guided tours, Maligne Canyon ice walks and guided trail biking.

Walks and Talks Jasper, 626 Connaught Dr, T780-852 4994, www.walksntalks.com. Interpretive guided hikes, walks and ice walks which focus on wildlife and the environment. Also offer guided ski and snowshoe tours.

Horse riding
Pyramid Riding Stables, T780-852 7106, www.mpljasper.com/jasper/pyramid_riding. 1-hr to 1-day horse rides above town on Pyramid Bench with views of the Athabasca Valley. Also offer carriage and wagon rides, and sleigh rides in the winter, T780-852 7433.
Skyline Trail Rides, T780-852 4215, www.skylinetrail.com. 3-day horseback trips to their Shovel Pass Lodge, $650 including food, lodging, horses and guides. Also daily rides from Jasper Park Lodge from 1 hr ($39) to 4½ hrs ($120).
Tonquin Valley Pack Trips, T780-852 1188, www.tonquinadventures.com. 2- ($425), 3- ($650), 4- ($850) or 5-day ($1050) horse riding trips up Tonquin Valley to their Amethyst Lake Lodge, with meals and accommodation included.

Icefield Tours
Brewster, T403-762 6700, www.sightseeing tourscanada.ca. Run the Icefield Glacier Experience tours onto the glacier in the Snowcoach, a specially built bus that moves at a snail's pace, doing the 5-km round trip in 90 mins. Tours leave every 15 mins Apr-Oct and cost $36, child $18. Also included in their 9-hr tour from Jasper ($111). They also run bus tours to Banff, Lake Louise, Maligne Lake and around town.

Ice-skating
Jasper Activity Centre, 303 Pyramid Av, T780-852 3381, has an indoor rink; **Lac Beauvert**, by Jasper Park Lodge; **Pyramid Lake**, Pyramid Lake Rd.

Rafting
All of the rafting companies offer similar trips and prices. 2-hr ($59) and 3-hr ($79) trips on the Athabasca River, with mellow Grade II runs and 4-hr trips on the Sunwapta River ($89) for more dramatic Grade III trips.
Maligne Rafting Adventures, T780-852 3370, www.mra.ab.ca, also run 5-hr trips

on the Fraser ($89) and multi-day trips on the Kakwa and Athabasca rivers; **Raven Rafting**, T780-852 4292, www.ravenad venture.com; **Rocky Mountain River Guides**, T780-852 3777, www.rmriverguides.com; **Whitewater Rafting Ltd**, T780-852 7238, www.whitewaterraftingjasper.com.

Rentals

Edge Control Ski & Outdoor Store, 626 Connaught Dr, T708-852 494, specializes in ski and snowboard equipment rentals; **Jasper Source for Sports**, 406 Patricia St, T780-852 3654; **On-Line Sport**, 600 Patricia St, T780-852 3630.

Skiing

Visit www.skijaspercanada.com, for general information. For Downhill skiing, see Marmot Basin Ski Hill, page 297. For cross-country skiing there are 20 km of groomed trails at Maligne Lake. The Bald Hills up above offer plenty of space for telemarking and touring, but the 480 m elevation gain over 5.5 km makes it hard work getting there. The 5 km Beaver/Summit Lake Trail, Km 27 on Maligne Lake Rd, gives easy access to the backcountry. There are 1- to 30-km trails at Pyramid Bench and around Patricia Lake. Jasper Park Lodge, on Lodge Rd just east of Jasper, also has a network of groomed loops from 5-10 km. The 4.5-km Whistlers Camp-ground loop is flat, easy and lit up at night. Moab Lake is a nice, easy 18-km trail with great views, 20 km south on Hwy 93A.

Tour operators

Air Jasper, T708-865 3616, www.airjasper. com. Flightseeing tours of the Icefield and Maligne Lake or Mt Robson and Amethyst Lakes in a Cessna (75 mins, $185 per person). The tours can be combined (105 mins, $270 per person). Price includes the shuttle to Hinton Airport.
Jasper Adventure Centre, 604 Connaught Dr (mid-May to mid-Sep); 306 Connaughts Dr (mid-Sep to mid-May), T780-852 5595, www.jasperadventurecentre.com. Repre-senting many of the other companies in this listing, these guys can set you up with any activity around Jasper. They also run 2-hr 'voyageur' canoe trips, walking and hiking trips and a number of van tours for those without transportation to places like Jasper

Tramway, Maligne Lake or Canyon and Miette Hotsprings.
Sun Dog Tours, T780-852 4056, www.sun dogtours.com. As well as providing shuttles, they can also book any tours you need.

Mount Robson Provincial Park *p301*
Headwaters Outfitting, T250-566 4718, www.davehenry.com. Backcountry skiing and hiking in Mt Robson.
Mount Robson Whitewater Rafting, T250-566 4879, www.mountrobsonwhitewater. com. Float trips (2½ hrs, $49) and white-water trips (3 hrs, $89) on the Fraser River
Snow Farmers, T250-566 9161, www.snow farmers.com. Guided horseback riding, 1 hr, $35 and ½-day, $85.

⊖ Transport

Jasper Townsite *p298, map p299*
Bus
Local Most of Jasper's important trails are far removed from the town. For those with-out their own transport the choices are to hitchhike or use one of the rather expensive shuttle services: **Jasper Adventure Centre**, T780-852 5595; **Walks and Talks Jasper**, T780-852 4945. From May-Oct the **Jasper Shuttle**, T780-852 3370, www.jaspershuttle. com, connects the townsite with Maligne Lake, leaving 616 Patricia St at 0830, 1130, 1415, 1630, leaving the lake at 1000, 1300, 1515, 1800. One-way $16, $10.70 to Maligne Canyon. Will also drop you at trailheads.
   Long distance Greyhound, T1800-661 8747, runs 4 daily buses to **Edmonton** (5 hrs, $58), 2 to **Vancouver** (11-12 hrs, $117) via **Kamloops** (5½ hrs, $61) and 1 to **Prince George** (5½ hrs, $62). Sun Dog Tours, T1888-786 3641, www.sundogtours. com, runs a shuttle to Banff ($59) and Calgary ($105).

Train
VIA Rail, T1888-842 7245, www.viarail.ca, operates 3 trains per week to **Edmonton** (5 hrs, from $112) and **Vancouver** (17½ hrs, from $155) or to **Prince Rupert** (31 hrs, from $107) with a night in **Prince George** (6½ hrs, from $50). **The Rocky Mountaineer** train, T604-606 7245, 1 nights and 2 days to **Vancouver**, starting at $809 including accommodation. A beautiful journey.

Mt Robson Provincial Park *p301*
Greyhound, T1800-661 8747, buses will drop you off at the Visitor Centre. 3 daily to Jasper (1½ hrs, $24), 1 daily to Prince George (3½ hrs, $46) and 2 from Kamloops (4½ hrs, $55).

● Directory

Jasper Townsite *p298, map p299*
Banks TD Bank, 606 Patricia Av, T708-

852 6270. **Internet** Library; Soft Rock Internet Café, 632 Connaught Dr, T708- 852 5850. **Laundry** Coin Clean Laundry, 607 Patricia Av, T708-852 3852, also has coin-operated showers. **Library** Jasper Municipal Library, 500 Robson St/Elm Av, T708-852 3652. **Medical services** Cottage Medical Clinic, 507 Turret St, T780-852 4885; Seton General Hospital, 518 Robson St, T780-852 3344. **Post office** Canada Post, 502 Patricia St, T708-852 3041.

Yoho National Park

Yoho is a Cree exclamation of awe and wonder, something like 'Wow!' The scenery in this park is indeed astounding, with many waterfalls and 28 peaks over 3000 m. Banff may be the most famous of the parks and Jasper the biggest, but get any Rocky Mountain aficionado talking and they'll soon start waxing passionate about Yoho. Comparatively small, it contains the greatest concentration of quality hikes in the range, mostly clustered in two major areas and one minor. Lake O'Hara has proved so popular that a complete traffic ban has been imposed and visitor numbers are now strictly limited. A good second choice, if that's too much hassle, Yoho Valley has the park's only hostel and a fabulous campground. Emerald Lake is a pretty destination and offers one very good hike. The pleasant little village of Field makes a good base for those not camping. ►► *For Sleeping, Eating and other listings, see pages 311-312.*

Ins and outs

Getting there and around
Field is on the TransCanada Highway and therefore receives three **Greyhound** ① *www.greyhound.ca*, buses from Vancouver, Calgary and all points in between, including Banff and Lake Louise. ►► *For further details, see Transport, page 312.*
There is no public road to Lake O'Hara and bikes are not allowed. A shuttle bus runs from mid-June to early October from the Lake O'Hara Fire Road parking lot, off Highway 1 15 km east of Field, 11 km west of Lake Louise. Buses leave at 0830, 1030, 1530 and 1730, departing from Lake O'Hara Lodge at 0930, 1130, 1430, 1630 and 1830. To get a place on the bus it is essential to reserve at T250-343 6433 up to three months in advance. You will need to know your plans, as bus, campground and reservation fees are all to be paid by credit card when booking. Six seats on the bus and three to five places in the campground are left open per day for bookings by phone the day before. The office opens at 0800 (Mountain time) and the fare is $15 return, with $12 reservation fee. Once up there a place on the return bus is first-come, first-served, but practically guaranteed at 1630 or 1830.

Tourist information
Unless you know specifically what you want to do, a sensible first port of call is to the village of Field which is close to all of Yoho's sights and contains the excellent **Visitor Centre/Parks Office** ① *T250-343 6783, www.field.ca, mid-May to mid-Sep daily 0900-1900, mid-Sep to mid-May daily 0900-1600 or 0900-1700, backcountry camping reservations T250-343 6433, $12.* They can help organize accommodation

and camping arrangements, give sound advice on what hikes to choose and issue the very useful backcountry guide, as well as maps. They also take backcountry camping reservations up to three months ahead, a must for Lake O'Hara.

Field ⬛🍴♦▲ ▸ pp311-312. Colour map 2, B3.

Field is a remarkably attractive one-horse town of 250 people built on the side of a mountain and dotted with beautiful flower gardens and makes a delightful base for day-hikes around the park. There are no sights as such, but Field Mountain, visible

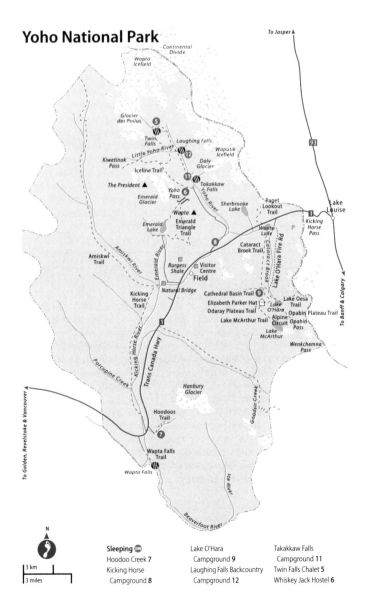

Yoho National Park

To Jasper

Continental Divide

Wapta Icefield

Glacier des Poilus 5

Twin Falls
Laughing Falls
Little Yoho River
Waputik Icefield

Kiwetinok Pass
Iceline Trail
Daly Glacier

The President ▲
12
11
Takakkaw Falls

Emerald Glacier
Yoho Pass 6
Wapta ▲

Emerald Lake
Emerald Triangle Trail
Sherbrooke Lake
Paget Lookout Trail

Amiskwi Trail
Amiskwi River
Emerald River
Yoho River
Wapta Lake
Lake O'Hara Fire Rd

8
Cataract Brook Trail

Burgess Shale
Visitor Centre
Field
Natural Bridge
Cathedral Basin Trail 9
Lake O'Hara
Laké Oesa Trail

Kicking Horse Trail
Elizabeth Parker Hut
Odaray Plateau Trail
Lake McArthur Trail
Alpine Circuit
Opabin Plateau Trail
Opabin Pass

Kicking Horse River
Lake McArthur
Wenkchemna Pass

Porcupine Creek
Trans Canada Hwy

Hanbury Glacier
Goodsir Creek

To Golden, Revelstoke & Vancouver

Hoodoos Trail

7
Wapta Falls Trail

Wapta Falls
Ice River

Beaverfoot River

Lake Louise
Kicking Horse Pass

To Banff & Calgary

93

N

3 km
3 miles

Sleeping
Hoodoo Creek 7
Kicking Horse Campground 8

Lake O'Hara Campground 9
Laughing Falls Backcountry Campground 12

Takakkaw Falls Campground 11
Twin Falls Chalet 5
Whiskey Jack Hostel 6

across the valley, is the site of the **Burgess Shale**, an ancient seabed that has yielded a host of 515 million-year-old fossils. Remains of more than 120 species of soft-bodied marine animals have been found, some so well preserved that scientists can tell what they ate just before they died. This is one of only three places in the world where such fossils are found. An excellent exhibit recreating the sea and explaining its inhabitants is one of the highlights of the Royal Tyrell Museum in Drumheller, Alberta (see page 263). There are also displays at the Field and Lake Louise Visitor Centres. Long and strenuous guided hikes to the fossil beds are run between July and mid-September by the **Yoho Burgess Shale Foundation** ⓘ *T1800-343 3006*. Numbers are limited to 15 per hike.

There is also a **viewpoint** ⓘ *8 km east of Field and 2 km up the Yoho Valley Rd*, for contemplating the Spiral Tunnels, two enormous figure-of-eight galleries blasted out of the mountains in 1909 in order to reduce the original 4.5% railway grade to a much safer 2.2%. For railway buffs, the sight of a long goods train tying itself in knots through these tunnels is an extraordinary phenomenon not to be missed.

Lake O'Hara 🏠 ⟫ *pp311-312. Colour map 2, B3.*

The camping fee here is $10 per person per night. Anybody can hike the 11 km trail to the lake, but it's still essential to have reserved a campsite. These days places in the Alpine Club of Canada's **Elizabeth Parker Hut** are allotted by a lottery, which only members can enter. ⟫ *For further details on getting there, see Ins and outs, page 307.*

The Lake

Exquisitely framed by the two lofty mountains, Victoria and Lefroy, that tower over Lake Louise on the other side of the Continental Divide, Lake O'Hara is a rare jewel even in the overflowing treasure chest of the Rockies. When it was first discovered by Canada's hiking community, news of its extraordinary natural beauty and network of quality day-hikes spread like wildfire and soon the area was too popular for its own good. Parks Canada have taken measures to protect it, so visiting can be difficult unless you book ahead. No traffic is allowed into the region, not even bikes.

Hikes from Lake O'Hara

Hiking in the Lake O'Hara region is among the most popular and rewarding in the Rockies. On the Continental Divide between here and Lake Louise are a number of the highest and most awe-inspiring peaks in the range. Within a relatively small area are 25 named lakes and an extensive, well-maintained network of trails that radiate out from Lake O'Hara like the spokes of a wheel. There are five main sub-regions that can be combined in any number of ways.

Lake Oesa ⓘ *5.8-km loop; 240 m elevation gain*. This is a short and easy hike to a stunning turquoise lake set in a rugged cirque. Towering above are the Continental Divide summits of Mounts Lefroy and Victoria, the other side of the stunning massif that towers so dramatically over Lake Louise.

Opabin Plateau ⓘ *7.2-km loop; 250 m elevation gain*. Set in a beautiful hanging valley, this easy hike offers many temptations for casual exploration among small flower-filled tundra meadows. The loop follows the east and west sides of the same valley. A 0.6-km side-trail leads from the west side to outstanding views from Opabin Prospect. From the east side, a detour leads along Yukness Ledge, a possible highline traverse to Lake Oesa.

Lake McArthur ⓘ *7 km return; 315 m elevation gain*. This half-day hike is one of the area's finest. The 1.5-km-long lake is the biggest in the area and an exquisite, deep blue colour due to its 65-m depth. Sheer cliffs rising straight up, more than 600 m above the water, make for a dramatic location.

Odaray Plateau ⓘ *7-10-km loops; 290-655 m elevation gain.* This is one of the most spectacular routes in the park, but is often closed, or visitor numbers are limited due to grizzly bears. The trail climbs quickly and steeply. Odaray Prospect offers a 180° panorama centred on Lake O'Hara, backed by the wall of high peaks that comprise the Great Divide. Further along, the trail branches off to Odaray Grandview, the only spot in the park from which all of its major lakes can be seen simultaneously. To achieve this prize you have to face a difficult 1.1-km scramble that requires endurance and some experience. At Km 4.5 a junction at McArthur Pass leads back to the start making a 6.5-km loop, or on to Lake McArthur as part of a 9.5-km loop.

Cathedral Basin ⓘ *13-15 km return; 300 m elevation gain.* This is one of the longest and least crowded day-hikes in the area, but is also one of the lowest and least dramatic. However, after skirting the pretty Linda and Cathedral Lakes, the trail starts to climb towards the mouth of the Cathedral Basin. The wonderful views all along this stretch peak at Cathedral Prospect, which offers one of the most complete overviews of the whole Lake O'Hara region. The climb to the Prospect is fairly steep on a poor, rocky surface.

Alpine Circuit ⓘ *9.8-12.4 km; 495 m elevation gain.* The classic way to combine some of the area's sights, this is one of the highlights of the Lake O'Hara region, but it's a fairly tough circuit, more route than trail, following cairns and paint-marks across scree slopes and along exposed ledges. Those scared of heights, worried about getting lost, or not in tip-top condition should probably choose another hike. Use a good trail description and carry a good map. Starting the circuit with the toughest section, the ascent to Wiwaxy Gap, is a good idea. Views from the gap are exceptional. The loop can be extended or shortened in a couple of places. The short detour to Opabin Prospect is worth the effort, while the ascent to All Souls' Prospect is an excellent conclusion to the hike.

Yoho Valley 🚌 ↠ *pp311-312. Colour map 2, B3.*

Logistically easier than Lake O'Hara and almost equally wonderful, is the Yoho Valley, which is lined with waterfalls, including the dramatic **Twin Falls** and the 380-m **Takakkaw Falls**, one of Canada's highest, whose name comes from a Stoney Indian word meaning 'magnificent'. This is also one of the most exceptional areas for glaciers: the enormous Wapta and Waputik Icefields are both easily visible, as is the beautiful Emerald Glacier. The valley is ringed with monster peaks. To get there, drive 3.7 km northeast of Field, or 12.5 km southwest of the Continental Divide, turn north on Yoho Valley Road and drive about 13 km up a very steep, winding road, not suitable for RVs or trailers.

Hikes in the Yoho Valley

Iceline ⓘ *12.8-21.3 km; 690 m elevation gain. Trailhead: Whiskey Jack Hostel.* The steep ascent of this popular hike takes you up to the Emerald Glacier, on a level with truly extraordinary scenery that includes the Daly Glacier and Takakkaw Falls opposite and the vast Wapta Icefield to the north. Once at the top, the hiking is high, easy and scenically uplifting. A return journey to the highpoint is 12.8 km. Circuits can be made by continuing to the Yoho Valley and possibly the Little Yoho Valley as well, though neither option adds anything that compares to the views from the top. A two-day backpack trip would entail a night at Little Yoho campground or the nearby

Stanley Mitchell hut (book with the Alpine Club, T403-678 3200, www.alpineclubof
canada.ca), a possible diversion to Kiwetinok Pass and a return via the stupendous
vantage point of the Whaleback.

Yoho Valley ① *16.4 km; 290 m elevation gain.* This flat trail through the trees leads
to a few waterfalls, ending at the dramatic Twin Falls. It is a nice enough stroll and
good for a rainy day, but otherwise there seems no point if you're capable of doing the
spectacular Iceline trail, which offers so much more.

Emerald Lake ⬤🍴▲ ›› *pp311-312.*

This is a lovely spot and the name is accurate, if lacking in imagination. To get here,
drive 2.6 km southwest of Field, then 8 km on Emerald Lake Road, passing on the way
the Natural Bridge, a giant rock that has been carved by the powerful Kicking
Horse River. In addition to those listed below, a number of longer trails are better
suited to mountain biking. The **Amiskwi Trail** ① *35 km one-way,* follows a river,
starting at Emerald Lake Road. The **Kicking Horse Trail** ① *19.5 km,* starts at the same
point or at the now-closed Chancellor Peak campground.

Emerald Triangle ① *19.7 km; 880 m elevation gain.* The clear-cut choice for a
day-hike. A satisfying loop, the climb is gentle (more gentle in a clockwise direction),
but the descent at the end is rapid. As well as the lake, views are of the glaciated
ramparts of The President, the sheer cliffs of Wapta Mountain, the Kicking Horse
Valley and the fossil-fields of the Burgess Shale.

Hikes (and biking) from the TransCanada Highway
Paget Lookout ① *7.4 km return, 520 m elevation gain. Trailhead: Wapta Lake Picnic
Area, 5.5 km southwest of BC/Alberta border.* This short but steep climb leads to
astounding views that include the mountains encircling Lake O'Hara and the Kicking
Horse Valley. Scramblers can ascend a further 430 m to Paget Peak for even better views.

Hoodoos ① *3.2 km, 455 m elevation gain. Trailhead: 22.7 km southwest of Field, before
campground entrance, 1.5 km to parking area.* A short but very steep hike leads to these
fascinating, elongated-mushroom-shaped rock formations. Follow the trail above them
for the best views. This can be enjoyed whatever the weather and combines nicely with
Wapta Falls ① *4.8 km, 45 m elevation gain. Trailhead: 25 km southwest of Field, 1.8 km
down Wapta Falls access road,* a powerful waterfall in a raw setting. The short, level hike
is good for spring or autumn, a rainy day, or just a leg-stretch to see the cascade.

● Sleeping

Field *p308*
Almost every residence in Field functions
as an informal guesthouse, offering self-
catering suites with kitchen for about $100.
Contact the Visitor Centre, which has a full,
up-to-date list, or check www.field.ca.
A Alpine Guesthouse, 2nd Av, T250-343
6878, www.alpineguesthouse.ca. Spacious
2-bedroom suite with private entrance and
kitchen. Incredible views.
B Kicking Horse Lodge, end of Kicking
Horse Av/Stephen Av, T250-343 6303,

www.kickinghorselodge.net. The only hotel
in town, with big rooms, kitchenettes for an
extra $14 and a nice restaurant.
B Canadian Rockies Inn, T250-343 6046,
www.bbcanada.com/7896. Has 3 suites,
all with private bathroom and living room,
1 with kitchen, and 2 bedrooms.
C Alpenglow B&B, 306 Kicking Horse Av,
T250-343 6356. Good rooms with shared
bath and no kitchen.
C Mount Burgess Guesthouse, T250-
343 6480, www.mtburgessguesthouse.ca.

2 great suites with kitchens, private bath and TV. Good value.

C Mount Stephen Guesthouse, T250-343 6441, www.mountstephen.com. 2 en suite rooms with kitchen.

Camping

Kicking Horse Campground, 3.7 km northeast at the Yoho Valley turn-off. 86 very nice private sites and good showers.

Lake O'Hara *p309*
Camping

Lake O'Hara Campground. Doesn't cater to RVs. For further details, see page 307.

Yoho Valley *p310*

D Twin Falls Chalet, at the far end of the valley, a 10-km hike, T403-228 7079, Jul-Aug only. A real backcountry experience, with no electricity or running hot water but wonderful meals included in the price.
E Whiskey Jack Hostel, on the way to the campground, T1800-762 4122, www.hi hostels.ca, late Jun-Sep. The park's only hostel and one of the best in the Rockies. Friendly and cosy, with 27 beds in 3 dorms. Kitchen, showers and great views from the front deck. Reservations recommended.

Camping

Laughing Falls Backcountry Campground, halfway to Twin Falls. Basic but private, with just 8 sites.
Takakkaw Falls Campground. Beyond the hostel, a group of car parks signals the end of the road. The campground is a 500-m walk from here and suitable for tents only. It combines the excitement of the backcountry with much of the convenience of less remote camping because there are wagons on which you can cart in as much food and equipment as you wish. The sites are fairly private and very beautifully located close to the falls, with a view of the Wapta Icefield. Some excellent hikes begin here.

● Eating

Field *p308*

¶¶ **The Roundhouse Pub and Grill**, in the Kicking Horse Lodge (see Sleeping, above). Good food at modest prices.
¶¶ **The Truffle Pigs Café and Bistro**, Kicking

Horse Av/Stephen Av, T250-343 6462. About the only shop in town, with a small but excellent and quite expensive restaurant. The food is fresh and they do gourmet dinner specials. Very good coffee.

Emerald Lake *p311*

¶¶ **Cilantro On the Lake Restaurant**, next door to the **Emerald Lake Lodge**, T1800-343 3006. Set in an impressive wood building on the water, this is a perfect spot for a splurge or at least a drink. The menu, inspired by Californian, West Coast and First Nations cuisine, incorporates lots of wild game and fish from the area. The atmosphere is that of a casual but upmarket bistro.

▲ Activities and tours

Field *p308*

There are plenty of trails for cross-country skiing from Field. The 12 km Tally Ho Trail winds its way round Mt Burgess to Emerald Lake. The Information Centre has maps.

There are some world class ice-climbing routes in the Field and Yoho Valleys, but you will have to look elsewhere (Jasper or Banff) for tour operators. A few old fire trails and longer hikes make for good mountain biking, but the closest rentals are in Lake Louise.
Alpine Rafting, T1888-599 5299, www.alp inerafting.com. Whitewater rafting on the Kicking Horse River. All levels.

Emerald Lake *p311*

The Emerald Lake Loop is a popular 5-km hiking trail. Fishing is good here and a portion of the lake is cleared in winter for ice-skating.
Emerald Sports and Gifts, T250-343 6000. Canoes, rowboats, fishing tackle and permits, cross-country skis, snowshoes and all gear.

● Transport

Field *p308*

3 **Greyhound** buses daily from the Visitor Centre running: east to **Lake Louise** (20-35 mins, $14), **Banff** (80 mins, $18) and **Calgary** (3 hrs, $34); west to **Golden** (1 hr, $13), **Revelstoke** (3-3½ hrs, $34), **Kamloops** (6-8 hrs, $62) and **Vancouver** (12-14 hrs, $111).

Kootenay National Park

Situated on the other side of the Continental Divide from Banff and bounded to the north by Yoho, it would be wrong to expect anything but spectacular scenery from Kootenay National Park, yet this is far and away the least visited of the big four. Besides the relative tranquillity, this park has two major assets: the Rockwall, which is one of the top five backpacking trips in the range; and a large number of short walks right from the highway, ideal for the less athletic, leading to diverse destinations including a forest fire burn and the Paint Pots, a series of multi-coloured mineral pools. A much more comprehensive overview of the Rockies can be gained by taking our suggested loop from Lake Louise through Yoho to Golden, down Highway 93, then through Kootenay Park arriving back near Banff. Entering from this direction, you'll be greeted by the dramatic red walls of Sinclair Canyon. ▶▶ *For Sleeping, Eating and other listings, see pages 316-317.*

Ins and outs

There is no public transport to or within the park. The only **Visitor Centre** ① *Jul-Aug daily 0900-1800, mid-May to Jun, Sep-early Oct daily 1000-1700*, in the park is in Kootenay Park Lodge at Vermilion Crossing. They hand out the *Backcountry Guide*, whose map and trail descriptions are all you need and issue backcountry passes ($9 per person per night). There is another, more helpful but less convenient **Parks Canada Visitor Centre** ① *7556 Main St E, T250-347 9505, T250-347 9331 for Chamber of Commerce, www.radiumhotsprings.com, mid-May to Jun daily 0900-1700, Jul-Aug daily 0900-1900, Sep-early Oct daily 0900-1600*, in the town of Radium Hot Springs.

Sights ◐◗ ▶▶ *p317.*

Radium Hot Springs → *Colour map 2, B3.*

Kootenay National Park's boundaries neatly parallel the winding course of the Banff-Windermere Parkway (Highway 93) as it makes its way from Castle Junction on Highway 1 to Radium Hot Springs in the East Kootenays. This rather brash and unpleasant town is little more than a string of cheesy motels, which tend to be full throughout the summer. The only thing to see is the **Thousand Faces Sculpture Gallery** ① *Hwy 93/Madsen Rd, T250-347 9208, www.radiumwoodcarver.com, $1.* This large collection of carvings and masks, many of them done with a chainsaw has a lot of legends and stories built into it. The eccentric artist, Rolf, is a curiosity himself. He has two pet goats Goofy and Spoofy – that live on his roof.

Those entering from the south are treated to a fine introduction to the park, as the road snakes its way through the steep and narrow Sinclair Canyon, its cliffs a rich red due to the high iron content. Just to the north are **Radium Hot Springs Pools** ① *T250-347 2100, May-Oct daily 0900-2300, Oct-Apr Sun-Thu 1200-2100, Fri-Sat 1200-2200, $6.30, child $5.40*, with a hot pool (39°C) and a cool pool (27°C) surrounded by rugged rocky scenery. These are packed in summer with up to 4000 people a day. You do not have to pay the National Park entry fee to enter the pools, but you do if you go any further. Note that the park is on Mountain Time, an hour ahead of most of BC. The park's other attractions are all reached via hikes, described below.

Hikes in Kootenay National Park 🌐🏃 *p317.*

Short hikes from north to south

Fireweed Trail ⓘ *1 km, Trailhead: just south of park boundary.* In 1968 a forest fire started by a single lightning bolt laid waste to a 24 sq km area just south of Vermilion Pass (1651 m). In 2003, the park's most active fire season in living memory, 12.6% of the park burned. This short trail talks you through the regeneration process and reveals how such fires are an integral part of the forest's natural cycle, to the point that lodgepole pine cones actually require the heat of a forest fire in order to open and spread their seeds. Already, a new forest has begun to appear within the blackened remains.

Marble Canyon ⓘ *800 m or more. Trailhead: 7 km south of park boundary.* An easy trail takes you to this lovely 600-m-long, 37-m-deep canyon which Tokumm Creek has carved out of the white dolomite limestone that was once mistaken for marble. The highlight is a striking view of a powerful waterfall where the creek forces its way through a narrow opening. In winter, the whole canyon turns into a magical palace of blue and green ice. This trail is currently closed.

The Paint Pots ⓘ *3 km return. Trailhead: 9.5 km south of park boundary.* This trail leads to a series of fascinating pools where iron-laden mineral springs push through clay sediments to create shades of red, orange and yellow. Native Americans came from far and wide to collect these coloured clays, which were then baked, ground into powder and added to fat or oil to make paint, which was then used in a number of creative and ceremonial ways.

Dog Lake ⓘ *5.2 km return. Trailhead: 500 m south of Mcleod Meadows campground.* About the best of the short hikes in the southern half of the park. This shallow, marsh-edged lake sits in one of the Rockies' most temperate valleys, making it a good spot for wildlife. Orchids also abound in early summer.

Longer hikes

The Rockwall ⓘ *54.8 km; 1490 m elevation gain. Trailhead: 22.5 km south of park boundary.* The Rockwall is the name of the Vermillion Mountains' eastern escarpment, a solid sheet of grey limestone whose sheer cliffs run for 35 km along the Great Divide. Instead of running along a ridge like some highline trails, this one goes up and down like a rollercoaster, crossing three alpine passes then plunging down into valleys, passing on the way a number of hanging glaciers, flower-strewn meadows, gorgeous lakes and stunning waterfalls. It is one of the most demanding but rewarding hikes in the Rockies and is comfortably done in four days. Four trails lead to the Rockwall, along Floe, Numa, Tumbling and Helmet Creeks. The optimum approach is to hike up Floe Creek, spending night one at Floe Lake campground (10.5 km), night two at Tumbling Falls (27.9 km) and night three at Helmet Falls (39.7 km). A few shorter hikes take in sections of the Rockwall, although the greatest reward is hiking the whole thing.

Floe Lake/Numa Pass ⓘ *21-26.4 km; 715-1030 m elevation gain. Trailhead: 22.5 km south of park boundary.* This is the best of the Rockwall day-hikes. Floe Lake is one of the most majestic sights in the Rockies: sheer cliffs rise 1000 m straight up from the azure blue waters, their ice floes mirrored on its crystal surface. The ascent is long, quite steep and mostly through forest, making this more suited to an overnighter than a day-hike. Views from Numa Pass, 2.7 km (one hour) further, are even more striking, another reason to spend an extra day. It's the best place to take in the lake and the

Kootenay National Park

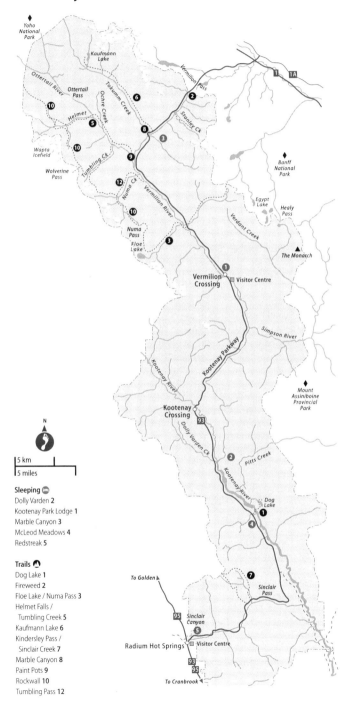

N

5 km
5 miles

Sleeping
Dolly Varden **2**
Kootenay Park Lodge **1**
Marble Canyon **3**
McLeod Meadows **4**
Redstreak **5**

Trails
Dog Lake **1**
Fireweed **2**
Floe Lake / Numa Pass **3**
Helmet Falls /
  Tumbling Creek **5**
Kaufmann Lake **6**
Kindersley Pass /
  Sinclair Creek **7**
Marble Canyon **8**
Paint Pots **9**
Rockwall **10**
Tumbling Pass **12**

rockwall that towers above it. From here, it is possible to descend to the highway via Numa Creek, making a total loop of 27.3 km, though it means hitching 8 km back to the trailhead.

Tumbling Pass ⓘ *24.4-km loop; 800 m elevation gain, 840 m loss. Trailhead: 9.5 km south of park boundary.* As a day-hike, this is extremely long and tough. It starts pleasantly enough by passing by the Paint Pots, but soon sets into a steady ascent with little reward until you reach Tumbling Falls at 9.4 km, where there is a nice campground. The pass is a tough 3.6 km further, but worth it for the awesome sight of the Rockwall and Tumbling Glacier. A 6-km detour to Wolverine Pass is also worth the effort, but as a day-hike there's no time. From the pass, return to the trailhead along Numa Creek, a steep but pleasant descent.

Helmet Falls/Tumbling Creek ⓘ *37-km loop. Trailhead: 9.5 km south of park boundary.* As a two-day trip, it is worth hiking up Ochre/Helmet Creeks to Helmet Falls at the north end of the Rockwall. This impressive cascade is one of the highest in Canada. It is possible to stay at the campground here then ascend through Rockwall Pass and exit to the trailhead along Tumbling Creek, though this is a tough second day.

Kindersley Pass/Sinclair Creek ⓘ *16.5-20.5-km loop, 1055 m elevation gain. Trailhead: across the highway from the parking area 9.5 km from the west gate at Radium.* This is one of the park's most scenic and most strenuous hikes. The trail ascends steadily for 8.4 km with little reward. From Kindersley Pass, views start to appear northward of the countless peaks of the Brisco Range. For the next 1.4 km to Kindersley Summit vistas of this ocean of summits keep getting better. From here the indistinct trail along Sinclair Creek makes for a convenient loop back to the Highway, though it leaves you 1.2 km northeast of your vehicle.

◉ Sleeping

Kootenay National Park *p313, map p315*
Apart from camping, most accommodation is in Radium Hot Springs.
B Chalet Europe, 5063 Madsen Rd, T250-347 9305 www.chaleteurope.com. This Swiss-style chalet is situated on a hill adjacent to the park entrance, a healthy 180 m above the madding crowd. The 6 very attractive suites have kitchens, and private balconies with telescopes to make the most of the incredible views. Sauna and jacuzzi.
C Kootenay Park Lodge, Vermilion Crossing, T250-762 9196, www.kootenayparklodge. com. Very small, fairly basic log cabins with front patios. The only beds in the park itself.
C Village Country Inn, 7557 Canyon Av, Radium Hot Springs, T250-347 9392, www.villagecountryinn.bc.ca. The nicest of many places to stay in town. Comfortable rooms with big beds and TVs.
C-D Rocky Mountain Springs Lodge, 5067 Madsen Rd, T250-285 9743, www.million dollarview.ca. Up on the hill above town by

the park entrance. Plain but decent sized rooms with balconies and great views. Very reasonable price and breakfast is included. Also serves the best food.
D-E Misty River Lodge and HI Hostel, Hwy 93, by the park entrance, T250-347 9912, www.radiumhostel.bc.ca. A small, friendly hostel with 11 dorm beds, 2 private rooms and 2 family rooms. Lounge, kitchen, deck with BBQ, and bike and canoe rental.

Camping
There are 8 campgrounds, mostly on the Rockwall and Kaufmann Lake trails.
Marble Canyon. The only campground in the more interesting northern part of the park, Jun-Sep. 61 sites.
McLeod Meadows, 25 km north of Radium. 98 basic sites on the river, May-Sep. Just to the north and only open in winter, is the tiny (free) Dolly Varden.
Redstreak, just north of Sinclair Canyon, T1877-737 3783, www.pccamping.ca,

May-Oct. The park's biggest campground and the only one that can be reserved, with 242 sites, showers and full hook-ups.

🅟 Eating

Kootenay National Park *p313, map p315*
🍴🍴🍴 **Old Salzburg**, 4943 Hwy 93, 2 km west of the park gates, T250-347 6553. Serves traditional Austrian food such as schnitzel and spaetzle, as well as seafood, steak and delicious desserts. Excellent food, service and atmosphere.

🍴 **Citadella Restaurant**, in Rocky Mountain Springs Lodge, 5067 Madsen Rd, T250-285 9743, www.milliondollarview.ca. Generous portions of delicious meat-based fair, with Hungarian specialities. There's also the amazing view.

🍴 **Horsethief Creek Pub and Eatery**, 7538 Main St, T250-347 6400. Good pub grub. Try the beef dip.

Waterton Lakes National Park

Despite its modest size, a mere 525 sq km – the most southerly of Canada's Rocky Mountain parks delivers landscapes and hiking to rival almost anything further north, but without the crowds. The scenery has a unique flavour of its own, a strange juxtaposition of prairies and mountain. The park's remarkable diversity of geographic zones – prairie, wetlands, aspen parkland, montane forest – has also led to a far greater variety of flora and fauna than any of Western Canada's other parks, with about 1200 plant species, including 55% of Alberta's wild flowers. In 1932, the park combined with Glacier National Park in Montana to become the world's first International Peace Park and was recognized as a Biosphere Reserve in 1979 and UNESCO World Heritage Site in 1995. ▸▸ *For Sleeping, Eating and other listings, see pages 321-322.*

Ins and outs

Getting there and around
The closest **Greyhound station** ⓘ *1018 Waterton Av, Pincher Creek, 51 km to the north, T403-627 2716*, receives daily buses from Vancouver via Highway 3 and from Calgary. The nearest **US border crossing** ⓘ *Jun-Aug daily 0700-2200, late May and Sep daily 0900-1800*, is at Chief Mountain on the park's eastern edge. At other times, the closest border crossing is east on Highway 2 at Carway, Alberta/Peigan, Montana, open year-round (daily 0700-2300).

A **Hiker Shuttle Service** from Tamarack Village Square, T403-859 2378, will take you to Cameron Lake, Red Rock Canyon and other trailheads. **Crypt Lake Water Shuttle Service** at the marina, T403-859 2362, delivers hikers to Crypt Lake Trailhead ($16 return) and points such as Rainbow Falls and Francis Lake.

Best time to visit
The park is open from the long weekend in May until Labour Day weekend in September, though many of the hikes are still under snow until well into June. Prairie flowers bloom in the spring and early summer, while higher elevation wild flowers arrive in late summer/autumn, which is also the best time to see animals such as bears and elk. Waterton receives Alberta's highest average annual precipitation levels and is one of the province's windiest places.

Tourist information
The **Parks Visitor Centre** ⓘ *Entrance Rd, T403-859 2445, www.watertonchamber.com, Jun-Aug daily 0800-2100, May and Sep daily 0900-1700*, is on the way into town. The rest of the year information is available at the **Parks Administration Office** ⓘ *215 Mt*

View Rd, T403-859 2477, Mon-Fri daily 0800-1600. Also useful is the **Waterton Natural History Association** ⓘ *117 Waterton Av, T403-8592624, www.wnha.ca,* which has exhibits, an art gallery, a museum and sells park-related books and maps. Hikers can buy a 1:50,000 map here or at the Visitor Centre, though for most people the free map will suffice. A park permit costs $6.80 per day, child $3.40.

Waterton Townsite 🍽🚲🚶❄🛏⛺🎒 ➻ *p321-322.*
Colour map 2, C4.

As a tribute to the herds that once roamed freely on this land, a Bison Paddock is maintained just north of the park entrance off Highway 6. As you approach the core of the park, the first thing you'll see is the magnificently grandiose **Prince of Wales Hotel**, a fascinating building erected by the Great Northern Railway in 1927, with a steeply sloping gabled roof, myriad balconies and an extraordinary post and beam lobby. Its location could hardly be more photogenic: high on a bluff overlooking broad expanses of crystal aquamarine surrounded by towering snowy peaks. Be sure to go in and explore.

Waterton Townsite cannot hope to live up to this opening gambit, but it's a pleasant enough spot that gains much from the lake setting. More resort than genuine

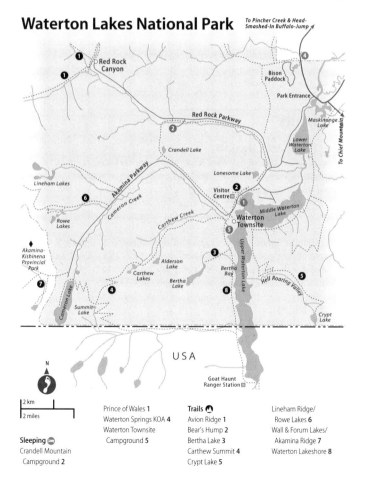

Waterton Lakes National Park

To Pincher Creek & Head-Smashed-In Buffalo-Jump

Prince of Wales **1**	**Trails** 🐾
Waterton Springs KOA **4**	Avion Ridge **1**
Waterton Townsite	Bear's Hump **2**
Campground **5**	Bertha Lake **3**
	Carthew Summit **4**
Sleeping 🛏	Crypt Lake **5**
Crandell Mountain	
Campground **2**	

Lineham Ridge/
Rowe Lakes **6**
Wall & Forum Lakes/
Akamina Ridge **7**
Waterton Lakeshore **8**

Canadian Rockies Waterton Lakes National Park Ins & outs

village, it still feels rather quaint, with mule deer and bighorn sheep wandering freely over the lawns and Cameron Falls just on the edge of town. Hiking is the main activity around here. Wonderful views are easily attained and a few of the many day-hikes lead right from the townsite. Thanks to the strong local winds, windsurfing is very popular on **Cameron Bay**, as are fishing (with a licence), canoeing and scuba-diving.

Hikes in Waterton Lakes National Park

Hikes from town

Crypt Lake ⓘ *17.2 km return; 685 m elevation gain. Trailhead: by boat.* This is one of the most popular and exciting trips in the park, with a bit of everything thrown in. You start with a boat trip across the lake, hike an undulating trail through Hell Roaring Valley, pass four waterfalls including the stunning Crypt Falls, stoop through a dark 20-m tunnel, then ascend a mountainside using a safety cable. The views are fine throughout and the emerald lake itself sits in a steep and dramatic cirque. You can expect to have plenty of company. There is a backcountry campground at Km 8.

Bear's Hump ⓘ *1.4 km; 200 m elevation gain. Trailhead: above Information Centre.* Short but steep, leading to great views of mountains, lake and townsite. Snow-free from late May.

Bertha Lake ⓘ *11 km return; 460 m elevation gain. Trailhead: car park opposite the town campground.* The popularity of this hike is due mainly to its being easy and conveniently located. The trail's highlight arrives at just Km 1.5, with views of the lake and distant prairie. A fork here leads right to Bertha Lake. The left fork descends to the Waterton Lakeshore Trail. This leads to the decent beach at Bertha Bay and beyond to Goat Haunt (15 km in total), where you can catch a boat back. This is only really recommended as a spring or autumn hike, as it's usually snow-free from April to October.

Hikes from the Akamina Parkway

Lineham Ridge/Rowe Lakes ⓘ *17-20 km return; 920-1,060 m elevation gain. Trailhead: Km 10.5 on the parkway.* This trail follows a creek up gentle slopes with valley views and through mature forest before cutting up bare, rocky slopes to the ridge. The pretty Row Lakes are a worthwhile side-trip best saved for the return leg if time and energy allow, because the highlight is Lineham Ridge, which offers excellent views of many of the jagged peaks in Waterton and Glacier Parks.

Wall and Forum lakes/Akamina Ridge ⓘ *10-20 km return; 915 m elevation gain. Trailhead: at Km 14.6 on the parkway.* There are three possible hikes in Akamina-Kishinena Provincial Park, adjacent to Waterton in British Columbia. Forum and Wall Lakes are distinct, easy hikes to pretty lakes at the base of sheer rock walls. Between the two is Akamina Ridge, the real prize for those not averse to a bit of scrambling, with great views into Waterton and Glacier Parks. The Forum-Ridge-Wall circuit is best done in this order. Be sure to get full details before attempting it and be ready for strong winds on the ridge.

Carthew Summit ⓘ *20 km one-way; 700 m elevation gain. Trailhead: at Km 15.7, the end of the road.* This is a one-way hike from Cameron Lake to Cameron Falls on the edge of Waterton Townsite, so is best done using a shuttle to the trailhead. The highlight is the view from Carthew Summit itself, with the steep peaks of Glacier National Park to the south and the curious sight of endless Alberta prairies stretching off to the northeast horizon. From here it's all down hill, in every respect.

Avion Ridge ⓘ *22.9-km loop, 944 m elevation gain. Trailhead: canyon car park at road's end.* This long, high, narrow ridge has few truly inspiring viewpoints, but offers panoramas whose very size makes an impression. The loop is best done clockwise, past Snowshoe Campground, over the ridge and down past Goat Lake. Otherwise, take the worthwhile 7-km detour from Snowshoe to Twin Lakes, the campground is much nicer.

Head-Smashed-In-Buffalo-Jump 🛏 ↠ *p321-322.*
Colour map 2, C4.

Native Americans had thousands of years to refine their techniques for the large-scale slaughter of bison, their ultimate method being the ruthlessly efficient 'buffalo jump'. Situated 18 km west of Fort Macleod on Highway 785, Head-Smashed-In-Buffalo-Jump was named a UNESCO World Heritage Site because it is one of the oldest and best preserved of its kind. Over 11 m of bone deposits at the base of the cliff bear witness to at least 5500 years of continual use.

A masterpiece of invention that blends into the sandstone cliff over which the herds were driven, the four-storey **Interpretive Centre** ⓘ *T1800-661 1222, www.head-smashed-in.com, mid-May to mid-Sep daily 0900-1800, mid-Sep to mid-May daily 1000-1700; $9, child $5, no public transport, taxis from Fort Macleod cost about $25*, uses archaeological evidence and the verbal records of the local First Nations to explain the functioning and history of the jump and its relation to the ecology, mythology, lifestyle and technology of the Blackffot people.

The process of the buffalo hunt presented by the centre includes: pre-hunt ceremonies; the **Gathering Basin** – a 40 sq km grazing area of plentiful grass and water to attract the herds; the network of **Drive Lanes**, consisting of stone cairns that helped hunters to funnel the bison towards the cliff; the **Kill Site**, which is just north of the centre, with another visible 1 km north; and the **Processing Area**, where the meat was sliced into thin strips and hung on racks to dry, much of it pounded with grease, marrow and berries to make pemmican. Displays also cover the lifestyle of prehistoric Plains people, their techniques of food gathering, social life and ceremonies; and the geography, climate, flora and fauna of the northwest plains.

Trails at the lower and upper level allow you to explore the site and have a good look at the Drive Lanes and cliff. Tours are conducted by Blackfoot guides and **drum and dance performances** ⓘ *Wed in Jul and Aug, 1100 and 1330*, are given on the Centre's Plaza.

Cardston ↠ *Colour map 2, C4.*

The obvious route between Waterton and Fort Macleod is via Highways 6 and 3, passing through Pincher Creek. An alternative route (and about the same length) is on Highways 5 and 2, which meet at Cardston, a small town with a couple of worthwhile attractions. The **Remington-Alberta Carriage Centre** ⓘ *623 Main St, T403-653 5139, www.remingtoncarriagemuseum.com, mid-May to mid-Sep daily 0900-1800, mid-Sep to mid-May daily 1000-1700, $6.30, child $3.50, free guided tours, carriage rides can be taken mid-May to mid-Jun, $4, child $2.50, 15-20 mins*, has over 250 horse-drawn carriages from around the turn of the 20th century, which are displayed in a superbly equipped, purpose-built museum. Most of the carriages are original and in tip-top condition. Videos, panels, displays and live demonstrations deal with the carriage business from factory to blacksmith to fire station.

While in town, the amazing **Alberta Temple of the Latter Day Saints** ⓘ *348 3rd St, T403-653 3552, mid-May to mid-Sep daily 0900-2000, free*, is well worth seeing. Built in 1912 from 3,680 tons of premium white gold-bearing granite quarried around

Kootenay Lake, this geometric structure successfully blends ancient and modern styles, with traces of the Temple of Solomon, Mayan-Aztec pyramids and the Prairie School of Frank Lloyd Wright. The inside sounds equally impressive, but non-Mormons cannot enter.

● Sleeping

Waterton Lakes National Park *p317, map p318*
Camping
There are 9 designated wilderness camp-grounds in the park. Limited spaces have resulted in a quota system, with reservations possible 90 days in advance, T403-859 5140 Apr to mid-May, then T403-859 5133. The full fee, $6.80, child $3.40 per person per night, plus a reservation fee of $6.80, child $3.40 per person, must be paid by credit card when booking. You'll need to know how many nights you intend to stay. Passes are issued at the Visitor Centre if there are places left.

Waterton Townsite *p318*
Accommodation in Waterton is expensive but embraces a few budget options. Call the Central Reservations Office for package deals, T1800-215 2395.
L Prince of Wales Hotel, T403-236 3400, www.glacierparkinc.com. A must for those who can afford it, this beautiful timber-frame building is brimming with character and a sense of history. Ask for a lake view. There's also a tea room lounge and gift shop.
A-B Waterton Lakes Resort, Windflower and Clematis Avenues, T403-859 6343, www.watertonlakeslodge.com. Many different types of appealing chalet-style rooms in 11 buildings, including the impressive lodge. There's a heated indoor pool, ping-pong tables and restaurant.
A-C Crandell Mountain Lodge, Mountain View Rd, T403-859 2288, www.crandell mountainlodge.com. An old-fashioned country cottage with a range of pleasant rooms and some suites with kitchenette.
B Kilmorey Lodge, Mountain View Rd, T403-859 2334, www.kilmoreylodge.com. Old-fashioned but comfortable rooms with big windows in an attractive building decorated with antiques. Has a restaurant.
B Northland Lodge, 408 Evergreen Av, T403-859 2353, www.northlandlodge canada.com. 8 colourful and distinctive rooms in a country-style home.

B-C Aspen Village Inn, Windflower Av, T403-859 2255, www.aspenvillageinn.com. Small but pleasant rooms with balconies. More attractive and more expensive cottages in an agreeable building. Use of hot tub.
C Bear Mountain Motel, 208 Mount View Rd, T403-859 2366, www.bearmountain motel.com. Plain rooms with 1-3 beds.
D HI Waterton Alpine Centre, 101 Clematis Av, T403-859 2150, www.hihostels.ca. 21 beds in dorms or private rooms in a choice wood lodge, with kitchen, sauna and café.

Camping
There are several walk-in sites and some private campgrounds north on Hwy 6 and east on Hwy 5.
Crandell Mountain Campground, 8 km west on Red Rock Canyon Rd. The nearest pleasant campground to town. 129 sites with fire pits and a kitchen.
Waterton Townsite Campground, T1877-737 3783, www.pccamping.ca. An ugly parking lot with 238 sites but in town. Only one that takes reservations.
Waterton Springs KOA, 3 km NE of gate on Hwy 6, T403-859 2247. Has the best facilities of those on the highway, with 190 sites, showers, laundry and a swimming pool.

Head-Smashed-In-Buffalo Jump *p320*
L Head-Smashed-In-Buffalo Jump, T403-553 2731, www.head-smashed-in.com, $325 for 4 or less, including dinner, breakfast, campfire storytelling and site entrance fee. Mid-May to mid-Sep, you can stay in a tepee and take part in various Blackfoot activities.

Camping
Buffalo Plains RV Park and Campground, 3 km east of town, T403-553 2592, www.buff aloplains.com. 30 pleasant sites with views and laundry, but no showers.

● Eating

Waterton Townsite *p318*
The better choices for food in Waterton are all hotel dining rooms.

Royal Stewart Dining Room, in the Prince of Wales (see Sleeping). European and Canadian dishes, decent but nothing exceptional. The views are superb.

Bighorn Grill, at Waterton Lakes Resort, Windflower and Clematis Avenues, T403-859 6343. Fairly predictable menu, but one of the nicer places to eat.

Glacier Café, in the Bayshore Inn, 111 Waterton Av, T403-859 2211. Good for breakfast, pizza and pasta.

Lamp Post, in the Kilmorey Lodge (see Sleeping), T403-859 2342. Exudes historic charm and has the best menu out of all the hotel dining rooms, includes some exotic options like ostrich, caribou and elk.

Pizza of Waterton, Fountain Av. Most appealing choice for good value food in attractive surroundings. The pizzas are good.

● Bars and clubs

Waterton Townsite *p318*
Gazebo Café, next to Kilmorey Lodge. Outdoor café with food and agood wine list.
Ram's Head Lounge, Kilmorey Lodge. The nicest spot for a quiet drink.
Windsor Lounge, Prince of Wales Hotel. Soak up the atmosphere by sipping a beer or glass of wine in the sophisticated lounge.

✪ Festivals and events

Waterton Townsite *p318*
Jun Waterton Wild Flower-Fest, www.wat ertonwildflowers.com. 9 days of events and guided excursions to see, photograph, paint and behold the park's plants and flowers.

○ Shopping

Waterton Townsite *p318*
Gust Gallery, 112A Waterton Av, T403-859 2535, www.gustgallery.com. 3 local artists.
Waterton Outdoor Adventures, T403-859 2378, Tamarack Village Sq. Camping and backpacking supplies, and trail maps.

▲ Activities and tours

Waterton Lakes National Park *p317,*
map p318
Hiking
There are over 200 km of trails in the park.

A hiker shuttle service to Cameron Lake, Red Rock Canyon and other trailheads is operated by **Waterton Outdoor Adventures**, Tamarack Village Sq, T403-859 2378, www.watertonvisitorservices.com. **Crypt Lake Water Shuttle Service**, at the marina, T403-859 2362, delivers hikers to Crypt Lake trailhead. After returning from a hike in spring and early summer, check for ticks.

Waterton Townsite *p318*
Tour operators
Alpine Stables, T403-859 2462, www.alpine stables.com. Horse riding and pack trips to many places in the park. 1 hr/$30, 3 hrs/$70, 8 hrs/$135.
Cameron Lake Boat Rentals, Cameron Lake, 17 km west. Canoes and row boats.
Hiker Shuttle Services, Tamarack Village Sq, T403-859 2378. Daily shuttle service to most of the trailheads.
Kimball River Sports, just south of Cardston, T1800-936 6474, www.raftalberta.ca. Rafting, canoeing, kayaking and fishing tours.
Mountain Meadow Trail Rides, Mountain View, halfway to Cardston, T403-653 2413, www.mountainmeadowtrailrides.com. Horseback adventures from 1½ hr rides to overnight pack trips. Also packages including canoeing or rafting.
Pat's Cycle Rental, Mountview Rd, T403-859 2266. Bike and scooter rentals, and sales.
Waterton Lakes Golf Course, T403-859 2114, www.watertonpark.com. Surely one of the most scenic in the country.
Waterton Inter-Nation Shoreline Cruise Co., T403-859 2362, www.watertoncruise. com. Interpretive tours of the lake. Also runs the all-important Crypt Lake Water Shuttle Service, daily 1000, Jul-Aug daily 0900, 1000 ($16 round trip).

❶ Directory

Waterton Townsite *p318*
ATM Tamarack Village Sq; Rocky Mountain Food, Windflower Av. **Currency Exchange** Tamarack Village Sq. **Emergencies** Ambulance T403-859 2636; Police T403-859 2244. **Laundry** 301 Windflower Av.
Medical services Closest hospitals are in Cardston, T403-653 4931 and Pincher Creek, T403-627 3333. **Post office** Canada Post, Corner Fountain Av/Windflower Av.

The Yukon

⁝ Footprint features

Introduction

The Yukon's landscapes are wide, magnificent and utterly unspoilt. Canada's highest mountains, most extensive non-polar ice fields and greatest concentration of grizzly bears are protected by Kluane National Park, famed for wonderful, uncrowded hiking trails and sensational white-water rafting. The territory, whose name means 'great river' in the native Loucheux language, is criss-crossed with rivers made for canoeing, while numerous circuits on backcountry roads lead through pristine wilderness to sleepy villages like the unfeasibly picturesque Atlin. The Dempster Highway, Canada's ultimate frontier road, passes desolate mountain ranges on its way to the frozen north. The laid-back capital, Whitehorse, is the place to plan excursions and then to relax afterwards.

The greatest Gold Rush of all time led thousands of treasure seekers to the goldfields of the Klondike. You can retrace their steps by hiking the Chilkoot Pass, panning for gold and visiting the renovated but still-living Wild West town of Dawson City, where clapboard houses, boardwalks and saloons line the dirt streets. Thriving First Nations culture and extensive wildlife are two more trump cards, but what keeps visitors coming back is the character and overwhelming friendliness of the Yukon people.

Beaufort Sea

Komakuk Beach
Herschel Is
Herschel
Ivvavik National Park
Shingle Point
Tuktoyaktuk
Richard Is
Tununuk
Kittigazuit

British Mountains

Mackenzie Delta
Aklavik
Inuvik

Old Crow

Old Crow Flats

Richardson Mountains

Whitefish Lake
Eagle
Cody

Fort McPherson
Arctic Red River
Mackenzie

Eagle Plains

NORTHWEST TERRITORIES

ALASKA USA
Dawson City
YUKON
Whitehorse
NORTHWEST TERRITORIES
BRITISH COLUMBIA
ALBERTA
Prince Rupert
Prince George
Rocky Mountains
Calgary
Vancouver
USA

Dempster Highway
Eagle Plains
5

Caribou
Peel
Bonnet Plume
Wind
Snake
Noisy

Peel Wilderness

ALASKA USA

Clinton Creek (abandoned)
5
Ogilvie Mountains

Top of the World Highway
Sixty Mile
9
Dawson City
4
Bear Creek
Rock Creek
Granville (abandoned)

Tok
Tetlin Junction

McQuesten Lake

Mackenzie Mountains
Backbone Range
Heritage Trail
Carcajou Range

White
Stewart River (abandoned)
McQuesten (abandoned)
Stewart Crossing
Silver Trail
Elsa
11
Keno
Mayo
Mayo Lake

Beaver Creek
Snag
Koidern
Yukon
Dawson Range
Fort Selkirk
Pelly Crossing
YUKON

Selwyn Mountains

Kluane Mountains
Alaska Highway
Minto

Pelly

Hess Mountains

Burwash Landing
1
Aishihik
Carmacks
Glenlyon Pk
Little Salmon Lake
Mt Sheldon
Ross

Kluane National Park
2
Destruction Bay
Aishihik Lake
Klondike Highway
Little Salmon
4
Faro
Robert Campbell Highway
Ross River

Mt Logan (5959m)
Sheep Mountain
Canyon (abandoned)
Big Salmon

Pelly Mountains

St Elias Mountains
Haines Junction
Champagne
2
Livingston (abandoned)
Canol Rd
McPherson Lake
Finlayson Highway
South Nahanni

Alsek
Dezadeash
Takhini Hot Springs
6

Haines Highway
Kluane Lake
Kluskhu
Robinson
Whitehorse

Tatshenshini-Alsek Wilderness Park
3
Kusawa Lake
Carcross
Tagish
Johnson's Crossing
Liard
Tutchitua

Tatshenshini River
3
Watson Bennett
Jake's Corner
Teslin
Alaska Highway

Klukwan
Fraser
Klondike Highway
Atlin Lake
Teslin Lake
Rancheria

Skagway
Atlin
1
Surprise

Cassiar Mountains

Upper Liard
11
Watson Lake

Haines

ALASKA USA

Gulf of Alaska

Inklin
Nakina

Lower Post
Smith River

Tulsequah
Nahilin
Cassiar (abandoned)
Good Hope Lake
Fireside
Coal River

Porter Landing
Liard River
Chee House
Muncho Lake

Callison Ranch
Sheslay
Laketon
Dease Lake
Stikine Ranges
Spatizi Plateau
Fort Halkett
Toad River

Coast Mountains
Grand Canyon of the Stikine
Glenora
Telegraph Creek
40 Mile Flat
97

Stikine
37
Tatoga

BRITISH COLUMBIA

N

50 km
50 miles

Whitehorse and the south

Although it's the provincial capital, Whitehorse is a very small, friendly town unlikely to evoke any strong reactions. Its riverside location is pleasant enough, but there's nothing like the atmosphere and excitement of Dawson City to the north. It's the best place to organize excursions and pick up supplies, and it offers a welcome dose of civilization after time in the bush. The canoe trip from here to Dawson City is the most popular in the Yukon and is suitable for all levels. Most of Whitehorse's sights are inspired by its river and history and there's a lot of very good art, much of it by local First Nations. On the way up from BC, Teslin is worth a stop and Carcross gives access to the famous Chilkat Trail hike. The ultimate diversion, however, is south to Atlin, possibly the most beautifully located town in Western Canada. ▶▶ *For Sleeping, Eating and other listings, see pages 333-340.*

Ins and outs

Getting there and around

Most visitors to the Yukon have their own vehicles, as public transport is almost non-existent. Buses follow the Alaska Highway (Highway 1) as far as Whitehorse but distances are vast and it is cheaper and quicker to fly. **Whitehorse Airport** (YXY) ① *www.gov.yk.ca/yxy*, is between Downtown and the Alaska Highway and there are regular buses to Downtown. **Air Canada** ① *T1888-247 2262, www.aircanada.ca*, and the much cheaper **Air North** ① *T867-668 2228, www.flynorth.com*, fly regularly from Vancouver, Calgary and Edmonton; fares start at $195 one-way with the former. The **Greyhound** station ① *2nd Av, T867-667 2223, www.greyhound.ca*, is a short walk north of Downtown, with daily buses from Dawson Creek via Watson Lake. During summer, two Alaskan companies provide services to and from Dawson City and from Tok, Alaska.

Whitehorse is small enough to explore on foot but there are local buses, most leave from the corner of Ogilvie and Third Avenues, running through town on Fourth and Second Avenues. Drivers can obtain a three-day complimentary parking pass at City Hall ① *2121 2nd Av, T867-668 8687.* ▶▶ *For further details, see Transport, page 340.*

Best time to visit

Being so far north, temperatures and daylight hours vary considerably throughout the year. In January the average temperature is -19°C with six hours of daylight, in July it's 19°C with 19 hours of daylight. Winter is the best time to experience the northern lights and the incredible resilience and friendliness of the Yukon people, but June is the best month for festivals. By mid-August, autumn is beginning, heralded by a triumph of wildflowers, especially fireweed.

Tourist information

The **Visitor Information Centre** ① *2nd Av/Hanson, T867-667 3084, www.visit whitehorse.com, www.travelyukon.com, May-Sep daily 0800-2000, Oct-Apr Mon-Fri 0830-1900, Sat 1000-1400*, is very helpful and professional, with information on the whole province. They put out a Whitehorse brochure and the very useful *Yukon Vacation Planner*. **Yukon First Nations Tourism Association** ① *1109 1st Av, T867-667 7698, www.yfnta.org*, publishes its own impressive brochure, *Welcome*.

⁞ White horses and wild rapids

The first Hudson Bay traders arrived in the area in 1843, followed 40 years later by men toting gold pans. After a lucky strike on Bonanza Creek sparked the Gold Rush of 1898, a stampede of hopefuls travelled upriver in makeshift boats. For the next 50 years, until the building of the Alaska Highway in 1942 and the Klondike Highway in the 1950s, the Yukon River remained the foremost means of transportation in the province. The city of Whitehorse was named after a set of fierce rapids, with thrashing waters that resemble the manes of galloping horses. This treacherous stretch of river, which claimed the lives of many men and vessels, began 7 km above today's city at Miles Canyon. Those wary of facing the rapids hauled their belongings around the obstruction on horse-drawn tramways. Makeshift tent settlements quickly developed at either end of the rapids, the one above was named Canyon City, the one below was named Whitehorse.

Whitehorse ⬛️🚹🚶🛏️✳️🅾️▲🅰️🅱️🆑 ⇥ *pp333-340. Colour map 4, B4.*

Yukon River

Approaching Whitehorse from the south, 3 km before town, Miles Canyon Road leads down to the site of the rapids, which were removed by the damming of the Yukon River in 1958. The diversion is still worthwhile, as **Miles Canyon** is now lined with fantastic basalt walls. Across the footbridge are a number of trails that are popular for mountain biking and skiing. One leads to the abandoned Canyon City, a nice walk, though there's not much to see.

Entering town on Robert Service Way, you can't miss the **SS Klondike** ① *300 Main St, T867-667 4511, www.pc.gc.ca/ssklondike, May-Sep daily 0900-1900, tours every 30 mins, $6*, the largest of the sternwheelers that played a vital role in the Yukon's early life. These shallow-bottomed vessels proved invaluable for transporting men, supplies and gold over the treacherous rock-strewn waters. As many as 250 such boats once plied the Yukon River; local forests were decimated to provide fuel for them.

Lewes Boulevard crosses the river from here, leading to a riverside trail and Nisutlin Drive, which both head to the dam. About 1 km below this is the 'intake', a tiny remainder of whitewater, popular with kayakers and canoeists. **Whitehorse Fishway** ① *95 Nisutlin Dr, T867-667 4263, Jun-early Sep, by donation*, is the longest wooden fish ladder in the world. You can tour the fishway and watch salmon through underwater viewing windows, a particularly dramatic sight between mid-July and mid-August.

Downtown

The sights of Downtown Whitehorse are mostly historical. **MacBride Museum** ① *1124 1st Av, T867-667 2709, www.macbridemuseum.com, mid-May to Aug daily 0900-1800, Sep to mid-May Tue-Sat 1200-1600, $7, child $3.50*, housed in a group of log cabins, reveals the stories of the Yukon's First Nations, the Gold Rush, the North West Mounted Police and early pioneers. Highlights include a replica of a 910 cm Tlingit canoe and a carving shed where demonstrations are given. You can also try your hand at gold panning. The **Yukon Archives** ① *500 College Dr, T867-667 5321*, contain a wealth of material relating to Yukon's First Nations history and culture, including films, photos and interviews with elders. You can even do genealogy research to find out if any of your relatives took part in the Gold Rush.

Whitehorse

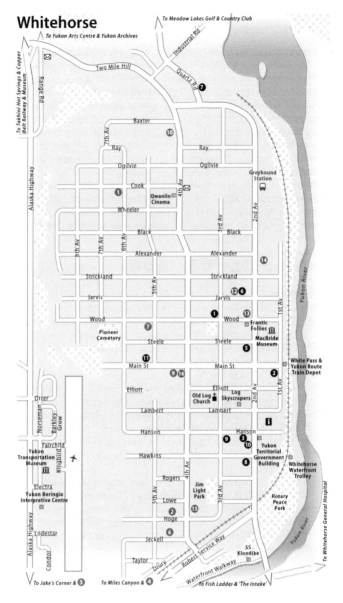

Sleeping
Beez Kneez Hostel 2
Historical House 7
Hostel Hide On Jeckell 6
MacKenzie's RV Park 3
Midnight Sun B&B 1
Robert Service
  Campground 4
Town & Mountain 9
Yukon Inn 10

Eating
Blackstone Café 1
Cellar Steakhouse &
  Wine Bar 2
Deli 3
Giorgio's Cuccina 6
Klondike Rib & Salmon
  BBQ 5
Midnight Sun Coffee
  Roasters 7
North Dragon 8

Sam & Andy's 11
Sanchez Mexican Deli 9
Talisman Café 10

Bars & clubs
Backwater Lounge 13
Lizards Lounge 16
Roadhouse Inn 14
Sam McGee's Bar & Grill 12
Yukon Mining Co 15

Many Klondike enthusiasts travel to Skagway (see page 333) on the **White Pass and Yukon Route Train** ⓘ *T867-633 5710, www.whitepassrailroad.com, US$130 one-way, tickets are available from the old depot on the waterfront at the bottom of Main St.* Note that only the last section, from Fraser to Skagway, is on the train and the rest is by bus. For a cheaper step back in time, the bright yellow **Whitehorse Waterfront Trolley** ⓘ *T867-667 6355, www.yukonrails.com, hourly 10000-1800, $3,* runs along the riverfront, leaving from Rotary Peace Park which is across from the *SS Klondike*. It's an interpretive ride, involving tales from Whitehorse's interesting waterfront history. One of the town's oldest buildings is the **Old Log Church** ⓘ *303 Elliott St, T867-668 2555, mid-May to Sep daily 0900-1800, $2.50,* built in 1900. It contains First Nations and Inuvialuit artefacts and photos documenting the impact of the white man's arrival on the native people. The **Log Skyscrapers** ⓘ *210 Lambert St, T867-633 2118,* are also worth a quick look.

Whitehorse is a good place for art-lovers. The best venue is the **Yukon Arts Centre and Gallery** ⓘ *Yukon College, north of town on Range Rd, T867-667 8575, www.yukonartscentre.com, Tue-Fri 1200-1800, Sat-Sun 1200-1700, by donation,* which hosts two or three temporary exhibitions of relevance to the Yukon, by local, national and international artists. The **Yukon Permanent Art Collection** is scattered throughout government buildings, ask at the Visitor Centre.

The **Yukon Territorial Government Building** ⓘ *2nd Av, T867-667 8589,* has some nice tapestries and murals. The free *Art Adventures on Yukon Time* brochure, available from the Visitor Centre, gives the addresses and numbers of artists' studios throughout the Yukon and **The Yukon Art Express** ⓘ *T867-667 8476, mid-May to mid-Sep daily 1100-1300, $15,* leaves from the White Pass building at Main and First Avenue.

On the Alaska Highway

During the last ice age, when glaciation caused sea levels to drop dramatically, Siberia was joined to Alaska by a great corridor of land that today is again submerged beneath the Bering Sea. This land bridge became a last refuge for thousands of species of plant and animal and among these were the giant woolly mammoth, scimitar cat and, of course, man. The **Yukon Beringia Interpretive Centre** ⓘ *T867-667 8855, www.beringia.com, mid-May to mid-Sep daily 00900-1800, mid-Sep to mid-May Sun 1300-1700, $6, child $4,* uses dioramas, murals, a film and life-sized reproductions of long-extinct wildlife to paint a picture of that frozen land and the people who managed to survive on it.

Just up the road, beside the airport, the **Yukon Transportation Museum** ⓘ *T867-668 4792, www.yukontransportationmuseum.ca, May-Sep daily 1000-1800, tours 1130 and 1600, $6, under 18 $4, under 12 $3, under 6 free,* documents provincial methods of movement, from moose-skin boats to modern aircraft. Enthusiasts could spend all day watching videos about the White Pass Railway, Alaska Highway, Sternwheelers and the Yukon Dog Sled Race. For most, the highlight is a scale model of the White Pass and Yukon Railway. On the way out of town heading north is the **Copper Belt Railway & Museum** ⓘ *91928 Alaska Hwy, T867-667 6355, www.yukonrails.com.* Ride the rails or check out a small collection of railway artefacts.

Takhini Hot Springs → *Colour map 4, B4.*

ⓘ *T867-633 2706, www.takhinihotsprings.yk.ca, mid-May to mid-Sep daily 0800-2200, mid-Sep to mid-May Mon, Wed 1200-1800, Thu-Sun 1200-2100, $7, child $5.25.*

About 10 km north of Whitehorse, the highway veers west towards Haines Junction and Kluane National Park, while the Klondike Highway continues north to Dawson City. Almost 10 km beyond the junction, a road heads 10 km west to **Takhini Hot Springs**. The waters are odourless and range from 45°C at one end to 35°C at the other. The main minerals are calcium, magnesium and iron, which gives the water a reddy-brown colour. There's a cedar sauna, campground, restaurant and trail rides.

⁑ The Northern Lights

Theories as to the exact science behind the aurora borealis, or northern lights, continue to evolve. Streams of charged particles from the sun are carried toward the earth by cosmic winds. As these interact with lines of the earth's magnetic field energy is produced. The result for those spectating is a light show, with eerie patterns projected over the sky, often seeming to spread out from a point and shifting like a kaleidoscope. The main colours are green, which comes from oxygen, and pink from nitrogen. Deep red auroras are rare, and were once seen as evil omens.

The aurora appears around the north and south poles simultaneously and symmetrically, though obviously it can only be witnessed at one as the other will always be in daylight. There is a 27-day cycle between the most brilliant displays, and also an 11-year cycle, which last peaked in 2002. Strong auroras can cause problems with radio signals, and even pipelines and transmission lines. Natives of the north were said to hear swishing sounds accompanying the lights, though these have never been recorded. They may be related to radio waves or static electricity.

Two kilometres before the Hot Springs is **Yukon Wildlife Preserve** ① *T867-633 2922, www.yukonwildlife.ca, May-Sep, $22, child $12, phone ahead to book tour, 1½ hrs*, where guided tours by vehicle offer the chance to observe caribou, moose, elk, muskoxen, wood bison, mountain goats and dall sheep in their natural habitat.

Watson Lake to Whitehorse 🍴🏨❄️⛰️🚌 ›› *pp333-340.*

Watson Lake

The Cassiar Highway (Highway 37) joins the Alaska Highway 22 km west of Watson Lake, where there is a useful petrol station. This is a relatively dull little town that fails to justify the 44-km diversion, unless you can make it in mid-July for the Watson Lake Rodeo. One reason to visit, however, is the extremely useful **Visitor Information Centre** ① *T867-536 7469, www.watsonlake.ca, mid-May to mid-Sep daily 0800-2000*, which can provide guides and maps. There are also displays and a slideshow about the Yukon and the construction of the Alaska Highway.

Before 30,000 US Army personnel arrived in 1942 to work on the highway, Watson Lake was just a tiny airport, part of the Northwest Staging Route Programme that tried to create a Great Circle Route connecting Alaska, Siberia and China. One homesick soldier put up a sign showing the distance and direction to his home town and, unwittingly, began a collection that now includes 53,000 such signs. This 'world famous' **Sign Post Forest**① *next to the Information Centre*, is the town's number one attraction. Across the highway is the only other attraction, the **Northern Lights Space and Science Centre** ① *T867-536 7827, www.northernlightscentre.ca, $10, child $6*, which shows 50-minute films that present the myths and reality of the aurora borealis and animal photos set to music.

Teslin → *Colour map 4, B5.*

After a brief, barely noticeable foray back into BC, the Alaska Highway joins the attractive shores of **Teslin Lake**, at the town of the same name. Teslin is home to a thriving community of native Tlingit, originally of coastal origin, who moved permanently to their inland summer home in the early 1900s, prompted by the quest for furs. The arts and crafts of their West Coast heritage migrated with them and provide a couple of good reasons to stop.

The largest collection of artefacts is found at the small but splendid **George Johnston Museum** ⓘ *off the highway, north side of town, T867-390 2550, www.gjmuseum.yk.net, May-Sep daily 0900-1800, $5, child $2.50*. This successful Tlingit trapper and entrepreneur opened the first aboriginal-owned store in town and bought its first car, a 1928 Chevrolet, exhibited in the museum. Of far greater interest is Johnston's collection of black and white prints that candidly document 50 years of Teslin's history. There's also a small theatre, showing films by and about the Tlingit people.

The best place to witness the work of talented local mask and totem carvers is further north on the highway at the striking **Teslin Tlingit Heritage Centre** ⓘ *T866-854 6438, www.ttc-teslin.com, May-Sep daily 0900-2100, $5*. Interpretive, audiovisual and art displays introduce the history and culture of the Tlinget and you can watch them at work in an outdoor carving shed.

Teslin Lake is noted for its fishing. Chinook salmon run late July to mid-August while spring and autumn are best for whitefish, trout, northern pike, Arctic grayling and inconnu. The **Nisutlin Delta National Wildlife Area** at the north end of the lake is a major waterfowl staging post, visited in autumn by thousands of ducks, swans and geese, and predators like peregrine falcon, fox, coyote and wolf. Canoeing is also popular. ▸▸ *For further details, see Activities and tours, page 339.*

Johnson's Crossing and Canol Road → *Colour map 4, B4.*

As well as a popular put-in spot for canoeing the Teslin River to access the Yukon, Johnson's Crossing is the junction with the **Canol Road** (Highway 6). The controversial Canol (Canadian Oil) Pipeline was built by the US in 1942 to pump oil from Norman Wells NWT to a refinery in Whitehorse. It was dismantled after just one year of use. Today, its southern section provides a chance to sample some of the Yukon's remote backcountry. The surface can be pretty rough but the effort is well rewarded by the last stunning stretch before **Ross River**, when the road skirts close to picturesque Pass Peak, then winds its way through the Lapie River Canyon. On the way are three small campgrounds. From Ross River, Highway 4 heads northwest through Faro to connect with the Klondike Highway near **Carmacks**, a very worthwhile alternative route to or from Dawson City, bypassing Whitehorse. The new **Dena Cho Trail** ⓘ *T867-969 2278*, is an 68-km hike from Ross River to Faro, with campsites and cabins along the way.

Jake's Corner and around → *Colour map 4, B4.*

There is little more of note on the highway to Whitehorse, but at **Jake's Corner** two possible diversions present themselves. Easily the more worthwhile follows Highway 7 south for 95 km to Atlin, BC. The other provides a loop on Highways 8 and 2, which takes in **Carcross**, a dull town but the gateway to the Chilkoot Trail and Skagway, Alaska (see page 333). Beyond Jake's Corner, the northern end of **Marsh Lake**, known as **McClintock Bay**, is a critical habitat for migrating waterfowl in April and May. The arrival of thousands of Tundra and Trumpeter swans is heralded annually by the **Celebration of Swans Festival**, held at the **Swan Haven Interpretive Centre** ⓘ 10 Burns Rd, T867-667 8291, which is only open in April. The viewing deck, however is open year-round and there are interpretive hikes and a campground.

Atlin, BC → *Colour map 4, C4.*

Highway 7 to Atlin is a rough dirt road that hugs the shore of BC's largest natural lake, also the headwater of the Yukon River. A few campgrounds line the road and Km 6 is the trailhead for the **Mount White Trail**, one of the Yukon's most rewarding day hikes. The path starts on the left at the back of a gravel pit and climbs to a plateau that offers fabulous views.

⁞ Hiking the Chilkoot Trail

The most common method for the 100,000 or so stampeders to get to the Klondike Gold Fields was to catch an ocean liner to Skagway, then make the gruelling trek over the dreaded Chilkoot Pass to the bottom end of Bennett Lake, from where they could proceed by boat. To make matters infinitely harder, the Canadian authorities, who felt threatened by this mass migration of unruly Americans, established a North West Mounted Police post at the pass to collect duty and make sure that every American had enough supplies to last them for a whole year. Together with tents and mining equipment, this usually added up to a load of over a ton. It took the average man as many as 40 ascents to the pass to do it, at least 90 days of strenuous hiking in harsh conditions through extreme weather.

Today, the Chilkoot Trail is Canada's largest National Historic Site, and a very popular hike. The 53-km route, which takes three to six tough days to complete, is lined with remnants of abandoned mining equipment and interpretive signs. Hikers should be very fit and prepared for extreme conditions. The trail can get very muddy and unclear in places, with rockslides not uncommon, and harsh weather is to be expected. There is often still snow at the pass well into July. Fifty hikers per day are allowed to start the hike.

Permits are $50, child $25, per person ($34, child $17 for the Canadian side only) and can be purchased by credit card from early January, T1800-6610 0486, T1867-667 3910 (from overseas). There is an $11.70 booking fee per person. At this time, hikers must specify exactly which designated campgrounds they will use, so plan your trip first by consulting the information on Parks Canada's website, www.pc.gc.ca/lhn-nhs/yt/chilkoot. Hikers must pick up reserved permits and register for customs at the **Trail Center**, Broadway/1st-2nd Aves, Skagway, T907-983 9234, by 1200 on the starting day. This office issues eight walk-in permits per day on a first come first served basis at 1300, they are valid for the following day. Again, campgrounds must be specified.

Atlin itself is a ramshackle little frontier-style village of funky houses, full of friendly, arty and eccentric characters. **Atlin Visitors Association** ⓘ *3rd St, T867-651 7522, www.atlin.net*, is in the historical museum. Almost devoid of sights and entertainment, Atlin enjoys a setting of unparalleled magnificence, in an unimaginably vast and timeless wilderness landscape. Rearing up behind broad Atlin Lake is a string of giant glaciated mountains belonging to the Coast Range. The one closest to town is actually on enormous **Teresa Island**, a bear sanctuary. Beyond and accessible only by boat, are **Atlin Provincial** and **Wilderness** parks. A third of the latter is covered in glaciers, including the massive **Llewellen Glacier**, best seen from the top of **Monarch Mountain**. This stiff 12-km return hike starts 5 km down Warm Bay Road, a rough gravel road which follows the lake to the south, giving access to several campgrounds, beaches and, at Km 24, the **Warm Springs**, a clear pool surrounded by watercress.

Carcross and around → *Colour map 4, B4.*

Atlin is part of a region touted as the **Southern Lakes** ⓘ *www.southernlakesyukon.com*, which contains more than 600 linear kilometres of thin lakes within an area of some 100 sq km. Canoeing, boating and fishing are major local activities and the winds are often strong enough for windsurfing. A loop on Highways 8 and 2 from Jake's Corner leads to the heart of this area, adding just 38 km to the journey to Whitehorse. Despite a lack of real attractions, many visitors make the diversion thanks to the important role the area played in the Klondike Gold Rush, see page 370. Skookum Jim Mason, who first sparked the stampede with his discovery of gold on what became known as Bonanza Creek, was a member of the Tagish First Nation, but there is little reason to stop in **Tagish**.

The hub of the region is **Carcross**, whose name was shortened from the more evocative Caribou Crossing. It sits at the north end of Bennett Lake, which has some large sandy beaches and is a favourite with windsurfers. Prospectors who made it over the Chilkoot Pass travelled up the lake to here. The town has clearly remained virtually unchanged since those heady days and is of interest mainly for its many historical buildings and general run-down frontier town atmosphere. Visitors can also retrace the steps of the many hopefuls on the **Chilkoot Trail**. The **Visitor Centre** ⓘ *T867-821 4431, May-Sep daily 0800-2000*, is in the restored train station.

The train played its own part in transporting prospectors, a role celebrated today by the **White Pass and Yukon Railway** ⓘ *T907-983 2217, www.whitepassrailroad.com*, which carries tourists along the historic route to **Skagway** ⓘ *6-hr train ride, non-Americans must clear customs in advance or get off at Fraser*. Buses also continue to Skagway, from where there is a scenic trip to Kluane Country via Haines, Alaska (see page 343).

Appropriately known as the **Klondike Highway**, Highway 2 follows the Gold Rush Trail north from Carcross through Whitehorse to Dawson City. The southern leg soon passes **Carcross Desert**, really a dried out lake bottom, very small and not especially impressive. A little further are the **Emerald** and **Spirit** lakes, where there is a very primitive and private campsite. Annie Lake Road branches west at the Robinson Roadhouse historic site and winds its way up the scenic Wheaton River Valley. There are lots of opportunities for hiking and mountain biking along here, such as the **Red Ridge** and **Two Horse Creek** trails, and experienced paddlers can canoe down the Wheaton or Watson Rivers to Bennett Lake.

● Sleeping

The *Yukon Vacation Planner* contains good listings, pick up a copy at a Visitor Centre.

Whitehorse *p327, map p328*
Whitehorse has 2 excellent hostels, both 15 mins' walk from the bus station.
B-C Fox Creek Wilderness B&B, 52 km north on Hwy 2, T867-333 3120, www.fox creekwild.com. If you're heading north, this is a beautiful place to stop. A big log house on a hillside surrounded by 65 ha, with views of Lake Laberge and the surrounding mountains, and a panorama of the Northern Lights. The 2 rooms are bright, very stylish and comfortable. There's a living room, sun deck and garden.
C Midnight Sun B&B, 6188 6th Av, T867-667 2255, www.midnightsunbb.com. 4 nice theme rooms in a large, central house owned by very hospitable hosts. Laundry, big common room and great breakfasts.

C Yukon Inn, 4220 4th Av, T867-667 2527, www.yukoninn.com. Fairly plain rooms in a very attractive, central, but quiet hotel.
C-D Town and Mountain Hotel, 401 Main St, T867-668 7644, www.townmountain. com. One of the cheapest hotels in town but with possibly the nicest rooms, which are spacious, bright and in keeping with the upbeat exterior. There's a restaurant and a bar and grill downstairs.
D Historical House, 5128 5th Av, T867-668 3907, www.yukongold.com. 2 reasonable rooms and a suite in a wooden home with lots of character, 2 blocks from the centre. Kitchen available and a stocked fridge to make your own breakfast.
E Beez Kneez Hostel, 408 Hoge St, T867-456 2333, www.bzkneez.com. Relaxed and homey atmosphere, with kitchen, 2 common rooms, a patio with BBQ, garden, laundry, and bikes. Free internet.

E **Hostel Hide On Jeckell**, 410 Jeckell, T867-633 4933, www.hide-on-jeckell.com. Very well organized. Each of the 4 dorms and 2 private rooms represent a different continent. There's a kitchen, games in the living room, lockable drawers, a garden, small deck and BBQ. Free internet, coffee and bike use. Library and book swap.

Camping

MacKenzie's RV Park, 18 Azure Rd, T867-633 2337. There are plenty of grim RV parks on the highway south of town, all resembling gravel car parks. This is the best of a bad bunch.
Robert Service Campground, 2 mins' drive east, or 20 mins' walk on the riverside Millennium Trail, T867-667 2846, www.robertservicecampground.com. A great location among the trees on the Yukon River, with a nice atmosphere, hot showers, specialty coffees and baked goods. For tents only.

Watson Lake *p330*

All of the motels are on the highway.
C **Belvedere Motor Hotel**, T867-536 7712, www.watsonlakehotels.com. Decent rooms and the town's most appealing restaurant.
C **Gateway Motor Inn**, T867-536 7744, www.watsonlakehotels.com. Acceptable rooms, a pizza restaurant and a bar that's full of Yukon character.
D **Big Horn Hotel**, T867-536 2020. The best rooms in town at very reasonable rates.
D **Cozy Nest Hideaway B&B**, 1175 Campbell Hwy, T867-536 2204, www.yukonalaska.com/cozynest. 2 rooms and a small cabin on the lake, with a common room and a lovely stone terrace. Close to cross-country skiing.

Camping

Campground Services, Km 1018 Alaska Hwy, just east of town, T867-536 7448. Not great, but it has showers and laundry and is much nicer than the RV car park in town.
Watson Lake Highway Campground, Km 984 Alaska Hwy, then 1.5 km on an access road. A nicer spot with 67 sites on the lake, including some pull-throughs.

Teslin *p330*

C **Yukon Motel**, Km 1293 Alaska Hwy, T867-390 2443, www.yukonmotel.com. A variety of surprisingly pleasant rooms

in an impressive log building right on the lake. Also has RV sites and a good restaurant.

Camping

Teslin Lake Campground, 10 km north at Km 1258 Alaska Hwy. 27 fairly good sites on the lake.

Johnson's Crossing and Canol Road *p331*

A **Inn on the River**, northeast of Johnson's Landing, T867-660 5253, www.visityukon.com/innontheriver. A stunning log building on the lake, surrounded by trees. 4 very tasteful, luxurious jacuzzi suites, with balconies/decks facing the river. Also 2 simpler cabin suites. Price includes breakfast and the hire of bikes, canoes and kayaks. Delicious but expensive dinner is prepared for guests by arrangement.
D **Johnson's Crossing Motel and Campground**, just west of Teslin River Bridge/Canol Rd Junction at Km 1346 Alaska Hwy, T867-390 2607. Small but pleasant rooms Also has camping.

Camping

Squanga Lake Campground, 22 km further north at Km 1368. A quiet spot with 12 sites. Good fishing and hiking trails.

Atlin, BC *p331*

B **Win's Place**, 1st St/Discovery, T250-651 7550. A cottage on the lake, charming and spacious. Lower rent for longer stays.
C **Atlin Inn & Kirkwood Cottages**, Lake St, T1800-682 8546. The most likely place to have vacancies. Small but attractive and comfortable rooms. Some slightly cheaper but rather shabby cabins close to the water. Restaurant with burgers, steak, fish and great views, as well as a pub and coffee shop.
C **Brewery Bay Chalet**, McBride Blvd, T250-651 0040, brewerybay@atlin.net. Probably the best place to stay in town. 8 pleasant 2-bedroom suites with kitchenette in an impressive wood construction on the lake. A big deck for taking in the view.
C **Quilts & Comforts B&B**, Pillman Rd, T1800-836 1818. Offers 3 very small, twee rooms. A beautiful perennial garden with deck and views, and a good breakfast.
D **Glacier View Cabins**, 12 km S, Warm Bay Rd, T250-651 7691, www.sidkatours.com.

3 beautiful log cabins with bedroom, living room/kitchen and decks with the best views of Llewellyn Glacier.

E Raven Hostel, T250-483 1287, www. raven hostel.com. Located at the south end of Tagish Lake, about 40 km from Atlin, accessible only by boat, kayak or floatplane. As remote as it gets. There are 4 dorm beds, 4 spaces in a heated wall tent, and tent pitches. Kitchen (bring your own food), common room, sauna and wood-fired bath-tub. Weekly rates (Thu-Thu), including transfer by boat to and from Atlin, $375 per person or $215 per person if there are 5 of you. One-way floatplane fare is $250 per person for 2 and $100 per person for 5. Strong kayakers could paddle from Atlin.

Camping

There are a couple of campgrounds north of town but the best bet is along Warm Bay Rd to the south. **Como Lake, Surprise Lake** and **Warm Bay**. There's a particularly nice spot right on the lake at Km 24.

Pine Creek, Km 5, Warm Bay Rd. Handy, but not as nice as the other forestry sites further on.

🍴 Eating

Whitehorse *p327, map p328*
🍴🍴 **Cellar Steakhouse & Wine Bar**, 101 Main St, T867-667 2572, www.edgewaterhotel. yk.ca. The town's most upmarket restaurant, serving tapas and classic steak and seafood dishes. The dim lighting, soft music and cocktails make for a romantic atmosphere.
🍴 **Giorgio's Cuccina**, 206 Jarvis St, T867-668 4050. One of the most popular choices for locals, offering a large menu of pasta, pizza, seafood, souvlaki, steaks and mesquite grilled dishes. The decor is over-the-top but likeable and there's a good choice of wines by the glass. Generous portions.
🍴 **Klondike Rib and Salmon BBQ**, 2116 2nd Av, T867-667 7554. Huge portions of halibut and chips, salmon, BBQ ribs, chowder or more exotic choices like muskox or caribou. The food is consistently delicious and the atmosphere down to earth and friendly. A true taste of Yukon hospitality.

🍴 **North Dragon Restaurant**, 2058 2nd Av, T867-456 2182. The best of many Chinese restaurants.
🍴 **The Deli**, 203 Hanson St, T867-667 7583. Great sandwiches with sausages made from buffalo, caribou and reindeer.
🍴 **Sam & Andy's**, 506 Main St, T867-668 6994. Mexican food, best enjoyed on the outdoor patio.
🍴 **Sanchez Mexican Deli**, 211 Hanson St, T867-668 5858. Authentic Mexican dishes, such as *pollo con mole*.
🍴 **Talisman Café**, 2112 2nd Av, T867-667 2736. Large portions of international vegetarian food.

Cafés
🍴 **Blackstone Café**, 302 Wood St, T867-667 6598. Good coffee and breakfast. A nice place to relax.
🍴 **Midnight Sun Coffee Roasters**, 9002 Quartz Rd, T867-633 4563. Not entirely convenient but the nicest place for coffee, which they roast themselves. The warm wood and stone decor features artwork by local artists.

Watson Lake *p330*
🍴🍴 **Belvedere Motor Hotel**, T867-536 7712. The best of the motel restaurants.
🍴🍴 **Wolf It Down Restaurant**, 26 km west. Good coffee, fresh baking and buffalo steak.

Teslin *p330*
🍴🍴 **Mukluk Annie's**, 13 km north of town, T867-390 2600. Salmon bake, made with delicious wild sockeye, is their speciality and is served with salad and tasty baked beans. A real bargain and what's more, it comes with a free houseboat cruise on Teslin Lake at 2000. All-you-can-eat breakfast until 1100. Free overnight parking for anyone, or very primitive cabins to rent. Showers and laundry available.

Jake's Corner and around *p331*
🍴 **Jake's Corner Bakery**. Famous for its cinnamon buns, but also sells fast food like chicken and ribs by the kilo.

🔴 *For an explanation of sleeping and eating price codes used in this guide, see inside*
🔴 *the front cover. Other relevant information is found in Essentials, see pages 28-31.*

When in Atlin, try the local smoked salmon.

¶¶ **Lakeshore Restaurant**, in the **Atlin Inn**, Lake St, T867-651 7546. The best option for food, with great views. The licensed lounge is more appealing, especially the patio.

¶¶ **Pine Tree Restaurant**, Discovery Av. Home cooking in a diner-style clapboard house. Breakfast available all day. Licensed.

¶ **Kershaws Coffee and Espresso Bar**, Pearl Av/1st St. Good coffee, baked goods, soup and sandwiches.

◑ Bars and clubs

Whitehorse *p327, map p328*
Every hotel in Downtown Whitehorse has its own bar, but many are sleazy or sterile.

Backwater Lounge, 102 Wood St, T867-667 2250. A decent, low-key place with Yukon beer on tap and regular live music.

Lizards Lounge, 401 Main St, T867-668 7644. A trendy lounge scene, with varied live music and dancing at weekends.

Roadhouse Inn, 2159 2nd Av/ Strickland, T867-667 6248. The locals' pub, full of character and people tapping their toes to the country and western music.

Sam McGee's Bar & Grill , in 202 Motor Inn, 206 Jarvis St, T867-668 4567. Live country music and line dancing at weekends.

Yukon Mining Co, in the **High Country Inn**, 4051 4th Av, T867-667 4471. The nicest spot for a drink and very popular. Excellent, locally made Yukon Brewing Co beers on tap.

◐ Entertainment

Whitehorse *p327, map p328*
Check out the daily *Whitehorse Star* for entertainment listings.

Arts Underground, 305 Main St, T867-667 6058. A great space for an extensive art gallery and gift shop.

Captain Martin House Gallery. Run by the Yukon Art Society, with local creations and a revolving exhibition space. Ask where (and if) it is open, as it recently moved out of the old premises.

Frantic Follies, in the Westmark Whitehorse Hotel, 27 2nd Av, T867-668 2042, www.frant icfollies.com, Mid-May to mid-Sep, 2030, $24, child $10. This turn-of-the-century-style vaudeville revue, a tribute to the gold-rush era, is one of Whitehorse's highlights. Aimed squarely at tourists but is well-executed and good fun for all.

Yukon Artists At Work, 3B Glacier Rd, 10 mins S of town, T867-393 4848, www.yaaw. com. An artist-run gallery exhibiting the work of 35 Yukon artists.

Yukon Arts Centre, College Dr, www.yuk onartscentre.com. The Yukon's main arts and entertainment facility has a large gallery with changing exhibits, a sculpture garden and a theatre that plays host to major visiting acts.

Yukon Gallery, 2054 2nd Av, T867-667 2391, www.yukongallery.ca. Original paintings by over 40 Northern artists, as well as antler sculptures, jewellery, pottery and more.

◉ Festivals and events

Whitehorse *p327, map p328*
Many of Whitehorse's festivals take place in Rotary Park on the Yukon River.

Feb Frostbite Music Festival, T867-668 4921, www.frostbitefest.ca. Celebrating its 30th anniversary in 2008, this 3-night event features local and national musicians, and other entertainment. **Yukon Quest International Sled Dog Race**, T867-668 7411, www.yukonquest.com. A 1600-km race along trap lines between Whitehorse and Fairbanks, Alaska. The race ends in Whitehorse (even years) and you can imagine the excitement when they arrive after such an epic journey. **Yukon Sourdough Rendezvous Festival**, T867-667 2148, www.yukon rendezvous.com. Winter sports, games and entertainment: a huge party Yukon-style.

Jun Aboriginal Day, T867-667 3937, www. yfnta.org. A day of First Nations celebrations towards the end of Jun. **Yukon River Quest Canoe and Kayak Race**, T867-333 5628, www.yukonriverquest.com. This is the world's longest annual canoe and kayak race, from Whitehorse to Dawson City.

Aug Yukon International Storytelling Festival, T867-633 7550, www.story telling.yk.net. Storytelling is an important part of native culture and a favourite pastime of the Yukon people. This is probably the highlight of the year. **Yukon River Bathtub Race**, T867-393 4467, www.yukon rendez vous.com. Apparently the longest and toughest bathtub race in the world, 776 km from Whitehorse to Dawson.

Watson Lake *p330*
Jun Kaska Days, T867-536 5200. A 3-day
First Nation celebration, featuring dancing,
drumming, singing, crafts and games.

Jake's Corner and around *p331*
Apr Celebration of Swans, T867-667 8291,
marks the arrival of thousands of swans on
their spring migration.

Atlin *p331*
Jul Atlin Arts and Music Festival, T250-651
2181, www.atlinfestival.ca. This is a small,
warm, friendly 3-day event in early Jul,
celebrating northern culture with music,
performing, visual and fine arts, crafts,
workshops and children's activities.

O Shopping

Whitehorse *p327, map p328*
Arts and crafts
Indian Craft Shop Ltd, 504 Main St. The
best of many retailers of aboriginal art.
Midnight Sun Gallery and Gifts, 205C
Main St, T867-668 4350. A wide range,
from jam to books to mastodon ivory.
Trappers Association, 4194 4th Av. Fur
goods and moccasins.

Books
Mac's Fireweed Books, 203 Main St, T867-
668 2434, www.macsbooks.ca, mid-May
to mid-Sep open till 2400. Maps and travel
books, large selection about the north.
Well-Read Books, 4194 4th Av, T867-
668 2434. Second-hand books.

Food
3 Beans Natural Foods, 308 Wood St. Bulk
foods, fresh juice and organic produce.
Wharf On Fourth, 4040 4th Av. Fresh fish
and seafood.

Sports equipment
Coast Mountain Sports, 2nd Floor, 305
Main St, T867-667 4074. Camping and
sports gear, clothing and footwear.

▲ Activities and tours

Whitehorse *p327, map p328*
To find operators for any activity here, visit
the excellent www.yukonwild.com.

Bird and wildlife watching
Boreal Biological Expeditions, 5 McQuesten
Rd, T867-668 7675. Year-round birdwatching
and wildlife viewing tours led by a biologist.

Canoeing, kayaking and rafting
Canoeing is the major activity in the Yukon.
On top of the 2-week trip to Dawson City, a
number of short canoe excursions can be
made. It is 40 km, or 1 day, to Marsh Lake, to
the south, via Miles Canyon. Another 1- or
2-day trip could be made to Lake Laberge to
the north. Carmacks is 320 km, or 5-6 days.
    Most of the canoe operators are around
2nd/1st Av and Strickland, by the river. Some
rent by the trip and others by the day. They
sell maps, gear and supplies, and offer a
shuttle/pick-up service (about $1/km). Some
can arrange air transport to remote put-ins.
Kanoe People, T867-668 4899, www.kanoe
people.com. A long-standing and highly
recommended choice for canoe and kayak
rentals. Standard rental is $30/day. Rental for
the Whitehorse to Dawson City trip is $350/
16 days for canoe, $495 for kayak, plus $75 if
you leave your canoe in Dawson City. Also
run guided trips ($1596, 8 days including
2 nights hotel accommodation), and rent
bikes and wilderness cabins.
Nahanni River Adventures, T867-668 3180,
www.nahanni.com. Specialists in long, and
consequently expensive, canoe, kayak or
rafting trips on all the best rivers throughout
the north. Also offer hiking trips.
Tatshenshini Expediting, T867-633 2742,
www.tatshenshiniyukon.com. The most
established whitewater rafting specialists.
1-day trips on the Tatshenshini, Tutshi (both
$125) or Liard Rivers. Also offer a number
of multi-day raft, canoe or kayak trips. Run
courses and rent kayaks, canoes and rafts,
and provide transportation for renters.

Climbing
Equinox Outdoor Learning Centre, T867-
633 6956, www.equinoxyukon.com. Operate
a climbing wall and zipline at Takhini Hot
Springs, ice climbing towers on the waterfront, and run rock climbing tours to Golden
and Spirit Canyons.

Dog sledding
Cathers Wilderness Adventures, T867-
333 2186, www.cathersadventures.com.

⁚ Canoeing the Yukon River

The 735-km canoe trip from Whitehorse to Dawson City is the most famous and popular route in the Yukon. It takes about two weeks to complete, and though the water is fast-flowing there are few rapids, making this a fairly safe trip even for beginners.

The scenery along the way is great and there are lots of First Nations and Gold Rush relics, as well as the wooden remains of settlements and trading posts from the 50-odd years when the river was the province's main transportation corridor. It's also worth noting that the so-called Thirty-Mile River from Lake Laberge to the confluence of the Teslin River is famous for its bald eagle population, and that Hootalinqua at the Teslin confluence is the site of an old NWMP post established in 1898.

The river crosses the Klondike Highway at Carmacks, a good place to stock up with provisions. The famous Five Finger Rapids, the river's biggest these days, are 38 km downstream, followed 8 km later by Rink Rapids. Below the confluence of the Pelly River is the important historic site of Fort Selkirk, the first white settlement on the upper Yukon, accessible only by river. Those who are still not satisfied can continue 155 km beyond Dawson City to the next take-out at Eagle, Alaska, accessed on the Top of the World Highway.

A number of operators in both cities make it very easy to do the Whitehorse-Dawson City run. It costs about $350 to rent a canoe for up to 16 days, which can then be left in Dawson for a fee (around $75). Transport back can be negotiated.

Multi-day dog-sledding trips, which can be combined with hiking. Also boating or canoeing tours.
Muktuk Kennels, T867-393 1799, www.muktuk.com. Dog-sledding trips from 2½ hrs ($175) or 1 day ($230) to much longer trips, or long term packages involving lodging and training.

Fishing
Spirit of the North Guides, T867-456 4339, www.spiritnorth.yk.ca. Based on Lake Laberge, specialists in guided sports fishing. Also offer boat, canoe, sea kayak or hiking tours and a shuttle service.

Golf
Meadow Lakes Golf & Country Club, 121 Copper Rd, T867-668 4653.
Mountain View Golf Club, 250 Skookum Dr, T867-633 6020, www.mountainview golf.ca.

Hiking
There are plenty of short hikes around Whitehorse. You can drive (4WD required) or mountain bike to Grey Mountain, then follow a ridge trail with views of the city. Pick up a copy of the trail map from Mac's Fireweed Bookstore. For walks closer to town, the Visitor Centre has a pamphlet, Whitehorse Trails. A useful book is Hikes and bikes: Whitehorse and area.
Fireweed Hikes and Bikes Pleasure Tours, T867-393 4276. Hiking and biking tours.
Yukon Conservation Society, T867-668 5678, Jul-Aug. Free guided 2- or 4-hr hikes in the Whitehorse area.

Horse riding
Yukon Horsepacking Adventures, T867-633 3659, www.yukonhorsepacking.com. Horse riding trips around Fox Lake or Lake Laberge. $35/1 hr, $110/4 hrs, $160/ 8 hrs or multi-day trips and riding combined with salmon bakes and picnics.

Skiing
There are plenty of cross-country trails, including Miles Canyon and Chadburn Lake Recreation Area.
Mount Sima, T867-668 4557, www.mount sima.com, $29, youth $22, child $15 per day.

A tiny ski hill 10 mins South, with 1 lift, a tow rope, snowshoeing trails, lessons and rental.

Tour operators

Adventure-Tours Yukon Wild Ltd, T867-668 5511, www.yukon-wild.com. Canoeing, hiking tours, horse riding, snowshoeing, dog sledding, snowshoeing, canoe rental and transportation and cabin rental.

Due North Journeys, T867-393 2244. Backpacking into Kluane Park, the Tombstone Mountains and the Arctic. Run canoe trips.

Gray Line Yukon, T867-668 3225, www.graylineyukon.com. Bus tours of the city and surrounding area.

MV Schwatka River Cruise, 68 Miles Canyon Rd, T867-668 4716, www.yukonrivercruises.com, May-early Sep daily 1400. Mid-Jun to mid-Aug daily 1400, 1600, $25, child $12.50. Boat tours to Miles Canyon.

Nature Tours of Yukon, T867-667 4868, www.naturetoursyukon.com. A variety of multi-day tours, mostly revolving around canoeing and hiking. They also rent canoes and camping equipment, and provide transportation for people and canoes.

Ruby Range Adventures, T867-667 2209, www.rubyrange.com Extensive van-based tours of the Yukon.

Sila Sojourns, 9 Kokanee Pl, T867-668 5032, www.silasojourns.com. A variety of trips of differing lengths that may involve hiking, canoeing, rafting or other activities. Focus is on self-reflection, creative expression and spirituality.

Up North Adventures, 103 Strickland St, T867-667 7035, www.upnorthadventures.com. Guided or self-guided canoeing, kayaking and boating trips. Also offers biking and skiing.

Yukon Adventure Company, T1866-417 7365, www.yukonadventurecompany.com. Dog sledding, aurora borealis chasing, snowshoeing, hiking, canoeing, mountain biking, ice fishing, snowshoeing and snowmobiling. Also rent canoes, kayaks, boats, bikes, camping gear and ski equipment, and provide courses and transportation.

Yukon Brewing Company, 102 Copper Rd, T867-668 4183. Free tours and samples.

Yukon Historical & Museums Society, T867-667 4704, Jul-Aug. Guides dressed in period costume lead 45-min tours of historic buildings, local landmarks and architecture.

Tours leave from Donnenworth House in LePage Park.

Yukon Wings Ltd, T867-668 4716, www.yukon-wings.com. Flightseeing tours, charged per mile.

Watson Lake *p330*

There are 80 km of hiking and skiing trails nearby, ask at the Information Centre.

Ceasar Lake Outfitters, T867-536 2174, www.ceaserlake.com. Wilderness trips with hunting, fishing or horse riding.

Greenway's Greens, Km 1033 Alaska Hwy, T867-536 2477. 9 holes, par 35. One of only 5 courses in the Yukon.

Teslin *p330*

Canoeing takes place on **Nisutlin River** or the lake. A fairly easy 4- to 5-day whitewater canoe or kayak trip on the Lower Nisutlin River starts 69 km up the South Canol Rd and ends in Teslin.

Nisutlin Outfitting, T867-390 2123, www.nisutlinoutfitting.com. Canoe rentals ($25/day), guided tours and shuttle (80c/km). Guided fishing tours and boat rentals ($150/day).

Atlin *p331*

www.atlin.net is a useful resource.

Atlin Centre, T250-651 7659, www.atlinart.com. This amazing organisation has 2 bases, the Atlin Centre on a plateau on Monarch Mountain and a base camp on an island in the lake. They offer 10-day artist workshops and 2 extensive adventure trips every summer, which include hiking, canoeing, camping and much more. Groups are small, so book early. Also offers winter retreats and pick-up and drop-off from Whitehorse.

Atlin's Happy Trails, T250-651 2211, on the lake, McBride Blvd. Rents bikes and fishing rods, sells topographical maps, fishing tackle and basic camping gear. Arranges all kinds of tour and generally knows everything you might want to know about Atlin.

Atlin Lake Houseboat Tours, T250-651 0030. Tours from the central dock to Teresa Island, or anywhere you like.

Atlin Wilderness Adventure, T250-651 7621. Sightseeing and fishing trips.

Diamond M Outfitters, T250-785 1240. Hunting, fishing, horseback trips or wildlife viewing trips.

Klondike Heliskiing, T1800-821 4429, www.atlinheliski.com. Heli-skiing in an untouched area of 5000 sq km. All-inclusive 7-day packages run from $6700.

Monkeyflower Adventures, T250- 651 2460. Guided 2-hr nature walks ($20/hr) and snowshoeing tours (Feb-Mar). Good for families.

Sidka Tours, T250-651 7691, www.sidka tours.com. Rents canoes ($25/day, $150/week) and kayaks ($35/day, $210/week) and runs 2- to 12-day canoe or kayak trips. They also run **Glacier View Cabins** (see Sleeping).

◒ Transport

Whitehorse *p327, map p328*

Air

For airport details, see page 326.

Air North, T1800-661 0407, www.flyairnorth.com, has daily flights to **Vancouver** (2½ hrs, $193 one-way) and regular flights to **Calgary** (3 hrs, $216) and **Edmonton** (1½ hrs, $216). **Air North** also flies to **Dawson City** (1½ hrs, $130) and indirectly to **Inuvik** (5½ hrs, $260). **Air Canada**, www.aircanada.com, has up to 3 flights daily to **Vancouver** (2½ hrs, $263), 7 to Calgary (from $263) and 7 to Edmonton ($263). **Air Condor**, www5.condor.com, has up to 2 direct flights per week from **Frankfurt**, Germany (from US$731 return).

Bus

Local For local transit information call T867-668 7433. Extensive service covering the whole city ($2). No service on Sun.

Long distance The Greyhound station is on 2nd Av, T1800-661 8747, a short walk north of Downtown, with 1 daily bus to **Dawson Creek** at 1330 (21 hrs, $211, from $140 with 14 days advance booking) via **Watson Lake** (5 hrs, $65). From mid-May to mid-Sep **Alaska/Yukon Trails**, T1888-600 6001, www.alaskashuttle.com, runs shuttles from Whitehorse train station on Mon, Wed and Fri at 1300 (8 hrs, $143). During the same months, **Alaska Direct**, T1800-770 6652, www.alaskadirectbusline.com, run a bus on Mon and Thu to Dawson City, leaving Whitehorse at 1100 ($150 one-way, 7 hrs). They also run a bus on Wed, Fri and Sun at 0600 to Tok, Alaska, stopping at Haines Junction and all locations west on the Alaska Hwy. **Alaskon Express**, run by

Gray Line Yukon, T867-668 3225, has a daily summer service to **Skagway**, departing the Westmark Hotel at 1330.

Taxis

5th Avenue/Yellow Cab, T867-393 2227; **Global Taxi**, 23 MacDonald Rd, T867-633 5300.

Vehicle rental

Can check road conditions at T1877-456 7623, www.gov.yk.ca/roadreport. **National Car and Truck Rental**, 213 Range Rd, T867-456 2277, www.nationalcar.ca. **RVs** Canadream, 17 Burns Rd, T867-668 3610, www.canadream.com. All sizes of unit. 1-way rentals available to Vancouver and Calgary.

Atlin *p331*

Bus

The **Atlin Express**, T867-651 7617, leaves Mon, Wed and Fri, from the Greyhound Station in **Whitehorse** at 1215 and leaves Atlin from the Atlin Inn on the same days at 0615 ($56 return).

Car

With your own transport you could explore the mining roads that cross the area. Otherwise you'll have to rely on tours or rent a canoe. Hitching might entail a long wait.

◑ Directory

Whitehorse *p327, map p328*

Currency exchange Bank of Montreal, 111 Main St, T867-668 4200; **Thomas Cook**, 2101A 2nd Av, T867-668 2867. **Internet** Library (free); Titan Gaming, 305 Main St, T867-668 5750. **Laundry** Norgetown Laundry, 4213 4th Av, T867-667 6113. **Library** Whitehorse Public Library, Govt Building, 2071 2nd Av, T867-667 5239. **Medical services** Pine Medical Centre, 5110 5th Av at Main St, T867-668 4353; **Whitehorse General Hospital**, 5 Hospital Rd, south side of river, T867-393 8700. **Post office** Canada Post, main office with General Delivery is at 300 Range Rd at the top of Two Mile Hill, T867-6682195; **Shoppers Drug Mart**, 211 Main St, T867-667 2485.

Kluane Country

Everything in Kluane National Park (pronounced Kloo-ah-nee) is of an exaggerated scale. Forming part of the largest protected area on Earth, Kluane encompasses both the world's second highest set of coastal mountains, the Saint Elias Range, which contains North America's highest peaks, and the largest non-polar ice fields on the planet. Together with the surprisingly lush lower valleys of the front ranges, these dramatic landscapes contain the greatest diversity of flora and fauna in northern Canada, including the world's greatest concentration of grizzly bears. The heart of the park is most easily experienced on a rafting trip down the Tatshenshini River, whereas the front ranges are ideal for hiking. In a land of awe-inspiring landscapes, the drive south to Haines, Alaska, is particularly scenic, while the Top of the World Highway is the most interesting route north to Dawson City.
▸▸ *For Sleeping, Eating and other listings, see pages 345-347.*

West of Whitehorse 🍴🎭❄🏔🚌 ▸▸ *pp345-347.*

Some 10 km outside Whitehorse, the Klondike Highway continues north towards Dawson City, while the Alaska Highway veers west. After 70 km, a good dirt road heads 20 km south to **Kusawa Lake**, a local favourite for hiking, fishing and canoeing. There is a small campground at Km 14.5 and a bigger one on the lake at Km 22.5. The latter is the start of popular Upper Tatshenshini canoe trip (see Activities and tours, page 346), ideal for beginners or intermediates. **Kwaday Dan Kenji** (Long Ago People's Place) ⓘ *Km 1566.5 Alaska Hwy, T867-667 6375, tours $10*, 23 km further on, is a traditional First Nations camp with displays on the history and culture of the Southern Tutchone people and a campground. Another 26 km along the highway, then 42 km on a dirt road, leads to the quiet and remote **Aishihik Lake**, a local fishing hole with a small campground. **Otter Falls**, on the way at Km 30, is home to a small herd of bison and some good mountain bike trails.

Haines Junction → *Colour map 4, B3.*

Haines Junction, 92 km further on, is an ugly little town but a vital stop for organizing excursions into **Kluane National Park**. The **Parks Office** ⓘ *T867-634 7207, www.pc.gc. ca/kluane, mid-May to mid-Sep daily 0900-1900, otherwise by appointment*, provides maps and information on trails and backcountry routes and takes the essential registrations. **Yukon Tourism** ⓘ *T867-634 7100, www.hainesjunction yukon.com, May-Sep daily 0800-2000*, deals with provincial enquiries. The junction itself, marked by what looks like a giant cupcake with cement animals crawling out of the icing, is an important one: Whitehorse is 158 km east; Kluane Lake some 60 km northwest and Haines, Alaska is 241 km south via one of the region's most stunning roads.

Kluane National Park 🏔 ▸▸ *pp347. Colour map 4, B3.*

This extraordinary park is just part of a vast UNESCO World Heritage Site. The Saint Elias Range contains North America's highest peak, **Mount McKinley** ⓘ *6193 m*, in Alaska, and Canada's highest, **Mount Logan** ⓘ *5959 m*. The ice fields here bear sheets of ice over 1.5 km thick, with glaciers extending up to 112 km. As well as harbouring healthy populations of mountain goats, moose, rare silver-blue glacier bears, wolves and dall sheep, this may well be the only protected area in North America large enough to ensure the long-term survival of the grizzly and the chances of stumbling upon one here are far greater than in more famous parks further south.

Access to most of the park is virtually impossible except by air, and only its eastern boundary is bordered by roads. The southern part, reached from the Haines Highway, tends to be greener and more lush and the northern part, accessed from the Alaska Highway, has the greater concentration of trails and is more arid. Stunning as the views may be, the really big mountains of the Saint Elias Range are almost perpetually hidden by the lower front ranges, with only the occasional glimpse offering the motorist a hint of what is being missed. Helicopter tours, rafting trips and overnight hikes are the only real ways to get closer. Mountain biking, cross-country skiing and mountaineering are other prime activities.

The park's main **Visitor Centre** is in Haines Junction (see above) but there's an office 71 km northwest, right in the park at **Sheep Mountain** ⓘ *mid-May to mid-September 0900-1600*. The *Kluane National Park Hiking Guide* by Vivien Lougheed can be picked up at either location. Hikers should be aware that most routes in the park involve difficult creek crossings with no bridges and extremely cold, fast-flowing water; so take a pair of creek-crossing shoes, such as old trainers. Registration for backcountry hiking is obligatory. A fee of $5 per person per night is charged for camping, which is allowed anywhere except on the Cottonwood Trail, which has designated sites. The normal no-trace ethical rules apply (see page 19).

Day hikes from the Haines Highway

King's Throne ⓘ *10 km return; 4 hrs; 1220 m elevation gain. Trailhead: Kathleen Lake day use area, 26 km south of Haines Junction.* A well-defined trail switchbacks fairly steeply to a saddle at Km 5, offering expansive views. The hike can be continued along a ridge, with ever-greater views. A possible 10-hour hike in all and one of the park's most popular.

Rock Glacier ⓘ *1.5 km; 30 mins. Trailhead: 44 km south of Haines Junction.* Short and easy hike on a former glacier, leading to good views.

Saint Elias Lake ⓘ *7.6 km; 3 hrs; 120 m elevation gain. Trailhead: 60 km south of Haines Junction.* A fairly easy but rewarding hike, can scramble to better views.

Day hikes from Sheep Mountain

Sheep Creek ⓘ *10 km; 4-5 hrs; 430 m elevation gain. Trailhead: Visitor Centre.* Exceptional views for such short a hike.

Sheep-Bullion Plateau ⓘ *24 km; 7-8 hrs; 880 m elevation gain. Trailhead: The Visitor Centre.* A beautiful area with diverse plant life as well as views of the valley, a glacier toe and the striking Red Castle Ridge. Home to bear families, so potentially dangerous. Could be treated as a two-day trip.

Soldiers Summit ⓘ *1 km; 30-40 mins; 90 m elevation gain. Trailhead: 1 km north of the Visitor Centre.* Easily the best very short hike.

Sheep Mountain Ridge ⓘ *11-km loop; 6-10 hrs; 1310 m elevation gain. Trailhead: 2 km north of Visitor Centre.* Wonderful views of the lake, Slims River Valley, mountains and glaciers, and the chance to see up to 200 sheep.

Overnight hikes (from south to north)

Cottonwood ⓘ *83-km loop; up to 6 days; 520 m elevation gain. Trailhead: 27 or 55 km south of Haines Junction.* A well-marked trail through more lush surroundings giving great views of towering mountains. Lots of creek crossings.

Alsek ① *52 km; 2-3 days; 90 m elevation gain. Trailhead: 10 km north of Haines* *Junction on Alaska Hwy*. Long but fairly easy trek down a spectacular valley. Good introduction for the inexperienced hiker.

Slims East ① *46 km; 2-4 days; 910 m elevation gain. Trailhead: 3 km south of the Visitor Centre*. Not quite as spectacular as the Slims West, but a better trail and certainly recommended. Also has lots of grizzlies.

Slims West ① *60 km; 3-5 days; 1340 m elevation gain. Trailhead: Sheep Mountain Visitor Centre*. The most popular overnight hike in the park, leading to Observation Peak and offering probably the best views of glaciers and mountains to be had without a guide or backcountry expertise. High concentration of grizzlies causes frequent closures.

Donjek Glacier ① *96-km loop; 6-10 days. Trailhead: Duke River, 9 km north of Burwash Landing*. A long and demanding hike. Very popular with experienced hikers, many of whom come to Kluane just to do it.

Heading south 🚌🚶▲🚏 ›› *pp347*.

Haines Highway
① *Km 170, US Customs post, 0800-2400*.
Haines Highway (Highway 3), heads south through glorious alpine terrain that slowly builds over a distance of 144 km to the crescendo of Chilkat Pass. At Km 26 is **Kathleen Lake**, the start of a number of hikes and home to the only campground within the park. At Km 62 is **Klukshu**, meaning 'coho place' in Tlingit (coho being a kind of salmon). Klukshu is a traditional First Nations salmon-fishing village which welcomes visitors with a small museum, a craft shop, smokehouses and signs detailing the people's traditional way of life. Slightly more authentic is **Dalton Post** (Shäwshe), 22 km further on then 5 km down a dirt road. Situated on the Tatshenshini River, this is a key site for rafts and kayaks. In BC, the road follows the eastern boundary of **Tatshenshini-Alsek Wilderness Park**, which is almost inaccessible except on a guided rafting trip.

Haines, Alaska
Just south of Klukwan on the Chilkat River is the **Chilkat Bald Eagle Reserve**. The waters here remain unfrozen in October and November and are full of spawned-out salmon at a time when food is scarce, attracting thousands of bald eagles from as far away as Washington State. From here, the road clings to the river, the massive Tsirku Glacier just 10 km away. It's a breathtaking introduction to Haines, which is cradled within the Y-shaped end of America's longest fjord. Friendly and uncrowded, Haines is ideal for aimless wandering, taking a tour or hiking to Mount Ripinsky or Seduction Point. The main sight is **Sheldon Museum and Cultural Centre** ① *11 Main St, T907-766 2368, www.sheldonmuseum.org, mid-May to mid-Sep Mon-Fri 1000-1700, Sat-Sun 1300-1600, mid-Sep to mid-May Mon-Fri 1300-1600, $3, child free*, with a collection of dioramas, Tlingit artefacts and exhibits on the town's pioneer history. To find out more about the area visit the **Visitor Information Centre** ① *2nd Av S near Willard St, T1800-458 3579, www.haines.ak.us, Mon-Fri 0800-1800, Sat-Sun 1000-1600*.

⁞ Tatshenshini and Alsek rivers

Two of the most beautiful and pristine rivers in North America, the Tatshenshini and Alsek both run through BC's Wilderness Reserve into Alaska. Their forested valleys provide the only corridors through the towering icy realm of the Saint Elias Mountains, a remote world few people ever get to see.

A rafting tour of the Tatshenshini (215 km, 10-14 days, class III-IV, Dalton Post to Dry Bay, near Yakutat, Alaska) is one of the most highly recommended experiences in Western Canada and suitable for all levels of experience. Yukon's most popular day trip is on the Upper Tatshenshini (40 km, 1-2 days, class III-IV, 110 km south of Haines Junction to Dalton Post), which can be reached via Blanchard River (26 km, including 15 km on the Tatshenshini, day trip, class II-III, 105 km south on the Haines Hwy to Dalton Post). Alsek River (290 km, 10-14 days, with class IV rapids. Dezadeash River, Haines Junction to Dry Bay, near Yakutat, Alaska) is a tough trip for experienced kayakers. See Activities and tours, page 346.

Heading north ⬤⬤ ▸ *pp345-347.*

Alaska Highway

Interpretive panels are dotted along this highway, but few are of real interest except to hard core history enthusiasts. Driving northwest from Haines Junction, the first reason to stop is the **Kluane Lake** viewpoint at Km 60, with winning views over the Yukon's largest lake. Anglers should note that Kluane is a Southern Tutchone word meaning 'lake with many fish'. Another 11 km brings you to the Visitor Centre at **Sheep Mountain**, which is often dotted with the herd of Dall sheep after which it is named, though they are best seen from September to early June when there are no people around to bother them. Nearby on the lake's south shore the Arctic Institute 's **Kluane Lake Research Station** ⓘ *T867-633 2018* has an interpretive room with details on expeditions and research in the Saint Elias icefields.

North to Dawson City via Alaska

The best reason to continue northwest is to make a loop through Alaska to Dawson City. **Burwash Landing** ⓘ *72 km past Sheep Mountain*, is an old community of 100 people, home to the **Kluane Museum of Natural History** ⓘ *T867-841 5561, mid-May to mid-Sep daily 0900-1830, by donation*. As well as fossils and minerals from the area, there is a decent collection of First Nations artefacts and a number of wildlife dioramas. The **Icefield Ranges** viewpoint, 57 km further on, is one of the best places to stop for rare views of the Saint Elias Mountains, as well as the dramatic Donjek River Valley.

Just before the border with Alaska is the tiny and grim village of **Beaver Creek**. The coldest temperature ever recorded in Canada was measured close to here at a place called **Snag**, it was -62.8°C. There is a **Visitor Centre** ⓘ *T867-862 7321, May-Sep daily 0800-2000*. The 24-hour border crossing up the road charges a US$8 visa fee, even for those heading straight back into Canada. Unless you want to sample the limited charms of Tok, bear north at **Tetlin Junction** onto Taylor Highway (Highway 5), a windy dirt road through a narrow valley, where gold panners can still be seen at work. The drive is unexceptional until you cross back into the Yukon at **Little Gold Creek** ⓘ *the border here is only open 0900-2100, with the US side 1 hr behind*. From here, the aptly named **Top of the World Highway** affords unspeakably gorgeous views, with bare, multicoloured hills in the foreground and mountain peaks lining up on the horizon. This is the ultimate way to enter Dawson City, 105 km away.

● Sleeping

Haines Junction *p341*

B-C Raven Hotel and Gourmet Dining, T867-634 2500, www.yukonweb.com/tourism/raven. The nicest place to stay, with 12 attractive rooms, a sun deck and a good restaurant. German-style breakfast included.
D Cozy Corner Motel, Alaska Hwy, north end of town, T867-634 2119. The best of many standard motels, also has a restaurant.

Camping

Pine Lake Campground, 7 km east of town. A lovely spot on the lake, with 42 sites. Playground, swimming and drinking water.

Haines Highway *p343*

C The Cabin B&B, just south of Kathleen Lake, 27 km from Haines Junction, T867-634 2600, www.thecabinyukon.com. 5 very nice cabins, nestled in the woods, with views of the mountains. Shared shower, sauna and picnic area with BBQ. Full cooked breakfast.

Camping

Kathleen Lake, 27 km S of Haines Junction. The only campground actually in the park, 39 sites, operated by Parks Canada.
Million Dollar Falls, 85 km S of Haines Junction. 33 sites including 8 for tents only.

Haines, Alaska *p343*

D A Sheltered Harbour, T616-527 2732, www.geocities.com/asheltered. 5 very nice, spacious rooms in an interesting waterfront building with a large wrap-around deck in the historic Fort Seward part of town. Hot buffet breakfast. Bike rentals.
D Summer Inn B&B, 117 2nd Av, www.summerinnbnb.com. Small but decent rooms in a house in the centre of town, with a deck and living room. Full breakfast included.
E-F Bear Creek Cabins & Hostel, T907-766 2259, www.bearcreekcabinsalaska.com. Dorm beds or rustic private cabins, also has camping. Short walk from town.

Camping

Chilkoot State Park, 16 km north of Haines off Lutak Rd. 32 sites in a very scenic location.
Portage Cove State Recreation Site, 1.5 km south on Beach Rd. Another very attractive spot, for tents only.

Heading north *p344*

C Westmark Hotel, Beaver Creek, T867-862 7501, www.westmarkhotels.com. The best place to stay, small but pleasant rooms. Bar, recreation room and restaurant with theatre in the evening. Also has camping.
D Burwash Landing Resort, off the highway on the lake, T403-841 4441. Well situated, close to Sheep Mountain. Standard rooms with old beds in a Wild West-style building with a striking log-beam interior and a restaurant with a reasonable menu. RV sites.
D Kluane B&B, south end of Kluane Lake, T867-841 4250, www.kluanecabins.com. Cute but basic A-frame cabins with showers and kitchen facilities, breakfast included. Very likeable owners.
D-F Kluane Base Camp, T867-841 2135, www.kluanebasecamp.com. A lovely wood lodge close to the lake, with bright, modern cabins, dorm beds and camping. Shared kitchen, washrooms and a deck with views.

Camping

Congdon Creek, 17 km west of Sheep Mountain. 81 sites and an interpretive trail.
Lake Creek, 131 km north of Sheep Mountain. 27 sites.
Snag Junction, 59 km further north of Sheep Mountain. 15 sites.

● Eating

Haines Junction *p341*

♈♈♈ Raven Hotel and Gourmet Dining, T867-634 2500. European-style fine dining, named the best restaurant in the Yukon.
♈ Village Bakery and Deli, opposite the Visitor Centre. Good bread, muffins, quiche, pizza, sandwiches and espresso. Every Fri night host live music and a salmon bake.

Haines, Alaska *p343*

♈♈ Bamboo Room, 2nd Av, near Main St, T907-766 2800. Relaxed, central and friendly. Famous for halibut and chips.
♈♈ The Commander's Room, in Hotel Halsingland, T1800-542 6363. Fine dining, with lots of seafood on the small menu.
♈♈ Fog Cutter Bar, Main St between 1st and 2nd Avenues, T907-766 2555. Lively, with pool tables, a dance floor and light food.

⚙ Festivals and events

Haines Junction *p341*
Jun Alsek Music Festival, T867-634 2520, www.alsekfest.com. 3-day outdoor event in early Jun, featuring music from the Yukon on 3 stages with the St Elias Mountain as an awesome backdrop. **Kluane Chilkat International Bike Rally**, T867-633 2579, www.kcibr.org. A 238-km relay race from Haines Junction to Haines.

⛰ Activities and tours

Haines Junction *p341*
Tour operators
Kluane Ecotours, Haines Rd, T867-634 2600, www.kluaneco.com. Custom day trips with an interpretive naturalist, or extended back-country canoe, kayak or hiking trips.
Paddle/Wheel Adventures, opposite the Visitor Centre, T867-634 2683, www.paddle wheeladventures.com. Rents bikes, canoes and cabins, and runs a number of trips. Offers ½-day ($45) and full day ($100) hiking trips, canoeing and fishing ($100) or tatshen-shini rafting ($125).
Trans North Helicopters, T867-634 2242, www.tntaheli.com. Glacier tours, flight-seeing and the best way to get into the most striking landscapes for activities.
Yukon Trail Riding, T867-634 2386. Horse riding excursions.

Kluane National Park *p341*
Biking and mountaineering
There are some excellent mountain bike routes in the park. Mush Lake Rd and the Alsek Trail are recommended. Mt Logan, Mt St Elias and Mt Steele are magnets for world-class mountaineering.

Cross-country skiing
This is first class, especially on the Cotton-wood and Dezadeash trails, or around the Chilkat Pass, where you can ski as late as Jun. The 15-km Auriol Trail, 7 km south of Haines Junction is also good for its ski trails.

Rafting
Both the Tatshenshini and Alsek rivers provide adrenaline feasts for kayakers and canoeists, but experience is essential. **Tatshenshini Expediting**, Whitehorse,

T867-633 2742, www.tatshenshiniyukon. com. 1- to 11-day trips through incredible scenery on a river that has the best reputation for whitewater rafting in the Yukon. $125 for 1 day.

Haines, Alaska *p343*
Tour operators
Alaska Mountain Guides, Fort Seward, T1800-766 3396, www.alaskamountain guides.com. Mountaineering courses, ice climbing, hiking, sea kayaking and rentals, skiing, and snowboarding. Trips are anything from ½-day to 14 days long.
Alaska Nature Tours, T907-766 2876, www.kcd.com/aknature. Guided hikes, birdwatching and wildlife photography in and around the Chilkat Bald Eagle Preserve.
Chilkat Cruises and Tours, T1888-766 2103, www.chilkatcruises.com. Kayak rentals and guided trips ($125).
Chilkat Guides, T907-766 2491, www.raft alaska.com. Daily rafting trips through the Chilkat Bald Eagle Preserve (US$89) and longer trips on the Tatshenshini, Alsek and Konqakut Rivers.
Sockeye Cycle Co, 24 Portage St, Fort Sewarm, T907-766 2869, www.cyclealaska .com. Daily guided bike tours ($75/3 hrs, $175/8 hrs) and extended or self-guided bike tours.

⊘ Transport

Haines Junction *p341*
Throughout the summer, **Alaska Direct**, T1800-770 6652, www.alaskadirectbus line.com, run a bus on Wed, Fri and Sun between Whitehorse and Tok, Alaska, leaving Whitehorse at 0600 arriving in Haines Junction at 0800 (US$65 one-way), then stopping at all locations west on the Alaska Hwy. On the way back it leaves Haines Junction at 2100, arriving in Whitehorse at 0100. They also run a service between Tok and Dawson City on Mon and Thu ($125).

Haines, Alaska *p343*
Regular ferries up the Taiya Inlet to **Skagway** with **Chilkat Cruises and Tours**, T1888-766 2103, www.chilkatcruises.com, 35 mins, US$30 one-way, $54 return; $123 one-way, $147 return when combined with a trip to the Chilkoot summit on the White Pass Train.

Alaska's Marine Highway, T1800-6420 066, www.dot.state.ak.us/amhs, also connects Haines with Skagway ($31, youth $15, vehicle $41).

Heading north *p344*
Throughout the summer, **Alaska Direct**, T1800-770 6652, www.alaskadirectbus line.com, run a bus on Wed, Fri and Sun to Tok, Alaska, leaving Whitehorse at 0600,

Haines Junction at 0800, Burwash Landing at 1000 ($70 for Whitehorse) and Beaver Creek at 1200 ($100), arriving in Tok at 14.30 ($125). Going the other way, it leaves Beaver Creek at 1800, Burwash Landing at 1900, Haines Junction at 2100, arriving in Whitehorse at 0100. They also run a service between Tok and Dawson City on Mon and Thu ($125 one-way).

Dawson City and the north

The unavoidable Gold Rush paraphernalia that can be found in every Yukon village reaches its apotheosis in Dawson City, the ultimate boomtown, site of the biggest stampede to the most productive gold fields of all time. Canadian history doesn't get any more exciting than this. In 1959, the gold all but exhausted, Dawson was declared a National Historic Site and saved from otherwise inevitable disintegration. Today, the perfectly restored buildings – with the help of costumed interpreters, boardwalks, dirt streets and a wealth of interesting sights – present the visitor with a unique slice of living Wild West history, half real town, half museum. There are a number of interesting diversions on the way up from Whitehorse, but nothing that comes close to the Dempster Highway, a genuine frontier road, which heads 740 km north to Inuvik, deep in the Arctic. From there, a handful of excursions lead still further into the remote frozen realm. ▸▸ *For Sleeping, Eating and other listings, see pages 355-360.*

Ins and outs

Getting there and around
Dawson City Airport (YDA) is 19 km southeast of town on the Klondike Highway. **Gold City Tours** ⓘ *T867-993 5175*, runs a shuttlebus to Downtown ($10) that meets all scheduled flights. **Dawson Courier Taxi** ⓘ *T867-993 6688*, charges $23. **Air North** ⓘ *T867-668 2228, www.flyairnorth.com*, has regular flights from Whitehorse and Fairbanks in Alaska.

Most people arrive in Dawson in their own vehicle. Entering from the Klondike Highway gives an idea of the extent to which the land has been plundered. For almost 10 km you pass through desolate wasteland, littered with huge boulders and abandoned mining equipment. A free ferry runs 24-hours daily from late May to mid-October across the Yukon River to connect the town with the Top of the World Highway, the best campground and a hostel. ▸▸ *For further details, see Transport, page 360.*

Best time to visit
Dawson City hibernates in winter, when average temperatures drop to -30°C. Most sights are only open mid-May to mid-September. The hottest months are July and August, when average temperatures rise to 15°C and the sun shines almost around the clock. However, at this time the streets throng with tourists, many of them stopping en route from the US to Alaska. June is a good compromise, with the bonus of an excellent festival (see Festivals, page 358). By late August the crowds begin to dwindle and the scenery takes on the magnificent colours of autumn.

The **Yukon Visitor Information Centre** ⓘ *Front and King St, T867-993 5566, www.dawsoncity.ca, mid-May to mid-Sep daily 0800-2000*, is by the river. Jointly operated by **Tourism Yukon** and **Parks Canada** ⓘ *T867-993 7200*, this first-class facility has a wealth of information and photos on the town's historical buildings. A popular 90-minute walking tour of town, conducted by guides in period costume, runs daily at 0930, 1100 and 1300. Across the road, located in the historic British Yukon Navigation Co.'s Ticket Office is the **Western Arctic Information Centre** ⓘ *T1800-661 0750, www.explorenwt.com, mid-May to mid-Sep daily 0900-2000*, a key stop for anyone planning on travelling up the Dempster Highway.

Dawson City ⊜⬤🚽🛏🚿❀🅿🛆🚌🚻 ⇥pp355-360. Colour map 5, C3.

Coming to the Yukon and not visiting Dawson City is like going to Agra and failing to see the Taj Mahal. At the heart of summer, when the atmosphere is more that of theme park than museum, you may feel that Dawson has been saved at the expense of its character and soul. To get the most out of a visit you have to enter into the spirit of the place. Submerging yourself in the history is essential, maybe by reading a work like Pierre Berton's bestseller *Klondike* (1958), the short stories of Jack London or poetry by Robert Service. More importantly, Dawson's soul remains that of a party town, so go gambling at Diamond Tooth Gertie's, have a few drinks in the saloon and dream of gold.

Heritage buildings

Most of the town's century-old buildings are still in use as hotels and saloons. Many more have been lovingly restored by Parks Canada and are visited on their tours. The first to be renovated, in 1960, was the wonderful **Palace Grand Theatre** on King Street. It was originally built in 1899 by Gold Rush legend Arizona Charlie Meadows from the hulks of two beached paddle steamers. The last such sternwheeler to ply the Yukon River, the 1922 *SS Keno*, is exhibited at Front Street and Queen Street.

The grandest building in town is the **Commissioner's Residence** ⓘ *daily 1500-1700, free, tours Jun to mid-Sep daily 1400, $6*, at the east end of Front Street. This elegant former home of the Queen's representative to the Yukon has been renovated to reflect the 1912-1916 era. Many of the best structures are on Third Avenue, such as the **1901 Post Office** ⓘ *3rd Av and King St*, which is still in operation. **Harrington's Store** ⓘ *nearby at 3rd Av and Princess St*, displays a collection of rare original photos and journal excerpts from the Gold Rush era entitled 'Dawson as they saw it'. Also worth seeing is the **Firefighters Museum** ⓘ *5th Av/ King St, mid-May to mid-Sep Mon-Sat 1230-1730, by donation*. The town's cemeteries make an interesting tour, ask for a free *Walking Tour* booklet at the Visitor Reception Centre.

Dawson City Museum

ⓘ *595 5th Av/Church St, T867-993 5291, www.dawsonmuseum.ca. May-Sep daily 1000-1800, $9, child $7. Daily tours 1100, 1300, 1700.*

Housed in the old territorial administration building, the town museum is an essential stop for soaking up some history. It's packed full of artefacts and photos, First Nations items, diaries and newspaper cuttings. One key highlight is the 27-minute *City of Gold*, a black and white documentary made by Pierre Berton, which underlines the town's sad demise and helped spur the federal government to action. Costumed staff help bring the history alive through demonstrations and re-enactments. Tours of the museum building take in the old court chambers, the archives and the visible storage area, where a fifth of the museum's 30,000 artefacts are displayed.

Diamond Tooth Gertie's Gambling Hall

ⓘ *4th Av/Queen St, T867-993 5575. Mon-Thu 1900-0200, Fri-Sun 1400-0200, $6 for 3 shows.*

An absolute must is a visit to Canada's first legal casino, housed in the old Arctic Brotherhood Hall which was built in 1899. The atmosphere is wonderful, with lots of good-natured gambling tables and three cancan shows every night. The midnight performance is a little more risqué. There are Yukon beers on tap and happy hour starts at midnight. Gambling proceeds go to the continued development of the town.

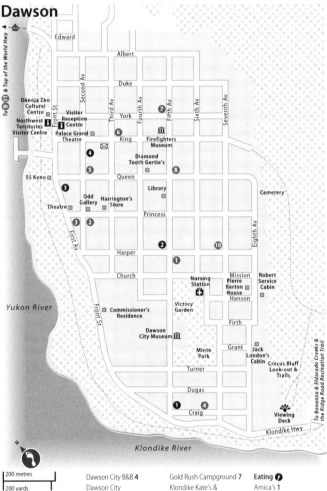

Dawson

| 200 metres |
| 200 yards |

Sleeping 🛏
Aurora Inn & La Table on 5th **1**
Bombay Peggy's Victorian Inn **2**

Dawson City B&B **4**
Dawson City Bunkhouse **3**
Dawson River City Hostel **9**
Downtown, Jack London Grill & Sourdough Saloon **5**

Gold Rush Campground **7**
Klondike Kate's & Restaurant **6**
Triple J **8**
Yukon River Campground **11**

Eating 🍴
Amica's **1**
Belinda's Dining at Westmark Inn **2**
Grubstake **4**
Riverwest Bistro Restaurant & Coffee Bar **3**

⁞ From rags to riches

When the gold prospectors arrived in Dawson City, the population swelled to 30,000, making this the biggest city north of Seattle. There were casinos and cabarets, showgirls, saloons, brothels and rag-time tunes. Fancy hotels, running water and electricity were all available for those who could pay. Prices ran amok and with gold dust used as currency it was not unknown for barkeepers who sifted the saloon floor sawdust to find up to $300 worth of dust.

For most, the reality was harsh squalor. Prospectors had to build fires to thaw the frozen ground, then spend weeks searching through the icy, rocky mud. The Native Americans became strangers in their own land and their culture was almost completely destroyed.

Less than a year after the masses arrived, all the accessible gold had been extracted. Dawson City sank into a terminal decline until Parks Canada began to intervene in the 1960s. They named the town a National Historic Site and set about restoring its century-old buildings. Today, the place is like a big living museum, a fossilized remnant of the Wild West, complete with false- fronted wooden houses, boardwalks, saloons and dirt streets.

Dänojà Zho Cultural Centre (Long Time Ago House)

ⓘ *Front St, T867-993 6768, www.trondek.com. May-Sep daily 1000-1800, slideshow at 1500, $5, under 18 $2.50, under 12 free.*

This striking contemporary building, nicely situated on the riverfront, seeks to provide a little balance by documenting the last hundred years from a First Nations perspective. Guided tours are given daily of the Hammerstone Gallery, where audio-visual displays, photos, dioramas, artefacts, arts and crafts, theatre, dance and slide shows bring alive the history and culture of the Tr'ondëk Hwëch'in people. There is a decent gift shop and you can also find out about other Tr'ondëk Hwëch'in sites in the area, including a hike to Moosehide village.

Authors On Eighth

Parks Canada runs daily tours down Eighth Avenue, where the former homes of three famous writers are conveniently clustered. The **Robert Service Cabin** ⓘ *daily 1300-1500, free, readings Front St/Princess St, daily 1500 and 2000, $8*, is a renovated version of the poet's abode, from the time when he worked here as a bank clerk in 1908. Born in Preston, England, Robert Service (1874-1958) became one of the most successful poets of his day, writing verses that romanticized the north but immortalized much of its mystique, charm and eccentricity. Ironically, most of his Gold Rush verse was written before he even set foot in the Yukon. A recital of verses like *The Cremation of Sam McGee* and *The Shooting of Dan McGrew* takes place in a theatre daily. Service's poems are very effective when read aloud.

Across the road from the cabin is Berton House, the boyhood home of author **Pierre Berton**, whose bestseller *Klondike* is the most compelling introduction to the era. Further down is **Jack London's Cabin** ⓘ *8th Av/Firth St, T867-993 5575, $2*, built using 'a few' logs from the writer's original, abandoned cabin 120 km to the south. Inside, photos, documents, newspaper articles and two resident costumed guides tell Jack London's story. He fell in love with the north and made it over the Chilkoot Pass during the stampede but failed to find any gold and, finding Dawson too expensive, ultimately left penniless after just a year. In that time however, he had gathered enough inspiration to forge literary gold, winning fame and acclaim with stories like *Call of the Wild* and *White Fang*. His version of the Yukon is tougher and more realistic than that of Service.

Goldfields

An integral part of the Dawson City experience is to witness **Bonanza** and **Eldorado creeks**, where most of the gold was mined. The action begins at Km 4 on the Klondike Highway, the start of Bonanza Creek Road. Near the turning is **Bear Creek**, a 25-ha site that supported the dredge teams until 1966. Tours take in the shops and the gold room where the dust was processed. On Bonanza Creek Road is the fascinating **Dredge No 4**, the largest bucket-line, wooden-hulled dredge in North America. Monsters like this one scooped up copious quantities of mud and rock and passed the material through their insides, where it was sifted for gold. Operated by just four men, it extracted a remarkable 25 kg of gold per day between 1913 and 1966. At Km 12 on this road is the cairn marking **Discovery Claim**, where the original lucky strike occurred. Every 150-m claim on this stretch went on to yield around 3500 kg of gold, worth about $25 million at 1900 prices.

The road forks here, the east spur leading along Eldorado Creek, which proved even more bountiful than Bonanza. The other branch runs up to the summit of **King Soloman Dome**. From here you can see the network of trails and roads, all of them littered with ramshackle buildings and the rusting remains of mining equipment. Hunker Road runs back from the summit to the highway. Enthusiasts could spend hours exploring these desolate landscapes, or you could try your hand at gold-panning. At about Km 15 on Bonanza Creek Road is **Claim No 6**, where you can usually pan for free ① *ask at the Visitor Reception Centre, or call T867-993 5575*. Pans can be rented at several places in town.

Hikes around Dawson City

Midnight Dome ① *8 km return*. Ask at the Visitors Centre for directions. The hill that rises behind Dawson City, is so named because it's a great place to watch the sun drop to the horizon then rise again at midnight on 21 June, an occasion for much drinking and festivity. The stiff hike to the summit is rewarded with superb views of the city, goldfields, Yukon River and rows of mountains.

Crocus Bluff Lookout Trail ① *Trailhead: follow King St, southeast above town*. A short walk leading to good views of the town.

Ridge Road Recreation Trail ① *32 km; 3 days. Trailhead: Upper Bonanza Creek*. This hike follows the ridge tops back to the Klondike Valley, with views all the way. There are two campsites on the route.

Klondike Highway to Dawson City ⊕🍴❄️▲▲

➥*pp355-360.*

By Yukon standards, the Klondike Highway north of Whitehorse is a pretty dull drive. The minor towns of Carmacks and Pelly Crossing offer little reason to stop. A worthwhile side-trip off the beaten track is down the **Silver Trail** ① *Hwy 11*, to the tiny, artist-dominated village of **Keno**. Just south of the turning, a dirt road leads to Ethel Lake, a beautiful camping and fishing spot for those seeking tranquility. Remainders of large forest fires along the highway offer the chance to hunt for morel mushrooms.

Carmacks and around → *Colour map 4, A4.*

The Yukon River crosses the Klondike Highway at **Carmacks**, making this a useful provisions stop for canoeists. The town's main sight is the **Tage Cho Hudan**

Interpretive Centre ① *T867-863 5830, free*, which has displays on First Nations culture and history, an interpretive trail and local handicrafts. This is also the best place to ask about the 2-km boardwalk, which runs along the river, and about local trails to areas good for seeking agates and other semi-precious stones.

It's well worth stopping at a viewpoint 23 km north of Carmacks, where a 1-km boardwalk leads to an observation deck offering views of **Five Fingers Rapids**, one of the most treacherous spots on the Yukon River. At **Pelly Crossing** is **Big Jonathan House** ① *T867-537 3150, May-Sep daily 1000-1900, free*, which contains displays of native artefacts, arts and crafts. It's a replica of a building still standing in **Fort Selkirk**, due west at the confluence of the Yukon and Pelly rivers, accessible only by water.

Robert Campbell Highway

The region east of Carmacks is named Campbell after **Robert Campbell**, a Hudson's Bay Company employee who was sent here in the 1840s to open up new fur trading routes. Following trails used by the Native Kaska Dena people, Campbell built a chain of trading posts culminating in Fort Selkirk. The highway that also bears his name (Highway 4) heads east just north of Carmacks, passing **Little Salmon Lake**, a fishing spot with two tiny picturesque campgrounds, on the way to **Faro**. This tiny town of 360 is situated on the remarkably broad **Tintina Trench**, an important wildlife corridor that attracts millions of migrating birds and has one of the highest concentrations of moose and wolves in the province. A breed of sheep unique to the region, the fannin, can be seen at **Mount Mye Sheep Centre** ① *10-km hike from the 1.5-km Van Gorder Falls Trail, or a 7.5-km drive*. Ask at the summer-only **Campbell Region Interpretive Centre** ① *T867-994 2728, www.faroyukon.ca, May-Sep daily 1000-1700*, which also contains an exhibition about the region's history, geology and wildlife. Many other activities are available in the area and free guided hikes are offered throughout the summer.

The Robert Campbell Highway can be used in conjunction with the South Canol Road, which it meets at Ross River, as a scenic route that bypasses Whitehorse and Carmacks. As a further refinement, the Tatchun/Frenchman Road cuts the corner between Highway 4 and the Klondike Highway, offering a remote diversion lined with small lakes and several lovely campgrounds. The **Dena Cho Trail** ① *67 km, T867-969 2278*, follows a historic gold prospector route between Faro and Ross River. It's a fantastic hike with four cabins along the way. Register at the Interpretive Centre, maps can be picked up there or downloaded from their website.

Silver Trail

The Yukon's first small gold rush occurred on the Stewart River in 1883, but ultimately the area proved more successful with its high-grade lead-silver ore. Better known as the Silver Trail, Highway 11 from **Stewart Crossing** is one of the Yukon's more worthwhile side-tracks, leading past abandoned homesteads and mining equipment to the sleepy, ramshackle communities of **Mayo** ① *Km 53*, **Elsa** ① *Km 96*, and **Keno** ① *Km 112*. Watch for moose on the first 15 km of the Silver Trail, as this is a calving habitat.

The road is paved to just beyond Mayo, whose **Interpretive Centre** ① *T867-996 2317*, is housed in historic Binet House, which also has a collection of historic photos and displays on local natural history, flora and fauna. There's a viewing deck overlooking the river. Minto Lake Road is a good place for genuine gold panning, ask the **Mayo Mining Recorder** ① *T867-996 2256*, which streams are open. **Elsa** is essentially a ghost town, though its United Keno Mine continued to operate until 1989. The dirt road deteriorates towards **Keno**, but this funky little village of 25 is the highlight of the trip. A small cluster of log cabins mainly populated by artists, miners and eccentrics, Keno's authentic character remains quirky and uncompromised. Partially housed in a boom-time dance hall, **Keno City Mining Museum** ① *T867-995 2792, www.kenocity.ca/museum, Jun-Sep*

⁞ Preparing for the Dempster Highway

First stop at the Western Arctic Information Centre, T1800-661 0750, www.explorenwt.com in Dawson City, which provides details on road conditions, weather and which petrol stations are open.

Drivers should fill up at Mackenzie Petroleum in Callison off the Klondike Highway, which is much cheaper. Note that petrol stations are scarce on the highway, so drivers must fill up every time they get the chance and those with a small tank should take a jerry can and keep it filled. Make sure your tyres are good and take at least two spares, preferably six-ply. Do any routine maintenance before heading out. Petrol and tyre repairs are usually only available at Eagle Plains (369 km), Fort McPherson (550 km) and Inuvik (736 km). There is no drinking water available until Fort McPherson.

For maps, road reports and information, visit www.yukoninfo.com/dempster.

daily 1000-1800, has an extensive collection of old photographs, mining artefacts and local alpine butterflies. A large number of butterflies congregate at Keno Hill, attracted by the many wild flowers. A network of hiking trails criss-crosses the surrounding area. Ask in Mayo, or visit www.kenocity.ca/trails. You can loop back to Mayo to visit a family-owned placer mine on Duncan Creek and pass Mayo Lake, good for fishing and boating.

The Silver Trail provides the easiest access to the **Peel Wilderness**, one of the most remote areas on earth. Local paddlers know that some of the Yukon's very best canoeing is down the pristine rivers of the Peel watershed, particularly the Wind, the Snake and the Bonnet Plume. The sanctity of these waters, which flow through the **Mackenzie Mountains** and harbour large animal populations, has been preserved by their very remoteness. Access is by floatplane.

Back on the Klondike Highway, 121 km north of Stewart Crossing, is the **Tintina Trench viewpoint**, with vistas of the Klondike River and a valley so big that it stands out clearly on satellite photos. The product of the largest geological fault in North America, the trench apparently provides visible proof of the concept of plate tectonics. The Dempster Highway branches off 20 km later and, 39 km beyond, you roll into the ultimate apotheosis of Gold Rush memorabilia, Dawson City.

Dempster Highway ⬤⬤⬤⬤⬤⬤⬤⬤ ▸▸*pp355-360.*

The 740-km Dempster Highway is Canada's only year-round public road to cross the Arctic Circle. Construction of a highway across the tundra was a great challenge, eventually solved by using a raised gravel pad to insulate the permafrost and keep it from melting. Driving the length of this rough frontier road is a challenge and an adventure, not to be entered into without adequate preparation (see above). Nevertheless, the effort is amply rewarded by ever-changing, wide-open views. Three very different mountain ranges are crossed and the continuous freeze and thaw adds a host of unusual features to the landscapes, with names like hummocks, tussocks, frost boils, ground slumping and polygons. In summer, perpetual sunshine causes the vegetation to burst into a riot of colour. Mid-August ushers in the autumn, the most beautiful time of all, when the scenery is filled to the horizon with vivid shades of red, orange, gold, purple and brown and hosts of berries are ready to be picked.

Tombstone Mountains

You don't have to go far to get the most out of the Dempster Highway. In fact its most beautiful and well-paved section is the first 100 km. A perfect destination is the **Tombstone Mountain Campground** ⓘ *Km 72*, a lovely spot and home to the **Dempster Interpretive Centre** ⓘ *mid-Jun to early Sep*. They can give you all the information you need on local wildlife, geology, First Nations culture and some of the most rewarding hikes in the west. The spectacular **Tombstone Mountain Range**, well known for its jagged black granite peaks and idyllic alpine lakes, is a long day's hike away but plenty of shorter trails lead to gorgeous views and there's a good chance of spotting dall sheep, grizzlies and the hart caribou herd. A useful publication is *Yukon's Tombstone Range and Blackstone Uplands: A Traveller's Guide*.

Hikes around Tombstone Mountains

Goldensides ⓘ *2½ hrs; 610 m elevation gain. Trailhead: 3 km north of the Interpretive Centre, turn right and drive to the radio tower.* From the top are views of the Klondike River Valley and Tombstone Mountains.

Angelcomb Mountain ⓘ *10 km return; 3 hrs; 580 m elevation gain. Trailhead: 9.5 km north of the Centre, park at the gravel pit on the east side of the highway.* A fairly easy and gradual ascent to the first peak, with wonderful views and a fair number of dall sheep and caribou.

Grizzly Valley ⓘ *8 km round trip; 2-4 hrs; 640 m elevation gain. Trailhead: 12.5 km north of the Centre on the west side.* This is the fastest route into the Tombstone Range and leads to a lookout with great views. To go all the way in is at least a 58.5-km return hike, with possible additional diversions to Divide Lake, Talus Lake or Tombstone Mountain itself (2192 m). A first-class adventure.

North to Inuvik

By the West Blackstone River at Km 115, take a look upstream. The two low, cone-shaped mounds about 8 km away are not volcanoes but pingoes, strange phenomena caused by mass movements of frost. These ones are thought to be more than 5000 years old. Further on, the highway eventually leads through the **Ogilvie Mountains**, whose peaks are markedly different from the scenic Tombstones. These bare, grey-black piles of shale make for bizarre landscapes. Beyond, you enter the broad flat horizons of the **Eagle Plains**, arriving eventually at a service centre (Km 369), where you can get petrol, tyre repairs and a bed for the night.

Just north, at Km 405, a set of quite interesting interpretive panels marks the 66°33' latitude line of the Arctic Circle. With the best of the scenery gone, this makes a good point to turn back. Should you be here between September and May, note that the stretch of road from Km 408 to the Richardson Mountains is part of the porcupine caribou herd's winter range. **Wright Pass** ⓘ *Km 465*, marks the Continental Divide and the border with the Northwest Territories. The **Richardson Mountains** are softer and rounder than those further south. A moderate hike up to the obvious summit via the ridge on its south side offers a chance to admire their gentle contours. On the other side, the road sweeps down to the Peel River Valley. Near the top, a viewing platform provides equally outstanding vistas. At Km 539 a free ferry crosses the river on demand from June to mid-October.

Nitainlaii Visitor Information Centre ⓘ *9 km before Fort McPherson, T867-777 3652, Jun-Aug daily 0900-2100*, has interpretive displays focusing on the life of the Gwich'in Dene people. The small native village of **Fort McPherson** has a mechanic, a hotel and usually petrol for filling up (but don't depend on it). From here the road gets even rougher and far less interesting. At Km 608 is the impressively broad **Mackenzie River**, the small village of **Tsiigehtchic (aka Arctic Red River)**, and another free ferry

that leaves hourly from June to mid-October. The end of the road is **Inuvik**, a grim little
town best used as a jumping-off point for even more remote northern communities
and parks that can only be reached from here and by plane.

Inuvik, NWT → *Colour map 5, B6.*

Inuvik is an unattractive town that may come as a disappointment after 736 gruelling
kilometres on a rough dirt road. Most visitors who come this far are planning on
continuing to one of the Arctic parks and isolated communities that can be reached
from here only by plane. The houses, identical but painted bright colours to add some
character, are built with steel poles drilled through to the stable layer of permafrost so
that they don't buckle in spring frost heaves.

On the way into town is the **Western Arctic Visitor Centre** ① *T867-777 4727,
www.inuvik.ca, www.explorenwt.com, Jun-Sep daily 0900-2000,* which has displays on
First Nations culture and a collection of interesting videos; if flying out on an excursion,
it's worth watching the video first. If you want to visit Vuntut, Ivvavik, Tuktut Nogait or
Aulavik National Parks, you must register at the **Parks Canada Office** ① *187 MacKenzie
Av, above the post office, T867-777 8800, inuvik.info@pc.qc.ca, May-Sep Mon-Fri
0830-1700.* Almost everything of interest is within four blocks on Mackenzie Road,
including the striking **Igloo Church** ① *T867-777 2236,* which can only be visited on tours
in the summer. At Mackenzie and Distributor Street is an inukshuk, a piled-stone
representation of a human with outstretched arms, a traditional Inuit symbol of
hospitality and friendship, now adopted as official symbol of the 2010 Winter Olympics.

A number of small communities and large parks are accessible only by air
from Inuvik. These are places where the 'true North' can still be experienced: rugged
landscapes, people who still live off the land and exotic animals such as musk oxen.
The most popular and logistically simple trip is to Tuktoyaktuk. On the flight there,
you pass over some 1400 pingoes, utterly conspicuous on the delta's otherwise
flat expanses. It's possible to get there alone but much easier and often cheaper to go
with a tour company. When making plans, remember that flights are at the mercy of
the changeable weather so keep your schedule flexible and be prepared to wait.

● Sleeping

Dawson City *p348, map p349*
There is a good list of lodgings with prices
and photos in the Visitor Centre.
A-B Bombay Peggy's Victorian Inn, 2nd
Av/Princess St, T867-993 6969, www.bomb
aypeggys.com. Hands down the nicest place
to stay in town. 7 elegant, classy rooms in a
house brimming with historic character.
B Aurora Inn, 5th Av/Harper St, T867-993
6860, www.aurorainn.ca. 18 bright, spacious
and very comfortable en suite rooms with
big beds, in a large pine-finished house that
also has a great leisure area for guests and
a restaurant.
C Dawson City B&B, 451 Craig St, T867-993
5649, www.dawsonbb.com. 7 rooms with
shared bath in an attractive home overlooking the Yukon and Klondike rivers.
Great hospitality.
C Downtown Hotel, 2nd Av/Queen St,
T867-993 5346, www.downtownhotel.ca.

Acceptable rooms in a building with lots
of Wild West character and located in the
thick of the action. The rooms across the
road from the office open out onto a plant-
filled courtyard with hot tub.
C Klondike Kate's, 3rd Av/King St, T867-
993 6527, www.klondikekates.ca. 15 pretty
log cabins, newly renovated and understandably popular.
C Triple J Hotel, 5th Av/Queen St, T867-
993 5323, www.triplejhotel.com. Cabins
with kitchenettes, plain motel rooms and
nice, spacious hotel rooms.
D Dawson City Bunkhouse, Front St/
Princess St, T867-993 6164, www.dawson
citybunkhouse.com. Simple but lovely rooms
with shared bath.
E Dawson River City Hostel, across the
river (on ferry), T867-993 6823, www.yuk
onhostels.com. HI-affiliated. Rustic accommodation in dorms or private rooms, with

a large common cabin, cooking facilities, a deck with good views of town, saunas and lockers. Free bike use. Some ugly tent sites.

Camping
Gold Rush Campground, in town on 5th Av/York St, T867-993 5247. The only place for RVs, but utterly devoid of charm. Coin-operated showers.
Klondike River Campground, 15 km east of town. Not as nice as the Yukon River site, but still a decent and quiet spot.
Yukon River Campground, across from the ferry, walking distance from town. The nicest campsite, with pitches by the river. Fills up, so arrive in the morning.

Klondike Highway to Dawson City
p351
Camping
The following are Yukon government sites, non-reservable and in gorgeous locations.
Fox Lake, Km 59. Has 33 sites, good for birds and muskrats.
Lake Laberge, 36 km north of Klondike/Alaska junction. Has 16 sites, good for birdwatching.
Twin Lakes, Km 119. Pretty, with 18 sites.

Carmacks and around *p351*
C **Hotel Carmacks** , T867-863 5221, www.hotelcarmacks.com. About the only place to stay, with standard rooms, cabins, RV sites, a lounge and a restaurant.

Camping
There are 3 lovely government camp-grounds on Tatchun/Frenchman Rd to the west. **Tatchun Creek**, 26 km N of Carmacks at the junction with that road. 12 very nice sites.

Robert Campbell Highway *p352*
C-D **Blue House B&B**, 440 Campbell St, Faro, T867-994 2106, www.nfyukon.com/e_b&b. A more intimate choice. 4 nice rooms, only 1 with en suite bath. A south-facing deck and garden, kitchen, living room, laundry and full breakfast included. Owners run an adventure tour company.
D **Faro Studio Hotel**, T867-994 3003, Dawson Dr, Faro. 16 suites with kitchen facilities, as well as a restaurant and lounge.

Camping
On the way are **Little Salmon Lake** and **Drury Creek** campgrounds; **Johnson Lake**, 3.5 km towards Faro from Hwy 4; **Lapie Canyon**, at Ross River.

Silver Trail *p352*
D **Bedrock Motel**, Mayo, T867-996 2290, www.bedrockmotel.yk.ca. 12 spacious rooms with continental breakfast included. Licensed lounge, laundry and camping.
D **Keno Cabins**, Keno, T867-995 2892, www.kenocity.ca/cabins. 2 very attractive and cosy self-contained units with kitchen, capable of sleeping 4. Shared bathroom.
D **North Star Motel**, Mayo, T867-996 2231. 9 rooms with kitchenettes and showers on a nicely landscaped property.

Camping
Five Mile Lake Campground, 7 km north-east of Mayo. If you have a tent, head for this government-run ground, with 20 sites, swimming, fishing and trail around the lake.
Keno City Campground, T867-995 2892. 7 sites on Lightning Creek.
Moose Creek, 25 km beyond, to the north of Stewart Crossing. 36 sites, 6 tent-only.
Whispering Willows, Mayo, T867-996 2284. In town and catering to RVs.

Dempster Highway *p353*
There are just 2 settlements for beds, food and even petrol on the Dempster Hwy.
A **Peel River Inn**, Fort McPherson, T867-952 2417, www.peelriverinn.com. 8 plain rooms with private bathroom. Also a guest lounge, restaurant, laundry, vehicle rental and petrol.
B **Eagle Plains Hotel**, Km 371 Dempster Hwy, T867-993 2453, www.eagleplainshotel.com. 32 standard rooms and a reasonably priced restaurant. Lounge, laundry, fuel and a basic campground.

Camping
Engineer Creek, at Km 193. Has 8 sites at the foot of an eroded limestone ridge, with good fishing.
Nitainlaii Territorial Park, at Km 541, just 5 km from the Peel River ferry. 23 sites and an interesting Visitor Centre open Jun-Aug.
Rock River, at Km 446. Has 20 sites, 3 tent-only, sheltered within a steep gorge of the Richardson Mountains.

Tombstone Mountain, at Km 71. Has 22 sites. A great spot and the base for hikes into the Tobstone Range.
Vadzaih Van Tshik Campground, at Km 692. Has 11 sites.

Inuvik, NWT *p355*

A **Capital Suites**, 198 Mackenzie Rd, T867-678 6300, www.capitalsuites.ca/inuvik. Reasonable suites with kitchens and a fitness room and laundry. The first new hotel to open here is many years.
A **Mackenzie Hotel**, 185 Mackenzie Rd, T867-777 2861, www.inuvikhotels.com. Decent, spacious rooms in a central location, with a restaurant, lounge and exercise room.
B **Nova Inn**, 300 Mackenzie Rd, T867-777 6682, www.novahotels.ca/inuvik. Fairly nice rooms with fireplaces and TVs. Breakfast and laundry.
B-C **Eskimo Inn**, 133 Mackenzie Rd, T867-777 2801, www.inuvikhotels.com. Pretty standard rooms. Restaurant, lounge, laundry.
C **Arctic Chalet**, 3 km before town on the highway, T867-777 3535, www.arctic chalet.com. Cosy little rooms in log cabins or in the splendid wood lodge. Most have en suite baths and kitchenettes. The owners offer dog-sled tours and rent kayaks, canoes and cars. The best choice.
C **Finto Lodge**, 288 Mackenzie Rd, at the south entrance to town, T867-777 2647, www.inuvikhotels.com. The quietest location, just outside town. The best rooms have a kitchenette.
C **Polar B&B**, 75 Mackenzie Rd, T867-777 2554. The 4 rooms that share a kitchen, bathroom and laundry.

Camping

Happy Valley, northwest end of town on Franklin Rd, T867-777 3652. Showers, views and nice sites. Drinking water.
Jak Park, south of town on the highway, T867-777 3613. Quieter, nicer in many ways and high enough to give good views. Coin-operated showers. Drinking water.

⊘ Eating

Dawson City *p348, map p349*
♦♦ **Amica's**, west end of 5th Av, T867-993 6800. Authentic Italian and Greek cuisine, a bit on the pricey side but highly regarded

and more interesting than most choices. Has more seafood and salads than you expect.
♦♦ **Belinda's Dining**, in the Westmark Inn at 5th Av/Harper, T867-993 5542. One of the better restaurants, with a deck and lounge, and some barbecues in the courtyard.
♦♦ **Jack London Grill**, Downtown Hotel, 2nd Av/Queen St, T867-993 5346. A broad menu featuring burgers, steak, fish and good cheesecake. Also has a heated patio.
♦♦ **Klondike Kate's**, 3rd Av/King St, T867-993 6527. An authentic 1904 heritage building, always quite busy. The reasonably priced menu features pasta and fish dishes.
♦♦ **La Table on 5th**, in the Aurora Inn at 5th Av/Harper, T867-993 6860. One of the better locations, making a reasonable compromise between French inspired fine dining and satisfying comfort food.
♦ **The Grubstake**, 1054 2nd Av. Subs and pizza. Internet access.
♦ **Riverwest Bistro Restaurant & Coffee Bar**, Front St, across from the *SS Keno*, T867-993 6339. Organic fairtrade coffee, home-made soups and wraps. Good atmosphere, with outdoor seating.

Silver Trail *p352*
♦ **Keno City Snack Bar**, Keno, T867-995 2409, mid-May to mid-Sep. Pizza, hot dogs, sandwiches and light meals.
♦ **Mayo Chinese Restaurant**, Mayo, T867-996 2939. Not very Chinese but the only restaurant in town.

Inuvik, NWT *p355*
Fish lovers should be try the delicious Arctic char. Each hotel has a restaurant.
♦♦ **Green Briar Dining Room**, in the Mackenzie Hotel, 185 Mackenzie, T867-777 2414. Basic food, good for steaks and for breakfast.
♦♦ **Peppermill Restaurant**, in the Finto Lodge, 288 Mackenzie Rd, T867-777 2647. The best ambience, with specialities like Arctic char and caribou.
♦ **Café Gallery**, 84 Mackenzie Rd, T867-777 2888. Good spot for coffee and baked treats.
♦ **To Go's**, 71 Mackenzie Rd, T867-777 3030. A casual and friendly spot, popular with locals and pretty good value for Inuvik. Muskox and caribou burgers are the speciality.
♦ **The Roost**, 108 Mackenzie Rd, T867-777 2727. Serves same kind of thing as **To Go's**.

♪ Bars and clubs

Dawson City *p348, map p349*
Bombay Peggy's Lounge, 2nd Av/Princess St, T867-993 6969. A beautiful, relaxed place for a pint that also boasts a good list of spirits. Some light food and a summer patio.
Diamond Tooth Gertie's Gambling Hall, see page 349. Yukon beers on tap, happy hour after midnight and a fun atmosphere.
Sourdough Saloon, in the **Downtown Hotel**, 2nd Av/Queen St, T867-993 5346. An atmospheric, authentic-feeling place that is the home of Dawson's most bizarre ritual: have a drink served with a real mummified human toe and join the 'Sourtoe cocktail club', www.sourtoecocktailclub.com.
Westmark Inn, 5th Av/Harper St, T867-993 5542. One of the nicer lounges, with an inviting deck and martinis.

Inuvik, NWT *p354*
Cabin Lounge, Motor Inn. Good for a drink and sometimes has live music.
The Mad Trapper Pub, Mackenzie Rd, T867-777 2785. A reasonable pub with a pool table and occasional live music.

⊚ Entertainment

Dawson City *p348, map p349*
Diamond Tooth Gertie's, see page 349 and Palace Grand Theatre, see 348; Odd Gallery, 2nd Av/Princess St, www.kiac.org, Dawson's primary location for visual arts, always Canadian and usually very good.

⊛ Festivals and events

Dawson City *p348, map p349*
Mar Dawson City International Short Film Festival, T867-993 5005, www.kiac.org/filmfest. Runs for 3 days in late Mar.
Jun Yukon River Quest Canoe and Kayak Race, T867-333 5628, www.yukonriverquest.com. The longest such race in the world and it ends here. Commissioner's Klondike Ball, T867-993 5575. Gives everyone an excuse to get dressed up in Gold Rush era clothes for food, drink and dancing. Aboriginal Day Celebrations, T867-993 6768, Dänojà Zho Cultural Centre, take place a week later.
Jul Yukon Gold Panning Championships, T867-993 5575. An exciting spectator sport,

takes place at the beginning of the month.
Dawson City Music Festival, T867-993 5584, www.dcmf.com. 3 days of music featuring the best up-and-coming Canadian talent. Extra camping is laid on and the atmosphere is fantastic. The biggest event of the year and is rated as one of the best in the west.
Aug Yukon Riverside Arts Festival, T867-993 5005, www.kiac.org. Mid-Aug is a weekend of arts, crafts, music, dancing and theatre on the banks of the river. Part of the Discovery Days Celebrations, T867-993 2350. A week of games, races and other fun events.

Robert Campbell Highway *p352*
May Crane and Sheep Viewing Festival, T867-994 2728. A good time to be in Faro, the sandhill cranes are returning and the local Fannin sheep are being born.
Aug Fireweed Festival, T867-994 2728. Faro is home to the jamboree, featuring a horticultural fair, arts and crafts, dances and more.

Inuvik, NWT *p354*
Jul Great Northern Arts Festival, T867-777 8638, www.gnaf.org. Celebrating its 20th anniversary in 2008, this 10-day bonanza features over 80 visual artists and 40 performers from north of the Arctic Circle. Given the challenges they face living in such isolation, it's an inspiring and humbling collection. Takes place mid-month.
Aug The End of the Road Music Festival, T867-678 2806, www.eotrmusic.com. 2 days of varied acts.

◐ Shopping

Dawson City *p348, map p349*
Bonanza Market, 2nd Av/Princess St, T867- 993 6567. Groceries and a deli.
Dawson City General Store, Front St, opposite the *SS Keno*, T867-993 5475. Good for most needs, with a bakery, groceries and newspapers.
Dawson Trading Post, Front St, T867-993 5316. Camping and fishing gear. The only outdoors shop in town.
Fortymile Gold, 3rd/York, T867-993 5690. More original than most of the other jewellers.
Klondike Nugget & Ivory Shop, Front St/Queen St, T867-993 9333. Jewellery made from gold nuggets or mammoth ivory.

❖ Flora and fauna in the north

The wildlife of the north includes old favourites like grizzly bears and dall sheep, and species such as musk oxen, polar bears, Arctic foxes and barren ground caribou. Each year, a herd of 120,000 porcupine caribou migrates from central Yukon to calving grounds on the Beaufort Coast, returning south in the autumn. Their migration path crosses the Dempster Highway and it can take hours for the herd to cross the road.

Plants have a particularly hard life up here. The average temperature is so low that the ground never thaws,

with only a thin top layer melting enough to sustain vegetation. Moreover, Arctic precipitation is so low that it is technically classified as desert. Yet a surprising amount of vegetation survives, such as sedges and dwarf birch, and goes absolutely crazy every summer. The growing season may be short, but it's rendered particularly intense by the constant sunshine. As a result, millions of birds are drawn north to feed on this nutrient-rich vegetation, such as long-tailed jaegar, Arctic tern and snowy owls.

Inuvik, NWT *p355*
Boreal Books, 75 Mackenzie Rd, T867-777 3748. Maps and books about the north.
Northern Images, 115 Mackenzie Rd, T867-777 2786. Inuit sculpture, sealskin slippers and prints.
Northern Store, 160 Mackenzie Rd, T867-777 2582. Groceries, clothing, sportswear, tacky souvenirs and pharmacy.

▲ Activities and tours

Dawson City *p348, map p349*
Canoeing
Castlerock Canoe, at the Trading Post on Front St, T867-993 5316. Hourly and weekly rentals, trips and shuttle service.
Dawson City River Hostel, T867-993 6823. Bike and canoe rentals.

Golf
Top of the World Golf Course, T867-993 5888, 9 holes. Offers the rare opportunity to tee off in the middle of the night and play a round beneath the midnight sun. Rentals also available.

Tour operators
Ancient Voices Wilderness Camp, T867-993 5605, kormendy@yknet.ca. First Nations camp with cabins and tents, offering cultural day trips and longer excursions with guides.
Gold Bottom Mine Tours, T867-993 5023, www.goldbottom.com, $20. Offers 2 90-min

daily tours of a still-operating placer mine on Hunker Creek Rd, followed by 1 hr of creek panning. Keep what you find. Extended tours also take in King Solomon Dome, Bonanza Cree and Dredge No 4.
Klondike Spirit, www.klondikespirit.com. Tickets from Triple J Hotel, 5th Av/Queen St, T867-993 5323. Tours on the Yukon River in a nostalgic paddle wheeler.
Trans North Helicopters, T867-993 5494, www.tntaheli.com. Flightseeing tours of the goldfields or Tombstone Mountains.
Yukon Queen II, T867-993 5599. Cruises on the Yukon River from Dawson City to Eagle, Alaska. Booking office at the Westmark Inn.

Robert Campbell Highway *p352*
Nature Friends Outdoor Adventures, 440 Campbell St, Faro, T867-994 3102, www.nf yukon.com. Guided hikes, dogsledding and canoe trips in and around Faro. 4-day hike on the Dena Cho Trail. Bike and canoe rental and free trail information.

Silver Trail *p352*
There is great hiking and mountain biking off the Silver Trail, with many mining roads to explore. A trail map is available at the Mayo Visitor Centre. For the best views, hike the Mt Haldane Trail, 6 hrs return, from Halfway Lakes between Mayo and Keno.
Mount Joy Wilderness Adventures, T403-997 7111, www.mountjoywilderness. com. Expensive multi-day boat trips on the

Stewart River and winter dog-sled trips.
An authentic experience with a trapper.

Dempster Highway *p353*
Bensen Creek Wilderness Adventure,
T867-993 5468, www.bensencreek.com.
Guided hiking or snowshoeing trips in the
Tombstone Mountains, canoe trips on the
Klondike River, Zodiac trips on the Yukon or
wildlife viewing around the Dempster Hwy.

Inuvik, NWT *p355*
Arctic Chalet, 3 km S on the Hwy, T867-777
3535, www.arcticchalet.com. Rents canoes
and kayaks and run highly recommended
dog-sledding trips, where you get the dog
team all to yourself ($225 per person for 3-
4 hrs, $350 for a day). Packages including
accommodation and some meals, $1290
for 3 people for 3 days.
Arctic Nature Tours, T867-777 3300,
www.arcticnaturetours.com. The biggest
operator in town. Inuvik town tours are
$35 for 2 hrs; tours to Tuktoyaktuk $280 for
3-4 hrs or $360 for 5-6 hrs; tours to Herschel
Island $420 for 5-6 hrs; Mackenzie Delta
eco-tours by boat, from $65 per person for
2-4 hrs; Babbage River on the edge of Ivvavik
National Park, $420 for 6 hrs.

● Transport

Dawson City *p348, map p349*
Air
For airport details, see page 347.
Air North, T867-668 2228, www.flyairnorth.
com, has regular flights to **Whitehorse**
(1¼ hrs, $130) , **Fairbanks**, Alaska (1½ hrs,
$208) and **Inuvik** (2½ hrs $195).

Bus
From mid-May to mid-Sep **Alaska/Yukon
Trails**, T1888-600 6001, www.alaskashuttle.
com, run shuttles from Whitehorse train
station on Mon, Wed and Fri at 1300, $143,
8 hrs. They also run a shuttle to **Fairbanks**,
Alaska on Mon, Wed and Fri ($162).

During the same months, **Alaska Direct**,
T1800-770 6652, www.alaskadirectbusline.
com, run a bus on Mon and Thu at 1100
from Whitehorse (7 hrs, $150 one-way).
They also run a bus on Mon and Thu to
Tok, Alaska, $125 one-way, call for times,

from where they have buses on Mon, Wed
and Sun to Whitehorse via the Alaska Hwy
through Kluane Country.

Inuvik, NWT *p355*
Air
Air North, T1800-661 0407, www.flyair
north.com, has flights from **Dawson City**
(2½ hrs, $195) and, indirectly, from
Whitehorse (4¼ hrs, $260).

Bus
MGM Bus Services, T867-777 4295, www.
mgmbusservices.ca, run chartered van
journeys with 8 passengers minimum
to **Dawson City** ($173 one-way, $294
return) and Whitehorse ($234 one-way,
$393 return).

Vehicle hire
Arctic Chalet, T867-777 3535, www.artic
chalet.com; Norcan Rentals, 60 Franklin Rd,
T1877-398 1338, www.norcan.yk.ca.

● Directory

Dawson City *p348, map p349*
Banks CIBC, Queen St between Front St/
2nd Av, with 24-hr ATM, T867-993 5447.
Emergency Ambulance, T867-993 4444;
Fire, T867-993 2222; Police, T867-993 5555.
Internet Library; Tastebyte Internet Café,
Front St, T867-993 6100. **Laundry** Gold
Rush Campground, 5th Av/York St, T867-
993 5247. **Library** 5th Av/Queen St and
Princess St, T867-993 5571. **Medical
services** Nursing Station, behind the
museum on Mission St, T867-993 4444.
Post office Canada Post, across from
the library on 5th St; Old Post Office at 3rd
Av/King St.

Inuvik, NWT *p355*
Banks CIBC, 134 Mackenzie Rd. 24-hr ATM,
T867-777 4539. **Internet** Library (free).
Laundry Happy Valley Campground,
T867-777 3652. **Library** Inuvik
Centennial Library, 100 Mackenzie Rd,
T867- 777 2749. **Medical services**
Regional Hospital, Inuvik Access Rd, on
the way into town, T867-979 2955. **Post
office** Canada Post 187 Mackenzie Rd,
T867-777 2252.

History

First Nations

Beringia

The generally accepted explanation of how North America's very first people arrived is that they crossed a temporary land bridge between Asia and Alaska. Though some sites in Alaska and the Yukon hint at occupation as long as 25,000 years ago, the most common theory is that this migration occurred about 15,000 years ago, when ice-age glaciation had lowered the world's sea levels dramatically, creating a whole continent called Beringia. Animals now long extinct, such as the woolly mammoth and giant beaver, fled to this vast oasis of green within a desert of ice looking for food, and human hunters with the same motives followed them.

Pre-history

At least 14,500 years passed before the first Europeans 'discovered' this New World, by which time aboriginal societies had spread throughout North and South America. In Canada alone, over 50 languages were spoken, a fact that prompted historian Olive Dickason to comment: "Canada has 55 founding nations rather than just the two that have been officially recognized". It is certainly useful to band Canada's First Nations together according to language groups or broad geographical areas, but to generalize about them is about as useful as speaking of Europeans as a single cultural unit.

People of the Plains

The stereotypical Hollywood-style image of the painted 'Red Indian' warrior with eagle-feather headdress, buffalo outfit, horse and rifle is based entirely on the tribes that lived on the Great Plains of Central Canada. Of these, the most militant and powerful were the Blackfoot Confederacy, who waged almost continual war with the Plains Cree and Assiniboine to the north and east, the Sioux and Crow to the south, and tribes such as the Kootenay and Shuswap who occupied the interior valleys of southern BC, but crossed the Rockies to hunt at certain times of year.

The whole way of life of the Plains Indians depended on the herds of buffalo that roamed the prairies in staggering numbers. Their meat provided the people with food; their hides were used to make clothes, blankets, rafts, and tepees that could be quickly dismantled and carried away when whole villages left to follow the buffalo's migrations. Painting on buffalo leather was the chief mode of artistic expression: tepees were lavishly decorated with naturalistic and geometric motifs, rawhide shields were symbolically painted with guardian spirits that would protect the warrior and buffalo robes were covered in designs ranging from abstract concentric patterns to representational images.

Ironically, the heyday of the Plains dwellers only came with the arrival of the Europeans and introduction of horses and rifles. But the white settlers also introduced the systematic and wholesale slaughter of the buffalo herds which they used as a means to rid themselves of the aboriginals.

The Pacific Northwest

By far the most densely populated area in Canada when the Europeans arrived, with about half of the country's inhabitants, was the Pacific Northwest. About 16 languages were spoken here, including two that were utterly unrelated to any others, making this one of the most linguistically rich regions in the history of the world. Radically different as they may have been, the West Coast nations had many cultural

⁝ The Northwest Passage

An interesting footnote in Canadian history is the story of Britain's obsession with finding the Northwest Passage which, it was originally hoped, would provide an alternative trade route to the Orient. One of the first to fall to the challenge was Martin Frobisher, a big, blustering, larger-than-life professional adventurer who made three voyages into the Arctic.

Henry Hudson set sail in 1610 to find the passage. He made it through the Strait that separates Québec from Baffin Island, and headed south across the vast bay that now bears his name. At the bottom of James Bay he hit a dead end, and spent what remained of the summer looking for a way through, before finally getting frozen in and passing the winter on starvation rations, eating moss to survive. When in the spring he wanted to continue rather than return, his crew mutinied and set him adrift, tied up, in a small boat.

Some two centuries later, despite the fact that the geography of the continent had been established, and it was clear that any existing Northwest Passage would be utterly unsuitable as a trade route, Captain John Franklin took up the old challenge. Having already made two attempts, one of which had ended in death, murder and cannibalism, he set off again in 1845, loading up the ships *Terror* and *Erebus* with 129 men. They were never seen again. The expeditions that followed rank as the longest, most extensive search in human history, and though Franklin was never found, a possible Northwest Passage was, by Robert McClure in 1851. Even then it was only conquered by ship in 1905 by Norwegian explorer Roald Amundsen.

similarities, although the Haida, from the isolated Queen Charlotte Islands, in Northern BC, were the fiercest, wealthiest, most extravagant and artistically gifted nation of all.

Thanks to a relatively mild climate and an abundant supply of food and materials, the coastal people had enough time and wealth to evolve into incredibly rich and complex societies. Extended families lived in vast, elaborately carved and decorated cedar plank houses, before which stood tall cedar poles covered in rich, anthropomorphic symbolism. People wore weavings, furs, leather footwear and exquisite jewellery, kept their possessions in sumptuously carved cedar boxes, and travelled in long dugout canoes that made them masters of the turbulent ocean and formidable fishermen. They dined on a rich diet of salmon, game, fruit, berries and roots, and enjoyed gambling, dancing, games, ceremonies, music and celebrations (see Culture, page 378). The coastal First Nations has a firmly entrenched sense of social class, with ranks including chiefs, commoners and slaves who were usually prisoners from conquered neighbours. Private ownership covered everything, even such essentials as fishing and hunting rights.

The Inuit and Inuvialuit

The people of Canada's Arctic occupy the very last region on earth to be inhabited by humans. The Inuit arrived from Siberia about 4000 or 5000 years ago, and speak the Inuktitut language in an area that stretches from Eastern Siberia to Greenland. Their survival is a testament to their formidable skills as hunters, and a triumph of human ingenuity and perseverance. The traditional Inuit abode, rarely seen today, is the igloo, a strong, elegant, complex structure that can be erected in little over an hour. Seals and whales were the buffalo of these Arctic dwellers, from which they crafted almost every tool for survival. Among other things, they invented the fur-lined parka, snowshoes, dog-sleds and the kayak. These incredible little vessels, made from skins stretched over a frame, are waterproof and virtually unsinkable.

The white man cometh

A complex network of trade had long-since been practised by most First Nations, and far from being easily duped innocents, they were from the start notoriously shrewd and tough in their dealings with the white man, and greatly appreciative of the iron, weapons and various tools that revolutionized their lives. The big problem originally was those other imports, the infectious diseases. Most European germs were utterly alien in the New World, so the natives had never developed a resistance to them. Smallpox, measles, influenza, even the common cold, decimated aboriginal populations. It has been estimated that the population of North America before the Europeans arrived was between 10 and 18 million, a number that fell by 95% in a mere 130 years.

Native bands were continually at war with their neighbours over territorial disputes and hunting and fishing rights; they raided and looted each other, taking slaves from among the defeated, and in some cases practised ritual cannabilism and torture. However, this situation only got out of hand with the introduction of European weapons, a problem further exacerbated by Christian missionaries, who divided bands, villages, even families, between those who had converted and those who had not.

First contacts

The debate is still open concerning which Europeans first reached the so-called New World. It may well have been a group of Irish monks led by St Brendan in AD 565. They almost certainly reached Iceland before the Vikings, and may well have visited the Northeast American Coast, but proof is yet to arrive. The Norsemen had island-hopped their way to Greenland by AD 1000, when sailors on a lost supply ship caught a glimpse of an unknown shore. Eric the Red's son Leif went in search of this mysterious land, stopping first at Baffin Island, then Labrador, then a heavily forested and pastured land, probably on Newfoundland, which he named Vinland, Land of Wine. His brother later returned and spent the winter getting into a battle with the people they called skraelings, meaning 'barbarians'. Little more came of it.

In 1497 John Cabot, searching for the 'backdoor' route to China, arrived in Newfoundland, or maybe Cape Breton, where he found so many cod that "they sometimes stayed his shippes". From then on hundreds of ships from all over Europe prowled the Newfoundland waters, but nobody was interested in settling the land.

In 1534 Jacques Cartier led the first of three expeditions to the new land looking for gold and diamonds. Stumbling across a group of Iroquoian natives on a fishing expedition, he set up a wooden cross in their presence and claimed the land for France, a symbolic act understood despite the language barrier by their chief Donnacona, who was enraged. On his third voyage Cartier returned to set up a colony but the understandable antagonism of the natives, together with the harshness of the weather, made him leave again for home, this time with a handful of 'gold' that turned out to be the fool's variety and 'diamonds' that were merely quartz.

It wasn't until 1608 that the first European settlement was established on Canadian soil. Samuel de Champlain set up his habitation at the site of today's Québec City and refused to give up, even when 20 of his 28 men died of scurvy in the first winter. Determined and energetic, this true founding father of Canada explored the waterways of the St Lawrence and Great Lakes, criss-crossing the ocean to promote his struggling colony. In 1609 the Montagnais Indians asked Champlain to accompany them on an expedition against the Iroquois to the south. It was the first time European weapons had been used against the natives and began a feud with the Iroquois, particularly the Mohawk, that would continue for generations, keeping the future land of 'New France' in a state of almost constant siege until a peace treaty was finally signed in 1701. From as early as 1615, Champlain invited the Récollet missionaries to come over and start converting the natives. He said it would "cement their commercial ties with the French as well as save them from eternal hell-fire in the next world". Their tactic was to relocate the natives on farms, dress them in European clothes and teach them French. It failed utterly. The Jesuits, however, lived among the natives, learned their language, and sought to convert them one at a time. The tactic was far more successful and ultimately perilous for the natives. Chief Dan George later lamented: "When the white man came, we had the land and they had the Bibles. Now they have the land and we have the Bibles".

Despite many vicissitudes, and thanks largely to the fur trade, New France survived, but it remained little more than a trading post until 1617, when Champlain asked one Louis Hébert to settle the land properly, by farming it. The first century was a tenuous time, during which the colony's very existence was constantly threatened by the powerful Iroquois Confederacy. In 1667, Louis XIV sent over 1100 of his best soldiers, whose very presence led to a truce and 20 years of peace during which the young colony flourished. At the same time, the king sent about 800 young female settlers, known as Filles du Roi, to redress the balance between males and females. This helped spark a population explosion, and today the majority of Canada's six million Québecois can trace their roots back to these adventurous women, who were mainly orphans, prostitutes and widows.

The fur trade

Coureurs de bois and voyageurs

It was the humble beaver that really allowed settlers on the East Coast to survive and expand westwards. In Europe, top hats were all the rage, and the best felt for their fabrication came from the soft underpelt of the beaver. Since the best fur came from the coldest regions, pursuit of the beaver led directly to the colonization of the north and west of this vast new continent. At first native trappers brought furs to trade with the French, but Champlain shrewdly began sending men to live among his native allies, learn their language and customs, and become familiar with the geography. As well as bridging a gap between the cultures, he wanted these coureurs de bois, runners of the woods, to help him chart the interior. They were forerunners of the voyageurs, intrepid adventurers who paddled deep into the continent each year in flotillas of canoes to collect furs.

The Hudson's Bay Company

Two coureurs de bois named Radisson and Groseilliers, maybe at the suggestion of the Cree trappers in the north, realized that instead of taking the longer route to the northwest via the St Lawrence River, ocean-going vessels could sail right into Hudson Bay and load up with furs brought straight to them by native trappers, thus cutting out the middlemen entirely. The French were not interested in the idea, so they took it to the English, and in 1668 two ships were sent to test the idea, one of which, the *Nonsuch*, made it through to the bottom of James Bay and set up a small trading post. This led to a Royal Charter being issued for a 'Company of Adventurers', who were given exclusive trading rights over the lands that drained into Hudson Bay. Named Rupert's Land, this vast area covered 40% of Canada's present territory. Founded in 1670, the Hudson's Bay Company (HBC) was the world's first corporation, very much in the shape of things to come. Historian Peter C Newman has pointed out that "at the peak of its expansion (the HBC) controlled nearly 3 million square miles of territory – nearly a twelfth of the earth's land surface and an area 10 times that of the Holy Roman Empire at its height".

War and revolution

The Seven Years' War
The battle for supremacy between the French and English continued for over 150 years, often during times of official peace, finally culminating in the so-called Seven Years' War (which lasted nine years in North America). The conflict began on the American frontier and eventually spread to Europe and beyond, spawning a web of alliances that fought on four continents, making this the first true World War. Though outnumbered three to one in ships, four to one in troops, and ten to one in money, the French actually seemed to be winning the war, until Britain was rescued by the election of Prime Minister William Pitt, for whom the war became an obsession. Ultimately, the war was won thousands of miles away, with the defeat of the French navy in Europe.

The American Revolution
The war against France had pushed Britain to the brink of financial ruin. Attempts to make the American colonies contribute towards clearing the imperial debt was the last straw for a people already ripe for self-dominion: the Thirteen Colonies of the Eastern Seaboard broke free from British rule and formed a new political union, the United States of America. The question is not why did they want to break free, but why did the northern colonies not choose to seize the moment. A very important part of the answer is that they were wary of the Americans, a factor that has recurred perennially throughout Canadian history to this very day. English settlers in Canada were happy to have access to so much land, the territory of Québec having just been expanded to include the Great Lakes and the Ohio Valley. The French had so far been well-treated by the English, who had done little to undermine their institutions and culture. As Henri Bourassa later put it: "It was all very simple; we had to choose between the English of Boston and the English of London. The English of London were farther away and we hated them less". Both sides considered their neighbours to the south a much less tolerant prospect than the present regime, so when the Americans attempted to take Québec by force in 1775, they were duly resisted, and the attempt degenerated into a fiasco.

Go West, Young Men!

Pierre de la Vérendrye
The differing styles of the opposing fur trading companies was apparent from the very beginning. While the English HBC encouraged native traders to bring furs to them, the French voyageurs went out into the land and learned to live like the natives. The first Canadian explorer to be born in Canada, Pierre de La Vérendrye, was also the first to push west of the Great Lakes and the Canadian Shield into the great Central Plains. In the 1730s and 1740s, he and four of his sons discovered the Saskatchewan River, whose twin branches turned out to be the key to the interior. They went on to found a string of trading posts, including Fort Rouge at the fork of the Red and Assiniboine Rivers, a junction now known as The Forks in the heart of Winnipeg.

The NorthWest Company

With the Company of the North destroyed by Britain's victory over France, a trading vacuum appeared that was quickly filled by Scottish and American merchants, who hired seasoned voyageurs and picked up where the French had left off. An American named Peter Pond had established a trading post near Lake Athabasca in Northern Alberta, opening up the deep north to the fur trade. Establishing themselves as the NorthWest Company, the Montréal traders dedicated themselves to expanding the fur trade still further, as far as the Pacific and the Arctic. It was their explorers who travelled, charting almost all of the vast land north and west of Ontario, opening it up to later settlement. Of these, three in particular have become household names.

Mackenzie, Fraser and Thompson

Alexander Mackenzie mistakenly followed the river later named after him, which he called the 'River of Disappointment', all the way to the Arctic Ocean. On his next expedition he became the first person to cross the continent north of Mexico. Following the Peace River into the Rockies, he battled his way across the mountains to the Pacific, where on a large boulder he left Canada's most famous bit of graffiti: Alexander Mackenzie, from Canada, by land, 22 July 1793. Simon Fraser was chosen to expand trade into the land west of the Rockies and explore the Columbia River. Between 1805 and 1807 he accomplished the first of these goals, establishing four forts at McLeod, Stuart and Fraser lakes, and Fort George, naming this vast and hitherto unexplored wilderness New Caledonia. The following year, believing it to be the Columbia, he followed the treacherous river that now bears his name all the way to the Pacific. David Thompson founded a series of important trading posts along BC's windy rivers (including the one named after him) in his pursuit to follow the Columbia River to the Pacific. He finally succeeded in 1811, only to find that the Americans had beaten him by a few weeks.

A mere matter of marching

While the English were fighting the 1812 war against Napolean, the Americans saw their chance of capturing Canada. With Britain preoccupied and the US population at 7.5 million compared to Canada's 80,000, Thomas Jefferson advised President Madison that it was "a mere matter of marching". On 18 June 1812 they promptly declared war on Britain and made plans for the Conquest of Canada. It was General Isaac Brock and the great Shawnee Chief Tecumseh who were to save Canada. In a series of battles in which they were greatly outnumbered, this dynamic duo scared the Americans into submission by exploiting their irrational fear of those wild Indian braves.

In the treaty that followed, Canada and the First Nations were excluded from negotiations, while Britain agreed to return the frontiers to their original positions, allowing the Americans to extend their borders into the Indian Territory that had previously been reserved as native lands. The First Nations had been shafted again, this time for good. No longer needed by the British as allies or a buffer zone, they were destined to be 'civilized' and assimilated, or slowly wiped out.

Once upon a time in the West

First landings

The first European to arrive on the Pacific Northwest coast was a Danish sea captain, named Vitus Bering, after whom the Strait was later named. Working for the Russian Czar he reached the islands off the coast of Alaska, and his crew returned with otter pelts whose value soon inspired the Russians to set up trading posts in the area. Hearing of this, the Spanish, who had claimed the whole Pacific Ocean for themselves, sent their own expedition to the region, and began trading with the Haida in 1774. Next to arrive were the British, in the form of Captain James Cook, who began charting the west coast of Vancouver Island. He traded with the friendly natives for otter pelts, which his crew later sold in China at a great profit. Cook himself had by then been killed by Hawaiian Polynesians. Word was out and the sea otter, like the beaver, would be hunted to the brink of extinction.

A Perfect Eden

Despite the burgeoning sea otter trade, and Captain George Vancouver's extensive charting of the coast, no attempt was made to settle the West until the HBC established Fort Langley (near today's Vancouver) in 1827, and Fort Victoria in the 1840s. The latter was a purely strategic manoeuvre. The border with the US had been drawn along the 49th parallel from the Great Lakes to the Rockies, but the HBC shrewdly recognized that if this line were ever extended, it would clip the south end off Vancouver Island. In an attempt to get there first, James Douglas was sent to survey prospective sites for a new fort and trading post, and chose a site which he called 'a perfect Eden'. Douglas was named governor of Vancouver Island on top of his title as Chief Factor of the HBC.

The Company's fears were soon vindicated. In 1844, US President James Polk was elected on the cry of "54.40 or fight", a brazen threat that the Union would claim the whole of the mountainous Oregon territory, including most of today's BC, right up to Alaska, taking it by force if necessary. The matter was ultimately decided by the 1846 Treaty of Oregon, signed by the US and Britain, which extended the 49th parallel straight across, ignoring the natural geography of north-south river valleys. The HBC was obliged to relocate its western HQ to the new Fort Victoria, greatly bolstering its importance.

Gold fever

If Canada as a whole owes its existence to the beaver, British Columbia came about thanks to the more obvious incentive of gold, the 1858 discovery of which in the Fraser Valley changed Fort Victoria almost overnight. For 25,000 stampeders en route to the gold fields, this was the only possible stop-over, and the town quickly swelled with shops and hotels, bars and brothels, politicians and newspapermen. Afraid of an American takeover, Governor Douglas issued a public proclamation that the gold fields were Crown property, forcing all miners to register and pay a fee. In doing so he had assumed control of the mainland, a blatant bluff. Britain pointed out that he was overstepping his authority, then backed him up anyway, creating a second Crown Colony called British Columbia in 1866, with Douglas as governor of both.

Soon the new colony was littered with desperate hopefuls panning every creek for traces of the yellow metal. When large deposits of gold were found in the Cariboo, Douglas commissioned the Cariboo Road, a 650-km marvel of engineering and daring, eventually used to haul out millions of tons of ore, much of it from the boomtown of Barkerville, which for many years took its turn as the biggest settlement north of San Francisco. More importantly, the road opened up the grassland valleys and rolling basins of the interior plateau to ranching.

Dominion from sea to sea

Two nations warring …

Many of Canada's problems can be traced back to the Constitutional Act of 1791, which cut the large province of Québec in two: Upper Canada in the west (now Ontario) would be English, Lower Canada in the east (now Québec once again) would be French. The problems caused by this apartheid smouldered for 40 years before flaring up as two minor rebellions in the 1830s which, though quickly smothered, had far-reaching effects. The British sent over Lord Durham, whose liberal leanings had earnt him the name 'Radical Jack'. He recommended that Upper and Lower Canada be united under one government in order to assimilate the French; that leaders of the elected assembly should henceforth assume the role of the governor's ruling advisors; and that the colonies be given authority over their own internal affairs. He blamed the unrest on an outdated colonial system in Upper Canada, and in Lower Canada talked of "two nations warring in the bosom of a single state". The two provinces were joined under one government by the 1841 Act of Union, and the 1848 election saw the victory of one of the greatest political alliances in Canadian history: Louis-Hippolyte La Fontaine and Robert Baldwin. The capital of the new single province of Canada was eventually decided by Queen Victoria. She chose a small unknown lumbertown called Ottawa. Strategically located on the river border between French and English Canada, it was inland from a possible American attack on the St Lawrence, yet linked to the Great Lakes by the defensive Rideau Canal.

Confederation

During the 1860s, several key elements came together to make the union of the northern colonies a reality. The emphasis in Britain had shifted to trade and profits rather than military glory and monopolies. The colonies were coming to be seen as financial burdens that had to grow up and take responsibility for themselves. At the same time, Britain's clear sympathy and tacit support of the southern states during the brutal Civil War of 1861-65 had angered the northern states, at times bringing Britain and the US to the brink of war, with Canada as the battlefield. Newspapers in Chicago and New York were warning Canada: "Just wait till this war is over. You're next!"

The Treaty of Reciprocity with the US that had helped Canada to survive when Britain ended its protective colonial tariff and began moving towards freer trade seemed unlikely to be renewed, so Canada had to look elsewhere, namely towards the land to the west. In this respect, the railways offered great promise, a possible response to the US threat, and also great profits. It is no coincidence that the leading proponents of Confederacy were also railway promoters. And one of the arguments they used was that of glory, the glory of expansion.

A federal system was eventually agreed on that borrowed from the British and American systems. Like the latter, it would have two levels of government, federal and provincial. But rather than electing a President by a separate vote, they chose to be led by a Prime Minister, who would be the leader of the party with the most seats in the House.

The Province of Canada said yes to union, though there was only a small majority among the French. New Brunswick eventually said yes. The Nova Scotia premier said yes, though without the consent of his people who were basically tricked into the deal. Newfoundland said no. Ironically, the first Canadian land to be inhabited by Europeans, or so we believe, was the last to join the union, holding out until 1949. Canada was called a Dominion after the Psalm 72 phrase "His dominion shall be from sea to sea", which also provided the national motto A Mari Usque Ad Mari. The very day after Queen Victoria signed the British North America Act in 1867, the Americans ominously purchased Alaska from the Russians.

The Canadian Pacific Railway

Asked to join the Confederation, BC requested a wagon trail from Manitoba to the coast. Cartier extravagently offered them a full-scale Trans-Continental railway instead, an offer they couldn't refuse. The Liberals called the building of the Canadian Pacific Railway (CPR) "an act of insane recklessness", and they were right, but glory knows no bounds. The railway skirted the edge of bankruptcy on several occasions. Crossing 5000 km it would become the longest railway on earth, and a marvel of

The Klondike Gold Rush

The Klondike bonanza began when George Washington Carmack and his native brothers-in-law Skookum Jim and Tagish Charley prospected on Rabbit Creek, a tributary of the Klondike River, following a tip from a Nova Scotian named Robert Henderson. Legend has it that on 17 August 1896, at the spot now named Discovery Claim on the creek now renamed Bonanza, Carmacks pulled out a nugget the size of his thumb, later talking about layers of gold between slabs of rock "like cheese sandwiches". The trio staked their claim and, when word got out, miners already in the vicinity staked every creek in the Klondike and Indian River watersheds, including the unthinkably bountiful Eldorado. By that winter, when snow and ice quarantined the region from the rest of the world, all the big money had already been secured by the fortunate few. A second wave of West Coast prospectors arrived the following spring to fight for the remaining scraps, but the real story was yet to begin.

In mid-July 1897, some of the newly rich were seen in San Francisco struggling from the Excelsior with more gold than they could carry. When the Portland docked in Seattle, the press were waiting, and the Post-Intelligencer's description of "a ton of gold" effectively sparked off the stampede. In an atmosphere of terrible economic depression, thousands suddenly sold off their possessions or used their hoarded funds to answer the call of adventure and fortune. It has been estimated that over a million souls left their homes, of which only 100,000 made it to the Yukon. Only 20% of these ever panned for gold, a fifth of that number actually found some, and very few made that elusive fortune.

In retrospect, it seems that the real point for many, like writer Jack London, was not finding the gold but being part of the quest. The richest travelled up the coast to the mouth of the Yukon in Alaska, and upriver from there. The unfortunate and gullible were hoodwinked into taking the bogus 'All Canadian' routes through Edmonton and BC, spending two years on hellish trails, if they made it at all. The majority took ocean liners to Skagway, laboured their way over the fearsome Chilkoot Pass and waited out the winter somewhere between Carcross and Whitehorse. They then constructed makeshift boats to cover the last 800 treacherous kilometres down the Yukon River. Those who could afford it took one of the 60 stern-wheelers that plied the river. Between them, these dreamers and schemers spent some $50 million reaching the Klondike, about an equal sum to what was extracted from the creeks in the first five years of mining. Almost every town in Western Canada was affected by the stampede, and the Yukon Territory itself was created in 1898 to assert sovereignty over the region.

modern engineering. Historian Will Ferguson says: "Ours was a country forged not in revolution but in a landscape traversed. Ours was a victory over sheer geography". In places the railway had to be blasted out of rock, costing thousands of lives.

How the West was won

British Columbia joined the Confederation in 1871, but the union was for some time an unhappy one. Governing a large mountainous area with few people was an expensive business, revenue from resources was low, and the hoped-for expansion of trade with East Asia following completion of the Canadian Pacific Railway was slow to arrive. The railway did, however, bring people to the port of Vancouver, which in 15 years already surpassed the population it had taken Victoria almost 60 to accrue.

The kind of settlers attracted to BC were very different from those drawn to the East and Prairies. Entrepreneurs with capital to invest came West around the turn of the 20th century to exploit the province's vast resources. A salmon-cannery industry was established along the coast. Sawmills sprang up around the shores of Georgia Strait and along eastern Vancouver Island. The first pulp and paper mill at Powell River wasn't completed until 1912 and significant expansion of the forest industry only occurred after the First World War, when the Panama Canal gave access to markets in the North Atlantic.

Missionary Father Pandosy's successful cultivation of apples in Kelowna had led to a string of orchards down the Okanagan Valley by the 1890s, and around the same time the discovery of gold, silver, copper and lead around Kootenay Lake led to a new wave of gold fever and subsequent settlement. Responding to railways that extended northward into the region from the US, the CPR built a line through the Crowsnest Pass in 1899 to extract coal from Fernie, constructed the Kettle Valley Railway from Hope, and blazed the Dewdney Trail, much of which was later converted into Highway 3. Throughout the mayhem of gold fever, which created or affected almost every community in BC, the province never turned into the kind of lawless free-for-all that California had earlier become. Much credit for this goes to the NWMP, and to the famous figure of Matthew Begbie, also known as 'the hangin' judge'.

The Gold Rush to end them all led tens of thousands of mostly Americans to the Klondike River near the overnight boomtown of Dawson City. For a full account, see page 370. The Yukon Territory was created in 1898 to assert Canadian sovereignty over the region. The building of the Grand Trunk Pacific Railway west from Edmonton through the Upper Fraser, Bulkley and Skeena valleys in 1907-14 was intended to give Canada a second gateway through the mountains to the Pacific Coast. Prince George then became a minor sawmill centre, servicing the growing housing market in the Prairies to the east.

From sea to frozen sea

Britain had meanwhile transferred jurisdiction over the Arctic Islands to Canada in 1880, but it wasn't until the early 20th century that Canada officially extended its boundary to the North Pole. A single mariner claimed the entire Arctic Archipelago for Canada in 1909, but it meant nothing until the area was surveyed in the mid-1930s. As a senior Ottawa bureaucrat noted: "The history of the Canadian North can be divided into two periods – before and after the airplane".

The 20th century

First World War

Canada catapulted itself onto the world stage with the accomplishments of its soldiers in the Great War, most famously at Vimy Ridge, Passchendaele, Amiens and the Hindenburg Line. Canada's contribution of over 620,000 men, 60,000 of whom died, with over 172,000 injured, was extremely high in relation to its population, a fact that further strengthened its international voice. In 1917, Prime Minister Robert Borden, along with South African Prime Minister Jan Smuts, demanded that the dominions be given full recognition as "autonomous nations of an Imperial commonwealth". He also insisted that Canada put its own signature on the Treaty of Versailles, and when the League of Nations was formed, Canada and the other dominions were given seats, much to the annoyance of the US, who saw it as a British ploy to secure more votes.

The inglorious side of the war, often glossed over, was the mass arrest of over 8500 'enemy aliens', including over 5000 Ukrainians who were interred and used as labour in the steel mills of Nova Scotia. In other respects the war years and following decade were a time of positive reform. The Labour and Women's movements in particular made great leaps forward: in 1916, women won the right to vote in Manitoba, Alberta and Saskatchewan, with BC and Ontario following the next year and Nova Scotia a year later. Other provinces followed suit, although Québec women were denied their rights until 1940.

The Great Depression

It's clear today that the prosperity of the 1920s was a colossal house of cards which provoked a domino effect of crises when it came tumbling down in 1929. When panic ensued, countries followed the example of the US and retreated behind walls of protectionist tariffs. As a nation whose economy was largely built on exports, Canada was one of, if not the, worst hit countries in the West. The Prairies suffered the most. A bumper crop flooded the market just as demand dried up, pushing prices to an all-time low, then a severe drought began with almost no rain at all for seven years. The Plains region became a dust bowl, afflicted with dirt storms, darkened skies and plagues of grasshoppers. More than 200,000 people were forced to leave their farms. Income in Canada as a whole fell by almost 50%, with 20% of the population living on relief handouts. The jobless rate rose from 4 to 27%. With warmer weather on the West Coast, many of the homeless gravitated towards Vancouver, where they seem to have set up permanent residence on Hastings Street. At this time a new party was formed in Calgary from farmers and unions. Called the Co-operative Commonwealth Fed (CCF) it later merged in 1961 with the Canadian Labour Congress to form the NDP.

Second World War

The most striking aspect of Canada's involvement in the Second World War was the way in which Canadian troops were so often used as cannon fodder. Churchill sent 1900 of them into Hong Kong as a hopeless 'symbolic' defence against the Japanese. In 1942, in what could be seen as a farcical dress rehearsal for the D-day landings, 6000 troops, including 5000 Canadians, were sent on an ill-conceived mission into Dieppe that turned into a bloody fiasco. Over a million Canadians served in all, of which 45,000 died and 55,000 were wounded.

The war had made Canada, along with the US, one of the two richest nations on earth, with the third largest navy and fourth largest air force. At the same time as the Citizenship Act of 1946 defined the people of Canada as Canadian citizens rather than British subjects, discriminatory immigration laws were set up to preserve "the fundamental character" of the country, making it very hard for blacks, Arabs, Asians and Jews to get in.

The Cold War

Surprisingly enough, Canada was where the Cold War began. It was a clerk at the Soviet Embassy in Ottawa, Igor Gouzenko, who revealed to British intelligence officers just how many spies had infiltrated their embassies, governments, and atomic research facilities. He had tried to approach Canadian officials, who refused to take him seriously. But the Cold War was a serious business for a country which, as one Soviet ambassador put it, was "the ham in the Soviet-American sandwich". During the 1950s, a series of expensive radar lines were built across Canadian Territory, including the Distant Early Warning line, which was entirely paid for by the US, who would not allow Canadian officials even to approach the sites without prior approval. In 1956, Canada's reputation as a peace-keeping force was cemented when diplomat (and later Prime Minister) Lester Pearson almost single-handedly defused the highly explosive Suez Crisis, for which he earnt the Nobel Peace Prize.

Trudeaumania
Pierre Elliott Trudeau was perhaps the all-time most famous icon of Canadian politics, and dominated the scene from 1968-84. Young, suave and free-spirited, he captured the optimistic spirit of the Sixties.

Though prone to be coldly intellectual, Pierre Trudeau mostly lived up to his purported liberalism. As Minister of Justice he had already brought in key changes that relaxed divorce laws and ended restrictions on homosexuality and access to abortion. In 1971 he introduced the Canadian Multicultural Act, emphasizing the equality of all 'cultural and ethnic groups'. A few years later, in a landmark piece of legislation, a proposed gas pipeline from Alaska to Alberta was shelved due to native land rights and environmental issues. And in a reversal of former policy, nearly 60,000 Indo-Chinese were allowed into Canada during the Vietnamese boat crisis.

With a great deal of squabbling and difficulty, Trudeau drew up a Canadian Constitution in 1982. Until then the Constitution was still under British jurisdiction. Included within it was the Charter of Rights and Freedoms, which delineates freedom of conscience and religion; freedom of expression (including that of the press); freedom of peaceful assembly; and freedom of association.

Separatism
Perhaps Trudeau's key contribution to Canadian politics, though, was his firm stance against separatism in Québec, a position that has been upheld by his colleague and fellow Québecois, Jean Chrétien.

In 1976 the Parti Québecois (PQ) was elected as Québec's government. The following year they passed Bill 101, which banned English on commercial signs and severely restricted access to English-language education. Ironically, a federal bill had already been passed making it compulsory for the rest of the country to have labels in both languages on items as trivial as a jar of jam. In 1980, the PQ held a referendum on separation in which 60% of Québecois voted against sovereignty, but this was far from the end of the affair. During the term of Albertan PM Brian Mulroney, the separatists' position strengthened due to the premier's constant pandering to Québec, which was cited as a major reason why dissatisfied conservatives from the West broke away to form the Reform Party in 1987.

The stakes were raised in 1990 when the Bloc Québecois was formed to campaign on a federal level. Another referendum was arranged by the PQ for 1995, and this time the nation held its breath. Just 50.6% of Québec voted against separation, the narrowest of escapes. The issue of two warring nations has been a perennial thread in Canada's political tapestry, and doesn't look like going away any time soon.

During and after the Second World War, a trend began by which Canada became more and more linked to the US both militarily and economically. The Ogdensburg Agreement of 1940 established a Permanent Joint Board to integrate North American defences, while the government started courting American money to a degree that was considered shameless. By signing the North American Air Defense Agreement (NORAD), John Diefenbaker pretty much put Canada's air defences under US control.

Trudeau became more and more concerned by US penetration into the Canadian economy, and made real efforts to increase ties to Britain and Europe, introducing some of the most unabashed examples of economic nationalism since Macdonald. But matters took a dramatic turn with the election of Brian Mulroney, an Albertan Conservative who started Investment Canada to encourage American investment. In 1987 he proposed the Free Trade Agreement with the States, removing almost every trade barrier between the countries, even though 80% of Canada's exports were already going south. He then won the 1988 election on a platform of closer economic ties with the US, the first time that had ever happened. The White House saw the FTA as "a major victory for the United States", one US trade rep even saying,

"The Canadians don't understand what they have signed. In 20 years they will be sucked into the US economy".

By 1993, Mulroney's popularity had fallen to a record low of 9%, and he was replaced in 1993 by Kim Campbell, Canada's first female prime minister, who only lasted a few months. Trudeau's old henchman Jean Chrétien was voted in, and has remained in power ever since. In January 1994, months after taking office, he signed the NAFTA agreement that greatly expanded the Mulroney agenda he claimed to oppose. The effects were immediate: while the US retail giant Walmart moved into every mall in the country, the ancient Canadian stalwart Eatons filed for bankruptcy.

Return of the natives

The third strand that has persisted throughout Canada's history is the plight and struggles of its First Nations. The Indian Act that followed the First World War aimed at nothing short of complete assimilation, forcing natives to relinquish all rights and status in order to vote or even own property. This once proud people had been racked by alien diseases, restricted to reserves, deprived of their traditional hunting grounds, taught in schools where they were discouraged from speaking their own languages, forbidden to continue ceremonies like the potlatch (see page 380), and denied basic rights such as a vote. In the 1920s it seemed that they were a dying breed.

Yet somehow they survived, with many of their traditions and languages intact. After the Second World War the government decided to revise the Indian Act, and for the first time natives were involved in the discussions. Little came of it, but at least they got the vote in 1960.

The struggle for native land claims began in the 1890s in British Columbia, where no treaties had ever been drawn up as they were further east. Nations like the Nisga'a of the Nass Valley near Terrace never signed their land away and were never conquered, so technically their land still belongs to them. Only in the last 25 years have such claims begun to be taken seriously. When the government of Québec wanted to build a hydro project in the north, they had to negotiate terms with the James Bay Cree and Inuit, who surrendered their rights to a million square kilometres of land in exchange for self government within their own communities, hunting, trapping and fishing rights, and a trust fund of $225 million. In 1987, the Sechelt Inlet Band became the first native group in Canada to be granted self-government within their own reserve lands.

In 1990, Mohawk protesters in the Oka region outside Montréal barricaded roads to a forest that was slated to be cut down, and in the resistance killed a police officer. This led to the formation in 1991 of the Royal Commission on Aboriginal Peoples. The report took five years to complete, and included 400 proposed changes, including the creation of an individual tribunal for land claims. It was finally recognized that the government could hardly be impartial in cases filed against itself. In 1999 the UN Human Rights Committee ruled that Canada was in violation of international law in its treatment of aboriginal rights. In 1999 the new territory of Nunavut was created. More than twice the size of BC it covers two million square kilometres, about a fifth of Canada's land mass. One of the most thinly populated areas on earth, it has just 25,000 people, 83% of whom are Inuit, who were allowed to retain ownership of 18% of the land. The territory was given self-government and a $1 billion cash settlement. It is the first time any single First Nations group will have a majority presence in a provincial or territorial government.

Modern Canada

An overview

Like most of the First World, Canada has become a consumer society, dominated by bad television, suburbs and malls. Fortunately, in Western Canada that grim summary only really applies to the two comparitively small pockets where the vast majority of people live: the Lower Mainland around Vancouver in BC, and the corridor between Calgary and Edmonton in Alberta. Elsewhere, life moves at a slower pace, and people still have time to ponder the age old mysteries and enjoy the natural beauty that surrounds them. The air is fresher, the water cleaner, the people more friendly, the atmosphere more relaxed. The UN declared Canada the best country in the world in which to live for almost a decade, but it dropped behind Norway and Sweden in 2001.

Politics

Canadians have always considered the Liberals their default political party, and have a penchant for Québecois leaders. Pierre Trudeau dominated the scene from 1968-1984, and Jean Chretien from 1993-2003. Paul Martin briefly took the helm for the liberals from 2003-5, but a messy and long-winded 'sponsorship scandal' toppled his government and brought the Conservatives to power in January 2006, led by ultra right-wing Stephen Harper. It was the weakest minority government in Canadian history yet, contrary to everyone's expectations, it has survived for over two years. Naturally, the Liberals – now the official opposition – have chosen another Québecois as their leader: Stephane Dion, who fended off famous writer and intellectual Michael Ignatieff in the leadership race, and has had to brush up on his English to fuflfil the role. Canada's third party is the more left-wing NDP, led by Jack Layton, who usually comes across as the most eligible of the three leaders. Traditionally popular in the West, but not the East where political fortunes are invariably decided, their strong emphasis on healthcare and the environment is now steadily gaining them support across the nation.

Sleeping with the elephant

Several key perennial issues continue to dominate Canadian politics. The issue of native rights, land claims and self-determination; the constant threat that the Parti Québecois will muster enough support to separate from the rest of the country; the inadequate state of the national health system; and the country's ambivalent relationship with its supersized neighbour to the south. In an address to the National Press Club of Washington, DC in March 1969, Pierre Elliot Trudeau said, "Living next to you is in some ways like sleeping with an elephant. No matter how friendly and even-tempered is the beast, if I can call it that, one is affected by every twitch and grunt". Canada continues to be defined by the fact that it is not the United States and it is amazing that the country can retain any sense of national identity while so completely overwhelmed by the centrifugal force of US money and ideology. Living next door to the world's number one superpower has never been easy, and though a land-grab seems less likely now than in the past, the threat of a more insidious cultural and economic takeover is as real as ever. Some 200 million people cross the border every year, and over $1 billion of trade crosses it every day. The latest chapter in the stoty involved the complete ban by the US on Alberta beef, as the result of one case of mad cow disease, costing the ranching industry millions of dollars; and a bogus (and allegedly illegal) embrago on softwood lumber, which cost BC's forestry industry millions of dollars. Stephen Harper is keen to remain on good terms with George W Bush and has committed Canada's troops to the wars in Iraq and Afghanistan, but there are many on both sides of the border who still feel that Canada is not doing enough.

Focus on the West

For all the righteous indignation of his opponents, Gordon Campbell's strategies appear to have borne some fruit. When he took over, British Columbia was considered a 'have-not' province: unemployment was rising, the economy was stagnating and a deficit was growing, despite ample natural resources. That situation has turned around. The economy is booming, unemployment has plummetted and the government is now in a position to sink millions of dollars into province-wide improvements to public transport. They are now working on a emissions tax on gasoline, ostensibly for environmental purposes, though it looks like just another money-grab.

Economy

Tourism is the fastest growing industry in Western Canada, as the world catches on to its unequalled expanses of unspoilt wilderness, superb recreation possibilities, and friendly, relaxed people. The process is accelerating as the global media spotlight is fixed on Vancouver and Whistler who will co-host the Winter Olympics in 2010. The challenge for the future will be protecting the wilderness from mining, oil exploration and irresponsible logging. The extremely costly extraction of oil from Oil Sands around Fort McMurray in Northern Alberta strikes many as a project that is irresponsibly harmful to the environment. Having raised the moratorium on grizzly-bear hunting as one of its first acts in power, the Campbell government, clearly valuing short-term gain over long-sighted preservation of the natural beauty that is clearly BC's trump card, is in the process of opening up the province's protected parks to exploitation, the thin edge of an extremely dangerous wedge. On the other hand, the Campbell government's recent plans to dedicate $14 billion to upgrading the province's transportation network, inspired in part by the 2010 Olympics, should benefit everyone, though it inevitably has its opponents. Meanwhile, the victory of the Tsilhqot'in and Xeni Gwet'in peoples in their treaty negotiations with the BC government led First Nations leaders from across British Columbia to issue a declaration affirming Aboriginal Title to their respective traditional territories.

British Columbia

Forestry has been the main component of BC's economy throughout this century. About 64% of the province is forested, and thanks to excellent growth conditions BC produces nearly 60% of Canada's sawn lumber, most of its plywood and 30% of its chemical pulp. This over-dependence on its softwood has caused the province major problems following tariffs introduced by the US, where most of the wood goes.

A wide range of metals has been discovered throughout the Cordilleran part of the province, including lead, zinc, gold, silver, copper and iron. The Peace River Lowland has a different geological base consisting of younger, sedimentary rocks which have been the sources of petroleum, natural gas and coal. Mining and mineral processing employ about 3% of the labour force but yield nearly 20% of the product value of BC's major industries. Most consumer-goods manufacturing, as well as management and financial activities concerned with resource developments, has remained concentrated in or near the ports of the southwest, whose activities contrast ever more clearly with the primary activities of the north coast and interior.

In 2001, $601 million worth of fish were harvested in BC and 20,100 were employed in the industry. The most valuable fishery is for the five species of Pacific salmon, which are caught by large, modern fishing vessels mostly near the mouths of the Fraser and Skeena rivers, a method of harvesting that has resulted in disastrously depleted fish stocks. Other important seafood include herring, halibut, cod and sole, and a large variety of shellfish, particularly oysters. In cultivated land as a percentage of total provincial area, BC ranks second lowest in Canada, behind Newfoundland. Its most productive official crops are vegetables, tobacco and ginseng, but these are probably dwarfed by the incalculable market value of BC's marijuana industry. The most important regions for agriculture are the Peace River area, which accounts for about 90% of BC's grain, the Okanagan Valley, one of Canada's three main fruit-growing regions, and the small but fertile farms of the Lower Fraser River. Cattle ranching on the grasslands of the southern Interior Plateau is relatively small-scale.

BC is well endowed with steep and rugged landforms and ample precipitation, which together produce enormous seasonal runoffs in numerous rivers and vast amounts of potential hydroelectric power. Dams along the Kootenay, Columbia, and Peace rivers in particular are among the country's most productive, producing energy for the Lower Mainland and the United States. The physical environment of BC is itself a valuable resource, attracting visitors from throughout the world. Above all, the province is renowned internationally for the extent and diversity of its opportunities for outdoor recreation. In 2005 tourism generated 4% of BC's GDP, providing 6% of jobs.

Alberta

Like the other Prairie provinces, Alberta was struggling with an economy reliant on the vicissitudes of the world's grain and cattle markets, until the discovery of oil in the Leduc field in 1947 transformed it overnight into Canada's most energy-rich province. A rapid rise in the world price of oil in the early 1970s drove the Alberta economy to unprecedented and frantic growth. While Edmonton became the centre for petroleum servicing, production and transmission, Calgary remained the exploration, administrative and financial centre. After a decade of financial boom, the nationwide recession of the 1980s was particularly severe in Alberta. The mid-1990s saw its fortunes rise again with higher world prices for oil and natural gas. The value of fuels in 1993 reached $18.5 billion, or 79.9% of total national value.

While proven remaining recoverable oil reserves are still considerable, Alberta holds some other aces. About 70% of Canada's proven remaining coal reserves lie within the province, estimated in 1995 at $34 billion. The natural gas industry is older than oil, dating from 1883 discoveries near Medicine Hat, and in 1994 Alberta's production was still 83% of the Canadian total. Two-thirds of the world's bitumen is located in the Fort McMurray region of Northern Alberta in the form of oil sands that cover more than 78,000 sq km, an area almost as big as Scotland. The 1.7 trillion barrels of bitumen represents one of the largest known hydrocarbon accumulations in the world. As conventional production declines, the oil sands could become the future for Canada's energy security in the next century. Alberta also has vast heavy oil reserves which exhibit the same general chemical characteristics as bitumen from the oil sands.

The success story of the petroleum industry had a knock-on effect that further benefitted Alberta's economy. As Canada's balance of financial power shifted westward, Calgary emerged as the third-largest head-office location after Toronto and Montreal for major Canadian companies and foreign banks. Between 1978 and 1986 the Calgary-based Alberta Stock Exchange increased its number of company listings by nearly 400, reaching 491. The construction industry in the two major cities also rides high on the province's booms.

Forests cover nearly three-quarters of Alberta, 67% of which is considered productive for forestry. Owing to the boom and bust cycle of the oil industry, the Alberta government has been aggressively promoting this sector of the economy since the late 1980s, and it now ranks as the province's second-largest industry. Agriculture and livestock husbandry also remain of vital importance. The black and brown soils of the mixed-grass prairie and parkland regions possess great potential for mixed farming. Away from this fertile crescent, especially in the southeast, lie the more specialized ranching and wheat operations, which compensate for their marginal soils with their large size. Over $40 billion worth of product is exported each year.

Tourism has become an increasingly important sector of Alberta's economy, thanks to the spectacular scenery and year-round recreational facilities of the Rocky Mountain National Parks, particularly Banff and Jasper, which attract hundreds of thousands of tourists annually from all over the world. The next most significant sector of the economy is manufacturing, principally food and beverages, chemical products, forest products, and petroleum products. Other sectors include the processing of minerals such as sulphur, and commercial fishing in the northern lakes.

The Yukon

Having been originally put on the map by the greatest Gold Rush the world has known, it comes as no surprise that mining has continued to play a vital part in the Yukon's survival, comprising more than 30% of the territory's economic base. This has made it extremely vulnerable to reversals. The closure of all the Yukon's major mines in the 1980s because of depressed world markets and depleting resources resulted in a serious economic crisis, but this trend reversed in 1986 with the re-opening of the Yukon's major lead-zinc mine and the setting of a 30-year record in placer gold production. Many large mineral deposits still remain and new mines have recently been developed which will bring significant increases in the production of copper, zinc, lead, gold and silver.

Tourism is the second most important industry in the Yukon, and continues to grow steadily. Other secondary but expanding sectors include agriculture, forestry, manufacturing and fishing.

Culture

Architecture

Apart from the cedar longhouses that can still occasionally be seen, particularly in Northern BC, most of Western Canada's architectural interest resides in Vancouver and Victoria. The former features a handful of undeniably innovative structures, while the latter is dominated by hulking Victorian-England style structures and streets lined with attractive brick and stone buildings. Otherwise, only the occasional town is of interest: some, like Nelson, for their turn-of-the-20th-century heritage buildings; others, like Stewart, for their appealing ramshackle eccentricity.

Francis Rattenbury

The man responsible for almost all of Victoria's important buildings, including the Empress Hotel and the Parliament Building was Francis Rattenbury. A first-class draftsman, Rattenbury was a master at manipulating the Château and Beaux-Arts styles that were so popular at the time. This brought him a great deal of work from employees such as the Canadian Pacific Railway, for whom he finished many buildings. He also completed a number of provincial courthouses, such as the ones at Nanaimo (1896), Victoria (1899), Nelson (1905-06) and Vancouver (1906-1911), this last one adapted by Arthur Erickson in 1978-83 for the Vancouver

Art Gallery. His main contribution to architecture in BC was not in the originality of his designs but rather his ability to bring a new level of sophistication to building technology and craftsmanship. After a scandal over his divorce and remarriage, Rattenbury returned to Britain in 1929, only to be murdered by his second wife's lover, who was also his chauffeur.

Arthur Erickson

If there is such a thing as a Vancouver style of architecture, Arthur Erickson is the man who invented it. Born in the city in 1924, he rose to prominence by winning the design competition for Simon Fraser University in 1963, and has many key buildings dotted around town. In keeping with the frequently overcast climate of the West Coast, which he believed could not take bright colours, Erickson became famous for creating dramatic structures out of potentially dull, mute colours, and concrete and glass canopies. Part of the secret of his success is a strong ability to blend a building into its landscape, as best evidenced by the extraordinary University building in Lethbridge. He also displays a rare knack for designing a building so as to make a statement about its purpose, as demonstrated by the Native Big House design of the UBC Museum of Anthropology (1973-6), and the deliberate openness of the Law Courts complex at Robson Square.

Arts and crafts

Native arts

The native people of Canada, and particularly the Pacific Northwest, excelled and continue to excel in all forms of art, but most particularly in the field of carving. The genius of Bill Reid (see page 53) can be seen in various venues around Vancouver. Throughout Western Canada there are many opportunities to experience native art, particularly in the UBC Museum of Anthropology in Vancouver, the Glenbow Museum in Calgary, the Kwagiulth Museum on Quadra Island, around the Hazletons in Northern BC, and on Haida Gwaii (Queen Charlotte Islands). A number of shops in Vancouver and Victoria also carry works by contemporary native artists, and a particularly fine private collection is on display in Swans Pub in Victoria.

The Group of Seven

While the turn-of-the-20th-century art scene was marked by such major figures as James Wilson Morrice, considered the father of Canadian modernism, a truly Canadian form of painting only arrived with the ascension of the Toronto-based Group of Seven, who sought to draw inspiration directly from the Canadian landscape. Like the European fin de siècle symbolists and post-impressionists, they steered clear of the naturalism that had defined the previous generation, attempting to capture nature's grandeur through the use of bold colours and decorative patterning.

The original members – Franklin Carmichael, Lawren Harris, AY Jackson, Franz Johnston, Arthur Lismer, JEH Macdonald and FH Varley – befriended each other in Toronto between 1911 and 1913, and often painted together, their work, romantic and with mystical tendencies, developing along somewhat similar lines. Tom Thomson, who died in 1917 before he could become a member of the group, also left behind a remarkable collection of paintings and oil sketches.

If the group had a leader it was Harris, who began to radically simplify the colour and layouts of his canvasses. By the mid-1920s he had reduced his paintings to a few simplified and nearly monochromatic forms. Ten years later he became the only member of the group, and one of the first Canadian artists, to turn to abstraction. By the time the group disbanded in 1933, however, it had in many ways become as entrenched and conservative as the art establishment it had overthrown.

Emily Carr

Born and raised in a disciplined, middle-class Victoria household, Emily Carr (1871-1945) was orphaned in her teens, and went in 1891 to study art at the California School of Design in San Francisco. Her most important of many early travels was to France in 1910, from where she returned with a post-impressionist style of painting. She then continued a tour of Native Canadian sites, rendering a service to humanity by capturing on canvass, ancient villages, longhouses and totem poles that would soon fall into complete neglect. Particularly important are her evocative paintings of what is now Gwaii Haanas National Park Reserve (see page 234).

It wasn't until 1928 that she slowly began to receive the kind of national exposure and critical recognition that she deserved, though financial success remained elusive. Most people agree that her late work is her best, when she returned to painting nature scenes inspired by the rugged West Coast, in a style that was more free-flowing and expressive. Large collections of her work are held at both the Vancouver and Victoria Art Galleries, and her Victoria house, where she lived with all kinds of animals, can also be visited.

First Nations Culture

Society

The most formidable of the First Nations was the Haida of Haida Gwaii, whose artwork is so distinctive as to be instantly recognizable. For more information about them, refer to page 235, and visit the Gwaii Haanas National Park to see their long-abandoned villages, one of the most moving experiences in Canada.

Extended families of 50 or more lived together in large, elaborately decorated longhouses, whose interiors were divided by hanging mats, with communal fires and cooking areas shared by all. Containers, clothing and utensils were fashioned from cedar bark, roots, reeds and animal skins and furs, while specialized equipment was designed for catching salmon, hunting deer and elk, snaring birds, and harpooning sea mammals such as seals and porpoises. These, along with gathered shellfish, fruits and roots, provided the people with a fairly broad diet. Ritual dancing, singing and drumming were a major part of life, as were feasts, story-telling and games. Spiritually, as has been well documented, the great animist tradition of the First Nations perceived the whole of Nature as alive with sacred significance.

Their complex social system divided people into two clans: Eagle and Raven among the Haida, Crow and Wolf in many other nations. These are further divided into hereditary kin groups. Marriage within a clan was considered incestuous, so Eagles would seek a Raven and vice versa. In this way there are always ties between clans and between people from distant places. Descent was through the female line, meaning that if a chief wanted to keep his property within the clan, he had to pass it on to his sister's sons.

The potlatch

Native Americans were (and are) fun-loving people. They would travel long distances to gather and socialize, and today's native pow-wows are always wonderful celebrations. The most famous ceremony of the coastal people was the potlatch, a celebration that marked major events, from births, deaths and marriages to the raising of a totem pole. The word potlatch derives from the verb 'to give', and this was an excuse for an individual to display their wealth by giving things away, be it art, land deeds or slaves. This was a means by which wealth was redistributed, but it was also an investment and a challenge, as those who received would be shamed if they failed to respond with a potlatch where they gave away even more. With the arrival of the Europeans, inequality between tribes and villages escalated to the point that the receivers were ruined both

financially and symbolically by their own inability to respond. As a result of these and 381
less noble considerations, like fear and ignorance, the Government outlawed the potlatch from 1884 to 1951. Many items were returned, on the condition that they be stored and displayed in museums. A collection of items resides at the Kwagiulth Museum on Quadra Island.

Mythology

West Coast mythology is rich and complex, and far too involved to treat with any justice here. A wealth of tales passed on verbally from one generation to the next served to provide the spiritual and social foundation of the group, imbuing existence with meaning and mystery, and helping each individual through the natural trials and rites to which every lifetime is subject. Spiritually, the First Nations perceive the whole of nature as interconnected and alive with sacred significance, thus fostering a loving relationship with the earth and a desire to live off the land without destoying it.

Most of these instructive, frequently humorous and often profound stories involve symbolic animals such as the bear or wolf, but the most important character is the raven or crow. Raven is the creator, as well as a trickster and transformer, making people laugh at themselves and cry simultaneously, by revealing how human greatness is tempered with pride and vanity, and subject to the whims of fate and chance. After the great flood, having gorged himself on shellfish, Raven discovered the remnant of the human race hiding in a clam shell on Rose Spit, Haida Gwaii and coaxed them out with his voice. At first he amused himself with these new playthings but then he helped them to build their culture. A sculpture of the scene by Bill Reid can be seen in the UBC Museum of Anthropology.

Art and crafts

Native art around Western Canada   The principal art of the Dene or Athapaskan people involved decoration of personal gear and clothing, such as caribou and moose hides embellished with porcupine quills, moosehair embroidery, and beads arranged in geometric and floral patterns. The Blackfoot and other Plains dwellers specialized in paintings on leather. This included tepees lavishly decorated with naturalistic and geometric motifs, rawhide shields symbolically painted with guardian spirits that would protect the warrior, and buffalo robes whose motifs ranged from the abstract to concentric sunburst patterns to representational images. The interior Salish of central BC's plateau region left behind a major body of prehistoric pictographs. The Lillooet, Thompson, Okanagan and Shuswap are noted for their finely crafted, watertight baskets made by the coiling technique and decorated with geometric motifs.

Pictographs, paintings executed with the finger in red ochre, and petroglyphs, carvings incised, abraded or ground by means of stone tools upon cliff walls, boulders and flat bedrock surfaces, have been discovered throughout Canada, and may constitute the continent's oldest and most widespread artistic tradition. The BC coast has many petroglyph sites, primarily on Vancouver Island, including Nanaimo and Gabriola Island. Other sites have been discovered as far north as Prince Rupert and along the Nass and Skeena River system, and there is an extensive series of small-scale petroglyphs incised on sandstone bluffs at Writing-On-Stone Provincial Park in southern Alberta.

Northwest Coast Art   Northwest Coast societies were unique in their ability to sustain a whole sub-class of professional male artists who were commissioned by wealthy patrons to produce works for potlatches and winter dances. Such artists were trained from youth as apprentices by master artists, usually their uncles or fathers. All men and women, however, would produce works of art and craft for their own home. For at least 2500 years native men have created carvings from a variety of media, including wood, stone, horn, copper, bone, antler, leather, ivory and abalone shells. The finest and best known of these are large-scale works in red cedar, including totem

Background First Nations Culture

poles, house posts and canoes. Sadly though, much of Canada's prehistoric art has been lost. On Haida Gwaii a type of soft shale called argillite is used, which can only be found in one spot, its location a jealously guarded secret. Silver and gold were used in historic times, and works in bronze have been made in recent years. Knives, adzes, chisels, gouges and awls were made of stone, shell and beaver teeth, with sculptural hafts. Bowls, dishes and ladles were fashioned from stone and wood. Boxes were made by a kerfing technique in which a single board is steamed and bent in three corner folds with a bottom and fourth corner attached by pegs. In weaving, almost every technique found elsewhere in North America was used.

Crests Crests were usually, but not always, composed of animal images (including some imaginary ones like the thunderbird), whose representation was given a conventional, stylized form. Details of the crest images vary widely, according to personal and stylistic preferences. Families and bands jealously guarded their crests, which were a legacy from the ancestors, acquired in mythic time from supernatural beings, and to be held in perpetuity by their descendants. Common crest-bearing artefacts are totem poles, painted housefronts and screens, ceremonial robes and headdresses, staffs, feast dishes, spoons and ladles. To display a crest of another group is an insult to their integrity and identity. As well as displaying crests, totem poles portrayed actual characters, often enemies of the family who were depicted to provoke ridicule and contempt from those passing by.

Formlines Objects made in the Northwest Coast traditions are so distinctive as to be instantly recognizable. The primary design element on which their artforms depend is called the formline, and by the turn of the 20th century its use had spread to the southern regions as well. Formlines are continuous, flowing, curvilinear lines that turn, swell and diminish in a prescribed manner. They are used for figure outlines, internal design elements and in abstract compositions. Traditionally figures were strongly coloured with primary black lines (charcoal and lignite), secondary red lines (ochres) and tertiary blue-green elements (copper minerals), though the colour palette has exploded since the 1980s to embrace the full spectrum. Pigments were mixed with a medium derived from dried salmon eggs, and paint brushes were made of porcupine hairs. Designs were rendered freehand, although templates were frequently used for the recurring ovoid shapes.

Contemporary Native Art Native art, like the people themselves, has enjoyed a recent resurgence, and covers the full spectrum from commercial and often trashy tourist kitsch to traditional artworks. Besides the legacy of Bill Reid, many key artists such as Robert Davidson, Joe David, Norman Tait, Tony Hunt Sr, Freda Diesing, Susan Point, and Dorothy Grant are training a new generation of artists who both sell to the collectors' market and make masks, blankets and other traditional objects and regalia, including totem poles, for use by their own people. Many new materials are utilized, including ceramics, glass, and clothing, with objects in the latter category ranging from sweatshirts to haute couture. To a large extent, tourist art only pretends to represent authentic native culture, catering as it does to the stereotypical expectations of the non-Native tourist market, and has been shown more often than not to misrepresent that culture. In fact many native artists see themselves primarily as artists, whose ancestry is secondary if not incidental.

Language

Of the 50 or so Native Canadian languages that existed when the Europeans arrived, only a few are still widely spoken enough to ensure a long-term future. To hear an

‼ Canadians you always thought were American

- → Dan Ackroyd
- → Pamela Anderson
- → Jim Carrey
- → Michael J Fox
- → Avril Lavigne
- → Christopher Plummer
- → Keanu Reeves
- → Keifer Sutherland

aboriginal dialect spoken is sadly rare, but most likely in remote areas of Northern BC or the Yukon, especially among older people. Canadian English is roughly halfway between that spoken in Britain and the United States. Québecois French, which you are likely to encounter at some point in the west, is very different from that spoken in France, riddled with slang, and almost incomprehensible when spoken at full speed. Vancouver is celebrated for its multiculturalism, with immigrants accounting for about a third of the population, and over half of the city's school-age children having been raised speaking a language other than English. The top 10 languages spoken in the city, in order, are: English, Cantonese, Punjabi, German, French, Tagalog (Phillipine), Italian, Spanish, Vietnamese and Polish.

Cinema

Many films are shot in Vancouver, but most of them are American and second-rate tosh. Some of the best are: *The Accused*, *Little Women*, *The X-Files*, *McCabe and Mrs Miller*, and Schwarzenegger's *The Sixth Day*. Films made by Canadians are less famous but often a lot better. The best-known are by Toronto director David Cronenberg, whose films tend to combine conventional elements of horror and science fiction with a wry commentary on contemporary life that hints at profound questions involving the relationship between mind and body, and the role of technology and science in modern life. These include: *Scanners* (1980); *Videodrome* (1980); *The Dead Zone* (1983); *The Fly* (1986), a hugely successful remake of the classic B-movie, starring Jeff Goldblum; *Dead Ringers* (1988), starring Jeremy Irons, considered by many to be his masterpiece; *Naked Lunch* (1991), based on the William Burroughs novel of the same name; *M Butterfly* (1993), based on the play by David Henry Hwang; his most controversial film, *Crash* (1996), modelled on the novel by JG Ballard, which won a Special Jury Prize at the Cannes Film Festival for 'originality, daring and audacity'; *eXistenZ* (1999), a virtual reality mind-trip with Jennifer Jason Leigh and Jude Law; *Spider* (2002) with Ralph Fiennes; *A History of Violence* (2005) with Viggo Mortensen; and the incredible *Eastern Promises* (2007) with Viggo again, Vincent Cassel and Armin Mueller-Stahl.

A generation of writer-directors to emerge in the 1980s included Guy Maddin, Denys Arcand (*Jesus of Montréal*), Bruce McDonald (*Road Kill, Last Night*), and Patricia Rozema who came to international recognition with her first feature film *I've Heard the Mermaids Singing* (1987), one of Canada's most successful films both critically and commercially. Probably the most acclaimed and influential is Atom Egoyan, who grew up in Victoria. *Speaking Parts* (1989) and *The Adjuster* (1991) were both invited to debut at the Cannes Film Festival in France. *Exotica* (1994) became the most successful English-Canadian movie export since *Porky's* in 1981. For most people his finest work to date is *The Sweet Hereafter* (1997), though *Where the Truth Lies* (2002), with Kevin Bacon and Colin Firth, is an understated masterpiece. Made by the Inuit collective Igloolik Isuma Productions, under the self-effacing leadership of director Zacharias Kanuk, prize-winning *Atanarjuat–The Fast Runner* (2002), is an epic in the old sense of the word: the enactment of primal, archetypal human issues on a mythic stage; set in real time but utterly timeless. The camerawork is exceptional, the story compelling and sometimes surreal. Their follow-up in 2005, *The Journals of Knud Rasmussen*, depicts a series of events that took place in 1922, when Shamanism was replaced by Christianity. As such, it was the first film to portray the Christianization of indigenous people from their own point of view.

Literature

Up to the mid-20th century

In the first century of Canadian writing, techniques tended to reflect literary fashions in England. The best-known book by an early settler is Susanna Moodie's *Roughing It in the Bush* (1852), which opens with a warning to prospective immigrants that Canada is not the Eden it is widely promoted as in England, and that the settlers' lot is a harsh one. Lurking behind the young lady's steadfast moral vision is a fascination with characters, an acute attention to detail, considerable psychological insight, and a good dose of genuine wit. Those writers best known for their portraits of the Northwest around the time of the Gold Rush were both foreigners: the British poet Robert Service, who romanticized the frozen north, and the American writer of short novels and stories, Jack London.

With Confederation came a quickened interest in the growth of a national culture, most often expressed through romantic rewritings of Canadian history. The most successful turn-of-the-20th-century works were both written for children: Margaret Marshall Saunders' *Beautiful Joe* (1894) and LM Montgomery's international best-seller *Anne of Green Gables* (1908). Around the same time, Stephen Leacock established an international reputation as a comic writer and lecturer in the Dickensian tradition with works such as *Sunshine Sketches of a Little Town* (1912) and *Arcadian Adventures with the Idle Rich* (1914). And native poet E Pauline Johnson produced a timeless work, *Legends of Vancouver*, a collection of stories based on legends recounted to her by Chief Joe Capilano of Vancouver.

Hugh McLennan, who won the prestigious Governor General's award an unequalled five times, is credited as the first major English-speaking writer to attempt a portrayal of Canada's national character. His 1941 novel *Barometer Rising* introduced a period of optimism towards the country's own culture, progress and role on the world stage. His classic *The Watch that Ends the Night* (1959) summarizes a new faith in the land, if not the politicians it spawns. Such themes, given impetus by the humanist and anticlerical stances of francophone writers such as Gabrielle Roy, were picked up by the likes of Pierre Berton, Roderick Haig-Brown and Farley Mowat.

Following a heart attack in 1937, renowned Victoria artist Emily Carr began devoting more of her time to writing. *Klee Wyck* (1941) won her a Governor General's Award, followed by *The Book of Small* (1942), and *The House of All Sorts* (1944). Her very readable journals *Growing Pains*, *The Heart of a Peacock*, *Pause*, and *Hundreds and Thousands* were published posthumously. Morley Callaghan's novels deal with two apparently irreconcilable worlds, the self-seeking empirical jungle, and the spiritual realm of trust and faith. Such heady themes are most timelessly treated in *Such is My Beloved* (1934), and *The Loved and the Lost* (1951), which is often considered his masterpiece. In 1960, American critic Edmund Wilson identified him as "unjustly neglected" and compared him to Chekhov and Turgenev. Ethel Wilson was born in South Africa, but lived in Vancouver, and is one of the first Canadian writers to truly capture the rugged and unsurpassed beauty of the BC landscape. A strong sense of place is evoked in the unpretentious and lucid style of books such as *Swamp Angel* (1954), while her characters consistently struggle with the paradox of the human condition. Around the same time, William Mitchell achieved instant recognition with his classic *Who has seen the Wind* (1947), which magically captures the characters and eccentrics, but especially the beauty and power of the Prairies.

Margaret Atwood

Margaret Atwood is probably Canada's most celebrated late 20th-century writer, and has written 15 novels, 13 books of poetry, and numerous other miscellaneous works. She first gained critical and popular acclaim, as well as a number of literary prizes, with *The Handmaid's Tale* (1985). A disturbing dystopia set in a post-nuclear wasteland run by a right-wing monotheocracy, it was made into a film in 1990. *Cat's Eye* (1988), shortlisted for the Booker Prize, broke literary ground in its exploration of the realm of childhood, replete with shifts of power, secrecies and betrayals. *The Robber Bride* (1993) focuses on the characters of three very different Toronto women and their evil nemesis. In *Alias Grace* (1996), which was very popular in Britain, Atwood looked back into the life and mind of one of the most enigmatic and notorious women in 19th-century Canada, Grace Marks. In 2000, Atwood finally won the Booker Prize with *The Blind Assassin*. In the highly acclaimed *Oryx and Crake* (2003), Atwood turns her talent to science fiction and the thorny issue of cloning. More prolific than ever, she has since written *The Penelopiad* (2005), *The Tent* (2006), and *Moral Disorder* (2006).

Pierre Berton

Pierre Berton, who was born and lived in Whitehorse, Yukon, and grew up in Dawson City amid the debris of the Stampede, is one of Canada's best-known living writers. Above all, he is renowned for his serious but highly readable popularizations of Canadian history, which combine patriotic verve, colourful detail, and a strong, driving narrative. His first important book was *Klondike* (1958), a classic account of the 1898 Gold Rush, whose left-overs he grew up with. Among other key moments in Canadian history, he turned his hand to the building of the CPR in *The National Dream* (1970) and *The Last Spike* (1971); the settling of the West in *The Promised Land* (1984); and the Canadian army's glorious First World War victory in *Vimy* (1986). *Winter* (1994), is a celebration of that season and the strength of character that allows Canada as a nation to overcome its harshness.

Robertson Davies

Canadian fiction's most rumbustious, larger-than-life character, Robertson Davies is best remembered as a prolific novelist, but for years he was an actor, playwright, essayist and teacher. His work demonstrates Canadian humour at its best, with wry social comment and witty observations on life often carrying greater importance than the slow-paced plot development. His breakthrough came with *Fifth Business* (1970), which remains one of the Canadian classics. In this and its two sequels, *The Manticore* (1972) and *World of Wonders* (1975) (known collectively as *The Deptford Trilogy*), he uses a deep knowledge of Jungian psychology and archetypes to show that matters of the spirit inform and transcend mere worldly concerns. The most highly recommended of Davies' vast oeuvre is the Cornish Trilogy, comprising *The Rebel Angels* (1981), a Rabelaisian satire of academia, *What's Bred in the Bone* (1985), a profound study on artistic inspiration, and *The Lyre of Orpheus* (1988). Published posthumously, *The Merry Heart* (1996) is a charming selection of speeches, reminiscences, parodies, book reviews and essays.

Timothy Findley

The openly gay and greatly loved writer Timothy Findley lived much of his life on Salt Spring Island. He was equally succesful as a playwright, and his novels were eclectic. *The Wars* (1977) is one of the greatest fictional treatments of the First World War; *Famous Last Words* (1981) deals with the rise of fascism and an international conspiracy during the Second World War; *Not Wanted on the Voyage* (1984) is a witty and inventive reworking of the Noah myth; *Headhunter* (1993) pictures a Toronto replete with upper-class violence and evil; *The Piano Man's Daughter* (1995) focuses on a young piano tuner forced to face the questions of his father's identity and his mother's madness.

Farley Mowat

On a field trip as a student biologist, Farley Mowat became outraged at the problems of the Inuit, all of which he attributed to white misunderstanding and exploitation. Such observations led to his first book, *People of the Deer* (1952), which made him an instant, albeit controversial, celebrity. Since then he has spent a lot of time living in the Arctic with the Inuit people, and has written 26 books, whose views are bitterly attacked by some and highly praised by others. The most famous are *Never Cry Wolf* (1963), which was made into a moving film, and the novel *Lost in the Barrens* (1956), written for younger readers. He has also written some very readable accounts of those crazy explorers who obsessively sought the Northwest Passage. Reputedly Canada's most widely read author, Mowat is a natural storyteller with a graceful, personal, and conversational tone, and his narratives and anecdotes are always fast-paced and compelling.

Alice Munro

Alice Munro is mostly a writer of short stories, but her best-known work is the novel *Who Do You Think You Are?* (1978), which concerns the tough life of a girl growing up in the Prairies. It was runner-up for the Booker Prize, and winner of the Governor General's Award, which she also received for *Dance of the Happy Shades* (1968), and *The Progress of Love* (1986). The latter represented a major distillation of her work thus far, exploring with increased profundity the problems of time, and the narrator's relation to it, in an instinctive prose that perfectly balances senses of wonder and compassion. Her two subsequent collections of stories, *Friend of My Youth* (1990) and *Open Secrets* (1994), built on these strengths and extended her fame far beyond Canada's borders. The latter won the 1995 W.H. Smith Award as the best book in any category published in Britain throughout the previous year. Her latest collections of stories, *Hateship, Friendship, Courtship, Loveship, Marriage* (2001), *Runaway* (2004), and *The View From Castle Rock* (2006) have also won a number of key awards, and continue to cement her reputation as one of the supreme crafters of short stories of our time .

Michael Ondaatje

Born in Sri Lanka, Michael Ondaatje was the forerunner of a burgeoning multicultural strata in Canadian literature. An editor, film-maker and teacher, Ondaatje was originally more a poet than novelist, with 11 books of verse to his name, including *The Cinnamon Peeler* (1992). His prose style also has an extremely poetic quality: lilting, dream-like, extremely cinematic at times, and textured with richly exotic imagery that gravitates towards the bizarre, the exaggerated, and the unlikely. Earlier works often combine documentary and fictional elements, such as *Coming Through Slaughter* (1976), which tells of real and imagined events in the life of New Orleans jazz cornetist Buddy Bolden. *In the Skin of a Lion* (1987), a novel set in Toronto's golden age, received great critical and national acclaim, but Ondaatje only reached international stardom with *The English Patient* (1992), which earned him a share of the prestigious Booker Prize (the first ever awarded to a Canadian), and was made into a film that garnered nine Oscars at the 1997 Academy Awards. *Anil's Ghost* (2000), set amidst the civil war that tore Sri Lanka apart, also won a handful of major literary prizes, and became an international bestseller. His latest work, *Divisadero* (2007), set in Northern California in the 1970's, won the Governor's General Award.

Other key players

The late Mordecai Richler established himself as one of Canada's foremost novelists with the publication of *The Apprenticeship of Duddy Kravitz* (1959) about a young Montréal-Jewish entrepreneur. Its dramatic scenes are complemented by a lively narrative pace, and profound characterisation. Other works include *St Urbain's Horseman* (1971), *Joshua Then and Now* (1980), and *Solomon Gursky Was Here* (1990), which won the Commonwealth Writers' prize. Thomas King is the best-known of Canada's First Nations writers. His most celebrated works are *Green Grass, Running Water* (1993), and a collection of short stories, *One Good Story, That One* (1993). He has also edited *The Native in Literature* (1987), a collection of critical essays, and *All My Relations* (1990), an anthology of native Canadian fiction. In Canada he is equally famous for penning the hilarious CBC radio show *Dead Dog Café* – a perfect introduction to native humour and issues.

Margaret Laurence's many novels, of which *The Stone Angel* (1964) is the most highly regarded, are wonderful treatments of life in rural Canada. The fiction of Jack Hodgins, while sometimes experimental, displays a playful love of narrative. His novels, such as *The Resurrection of Joseph Bourne* (1979), deal with characters reconstructed from the his Vancouver Island childhood. In his hands, they are eccentric but realistic characters, deployed with stylistic suppleness in life-affirming situations. Leonard Cohen is best known as a singer, but he started life as an exceptionally gifted poet. *Stranger Music* (1993) gives a good overview of his verse and lyrics. He also wrote two very fine novels, *The Favourite Game* (1963) and *Beautiful Losers* (1966). In 2005, he brought out a new collection of poems, *Dance me to the End of Love*, with illustrations by Henri Matisse.

The New Breed

At the start of the new millennium, a fresh breed of Canadian writers is winning international awards and conquering the international market. The trend began with Douglas Coupland's *Generation X: Tales for an Accelerated Culture* (1991), which came to crystallize the entire post-boomer generation born in the late 1950s and the 1960s. Most popular of the follow-ups are *Girlfriend In A Coma* (1998), and *All Families are Psychotic* (2001). In 2001 he put together an interesting book of anecdotes and photos about his native Vancouver, *City of Glass*. Since then the floodgates have opened. Jane Urquhart has been tremendously successful with *The Underpainter* (1997), which won the Governor General's Award and *The Stone Carvers* (2001), also a world-wide bestseller. But her best work is probably still *Away* (1993), in which she juxtaposed the Irish potato famine of the 1840s with pioneer homesteaders in 19th-century Ontario to explore the transplanting of Old World myths to the new land. She has also published a book of short stories, *Storm Glass* (1987) and three books of poetry.

Carol Shields won several prizes, including the Pulitzer Prize with her classic *The Stone Diaries* (1993). Other favourites are *Larry's Party* (1997), and *Unless* (2002), which has received rave reviews. Rohinton Mistry has been greeted with tremendous international acclaim. Set in India, his novels *Such A Long Journey* (1991), *A Fine Balance* (1995) and *Family Matters* (2002) have won many literary awards, including a nomination for the Booker Prize. David Adams Richards has built a reputation as one of the country's most gifted writers with novels like *Nights Below Station Street* (1988), and *Mercy Among the Children* (2000). John Ralston Saul caused quite a stir in the intellectual world with *Voltaire's Bastards* (1992), a brilliant treatise on the problems caused by modern man's excessive devotion to reason. Other highly recommended international bestsellers are *The Cure For Death By Lightning* (1996) and *A Recipe for Bees* (1998) by Alberta novelist Gail Anderson-Dargatz, *At the Full and Change of the Moon* (1999) by the highly gifted Dionne Brand, and Anne-Marie MacDonald's fashionably miserable *I Fall On My Knees*. Popular on the home front are

Anne Michaels' *Fugitive Pieces* (1996), Nino Ricci's superb *Lives of the Saints* (1990), and novels by Galiano Island resident Jane Rule, including *Memory Board* (1987) and *After the Fire* (1989). And most recent of all is Yann Martel's *Life of Pi*, which won the 2002 Booker Prize.

For a collection of short modern fiction by BC writers, there's *West by Northwest: BC Short Stories* (1998), edited by D Stouck and M Wilkinson (Polestar). And finally, George Bowering, *Selected Poems 1961-92* is an overview of the work of a Vancouver poet who was named Canada's first poet laureate in 2002.

Music

It comes as no surprise that those Canadian musicians and bands who have achieved a degree of international recognition are usually mistaken as Americans. Many of these are singer-songwriters such as Joni Mitchell, Neil Young, Leonard Cohen, Tom Cochrane, Bruce Cockburn, Paul Anka, Ann Murray, Gordon Lightfoot, and Buffy Sainte-Marie. Certain others, utterly unknown abroad, are veritable institutions here in Canada, especially Valdi and the irrepressible Stompin' Tom Connors. There have also been a few big rock groups such as Bachman Turner Overdrive, Steppenwolf, The Guess Who, Rush, and most of The Band, including Robbie Robertson.

The trend of solo artists has continued more recently with big names like Avril Lavigne, Nelly Furtado, Feist, Sarah McLachlan, KD Laing, Alanis Morissette, Jann Arden, Jane Siberry, Céline Dion, and Loreena McKennitt. The latter is the most internationally successful of a large number of musicians who delve into their Celtic roots. To these should be added Vancouver-boy Brian Adams, and Daniel Lanois, who is more famous for producing bands like U2, and national favourites like Bif Naked, Veda Hille, Kinnie Starr, and Hawksley Workman. Some of the more successful modern Canadian bands include The Tragically Hip, Crash Test Dummies, Cowboy Junkies, The Rankin Family, Spirit of the West, Blue Rodeo and Barenaked Ladies. The best-known singer in the Country genre that dominates Alberta and the Prairies is Shania Twain. Canadian jazz musicians include the hugely popular singer Diana Krall, maestro pianist Oscar Peterson, the ebullient big band-style trumpeter Maynard Ferguson, superb ECM trumpeter Kenny Wheeler and alto-sax master David Sanborn. Metalwood, a modern, funky quartet from Vancouver, have five very good albums to their name. Roots is the real music of Canada, enjoying a resurgence today thanks to artists like BC's excellent Zubot and Dawson.

Religion

Most people in Canada are of British national origin and English-speaking, so it's not surprising that they are predominantly Christian, belonging to the United, Anglican or Roman Catholic churches. The variety of other cultures and second languages can be seen in the relative significance of other religions such as Buddhism, Sikkhism and Islam, which are far more significant in Vancouver than anywhere else in Western Canada. It must also be remembered that Canada, and the Prairies in particular, has in certain eras received large influxes of minor religious groups such as the Mormons, Mennonites, Hutterites and Doukhobours. The latter group are particularly well-represented in the Okanagan-Boundary and West Kootenay regions of BC. Many native people converted to Christianity and often take the religion more seriously than their white neighbours, but it should not be forgotten that the older, animist-style spirituality of Canada's First Nations is still alive and in a position to make a come-back.

Land and environment

Geography

The Canadian Shield

Canada consists of six geological regions, five of which are arranged roughly concentrically around, and partly on top of, the sixth. Far older than the others this central core is the Canadian Shield, which is of Precambrian age, more than 570 million years old. Itself a mosaic of geological sub-regions centred around Archean age rocks (more than 2.5 billion years old), the Shield covers an area of about 4.8 million sq km stretching in a broad band from the Northwest Territories down to the Great Lakes of southern Ontario. Repeated advances of glacial ice have scoured its surface and left it covered with hundreds of lakes and rivers, including the biggest on the continent, making it very easily identified on any map. Also dominating this vast region's landscapes are slabs of protruding basement rock. Originally formed during rounds of mountain-building activity, these are now among the most stable, and oldest, on Earth. This bare rock, together with its thin soils, muskeg, and insects, has presented a constant barrier to settlement. The agricultural frontier of the prairie provinces and eastern Canada end abruptly at its perimeter. The railway link to the West literally had to be blasted through Shield rock, which also revealed its treasures of gold, silver, nickel, cobalt, zinc, copper and iron ore.

The Canadian Cordillera

Of the younger geological regions that border the Shield, almost all of the area covered in this book is part of the Canadian Cordillera, meaning the landscapes are utterly dominated by mountain ranges. British Columbia has two main regions, loosely called the Coast and the Interior, each containing many contrasting sub-regions. The Peace River Lowland of the northeast is the only part of BC not on the Cordillera. An extension of the Interior Plains, it belongs in character to neighbouring Alberta.

The Coast

The western section of the Cordillera is dominated by the lofty Coast Mountains and the offshore Insular Mountains. The Cascade Mountains of Washington State end at the Fraser River, then the high, snow- and ice-covered peaks of the Coast Mountains extend northward along the Alaskan Panhandle into the Yukon. These gloriously scenic mountains have peaks, rising to 3000 m in the southern part, while northern peaks such as Mount Waddington rise to over 4000 m. Numerous long, twisting, deep fjords penetrate into the mountain mass along the coast. Only three major rivers, the Fraser, Skeena and Stikine, have managed to cut through the Coast Mountain barrier, the first two of which have provided vital funnels for the only roads and railway lines to reach the Ocean. Northwest of the Coast Range the St Elias Mountains straddle BC, the Yukon and Alaska, containing North America's mightiest peaks, including the highest in BC, Fairweather Mountain (4663 m), and the highest in Canada, Mount Logan (6050 m). The offshore Insular Mountains, whose highest peak is Strathcona Park's Golden Hinde at 2200 m, are the partially submerged northern continuation of the Olympic Mountains and Coast Ranges of Washington State. They provide the land mass for both Vancouver Island and the Queen Charlotte Islands.

Almost all of BC's population resides in its southwestern corner. The so-called Lower Mainland, dominated by metropolitan Vancouver, contains almost half of the province's population, and represents its commercial, cultural and industrial core.

Together with Victoria and the southeast coast of Vancouver Island, this zone is also sometimes called the Georgia Strait region, which holds a whole 70% of BC's population.

The Interior

British Columbia's vast interior is equally dominated by mountains. In the south are three parallel, north-south oriented ranges known collectively as the Columbia Mountains. The backbone is the Selkirk Range, flanked by the Purcells to the east and the Monashees to the west. Between them, carved out by lakes and rivers, are great valleys such as the Okanagan and the Kootenay, along which most of the population is strung. These tend to have radically differing characteristics of landscape and climate dependant on such factors as the rain-shadows which keep the Okanagan and Thompson Valleys so very dry.

Further northwest is a fourth range of the Columbias, the Cariboo Mountains. Between these and the Coast Range lie the broad, gently rolling uplands of the Interior Plateau that covers much of central BC. This region can be considered a basin because it is surrounded by higher mountains, though its average elevation is still about 1000 m above sea level. Some of BC's bigger but less interesting towns, such as Kamloops and Prince George, have grown as transportation and service hubs for the isolated subregions that surround them. The northern half of the province is barely inhabited away from the Yellowhead Highway, and beyond Prince Rupert is cut off from the Pacific by the Alaska Panhandle. The Cassiar-Omineca Mountains run between the Coast and Rocky Ranges, broken up by a second relatively flat expanse, the Spasizi Plateau.

The Canadian Rockies

The Rocky Mountains rise abruptly about 1000-1500 m above the foothills of Alberta, and some of their snow-capped peaks tower more than 3000 m above sea level, the highest being BC's Mount Robson at 3954 m. The range ends south of the Liard River in northeastern BC, its western boundary marked by the Rocky Mountain Trench, which extends 1400 km from Montana to the Yukon, making it the longest valley in North America. Out of the trench flow the headwaters of many rivers, including the Kootenay, Columbia, Fraser and Liard. For details on the formation of the Rockies, see Geology.

The Yukon

The Yukon constitutes the northernmost part of the Cordilleran region. Much of its area is covered by a high subarctic plateau with an average elevation of 1200 m, frequently interrupted by predominantly northwest-southeast oriented mountain ranges and deep valleys. To the east the Yukon Plateau is bounded by the Selwyn and Mackenzie mountains. To the south an area of lower terrain near the 60th parallel separates it from the mountainous areas of northern BC. The territory's southwest is dominated by the spectacular St Elias and Coast mountains mentioned above, many of them covered by extensive permanent ice caps, including the largest nonpolar icefields in North America. These mighty peaks cut off direct access to the Pacific Ocean, despite its relative proximity. The 2400 m Ogilvie Mountains in the north separate the Yukon and Porcupine Plateaus, the latter hemmed in by the British Mountains to the north and Richardson Mountains to the east. The Arctic Coastal Plain is a narrower eastward continuation of the same region in Alaska, which slopes down to the Beaufort Sea from the British Mountains inland. Much of the north and northwest was part of the Ice Age continent of Beringia, which escaped glaciation despite its northern latitude.

The Interior Plains

East of the Rockies, the foothills quickly slope down to the broad, comparitively flat eco-region of the Interior Plains, which stretches right across Saskatchewan and Manitoba. Alberta can be divided into into four biophysical regions according to physiography, climate, soil and vegetation. The prairie region includes most of southern Alberta, more precisely the land south and east of an arc stretching from Waterton in the southwest to a point along the Saskatchewan border east of Red Deer. This gently rolling grassland is relatively dry and mostly treeless. The terrain varies locally, in places broken by deep river valleys, and rising from less than 300 m in the northeast to over 1460 m in the southeastern Cypress Hills. The parkland region predominates in central Alberta, forming a crescent to the west and north of the prairie region and including most of the North Saskatchewan River drainage basin. This area varies from the flatland of old lake bottoms to rolling landscapes with numerous lakes and depressions. It contains both forested and grassy terrain, with soil and climatic factors favourable to agriculture. West of the plains an area of foothill ridges rises fairly rapidly towards the Rockies. The northern half of the province is covered by boreal forest. Here great rivers and lakes dominate the landscape, draining northward to the Arctic Ocean. Soil and climatic factors make agriculture unprofitable except in the northwestern Peace River region that extends into BC, where parkland conditions create the world's most northerly grain-growing area.

In sociocultural terms, the province's more populated lower half can be further divided into two distinct regions, with Calgary and Edmonton as their respective focal points. This is a long-standing division dating to the times when the powerful Blackfoot Confederacy dominated the south, with the Cree and Assiniboine inhabiting the north. In the early days of white settlement, grain farmers opened up the central fertile zone, while the south was more suitable for cattle-rearing on large-scale ranches, a fact that has led to the cowboy culture of Calgary, its nickname of Cow-town, and the famous Stampede. Calgary and southern Alberta were first linked to the east by the Canadian Pacific Railway, Edmonton and the north by the Grand Trunk Pacific and Canadian Northern railways. Later, Calgary became the administrative and financial headquarters for the province's petroleum industry, Edmonton its exploration and production centre.

Geology

The Cordillera
The continent now known as North America was covered by vast granite mountains up to roughly 600 million years ago. The greatly eroded lake-dotted remains of this rock now constitute the Canadian Shield, which stretches from Great Bear Lake in the Northwest Territories to the Great Lakes of Ontario. As the Shield had a slight tilt, all the eroded debris was carried westward by streams and rivers, and dumped into the Ocean, slowly building up a 'continental slope' that reached a depth of 20 km over 400 million years. The weight of this sediment turned mud to stone, sand to sandstone, and the lime-heavy sea-debris into limestone.

Roughly 200 million years ago, two distinct, equally vast chains of volcanic islands were carried eastwards by the shifting Pacific Plate towards the continent's west coast. When this 50-km thick platform eventually collided with the North American Plate, it slid underneath it, plunging into the earth's molten interior. At the same time, the first island chain was broken apart from the heavier plate and smashed violently into, over and through the continental rock, causing it to lift, crumple, buckle and twist itself into the myriad fascinating shapes of BC's interior mountain ranges. Over a period of 75 million years, the aftershock of this awesome collision caused further ripples of upheaval, as the incoming islands continued to smash into the ancient rock, creating the Western Ranges of the Rockies that are mostly contained in Yoho and Kootenay National Parks. Eventually, they bulldozed their way still further east, building the Eastern Ranges, such as those around Lake Louise.

When the second Pacific island chain smashed into the continent, further chaos was unleashed: a new round of lifting, distorting, rupturing and co-mingling resulted in the Rockies' easternmost Front Ranges, the rockwall that rears up from the Albertan Prairies, together with the lower foothills. A series of ice-ages (at least three) in the last 240,000 years, have added their own contributions to this on-going work of art, sculpting, shattering, eroding and re-shaping of the mountain contours.

The Columbia Mountains consist mainly of sedimentary and intrusive rocks of Cretaceous, Triassic and Jurassic ages, and they have been well mineralized. The exception is the Cariboo Range, which is composed of sedimentary rocks of Proterozoic age that appear to be less mineralized. Many of the rocks of the interior plateau are lavas of Cretaceous and Tertiary geological ages with apparently little mineralization except around the plateau edges. The Coast Mountain rocks are mostly granitic intrusions of Cretaceous and Tertiary ages and there are some recent volcanoes. The Yukon is geologically very complex but includes three parallel sectors oriented northwest-southeast. In the east, folded sedimentary Paleozoic and Mesozoic formations are set off sharply from the Mackenzie Valley by great faults. The middle sector includes sedimentaries, metamorphics and volcanics ranging from Precambrian to Mesozoic age. Massive plutonic Mesozoic and Tertiary granites make up the core of the western sector.

Alberta

Alberta's oldest surface landscape is a small outcrop of the Canadian Shield in its extreme northeastern part. This does not end in the northeast, for its rocks form a basement under the rest of the province, sloping down to 6,000 m in the southwest. During the Paleozoic era (544-250 million years ago), Alberta alternated between dry land and sea, and life evolved from simple plants and animals to vertebrates and dryland vegetation. The decay of this plant and animal life, especially during the Devonian period (410-353 million years ago), formed the basis of most of the province's oil and natural gas deposits. Alternating upraisings of the land and infloodings of ocean waters affected the province during the Mesozoic era (250-65 million years ago). This was the era of the dinosaurs, the period that shaped the badland formations of the Red Deer River valley, and laid down most of the province's coal resources. The Cenozoic era (65 million years ago to the present) saw the uplifting of the Rocky Mountains, then about 25,000 years ago the last advance of continental ice scoured the terrain, covering the entire province apart from the highest parts of the Rockies, the Cypress Hills and the Porcupine Hills. The final retreat of the ice age, created the current river systems and soils.

Glaciation

During the last ice age, almost all of Western Canada was covered by a thick sheet of ice until about 12,000-15,000 years ago in the coastal lowlands and some interior valleys, and as late as 7000 years ago at higher elevations. The results of continental and alpine glaciation are seen throughout the region in coastal fjords, mountain cirques, ground moraines across the Interior Plateau, and terraces and benches along the interior rivers. Many features commonly produced by glaciers can be observed on or near the Athabasca Glacier in the Rocky Mountains. These include: crevasses; fissures that form from tensile stress in the glacier surface; icefalls, resulting from crevasses formed where the glacier hangs over a bedrock protuberance; and a medial moraine, composed of debris and ice, which is formed where two valley glaciers coalesce. Other features that were formed during the retreat of the glacier (and can be seen nearby) include lateral moraines, formed by debris deposited along the glacier terminus. In addition, glacier meltwater carries and deposits debris, forming such features as deltas and glacial-outwash plains composed of sand and gravel. The Bow Valley itself is also a classic example of the

Climate

Western Canada is a vast region of complex geography, with many different micro-climates. The single most obvious variable at play is latitude, which has a great effect on the quantity and strength of sunlight. In December, southern Canada receives eight hours of daylight, whereas the far north gets none at all. The north compensates for its short summer season with almost continuous sunshine.

British Columbia and the Rockies

The second most crucial factor for climate is distance from the ocean, with the most marked differences existing between the coast and interior. Relatively warm air masses from the Pacific Ocean keep coastal temperatures mild in the winter, while cold water keeps it cool in the summer. The barrier of the Coast Mountains prevents such moderating conditions from reaching the interior, which tends to have cold winters and hot summers. Average January temperatures are above 0°C at most coastal stations – the mildest in Canada – and July averages are about 15°C in the north and 18°C in the sheltered Georgia Strait region. In contrast, the interior may be covered in winter by cold air masses pushing south from the Yukon or Alaska, particularly in the northern part of the province. Average daily January temperatures are -10°C to -15°C across the central interior and are a cold -20°C or more on the northeastern plains. The southern interior valleys tend to heat up during the summer, with average July temperatures of more than 20°C, sometimes considerably more. The frost-free season on the coast is the longest in Canada, averaging more than 200 days, whereas the central Interior Plateau receives only about 75-100 frost-free days.

The air masses which cross the Pacific also bring ample rainfall to the coast, particularly in the autumn and winter. Much of this is dumped on the western slopes of mountain ranges, with the eastern (lee) sides often sitting in what is called a rain shadow, deprived of moisture. The western slopes of the Coast Mountains, for instance, accumulate 1000 to 3000 mm of precipitation annually, of which a high percentage is snowfall, whereas the Okanagan Valley receives a mere 250 mm per year. Weather in the Rockies and BC's various mountain ranges is notoriously unpredictable, with snow and hail always possible at high elevations even on the hottest days of July.

Alberta

As a whole, Alberta is characterized by cold winters and relatively short, cool summers. The most important factors in determining both temperatures and precipitation are the height and width of the Rocky Mountains and the direction of the prevailing winds. As the Rockies' eastern slopes sit in a rain shadow, Alberta's skies are predom- inantly clear. Precipitation is generally low, ranging from about 300 mm annually in the southeast to 400-450 mm in the north, with a little more in the foot-hills region. The dry clear air provides Albertans with plenty of sunshine, ranging from 1900 annual hours in the north to 2300 in the south. Air funnelling through the Rockies also produces the warm, dry chinook winds which can raise temperatures dramatically within hours. In eastern Alberta, the influence of the Pacific air mass gives way to continental conditions originating in the Arctic and mid-western US. These air masses bring mean temperatures in January ranging from -8°C in the south to -24°C in the north, and July mean temperatures ranging from 20°C in the south to

16°C in the north. The growing season lasts about 120 days in southern Alberta, decreasing to 60 days in the north.

The Yukon

The climate of the Yukon is continental, as its steep mountain ramparts seal it off from the moderating Pacific Ocean. Winters are very cold most of the time, with Canada's lowest ever recorded temperature (-62.8°C) occurring at Snag, northwest of Kluane Lake, in 1947. At times, Pacific air may edge into the southwestern sectors resulting in short intervals of milder temperatures. Summers are warm and frequently hot (35°C has been recorded at Dawson City) but cooler air from the Arctic can push southward. Precipitation is generally low because the high mountains in the southwest seal off access to the moister air. The Arctic receives so little moisture that it technically qualifies as a desert.

Vegetation

West Coast forest

The coniferous trees of coastal British Columbia are the tallest, broadest trees in Canada. The outer island and exposed mainland coasts are predominantly covered in giant Douglas fir, western red cedar, western hemlock, yellow cypress, Sitka spruce, shore pine, and occasionally western yew. The principal deciduous hardwoods are red alder and Scouler willow. The main undergrowth shrubs in these regions are salal, skunk cabbage, salmonberry, bilberry and huckleberry, along with assorted mosses, ferns, lichens, liverworts, and orchids. The Georgia Strait area on the east coast of Vancouver Island and the adjacent mainland have a drier, Mediterranean climate, with a hot, dry summer spell that can last up to eight weeks. Vegetation here is characterized by a colourful spring flora with several annual herbaceous species. Arbutus, western flowering dogwood and Garry oak reach their northern limits in this region. Other forest species include Douglas fir, western hemlock, grand fir, bigleaf maple, western red cedar and bitter cherry. The copious undergrowth includes thimbleberry, red elderberry, blackberry, Nootka rose, ocean spray, snowberry, western sword fern and deer fern.

Cordillera

Vegetation of the Canadian Cordillera is very diverse, depending on differences in elevation and latitude. Many additional variations in vegetation are the result of parallel mountain ranges that run at right-angles to the easterly flow of weather systems, causing 'rainshadows' that keep the mountains' eastern slopes dry. The lower slopes of BC's interior mountains and the Rockies, known as Columbia (or Interior) forest are mostly dominated, like the coast, by Douglas fir, western red cedar and western hemlock, though you will also see many pines, larch and spruce, as well as deciduous trees such as alder, birch, aspen, and giant cottonwood. The undergrowth here includes devil's club, azaleas, black and red twinberry, salmonberry and redberry alder. Common flowers include mountain lily, columbine, bunchberry and heartleaf arnica. The more southerly and sheltered reaches of the Rockies, and the plateaux of interior BC, are covered by less attractive montane forest comprised mostly of ponderosa and lodgepole pine, along with more spindly Douglas fir and western larch. Most of the hillsides in the Thompson and Okanagan Valleys have a sparse scattering of occasional trees, between which grows vegetation typical of such arid landscapes: sage, antelope grass and even cacti.

The next major zone is the sub-alpine, from 1300 to 2200 m, where forests are typically made up of lodgepole and whitebark pines, subalpine larch, Engelmann spruce and subalpine fir. The common understorey plants are white-flowered rhododendron, false azalea, black huckleberry, Sitka alder, oak fern, mountain arnica and leafy liverwort. The zone above the treeline, known as the alpine, is mainly covered with grasses, sedges, dwarf willows, mosses, lichens and other low woody and herbaceous plants. Meadows at this elevation compensate for the lack of forest with dazzling displays of wild flowers throughout the summer, including lilies, anemones, Indian paintbrush, lupins, arnica, cinquefoil, and glacier lily.

Grasslands

The prairie region of southern Alberta includes both short-grass and mixed-grass characteristics. The short-grass area of the southeastern corner features short, drought-resistant grasses such as blue grama. The mixed-grass area, forming an arc to the west and north of the short-grass region, contains more fertile, dark brown soil, with western wheat grass and other taller grasses providing the natural vegetation. The parkland regions of central Alberta and the Peace River country are characterized by a natural vegetation cover of tall grasses and aspen tress.

Boreal forest

The boreal forest that runs in a broad band across Northern Canada is dominated by plants that are capable of surviving cool, short summers and long, cold winters. The southern half is typified by canopied forests composed of both pure and mixed stands of deciduous and coniferous trees, mostly aspen, balsam poplar and white spruce. The undergrowth is usually a mixture of herbs and deciduous shrubs, while dry sites with less tree cover have a ground storey dominated by bearberry, blueberry and lichens. The northern boreal forest tends to be composed of stunted (5-7 m tall) coniferous trees of which black spruce and balsam fir are the most common, with white spruce, paper birch and jack pine occurring on warm dry sites. Between the dwarfed trees grow shrubs such as dwarf birch and Labrador tea or mats of lichens and mosses. About a quarter of the boreal forest is covered in poorly drained areas, sometimes filled with organic deposits (peatlands). These ecosystems are called fens or bogs depending upon whether they are nutrient-rich or poor. Species such as black spruce, larch, eastern red cedar (eastern and southern portion only), willows, Labrador tea, bog rosemary, cloudberry, sedges, sphagnum and mosses are typical members of wetland communities. Sedges, horsetails and spike rushes are common plants in peatlands.

Tundra

The arctic tundra which covers much of the Yukon is the second-largest vegetation region in the country, with a greater range of latitude than any other. Only a few birch, willow and trembling aspen can survive the cold temperatures and short growing season this far north, and these rarely reach more than a metre in height. Grasses and sedges abound, along with small flowering annuals, mosses, lichens and shrubs. Wild flowers include purple mountain saxifrage, yellow Arctic poppy, and Jacob's Ladder. Purple wild crocuses arrive in May, followed by lupine, wild rose and wild sweet pea in June. Mountain meadows break out in rashes of alpine forget-me-nots, pink moss campion and yellow mountain avens the following month, then August brings an explosion of reds and purples as the provincial flower, fireweed, sets every roadside ablaze. In summer and autumn, these treeless expanses represent some of the most beautiful landscapes in Canada, bursting into colourful life, encouraged by the sheer lack of time and the lengthy hours of sunshine. The transition zone from boreal forest to tundra consists of ribbons or islands of stunted black and white spruce trees in a sea of tundra vegetation.

Arctic

Most of the Arctic region covered by this book, called Low Arctic, is characterized by nearly complete plant cover and abundant low and dwarf woody shrubs. Along rivers, streams and lakeshores, and on steep slopes the major plant communities include tall (2-3 m) shrub tundra of alder, scrub birch and willows. On medium-drained slopes the vegetation is lower (30-60 cm), consisting of willow, dwarf birch, dwarf heath shrubs, numerous sedges and small herbaceous species, and abundant lichens and mosses. The poorly drained soils of low rolling hills are covered in tussock sedge, dwarf heath shrubs, mosses and lichens, while various combinations of sedges, a few grasses and herbs, and abundant mosses dominate the poorly drained flat- land soils. Again, this vegetation celebrates its short life with dazzling displays of colour in July and August.

Wildlife

Visit Environment Canada at www.ec.gc.ca. Western Canada is one of the least disrupted regions in the world, with vast areas of remaining wilderness covered by diverse forests and lakes. Some of the planet's most productive ecosystems are found here, including great swaths of wetlands and temperate rainforest. The Pacific Ocean region has the largest number of marine mammal species in Canada, while British Columbia contains the country's greatest number of terrestrial mammal species and bird species. To the latter must be added a large number of migrating or 'accidental' species. Below is a brief look at what animals you are most likely to see in the key eco-regions, but as many creatures are found throughout much of Western Canada, this is preceded by an A-Z of the most important species.

A-Z of species

Beaver

For an illustrated overview of Canadian species, www.cws-scf.ec.gc.ca/hww-fap. The beaver was the obvious choice as Canada's national animal, as it had a greater impact on the country's history than any other animal or plant. The reason: beaver underfur is warm, soft and waterproof, the perfect material for making the kind of felt used in top hats. To make the fur softer still, hatters used nitrate of mercury, continued exposure to which made them go mad, hence the expression. With beaver pelts fetching the highest prices, pursuit of the rodents was the leading motive of early colonizers, and led to explorations which opened up most of the northwestern hinterland to settlement. In the process, the beaver population was reduced from ten million to near extinction.

Ten thousand years ago, Beringia was inhabited by giant beavers the size of bears with lower incisors 25 cm long. Today they are still the largest member of the rodent family. Beavers are monogamous and mate for life. Their tails are horizontal, flattened, paddle-shaped and scaly. As well as eye membranes and ear valves, they have structural adaptations at the back of their mouths to stop water from entering the lungs, meaning they can gnaw and carry branches when submerged. They typically inhabit slow-moving streams, where they construct dams, making them one of the only animals beside humans that can build their own environment. Beaver lodges are made of intricately interlaced branches, with mud and grass plastered on the outside, and are almost impenetrable. Rather than hibernating, they stay in their lodges, whose clever design keeps temperatures at an even 8-12°C even when it is -40°C outside. A cache of food is kept nearby, submerged to preserve it. Mainly nocturnal, this most hard-working of animals can usually be seen swimming busily around at dusk.

Without beaver dams, much of Canada's water would flow unchecked. The beavers thin out dense woods, creating opportunities for a variety of animals and plants. They are therefore a keystone species in temperate and boreal forest aquatic ecosystems.

Birds

The list of birds native to Western Canada is extensive. This is a summary of the most notable species. Waterbirds Common and red-throated loon, horned and red-necked grebe, cormorant, various species of swan including the trumpeter, geese, American widgeon, mallard, northern pintail, green-winged teal, common eider, various ducks including the harlequin, Barrow's goldeneye, merganser. Raptors Osprey, northern harrier, bald and golden eagles, various hawks and kestrels, peregrine falcon, gyrfalcon. Shorebirds American golden plover, lesser yellowlegs, wandering tattler, spotted and upland sandpiper, whimbrel, red-necked pharalope, long-tailed jaeger, various gulls, Arctic tern, black guillemot, belted kingfisher. Owls Great grey, snowy, northern hawk, short-eared. Perching birds Various jays including blue and grey, raven, numerous swallows including tree, violet-green, bank, barn and cliff, chickadees, American dipper, ruby-crowned kinglet, northern wheater, Townsend's solitaire, various thrushes including grey-cheeked and Swainson's, American pipit, Tennessee, Wilson's and yellow warblers, common yellowthroat, numerous sparrows, junco, snow bunting, Lapland and Smith's longspur, redpolls. Other Spruce and sharp-tailed grouse, ptarmigan, sora, American coot, sandhill crane, northern flicker, assorted woodpeckers and many hummingbirds.

Bears

Black bears Black bears are bulky, thickset animals about 150 cm long and 100-120 cm high at the shoulder. Adult males weigh about 135 kg, although exceptionally large animals weighing over 290 kg have been recorded. Females are much smaller, averaging 70 kg. Although black is the most common colour, other colour phases such as brown, dark brown, cinnamon, blue black, and even white also occur. A black bear walks like a human being with the entire bottom portion of the foot touching the ground, and will often stand on two legs with its nose in the air. Since the eyesight of bears is poor, they rely heavily on well-developed senses of hearing and smell, and will usually attempt to get downwind from an intruder to make an identification by smell. Contrary to common misconceptions, bears are shy, timid animals who want nothing more than to be left alone. They are mostly vegetarians, particularly fond of berries, though they will also happily devour a whole nest of ants.

Black bears appear awkward as they shuffle along, but can move with amazing speed when necessary. For short distances they have been clocked at speeds of up to 55 kmph. They are good swimmers and frequently cross rivers and small lakes. Climbing is second nature to a black bear. Young animals readily take to trees when frightened. They climb with a series of quick bounds, grasping the tree with their forepaws and pushing with their hind legs. The black bear has several distinct calls, including a growl of anger, a whining call, and sniffs of many sorts. A female with cubs may warn them of danger with a loud woof-woof and call them in with a whining or whimpering sound. The cry of a young cub in trouble is similar to the crying of a human baby.

Grizzly bear The brown, or grizzly, bear has always been something of a feared, misunderstood and mythologized enigma, its habits only becoming known following extensive studies in Canada and the United States during the 1960s. As human populations have grown, the grizzly's range has gradually shrunk back to north-western North America, and even here you are far more likely to see a black bear. Although grizzly bears have been known to weigh as much as 500 kg, the average male weighs 250-350 kg and the female about half that. Like black bears, grizzlies are mostly vegetarian, though they have a great love of salmon. Watching them fishing during salmon season, at places like Hyder near Stewart, is a particularly rewarding experience. Despite their reclusive tendencies, grizzlies are much feared by many people, the more ignorant of whom will shoot them for pleasure or 'sport'.

As a result, the grizzly is becoming a greatly endangered species, and a moratorium (suspension of hunting) was declared to protect them. This, however has been lifted by BC premier Gordon Campbell.

The usual obvious way to distinguish between black and grizzly bears is by size and colour. Such methods are unreliable, not accounting for big black bears, younger, smaller grizzlies, and the tendency of both bears to come in a variety of shades. To be certain, look at the faces: black bears have a 'Roman' (straight) facial profile, whereas Grizzlies have dish-shaped (concave) profiles. Grizzlies have a large shoulder hump lacking in black bears, and much longer front claws which prevent them from climbing trees. You are most likely to see a grizzly where there are few humans, such as in the Yukon's Kluane National Park, or very remote spots such as Bella Coola. Sadly, the most reliable place of all to see either bear is around municipal garbage dumps.

Buffalo (bison)

The bison is the largest land animal in North America. A bull can stand 2 m high and weigh more than a tonne. It has curved black horns on the sides of its head, a high hump at the shoulders, a short tail with a tassel, and dense shaggy dark brown and black hair around the head and neck. Another distinctive feature of the buffalo is its beard. Two hundred years ago, the Great Plains aboriginal people relied heavily on the great herds of 30 to 70 million bison that roamed free in North America. By the end of the 1800s, the species was on the verge of extinction. Since then numbers have increased, but the great free-ranging herds have gone forever. Today's wild herds move freely only within parks and fenced wildlife sanctuaries.

There are two living subspecies of wild bison in North America: the plains bison and the wood bison. Today, there are few plains bison, though some of their traditional routes are still visible from the air in the form of deep paths worn over the years by millions of passing hooves. A herd of about 600 lives at Elk Island National Park, 64 km east of Edmonton, and there are small numbers at Waterton Lakes National Park in Alberta. Some commercial ranchers have bred the plains buffalo with cows, resulting in 'beefalo'.

In historic times, the range of the wood bison was further north, centred in northern Alberta and adjacent parts of BC, the Northwest Territories, and Saskatchewan. In general, the wood bison is darker in colour, less stocky and long-legged, but heavier. Never as abundant as its southern cousin, the total number in North America was probably never more than 170,000. Today the largest free-roaming herds of both breeds is in Wood Buffalo National Park, on the Alberta/NWT border, where there are about 2000 animals. Bison have keen senses of smell and hearing, able to distinguish smells from 3 km away, and are quick to detect changes in their environment.

Caribou

One of Canada's most widely distributed large mammals, the caribou is the only member of the deer family whose males and females both carry antlers. They are similar to, and belong to the same species as, the reindeer of Eurasia. Their ability to use lichens as a primary food distinguishes them from all other large mammals, and has enabled them to survive on harsh northern rangeland. An excellent sense of smell enables them to locate lichens under the snow. Large, concave hooves splay widely to support the caribou in snow or muskeg, and also function well as paddles, making them excellent swimmers. In fact, a herd of caribou will often swim across even the widest of lakes rather than walk around them, and often do so to gain some respite from the swarms of insects that make their lives a misery in summer.

Woodland caribou are large, dark animals usually found in small herds in northern boreal forests. Average weights are 180 kg for bulls and 135 kg for cows. In the mountainous areas of Western Canada, they make seasonal movements from winter range in forested valleys to summer range on high, alpine tundra. Clearing of

⦙ Bear essentials

Bears are shy, reclusive creatures who will usually take off if warned of your presence. Your voice is the best way to do so. In areas where forest or brush limits visibility, especially if you are hiking into the wind or close to a stream, sing and shout loudly. The little bells you see some people wearing are not loud enough to be effective. Be particularly wary in areas where bears are known to live, if there are lots of berry bushes around, or if you have seen bear droppings (it looks like what it is: mushed up berries). When camping, never leave food in or close to your tent.

Only in very rare cases have bears preyed on humans, or attacked in a premeditated way. If you catch a bear by surprise, however, it may attack out of fear, especially if it's a sow with cubs to defend. If you see a bear, avoid looking it in the eyes as this could be seen as a challenge.

Resist the temptation to run: like most animals, bears are more likely to pursue a fleeing target, and they run much faster than humans. They are also strong swimmers, and black bears are consummate climbers of trees. Generally the best advice is to stay calm and still, moving in slow motion if at all. Stand your ground making soothing, non-threatening sounds, then retreat slowly. If a lone black bear attacks, fighting back and screaming at it might be effective. If it's a grizzly, try climbing a tree, otherwise lie face down with your legs apart and your hands clasped behind your neck. This position makes it hard for the bear to flip you over. Once the bear feels you are no longer a threat it is likely to leave you alone. Only move when you are sure the bear has left the area, then get up slowly and quietly and walk away.

land for agriculture has sadly destroyed much of their habitat, with new growth forest a much more suitable environment for moose and deer. Barren-ground caribou are smaller and lighter coloured, and spend much or all of the year on the tundra. Most of those in Western Canada belong to the porcupine and bluenose herds which migrate seasonally across the Yukon from the tundra to the sparsely wooded northern coniferous forests, known as taiga. They are excellent navigators, unerringly walking hundreds of kilometres in spring to their relatively small calving areas, led by the pregnant cows. In fact, their migration routes have always been so well established that, in past years, native hunters would lay in wait at certain places, knowing the caribou would come. The annual crossing of the Dempster Highway by the porcupine herd in autumn is one of the most spectacular sights imaginable.

Cougar

The cougar's range has decreased since European settlement, but is still the most extensive of any terrestrial mammal in the western hemisphere, extending from the Yukon to Patagonia. In Canada this large predator, which can also go my the names mountain lion, puma, and panther, is now common only in western forested regions, where three subspecies occur: one in southwestern Alberta and interior BC, one in the Coast Mountains, and one only on Vancouver Island. The cougar is the second largest cat in the New World after the jaguar, with a body length of around 2 m, and weights of about 71 kg and 40 kg for males and females respectively. One of the cougar's distinctive characteristics is its long tail, which is useful for balance. Like all cats, cougars are formidable hunters, very secretive, and almost entirely nocturnal, so the chances of seeing one are almost nil.

Deer

Of all North America's large animals, the white-tailed deer is the most widely distributed and the most numerous. Its range extends from the southern tip of the continent well into the northern boreal forest. Far from being endangered, these deers are excessively numerous, and you are almost guaranteed to see their distinctive white rears bouncing away into the bush, or running out in front of your vehicle. Even more common west of the Continental Divide is the almost identical black-tailed deer, which has similar antlers and will sometimes show the characteristic 'flag' of the white tail, though usually with less flare. Mule deer can be distinguished by a small white tail with a black-tip, antlers that divide and redivide into paired beams and points, and large ears that resemble those of their namesake.

Elk

In general appearance elk, also known as wapiti, are obviously kin to these deer, but considerably larger. An adult bull elk stands about 150 cm tall at the shoulder and weighs around 300-350 kg, with some large bulls approaching 500 kg in late summer. The colour of the elk's coat ranges from reddish brown in summer to dark brown in winter. They have long, blackish hair on the neck that is referred to as a mane. Male elk are notable for their impressively large antlers, which are grown new each year in just a few months. In summer these are encased by a protective layer of 'velvet'. Elk are sociable and talkative animals, communicating through frequent grunts and squeals. They are also long-lived, with males surviving to an average of 14 years, and females living as long as 24 years. In autumn the males go into rut as they prepare to mate, at which time they can be extremely aggressive, and should be avoided. While elk inhabit almost the entire region, you are most likely to see them wandering through campgrounds in the Rockies, or grazing in northern wetlands.

Insects

Unfortunately, the creatures you are most likely to encounter are voracious biting insects. Though the Tropics are more famous for their mosquitoes, nowhere in the world has bugs worse than those found in Canada. Naturally, such beasties only thrive at certain temperatures, so the further north you go the shorter their season, and places like the Okanagan are too hot for them in summer. Most of Western Canada has horrible bugs for at least a few weeks of the summer. Central BC is particularly brutal, and the whole of the north is afflicted with appallingly vicious insects for a shorter time span. Mosquitoes are annoying mostly for their persistence and whining sound, but black flies can be an even greater torment as they are numerous, harder to kill, and like to go for your eyes. They can be horrible in the Coast Mountains. No-see-ums are so named because you can't see them, making these a formidable enemy. They're small enough to get through protective netting, and their bites are extremely painful. Towards the end of the summer, deer flies and horse flies have a brief season. Both are big enough to take a nasty chunk out of you, but they're slow and fairly easy to kill. For a couple of weeks in spring, the most heinous bugs of all have a brief season in certain regions that includes the Rockies: ticks. Ticks attach themselves to your flesh and suck your blood. They particularly like to hang out in long grass. Signs normally warn hapless hikers of the danger, so do a full body (and hair) check at the end of the day, and wear long trousers. The best way to remove them is very delicately with a pair of tweezers, making sure that no parts of the insect break off inside. The very tiny ticks that carry Lymes disease are practically non-existent in Canada.

Lynx and bobcat

Of the three Canadian wild cats, the lynx and bobcat are most alike and most closely related, both probably having descended from the Eurasian lynx. They resemble a

large domestic cat, with a short tail, long legs, large feet, and prominent ear tufts.
Both cats have large eyes and ears, and depend on acute sight and hearing when hunting. Secretive and nocturnal, these too are rarely seen in the wild, generally inhabiting forested wilderness areas, particularly old-growth boreal forests with a dense undercover of thickets and windfalls. The lynx preys almost exclusively on the snowshoe hare, and numbers of lynx are known to fluctuate dramatically due to this hare's 10-year population cycle.

Moose

Moose are the largest members of the deer family. An estimated half to one million of them live throughout Canada's forests, though you are most likely to see them in boreal forest, or marshy areas of Northern BC. A bull moose with a full rack of antlers is arguably the continent's most formidable animal, standing taller than the largest horse, and weighing up to 600 kg, or 800 kg in the Yukon. For all that, the moose is an ungainly, rather whimsical looking beast. Its body is deep at the shoulders, where massive muscles result in a humped appearance. The slim hindquarters and spindly legs look inadequate for the task of supporting so massive a bulk. The head is heavy and huge, its ears similar to a mule's, its long nose lending the beast a perpetual mournful expression. The upper lip is drooping and flexible, and from its throat hangs a pendant of fur-covered skin, some 30 cm long, called a bell. In colour the moose varies from dark brown, almost black, to reddish or greyish brown, with grey or white leg 'stockings'.

In late summer and autumn, a mature bull carries a great rack of antlers which may reach a span of 180 cm. The heavy main beams broaden into large palms which are fringed with a series of spikes usually less than 30 cm long. At this time, like the elk, bull moose enter their rutting season, at which time they are extremely dangerous. The eyesight of the moose is extremely poor, but its senses of smell and hearing compensate for this. On obscure forest roads, moose have a habit of getting in front of a car and walking or running along the road for long distances. Few motorists seem to mind.

Mountain goat

Mountain goats are found throughout the mountain ranges of the Cordillera, at elevations where they feel safe from humans and other predators. Their ability to negotiate steep, rocky terrain is unequalled. Pure white of colour, with short, pointed horns, these bearded goats have long, thin faces that seem to wear perpetual expressions of benign intelligence and mild amusement, no doubt one of the reasons for their great popularity with visitors. Though they do not stoop to begging at roadsides like the sheep, your chances of encountering these creatures in the Rockies are very high.

Mountain sheep

The wild, or mountain, sheep is a stocky, hoofed mammal, about one and a half times as large as a domestic sheep. The most distinctive characteristic of the males is their massive horns, which spiral back, out, and then forward, in an arc. Adult females have slightly curved horns about 30 cm long. North American wild sheep are related both to domestic sheep, which were imported from Europe by early settlers, and to the native sheep of Asia, which is thought to have migrated across the Bering land bridge about half a million years ago. As the great ice-age glaciers moved south from the pole, those animals became isolated in two ice-free areas, one in central Alaska, the other in the United States. The former evolved into the slender-horned Dall sheep, those farther south into the heavy-horned Rocky Mountain and desert bighorns. Today the white Dall sheep is found in mid and north Yukon, while its almost black cousin, the Stone, or black Dall sheep, makes its home in northern BC and southern

Yukon. In the Pelly Mountain area of the Yukon, the two breeds merged gradually with each other, resulting in the Fannin sheep of the Faro region.

The southern sheep evolved into seven races, two of which returned to Canada after the retreat of the glaciers. Rocky Mountain bighorns moved north into the Rockies of BC and Alberta. California bighorns expanded into southwestern BC, colonizing the arid mountains and river valleys of the Okanagan and Chilcotin areas. Once a year, around about June or July, the bighorns shed their hair, resulting in a scruffy, bedraggled appearance until the new coat grows in.

Musk ox

Superficially the musk ox resembles the bison, its humped shoulders and long black coat accentuating the shortness of its legs. In fact, it is more closely related to sheep and goats. Although not very tall, musk oxen are relatively heavy owing to their stocky and compact build. Adult bulls weigh 270-315 kg and cows about 90 kg less. Both have impressive, very distinctive horns, which curve downward toward the face then out and up at the slender tips. On the bulls, the base of each horn extends across the forehead to meet as a solid 'boss' of horn and bone up to 10 cm thick. Superbly equipped to withstand frigid temperatures, the musk ox remains on the Arctic tundra year round. Fossil evidence suggests that their ancestors crossed the Bering land bridge to North America about 90,000 years ago. An ability to function normally in temperatures of -40°C in high winds and blowing snow is mainly due to the muskox's amazing coat, which has layers of wool and hair. The insulating woolly layer next to the animal's skin is stronger than sheep's wool, eight times warmer, and finer than cashmere. The coarser hairy layer that covers and protects the wool grows to be the longest hair of any mammal in North America. The Inuit name for muskox is omingmak, "the animal with skin like a beard".

Polar bear

The polar bear is North America's largest land carnivore. Adult males measure 240-260 cm in total length and usually weigh 400-600 kg, although they can weigh up to 800 kg, about as much as a small car. Adult females weigh 150-250 kg. Polar bears have longer necks, skulls and bodies than their southern cousins, and a 'Roman' nose like black bears. Though it looks white, or lemon yellow under a rising sun, polar bear hair is translucent, and reflects the heat from the sun down to the base of the hair, where it is absorbed by the black skin. It sheds water easily, so that after a swim the bear can shake itself dry like a dog. Polar bears are considered to be marine mammals because they depend upon seals and the marine environment for their existence. They feed mostly on ringed seals, but they also catch bearded seals, harp seals, hooded seals, and harbour seals, occasionally also killing walruses, belugas or white whales, and narwhals.

Along with eyesight and hearing believed to be similar to those of a human, polar bears have an exceptional sense of smell, and sniff constantly, testing the air for scent from ringed seal breathing holes, which they can detect through layers of ice and snow 90 cm or more thick up to a kilometre away. When the seal comes up to the breathing hole for air, the polar bear kills it and flips it out of the water with a single blow of its large front paws, which also double up as powerful oars. During spring and early summer, when seals are most accessible, a bear may catch one every 4-5 days. Whatever the time of year, they can slow down their metabolism at will if food is short. Polar bears can be seen around the Beaufort Sea in winter, but the best place to see them is Churchill, Manitoba.

Wolverine

Few people, even those who spend a lot of time outdoors, have seen wolverines in the wild. This contributes to their mysterious reputation and explains why they are the

most misunderstood of Canada's wild animals. The wolverine belongs to the weasel
family, and has been described as the fiercest creature on earth, a fearlessly aggressive
fighter that will drive bears away from their kills. The wolverine is not long and lean, like
a weasel, but short and thick, like a small bear. An adult is about the size of a
medium-sized dog, and weighs 12-18 kg, 8-12 kg for females. The typically glossy, dark
brown pelt of the wolverine is striking. Two yellow stripes originate at the nape of its
neck and sweep along each flank to merge at the base of its long, bushy tail.

Wildlife by region

Pacific Ocean

When Captain Cook first visited these shores, the waters teemed with the kind of cute
sea otters that like to lay around on their backs adroitly opening up shellfish with their
skillful little hands. Alas, the brisk trade in their pelts that followed this first sojourn of
a European led the otters to be hunted to near extinction, a crisis from which they
have recovered less well than the inland beaver. They can still be seen, though the
Vancouver Aquarium is the most likely spot. Colonies of seals and sealions are a
more likely spectacle, especially for sea kayakers off the West Coast of Vancouver
Island or Haida Gwaii.

Some 22,000 grey whales migrate past the West Coast every year from March
to May. Orca (killer whales) are year-round residents, and can often be seen from the
Vancouver Island shore, especially in Victoria. The world's third largest residence of
orca pods is in the Johnstone Strait close to Telegraph Cove. Humpback whales are
also frequently seen in the Pacific, and further north are blue, beluga and right
whales. Dolphins are also spotted. Of the many fish species, the most remarkable
is salmon. Divers come to these shores to see the likes of giant octopuses and
massive wolf eels. At low tide a large number of colourful critters can be seen in tide
pools, especially in sheltered waters such as on the Gulf Islands. The starfish are big,
numerous, and come in many colours.

West Coast forest

As well as bears, cougars, deer and elk, and the usual collection of smaller mammals,
the temperate rainforests of the West Coast are home to many bird species, including
a wealth of woodland species, such as Townsend's, Wilson's and orange-crowned
warblers, junco, Swainson's thrush, and golden-crowned kinglet. Rarer birds include
the rufous hummingbird. The Gulf Islands are very good places to see golden and
bald eagles, but the best place for the latter is Brackendale near Squamish, which
plays host to thousands of the salmon-hungry birds every January.

Columbia forest

The lower slopes of BC's interior mountains and the Rockies also support healthy
populations of the widespread large mammals, as well as many smaller creatures
such as coyotes and weasels, porcupines, red and grey squirrels, and chipmunks.
Birds are numerous, especially hawks and owls.

Montane forest

The more southerly and sheltered reaches of the Rockies and the dry plateaux of
interior BC are home to a lot of coyotes, who thrive on the large numbers of voles and
small rodents. Parts of the Okanagan are home to desert species such as the rattlesnake and certain rare amphibians. This is a good area for birds such as warblers,
woodpeckers, nuthatches, chickadees and the ruby-crowned kinglet. Birds of prey
include goshawks and Swainson's hawks. Ducks such as mallard, shoveler, and
widgeon are common, and rarer birds such as the cinnamon teal can also be seen.

Sub-alpine forest

Forests between 1300-2200 m throughout the Rockies' interior ranges in BC are teeming with deer and elk. Smaller mammals include the golden-mantled ground squirrel, and bird species include Clark's nutcracker.

Alpine

Alpine zones above the treeline are less inhabited by man, and so popular with animal species. Elk and mule deer are resident only in summer, whereas Dall and bighorn sheep and mountain goats can be seen year-round. Among smaller mammals, a particular favourite is the marmot, a large rodent that often lives on rock-slides in the mountains. These can become tame and curious, approaching humans for hand-outs. Often seen, they are more frequently heard, producing a shrill whistle to warn each other of intruders. The pika is a seldom seen little relative of the rabbit. Birds at this elevation include rosy finches, pipits, and blue grouse. The white-tailed ptarmigan, similar to a partridge, is resident throughout the year.

Grasslands

The grasslands of Alberta and BC's Peace River district are the traditional home of bison and the pronghorn, a tawny-gold species of antelope. The size of a large dog, but with a heart twice the size and eyes larger than a horse, pronghorns are the fastest animals in North America, capable of speeds over 100 kmph. The traditional predators of such cattle are wolves and coyotes, both of which you are much more likely to hear than see. What you are guaranteed to witness are large numbers of small mammals such as gophers, groundsquirrels and jackrabbits, which have bred out of control and are much hated by farmers. Occasional ponds or 'sloughs' on the plains are important breeding grounds for ducks, grebes, herons, pelicans, rails and many more. Other common birds are the marbled godwit, the curlew, and the prairie falcon, which is a close relative of the peregrine falcon.

Boreal forest

The boreal forest that runs in a broad band across much of Canada is one of the best places to see many of the species mentioned above, particularly caribou and moose. Thanks to their unmerited reputation, most of the west's population of wolves has been driven back to these sparsely populated northern forests. Beavers can be seen in any wet forest environment, but are especially common here. Small mammals include muskrat, varying hare, red squirrel, deer mouse and red-backed vole. Frequently seen birds are jays, ravens and grouse. Forest wetlands offer a refuge to ducks, geese and herons, including the great blue heron, with loons, grebes and songbirds attracted to the surrounding undergrowth. There are also plenty of raptors, including numerous types of hawk, and Canada's largest owl, the great grey. There is a good chance of seeing ruffed and spruce grouse, belted kingfisher, grey jay, robin and other thrushes, black-capped and boreal chickadees, waxwings and finches, several nuthatches, vireos and grosbeaks, and many species of warblers and sparrows. The zone is also justly infamous for supporting some of the world's most voracious and copious biting insects, including the ubiquitous mosquitoes, black flies and no-see-ums.

Tundra

The apparently harsh environment of the Arctic tundra is nevertheless rich in animal life and is the best place to see caribou and smaller mammals such as Arctic ground squirrels, and lemmings, ermines and weasels, Arctic white foxes and Arctic hares.

The far north is home to Muskoxen and polar bears, while the Beaufort Sea is home to ringed and bearded seals, and the incredibly graceful beluga whales. Lots of ravens inhabit the north, earning their reputation as crafty tricksters. Predators including the gyrfalcon, the largest falcon in the world, jaegars, hawks, gulls and owls, including the snowy owl. Of the hundred or so bird species to be spotted, most are migratory, including numerous swans, geese and loons. The Arctic tern makes a 32,000 km return migration from the Antarctic, the longest annual migration of any creature.

Conservation

The first European explorers and settlers in Canada found wildlife in abundance. Believing natural resources to be unlimited, they saw no need to practise conservation. Wildlife, fish and timber were free for the taking. The result of this attitude became apparent in the latter half of the 19th century with the near extinction of animals like buffalo and elk that once numbered many millions. Even then, western and northern Canada were still held to be boundless frontiers. The British North America act of 1867 assigned resource-management responsibilities to governments, with wildlife conspicuous by its omission, lumped under 'matters of private and local nature'. Wildlife enthusiasts of the 1880s solemnly predicted the extinction of most large North American mammals, but the next two decades marked a significant turning point in Canadian wildlife history. Following Confederation and the assumption of resource- management control by the original provinces, a move was made to develop wildlife conservation laws. Banff National Park, the first in Canada (established 1885), was created to make money rather than protect wildlife, but this would become one of its significant functions. Others, such as Wood Buffalo National Park, were created solely for that purpose.

From 1920 to 1970, the concerns of society led to the formation of non-profit organizations such as the Canadian Wildlife Federation, Canadian Nature Federation, Ducks Unlimited (Canada), World Wildlife Fund (Canada) and the Nature Conservancy of Canada, as well as government conservation agencies like the Canadian Wildlife Service of Environment Canada. Many parks and conservation areas were created to protect particular animals and ecosystems, and thanks to the wide distribution of most species, relatively few have actually been lost compared with what has occurred in tropical regions. The most significant exceptions were the great auk, passenger pigeon, Labrador duck, Dawson caribou and sea mink.

Many forms of wildlife are more abundant now than they were a century ago, but a number of species have continued to decline to threatened levels or are in danger of extinction, and this includes some very significant animals such as the grizzly bear. Over-hunting or harvesting is often to blame, but the real problem is usually the extensive alteration of ecological regions because of competing land uses such as forestry, agriculture and urbanization. Despite its obvious importance and irreplacable status, the unlogged temperate West Coast rainforest keeps shrinking; hardly any of Canada's only living desert around Osoyoos has survived the wholesale conversion of land into orchards and vineyards; and only a few hectares of the resilient tallgrass prairie remain intact, the rest having been degraded to the point of increasing worthlessness by short-sighted agricultural methods. Wetland drainage permanently removes the habitat required by many species.

Western Canada is lucky because it has only been subjected to a century and a half of abuse by modern man. Given time and increasing over-population of the globe, however, there is no reason to believe that its vast tracts of wilderness will not eventually go the same way as most of Europe, which has lost almost all of its forests and indigenous wildlife, unless a fundamental shift in human priorities occurs. Pollution of rivers and estuaries will render them unfit for wildlife survival; acid rain will sterilize vast tracts of land and waterways; marine birds and mammals will increasingly face the threat of offshore oil spills, general pollution of the oceans, and the gradual depletion of marine life due to over-fishing. The direct threat of uncontrolled harvests, so devastating in the 19th century, has been replaced by the indirect, insidious but permanent threat of environmental degradation that is characteristic of the 20th century. Certainly, provincial governments seem just as happy to sell off chunks of priceless and irreplaceable temperate rainforest to the big money of logging companies unless their people kick up enough of a fuss to deter them. So often, such environmental trouble-makers have been led by native people whose relatives have witnessed the undoing in little more than a century of a happy natural balance their ancestors had managed to sustain more or less intact for some 15,000 years.

Protected areas

National parks

Following the discovery of the Cave and Basin Hot Springs by railway workers in today's Banff National Park, the government was flooded with offers but chose not to grant private title to the lands. Instead, it was decided that the region should be preserved for the benefit of all Canadians. A report by the commissioner of Dominion Lands that "a large tract of country lying outside of the original reservation presented features of the greatest beauty, and was admirably adapted for a national park" led to the creation of Canada's first national park in 1887. Within eight years, three new mountain reserves were set aside, unavailable for "sale, settlement or squatting". These later became Yoho, Glacier and Waterton Lakes National Parks.

The world's first distinct bureau of national parks, the Dominion Parks Branch, was formed in 1911, and led by JB Harkin from 1911-36. During this time nine national parks were established, including Elk Island (1913), Mount Revelstoke (1914), Kootenay (1920), and Wood Buffalo (1922), and "hereby dedicated to the people of Canada, for their benefit, education and enjoyment". Further park establishment was sporadic until, in 1961, John I. Nicol became director of the National and Historic Parks Branch. Under his administration, 10 new national parks were created, and the emphasis shifted to the preservation of natural ecological processes above all else. Current policy has continued this shift in emphasis and now stresses the importance of minimal interference from people. These days, if a grizzly mother wants to set up home with her cubs in a Banff campsite that normally caters to 200 people, the campsite closes. National parks are also protected by federal legislation from all forms of extractive resource use such as mining, forestry, agriculture and sport hunting, though fishing is still allowed with a special licence.

By 1970, 20 national parks had either been established or negotiated, but opportunistically, without a vision or long-term goal. This vision was provided in the early 1970s by the National Park System Plan, which sought to develop a system of national parks using the principle of 'representativeness'. Canada is thus divided into 39 natural regions, each containing a unique set of geological, biological and ecological characteristics, each to be represented by at least one national park. At the moment, 24 natural regions are thus represented, with no progress since 1999. Parks Canada are currently considering the feasibility of creating a National Park Reserve in the South Okanagan-Lower Similkameen area, which would represent one of the missing 15 regions.

British Columbia's national parks are: Pacific Rim, Gwaii Haanas, Mount Revelstoke, Glacier, Yoho, the Gulf Islands and Kootenay. Alberta's are Banff, Jasper, Waterton lakes, Elk Island, and Wood Buffalo. In the Yukon are Kluane, Ivvavik and Vuntut. All of these have their own fees. An annual pass for 27 parks, including all of the above, currently costs $61.80, $53 senior, $31.40 youth (6-16), and $122.60 family (up to 7). An annual pass for all 78 Parks-run historic sites is $48/41.20/24.50/97.10. The two combined, called a Discovery package, is $76.50/65.70/$38.20/$154.

⁞ Greenpeace

Greenpeace was born in Vancouver in 1969, a few days after the US detonated a nuclear bomb at Amchitka Island in the Alaskan Aleutians. A small group, varied in age and profession but equally concerned for the environment, formed the Don't Make a Wave Committee. At the end of a meeting one of the oldest members is said to have uttered the traditional "Peace" as he left, and one of the youngest replied "Make it a Green Peace". At first the name was given to the fishing boat which the group chartered to head for the detonation site, but which bad weather forced to turn back. A bigger boat, *Greenpeace Too* suffered the same fate and the bomb was detonated. The foundation persisted, however, adopting its new name and expanding its efforts to combat whaling, sealing and eventually such broader concerns as toxic pollution and the destruction of rainforests.

UNESCO World Heritage Sites

UNESCO recognizes the responsibility of all nations to protect places of such unique natural and cultural value and that they are considered part of the heritage of all mankind. In Western Canada Kluane, Nahanni (NWT), Wood Buffalo, the Burgess Shale of Yoho National Park, and Anthony Island (Gwaii Haanas Park National Park Reserve) have been designated World Heritage Sites. The combined boundaries of Yoho, Jasper, Banff and Kootenay national parks and Mount Robson, Mount Assiniboine and Hamber PPs (BC) make up the Canadian Rocky Mountain Parks World Heritage Site. Waterton Lakes National Park has been chosen as a Biosphere Reserve, which designates outstanding examples of natural ecosystems throughout the world.

Provincial Parks

The term provincial park is misleading as it can equally refer to a five-site campground by a strip of highway or a vast area of outstanding wilderness which is every bit the equal of one of the more high profile national parks. This is especially true in British Columbia, the first western province to create provincial parks. Strathcona on Vancouver Island gained park status in 1911 as a result of public support from such groups as the Alpine Club of Canada. Attention then focused on the mountains and glaciers of eastern BC, Mount Robson being declared a provincial park in 1913, followed by Garibaldi in 1920, and Mount Assiniboine and Kokanee Glacier in 1922. The province's largest park, Tweedsmuir (9810 sq km), gained park status in 1938; Wells Gray, in 1939. As of June 2007, BC had 893 provincial parks and other protected areas, covering 13.09 million hectares, or 13.8% of the province. This is the largest provincial park system in the country, with 340 campgrounds, 11,000 campsites and 6000 km of hiking trails. Alberta has 67 provincial parks, 3 wilderness areas, over 300 recreation areas, 14 ecological reserves and Willmore Wilderness, together encompassing over 10,000 sq km.

Books

Guide books and reference

Bushnell, V. *Kids' Vancouver* (Raincoast Books, 2000).
Devine, B. *Western Canada: National Geographic Guide to America Outdoors* (National Geographic, 2002). Full of gorgeous photos.
Spalding, D and A et al. *Southern Gulf Islands* (Altitude, 1995). Useful guide to the islands with lots of pictures.

Cavanaugh, C. *Making western Canada: Essays on European colonization and settlement* (Garamond, 1996). An intelligent, gripping account of Western Canada's tumultuous history.

Vogel, A and Wyse, D. *Vancouver: A History in Photos* (Altitude, 1993). A visual approach to the city's past, captured in vintage black and white.

Natural history and environment

Baron, N and Acorn, J. *Birds of the Pacific Northwest Coast* (Lone Pine, 1997). Thorough and well illustrated.

Eyles, N and Miall, A. *Canada Rocks: The Geologic Journey* (Fitzhenry and Whiteside 2007). A fascinating journey through Canada's surprising geological history.

Harbour. Kramer, P. *Gardens of British Columbia* (Altitude, 1998). Lots of sumptuous photos.

Sheldon, I. *Seashore of British Columbia* (Lone Pine, 1998). An exploration of coastal flora and fauna with decent drawings.

Outdoor activities

Copeland, K. & C. *Don't Waste Your Time in the Canadian Rockies, 5th Ed.* (2006).

Cousins, J. *Easy Hiking around Vancouver* (1980, updated 2001).

Dunn, S. *Mountain Biking BC* (Rip It Up Publications, 2001).

Ed McGee, P. *Kayak Routes of the Pacific Northwest Coast* (Greystone Books, 1998).

Greystone. Cousins, J and N. *Easy Cycling Around Vancouver* (Greystone Books, 2002).

Hanna, D. *Easy Hikes and Walks of Southwest BC* (Lone Pine, 2002). A useful resource for those who want to home in on less demanding hiking.

Kimantas, J. *The Wild Coast 3: A kayaking, hiking, and recreation guide for BC's South Coast and East Vancouver Island* (Whitecap Books, 2007).

Nomad, L. & S. *Gotta Hike BC: Premier Trails in southern British Columbia* (2001)

Stedham, Glen. *The Vancouver Paddler* (Self-published, 1999).

Pictorial

Douglas Coupland. *Souvenir of Canada* (Douglas & MacIntyre, 2002). This time the author presents a collection of quirky photos and observant witicisms about the country as a whole.

Berton, P. *Pierre Berton's Canada: The land and the People* (Stoddart, 1999). A gorgeous coffee-table book with text by an acclaimed local authority.

Coupland, D. *City of Glass* (Douglas & MacIntyre, 2001). An interesting book of anecdotes and photos about Vancouver by this celebrated local.

Hines, Sherman. *British Columbia* (Nimbus, 1988). Coffee-table book with a collection of nice photographs.

Horwood, D & Parkin, T. *Haida Gwaii: The Queen Charlotte Islands* (Heritage House Pub, 2006).

Leighton, D. *The Canadian Rockies* (Altitude, 1993). One of a few similar coffee-table offerings of the range.

Lynch, W. *Wild Alberta: A Visual Celebration* (Fifth House, 2005). Fantastic colour photos of Alberta's surprisingly varied landscapes.

McAllister, I & K. *The Great Bear Rainforest: Canada's Forgotten Coast* (Sierra Club Books , 1998). Stunning shots of the wild and rugged coast from north of Vancouver Island to Alaska.

Pistolesi, Andrea. *Vancouver: Sunrise to Sunset* (Bonechi, 1998). Collection of glossy photos depicting this photogenic city.

Spalding, DAE & Oke, K. *Enchanted Isles: The Southern Gulf Islands* (Harbour, 2007). Visually enchanting, and somehow manages to capture the rich flavour of the islands' inhabitants.

Travelogues & biographies

Coffey, M and Goering, D. *Visions of the Wild: A Voyage by Kayak around Vancouver Island* (Harbour, 2001). An account of a personal odyssey, with beautiful photos.

Danlock, T. *In the Wilds of Western Canada* (Trafford, 2005). A collection of real life short stories, documenting the psychological and spiritual impact.of one man's many electrifying encounters with Nature.

Gordon, Charles. *The Canada Trip* (Douglas Gibson, 1997). About the only example of humourous travel writing on the country, but only a few chapters on Western Canada.

Footnotes

Index → Entries in **bold** *refer to maps.*

Credits

Editor: Sara Chare
Map editor: Sarah Sorensen
Picture editor: Kevin Feeney, Robert Lunn

Managing Director: Andy Riddle
Publisher: Patrick Dawson
Editorial: Alan Murphy, Felicity Laughton,
Nicola Gibbs, Ria Gane
Cartography: Robert Lunn, Kevin Feeney,
Emma Bryers
Cover design: Robert Lunn
Design: Mytton Williams
Sales and marketing: Zoë Jackson,
Hannah Bonnell
Advertising sales manager: Renu Sibal
Finance and administration: Elizabeth Taylor

Photography credits
Front cover: Carson Ganci/Design Pics
Back cover: Al Harvey/Slide Farm
Inside colour section: Matthew Gardner;
Alison Bigg; Andy Bell www.ticket2ride.com;
Al Harvey www.slidefarm.com; Ian Wilson,
Bev Ramm, Karoline Cullen, Goncalo Veloso
de Figuieredo/Shutterstock; age fotostock,
Hemis.fr/Superstock, Terry W Ryder/
Superstock; kwest/Superstock; robcocquyt/
Superstock, Sam Cornwell/Superstock.

Print
Manufactured by Nutech
Photolithographers, Delhi, India.
Pulp from sustainable forests.

Footprint feedback
We try as hard as we can to make each
Footprint guide as up to date as possible
but, of course, things always change. If you
want to let us know about your experiences –
good, bad or ugly – then don't delay, go to
www.footprintbooks.com and send in
your comments.

Publishing information
Footprint Western Canada
3rd edition
© Footprint Handbooks Ltd
June 2008
ISBN 978 1 906098 26 1
CIP DATA: A catalogue record for this book
is available from the British Library
® Footprint Handbooks and the Footprint
mark are a registered trademark of
Footprint Handbooks Ltd

Published by Footprint
6 Riverside Court
Lower Bristol Road
Bath BA2 3DZ, UK
T +44 (0)1225 469141
F +44 (0)1225 469461
discover@footprintbooks.com
www.footprintbooks.com

Neither the black and white nor coloured
maps are intended to have any political
significance.

Every effort has been made to ensure that
the facts in this guidebook are accurate.
However, travellers should still obtain advice
about travel and visa requirements before
travelling. Hotel and restaurant price codes
should only be taken as a guide to the prices
and facilities offered by the establishment.
It is with the discretion of the owners to
vary them from time to time. The authors
and publishers cannot accept responsibility
for any loss, injury or inconvenience however
caused.

Western Canada

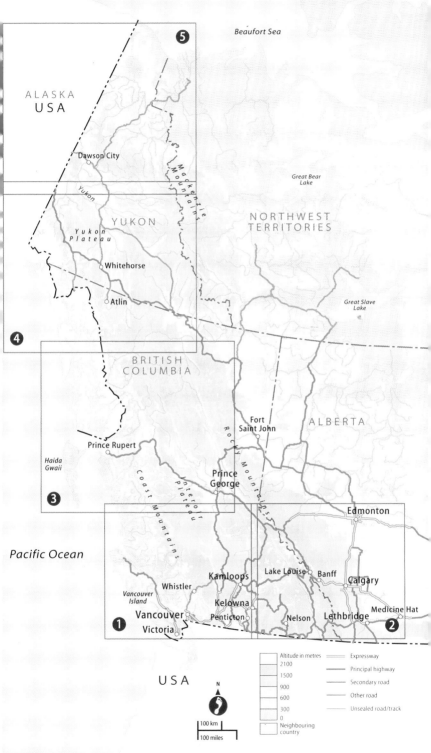

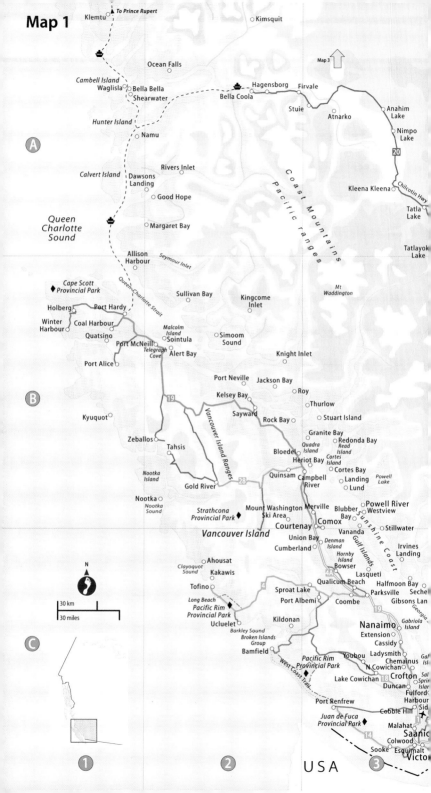

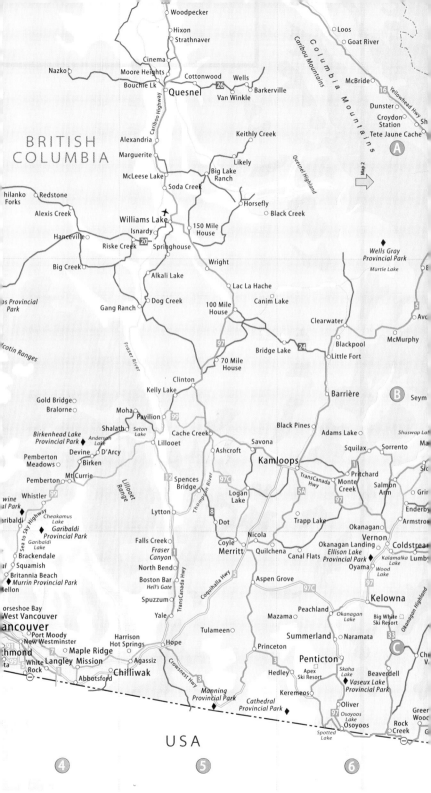

Map 2

30 km
30 miles

Whitecourt

Grande Cache

loos

Goat River

McBride

16 Yellowhead Hwy

Dunster

Croydon
Station

Shere

Tete Jaune
Cache

16

Valemount

Albreda

Lempriere

Thunder River

Wells Gray
Provincial Park

Murtle Lake

Blue River

Mica Creek

Avola

McMurphy

lackpool

ttle Fort

rrière

as Lake

Squilax

Sorrento

Pritchard

Monte
Creek

7

Salmon
Arm

Sicamous

Grindrod

Enderby

Armstrong

Vernon

Okanagan
Landing

Oyama

Kalamalka
Lake

Wood
Lake

97

Kelowna

Okanagan
Lake

Naramata

Skaha
Lake

Vaseux Lake
Provincial Park

97

Oliver

Osoyoos
Lake

Osoyoos

Rock
Creek

Green
Wood

Grand Forks

Cascade

Seymour Arm

Shuswap Lake

Malakwa

Taft

Three Valley

Revelstoke

Greenslide

Beaton

Shelter Bay

Galena

Ferguson

Trout Lake

Gerrard

Saint Leon

Goat Range
Provincial Park

Nakusp

Needles

Fauquier

Edgewood

New Denver

Silverton

Valhalla
Provincial Park

Slocan
Lake

Slocan

Kokanee Glacier
Provincial Park

Vallican

Winlaw

Gladstone
Provincial Park

Castlegar

Christina
Lake

Genelle

Trail

Rossland

Fruitvale

Nelway

Salmo

Mabel Lake

Cherryville

Lumby

Coldstream

6

Christian
Valley

33

Big White
Ski Resort

Beaverdell

Monashee
Mountains

Selkirk
Mountains

BRITISH
COLUMBIA

Kicking
Horse
Mountain

Rogers Pass

Glacier

Glacier
National Park

1

23

Rogers

Beavermouth

Yoho
National Park

Field

Golden

Lake Louise

Lake O'Hara

Banff
National Park

Castle
Mountain

Mt Ayl

Bow Valley
Parkway

Purcell
Mountains

Parson

95

Spillimacheen

Bugaboo
Provincial Park

Brisco

Radium
Hot Springs

Invermere

Windermere

Poplar Creek

Howser

Argenta

Lardeau

Retallack

Sandon

Kaslo

Riondel

Kootenay Bay

Gray Creek

Procter

Balfour

Ainsworth

Nelson

Shoreacres

Boswell

Kootenay
Lake

Kootenay
Landing

Sirdar

Creston

Kingsgate

Purcell Wilderness
Provincial Park

Fairmont
Hot Springs

Canal Flats

93
95

Elkw

Skookumchuck

Ta Ta Creek

Wasa

Kimberley

Marysville

Cranbrook

Fort Steele

93

Bull River

Wardner

Moyie

93

Elko

Yhak

McConnel

3

Newgate

Roosville

Hos

Fernie

Hosm

3

Roosville

Maligne Mountains

Icefields Pkwy

Columbia Icefield

Columbia Icefield

Saskatchewan
River Crossing

93

Abraham
Lake

Rocky Mountains

Rocky Mountain Foothills

11

Nordegg

Hort

Whitecourt

Peers

Mackay

Nitton
Junction

Edson

Yellowhead Highway

Obed

Marlboro

Bickerdike

Hinton

40

Entrance

Brûlé

Erith

Robb

Pocahontas

Miette
Hot Springs

16

Jasper
National Park

Jasper

Cadomin

Mount Robson
Provincial Park

Mt Assiniboine
Provincial Park

Kananas

Kootenay
National Park

Sunshine

93

Canmore

Banff

Se

Map 1

1

2

3

A

B

C

Map 3

Sheslay

Map 4

Glenora Grand Canyon of the St

Stikine Telegraph
Creek

Stikine Bob Quinn
Lake

N

30 km
30 miles

Premier
Mezia
Junct
Hyder Stewart

Anyox Alice Ar

Na
Ca

Kincolith Nass Aiyans
Nisga's
Greenville Memori
Lava Bed P

Dixon Entrance Portland Canal

Lax Kw'alaams
(Port Simpson) Rosswood

Masset Metlakatla **Prince**
Graham Island **Rupert**
Port Edward Copper R
Hunts Inlet Skeena Exstew Terrace
Juskatla Port Clements Porcher 16 Skeena Lakelse
Island Port
Tlell Oona River Essington
Queen Kitkatla
Charlotte Lawnhill
Skidegate Kitimat
Haida Gwai: Sandspit Kitimat Village
Queen Alliford
Charlotte Bay
Islands Hecate Strait Pitt
Sewell Inlet Island
Tatsu Banks Hartley Bay
Moresby Island
Island Gill
Island
Estevan Group Coast Ra
Campania Butedale
Island

Gwai Haanas
National Parl

Jedway

Aristazabal Is Klemtu King Is
Swindle Is
Price Is

Ocean Falls
Bella Bella

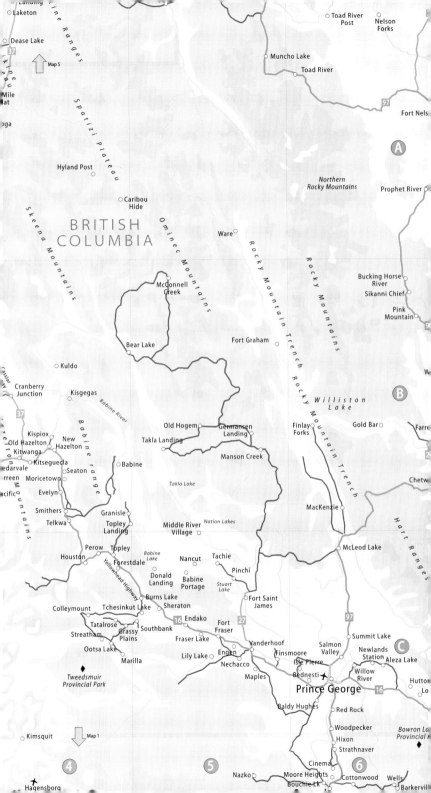

Map 4

Map 5

Stewart River
(abandoned)

White

Yukon

Dawson Rd

Beaver Creek

Snag

Koidern

ALASKA
USA

Kluane Mountains

Alaska Highway

1

Ruby Range

Yukon Plat

Burwash Landing

Destruction Bay

Aishihik

Aish
La

A

St Elias Mountains

▲ Mt Logan
(5959m)

Kluane National Park ◆

Sheep Mountain

Canyo
(abandor

Haines Junction

Champa

N

30 km
30 miles

Alsek

*Kathleen
Lake*

Dezadea
Klukshu

*Kusawa
Lake*

B

Tatshenshini

Tatshenshini-Alsek
Wilderness Park

Haines Highway

3

Klukwan

Gulf of Alaska

Hain

C

Map 3

1　　　**2**　　　**3**

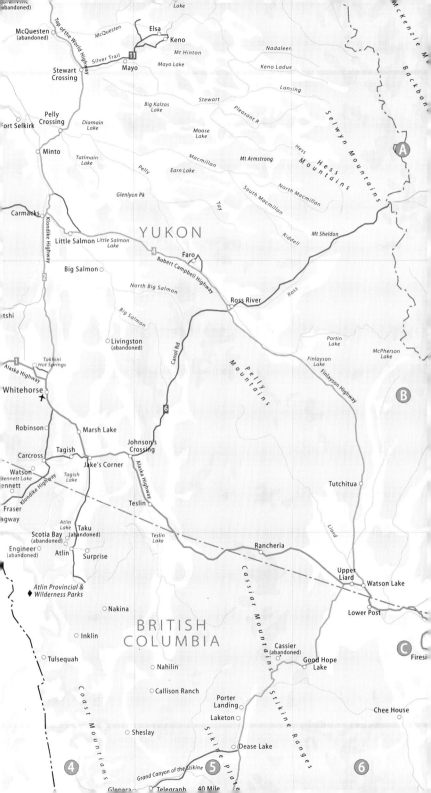

Map 5

N

30 km
30 miles

A

B

ALASKA
USA

Mt ...

C

Mt Harpe

Clinton Creek
(abandoned)

Top of the World Highway

○ Tok

○ Tetlin Junction

Sixty Mile

Dawson City

Rock
Creek

Bear Creek

Granville
(abandoned)

Map 4

Stewart River
(abandoned)

White

Yukon

1

2

3

Beaver Creek

Snag

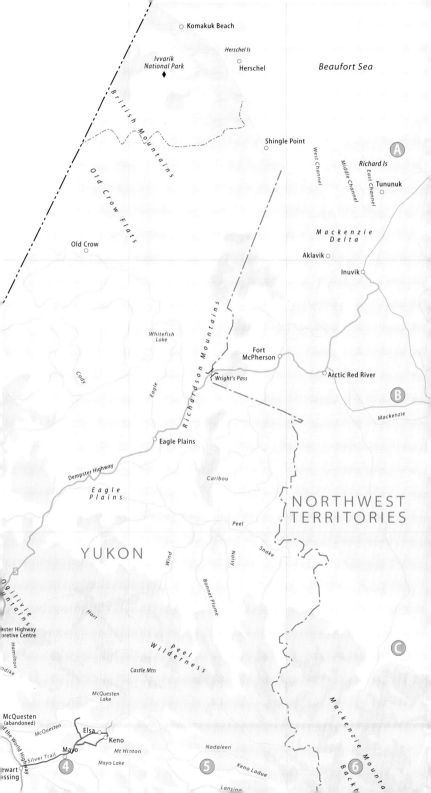

Map symbols

Administration

- □ Capital city
- ○ Other city, town
- International border
- Regional border
- ⊖ Customs

Roads and travel

- Motorway
- Main road
- Minor road
- Track
- Footpath
- Railway
- Railway with station
- ✈ Airport
- 🚌 Bus station
- Ⓜ Metro station
- Cable car
- ╫╫╫╫ Funicular
- ⛴ Ferry

Water features

- River, canal
- Lake, ocean
- Seasonal marshland
- Beach, sandbank
- Waterfall
- Reef

Topographical features

- Contours (approx)
- ▲ Mountain, volcano
- Mountain pass
- Escarpment
- Gorge
- Glacier
- Salt flat
- Rocks

Cities and towns

- Main through route
- Main street
- Minor street

- Pedestrianized street
-) (Tunnel
- Track
- Footpath
- → One way-street
- Steps
- ⥾ Bridge
- Fortified wall
- Park, garden, stadium
- 😴 Sleeping
- 🍴 Eating
- 🍸 Bars & clubs
- Building
- ▫ Sight
- ✝✝ Cathedral, church
- 🏮 Chinese temple
- Hindu temple
- Meru
- Mosque
- △ Stupa
- ✡ Synagogue
- ℹ Tourist office
- 🏛 Museum
- ✉ Post office
- Police
- Ⓢ Bank
- @ Internet
- ♪ Telephone
- Market
- ✚ Medical services
- 🅿 Parking
- Petrol
- Golf
- A Detail map
- A Related map

Other symbols

- ∴ Archaeological site
- ♦ National park, wildlife reserve
- Viewing point
- ∧ Campsite
- Refuge, lodge
- Castle, fort
- Diving
- Deciduous, coniferous, palm trees
- Hide
- Vineyard, winery
- Shipwreck
- ✕ Historic battlefield

Footnotes

Complete title listing

Footprint publishes travel guides to over 150 destinations worldwide. Each guide is packed with practical, concise and colourful information for everybody from first-time travellers to travel aficionados. The list is growing fast and current titles are noted below.
Available from all good bookshops and online at www.footprintbooks.com

(P) denotes pocket guide

Latin America and Caribbean

Argentina
Barbados (P)
Belize, Guatemala &
  Southern Mexico
Bolivia
Brazil
Caribbean Islands
Central America & Mexico
Chile
Colombia
Costa Rica
Cuba

Cusco & the Inca Trail
Dominican Republic (P)
Ecuador & Galápagos
Guatemala
Havana (P)
Mexico
Nicaragua
Patagonia
Peru
Peru, Bolivia & Ecuador
Rio de Janeiro
Rio de Janeiro (P)
South American Handbook
St Lucia (P)
Venezuela

North America

Vancouver (P)
New York (P)
Western Canada

Africa

Cape Town (P)
East Africa
Egypt
Libya
Marrakech (P)
Morocco
Namibia
South Africa
Tanzania
Tunisia
Uganda

Middle East

Dubai (P)
Israel
Jordan
Syria & Lebanon

Australasia

Australia
East Coast Australia
New Zealand
Sydney (P)
West Coast Australia

Asia

Bali
Bangkok & the Beaches
Bhutan
Cambodia
Goa
Hong Kong (P)
India
Indian Himalaya
Indonesia
Laos
Malaysia & Singapore
Nepal
Northern Pakistan
Pakistan
Rajasthan
South India
Sri Lanka
Sumatra
Thailand
Tibet
Vietnam

Europe

Andalucía
Barcelona (P)
Belfast (P)
Berlin (P)
Bilbao (P)
Bologna (P)
Britain
Cardiff (P)
Copenhagen (P)
Croatia

Dublin (P)
Edinburgh (P)
England
Glasgow (P)
Ireland
Lisbon (P)
London
London (P)
Madrid (P)
Naples (P)
Northern Spain
Paris (P)
Reykjavík (P)
Scotland
Scotland Highlands & Islands
Seville (P)
Siena (P)
Spain
Tallinn (P)
Turin (P)
Turkey
Valencia (P)
Verona (P)
Wales

Lifestyle guides

Surfing Britain
Surfing Europe

Also available:
Traveller's Handbook (WEXAS)
Traveller's Healthbook (WEXAS)
Traveller's Internet Guide (WEXAS)